Sylvia Langfield and Dave Duddell

Cambridge International AS and A level **Computer Science** Coursebook

CAMBRIDGE
UNIVERSITY PRESS

University Printing House, Cambridge CB2 8BS, United Kingdom

One Liberty Plaza, 20th Floor, New York, NY 10006, USA

477 Williamstown Road, Port Melbourne, VIC 3207, Australia

314–321, 3rd Floor, Plot 3, Splendor Forum, Jasola District Centre, New Delhi – 110025, India

79 Anson Road, #06–04/06, Singapore 079906

Cambridge University Press is part of the University of Cambridge.

It furthers the University's mission by disseminating knowledge in the pursuit of education, learning and research at the highest international levels of excellence.

www.cambridge.org
Information on this title: www.cambridge.org/9781107546738

First published 2015

20 19 18 17 16 15 14 13 12 11 10 9 8 7 6

Printed in Dubai by Oriental Press

A catalogue record for this publication is available from the British Library

ISBN 978-1-107-54673-8 Paperback

The past paper questions on pages 107-108 and 316 are taken from the 9608 Specimen papers 1 and 3 respectively and are reproduced with the permission of Cambridge International Examinations.

All other examination-style questions and comments that appear in this book were written by the authors.

Contents

PART 4 FURTHER PROBLEM-SOLVING AND PROGRAMMING SKILLS

Introduction

This full-colour, illustrated textbook has been written by experienced authors specifically for the Cambridge International AS and A Level Computer Science syllabus (9608).

The presentation of the chapters in this book reflects the content of the syllabus:

- The book is divided into four parts, each of which is closely matched to the corresponding part of the syllabus.
- Each chapter defines a set of learning objectives which closely match the learning objectives set out in the syllabus.
- The syllabus defines two assessment objectives: A01 Knowledge with understanding and A02 Skills. Papers 1 and 3 have a major focus on A01 and Papers 2 and 4 have a major focus on A02. The chapters in Parts 1 and 3 have been written with emphasis on the promotion of knowledge and understanding. The chapters in Parts 2 and 4 have been written with an emphasis on skill development.

The chapters in Parts 1 and 3 have a narrative. We would encourage students to read the whole chapter first before going back to revisit the individual sections.

The chapters in Parts 2 and 4 contain many more tasks. We would encourage students to approach these chapters step-by-step. Whenever a task is presented, this should be carried out before progressing further.

In particular, Chapter 11 (Algorithm design and problem-solving) may be worked through in parallel with Chapter 13 (Programming and data representation). For example, Task 13.03 is based on Worked Example 11.03. After studying this worked example, students may wish to cover the first part of Chapter 13 and write the program for Task 13.03. This will give the student the opportunity to test their understanding of an algorithm by implementing it in their chosen programming language. Then further study of Chapter 11 is recommended before attempting further tasks in Chapter 13.

How to use this book: a guided tour

Chapter – each chapter begins with a short list of the learning objectives and concepts that are explained in it.

Chapter 1
Information Representation

Learning objectives

By the end of this chapter you should be able to:

- show understanding of the basis of different number systems
- show understanding of, and be able to represent, character data in its internal binary form
- show understanding of how data for a bitmapped or vector graphic image is encoded
- show understanding of how sound is represented and encoded
- show understanding of the characteristics of video streams
- show understanding of how digital data can be compressed.

Key Term – clear and straightforward explanations of the most important terms in each chapter.

KEY TERMS

Byte: a group of eight bits treated as a single unit

Task – exercises for the student to test their skills.

TASK 1.01

Convert the denary number 374 into a hexadecimal number.

Convert the hexadecimal number 3A2C to a denary number.

Question – questions for the student to test their knowledge and understanding.

Question:

Construct a partial drawing list for the graphic shown in figure 1.06. You can take measurements from the image and use the bottom left corner of the box as the origin of a coordinate system. You can invent your own format for the drawing list.

Discussion Point – discussion points intended for class discussion.

Discussion Point

What is the two's complement of the binary value 1000? Are you surprised by this?

Extension Question – extended questions for consideration of more advanced aspects or topics beyond the immediate scope of the Cambridge International AS and A Level syllabus.

Extension Question:

Graphic files can be stored in a number of formats. For example, JPEG, GIF, PNG and TIFF are just a few of the possibilities. What compression techniques, if any, do these use?

Tip – quick notes to highlight key facts and important points.

TIP

For multiples of bytes, the terminology used has recently changed. Traditionally, computer scientists have used the terminology kilobyte, megabyte, gigabyte etc. in a way that conflicted with the definition of these prefixes established by the International System of Units (SI). Following the SI convention, one kilobyte would represent 1000 bytes. Computer scientists have used one kilobyte to represent 1024 bytes. There have been a number of variations on how this was written, for example Kbyte, KB or kB but the basic contradiction remained. In order to resolve this unsatisfactory situation, the International Electrotechnical Commission (IEC) in 1998 proposed a new set of definitions for such quantities. 1024 bytes is now identified as one kibibyte where the kibi can be considered as representing kilobinary. This proposal has been accepted by other international standards bodies.

Worked Example – step-by-step examples of solving problems or implementing specific techniques.

WORKED EXAMPLE 1.01

Converting a negative number expressed in two's complement form to the corresponding denary number.

Consider the two's complement binary number 10110001.

Method 1. Convert to the corresponding positive binary number then find the denary value

Converting to two's complement leaves unchanged the 1 in the least significant bit position then changes all of the remaining bits to produce 01001111.

Summary

- A binary code or a binary number can be documented as a hexadecimal number.
- Internal coding of signed integers is usually based on a two's complement representation.
- BCD is a convenient coding scheme for single denary digits.
- ASCII and Unicode are standardised coding schemes for text characters.
- An image can be stored either in a vector graphic file or in a bitmap file.
- An ADC works by sampling a continuous waveform.
- Lossless compression allows an original file to be recovered by a decoder; lossy compression irretrievably loses some information.

Summary Checklist – at the end of each chapter to review what the student has learned.

Exam-style Questions

1 A file contains binary coding. The following are two successive bytes in the file:

10010101	00110011

a One possibility for the information stored is that the two bytes together represent one unsigned integer binary number.

i Give the denary number corresponding to this. Show your working. [2]

ii Give the hexadecimal number corresponding to this. Show your working. [2]

b Give one example of when a hexadecimal representation is used. [1]

Exam-style Questions – Exam-style questions for the student to test their skills, knowledge and understanding at the end of each chapter

Part 1 Theory Fundamentals

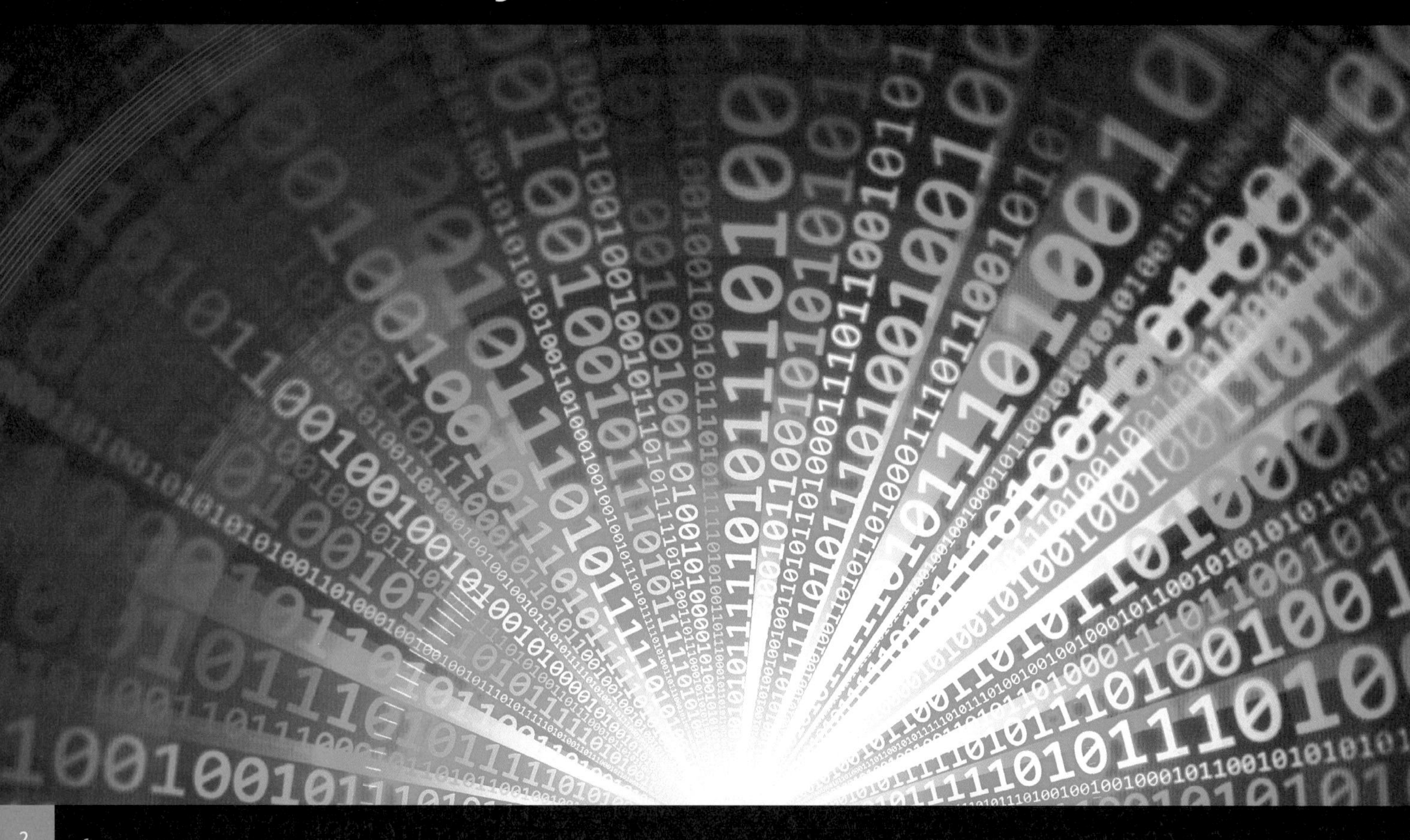

Chapter 1
Information Representation

Learning objectives

By the end of this chapter you should be able to:

- show understanding of the basis of different number systems
- show understanding of, and be able to represent, character data in its internal binary form
- show understanding of how data for a bitmapped or vector graphic image is encoded
- show understanding of how sound is represented and encoded
- show understanding of the characteristics of video streams
- show understanding of how digital data can be compressed.

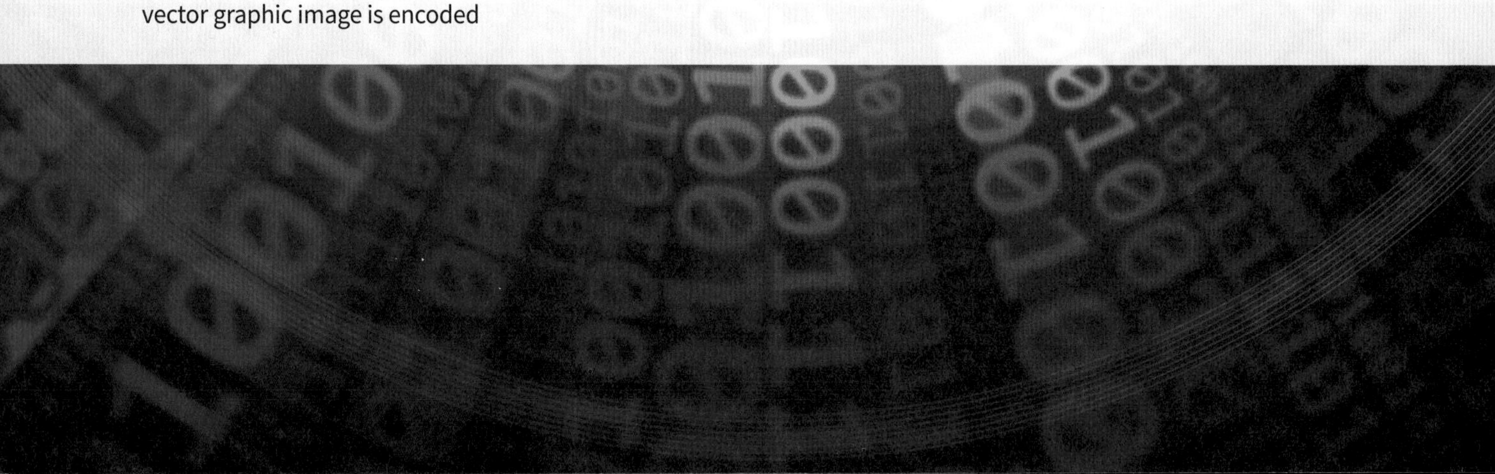

1.01 Number systems

As a child we first encounter numbers when learning to count. Specifically we learn to count using 1, 2, 3, 4, 5, 6, 7, 8, 9, 10. These are natural numbers expressed in what can be described as the denary, decimal or base-10 system of numbers. Had we learned to count using 0, 1, 2, 3, 4, 5, 6, 7, 8, 9 we would have more clearly understood that the number system was base-10 because there are 10 individual, distinct symbols or digits available to express a number.

A little later we learn that the representation of a number has the least significant digit at the right-hand end. For example, writing a denary number as 346 has the meaning:

$$3 \times 10^2 + 4 \times 10^1 + 6 \times 10^0$$

All computer technology is engineered with components that represent or recognise only two states. For this reason, familiarity with the binary number system is essential for an understanding of computing systems. The binary number system is a base-2 system which uses just two symbols, 0 and 1. These binary digits are usually referred to as 'bits'.

All data inside a computer system are stored and manipulated using a binary code. However, if there is ever a need to document some of this binary code outside of the computer system it is not helpful to use the internal code.

Instead, it is far better to use a hexadecimal representation for documentation purposes. Whether or not a code represents a binary number, it can be treated as such and converted to the corresponding hexadecimal number. This makes the representation more compact and, as a result, more intelligible.

Hexadecimal numbers are in the base-16 system and therefore require 16 individual symbols to represent a number. The symbols chosen are 0–9 supplemented with A–F. A few examples of the hexadecimal representation of binary numbers represented by eight bits are shown in Table 1.01.

Binary	Hexadecimal	Denary
00001000	08	8
00001010	0A	10
00001111	0F	15
11111111	FF	255

Table 1.01 Hexadecimal representations of binary numbers and the denary values

Note that each grouping of four bits is represented by one hexadecimal symbol. Also note that it is common practice to include leading zeros in a hexadecimal number when used in this way.

Question 1.01

Does a computer ever use hexadecimal numbers?

Converting between binary and denary numbers

To convert a binary number to a denary number the straightforward method is to sum the individual position values knowing that the least significant bit represents 2^0, the next one 2^1 and so on. This is illustrated by conversion of the binary number 11001 as shown in Figure 1.01.

Position values	$2^4 = 16$	$2^3 = 8$	$2^2 = 4$	$2^1 = 2$	$2^0 = 1$
Binary digits	1	1	0	0	1

Figure 1.01 Position values for a binary number

Starting from the least significant bit, the denary equivalent is 1 + 0 + 0 + 8 + 16 = 25.

An alternative method is to use the fact that 1 × 16 is equal to 2 × 8 and so on. To carry out the conversion you start at the most significant bit and successively multiply by two and add the result to the next digit:

```
                  1 × 2 =  2
add 2 to 1, then  2 × 3 =  6
add 6 to 0, then  2 × 6 = 12
add 12 to 0, then 2 × 12 = 24
add 24 to 1 to give 25.
```

When converting a denary number to binary the procedure is successive division by two with the remainder noted at each stage. The converted number is then given as the set of remainders in reverse order.

This is illustrated by the conversion of denary 246 to binary:

```
246 ÷ 2 → 123 with remainder 0
123 ÷ 2 →  61 with remainder 1
 61 ÷ 2 →  30 with remainder 1
 30 ÷ 2 →  15 with remainder 0
 15 ÷ 2 →   7 with remainder 1
  7 ÷ 2 →   3 with remainder 1
  3 ÷ 2 →   1 with remainder 1
  1 ÷ 2 →   0 with remainder 1
```


Thus the binary equivalent of denary 246 is 11110110. As a check that the answer is sensible, you should remember that you are expecting an 8-bit binary number because the largest denary number that can be represented in seven bits is $2^7 - 1$ which is 127. Eight bits can represent values from 0 to $2^8 - 1$ which is 255.

Converting hexadecimal numbers

To convert a hexadecimal number to binary, each digit is treated separately and converted into a 4-bit binary equivalent, remembering that F converts to 1111, E converts to 1110 and so on. Subsequent conversion of the resulting binary to denary can then be done if needed.

To convert a binary number to hexadecimal you start with the four least significant bits and convert them to one hexadecimal digit. You then proceed upwards towards the most significant bit, successively taking groupings of four bits and converting each grouping to the corresponding hexadecimal digit.

It is possible to convert a denary number directly to hexadecimal but it is easier to convert first to binary before completing the conversion.

TASK 1.01

Convert the denary number 374 into a hexadecimal number.

Convert the hexadecimal number 3A2C to a denary number.

1.02 Internal coding of numbers

The discussion here relates only to the coding of integer values. The coding of non-integer numeric values (real numbers) is considered in Chapter 16 (Section 16.03).

It is convenient at this point to emphasise that the coding used in a computer system is almost exclusively based on bits being grouped together with eight bits representing a **byte**. A byte, or a group of bytes, might represent a binary value but equally might represent a code. For either case, the right-hand bit is referred to as the least significant and the left-hand bit as the most significant or top bit. Furthermore, the bits in a byte are numbered right to left starting at bit 0 and ending at bit 7.

KEY TERMS

Byte: a group of eight bits treated as a single unit

Coding for integers

Computers have to store integer values for a number of purposes. Sometimes the requirement is only for an unsigned integer to be stored. However, in many cases a signed integer is needed where the coding has to identify whether the number is positive or negative.

An unsigned integer can be stored simply as a binary number. The only decision to be made is how many bytes should be used. If the choice is to use two bytes (16 bits) then the range of values that can be represented is 0 to $2^{16} - 1$ which is 0 to 65535.

If a signed integer is to be represented, the obvious choice is to use one bit to represent the + or – sign. The remaining bits then represent the value. This is referred to as 'sign and magnitude representation'. However, there are a number of disadvantages in using this format.

The approach generally used is to store signed integers in **two's complement** form. Here we need two definitions. The **one's complement** of a binary number is defined as the binary number obtained if each binary digit is individually subtracted from 1 which, in practice, means that each 0 is switched to 1 and each 1 switched to 0. The two's complement is defined as the binary number obtained if 1 is added to the one's complement number.

KEY TERMS

One's complement: the binary number obtained by subtracting each digit in a binary number from 1

Two's complement: the one's complement of a binary number plus 1

If you need to convert a binary number to its two's complement form you can use the method indicated by the definition but there is a quicker method. For this you start at the least significant bit and move left ignoring any zeros up to the first 1 which is also ignored. Any remaining bits are then changed from 0 to 1 or from 1 to 0.

For example, expressing the number 10100100 in two's complement form leaves the right-hand 100 unchanged then the remaining 10100 changes to 01011 so the result is 01011100.

The differences between a sign and magnitude representation and a two's complement representation are illustrated in Table 1.02. For simplicity we consider only the values that can be stored in four bits (referred to as a 'nibble').

Signed denary number to be represented	Sign and magnitude representation	Two's complement representation
+7	0111	0111
+6	0110	0110
+5	0101	0101
+4	0100	0100
+3	0011	0011
+2	0010	0010
+1	0001	0001
+0	0000	0000
–0	1000	Not represented
–1	1001	1111
–2	1010	1110
–3	1011	1101
–4	1100	1100
–5	1101	1011
–6	1110	1010
–7	1111	1001
–8	Not represented	1000

Table 1.02 Representations of signed integers

There are several points to note here. The first is that sign and magnitude representation has a positive and a negative zero which could cause a problem if comparing values. The second, somewhat trivial, point is that there is an extra negative value represented in two's complement.

The third and most important point is that the representations in two's complement are such that starting from the lowest negative value each successive higher value is obtained by adding 1 to the binary code. In particular, when all digits are 1 the next step is to roll over to an all-zero code. This is the same as any digital display would do when each digit has reached its maximum value.

It can be seen that the codes for positive values in the two's complement form are the same as the sign and magnitude codes. However, this fact rather hides the truth that the two's complement code is self-complementary. If a negative number is in two's complement form then the binary code for the corresponding positive number can be obtained by taking the two's complement of the binary code representing the negative number.

TASK 1.02

Take the two's complement of the binary code for –5 and show that you get the code for +5.

WORKED EXAMPLE 1.01

Converting a negative number expressed in two's complement form to the corresponding denary number.

Consider the two's complement binary number 10110001.

Method 1. Convert to the corresponding positive binary number then find the denary value

Converting to two's complement leaves unchanged the 1 in the least significant bit position then changes all of the remaining bits to produce 01001111.

Now using the 'successive multiplication by two' method we get (ignoring the 0 in the most significant bit position):

	2 × 1 = 2
add 2 to 0, then	2 × 2 = 4
add 4 to 0, then	2 × 4 = 8
add 8 to 1, then	2 × 9 = 18
add 18 to 1, then	2 × 19 = 38
add 38 to 1, then	2 × 39 = 78
add 78 to 1 to give 79	

So the original number is –79 in denary.

Method 2. Sum the individual position values but treat the most significant bit as a negative value

From the original binary number 10110001 this produces the following:

$$-2^7 + 0 + 2^5 + 2^4 + 0 + 0 + 0 + 1 =$$

$$-128 + 0 + 32 + 16 + 0 + 0 + 0 + 1 = -79.$$

Discussion Point:

What is the two's complement of the binary value 1000? Are you surprised by this?

One final point to make here is that the reason for using two's complement representations is to simplify the processes for arithmetic calculations. The most important example of this is that the process used for subtracting one signed integer from another is to convert the number being subtracted to its two's complement form and then to add this to the other number.

TASK 1.03

Using a byte to represent each value, carry out the subtraction of denary 35 from denary 67 using binary arithmetic with two's complement representations.

Binary coded decimal (BCD)

One exception to grouping bits in bytes to represent integers is the binary coded decimal (BCD) scheme. If there is an application where single denary digits are required to be stored or transmitted, BCD offers an efficient solution. The BCD code uses four bits (a nibble) to represent a denary digit. A four-bit code can represent 16 different values so there is scope for a variety of schemes. This discussion only considers the simplest BCD coding which expresses the value directly as a binary number.

If a denary number with more than one digit is to be converted to BCD there has to be a group of four bits for each denary digit. There are, however, two options for BCD; the first is to store one BCD code in one byte leaving four bits unused. The other option is packed BCD where two 4-bit codes are stored in one byte. Thus, for example, the denary digits 8503 could be represented by either of the codes shown in Figure 1.02.

One BCD digit per byte	00001000	00000101	00000000	00000011
Two BCD digits per byte	10000101	00000011		

Figure 1.02 Alternative BCD representations of the denary digits 8503

There are a number of applications where BCD can be used. The obvious type of application is where denary digits are to be displayed, for instance on the screen of a calculator or in a digital time display. A somewhat unexpected application is for the representation of currency values. When a currency value is written in a format such as $300.25 it is as a fixed-point decimal number (ignoring the dollar sign). It might be expected that such values would be stored as real numbers but this cannot be done accurately (this type of problem is discussed in more detail in Chapter 16 (Section 16.03). One solution to the problem is to store each denary digit in a BCD code.

It is instructive to consider how BCD arithmetic might be performed by a computer if fixed-point decimal values were stored as BCD values. Let's consider a simple example of addition to illustrate the potential problem. We will assume a two-byte representation. The first byte represents two denary digits for the whole part of the number and the second byte represents two denary digits for the fractional part. If the two values are $0.26 and $0.85 then the result should be $1.11. Applying simple binary addition of the BCD codes will produce the result shown in Figure 1.03.

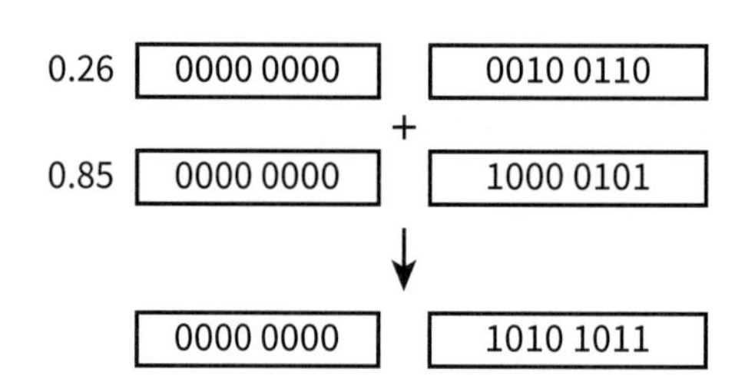

Figure 1.03 Erroneous addition using BCD coding

In the first decimal place position, the 2 has been added to the 8 to get 10 but the BCD scheme only recognises binary codes for a single-digit denary number so the addition has failed. The same problem has occurred in the addition for the second decimal place values. The result shown is 'point ten eleven', which is meaningless in denary numbers. The 'carry' of a digit from one decimal place to the next has been ignored.

To counteract this in BCD arithmetic, the processor needs to recognise that an impossible value has been produced and apply a method to remedy this. We will not consider the recognition method. The remedy is to add 0110 whenever the problem is detected.

Starting with the least significant nibble (see Figure 1.04), adding 0110 to 1011 gives 10001 which is a four-bit value plus a carry bit. The carry bit has to be added to the next nibble as well as adding the 0110 to correct the error. Adding 1 to 1010 and then adding 0110 gives 10001. Again the carry bit is added to the next nibble to give the correct result of $1.11 for the sum of $0.26 and $0.85.

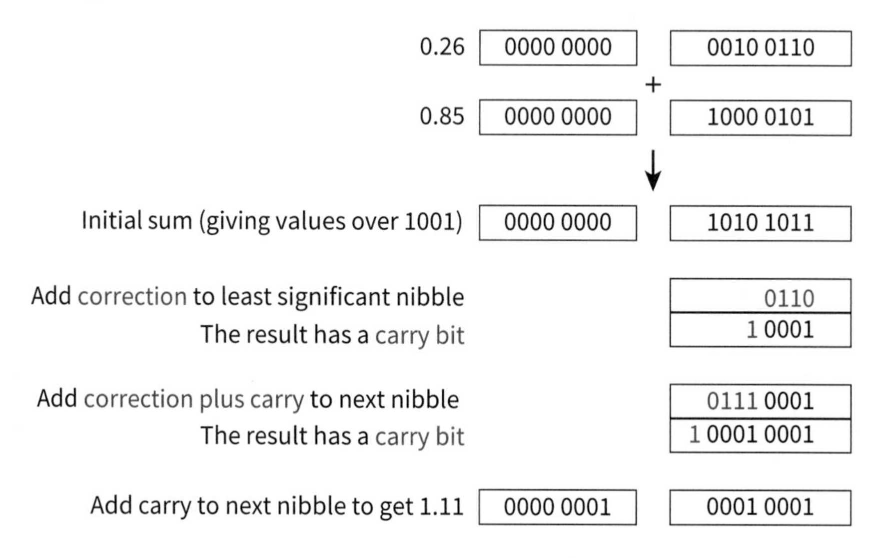

Figure 1.04 Correct representation of the BCD code for 1.11

In Chapter 5 (Section 5.02) there is a brief discussion of how a processor can recognise problems arising from arithmetic operations using numbers coded as binary values.

1.03 Internal coding of text

ASCII code

If text is to be stored in a computer it is necessary to have a coding scheme that provides a unique binary code for each distinct individual component item of the text. Such a code is referred to as a character code. There have been three significant coding schemes used in computing. One of these, which is only mentioned here in passing, is the EBCDIC code used by IBM in their computer systems.

The scheme which has been used for the longest time is the ASCII (American Standard Code for Information Interchange) coding scheme. This is an internationally agreed standard. There are some variations on ASCII coding schemes but the major one is the 7-bit code. It is customary to present the codes in a table for which a number of different designs have been used.

Table 1.03 shows an edited version with just a few of the codes. The first column contains the binary code which would be stored in one byte, with the most significant bit set to zero and the remaining bits representing the character code. The second column presents the hexadecimal equivalent as an illustration of when it can be useful to use such a representation.

Binary code	Hexadecimal equivalent	Character	Description
00000000	00	NUL	Null character
00000001	01	SOH	Start of heading
00000010	02	STX	Start of text
00100000	20		Space
00100001	21	!	Exclamation mark
00100100	24	$	Dollar
00101011	2B	+	Plus
00101111	2F	/	Forward slash
00110000	30	0	Zero
00110001	31	1	One
00110010	32	2	Two
01000001	41	A	Uppercase A
01000010	42	B	Uppercase B
01000011	43	C	Uppercase C
01100001	61	a	Lowercase a
01100010	62	b	Lowercase b
01100011	63	c	Lowercase c

Table 1.03 Some examples of ASCII codes

The full table shows the 2^7 (128) different codes available for a 7-bit code. You should not try to remember any of the individual codes but there are certain aspects of the coding scheme which you need to understand.

Firstly, you can see that the majority of the codes are for printing or graphic characters. However, the first few codes represent non-printing or control characters. These were introduced to assist in data transmission or in entering data at a computer terminal. It is fair to say that these codes have very limited use in the modern computer world so they need no further consideration.

Secondly, it can be seen that the obvious types of character that could be expected to be used in a text based on the English language have been included. Specifically there are upper- and lower-case letters, punctuation symbols, numerals and arithmetic symbols in the coding tables.

It is worth emphasising here that these codes for numbers are exclusively for use in the context of stored, displayed or printed text. All of the other coding schemes for numbers are for internal use in a computer system and would not be used in a text.

There are some special features that make the coding scheme easy to use in certain circumstances. The first is that the codes for numbers and for letters are in sequence in each case so that, for example, if 1 is added to the code for seven the code for eight is produced. The second is that the codes for the upper-case letters differ from the codes for the corresponding lower-case letters only in the value of bit 5. This makes conversion of upper case to lower case, or the reverse, a simple operation.

Unicode

Despite still being widely used, the ASCII codes are far from adequate for many purposes. For this reason new coding schemes have been developed and continue to be developed further. The discussion here describes the Unicode schemes but it should be noted that these have been developed in tandem with the Universal Character Set (UCS) scheme; the only differences between these schemes are the identifying names given to them. The aim of Unicode is to be able to represent any possible text in code form. In particular this includes all languages in the world. However, Unicode is designed so that once a coding set has been defined it is never changed. In particular, the first 128 characters in Unicode are the ASCII codes.

Unicode has its own special terminology. For example, a character code is referred to as a 'code point'. In any documentation there is a special way of identifying a code point. An example is U+0041 which is the code point corresponding to the alphabetic character A. The 0041 are hexadecimal characters representing two bytes. The interesting point is that in a text where the coding has been identified as Unicode it is only necessary to use a one-byte representation for the 128 codes corresponding to ASCII. To ensure such a code cannot be misinterpreted, the codes where more than one byte is needed have restrictions applied. Figure 1.05 shows the format used for a two-byte code.

11??????	10??????

Figure 1.05 Unicode two-byte code format

The most significant bit for an ASCII code is always 0 so neither of the two-byte representations here can cause confusion.

1.04 Images

Images can be stored in a computer system for the eventual purpose of displaying the image on a screen or for presenting it on paper, usually as a component of a document. Such an image can be created by using an appropriate drawing package. Alternatively, when an image already exists independently of the computer system, the image can be captured by using photography or by scanning.

Vector graphics

It is normal for an image that is created by a drawing package or a computer-aided design (CAD) package to consist of a number of geometric objects. The outcome is then usually for the image to be stored as a **vector graphic** file.

KEY TERMS

Vector graphic: a graphic consisting of components defined by geometric formulae and associated properties, such as line colour and style

We do not need to consider how an image of this type would be created. We do need to consider how the data is stored after the image has been created. A vector graphic file contains a drawing list. The list contains a command for each object included in the image. Each command has a list of attributes that define the properties of the object. The properties include the basic geometric data such as, for a circle, the position of the centre and its radius. In addition properties such as the thickness and style of a line, the colour of a line and the colour that fills the shape, if that is appropriate, are defined. An example of what could be created as a vector graphic file is shown in Figure 1.06.

Figure 1.06 A simple example of a vector graphic image

The most important property of a vector graphic image is that the dimensions of the objects are not defined explicitly but instead are defined relative to an imaginary drawing canvas. In other words, the image is scalable. Whenever the image is to be displayed the file is read, the appropriate calculations are made and the objects are drawn to a suitable scale. If the user then requests that the image is redrawn at a larger scale the file is read again and another set of calculations are made before the image is displayed. This process cannot of itself cause distortion of the image.

TASK 1.04

Construct a partial drawing list for the graphic shown in Figure 1.06. You can take measurements from the image and use the bottom left corner of the box as the origin of a coordinate system. You can invent your own format for the drawing list.

A vector graphic file can only be displayed directly on a graph plotter, which is an expensive specialised piece of hardware. Otherwise the file has to be converted to a bitmap before presentation.

Bitmaps

Most images do not consist of geometrically defined shapes so a vector graphic representation is inappropriate. The general purpose approach is to store an image as a bitmap. Typical uses are when capturing an existing image by scanning or perhaps by taking a screen-shot. Alternatively, an image can be created by using a simple drawing package.

The fundamental concept underlying the creation of a bitmap file is that the **picture element (pixel)** is the smallest identifiable component of a bitmap image. The image is stored as a two-dimensional matrix of pixels. The pixel itself is a very simple construct; it has a position in the matrix and it has a colour.

KEY TERMS

Picture element (pixel): the smallest identifiable component of a bitmap image, defined by just two properties: its position in the bitmap matrix and its colour

It is of no consequence as to whether it is considered to be a small rectangle, a small circle or a dot. However, the scheme used to represent the colour has to be decided and this can be quite detailed. The simplest option is to use one bit to represent the colour, so that the pixel is either black or white. Storage of the colour in four bits would allow simple greyscale colouring. At least eight bits per pixel are necessary to code a coloured image. The number of bits per pixel is sometimes referred to as the colour depth.

The other decision that has to be made concerns the resolution of the image which can be represented as the product of the number of pixels per row times the number of rows. When considering resolution it is important to distinguish between the resolution of a stored image and the resolution of a monitor screen that might be used to display the image. Both of these have to be considered if a screen display is being designed.

From the above discussion it can be seen that a bitmap file does not define the physical size of a pixel or of the whole image. The image is therefore scalable but when the image is scaled the number of pixels in it does not change. If a well-designed image is presented on a suitable screen the human eye cannot distinguish the individual pixels. However, if the image is magnified too far the quality of the display will deteriorate and the individual pixels will be evident. This is illustrated in Figure 1.07 which shows an original small image, a magnified version of this small image and a larger image created with a more sensible, higher resolution.

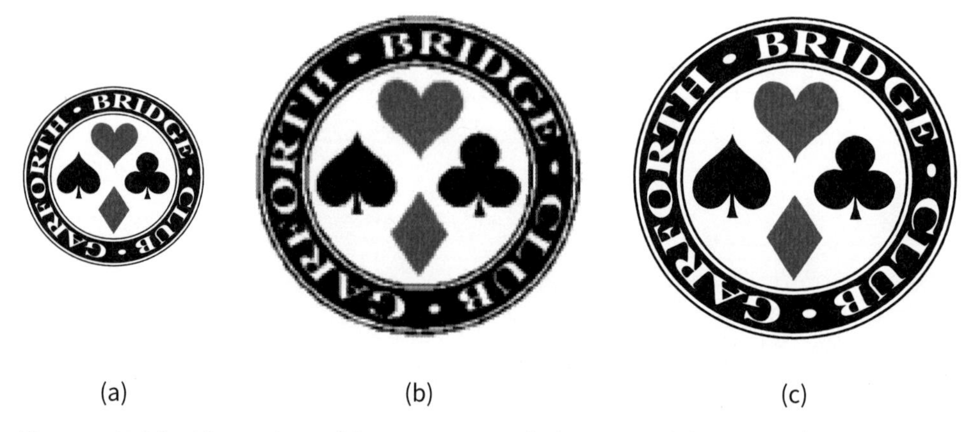

Figure 1.07 (a) a bitmap logo; (b) an over-magnified version of the image; (c) a sensible larger version

Bitmap file size

The above account has considered the two approaches for storing images and when they are appropriate.

File size is always an issue with an image file. A large file occupies more memory space and takes longer to display or to be transmitted across a network. A vector graphic file will have a smaller size than a corresponding bitmap file. A bitmap file has to store the pixel data but the file must also have a header that defines the resolution of the image and the coding scheme for the pixel colour.

You can calculate the minimum size (the size not including the header) of a bitmap file knowing the resolution and the colour depth. As an example, consider that a bitmap file is needed to fill a laptop screen where the resolution is 1366 by 768. If the colour depth is to be 24 then the number of bits needed is:

$$1366 \times 768 \times 24 = 25\,178\,112 \text{ bits}$$

The result of this calculation shows the number of bits but a file size is always quoted as a number of bytes or multiples of bytes. Thus our file size could be quoted as:

$$\begin{aligned} 25\,178\,112 \text{ bits} &= 25\,178\,112 \div 8 = 3\,147\,264 \text{ bytes} \\ &= 3\,147\,264 \div 1024 = 3073.5 \text{ kibibytes (3073.5 KiB)} \\ &= 3073.5 \div 1024 = \text{approximately 3 MiB} \end{aligned}$$

KEY TERMS

Kibi: a prefix representing the factor 2^{10} (1024) written as the symbol Ki

Mebi: a prefix representing the factor 2^{20} (1048 576) written as the symbol Mi

Gibi: a prefix representing the factor 2^{30} written as the symbol Gi

TIP

For multiples of bytes, the terminology used has recently changed. Traditionally, computer scientists have used the terminology kilobyte, megabyte, gigabyte etc. in a way that conflicted with the definition of these prefixes established by the International System of Units (SI). Following the SI convention, one kilobyte would represent 1000 bytes. Computer scientists have used one kilobyte to represent 1024 bytes. There have been a number of variations on how this was written, for example Kbyte, KB or kB but the basic contradiction remained. In order to resolve this unsatisfactory situation, the International Electrotechnical Commission (IEC) in 1998 proposed a new set of definitions for such quantities. 1024 bytes is now identified as one kibibyte where the kibi can be considered as representing kilobinary. This proposal has been accepted by other international standards bodies.

1.05 Sound

Natural sound consists of variations in pressure which are detected by the human ear. A typical sound contains a large number of individual waves each with a defined frequency. The result is a wave form in which the amplitude of the sound varies in a continuous but irregular pattern.

If there is a need to store sound or transmit it electronically the original analogue sound signal has to be converted to a binary code. A sound encoder has two components. The first is a band-limiting filter. This is needed to remove high-frequency components. The ear would not be able to detect these and they could cause problems for the coding if not removed. The other component in the encoder is an analogue-to-digital converter (ADC).

The method of operation of the ADC is described with reference to Figure 1.08. The amplitude of the wave (the red line) has to be sampled at regular intervals. The blue vertical lines indicate the sampling times. The amplitude cannot be measured exactly; instead the amplitude is approximated by the closest of the defined amplitudes represented by the horizontal lines. In Figure 1.08, sample values 1 and 4 will be an accurate estimate of the actual amplitude because the wave is touching an amplitude line. In contrast, samples 5 and 6 will not be accurate because the actual amplitude is approximately half way between the two closest defined values.

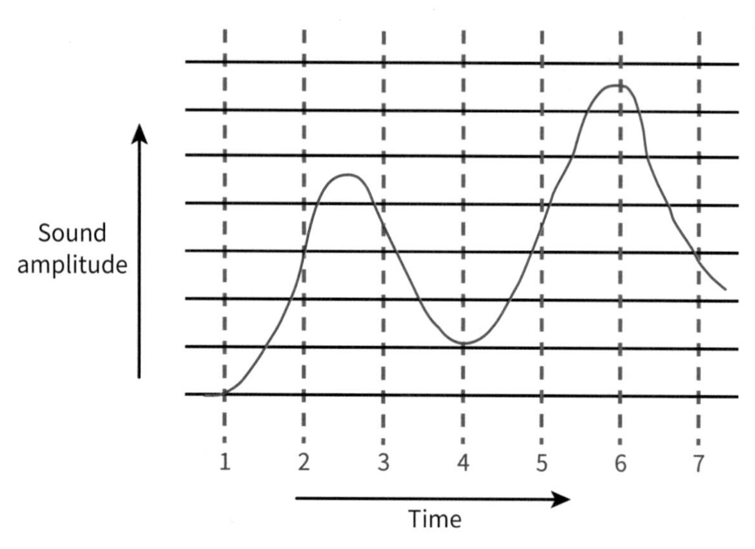

Figure 1.08 ADC sampling

In practice, for coding sound, two decisions have to be made. The first is the number of bits to be used to store the amplitude values, which defines the sampling resolution. If only three bits are used then eight levels can be defined as shown in Figure 1.08. If too few are used there will be a significant quantisation error. In practice 16 bits will provide reasonable accuracy for the digitised sound.

The other decision concerns the choice of the sampling rate, which is the number of samples taken per second. This should be in accordance with Nyquist's theorem which states that sampling must be done at a frequency at least twice the highest frequency in the sample.

Once again file size can be an issue. Clearly an increased sampling rate and an increased sampling resolution will both cause an increase in file size.

Simply recording sound and storing a digital representation is not enough for many applications. Once a digital representation of the sound has been stored in a file, it can be manipulated using sound-editing software. This will typically have features for:

- combining sound from different sources
- fading in or fading out the sound
- editing the sound to remove noise and other imperfections.

1.06 Video

The emphasis here is on the visual aspect of a video recording and, in particular, how the image is displayed on a screen. It might be imagined that a video would be stored very simply as a succession of still images or frames and the only concern would be the frame rate defined as the number of frames displayed per second. In practice the issues are far more complex. They have not been made any more simple by the recent changes that have taken place with regards to screen technology.

The basic principle of operation is that the display of an individual frame is created line by line. One of the issues is the choice of resolution. The resolution can be defined in terms of the number of lines per frame and the number of pixels per line. There needs to be compatibility between the resolution of the stored image and the resolution of the display screen. However, the technology used has to be chosen with regard to the sensitivity of the human eye. One constraint is that unless the screen is refreshed at least 50 times per second the eye will notice the flicker. However, provided that the refresh rate is 25 times per second the eye cannot see that any motion on the screen is not actually continuous.

The traditional solution to this problem has been to use interlaced encoding. This was used in television broadcasting and then adapted for video recordings. The image for each frame is split into two halves, one containing the odd numbered lines and the other the even. The first half is displayed completely then the second half follows. This produces what appears to the eye as being a high refresh rate but is halving the transmission bandwidth requirements. The alternative approach is to use progressive encoding where a full frame is displayed each time. As improved transmission bandwidths become more generally available it is likely that progressive encoding will become the norm.

1.07 Compression techniques and packaging of multimedia content

For another time the issue of file size will be discussed, this time in the context of starting with a file that needs to have its size reduced to reduce memory storage requirements and improve transmission rates.

There are two categories of compression. The first is **lossless compression** where the file size is reduced but no information is lost and when necessary the process can be reversed to re-create the original file. The second is **lossy compression** where the file size is reduced with some loss of information and the original file can never be recovered. In many applications a combination of lossless and lossy methods may be used.

KEY TERMS

Lossless compression: coding techniques that allow subsequent decoding to recreate exactly the original file

Lossy compression: coding techniques that cause some information to be lost so that the exact original file cannot be recovered in subsequent decoding

If a file contains text then compression must be lossless because it is not sensible to allow any loss of information. One possible compression method would be Huffman coding. The procedure used to carry out the compression is quite detailed but the principle is straightforward. Instead of having each character coded in one byte an analysis is carried out to find the most often used characters. These are then given shorter codes. The original stream of bytes becomes a bit stream. A possible set of codes if a text contained only eight different letters is shown in Table 1.04.

Code	Character
10	e
01	t
111	o
110	h
0001	l
0000	p
0011	w
0010	z

Table 1.04 An example of Huffman coding

The important point to note here is the prefix property. None of the codes begins with the sequence of bits representing a shorter code. Thus there can be no ambiguity when the transmitted compressed file has to be converted back to the original text.

A different lossless compression technique is run-length encoding. This can be particularly effective for compressing a bitmap file. The compression converts sequences of the same bit pattern into a code that defines the bit pattern and the number of times it is repeated.

Lossy compression can be used in circumstances where a sound file or an image file can have some of the detailed coding removed or modified when it is likely that the human ear or eye will hardly notice any difference. One example would be to reduce the colour depth for the coding of a bitmap.

Extension Question 1.01

Graphic files can be stored in a number of formats. For example, JPEG, GIF, PNG and TIFF are just a few of the possibilities. What compression techniques, if any, do these use?

If the image coding for a video is to be compressed, one approach is to tackle the spatial redundancy in individual frames using techniques applicable to an image file. However, this is unlikely to be an efficient technique because, in general, one frame is very similar to the preceding one. It will be more effective to tackle this temporal redundancy by changing the frame by frame coding to one which mainly records differences between adjacent frames.

A video contains images and sound but these do not go to the same part of any receiving and displaying system. Clearly the audio and visual parts of a video must be handled independently but in a way that guarantees synchronisation. The solution to this is to package the audio and visual components in what is known as a multimedia container format. This concept is currently being developed by several different organisations or companies. The use is not restricted to one video file and one sound file. Rather, one multimedia container file will have many audio and video streams plus other streams, perhaps for subtitles or chapter headings.

Summary

- A binary code or a binary number can be documented as a hexadecimal number.
- Internal coding of signed integers is usually based on a two's complement representation.
- BCD is a convenient coding scheme for single denary digits.
- ASCII and Unicode are standardised coding schemes for text characters.
- An image can be stored either in a vector graphic file or in a bitmap file.
- An ADC works by sampling a continuous waveform.
- Lossless compression allows an original file to be recovered by a decoder; lossy compression irretrievably loses some information.

Exam-style Questions

1 A file contains binary coding. The following are two successive bytes in the file:

10010101	00110011

a One possibility for the information stored is that the two bytes together represent one unsigned integer binary number.

i Give the denary number corresponding to this. Show your working. [2]

ii Give the hexadecimal number corresponding to this. Show your working. [2]

b Give one example of when a hexadecimal representation is used. [1]

c Another possibility for the information stored is that the two bytes individually represent two signed integer binary numbers in two's complement form.

i State which byte represents a negative number and explain the reason for your choice.

ii Give the denary number corresponding to each byte. Show your working. [3]

d Give two advantages from representing signed integers in two's complement form rather than using a sign and magnitude representation. [2]

e Give three different examples of other options for the types of information that could be represented by two bytes. For each example, state whether a representation requires two bytes each time, just one byte or only part of a byte each time. [3]

2 A designer wishes to include some multimedia components on a web page.

a If the designer has some images stored in files there are two possible formats for the files.

i Describe the approach used if a graphic is stored in a vector graphic file. [2]

ii Describe the approach used if a graphic is stored in a bitmap file. [2]

iii State which format gives better image quality if the image has to be magnified and explain why. [2]

b The designer is concerned about the size of some bitmap files.

i If the resolution is to be 640 × 480 and the colour depth is to be 16, calculate an approximate size for the bitmap file. Show your working and express the size using sensible units. [2]

ii Explain why this calculation only gives an approximate file size. [1]

c The designer decides that the bitmap files need compressing.

i Explain how a simple form of lossless compression could be used. [2]

ii Explain one possible approach to lossy compression that could be used. [2]

3 An audio encoder is to be used to create a recording of a song. The encoder has two components.

a One of the components is an analogue-to-digital converter (ADC).

i Explain why this is needed. [2]

ii Two important factors associated with the use of an ADC are the sampling rate and the sampling resolution. Explain the two terms. Use a diagram if this will help your explanation. [5]

b The other component of an audio encoder has to be used before the ADC is used.

i Identify this component. [1]

ii Explain why it is used. [2]

c The recorded song is to be incorporated into a video. Sound-editing software is to be used as part of this process. Describe two techniques that the sound-editing software could provide. [3]

Chapter 2
Communication and Internet Technologies

Learning objectives

By the end of this chapter you should be able to:

- explain the client–server model of networked computers
- give examples of applications which use the client–server model
- describe what is meant by the World Wide Web (WWW) and the Internet
- explain how hardware and communication systems are used to support the Internet
- explain the benefits and drawbacks of using copper cable, fibre-optic cabling, radio waves, microwaves, satellites
- show understanding of bit streaming and the importance of bit rates/broadband speed on bit streaming
- explain the format of an IP address and how an IP address is associated with a device on a network
- explain the difference between a public IP address and a private IP address and the implication for security
- explain how a Uniform Resource Locator (URL) is used to locate a resource on the WWW and the role of the Domain Name Service
- describe the sequence of events executed by the client computer and web server when a web page consisting only of HTML tags is requested and displayed by a browser
- recognise and identify the purpose of some simple JavaScript and PHP code and show understanding of the typical use of client-side code in the design of an application.

2.01 Transmission media

Cable

The options for a cable are twisted pair, coaxial or fibre-optic. (The first two use copper for the transmission medium.) In discussing suitability for a given application there are a number of factors to consider. One is the cost of the cable and connecting devices. Another is the bandwidth achievable, which governs the possible data transmission rate. There are then two factors that can cause poor performance: the likelihood of interference affecting transmitted signals and the extent of attenuation (deterioration of the signal) when high frequencies are transmitted. These two factors affect the need for repeaters or amplifiers in transmission lines. Table 2.01 shows some comparisons of the different cable types.

	Twisted pair	Coaxial	Fibre-optic
Cost	Lowest	Higher	Highest
Bandwidth or data rate	Lowest	Higher	Much higher
Attenuation at high frequency	Affected	Most affected	Least affected
Interference	Worst affected	Less affected	Least affected
Need for repeaters	More often	More often	Less often

Table 2.01 Comparisons between cable types

It should be understood that for each of the three types of cabling there are defined standards for different grades of cable which must be considered when a final decision is made. However, it can be seen that fibre-optic cable performs best but does cost more than the other technologies. For a new installation the improved performance of fibre-optic cable is likely to be the factor that governs the choice. However, where copper cable is already installed the cost of replacement by fibre-optic cable may not be justified.

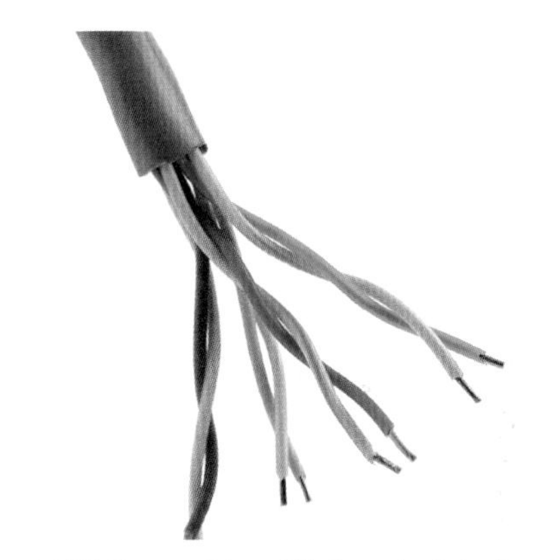

Figure 2.01 One cable with four twisted pairs with differing twist rates to reduce interference

Currently, twisted pair cable is still in use almost universally for connecting a telephone handset to a telephone line. This type of cable is illustrated in Figure 2.01. It is also the technology of choice for high-speed local area networks.

Coaxial cable has mainly been replaced for use in long-distance telephone cabling but is still used extensively by cable television companies and is often used in metropolitan area networks. Fibre-optic cable is the technology of choice for long-distance cabling. As shown in Figure 2.02, coaxial cable is not bundled but a fibre-optic cable contains many individual fibres.

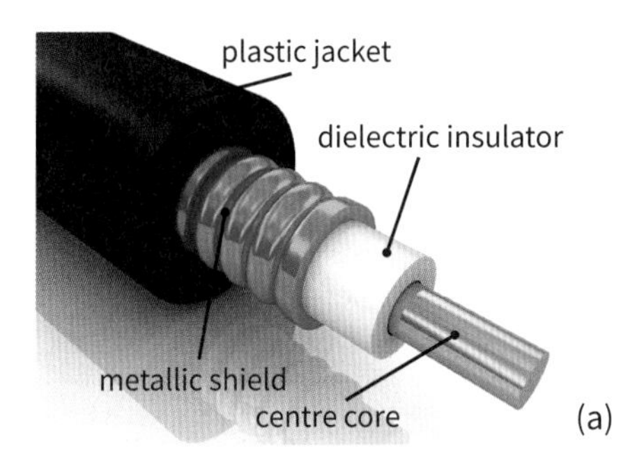

(a)

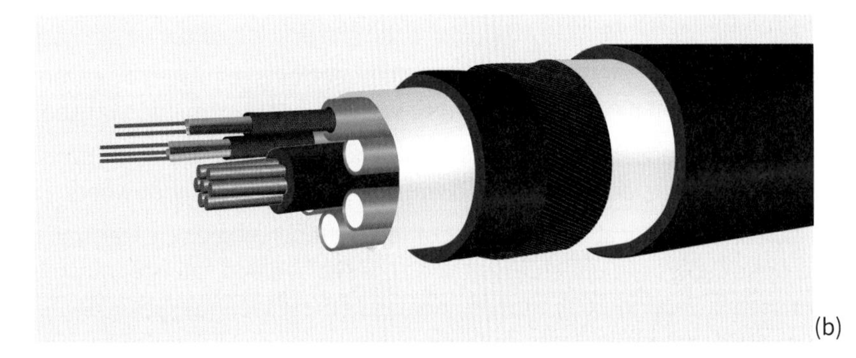

(b)

Figure 2.02 (a) Coaxial cable and (b) a bundled fibre-optic cable

Wireless

The alternative to cable is wireless transmission. The three options here are radio, microwave or infrared, which are all examples of electromagnetic radiation; the only intrinsic difference between the three types is the frequency of the waves.

When making a choice of which wireless option to use, all of the factors discussed when comparing cable media need to be considered again. In addition, the ability for the radiation to transmit through a solid barrier is an important factor. Also the extent to which the transmission can be focused in a specific direction needs to be considered. Figure 2.03 shows the approximate frequency ranges for the three types of radiation. The factors listed on the left increase in the direction of the arrow, so the bandwidth increases through radio and microwave to infrared but the ability of the waves to penetrate solid objects is greatest for radio waves. Interference is not consistently affected by the frequency.

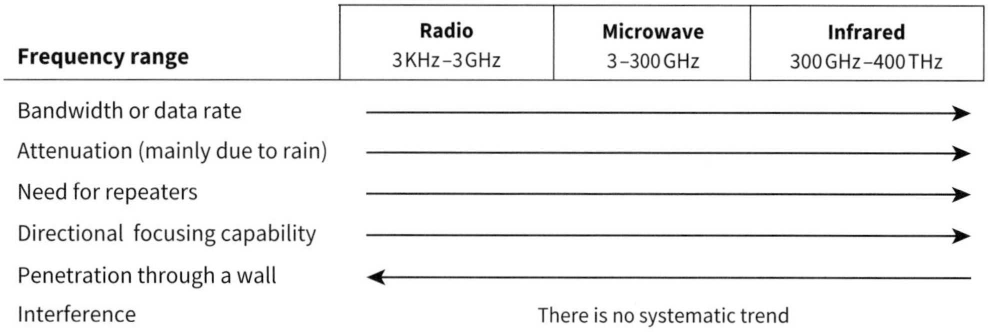

Frequency range	**Radio** 3 KHz–3 GHz	**Microwave** 3–300 GHz	**Infrared** 300 GHz–400 THz
Bandwidth or data rate	⟶	⟶	⟶
Attenuation (mainly due to rain)	⟶	⟶	⟶
Need for repeaters	⟶	⟶	⟶
Directional focusing capability	⟶	⟶	⟶
Penetration through a wall	⟵	⟵	⟵
Interference		There is no systematic trend	

Figure 2.03 Frequency ranges and frequency dependency of factors affecting wireless transmission

The increased attenuation for infrared transmission, which has the highest frequency, leads to it only being suitable for indoor applications. The fact that it will not penetrate through a wall is then of benefit because the transmission cannot escape and cause unwanted interference elsewhere. For most applications, microwave transmission is the option of choice with the improvement in bandwidth being the determining factor.

Comparing cable and wireless transmission

It is worth noting that cables are often referred to as 'guided media' and wireless as 'unguided media'. This is slightly misleading because only radio wave transmission fits this description. It is possible with microwaves or infrared to direct a transmission towards a receiver (as suggested in Figure 2.03).

There are a number of points to make when considering the relative advantages of transmission through a cable or wireless transmission:

- The use of specific wireless transmission frequencies is regulated by government agencies and so permission has to be obtained before wireless transmission is used.
- Outside these frequencies, no permission is needed to use the air for transmission but cables can only be laid in the ground with the permission of landowners.
- For global communications, the two competing technologies are transmission through fibre-optic cables laid underground or on the sea bed and satellite transmission (discussed in Section 2.02); currently neither of these technologies is dominant.
- Interference is much more significant for wireless transmission and its extent is dependent on which frequencies are being used for different applications.

- Repeaters are needed less often for wireless transmission.
- Mobile (cell) phones now dominate Internet use and for these only wireless transmission is possible.
- For home or small office use, wired or wireless transmission is equally efficient; the lack of cabling requirement is the one factor that favours wireless connections for a small network.

2.02 The Internet

Prior to the existence of the Internet there were two major periods of networking development. The first occurred in the 1970s when what are now referred to as wide area networks (WANs) were created. The ARPANET in the USA is the one usually mentioned first in this context. The second period of development was triggered by the arrival of the PC in the 1980s which led to the creation of the first examples of what are now referred to as local area networks (LANs). These developments continued into the 1990s (with, along the way, the addition of metropolitan networks (MANs)) but most importantly with the increasing aim of connecting up what were originally designed and created as independent, stand-alone networks. The era of internetworking had arrived and, in particular, the Internet started to take shape.

It is important to understand that the Internet is not a WAN; it is the biggest internetwork in existence. Furthermore, it has never been designed as a coherent entity; it has just evolved to reach its current form and is still evolving to whatever future form it will take. One of the consequences of the Internet not having been designed is that there is no agreed definition of its structure. However, there is a hierarchical aspect to the structure particularly with respect to the role of an Internet Service Provider (ISP). The initial function of the ISP was to give Internet access to an individual or company. This function is now performed by what may be described as an 'access ISP'. Such ISPs might then connect to what might be called 'middle tier' or regional ISPs which in turn are connected to tier 1 ISPs which may alternatively be termed 'backbone' ISPs. An ISP is a network and connections between ISPs are handled by Internet Exchange Points (IXPs). The other networks which can be considered to share the top of the hierarchy with tier 1 ISPs are the major content providers.

Discussion Point:

How many ISPs or major Internet providers are you familiar with?

Communication systems not originally designed for computer networking provide significant infrastructure support for the Internet. The longest standing example is what is often referred to as POTS (plain old telephone service) but is more formally described as a PSTN (public switched telephone network). At the time of the early period of networking the telephone network carried analogue voice data but digital data could be transmitted provided that a modem was used to convert the digital data to analogue with a further modem used to reverse the process at the receiving end. A dial-up network connection was available which provided modest-speed, shared access when required. However, an organisation could instead pay for a leased line service which would provide a dedicated link with guaranteed transmission speed which was permanently connected. Typically, organisations have made use of leased lines to establish MANs or WANs.

More recently, the PSTNs have upgraded their main communication lines to fibre-optic cable employing digital technology. This has allowed them to offer improved leased line services to ISPs but has also given them the opportunity to provide their own ISP services. In this guise they provide two types of connectivity service. The first is a broadband network connection for traditional network access. The second is WiFi hotspot technology, in which a public place or area is equipped with an access point which has a connection to a wired network that provides Internet access. Mobile devices in the vicinity of the access point can connect to it wirelessly and from this connection gain Internet access.

For users of devices with mobile (cell) phone capability there is an alternative method for gaining Internet access. This is provided by mobile phone companies acting as ISPs. The mobile phone equipped with the appropriate software communicates with a standard cell tower to access the wireless telephone network which in turn can provide a connection to the Internet.

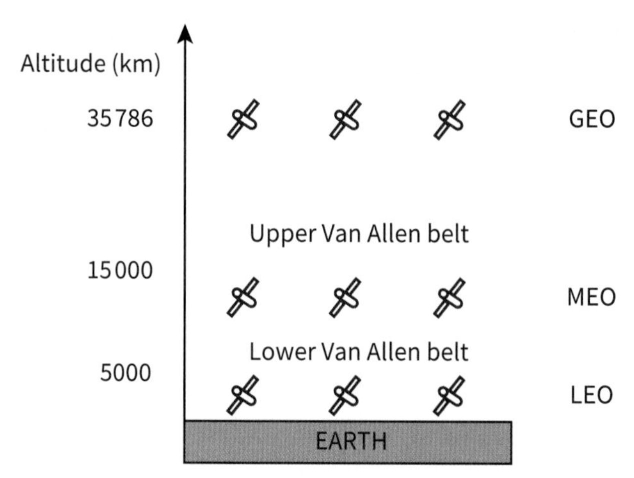

Figure 2.04 Satellite altitudes

Satellites are important components of modern communication systems. Three types of satellite are identified by the altitude at which they orbit. Figure 2.04 shows the positioning with respect to altitude of the different types of satellite. The Van Allen belts are no-go areas full of charged particles.

The highest altitude satellites are in geostationary Earth orbit (GEO) over the equator and these are used to provide long-distance telephone and computer network communication. Only three GEO satellites are needed for full global coverage. Closer to Earth are a group of medium-Earth-orbit (MEO) satellites some of which provide the global positioning system (GPS). Ten MEO satellites are needed for global coverage. Finally, low-Earth-orbit (LEO) satellites work in 'constellations' to supplement the mobile phone networks. Fifty LEO satellites are needed for full global coverage but currently there are several hundreds of them up there.

Because of its height above the ground a satellite has the advantage that it can act as a component in a network and can connect with other components that are separated by greater distances than would be possible if only ground-based components were used. The disadvantage is that the greater transmission distance causes transmission delays which can cause problems for the underlying technology supporting network operation.

2.03 The World Wide Web (WWW)

It is common practice to talk about 'using the web' or 'using the Internet' as though these were just two different ways of saying the same thing. This is not true. The Internet is, as has been described above, an internetwork. By contrast, the World Wide Web (WWW) is a distributed application which is available on the Internet.

Specifically, the web consists of an enormous collection of websites each having one or more web pages. The special feature of a web page is that it can contain hyperlinks which, when clicked, give direct and essentially immediate access to other web pages.

2.04 Internet-supporting hardware

Although the Internet has a structure which is in part hierarchical it is at heart a mesh structure. The device that acts as a node in this mesh is the **router**. Routers are found in what can be described as the backbone fabric of the Internet as well as in the ISP networks. The details of how a router works are discussed in Chapter 17 (Sections 17.03 and 17.04).

At the periphery of the Internet there are different types of network. Whenever networks of a different underlying technology need to communicate, the device needed is a **gateway**. Part of the functionality provided by a gateway can be the same as that provided by a router.

One definition of a **server** is a specialised type of computer hardware designed to provide functionality when connected to a network. A server does not contribute to the functioning of the network itself but, rather, it is a means of providing services via the network. In the context of the Internet, a server may act as any of the following:

- an application server (see Section 2.05)
- a web server (see Section 2.05)
- a domain name server (see Section 2.08)
- a file server
- a proxy server.

KEY TERMS

Router: a device that acts as a node on the Internet

Gateway: a device that connects networks of different underlying technologies

Server: a device that provides services via a network

File server functionality is very often provided by what is called a 'server farm', in which a very large numbers of servers work together in a clustered configuration. Tier 1 content providers use server farms and they are also used in the provision of cloud storage, which an ISP can offer as part of its service portfolio.

One example of the use of a proxy server is when a web server could become overwhelmed by web page requests. When a web page is requested for the first time the proxy server saves a copy in a cache. Then, whenever a subsequent request arrives, it can provide the web page without having to search through the filestore of the main server. At the same time a proxy server can act as a firewall and provide some security against malicious attacks on the server. Security is discussed further in Chapter 8 (Section 8.02).

2.05 Client–server architecture

Following the arrival of the PC in the 1980s it was soon realised that the use of stand-alone PCs was not viable in any large organisation. In order to provide sufficient resource to any individual PC it had to be connected to a network. Initially servers were used to provide extra facilities that the PCs shared (such as filestore, software applications or printing). A further development was the implementation of what came to be known as the 'client–server' architecture. At the time, the traditional architecture of a mainframe computer with connected terminals was still in common use and the client–server approach was seen as a competitor in which networked PCs (the clients) had access to one or more powerful minicomputers acting as servers.

The essence of the client–server architecture as it was first conceived is a distributed computer system where a client carries out part of the processing and a server carries out another part. In order for the client and server to cooperate, software called 'middleware' has to be present. This basic concept still holds in present-day client–server applications but the language used to describe how they operate has changed.

The server is now a 'web server' which is a suite of software that can be installed on virtually any computer system. A web server provides access to a web application. The client is the web browser software. The middleware is now the software that supports the transmission of data across a network together with the provision for scripting (see Section 2.09).

It is worth emphasising that the original uses of the web involved a browser displaying web pages which contained information. There was provision for downloading of this information but the web pages were essentially static. For a client–server application, the web page is 'dynamic' which means that what is displayed is determined by the request made by the client. In this context, there is almost no limit to the variety of applications that can be supported. The only requirement is that the application involves user interaction. The most obvious examples of a client–server application can be categorised as 'ecommerce' where a customer buys products online from a company. Other examples are: e-business, email, searching library catalogues, online banking or obtaining travel timetable information. Most applications require a 'web-enabled' database to be installed on the server or accessible from the server. In contrast, the monthly payroll run typifies the type of application which is unsuitable for implementation as a dynamic web application and will continue to be handled by batch processing.

2.06 Bit streaming

Streaming media are a major component of the use of the Internet for leisure activities like listening to music or watching a video. Before discussing such applications the use of the term bit stream needs an explanation. In general, data prior to transmission is stored in bytes and it is possible to transmit this as a 'byte stream'. However, streamed media is always compressed using techniques discussed in Chapter 1 (Section 1.07). Some compression techniques involve converting each byte into a representation with fewer bits. Thus, to allow the decoding process at the receiver end to work properly, the data must be transferred as a bit stream. So, to summarise, any reference to streaming media would normally imply that bit streaming is used.

For one category of streaming media, the source is a website that has the media already stored. One option in this case is for the user to download a file then listen to it or watch it at some future convenient time. However, when the user does not wish to wait that long there is the streaming option. This option is described as viewing or listening on demand. In this case the delivery of the media and the playing of the media are two separate processes. The incoming media data are received into a buffer created on the user's computer. The user's machine has media player software that takes the media data from the buffer and plays it.

The other category of streaming media is real-time or live transmission. In this case the content is being generated as it is being delivered such as when viewing a sporting event. At the receiver end the technology is the same as before. The major problem is at the delivery end because a very large number of users may be watching simultaneously. The way forward now is to transmit the media initially to a large number of content provider servers which then transmit onwards to individual users.

A crucial point with media streaming is whether the technology has sufficient power to provide a satisfactory user experience. When the media is created it is the intention that the media is to be delivered to the user at precisely the same speed as used for the creation; a song that lasted four minutes when sung for the recording will sound very peculiar if, when it is received by a user, it lasts six minutes. More specifically, the process of delivering the content will be quantified by the bit rate. For example, a relatively poor-quality video can be delivered at a bit rate of 300 kbps but a reasonably good-quality audio file only requires delivery at 128 kbps. Figure 2.05 shows a simple schematic diagram of the components involved in the streaming.

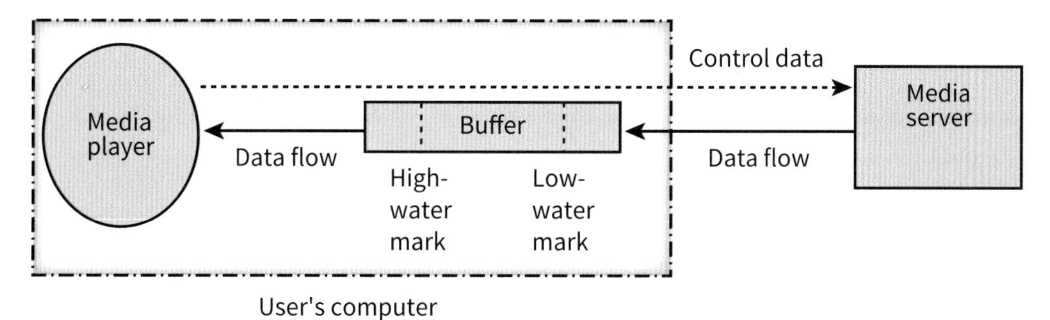

Figure 2.05 Schematic diagram of bit streaming

The bit rate for delivery to the user from the buffer must match the defined rate for the specific media in use but the planned transmission rate to the buffer should be higher to allow for unexpected delays. These rates are controlled by the media player by continuous monitoring of the extent of filling of the buffer in relation to the defined high- and low-water marks. It is essential to have a buffer size that is sufficiently large for it never to get filled.

The rate of transmission to the buffer is limited by the bandwidth of the network connection. For a connection via a PSTN, a broadband link is essential. For good-quality movie presentation the broadband requirement is about 2.5 Mbps. Because this will not be available for all users it is often the practice that an individual video is made available at different levels of compression. The most highly compressed version will be the poorest quality but the bit rate may be sufficiently low for a reasonable presentation with a relatively low bandwidth Internet connection.

TASK 2.01

Consider a bit-streaming scenario for a video where the following values apply:

- The buffer size is 1 MiB
- The low watermark is set at 100 KiB
- The high watermark is set at 900 KiB
- The incoming data rate is 1 Mbps.
- The video display rate is 300 Kbps.

Assume that the video is playing and that the buffer content has dropped to the low-water mark. The media player sets the controls for data input to begin again.

Calculate the amount of data that will be input in two seconds to the buffer and the amount of data that will be removed from the buffer in the same time period.

Repeat the calculation for 4, 6, 8, 10 and 12 seconds.

From this data, estimate when the buffer will have filled up to the high-water mark.

Assuming that the incoming transmission is halted at this time, calculate how long it will be before the buffer content has again fallen to the low-water mark level.

2.07 IP addressing

The functioning of the Internet is based on the implementation of the TCP/IP protocol suite as will be explained in Chapter 17 (Section 17.04). One aspect of this is IP addressing which is used to define from where and to where data is being transmitted.

IPv4 addressing

Currently the Internet functions with IP version 4 (IPv4) addressing. The reason for the strange name is of no consequence but the fact that this was devised in the late 1970s is of considerable consequence. Had the PC and the mobile phone not been invented, the scheme would be still sufficient for needs. Unfortunately for this scheme, these developments did take place and have come to dominate Internet usage.

The IPv4 addressing scheme is based on 32 bits (four bytes) being used to define an **IPv4 address**. It is worth putting this into context. The 32 bits allow 2^{32} different addresses. For big numbers like this it is worth remembering that 2^{10} is approximately 1000 in denary so the 32 bits provide for approximately four billion addresses. The population of the world is about seven billion and it is estimated that approaching half of the world's population has Internet access. From this we can see that if there was a need to supply one IP address per Internet user the scheme would just about be adequate. However, things are not that simple.

KEY TERMS

IPv4 address: a 32-bit long, hierarchical address of a device on the Internet

The original addressing scheme was designed on the basis of a hierarchical address with a group of bits defining a network (a netID) and another group of bits defining a host on that network (a hostID). The aim was to assign a unique universally recognised address for each device on the Internet. The separation into two parts allows the initial transmission to be routed according to the netID. The hostID only needs to be examined on arrival at the identified network. Before proceeding, it is important to note that the term 'host' is a little misleading because some devices, particularly routers, have more than one network interface and each interface requires a different IP address.

The other feature of the original scheme was that allocated addresses were based on the concept of different classes of networks. There were five classes but only the first three need concern us here. The structures used for the addresses are shown in Table 2.02.

Class	Class identifier	Number of bits for netID	Number of bits for hostID
Class A	0	7	24
Class B	10	14	16
Class C	110	21	8

Table 2.02 Address structure for three classes of IPv4 address

It can be seen from Table 2.02 that the most significant bit or bits identify the class. A group of the next most significant bits define the netID and the remaining, least significant, bits define the hostID. The rationale was straightforward. The largest organisations would be allocated to Class A. There could only be 2^7 i.e. 128 of these but there could be 2^{24} distinct hosts for each of them. This compared with 2^{21}, approximately two million, organisations that could be allocated to Class C but each of these could only support 2^8 i.e. 256 hosts.

The problems with this scheme arose once LANs supporting PCs became commonplace. The number of Class B netIDs available was insufficient but if organisations were allocated to Class C the number of hostIDs available was too small. There have been a number of different modifications made available to solve this problem.

Before considering some of these, the representation used for an IP address needs to be introduced. During transmission, the technology is based on the 32-bit binary code for the address; for documentation purposes, a dotted decimal notation is used. Each byte is written as the denary equivalent of the binary number represented by the binary code. For example, the 32 bit code:

10000000 00001100 00000010 00011110

is written in dotted decimal notation as:

128.12.2.30

Classless inter-domain routing (CIDR)

The first approach developed for improving the addressing scheme is called 'classless inter-domain routing' (CIDR). This retains the concept of a netID and a hostID but removes the rigid structure and allows the split between the netID and the hostID to be varied to suit individual need. The simple method used to achieve this is to add an 8-bit suffix to the address that specifies the number of bits for the netID. If, for instance, we define the suffix as 21, that means that 21 bits are used for the netID and there are 11 bits remaining (of a 32-bit address) to specify hostIDs allowing 2^{11}, i.e. 2048, hosts. One example of an IP address using this scheme is shown in Figure 2.06. The 21 bits representing the netID have been highlighted. The remaining 11 bits represent the hostID which would therefore have the binary value 11000001110.

Binary code: **110000110000110000000**11000001110/00010101

netID suffix

Dotted decimal notation: 195.12.6.14/21

Figure 2.06 A CIDR IPv4 address

It should be noted that with this scheme there is no longer any need to use the most significant bit or bits to define the class. However, it does allow already existing Class A, B or C addresses to be used with suffixes 8, 16 or 24, respectively.

TASK 2.02

Create an example of the binary code for a Class C address expressed in CIDR format. Give the corresponding dotted decimal representation.

Sub-netting

A quite different approach, sub-netting, allows further structure in the addressing.

To illustrate an example of this we can consider a medium-sized organisation with about 150 employees each with their own computer workstation. Let's assume that there are six individual department LANs and one head-office LAN. Figure 2.07 shows a schematic diagram of how the LANs would be connected to the Internet if the original scheme were used. The organisation would need seven individual Class C netIDs. Each of these would point to one of the LAN gateways (which have to function as routers). Each netID would be associated with 256 hosts so an organisation with just 150 computer workstations would leave 1642 IP addresses unused and unavailable for use by any other organisation.

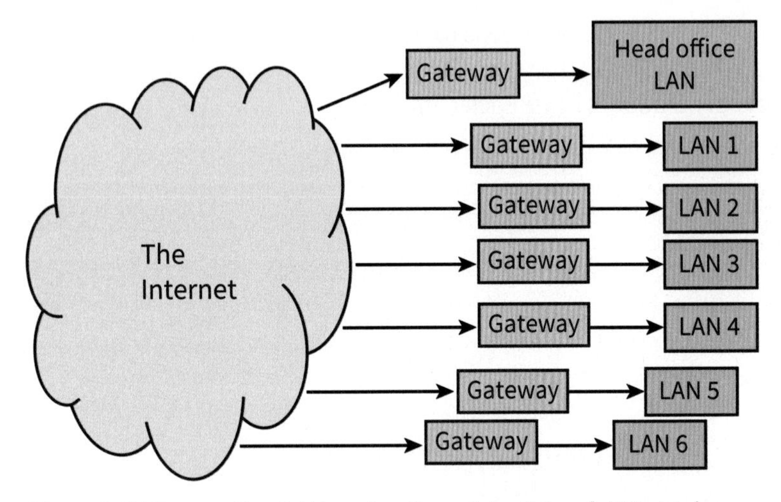

Figure 2.07 Connecting LANs using the original classful IPv4 scheme

The sub-netting solution for this organisation would require allocating just one Class C netID. For example, the IP addresses allocated might be 194.10.9.0 to 194.10.9.255 where the netID comprises the first three bytes, represented by the decimal values 194, 10 and 9.

The sub-netting now works by having a defined structure for the 256 codes constituting the hostID. A sensible solution for this organisation is to use the top three bits as a code for the individual LANs and the remaining five bits as codes for the individual workstations. Figure 2.08 shows a schematic diagram of this arrangement.

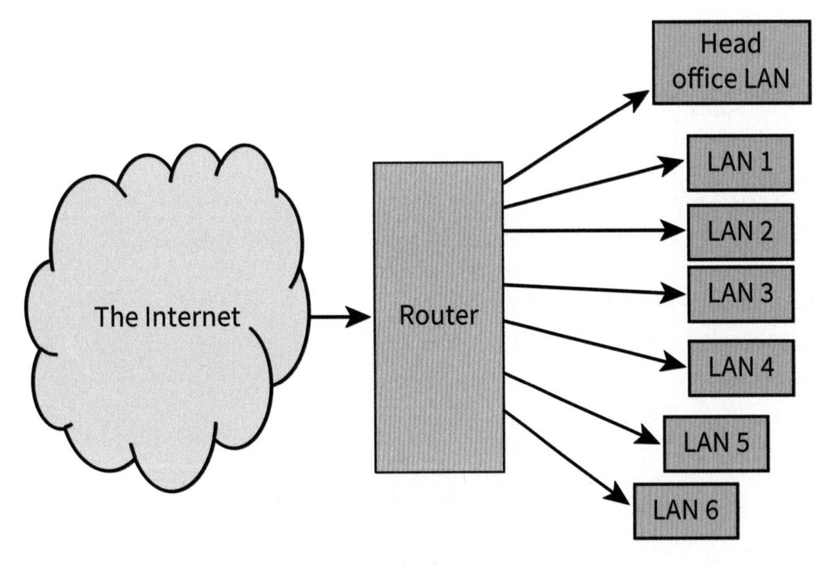

Figure 2.08 Connecting LANS using sub-netting

On the Internet, all of the allocated IP addresses have a netID pointing to the router. The router then has to interpret the hostID to direct the transmission to the appropriate host on one of the LANS. For example:

- hostID code 00001110 could be the address for workstation 14 on the head office LAN (LAN 000).
- hostID code 01110000 would be the address for workstation 16 on LAN 3 (LAN 011).

With 150 workstations the organisation hasn't used all of the 256 allocated IP addresses. However, there are only 106 unused which is a reasonable number to have available in case of future expansion.

Network address translation (NAT)

The final scheme to be considered is different in that it deviates from the principle that every IP address should be unique. In this scheme, provision has been made for large organisations to have private networks (intranets) which use the same protocols as those used for the Internet. One justification for using a private network has always been that this provides extra security because of the isolation from the Internet. However, this is no longer normal practice. Organisations want private networks but they also want Internet connectivity.

The solution for dealing with the addressing is to use network address translation (NAT). Figure 2.09 shows a schematic diagram of how this can be used. The NAT box has one IP address which is visible over the Internet so can be used as a sending address or as a receiving address. Internally the IP addresses have to be chosen from one of the three ranges of IP addresses shown in Table 2.03 that have been allocated for such networks. (You do not need to remember these numbers!)

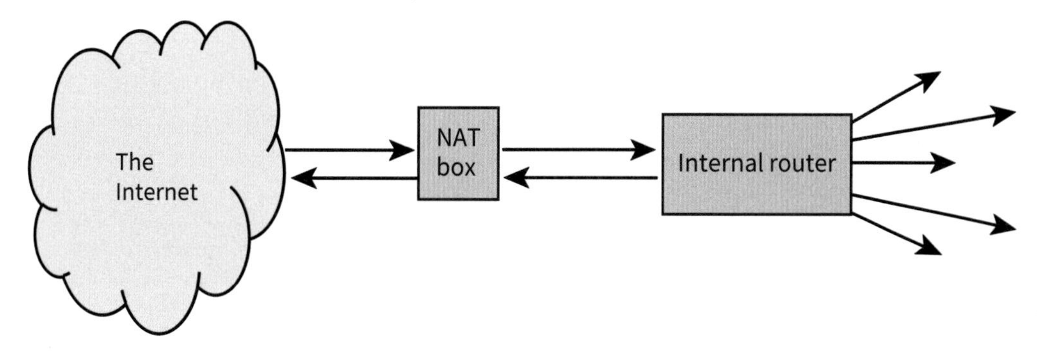

Figure 2.09 An intranet connected to the Internet using a NAT box

Lower bound	Upper bound
10.0.0.0	10.255.255.255
172.16.0.0	172.31.255.255
192.168.0.0	192.168.255.255

Table 2.03 IPv4 addresses to be used in private networks

The important point is that each address can be simultaneously used by any number of different private networks. There is no knowledge of such use on the Internet itself or in any other private network. The interface in the NAT box has software installed to examine each incoming or outgoing transmission. There can be a security check before an incoming transmission is directed to the correct internal address. The diagram shows undefined arrows from the router connected to the NAT box. These indicate that the network structure within the organisation could take many different forms.

Discussion Point:

Can you find out which IP addressing scheme is being used when you are connected to the Internet?

IPv6 addressing

Today there are combinations of IPv4 approaches in use and these allow the Internet to continue to function. Respected sources argue that this cannot continue beyond the current decade. There must soon be a migration to IP version 6 (IPv6), which uses a 128-bit addressing scheme allowing 2^{128} different addresses, a huge number! In practice, this will allow more complex structuring of addresses. Documenting these addresses is not going to be fun. The addresses are written in a colon hexadecimal notation. The code is broken into 16-bit parts with each of these represented by four hexadecimal characters. Fortunately, some abbreviations are allowed. A few examples are given in Table 2.04.

IPv6 address	Comment
68E6:7C48:FFFE:FFFF:3D20:1180:695A:FF01	A full address
72E6::CFFE:3D20:1180:295A:FF01	:0000:0000: has been replaced by ::
6C48:23:FFFE:FFFF:3D20:1180:95A:FF01	Leading zeros omitted
::192.31.20.46	An IPv4 address used in IPv6

Table 2.04 Some examples of IPv6 addresses

Extension Question 2.01

If IPv6 addressing is used, how many addresses would be available per square metre of the Earth's surface? Do you think there will be enough to go round?

2.08 Domain names

In everyday use of the Internet, a user needs to identify a particular web page or email box. The user will not wish to have to identify an IP address using its dotted decimal value. To get round this problem the **domain name system (DNS)** was invented in 1983. The DNS system allocates readable domain names for Internet hosts and provides a system for finding the IP address for an individual domain name.

KEY TERMS

Domain name system (DNS): a hierarchical distributed database installed on domain name servers that is responsible for mapping a domain name to an IP address

The system is implemented as a hierarchical distributed database which is installed on a large number of domain name servers covering the whole of the Internet. The domain name servers are connected in a hierarchy, with powerful replicated root servers at the top of the hierarchy supporting the whole Internet. DNS name space is then divided into non-overlapping zones. Each zone has a primary name server with the database stored on it. Secondary servers get information from this primary server.

As a result the naming system is hierarchical. There are more than 250 top-level domains which are either generic (e.g. .com, .edu, and .gov) or represent countries (e.g. .uk and .nl).

The domain name is included in a universal resource allocator (URL), which identifies a web page, or an email address. A domain is named by the path upward from it. For example, .eng.cisco.com. refers to the .eng subdomain in the .cisco domain of the .com top-level domain (which is the reverse of that used for a pathname of a file).

Looking up a domain name to find an IP address is called 'name resolution'. For such a query there are three possible outcomes:

- If the domain is under the jurisdiction of the server to which the query is sent then an authoritative and correct IP address is returned.
- If the domain is not under the jurisdiction of the server, an IP address can still be returned if it is stored in a cache of recently requested addresses but it might be out of date.
- If the domain in the query is remote then the query is sent to a root server which can provide an address for the name server of the appropriate top-level domain which in turn can provide the address for the name server in the next lower domain. This continues until the query reaches a name server that can provide an authoritative IP address.

2.09 Scripting and HTML in a client–server application

It is possible for an individual to create a client–server-based web application for personal use on an individual computer. This would require downloading appropriate server software, installing the application and using the computer's browser to access the application. However, a better understanding is gained by considering a scenario where a developer has created a web application and made it available for use by remote users.

The application developer has to create the application as one or more web pages. This is a three-stage process. Firstly, for each web page a file has to be created which is written in HTML (HyperText Markup Language). Secondly, a domain name has to be obtained from a web-hosting organisation. Finally, the HTML files have to be uploaded to the server provided by the web-hosting organisation.

The following is the simplest sequence of events associated with a user accessing the application:

1. The user opens up a browser on the client computer.
2. The user types in the URL of the web application or selects it from the bookmark list.
3. The browser asks the DNS system for the IP address.
4. The browser connects to the IP address and sends a request for the web page.
5. The page is sent by the server to the browser.
6. The browser displays the page.

Once the page is displayed the user can activate the application by clicking on a suitable feature or by entering data as appropriate.

HTML

We now need to consider the framework for creating a file using HTML. This is a text file constructed using pairs of what are referred to as 'tags'. The basic overall structure can be represented as:

```
<html>
<head>
</head>
<body>
...
</body>
</html>
```

In between each pair of opening and closing tags there can be any number of lines of text. These can be used to display on the browser screen any or all of the following: text, images, videos, forms, hyperlinks, icons and so on.

The facilities offered by HTML can be supplemented by the inclusion of scripted code, written in JavaScript or PHP.

JavaScript

JavaScript is written by the application developer into the HTML text but its effect is to allow the user at the client end to interact with the application and to cause processing to take place on the client computer. For this to work the browser must have JavaScript enabled. In the early days of the use of JavaScript it was necessary to ensure this and to include explicit reference to the use of JavaScript in the HTML file. However, JavaScript is now the default scripting language so a script runs automatically. The important point is that this has nothing to do with what is installed on the server.

One way to incorporate JavaScript is to write the code in a separate file which is then called from within the HTML. Here we only consider the case when JavaScript code is contained within the HTML itself. This is easily done (and easily recognised in an example HTML file) by containing the script in `script` tags:

```
<script>
...
// Lines of JavaScript code
...
</script>
```


If the developer wants the script to be accessed immediately when the web page is displayed the script tags are included in the HTML header section.

JavaScript is a full-blown computer programming language. Below is an example script which indicates how easy it is to identify some JavaScript within HTML and to see what it is doing. It uses variables (see Section 13.02 for more information about variables) to convert a temperature value input in Celsius to a value output as Fahrenheit. The input uses the `prompt` construct, which provides text to guide the user as to what should be input, and the `alert` construct, which displays an explanatory text with the output value.

```
<!DOCTYPE html>
<html>
<body>
<h1>You can input a value in Celsius and this will be converted to Fahrenheit.</h1>
<script>
var tempC = prompt("Please enter the Celsius value", "");
var tempF = (tempC * 1.8) + 32;
alert("The Fahrenheit value is " + tempF)
</script>
</body>
</html>
```

The question now is when would a developer want to use JavaScript? The answer to this is 'whenever the developer wants the user to have processing carried out on the client computer which does not involve the software running on the server'. This might involve running a program as illustrated by the above simple example. More often the JavaScript is used for collecting data which is to be used by a program running on the server. In particular, data validation and verification can be handled using JavaScript (see Chapter 8, Section 8.04).

PHP

PHP is also a full-blown computer programming language. The difference is that any PHP script is processed on the server. As for JavaScript, the PHP can be contained in a separate file accessed by the HTML. The example considered here will have the script written inside the file containing the HTML. In this case the HTML file must be named with a .php extension rather than the usual .html extension. The PHP code is included within special tags:

```
<?php
...
// Lines of PHP code
...
?>
```

The JavaScript program shown in the previous section could be converted to PHP to run on the server in the following way:

```
<!DOCTYPE html>
<html>
<body>
<?php
 $tempC = $ _ GET["value"];
 $tempF = ($tempC * 2) + 30;
 Echo ("The Fahrenheit value is ");
 Echo $tempF;
?>
</body>
</html>
```


This particular example has to be run by supplying the value for `$tempC` as a parameter to the URL for the file. This is done when the URL is entered into the address bar of the browser. To provide the value 25 the format is to append `?value=25` to the URL following the .php file extension (e.g. `index.php?value=25`).

As before this simple example shows how to identify some PHP code within HTML and see what it is doing. It is worth noting that variables start with $ and they are case sensitive. The first character has to be in lower case so `$ _ GET`, which is the method for getting the parameter value, can be recognised as not being a variable.

The main question is, again, why would a developer choose to include PHP script in some HTML? The answer is that an application will not run quickly if it is constantly transmitting data back and forward between the client computer and the server. For the particular case of a database application it is imperative that the database remains on the server (or within the system of which the server is part) and that only the results of queries are displayed on a browser screen. Also any SQL associated with the use of the database needs to be running on the server not on the client. An example of this will be considered after SQL has been introduced in Chapter 10 (Section 10.6).

Summary

- The main transmission media are copper (twisted pair, coaxial) cables, fibre-optic cables and wireless (radio, microwave, infrared).
- Factors to consider are bandwidth, attenuation, interference and the need for repeaters.
- The Internet is the largest internetwork in existence.
- The World Wide Web is a distributed application accessible on the Internet.
- ISPs provide access to the Internet.
- Internet infrastructure is supported by PSTNs and cell phone companies.
- Client–server architecture is established using a web server and a client browser.
- The current addressing scheme is IPv4, with IPv6 a future contender.
- The DNS resolves a domain name to an IP address.
- JavaScript is used to provide client-side processing.
- PHP is used to provide server-side processing.

Exam-style Questions

1 A new company has been established. It has bought some new premises which consist of a number of buildings on a single site. It has decided that all of the computer workstations in the different buildings need to be networked. They are considering ways in which the network might be set up.

a One option they are considering is to use cabling for the network and to install it themselves.

i Name the three types of cabling that they might consider. [2]

ii Explain two factors, other than cost, that they need to consider when choosing suitable cabling. [4]

b Another option they are considering is to use wireless technology for at least part of the network.

i Explain one option that might be suitable for wireless networking. [2]

ii Identify one advantage, other than cost, of using wireless rather than cable networking. [1]

iii Identify one disadvantage (other than cost) of using wireless rather than cable networking. [1]

c The final option they are considering is to use the services of a PSTN.

i Define what a PSTN is or does. [1]

ii Explain how a PSTN could provide a network for the company. [3]

2 a The Domain Name System is vitally important for Internet users.

i Name the type of software used by the system and the type of hardware on which the software is installed. [2]

ii Name two types of application that use the Domain Name System and for each give a brief description of how it is used. [4]

b In the classful IPv4 addressing scheme, the 32-bit binary code for the address has the top (most significant) bit set to 0 if it is of class A, the top two bits set to 10 if class B or the top three bits set to 110 if class C. In a document an IPv4 address has been written as 205.124.16.152.

i Give the name for this notation for an IP address and explain how it relates to the 32-bit binary code. [2]

ii Identify the class of the address and explain your reason. [2]

iii Explain why an IPv4 address defines a netID and a hostID. [3]

c If the CIDR scheme for an IPv4 address is used the IP address 205.124.16.152 would be written as:

205.124.16.152/24

State the binary code for the hostID in this address with a reason. [2]

3 a A client–server web application has been developed which uses a file containing the following code:

```
<!DOCTYPE html>
<html>
<body>
<h1>We can give you an estimate of how many you will need if you are tiling a floor
with our tiles.
You need to tell us the length and the width of the room
(in metres).</h1>
<script>
var length = prompt("enter the room length", "");
var width = prompt("enter the room width", "");
var tileSize = 0.25;
var numberOfTiles = (length * width)/tileSize;
alert ("The estimate for the number of tiles needed is " + numberOfTiles);
</script>
</body>
</html>
```

i Name the role of the person who would create this file. [1]

ii Identify where this file would be stored. [1]

iii A browser is needed to run the application. State where the browser software is installed. [1]

b The file uses JavaScript.

i Identify two component parts of the file which involve JavaScript and explain their purpose. [4]

ii Explain the sequence of events executed by the client computer and the web server when this application is used. [6]

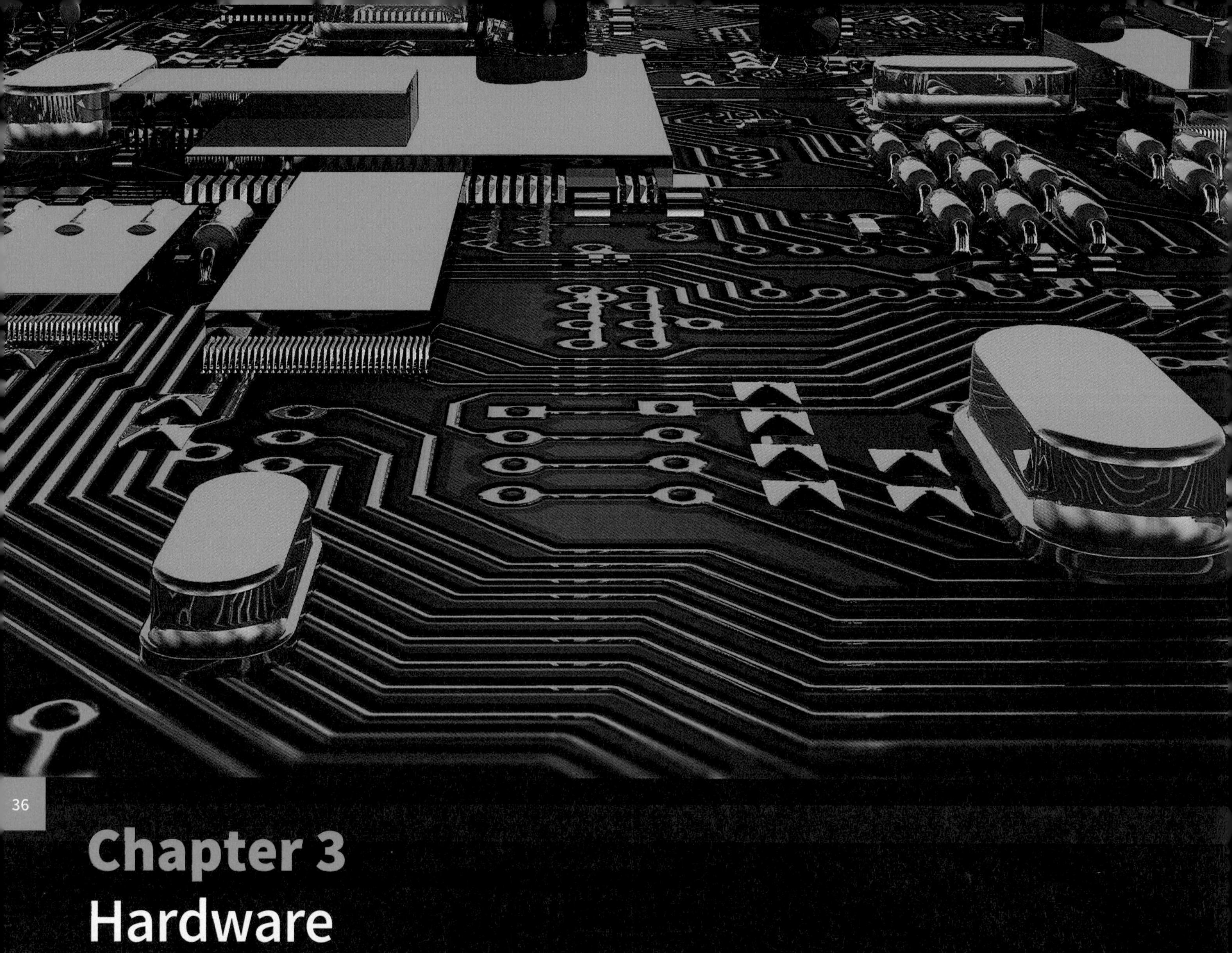

Chapter 3
Hardware

Learning objectives

By the end of this chapter you should be able to:

- show understanding of the need for primary storage
- show understanding of the need for secondary (including removable) storage
- identify hardware devices used for input, output, secondary storage
- show understanding of the basic internal operation of specific types of device.

3.01 The memory system

As a broad generalisation it can be said that there are two main uses of a computer system. The first is to run programs.

In the discussion of computer system architecture in Chapter 5 (Section 5.01) you will see that the simplest model consists of a processor with access to a stored program. The history of computing is one of increasing performance. In the context of increasing performance of the system in running programs, the first requirement is for the speed of the processor to increase. However, this potential for improvement can only be realised if the time taken for the processor to access the stored program decreases to match the increased processor speed. The reality so far has been that access speeds have improved but they haven't kept pace fully with the improvement in processor speeds.

The second main use of a computer system is to store data. Here the major issues with regards to increasing performance are capacity and cost; access speeds are not so important.

The terminology used to describe components for storing programs and data is not always consistent. One variation is to distinguish between memory as the component which the processor can access directly and the (file-) store used for long-term storage. An alternative is to distinguish between the primary and the secondary storage.

The memory system hierarchy is a useful concept for considering the choice of components in a memory system. Figure 3.01 uses a simplified version of a memory system hierarchy to show the trends in the important factors affecting this choice. The factors increase in the direction of the arrow.

Component	Category
Register	Processor component
Cache memory	Primary storage
Main memory	
Hard disk	Secondary storage
Auxiliary storage	

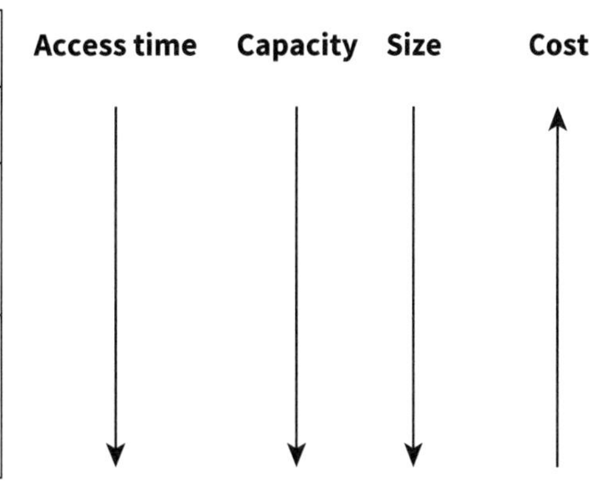

Figure 3.01 Trends in the factors affecting the choice of memory components

The individual entries in the Component column are discussed in Sections 3.02 and 3.03. Computer users would really like to have a large amount of primary storage that costs little and allows quick access. This is not possible; the fastest components cost more and have limited capacity. In practice, the choice made is a compromise.

It could be argued that there is a need for secondary storage because the use of only primary storage would be far too expensive. However, it is more sensible simply to recognise that long-term storage of data requires separate dedicated components.

3.02 Memory components

The processor has direct access to three types of storage component. The registers, as discussed in Chapter 5 (Section 5.02), are contained within the processor. External to the processor there is cache memory and main memory, which together constitute the primary storage. Cache memory is used to store data that at any time is the most likely to be needed again by the processor.

There is another way of categorising memory components. The first category is called **random-access memory (RAM)**. This is a potentially misleading term because a programmer does not expect a program to make random decisions about which memory location should be accessed.

KEY TERMS

Random-access memory (RAM): volatile memory that can be read from or written to any number of times

Read-only memory (ROM): non-volatile memory that cannot be written to but can be read from any number of times

The name has been chosen because such memory can be accessed at any location independently of which previous location was used (it might have been better called 'direct-access memory'). A better description is read–write memory because RAM can be repeatedly read from or written to. Another distinguishing characteristic of RAM is that it is volatile which means that when the computer system is switched off the contents of the memory are lost.

There are two general types of RAM technology. Dynamic RAM (DRAM) is constructed from capacitors which leak electricity and therefore need regularly recharging (every few milliseconds) to maintain the identity of the data stored. Static RAM (SRAM) is constructed from flip-flops (discussed in Chapter 18 (Section 18.02)) which continue to store data indefinitely while the computer system is switched on.

SRAM provides shorter access time but unfortunately it compares unfavourably with DRAM in all other aspects. DRAM is less expensive to make, it can store more bits per chip and despite the need for recharging it requires less power to operate. So, once more, a compromise is needed. The norm is for cache memory to be provided by SRAM with the main memory being constructed from DRAM technology.

The second category of memory component is called **read-only memory (ROM)**. Again this name does not give a full picture of the characteristics of this type of component. ROM shares the random-access or direct-access properties of RAM except that it cannot be written to. The other important characteristic is that the data in ROM is not lost when the computer system is switched off; the memory is non-volatile.

ROM has specialised uses involving the storage of data or programs that are going to be used unchanged over and over again. ROM may be programmable (PROM) or erasable PROM (EPROM) or even electrically erasable PROM (EEPROM). These terms relate to the manufacture and installation of the ROM and do not impact on its basic use in a computer system.

Discussion Point:

Can you find out what memory components are in the computer system you are using and any details about them such as the type and storage capacity?

3.03 Secondary storage devices

Before discussing storage devices it is appropriate to discuss some terminology that can confuse. For any hardware device, whether an integral part of the computer system or a connected peripheral, its operation requires appropriate software to be installed. This software is referred to as the 'device driver'. This should not be confused with the term 'drive' associated specifically with a storage device. Furthermore, the term 'drive' was initially introduced to refer to the hardware that housed a storage medium item and provided the physical mechanism for transferring data to it or reading data from it. However, as so often happens, such distinctions are often ignored. As a result, for example, references to a 'hard disk', a 'hard disk drive' and to a 'hard drive' have the same meaning.

Magnetic media

Magnetic media have been the mainstay of filestore technology for a very long time. The invention of magnetic tape for sound recording pre-dates the invention of the computer by many years so, not unexpectedly, this technology was the first to be utilised as a storage device. In contrast the hard disk was invented as a technology specifically for computer storage, arriving a few years later than the first use of magnetic tape.

For either type of magnetic media the interaction with it is controlled by a read head and a write head. A read head uses the basic law of physics that a state of magnetisation will affect an electrical property; a write head uses the reverse law. Although they are separate devices the two heads are combined in a read–write head. The two alternative states of magnetisation are interpreted as a 1 or 0.

A schematic diagram of a hard disk is shown in Figure 3.02. Points to note about the physical construction are that there is more than one platter (disk) and that each platter has a read–write head for each side. The platters spin in unison. The read–write heads are attached to actuator arms which allow the heads to move over the surfaces of the platters. The motion of each actuator head is synchronised with the motion of the other heads. A cushion of air ensures that a head does not touch a platter surface.

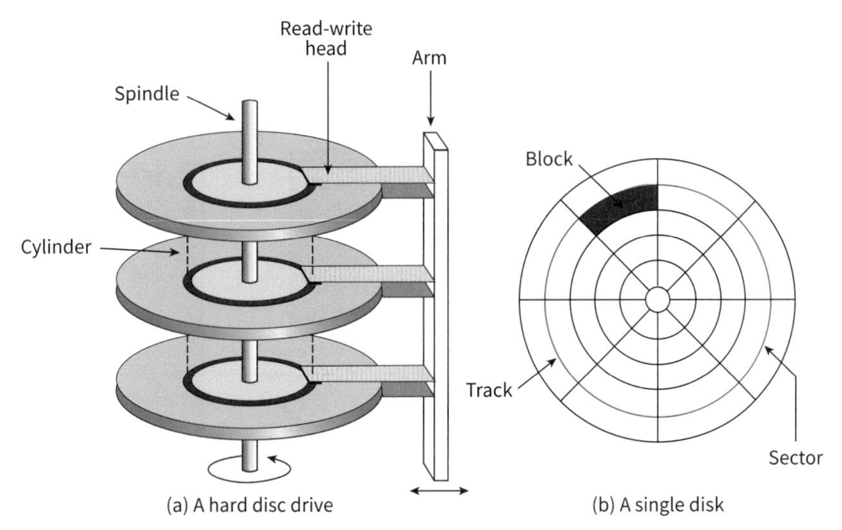

Figure 3.02 A schematic drawing of the components of a hard disk drive

The logical construction is that data is stored in concentric tracks. Each track consists of a sequence of bits but these are formatted into sectors where each sector contains a defined number of bytes. The sector becomes the smallest unit of storage. To store a file, a sufficient number of sectors have to be allocated but these may or may not be adjacent to each other. As files are created and subsequently deleted or edited the use of the sectors becomes increasingly fragmented which degrades the performance of the disk. A defragmentation program can reorganise the allocation of sectors to files to restore performance. This is discussed in Chapter 7 (Section 7.03).

A hard drive is considered to be a direct-access read–write device because any sector can be chosen for reading or writing. However, the data in a sector has to be read sequentially.

The above account only gives a simplified version of hard drive technology. One particular omission is consideration of how manufacturers can effectively deal with the fact that the physical length of a track increases from the innermost track to the outermost track. If this fact is ignored the data storage capacity must be less than it potentially could be. The other omission is the simple fact that the storage capacity of disk drives has continued to improve and sizes have continued to shrink. There is every reason to believe that this performance improvement is due to continue for some time.

There has always been a need for a storage device that can be removed from the computer system. For large installations an organisation's requirement is normally driven by security concerns and the need for suitable back-up procedures. For individuals the need may be the storage of personal data or personally owned programs or simple transfer of data between computers or between a computer and, for example, a camera. The first technology to dominate the use by individuals was the floppy disk but this was *superseded* by optical storage.

Optical media

As with the magnetic tape medium, optical storage was developed from existing technology not associated with computing systems. The compact disc (CD) evolved into CD digital audio (CD-DA) and this became the technology used in the CD-ROM. This was extensively used for distributing software but was of no value as a replacement for the floppy disk. The read–write version (CD-RW) which came later provided the needed write functionality. However, the CD has now given way to the DVD (originally 'digital video disc' but later renamed as 'digital versatile disc'). The latest and most powerful technology is the Blu-ray disc (BD).

A schematic diagram of an optical disc drive is shown in Figure 3.03. The disc spins and the laser beam is reflected from a surface which is sandwiched between a substrate and a protective outer coating. For a CD-ROM, the reflective surface is manufactured with indentations, called 'pits', separated by what are referred to as 'lands'. When the disc is being read, the travel of the laser beam to a pit causes a difference in phase compared to reflection from a land. This phase difference is recognised by the photodiode detector and attached circuitry and interpreted as a 1 or 0. For CD-RW and DVD-RW technologies, the reflective surface is a special alloy material. When data is being written to the disc (the 'burn' process) the heat generated by the absorption of the laser light changes the material to liquid form. Depending on the intensity of the laser light the material reverts to either a crystalline or an amorphous solid form when it cools. When the disc is read, the laser light is reflected from the crystalline solid but not from the amorphous solid allowing the coding of a 1 or 0.

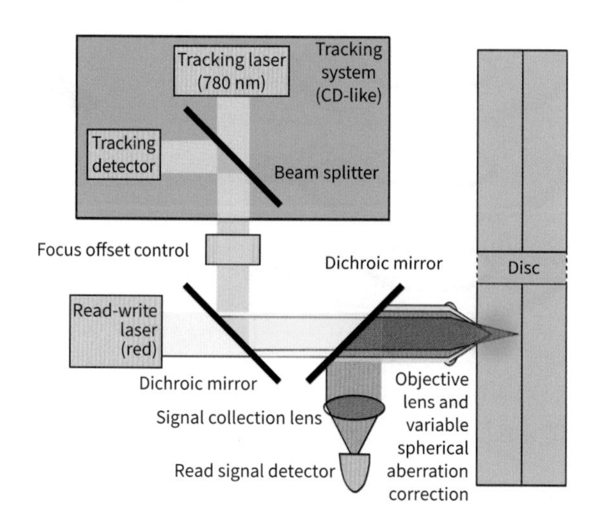

Figure 3.03 A schematic drawing of an optical disc drive

While the disc is spinning the optical head that directs the laser beam is made to move so that the point of contact of the laser beam with the disc follows a single spiral path from the centre of the disc to the periphery. Despite there only being this one path the formatting of the data into sectors allows the disc to be used as a direct-access device just as is the case for a magnetic hard disk.

Another similarity with magnetic disk technology is that the storage capacity is dependent on how close together individual physical representations of a binary digit can get. There are two aspects governing this for an optical disc. The first is that if the disc is spinning at constant revolutions per second the outer part of the disc travels faster than the inner part. Early technology counteracted this by spinning at a constantly changing speed keeping the bit density constant along the spiral path. The second is that the wavelength of the light controls how well the light can be focused; the shorter the wavelength the better the focus. The original infrared diode laser used in a CD-ROM has much longer wavelength than the red laser light used in a DVD. The more recently used blue laser light has an even shorter wavelength. This change in wavelength is one of the reasons for the improvements in the storage capacity of the modern technology.

Solid-state media

Despite the continued improvement in optical technology there is now a powerful competitor in solid-state storage. The basis for this is 'flash' memory which is often said to be a form of EEPROM but where the programmable aspect is part of the normal use. Flash memory is a semiconductor technology with no moving parts. The circuits consist of arrays of transistors acting as memory cells. The most frequently used technology is called 'NAND' because the basic circuitry resembles that of a NAND logic gate (see Section 4.03) with the memory cells connected in series. The special feature is that blocks of memory cells can have their contents erased all at once 'in a flash'. Furthermore, before data can be written to a block of cells in the memory the data in the block first has to be erased. When data is read, a whole block of data has to be read in one operation.

The technology can be used for 'solid-state' drives, which can replace hard disk drives. The more frequent use is either in a memory card or in a USB flash drive. In the latter case the flash memory is incorporated in a device with the memory chip connected to a standard USB connector. This is currently the technology of choice for removable data storage but how long this will remain so is very uncertain with alternative technologies such as phase-change random access memory (PRAM) already under development.

Extension Question 3.01

Carry out some research into the technologies currently available for storage.

Consider first the options available for the storage device inside a laptop computer. Create a table showing cost, storage capacity and access speed for typical examples. Then consider the options available for peripheral storage devices. Create a similar table for these.

Can you identify which technologies remain viable and which ones are becoming uncompetitive? Are there any new technologies likely to come into common use?

3.04 Computer graphics

The technologies associated with presenting a computer graphic as a screen display or as a printed page share common limitations. The nature of these was well understood by the newspaper printing industry many years before computers were invented. The issue was how to include pictures that were originally photographs. A photograph has continuous tones but a printer at any position on a page could only print black or nothing. The solution to this was halftoning. This technique approximated a grey tone by printing an array of black dots; varying the size of the dots changed the tone displayed. The technique, of course, relies on the limitations of the human eye which does not register the individual dots if they are sufficiently small.

A variation of this technique is used in computer graphic presentation. Normally, neither screen nor printer technology can produce varying size dots but the same effect can be produced by varying the number of dots created in what can be described as a halftone cell. It is now standard practice for grey-scale images or colour images to be presented using a halftoning technology. This requires a raster image processor, which can be a combination of hardware and software, to control the conversion of data stored in a graphics file to the physical screen display or printed page.

3.05 Screens and associated technologies

Screen technology associated with computer systems has a long evolutionary history. For many years the only example was the visual display unit (VDU) which was used as a computer monitor or terminal. The VDU employed the cathode ray tube (CRT) technology used in a television set but the functionality offered by the device was limited to recording keyboard input and displaying text output.

Computer mouse

A significant step forward came with the introduction of graphical user interfaces (GUIs) as standard features for microcomputer systems in the 1980s. The screen technology remained the same but the functionality was completely transformed by the arrival of screen windows and icons. To use the GUI effectively, the user needed a pointing device. The computer mouse was introduced for this purpose. The screen became not just an output device but also an input device activated by a mouse click.

There are two aspects to computer mouse technology. The first is the behaviour instigated by a button click which needs no further discussion; the second is the operation of the mouse in controlling a screen cursor. The important point to emphasise here is that a mouse has no knowledge of an absolute position; all it can do is allow a relative movement to be recorded so that it can influence the screen cursor position.

The computer mouse introduced initially contained a rubber ball held in contact with two rollers set perpendicularly to each other. Figure 3.04 shows a schematic diagram. As the mouse moves the rubber ball rotates causing one or both rollers to rotate. Each roller is attached to a spindle on which there is a disc with holes arranged around the outer edge. A light beam and detector are arranged so that the intermittent transmission of the light through the holes in the disc is recorded as the disc rotates and the circuitry attached to the pair of detectors then sends the appropriate data to the computer to activate movement of the screen cursor.

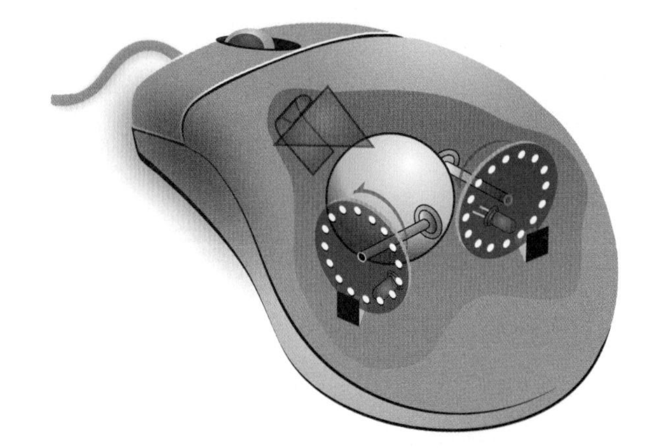

Figure 3.04 The components of a mechanical mouse

More recently the tracker ball mouse was phased out and the optical mouse was introduced. This technology dispenses with the mechanical aspects associated with the movement of a rubber ball. The mouse shines a light beam from a light emitting diode down onto the surface the mouse is resting on. This light is reflected back on to a sensor fitted to the underside of the mouse. As the mouse is moved along the surface the sensor acts like a camera taking successive images of the surface. Image processing software then interprets these images to establish the movement that has taken place and this data is transmitted to the computer as before.

Screen display

We can now consider the technology associated with the creation of a screen display. Chapter 1 (Section 1.04) described how an image could be stored as a bitmap built up from pixels. Screen displays are also based on the pixel concept but with one major difference: a screen pixel consists of three sub-pixels typically one each for red, green and blue. Varying the level of light emitted from the individual sub-pixels allows a full range of colours to be displayed.

There have been a number of very different technologies used to create a pixel. In the original cathode ray tube (CRT) technology, there is no individual component for a pixel. The inner surface of the screen is covered with phosphor, which is a material that emits light when irradiated. An individual pixel is created by controlling the direction of the electron beam irradiating the phosphor. This is modified for colour displays where individual red, green and blue phosphors are arranged so as to create an array of pixels.

Phosphors are also used in one of the major flat-screen technologies, the plasma screen. There is now a construction based on individual cells constituting a matrix of pixels. Each cell contains plasma and a phosphor. When an electrical charge is applied to the plasma it releases radiation that hits the phosphor and causes light emission. Each pixel or, more accurately, each sub-pixel is a light source. The sub-pixel emits one of red, green or blue light.

KEY TERMS

Liquid-crystal display (LCD): a screen back-lit by light-emitting diodes and with liquid crystal cells sandwiched between polarisers

In the flat-screen technology that is most used at present, the pixel is not a light source. The **liquid-crystal display (LCD)** screen has individual cells containing a liquid crystal to create the pixel matrix but these do not emit light. The pixel matrix is illuminated by back-lighting and each pixel can affect the transmission of this light to cause the on-screen display. A typical arrangement is shown in Figure 3.05.

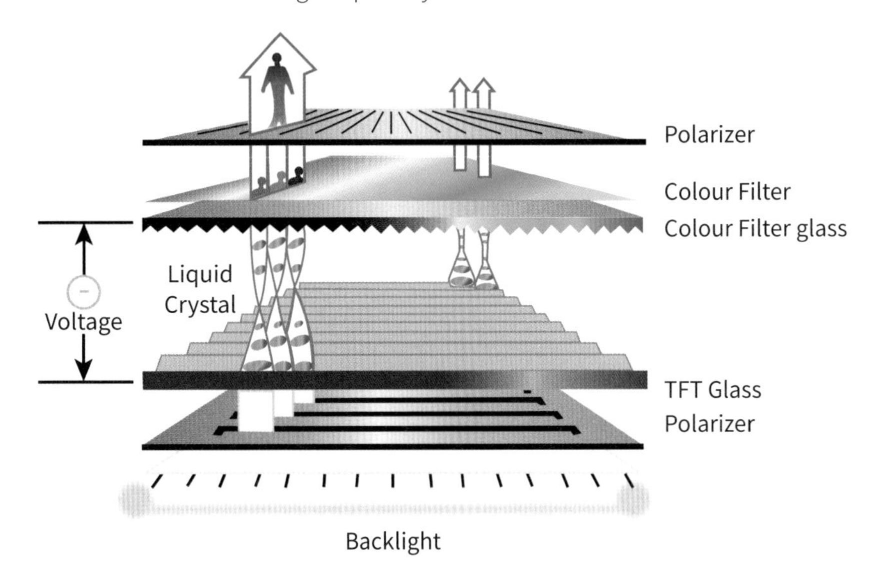

Figure 3.05 The components of a liquid-crystal display screen

The back-lighting is usually provided by light-emitting diodes (LEDs). The important feature is the use of polarised light directed towards the pixel matrix and the use of a further polariser between the pixel matrix and the screen. If a voltage is applied to an individual pixel cell the alignment of the liquid crystal molecules is affected and in turn this can change the polarisation of the light and therefore affect what is displayed on the screen. There are a number of different technologies but the principle of their functioning is the same and colour displays use red, green and blue combinations as before.

More recently, a different technology has been introduced. This is based on the use of an organic light-emitting diode (OLED) to create the pixel. The OLED is used directly as a light source so this technology requires no back-lighting.

Touch screens

As well as providing improved display capability, flat-screen technology has allowed a new mechanism for interaction with the display. Touch-screen technology is now a major feature of a whole range of computer-based products.

Extension Question 3.02

Consider the different possibilities for interacting with a screen display. Create a table showing the advantages and disadvantages for each technique.

The modern version of a touch-sensitive screen has the layers of technology providing the display with extra layers of technology added immediately beneath the surface of the screen. There have been two approaches used. The first is the **resistive touch screen**. This type has two layers separated by a thin space beneath the screen surface. The screen is not rigid so when a finger presses on to the screen the pressure moves the topmost of these two separated layers so that it makes contact with the lower layer. The point of contact creates a voltage divider in the horizontal and vertical directions. These allow the position of the point of contact to be transmitted to the processor.

The second technology is the **capacitive touch screen**. This does not require a soft screen but instead makes use of the fact that a finger touching a glass screen can cause a capacitance change in a circuit component immediately below the screen. The most effective technology is projective capacitive touch (PCT) with mutual capacitance. This has a circuit beneath the screen which contains an array of capacitors. This enables multi-touch technology, which allows more functionality than just pointing at one location on a screen.

KEY TERMS

Resistive touch screen: a flexible surface which causes contact between electrically resistive layers beneath when touched

Capacitive touch screen: a rigid surface above a conductive layer which undergoes a change in electrical state when a finger touches the screen

Discussion Point:

Investigate which flat-screen technologies are used in any computer, laptop, tablet or mobile/cell phone that you use. Discuss the benefits and drawbacks associated with their use.

3.06 Keyboards and keypads

The standard method of inputting significant amounts of text data into a computer system has always been to use a QWERTY keyboard (named after the top left row of alphabetic characters). The central part of the keyboard layout matches that of a standard typewriter, allowing skilled typists to continue to function effectively. When numbers only need to be input a skilled operator will use a numeric keypad. What might be described as a traditional mobile phone has a different type of keypad which can be used to input text data. The technology underpinning all of these devices is the same assuming that there are actual physical keys to be used.

When the keyboard is being used to input text it appears as though a key press immediately transfers the appropriate character to the computer screen but this is an illusion. The key press has to be converted to a character code which is transmitted to the processor. The processor, under the control of the operating system, ensures that the text character is displayed on the screen. The same process takes place if the keyboard is used to initiate some action, perhaps by using a shortcut key combination, except that the processor has to respond by taking the requested action.

To achieve this functionality the keyboard has electrical circuitry together with its own microprocessor and a ROM chip. The keys are positioned above a key matrix which consists of a set of rows of wires and another set of columns of wires. Pressing a key causes contact at a specific intersection. The microprocessor continuously tests to see if any electrical circuit involving a row wire and a column wire has become closed. When the microprocessor recognises that a circuit has become closed, it can identify the particular intersection that is causing this. It then uses data stored in the ROM to create the appropriate character code relating to the key associated with that intersection and sends this code to the processor. The same principles apply if two keys are pressed simultaneously.

3.07 Printers, scanners and plotters

Inkjet printer

Two technologies have come to dominate the printing of documents from data stored in a computer system. The technologies can be used irrespective of whether text or an image is being printed. The technology that is cheapest to buy is the inkjet printer but the purchase price is soon dwarfed by the cost of replacement ink. A genuine advantage of an inkjet printer is its relatively small size.

The working principle of an inkjet printer is very simply explained: a sheet of paper is fed in; the printhead moves across the sheet depositing ink on to the paper; the paper is moved forward a fraction and the printhead carries out another traversal and so on until the sheet has been fully printed. The precision of the mechanical operations involved is one of the factors governing the quality of the printing. The other factor is the accuracy of the process of applying the ink to the paper. The printhead consists of nozzles that spray droplets on to the paper. The number of nozzles in a printhead is truly amazing, running into the thousands. This is only possible because the manufacturing process can produce an individual nozzle with a diameter considerably less than that of a human hair. There are two alternative technologies for causing the ejection of the ink droplet (thermal bubble or piezoelectric) but neither has significant advantages or disadvantages.

Ink is supplied to the printhead from one or more ink cartridges. Often the printhead is part of the cartridge. For black and white printing only one cartridge is required but for colour printing more are needed. The simplest technology for colour printing uses three colour cartridges (one for each of the subtractive primaries: cyan, magenta and yellow) in addition to the black cartridge. Suitable positioning of combinations of overlapping droplets in principle allows any colour to be created. Good quality printing requires a printing resolution of several hundred dots per inch which is achievable because of the large number and small size of the nozzles. The number of dots per inch is defined by the printhead geometry and cannot be changed but the number of dots per pixel can be dictated by the controlling software. Increasing the number gives better colour definition for the pixel but the pixel size is increased giving poorer resolution for the image. Better resolution can only be achieved with poorer colour definition.

Laser printer

The alternative technology is the laser printer. Laser printers have always been more expensive to buy and used to offer much higher-quality printing but the comparison is no longer so clear cut.

A schematic diagram of the workings of a laser printer is shown in Figure 3.06. The operation can be summarised as follows:

1. The drum is given an electric charge.
2. The drum starts to revolve step by step.
3. At each step a laser beam is directed by the mirror and lens assembly to a sequence of positions across the width of the drum.
4. At each position the laser is either switched off to leave the charge on the drum or switched on to discharge the position.
5. This process repeats until a full page electrostatic image has been created.
6. The drum is coated with a charged toner which only sticks to positions where the drum has been discharged.
7. The drum rolls over a sheet of paper which is initially given an electric charge.
8. The sheet of paper is discharged and then is passed through heated rollers to fuse the toner particles and seal the image on the paper surface.
9. The drum is discharged before the process starts again for the next page.

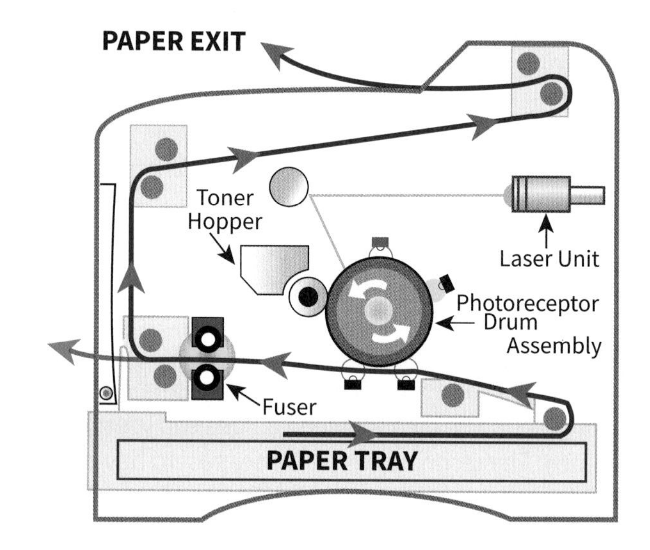

Figure 3.06 A schematic diagram of a laser printer

The above sequence represents black and white printing. For colour printing, separate toners are required for the colours and the process has to take place for each colour. Although the technology is completely different the logical aspect of the printing is the same as that for inkjet printing. Colours are created from cyan, magenta, yellow and black. The technology produces dots; quality depends on the number of dots per inch and software can control the number of dots per pixel.

It is normal nowadays for a laser printer or an inkjet printer to be a multi-functional device. It will have the capability to act as a flatbed scanner with the option for this also to provide a photocopying facility. Effectively, a scanner reverses the printing process in that it takes an image and creates from it a digital representation rather than the digital representation being used to create an image on paper. The principles of the operation of a typical scanner are straightforward. The sheet of paper is held in a fixed position and a light source covering the width of the paper moves from one end of the sheet to the other. The reflected light is directed by a system of mirrors and lenses on to a charge-coupled device (CCD). The finer details of how a CCD works are not important but the three aspects to note are:

- It consists of an array of photo-sensitive cells.
- It produces for each cell an electrical response proportional to the light intensity.
- It needs an analogue-to-digital converter to create a digital value to be stored.

Graphics plotter and 3D printer

In Chapter 1 (Section 1.04) the difference between a bitmap and a vector graphic was discussed. If a vector graphic file has been created the image can be displayed on a screen or printed by first converting the file to a bitmap version. However, specialised technical applications often require a more accurate representation to be created on paper. This requires the use of a graphics plotter. A plotter uses pens to write, usually, on a large sheet of paper constrained by sprockets along one pair of sides. The sprockets can move the paper forwards or backwards and pens can either be parked or in use at any given time. The controlling circuitry and software can create the drawing directly from the original vector graphic file.

Engineers and designers working in manufacturing are potential users of graph plotters. They are also potential users of the 3D printer. The name could be said to be a little misleading but its meaning is generally understood. It is a device that offers an alternative technology for computer-aided manufacture (CAM).

The original concept was that the starting point is a 3D design created in a suitable computer-aided design (CAD) package. The design is split into layers. The data for the first layer is transmitted to the 3D printer. Rather than using ink to draw the layer, the 3D printer uses a nozzle to squirt material on to the printer bed to create a physical layer to match the design. This process is repeated for successive layers. When the whole object has been formed it has to be cured in some way to ensure that the layers are, in effect, welded together and the material has been converted to the form required for the finished product.

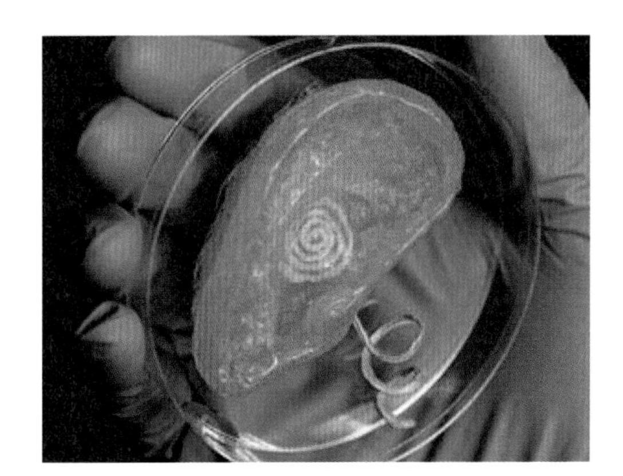

Figure 3.07 A bionic ear created using a 3D printer

The technology is very versatile and still under development. Figure 3.07 shows a striking example. This bionic ear was constructed with three 'inks'. Silicone was used for the basic structure, a gel containing chondrocyte cells and silicone infused with silver nanoparticles were the other two 'inks'. The final curing step involved incubation in a culture medium to allow the chondrocyte cells to produce cartilage. The only missing component was skin.

3.08 Input and output of sound

IP telephony and video conferencing are the two obvious technologies requiring voice input to a computer system and voice output from a computer system. Voice recognition is an alternative technique for data input to a computer.

For input, a microphone is needed. This is a device that has a diaphragm, a flexible material which is caused to vibrate by an incoming sound. If the diaphragm is connected to suitable circuitry the vibration can cause a change in an electrical signal. A condenser microphone uses capacitance change as the mechanism; an alternative is to use a piezoelectric crystal. The electrical signal has to be converted to a digital signal by an analogue-to-digital converter before it can be processed by a sound (audio) card inside the computer.

For output, a loudspeaker or speaker is needed. This is involved in what is effectively the reverse process to that for input. The computer sound card produces a digital signal which is converted to analogue by a digital-to-analogue converter. The analogue signal is fed to the speaker. In the traditional technology the current flows through a coil suspended within the magnetic field provided by a permanent magnet in the speaker. As the direction of the current keeps reversing, the coil moves backwards and forwards. This movement controls the movement of a diaphragm which causes sound to be created.

Summary

- Primary storage is main memory, consisting of RAM (DRAM or SRAM) and ROM.
- Secondary storage includes magnetic, optical and solid-state media.
- Input devices include the mouse, keyboard, scanner and microphone.
- Output devices include screens (CRT, plasma, LCD, OLED), printers (inkjet, laser and 3D), plotters and speakers.
- Touch screens (capacitive or resistive) are used for both input and output.

Exam-style Questions

1 a A typical computer will have RAM and ROM.

i Describe two differences between RAM and ROM. [4]

ii Name one similarity between RAM and ROM. [1]

iii RAM may be either DRAM or SRAM. Explain the difference between these. [2]

b Secondary storage can be magnetic, optical or solid state.

i For each type of storage identify one feature of the basic internal operation which is different from that of the other two types. [3]

ii For two of the three types of storage identify two similarities in the basic internal operation. [2]

2 a Pressing a key on a computer keyboard can cause a character to be displayed on the computer screen.

i Identify four aspects of the basic internal operation of a keyboard that makes this happen. [4]

ii Describe an alternative method for a user to enter some text into a computer system. [2]

b There are two types of printer commonly used with a PC.

i Describe two differences between how an inkjet printer works and how a laser printer works. [4]

ii Identify two similarities in the logical approach used in these two types of printer. [2]

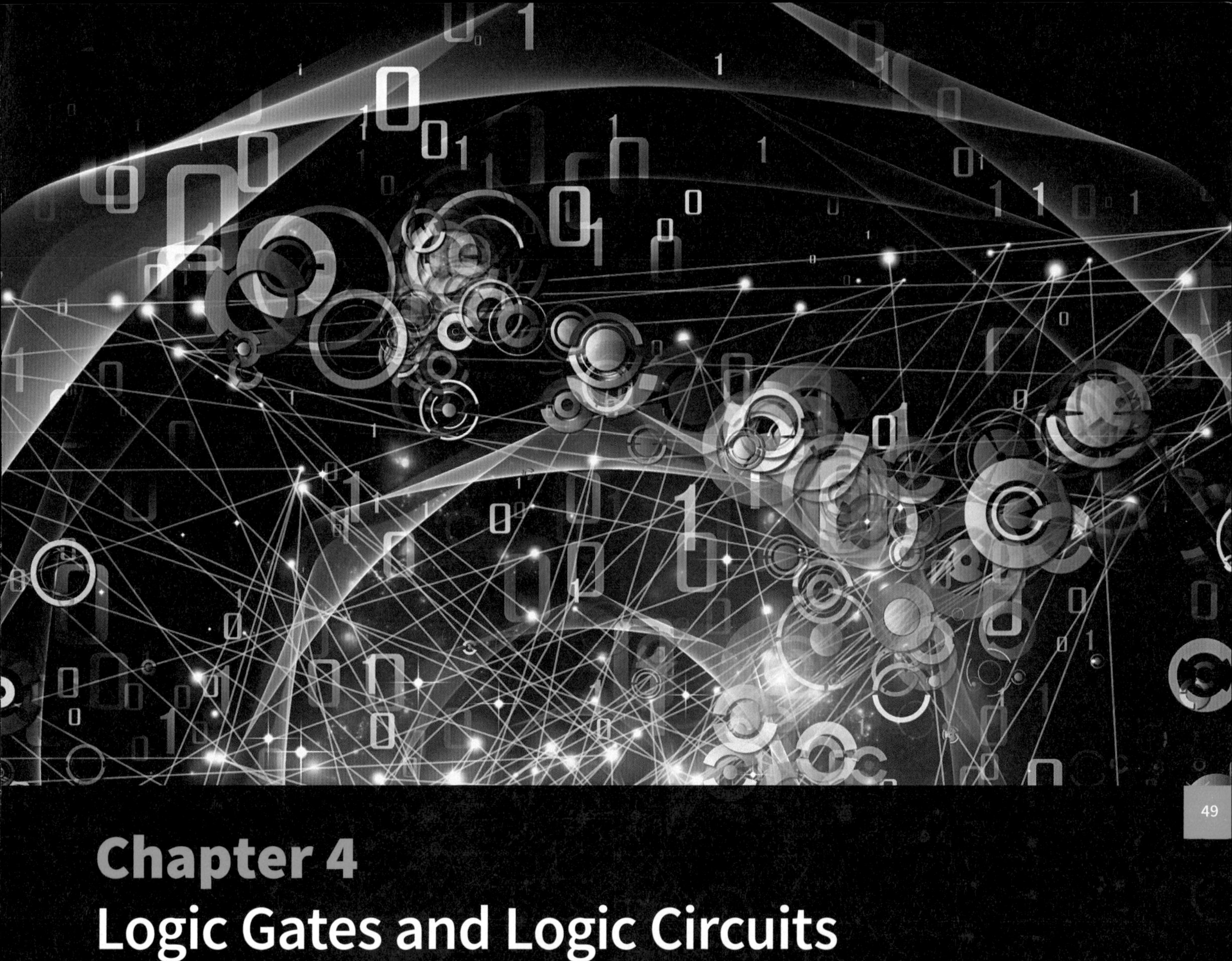

Chapter 4
Logic Gates and Logic Circuits

Learning objectives

By the end of this chapter you should be able to:

- use logic gate symbols
- understand and define the functions of NOT, AND, OR, NAND, NOR and XOR (EOR) gates
- construct the truth table for each of the logic gates above
- construct a logic circuit from:
  - a problem statement
  - a logic expression
- construct a truth table from:
  - a logic circuit
  - a logic expression
- show understanding that some circuits can be constructed from fewer gates to produce the same outputs.

4.01 Boolean logic and problem statements

Consider the following question:

Is Colombo further north than Singapore?

In everyday language the answer will be either yes or no. ('Yes', in fact.) However, the question could be rephrased to make use of the language of Boolean logic:

Colombo is further north than Singapore TRUE or FALSE?

More formally, the statement:

Colombo is further north than Singapore.

can be described as an example of a logic assertion or a **logic proposition** that can have only one of the two alternative Boolean logic values TRUE or FALSE.

KEY TERMS

Logic proposition: a statement that is either TRUE or FALSE

Now consider the following two individual statements:

- You should take an umbrella *if it is raining* or *if the weather forecast is for rain later.*
- The air-conditioning system is set to come on in an office *only during working hours* but also *only if the temperature rises to above 25°C.*

Each of these statements contains two logic propositions which are highlighted. In each statement these logic propositions are combined in some way. Finally, each statement has the addition of an outcome which is dependent on the combination of the two propositions. Each of these is, therefore, an individual example of a **problem statement**.

KEY TERMS

Problem statement: an informal definition of an outcome which is dependent on one logic proposition or a combination of two or more logic propositions

4.02 Boolean operators

The problem statements identified above can be more formally expressed in a form that is suitable for handling with Boolean logic. To do this it is necessary to use Boolean operators. The three basic Boolean operators are AND, OR and NOT.

The definition for AND can be expressed as:

A AND B is TRUE if A is TRUE and B is TRUE

Here, both A and B represent any logic proposition or assertion that has a value TRUE or FALSE.

In a similar way the definition for OR is:

A OR B is TRUE if A is TRUE or B is TRUE

The two problem statements above might be rephrased as follows:

- Take_umbrella = TRUE IF (raining = TRUE) OR (rain_forecast = TRUE)
- System_on = TRUE IF (office hours = TRUE) AND (temperature > 25°C)

Each original problem statement has now been rephrased as a form of **logic expression** with a defined outcome. The format of each expression here does not follow any formally defined convention but the structure does allow the underlying logic to be understood. In general, a logic expression consists of logic propositions combined using Boolean operators and the expression optionally may be stated with a defined output.

KEY TERMS

Logic expression: logic propositions combined using Boolean operators, which may be written with a defined outcome

TASK 4.01

Convert the following problem statement into a simple logic expression:

A document can only be copied if it is not covered by copyright or if there is copyright and permission has been obtained.

Any logic expression can be constructed using only the Boolean operators AND, OR and NOT but it is often convenient to use other operators. Here are the definitions for the six operators with which you need to be familiar:

- NOT A is TRUE if A is FALSE
- A AND B is TRUE if A is TRUE and B is TRUE
- A OR B is TRUE if A is TRUE or B is TRUE
- A NAND B is TRUE if A is FALSE or B is FALSE
- A NOR B is TRUE if A is FALSE and B is FALSE
- A XOR B is TRUE if A is TRUE or B is true but not both of them

4.03 Truth tables

The truth table is a simple but powerful technique for representing any logic expression or for describing the possible outputs from a logic circuit.

A truth table is presented by making use of the convention that TRUE can be represented as 1 and FALSE can be represented as 0. The simplest use of a truth table is to represent the logic associated with a Boolean operator.

As an example let us consider the AND operator. The labelling of the truth table follows the convention that the initially defined values are represented by A and B and the value obtained from the simple expression using the AND operator is represented by X. In other words we write the truth table for X = A AND B. Remembering that AND only returns true if both A and B are true we expect a truth table with only one instance of X having the value 1. The truth table is shown in Table 4.01.

A	B	X
0	0	0
0	1	0
1	0	0
1	1	1

Table 4.01 The truth table for the AND operator

The truth table has four rows corresponding to the four combinations of the truth values for A and B. Three of these lead to a 0 in the X column as expected.

TASK 4.02

Without looking further on in the chapter, construct the truth table for the OR operator.

4.04 Logic circuits and logic gates

The digital circuits that constitute the inner workings of a computer system all operate on the basis that at any one time an individual part of the circuit is either in an 'on' state, which can be represented by a 1, or in an 'off' state, represented by a 0. The physical circuitry consists of integrated circuits constructed from transistors. There can be billions of transistors in a single integrated circuit.

We will view a logic circuit as comprising component parts called **logic gates.** Each different logic gate has an operation that matches a Boolean operator.

KEY TERMS

Logic gate: a component of a logic circuit that has an operation matching that of a Boolean operator

Discussion Point:

There will be no further discussion of integrated circuits in this book but you might wish to do some research and have a look at the structure of a small-scale integration chip.

When drawing a circuit, standard symbols are used for the logic gates. As an example, the symbol shown in Figure 4.01 represents an AND gate.

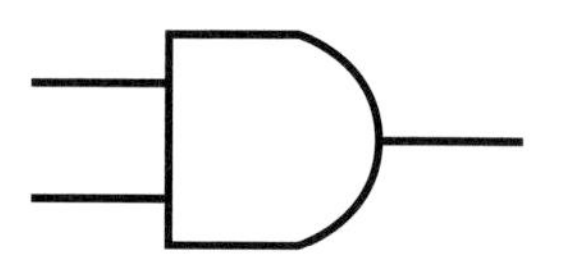

Figure 4.01 The symbol for the AND logic gate

The first point to note here is that the shape defines the type of gate. The second point is that the inputs are on the left-hand side and the output is on the right-hand side. In general, the number of inputs is not limited to two but the discussion in this book will only consider circuits where the number of inputs does not exceed two.

Figure 4.02 shows the logic gate symbols and the associated truth tables for each of the six Boolean operators introduced in Section 4.02.

NOT

A	X
0	1
1	0

AND

A	B	X
0	0	0
0	1	0
1	0	0
1	1	1

OR

A	B	X
0	0	0
0	1	1
1	0	1
1	1	1

NAND

A	B	X
0	0	1
0	1	1
1	0	1
1	1	0

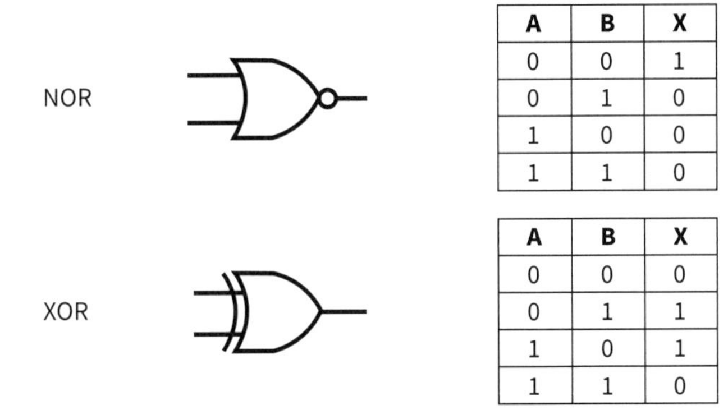

NOR

A	B	X
0	0	1
0	1	0
1	0	0
1	1	0

XOR

A	B	X
0	0	0
0	1	1
1	0	1
1	1	0

Figure 4.02 Logic gate symbols and their associated truth tables

There are two other points to note here. The NOT gate is a special case having only one input. The NAND and NOR gates are each a combination of a gate and the NOT gate so they produce complementary output to that produced by the AND and OR gates.

TASK 4.03

Draw a circuit where A and B are input to an AND gate from which the output is carried to a NOT gate from which there is an output X. Show that this has the same outcome as having one NAND gate.

Extension question 4.01

Could the same outcome be produced by positioning a NOT gate before the AND gate?

You need to remember the symbol for each of these gates. A good start here is to remember that AN **D** has the proper **D** symbol and OR has the curvy one. You also need to remember the definitions for the gates so that you can construct the corresponding truth table for each gate.

Question 4.01

Can you recall from memory the symbols and definitions of the six logic gates introduced in this chapter?

WORKED EXAMPLE 4.01

Constructing a logic circuit from a problem statement or logic expression

You need to be able to construct a logic circuit from either a problem statement or from a logic expression. If you are given a problem statement the best approach is to first convert it to a logic expression and then to identify the individual Boolean operations in the logic expression. This approach will be illustrated here.

Consider the following problem statement: A bank offers a special lending rate to customers subject to certain conditions. To qualify, a customer must satisfy certain criteria:

- The customer has been with the bank for two years.
- Two of the following conditions must also apply:
  - The customer is married.
  - The customer is aged 25 years or older.
  - The customer's parents are customers of the bank.

To convert this statement to a logic expression you need to represent each condition by a symbol (in the same way that a problem might be tackled in normal algebra):

- Let A represent an account held for two years.
- Let B represent that the customer is married.
- Let C represent that the customer's is age 25 years or more.
- Let D represent that the customer's parents have an account.

The logic expression can then be written as:

A AND (((B AND C) OR (B AND D)) OR (C AND D))

This could alternatively be presented with an outcome:

Special_rate IF A AND (((B AND C) OR (B AND D)) OR (C AND D))

Note the use of brackets to ensure that the meaning is clear. You may think that not all of the brackets are needed. In this example, an extra pair has been included to guide the construction of the circuit where only two inputs are allowed for any of the gates.

It can be seen, therefore, that the logic circuit corresponding to this logic expression derived from the original problem statement could be constructed using four AND gates and two OR gates as shown in Figure 4.03.

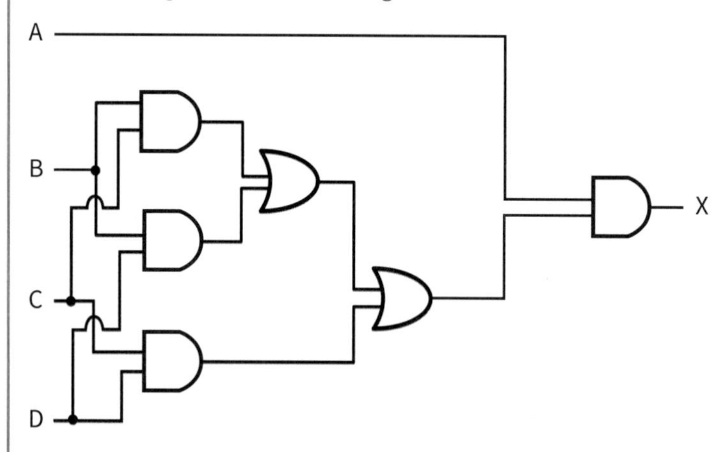

Figure 4.03 A logic circuit constructed from a problem statement

WORKED EXAMPLE 4.02

Constructing a truth table from a logic expression or logic circuit

You also need to be able to construct a truth table from either a logic expression or a logic circuit. We might have continued with the problem in Worked Example 4.01 but four inputs will lead to 16 rows in the truth table. Instead, we consider a slightly simpler problem with only three inputs and therefore only eight rows in the truth table. We will start with the circuit shown in Figure 4.04.

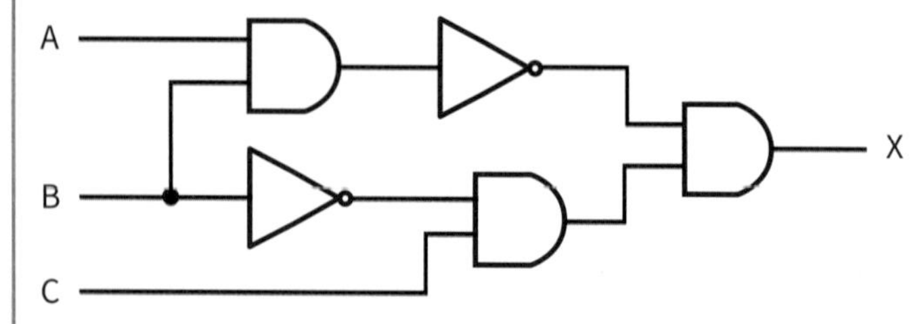

Figure 4.04 A circuit with three inputs for conversion to a truth table

Table 4.02 shows how the truth table needs to be set up initially. There are several points to note here. The first is that you must take care to include all of the eight different possible combinations of the input values. Therefore, you present the values in increasing binary number value from 000 to 111. The second point is that for such a circuit it is not sensible to try to work out the outputs directly from the input values. Instead a systematic approach should be used. This involves identifying intermediate points in the circuit and recording the values at each of them in the columns headed 'Workspace' in Table 4.02.

Inputs			Workspace				Output
A	B	C					X
0	0	0					
0	0	1					
0	1	0					
0	1	1					
1	0	0					
1	0	1					
1	1	0					
1	1	1					

Table 4.02 The initial empty truth table

Figure 4.05 shows the same circuit but with four intermediate points labelled M, N, P and Q identified. Each one has been inserted on the output side of a logic gate.

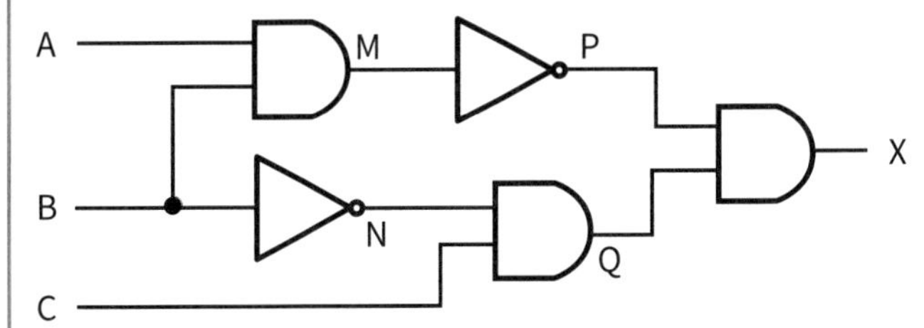

Figure 4.05 The circuit in Figure 4.04 with intermediate points identified

Now you need to work systematically through the intermediate points. You start by filling in the columns for M and N. Then you fill in the columns for P and Q which feed into the final AND gate. The final truth table is shown as Table 4.03. The circuit has two combinations of inputs that lead to a TRUE output from the circuit.

The columns containing the intermediate values (the workspace) could be deleted at this stage.

Inputs			Workspace				Output
A	B	C	M	N	P	Q	X
0	0	0	0	1	1	0	0
0	0	1	0	1	1	1	1
0	1	0	0	0	1	0	0
0	1	1	0	0	1	0	0
1	0	0	0	1	1	0	0
1	0	1	0	1	1	1	1
1	1	0	1	0	0	0	0
1	1	1	1	0	0	0	0

Table 4.03 The truth table for the circuit shown in Figure 4.05

One final point to make here is that you may be able to check part of your final solution by looking at just part of the circuit. For this example, if you look at the circuit you will see that the path from input C to the output passes through two AND gates. It follows, therefore, that for all combinations with C having value 0 the output must be 0. Therefore, in order to check your final solution you only need to examine the other four combinations of input values where C has value 1.

TASK 4.04

An oven has a number of components which should all be working properly. For each component there is a signalling mechanism that informs a management system if all is well or if there is a problem when the oven is being used. Table 4.04 summarises the signal values that record the status for each component.

Signal	Value	Component condition
A	0	Fan not working
	1	Fan working properly
B	0	Internal light not working
	1	Internal light working properly
C	0	Thermometer reading too high
	1	Thermometer reading in range

Table 4.04 Signals from the oven components

If the thermometer reading is in range but either or both the fan and light are not working, the management system has to output a signal to activate a warning light on the control panel. Draw a logic circuit for this fault condition.

4.05 Alternative circuits

For any given logic problem there will be different circuits that deliver the same output values from a given set of inputs. In some cases it will be possible to simplify an initial circuit design by reducing the number of logic gates. As a trivial example you may have noticed that the circuit in Figure 4.04 includes an AND gate immediately followed by a NOT gate. These could have been combined as a NAND gate. For more complex examples, there are techniques available which will be discussed in Chapter 18 (Sections 18.03 and 18.04).

However, reducing complexity is not just about reducing the number of logic gates. Logic circuit manufacturers can reduce costs by building circuits that contain only one type of logic gate; one that is itself cheap to manufacture. The NAND gate is an example of a universal gate which fits this requirement (the NOR gate is the other possibility). Manufacturers may find it cheaper to build a circuit with just NAND gates even though the circuit contains more components than alternatives containing different gates. To illustrate the concept of the universal NAND gate the circuit in Figure 4.06 has the same functionality as an OR gate.

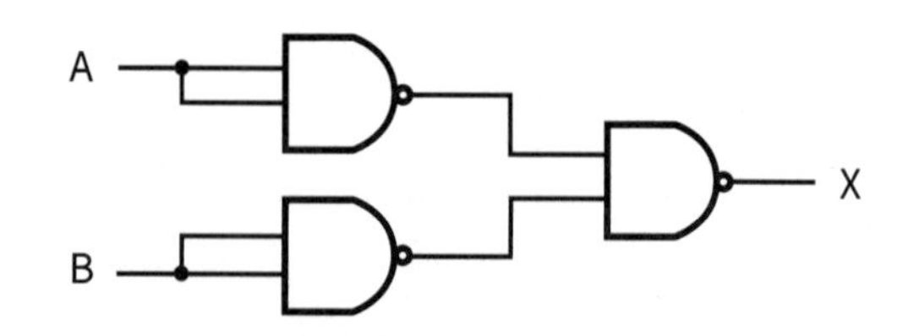

Figure 4.06 A circuit containing only NAND gates which is equivalent to an OR gate

Extension question 4.02

Create the truth table for the circuit shown in Figure 4.06 and show that it is the same as that for an OR gate.

Summary

- A logic scenario can be described by a problem statement or a logic expression.
- A logic expression comprises logic propositions and Boolean operators.
- Logic circuits are constructed from logic gates.
- The operation of a logic gate matches that of a Boolean operator.
- The outcome of a logic expression or a logic circuit can be expressed as a truth table.

Exam-style Questions

1 a The following are the symbols for three different logic gates.

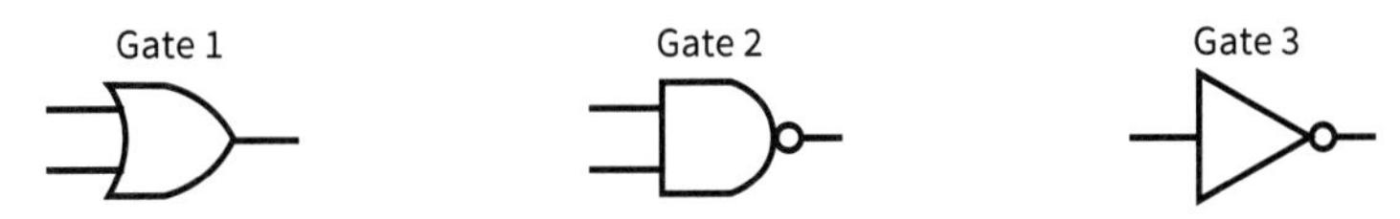

i Identify each of the logic gates. [3]

ii Draw the truth table for either Gate 1 or Gate 2. [2]

b Consider the following circuit:

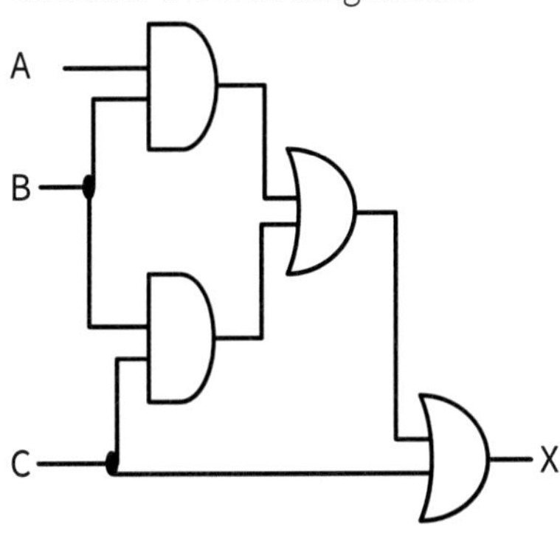

i Construct the truth table for the circuit using the following template:

Inputs			Workspace			Output
A	B	C				X
0	0	0				
0	0	1				
0	1	0				
0	1	1				
1	0	0				
1	0	1				
1	1	0				
1	1	1				

[8]

ii There is an element of redundancy in this diagram. Explain what the problem is. [2]

2 a The definition of the NAND gate can be expressed as:

A NAND B is TRUE if A is FALSE or B is FALSE

Draw the truth table for a NAND gate [4]

b Consider the following statement:

In a competition, two teams play two matches against each other. One of the teams is declared the winner if one of the following results occurs:

- The team wins both matches.
- The team wins one match and loses the other but has the highest total score.

i Identify the three logic propositions in this statement. [3]

ii By assigning the symbols A, B and C to these three propositions express the outcome of the competition as a logic expression. [3]

iii Construct a logic circuit to match this logic expression. [4]

3 A domestic heating system has a hot water tank and a number of radiators. There is a computerised management system which receives signals dependent on whether or not the conditions for components are as they should be. The following table summarises the signals received:

Signal	Value	Component condition
A	0	Water flow in the radiators is too low
	1	Water flow in the radiators is within limits
B	0	Hot water tank temperature too high
	1	Hot water tank temperature within limits
C	0	Water level in hot water tank too low
	1	Water level in hot water tank within limits

a Consider the following fault condition. The water level in the hot water tank is too low and the temperature in the hot water tank is too high. The management system must output a signal to switch off the system.

i Construct a truth table for this fault condition including the A, B and C signals. [4]

ii Construct the circuit diagram for this fault condition to match this truth table. [5]

b Consider the fault condition where the hot water tank temperature is within limits but the water flow in the radiators is too low and the water level in the hot water tank is too low. Construct the circuit diagram for this fault condition which requires the management system to output a signal to increase water pressure. [5]

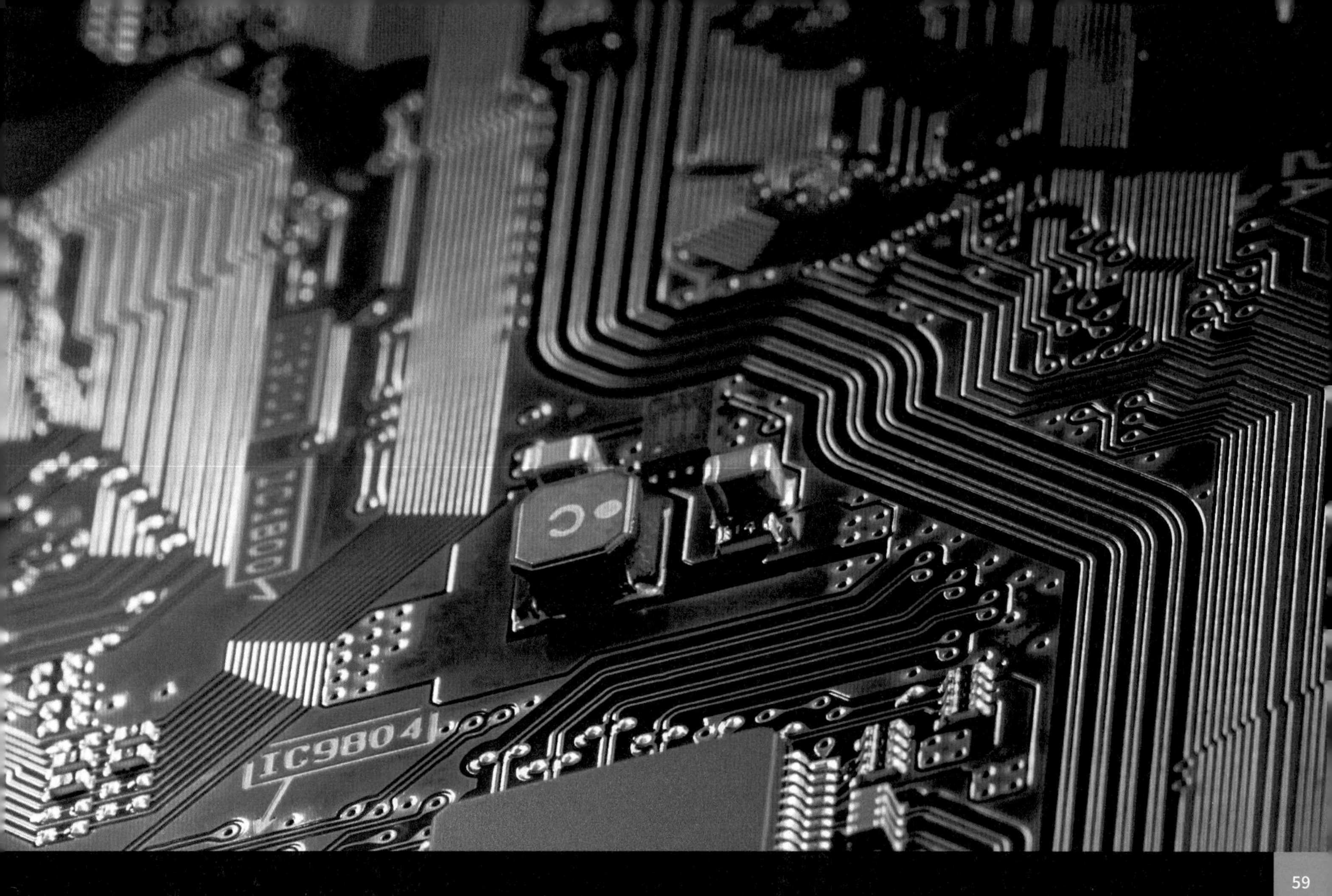

Chapter 5
Processor Fundamentals

Learning objectives

By the end of this chapter you should be able to:

- show understanding of the basic Von Neumann model
- show understanding of the roles carried out by registers
- show understanding of the roles carried out by the Arithmetic and Logic Unit (ALU), Control Unit and system clock
- show understanding of how data are transferred between various components of the computer system using the address bus, data bus and control bus
- show understanding of how the bus width and clock speed are factors that contribute to the performance of the computer system
- show understanding of the need for ports
- describe the stages of the fetch–execute cycle
- show understanding of 'register transfer' notation
- describe how interrupts are handled.

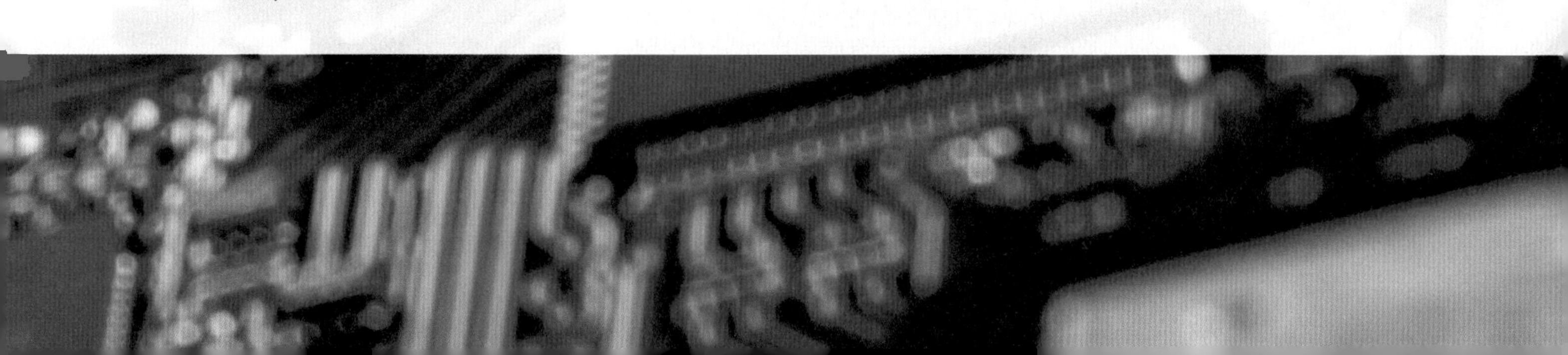

5.01 The Von Neumann model of a computer system

The simplest form of what might be described as a computer system model or computer system architecture is usually attributed to John von Neumann. This recognises the fact that he was the first to describe the basic principles in a publication.

The model has the following basic features:

- There is a processor, a central processing unit.
- The processor has direct access to a memory.
- The memory contains a 'stored program' (which can be replaced by another at any time) and the data required by the program.
- The stored program consists of individual instructions.
- The processor executes instructions sequentially.

5.02 Central processing unit (CPU) architecture

Modern processors are extremely complex; some of the complexities will be discussed in Chapter 19 (Sections 19.02 and 19.03). In this chapter the focus is on the fundamentals of the operation of an up-to-date version of a simple von Neumann computer system.

Figure 5.01 gives a simplified schematic diagram of a processor that could be part of this simple system. The dotted outline shows the boundary of the processor. The logical arrangement of some of the processor components is indicated. The arrows show possible directions of flow of data. As the following discussion will show, the data for some of the arrows is specifically an address or an instruction. However, in general, data might be an instruction, an address or a value.

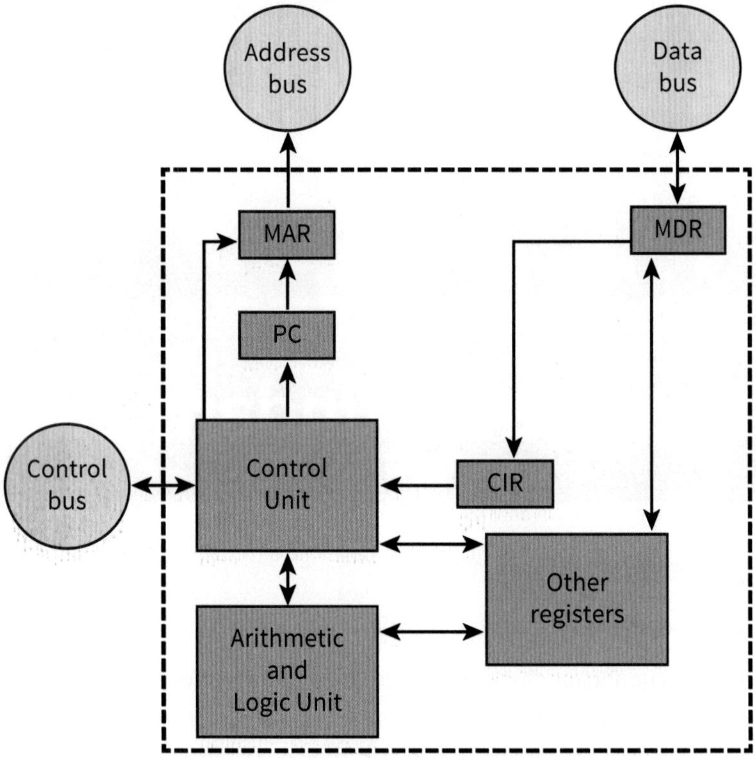

Figure 5.01 A schematic diagram of the architecture of a simple CPU

Components of the CPU

The two major components of the CPU are the arithmetic and logic unit (ALU) (or Arithmetic Logic Unit) and the control unit. As its name implies, the ALU is responsible for any arithmetic or logic processing that might be needed when a program is running. The functions of the control unit are more diverse. One aspect is controlling the flow of data throughout the processor and, indeed, throughout the whole computer system. Another is ensuring that program instructions are handled correctly. A vital part of the control unit is a clock which is used by the unit to synchronise processes. Strictly speaking there are two clocks. The first is an internal clock which controls the cycles of activity within the processor. The other is the system clock which controls activities outside the processor. The CPU will have a defined frequency for its clock cycle, which is usually referred to as the clock speed. The frequency defines the minimum period of time that separates successive activities within the system.

Extension question 5.01

In an advertisement for a laptop computer, the system is described as 4 GB, 1 TB, 1.7 GHz.

1 Which three components are being referred to here?
2 Have the values quoted been presented correctly? To answer this you need to refer back to the discussion in Chapter 1 (Section 1.04) about terminology.
3 Calculate the minimum time period that could separate successive activities on this system.

Registers

The other components of the CPU are the registers. These are storage components which, because of their proximity to the ALU, allow very short access times. Each register has limited storage capacity, typically 16, 32 or 64 bits. A register is either general purpose or special purpose. If there is only one general-purpose register it is referred to as the **accumulator**. For the rest of this discussion and for the discussion in Chapter 6, the assumption will be that the processor does have just this one general-purpose register. The Accumulator is used to store a single value at any one time. A value is stored in the Accumulator that is to be used by the ALU for the execution of an instruction. The ALU can then store a different value in the Accumulator after the execution of the instruction.

KEY TERMS

Accumulator: a general-purpose register that stores a value before and after the execution of an instruction by the ALU

Figure 5.01 shows some of the special-purpose registers as individual components. The box labelled 'Other registers' can be considered to comprise the Accumulator plus the special-purpose registers not identified individually. The full names of the special-purpose registers included in the simple CPU which we are going to discuss are given in Table 5.01 with a brief description of their function.

Register name	Abbreviation	Register's function
Current instruction register	CIR	Stores the current instruction while it is being decoded and executed
Index register	IX	Stores a value; only used for indexed addressing
Memory address register	MAR	Stores the address of a memory location which is about to have a value read from or written to
Memory data register (memory buffer register)	MDR (MBR)	Stores data that has just been read from memory or is just about to be written to memory
Program counter	PC	Stores the address of where the next instruction is to be read from
Status register	SR	Contains individual bits that are either set or cleared

Table 5.01 Registers in a simple CPU

Two points are worth making at this point. The first is that the alternative name for the MDR emphasises that this particular register must act as a buffer because transfers of data within the processor take place much more quickly than transfers outside the processor. This statement has to be slightly qualified because the transfer could be to or from cache memory which would be a fast process but it is otherwise generally applicable. The mention of cache memory brings us to the second point which is that all discussion in this chapter and Chapter 6 ignores the fact that cache memory exists. All references are simply to memory as in Table 5.01.

A further point to note here is that the index register (IX) can be abbreviated as IR but in some sources the current instruction register (CIR) is abbreviated as 'IR', which is an unnecessary potential cause of confusion. In this book, the index register is always IX and the current instruction register is CIR. Finally, there is also possible confusion if the abbreviation PC is used. This will only be used in this book when register transfer notation is being used as you will see later in the chapter. Everywhere else, a PC is a computer.

The SR is used when an instruction requires arithmetic or logic processing. Each individual bit in the SR operates as a flag. The bit is set to 1 if a condition is detected. As an example, the use of the following three flags will be illustrated:

- The carry flag, identified as C, is set to 1 if there is a carry.
- The negative flag, identified as N, is set to 1 if a result is negative.
- The overflow flag, identified as V, is set to 1 if overflow is detected.

WORKED EXAMPLE 5.01

Using the status register during an arithmetic operation

1 Consider the addition of two positive values where the sum of the two produces an answer that is too large to be correctly identified with the limited number of bits used to represent the values. For, example if an eight-bit binary integer representation is being used and an attempt is made to add denary 66 to denary 68 the following happens:

The value produced as an answer is denary – 122. Two positive numbers have been added to get a negative number. This impossibility is detected by the combination of the negative flag and the overflow flag being set to 1. The processor has identified the problem and can therefore send out an appropriate message.

2 Consider using the same eight-bit binary integer representation but this time two negative numbers (–66 and –68 in denary) are added:

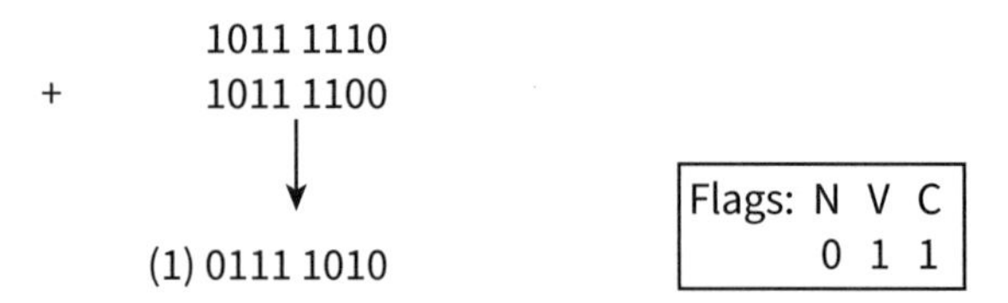

This time we get the answer +122. This impossibility is detected by the combination of the negative flag not being set and both the overflow and the carry flag being set to 1.

Extension question 5.02

Carry out a comparable calculation for the addition in binary of –66 to +68. What do you think the processor should do with the carry bit?

5.03 The system bus

A bus is a parallel transmission component with each separate wire carrying a single bit. It is important not to describe a bus as a storage device. A bus does not hold data. Instead it is a mechanism for data to be transferred from one system component to another.

In the simple computer system described in this chapter there will be a system bus that comprises three distinct components: the address bus, the data bus and the control bus. The schematic diagram of the CPU in Figure 5.01 shows the logical connection between each bus and a CPU component. The address bus is connected to the MAR; the data bus to the MDR; and the control bus to the control unit.

The system bus allows data flow between the CPU, the memory, and input or output (I/O) devices as shown in the schematic diagram in Figure 5.02.

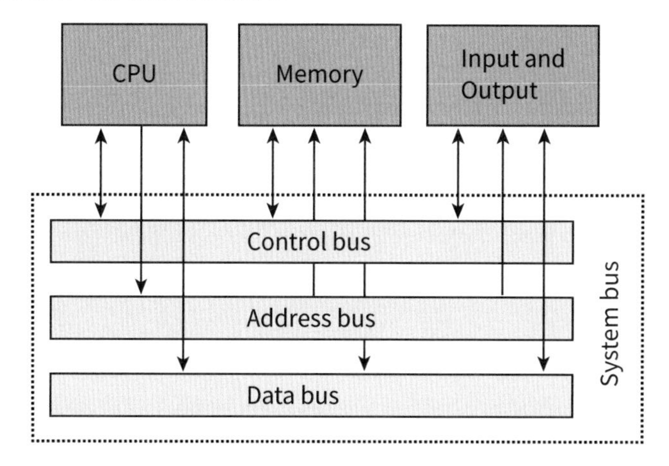

Figure 5.02 A schematic diagram of the system bus

The address bus

The sole function of the **address bus** is to carry an address. This address is loaded on to the bus from the MAR as and when directed by the control unit. The address specifies a location in memory which is due to receive data or from which data is to be read. The address bus is a 'one-way street'. It can only be used to send an address to a memory controller. It cannot be used to carry an address from the memory controller back to the CPU.

KEY TERMS

Address bus: a component that carries an address to the memory controller to identify a location in memory which is to be read from or written to

The crucial aspect of the address bus is the 'bus width', which is the number of separate wires in the bus. The number of wires defines the number of bits in the address's binary code. In the simple computer system considered here we will assume that the bus width is 16 bits allowing 65 536 memory locations to be directly addressed. Such a memory size would, of course, be totally inadequate for a modern computer system. Even doubling the address bus width to 32 bits would only allow the direct addressing of a little over four billion addresses. If the memory size is too large special techniques have to be used.

The data bus

The function of the **data bus** is to carry data. This might be an instruction, an address or a value. As can be seen from Figure 5.02, the data bus might be carrying the data from CPU to memory or from memory to CPU.

However, another option is to carry data to or from an I/O device. The diagram does not make clear whether, for instance, data coming from an input device is carried first to the CPU or directly to the memory. There is a good reason for this. Some computer systems will only allow input to the CPU before the data can be stored in memory. Other systems will allow direct transfer to memory.

Bus width is again an important factor in considering how the data bus is used. Before discussing this, it is useful to introduce the concept of a **word**. A word consists of a number of bytes and for any system the word length is defined. The significance of the word length is that it defines a grouping that the system will handle as one unit. The word length might be stated as a number of bytes or as a number of bits. Typical word lengths are 16, 32 or 64 bits that is, 2, 4 or 8 bytes respectively. For a given computer system, the bus width is ideally the same as the word length. If this is not possible the bus width can be half the word length so that a full word can be transmitted by two consecutive data transfers. For our simple system we assume a data bus width of 16 bits and a word length of two bytes to match this.

KEY TERMS

Data bus: a component that carries data to and from the processor

Word: a small number of bytes handled as a unit by the computer system

Extension question 5.03

Can you find out the bus widths used in the computer system you are using?

The control bus

The control bus is another bidirectional bus which transmits a signal from the control unit to any other system component or transmits a signal to the control unit. There is no need for extended width so the control bus typically has just eight wires. A major use of the control bus is to carry timing signals. As described in Section 5.02, the system clock in the control unit defines the clock cycle for the computer system. The control bus carries timing signals at time intervals dictated by the clock cycle. This ensures that the time that one component transmits data is synchronised with the time that another component reads it.

The clock speed is the most important factor governing the processing speed of the system. However, it is not the only factor. The performance will be limited if the bus widths are insufficient for the whole of a data value to be transferred in one clock cycle. For optimum performance it is also particularly important that memory access is as efficient as possible.

The schematic diagram in Figure 5.02 slightly misrepresents the situation because it looks as if the CPU, the memory and the I/O devices have similar access to the data and control buses. The reality is different. Each I/O device is connected to an interface called a port. Each port is connected to the I/O or device controller. This controller handles the interaction between the CPU and an I/O device. A port is described as 'internal' if the connected I/O device is an integral part of the computer system. An external port allows the computer user to connect a peripheral I/O device.

The universal serial bus (USB)

In the early days of the PC, the process of connecting a peripheral was time-consuming and required technical expertise. The aim of the plug-and-play concept was to remove the need for technical knowledge so that any computer user could connect a peripheral and start using it straight away. The plug-and-play concept was only fully realised by the creation of the USB (Universal Serial Bus) standard. Nowadays anyone buying a new peripheral device will expect it to connect to a USB port. There is an alternative technology known as FireWire but this is not so commonly used in computer systems.

Some information about the USB standard:

- A hierarchy of connections is supported.
- The computer is at the root of this hierarchy and can handle 127 attached devices.
- Devices can be attached while the computer is switched on and are automatically configured for use.
- The standard has evolved, with USB 3.0 being the latest version.

Discussion Point:

Carry out an investigation into storage devices that could be connected as a peripheral to a PC using the USB port.

For two representative devices find out which specific USB technology is being used and what the potential data transfer speed is. How do these speeds compare with the speed of access of a hard drive installed inside the computer?

5.04 The fetch–execute cycle

The full name for this is the fetch, decode and execute cycle. This is illustrated by the flowchart in Figure 5.03.

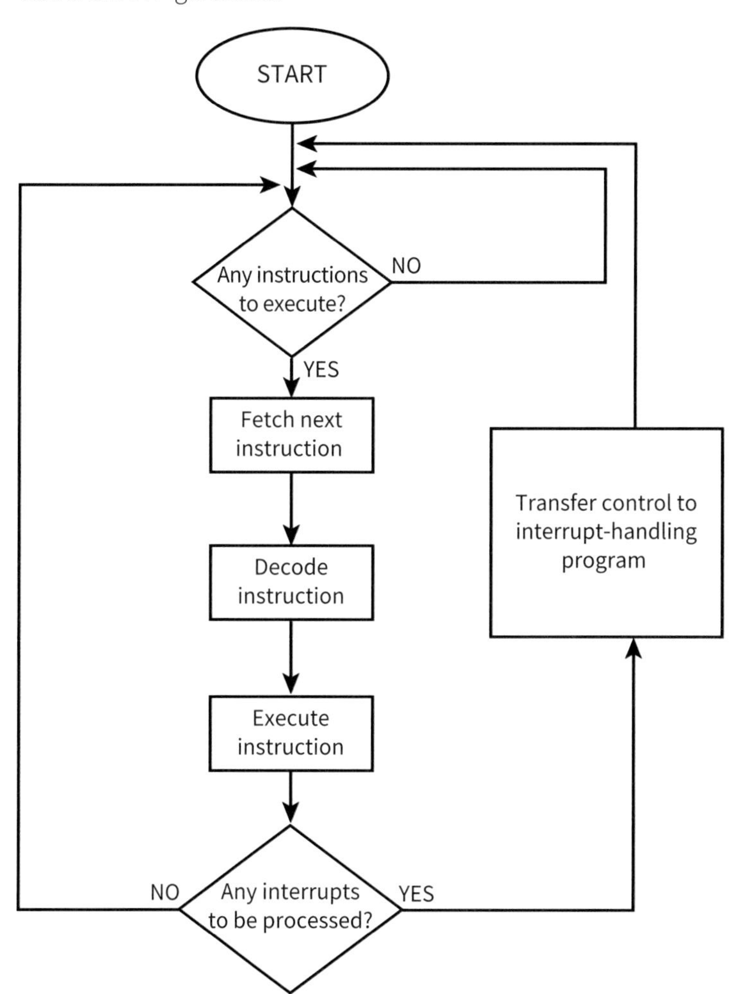

Figure 5.03 Flowchart for the fetch, decode and execute cycle

If we assume that a program is already running then the program counter already holds the address of an instruction. In the fetch stage, the following steps happen:

1 This address in the program counter is transferred within the CPU to the MAR.
2 During the next clock cycle two things happen simultaneously:
   - the instruction held in the address pointed to by the MAR is fetched into the MDR
   - the address stored in the program counter is incremented.
3 The instruction stored in the MDR is transferred within the CPU to the CIR.

For our simple system the program counter will be incremented by 1. However, it should be noted that the instruction just loaded might be a jump instruction. In this case, the program counter contents will have to be updated in accordance with the jump condition. This can only happen after the instruction has been decoded.

In the decode stage, the instruction stored in the CIR is received as input by the circuitry within the control unit. Depending on the type of instruction, the control unit will send signals to the appropriate components so that the execute stage can begin. At this stage, the ALU will be activated if the instruction requires arithmetic or logic processing.

The description of the execute stage is postponed until Chapter 6, in which a simple instruction set is introduced and discussed.

5.05 Register transfer notation

Operations involving registers can be described by register transfer notation. The simplest form of this can be illustrated by the following representation of the fetch stage of the fetch–execute cycle:

```
MAR ← [PC]
PC ← [PC] + 1; MDR ← [[MAR]]
CIR ← [MDR]
```

The basic format for an individual data transfer is similar to that for variable assignment. The first item is the destination of the data. Here the appropriate abbreviation is used to identify the particular register. To the right of the arrow showing the transmission of data is the definition of this data. In this definition, the square brackets around a register abbreviation show that the content of the register is being moved possibly with some arithmetic operation being applied. When two data operations are placed on the same line separated by a semi-colon this means that the two transfers take place simultaneously. The double pair of brackets around MAR on the second line needs careful interpretation. The content of the MAR is an address; it is the content of that address which is being transferred to the MDR.

5.06 Interrupt handling

There are many different reasons for an interrupt to be generated. Some examples are:

- a fatal error in a program
- a hardware fault
- a need for I/O processing to begin
- user interaction
- a timer signal.

There are a number of different approaches possible for the detailed mechanisms used to handle interrupts but the overriding principles are clearly defined. Each different interrupt needs to be handled appropriately and different interrupts might possibly have different priorities. Therefore, the processor must have a means of identifying the type of interrupt. One way is to have an interrupt register in the CPU that works like the status register, with each individual bit operating as a flag for a specific type of interrupt.

As the flowchart in Figure 5.03 shows, the existence of an interrupt is only detected at the end of a fetch–execute cycle. This allows the current program to be interrupted and left in a defined state which can be returned to later. The first step in handling the interrupt is to store the contents of the program counter and any other registers somewhere safe in memory.

Following this, the appropriate interrupt handler or interrupt service routine (ISR) program is initiated by loading its start address into the program counter. When the ISR program has been executed there needs to be an immediate check to see if further interrupts need handling. If there are none, the safely stored contents of the registers are restored to the CPU and the originally running program is resumed.

Summary

- **The von Neumann architecture for a computer system is based on the stored program concept.**
- **The CPU contains a control unit, an arithmetic and logic unit, and registers.**
- **Registers can be special purpose or general purpose.**
- **The status register has individual bits acting as condition flags.**
- **The system bus contains the data, address and control buses.**
- **A universal serial bus (USB) port can be used to attach peripheral devices.**
- **Instructions are handled by the fetch–execute cycle.**
- **Register transfer notation is used to describe data transfers.**
- **If an interrupt is detected, control passes to an interrupt-handling routine.**

Exam-style Questions

1 **a** A processor has just one general-purpose register. Give the name of this register. [1]

b The memory address register (MAR) is a special-purpose register. State:

i its function

ii the type of data stored in it

iii the register that supplies this data at the start of the fetch stage of the fetch–execute cycle. [3]

c The current instruction register (CIR) is another special-purpose register. State:

i its function

ii the type of data stored in it

iii the register that supplies this data at the end of the fetch stage of the fetch–execute cycle. [3]

d Explain three differences between the memory address register and the memory data register. [5]

2 The system bus comprises three individual buses: the data bus, the address bus and the control bus.

a For each bus give a brief explanation of its use. [6]

b Each bus has a defined bus width.

i State what determines the width of a bus. [1]

ii Explain which bus will have the least width. [2]

iii Explain the effect of changing the address bus from a 32-bit bus to a 64-bit bus. [3]

3 The fetch stage of the fetch–decode–execute cycle can be represented by the following statements using register transfer notation:

```
MAR ← [PC]
PC ← [PC] + 1; MDR ← [[MAR]]
CIR ← [MDR]
```


a Explain the meaning of each statement. The explanation must include definitions of the following items: MAR, PC, [ ], ←, MDR, [[ ]], CIR. [10]

b Explain the use of the address bus and the data bus for two of the statements. [4]

Chapter 6
Assembly Language Programming

Learning objectives

By the end of this chapter you should be able to:

- show understanding that the set of instructions are grouped into instructions for:
  - data movement
  - input and output of data
  - arithmetic operations
  - unconditional and conditional jump instructions
  - compare instructions
  - modes of addressing
- show understanding of the relationship between assembly language and machine code
- trace a given simple assembly language program.

6.01 Machine code instructions

The only language that the CPU recognises is machine code. Therefore, when a program is running and an instruction is fetched from memory this has to be in the format of a binary code that matches the specific machine code that the CPU uses.

Different processors have different instruction sets associated with them. Even if two different processors have the same instruction, the machine codes for them will be different but the structure of the code for an instruction will be similar for different processors.

For a particular processor, the following components are defined for an individual **machine code instruction:**

- the total number of bits or bytes for the whole instruction
- the number of bits that define the opcode
- the number of operands that are defined in the remaining bits
- whether the opcode occupies the most significant or the least significant bits.

In general, there can be anything up to three operands for an instruction. However, following on from the approach in Chapter 5, we consider a simple system where there is either one or zero operands.

KEY TERMS

Machine code instruction: a binary code with a defined number of bits that comprises an opcode and, most often, one operand

The number of bits needed for the opcode depends on the number of different opcodes in the instruction set for the processor. The opcode is structured with the first few bits defining the operation and the remaining bits associated with addressing. A sensible instruction format for our simple processor is shown in Figure 6.01.

Opcode			Operand
Operation	**Address mode**	**Register addressing**	
4 bits	2 bits	2 bits	16 bits

Figure 6.01 A simple instruction format

This has an eight-bit opcode consisting of four bits for the operation, two bits for the address mode (discussed in Section 6.03) and the remaining two bits for addressing registers. This allows 16 different operations each with one of four addressing modes. This opcode will occupy the most significant bits in the instruction. Because in some circumstances the operand will be a memory address it is sensible to allocate 16 bits for it. This is in keeping with the 16-bit address bus.

Because an instruction has two components, a slight modification to register transfer notation (see Section 5.05) is needed. As an example the first step in the decode stage of the fetch–execute cycle could be written as:

```
CU ← [CIR(23:16)]
```

Indicating that only bits 16 to 23 from the contents of the CIR have been transferred to the control unit; bits 0 to 15 are not needed in this first step.

6.02 Assembly language

A programmer might wish to write a program where the actions taken by the processor are directly controlled. It is argued that this can produce optimum efficiency in a program. However, writing a program as a sequence of machine code instructions would be a very time-consuming and error-prone process. The solution for this type of programming is to use assembly language. As well as having a uniquely defined machine code language each processor has its own assembly language.

The essence of assembly language is that for each machine code instruction there is an equivalent assembly language instruction which comprises:

- a mnemonic (a symbolic abbreviation) for the opcode
- a character representation for the operand.

If a program has been written in assembly language it has to be translated into machine code before it can be executed by the processor. The translation program is called an 'assembler', of which some details will be discussed in Chapter 7 (Section 7.05). The fact that an assembler is to be used allows a programmer to include some special features in an assembly language program. Examples of these are:

- comments
- symbolic names for constants
- labels for addresses
- macros
- subroutines
- directives
- system calls.

The first three items on this list are there to directly assist the programmer in writing the program. Of these, comments are removed by the assembler and symbolic names and labels require a conversion to binary code by the assembler. A macro or a subroutine contains a sequence of instructions that is to be used more than once in a program.

Directives and system calls are instructions to the assembler as to how it should construct the final executable machine code. They can involve directing how memory should be used or defining files or procedures that will be used. They do not have to be converted into binary code.

KEY TERMS

Directive: an instruction to the assembler program

6.03 Addressing modes

When an instruction requires a value to be loaded into a register there are different ways of identifying the value. These different ways are described as the 'addressing modes'. In Section 6.01, it was stated that, for our simple processor, two bits of the opcode in a machine code instruction would be used to define the addressing mode. This allows four different modes which are described in Table 6.01.

Addressing mode	Operand
Immediate	The value to be used in the instruction
Direct	An address which holds the value to be used in the instruction
Indirect	An address which holds the address which holds the value to be used in the instruction
Indexed	An address to which must be added what is currently in the index register (IX) to get the address which holds the value in the instruction

Table 6.01 Addressing modes

6.04 Assembly language instructions

The examples described here do not correspond directly to those found in the assembly language for any specific processor. Individual instructions will have a match in more than one real-life set. The important point is that these examples are representative. In particular, there are examples of the most common categories of instruction.

Data movement

These types of instruction can involve loading data into a register or storing data in memory. Table 6.02 contains a few examples of the format of the instructions with explanations.

It should be understood that an actual instance of an instruction would have an actual address where `<address>` is shown, a register abbreviation where `<register>` is shown and a denary value for *n* where #n is shown. The explanations use ACC to indicate the accumulator.

Instruction opcode	Instruction operand	Explanation
LDM	#n	Immediate addressing loading *n* to ACC
LDR	#n	Immediate addressing loading *n* to IX
LDD	<address>	Direct addressing, loading to ACC
LDI	<address>	Indirect addressing, loading to ACC
LDX	<address>	Indexed addressing, loading to ACC
STO	<address>	Storing the contents of ACC

Table 6.02 Some instruction formats for data movement

The important point to notice is that the mnemonic defines the instruction type including which register is involved and, where appropriate, the addressing mode. It is important to read the mnemonic carefully! The explanations for LDD, LDI and LDX need reference back to Table 6.01.

It is possible to use register transfer notation to describe the execution of an instruction. For example, the LDD instruction is described by:

```
ACC ← [[CIR(15:0)]]
```

The instruction is in the CIR and only the 16-bit address needs to be examined to identify the location of the data in memory. The contents of that location are transferred into the accumulator.

TASK 6.01
Use register transfer notation to describe the execution of an LDI instruction.

Arithmetic operations

Table 6.03 contains a few examples of instruction formats used for arithmetic operations.

Instruction opcode	Instruction operand	Explanation
ADD	<address>	Add the address content to the content in the ACC
INC	<register>	Add 1 to the value stored in the specified register
DEC	<register>	Subtract 1 from the value stored in the specified register

Table 6.03 Some instruction formats for arithmetic operations

Question 6.01
What would you need to do if, for example, you wanted to add 5 to the content in the accumulator?

Comparisons and jumps

A program might require an unconditional jump or might only need a jump if a condition is met. In the latter case, a compare instruction is executed first and the result of the comparison is recorded by a flag in the status register. The execution of the conditional jump instruction begins by checking whether or not the flag bit has been set. Table 6.04 shows the format for these types of instruction.

Instruction opcode	Instruction operand	Explanation
JMP	<address>	Jump to the address specified
CMP	<address>	Compare the ACC content with the address content
CMP	#n	Compare the ACC content with *n*
JPE	<address>	Jump to the address if the result of the previous comparison was TRUE
JPN	<address>	Jump to the address if the result of the previous comparison was FALSE

Table 6.04 Some jump and compare instruction formats

Note that the two compare instructions have the same opcode. For the second one, the immediate addressing is identified by the # symbol preceding the number. In the absence of the # the operand is interpreted as an address. Note also that the comparison is restricted to asking if two values are equal.

The other point to note is that a jump instruction does not cause an actual immediate jump. Rather, it causes a new value to be supplied to the program counter so that the next instruction is fetched from this newly specified address. The incrementing of the program counter that took place automatically when the instruction was fetched is overwritten.

Input and output

The two examples here are instructions for a single character to be input or output. In each case the instruction has only an opcode; there is no operand:

- The instruction with opcode `IN` is used to store in the ACC the ASCII value of a character typed at the keyboard.
- The instruction with opcode `OUT` is used to display on the screen the character for which the ASCII code is stored in the ACC.

WORKED EXAMPLE 6.01

Tracing an assembly language program

Consider some program instructions are contained in memory locations from 100 and some eight-bit binary data values are contained in memory locations 200 and onwards. For illustrative purposes the instructions are shown in assembly language form. At the start of a part of the program, the memory contents are as shown in Figure 6.02.

Address	Contents	Address	Contents
100	LDD 201	200	0000 0000
101	INC ACC	201	0000 0001
102	ADD 203	202	0000 0010
103	CMP 205	203	0000 0011
104	JPE 106	204	0000 0100
105	DEC ACC	205	0000 0101
106	INC ACC	206	0000 0111
107	STO 206	207	0000 0000

Figure 6.02 The contents of memory addresses before execution of the program begins

The values stored in the program counter and in the accumulator as the program instructions are executed are shown in Figure 6.03.

	Program counter	Accumulator
At the start of the execution	100	0000 0000
After the instruction in 100 has been executed	101	0000 0001
After the instruction in 101 has been executed	102	0000 0010
After the instruction in 102 has been executed	103	0000 0101
After the instruction in 103 has been executed	104	0000 0101
After the instruction in 104 has been executed	106	0000 0101
After the instruction in 106 has been executed	107	0000 0110
After the instruction in 107 has been executed	108	0000 0110

Figure 6.03 The contents of the program counter and accumulator during program execution

Question 6.02

Can you follow through the changes in the values in the two registers in Worked Example 6.01? Are there any changes to the contents of memory locations 100 to 107 or 200 to 207 while the program is executing?

Summary

- A machine code instruction consists of an opcode and an operand.
- An assembly language program contains assembly language instructions plus directives that provide information to the assembler.
- Processor addressing modes can be: immediate, direct, indirect or indexed.
- Assembly language instructions can be categorised as: data movement, arithmetic, compare, jump and input/output.

Exam-style Questions

1 Three instructions for a processor with an accumulator as the single general purpose register are:

`LDD <address>` for direct addressing

`LDI <address>` for indirect addressing

`LDX <address>` for indexed addressing

In the diagrams below, the instruction operands, the register content, memory addresses and the memory contents are all shown as denary values.

a Consider the instruction `LDD 103`.

i Draw arrows on a copy of the diagram below to explain execution of the instruction. [2]

Memory address	Memory content
100	116
101	114
102	112
103	110
104	108
105	106
106	104
107	102

Accumulator

Index register

3

ii Show the contents of the accumulator as a denary value after execution of the instruction. [1]

b Consider the instruction `LDI 107`.

i Draw arrows on a copy of the diagram below to explain execution of the instruction. [3]

Memory address	Memory content
100	116
101	114
102	112
103	110
104	108
105	106
106	104
107	102

Accumulator

Index register

3

ii Show the contents of the accumulator as a denary value after execution of the instruction. [1]

c **i** Draw arrows on a copy of the diagram below to explain the execution of the instruction `LDX 103`. [3]

Memory address	Memory content
100	116
101	114
102	112
103	110
104	108
105	106
106	104
107	102

Accumulator

Index register

3

ii Show the contents of the accumulator as a denary value after the execution. [1]

2 Every machine code instruction has an equivalent in assembly language. An assembly language program will contain assembly language instructions. An assembly language program also contains components not directly transformed into machine code instructions when the program is assembled.

a Name three types of component of an assembly language program that are not intended to be directly transformed into machine code by the assembler. For one component, state its purpose. [4]

b Trace the following assembly language program using a copy of the trace table provided. Note that the LDI instruction uses indirect addressing. [6]

Assembly language program

Memory address	Memory content
100	`LDD 201`
101	`INC ACC`
102	`STO 202`
103	`LDI 203`
104	`DEC ACC`
105	`STO 201`
105	`ADD 204`
107	`STO 201`
108	`END`
∫	
201	`10`
202	`0`
203	`204`
204	`5`

Accumulator
0

Memory addresses			
201	**202**	**203**	**204**
10	0	204	5

Chapter 7
System Software

Learning objectives

By the end of this chapter you should be able to:

- describe why a computer system requires an operating system
- explain the key management tasks carried out by the operating system
- show an understanding of the need for typical utility software used by a PC computer system
- show an understanding that software under development is often constructed using existing code from program libraries
- describe the benefits to the developer of software constructed using library files, including Dynamic Link Library (DLL) files
- draw on experience of the writing of programs which include library routines
- show an understanding of the need for assembler software, a compiler and an interpreter
- describe the different stages of the assembly process for a 'two-pass' assembler
- explain the benefits and drawbacks of using either a compiler or an interpreter
- show awareness that high-level language programs may be partially compiled and partially interpreted, such as those written in Java.

7.01 System software

In the 1960s, the likely scenario for using a computer would be something like this:

1. Enter machine room with deck of punched cards and a punched paper tape reel.
2. Switch on computer.
3. Put deck of cards into card reader and press button.
4. Put paper tape into tape reader and press button.
5. Press button to run the program, entered into memory from the punched cards, which uses the data entered into memory from the paper tape.
6. Press button to get output printed on the line-printer.
7. Switch off computer.
8. Leave machine room with deck of cards, paper tape and line-printer output.

What happened is that the user controlled the computer hardware by pressing buttons. Just try to imagine how many buttons would be needed if you had to control a computer in the same way today.

The missing component from the 1960s computer was, of course, an **operating system**; in other words some software to control the hardware. An operating system is an example of a type of software called 'system software'. This distinguishes it from application software which is created to perform a specific task for a computer user rather than just helping to run the system.

KEY TERMS

Operating system: a software platform that provides facilities for programs to be run which are of benefit to a user

7.02 Operating system activities

Operating systems are extremely complex and it is not possible to give an all-embracing description of what an operating system is. However, what an operating system does can be generalised by saying that it provides an environment within which programs can be run that are of benefit to a user.

The activities of an operating system can be sub-divided into different categories. There is overlap between many of these but the classification is worthwhile. The following account provides a very brief explanation of each of the various tasks carried out by the operating system. Details of how some of them are carried out are discussed in Chapter 20 (Sections 20.01, 20.02 and 20.03).

User–system interface

A user interface is needed to allow the user to get the software and hardware to do something useful. An operating system should provide at least the following for user input and output:

- a command-line interface
- a graphical user interface (GUI).

Discussion Point:
Have you any experience of using a command-line interface?

Program–hardware interface

Programmers write software and users run this software. The software uses the hardware. The operating system has to ensure that the hardware does what the software wants it to do. Program development tools associated with a programming language allow a programmer to write a program without needing to know the details of how the hardware, particularly the processor, actually works. The operating system then has to provide the mechanism for the execution of the developed program.

Resource management

When the execution of a program has begun it is described as a **process**. In a modern computer system, a process will not be able to run to completion without interruption. At any time there will be many processes running on the computer system. Each process needs access to the resources provided by the computer system.

KEY TERMS

Process: a program that has begun execution

The resource management provided by the operating system aims to achieve optimum efficiency in computer system use. The two most important aspects of this are:

- scheduling of processes
- resolution of conflicts when two processes require the same resource.

Memory management

There are three important aspects of memory management:

- Memory protection ensures that one program does not try to use the same memory locations as another program.
- The memory organisation scheme is chosen to achieve optimum usage of a limited memory size, for example, virtual memory involving paging or segmentation.
- Memory usage optimisation involves decisions about which processes should be in main memory at any one time and where they are stored in this memory.

Device management

Every computer system has a variety of components that are categorised as 'devices'. Examples include the monitor screen, the keyboard, the printer and the webcam. The management of these requires:

- installation of the appropriate device driver software
- control of usage by processes.

File management

Three major features here are the provision of:

- file naming conventions
- directory (folder) structures
- access control mechanisms.

Security management

Chapters 8 (Section 8.02) and 21 (Section 21.04) discuss details of security issues. There are several aspects of security management which include:

- provision for recovery when data is lost
- prevention of intrusion
- ensuring data privacy.

Error detection and recovery

Errors can arise in the execution of a program either because it was badly written or because it has been supplied with inappropriate data. Other errors are associated with devices not working correctly. Whatever the cause of an error, the operating system should have the capability to interrupt a running process and provide error diagnostics where appropriate. In extreme cases, the operating system needs to be able to shut down the system in an organised fashion without loss of data.

TASK 7.01

For each of the above categories of operating system task, the individual points mentioned could often be mentioned in a different category. Make an abbreviated list of these categories and add arrows to indicate alternative places where items could be placed.

Question 7.01

It is useful to describe the management tasks carried out by an operating system as being primarily one of the following types:

- those assisting the user of the system
- those concerned with the running of the system.

Considering the management tasks that have already been categorised, can you identify them as belonging to one or other of the above types? Are there any problems in doing this?

7.03 Utility programs used by a PC

A utility program is one that might be provided by the operating system but it might also be one that is installed as a separate entity. It is a program that is not executed as part of the normal routine of operating system utilisation. Rather it is a program that the user can decide to run when needed or possibly a program that the operating system might decide to run in certain circumstances. Some utility programs are associated with hard disk usage.

Hard disk formatter and checker

A disk formatter will typically carry out the following tasks:

- removing existing data from a disk that has been used previously
- setting up the file system on the disk, based on a table of contents that allows a file recognised by the operating system to be associated with a specific physical part of the disk
- partitioning the disk into logical drives if this is required.

Another utility program, which might be a component of a disk formatter, performs disk contents analysis and, if possible, disk repair when needed. The program first checks for errors on the disk. Some errors arise from a physical defect resulting in what is called a 'bad sector'. There are a number of possible causes of bad sectors. However, they usually arise either during manufacture or from mishandling of the system. An example is moving the computer without ensuring that the disk heads are secured away from the disk surface.

Other errors arise from some abnormal event such as a loss of power or an error causing sudden system shutdown. As a result some of the files stored on the disk might no longer be in an identifiable state. A disk repair utility program can mark bad sectors as such and ensure that the file system no longer tries to use them. When the integrity of files has been affected, the utility might be able to recover some of the data but otherwise it has to delete the files from the file system.

Hard disk defragmenter

A disk defragmenter utility could possibly be part of a disk repair utility program but it is not primarily concerned with errors. A perfectly functioning disk will, while in use, gradually become less efficient because the constant creation, editing and deletion of files leaves them in a fragmented state. The cause of this is the logical arrangement of data in sectors as discussed in Chapter 3 (Section 3.03), which does not allow a file to be stored as a contiguous entity.

A simple illustration of the problem is shown in Figure 7.01. Initially file A occupies three sectors fully and part of a fourth one. File B is small so occupies only part of a sector. File C occupies two sectors fully and part of a third. When File B is deleted, the sector remains unfilled because it would require too much system overhead to rearrange the file organisation every time there is a change. When File A is extended it completely fills the first four sectors and the remainder of the extended file is stored in all of Sector 8 and part of Sector 9. Sector 4 will only be used again if a small file is created or if the disk fills up, when it might store the first part of a longer file.

	Sectors 0-3	Sector 4	Sectors 5-7	Sectors 8-9
Initlial position	File A	File B	File C	
File B is deleted	File A		File C	
File A is extended	File A		File C	File A

Figure 7.01 File fragmentation on a hard disk

A defragmenter utility program reorganises the file storage to return it to a state where all files are stored in contiguous sectors. For a large disk this will take some time. It will be impossible if the disk is too full because of the lack of working space for the rearrangement.

TASK 7.02

If you have never used a disk defragmenter or disk repair utility program can you get access to a system where you can use one? If so, note the changes that are carried out and recorded by the utility program.

Backup software

It is quite likely that you perform a manual backup every now and then using a flash memory stick. However, a safer and more reliable approach is to have a backup utility program do this for you. You can still use the memory stick to store the backed-up data but the utility program will control the process. In particular it can do two things:

- establish a schedule for backups
- only create a new backup file when there has been a change.

File compression

A file compression utility program can be used as a matter of routine by an operating system to minimise hard disk storage requirements. If the operating system does not do this, a user can still choose to implement a suitable program. However, as was discussed in Chapter 1 (Section 1.07), file compression is most important when transmitting data. In particular, it makes sense to compress (or 'zip') a file before attaching it to an email.

Virus checker

A virus-checking program should be installed as a permanent facility to protect a computer system. In an ideal world, it would only need to be used to scan a file when the file initially entered the system. Unfortunately this ideal state can never be realised. When a new virus comes along there is a delay before it is recognised and a further delay before a virus checker has been updated to deal with it. As a result it is necessary for a virus checker to be regularly updated and for it to scan all files on a computer system as a matter of routine.

7.04 Library programs

A library program can be defined as a program contained in a program library but both 'library program' and 'program library' are misleading terms. There may be programs in a program library but more often they are subroutines that programmers can use in their programs.

There is no advantage to a programmer in 'reinventing the wheel'. If a routine exists in a library a programmer would be very unwise to write his or her own routine. Existing library routines will have been extensively tested before release. Even if some residual bugs did exist following testing, the regular use of the routines would almost inevitably lead to their detection.

The most obvious examples of library routines are the built-in functions available for use when programming in a particular language. Examples of these are discussed in Chapter 13 (Section 13.08). Another example is the collection of over 1600 procedures for mathematical and statistics processing available from the Numerical Algorithms Group (NAG) library. This organisation has been creating routines since 1971 and they are universally accepted as being as reliable as software ever can be.

In Section 7.05, the methods available for translation of source code are discussed. For the purpose of the discussion here you just need an overview of what happens. The source code is written in a programming language of choice. If a compiler is used for the translation and no errors are found, the compiler produces object code (machine code). This code cannot be executed by itself. Instead it has to be linked with the code for any subroutines used by it. It is possible to carry out the linking before loading the composite code into memory and running it.

By contrast, dynamic linking has the routines from a dynamic link library (DLL) already in memory. While the code is running, it links to the DLL routine that it needs. A DLL is created so that its routines can be shared. More than one process can dynamically link to a DLL file at any one time.

7.05 Language translators

As with much of this chapter, the discussion will contain few details of how translators work because they are dealt with in Chapter 20 (Section 20.05). The need for a language translator is easy to explain and, indeed, is explained in Chapter 6 (Section 6.02). Writing a program directly in machine code would take a very long time and undoubtedly would lead to a multitude of errors.

Assemblers

If a programmer has decided to write a program, or perhaps a procedure, in assembly language there is a need for a program to translate this into machine code. The program needed is called an assembler. If the program was written in a very simple form the conversion would require straightforward conversion of the instructions written in mnemonic form to the machine code version. However, in most instances more is required.

A 'two-pass' assembler is not an essential requirement but it does clearly differentiate between the two stages that are required in translation. As was discussed in Chapter 6, an assembly language program will contain features that are used to help the programmer and others that are used to inform the assembler program. In the first pass of a two-pass assembler all of these features are either removed or acted upon. Typical actions are:

- removal of comments
- creation of a symbol table containing the binary codes for symbolic names and labels
- creation of a literal table if the programmer has used constants in the program
- expansion of macros
- identification of system calls and subroutines used.

If errors are not found, the second pass of the assembler generates the object code. This involves replacing symbolic addresses with absolute addresses.

As noted above, object code is not an executable code. The creation of executable code requires a linker to be used to ensure that the object code for the program and the object codes for associated procedures are transferrable into memory with mutually consistent memory locations. The actual transfer into memory is carried out by a loader or the loader element of a link-loader. This carries out any final adjustment of memory addresses that might be necessary.

Compilers and interpreters

The starting point for using either a compiler or an interpreter is a file containing source code, which is a program written in a high-level language.

For an interpreter the following steps apply:

1. The interpreter program, the source code file and the data to be used by the source code program are all made available.
2. The interpreter program begins execution.
3. The first line of the source code is read.
4. The line is analysed.
5. If an error is found this is reported and the interpreter program halts execution.
6. If no error is found the line of source code is converted to an intermediate code.
7. The interpreter program uses this intermediate code to execute the required action.
8. The next line of source code is read and Steps 4–8 are repeated.

For a compiler the following steps apply:

1. The compiler program and the source code file are made available but no data is needed.
2. The compiler program begins execution.
3. The first line of the source code is read.
4. The line is analysed.
5. If an error is found this is recorded.
6. If no error is found the line of source code is converted to an intermediate code.
7. The next line of source code is read and Steps 4–7 are repeated.
8. when the whole of the source code has been dealt with one of the following happens:
   - If no error is found in the whole source code the complete intermediate code is converted into object code.
   - If any errors are found a list of these is output and no object code is produced.

Execution of the program can only begin when the compilation has shown no errors. This can take place automatically under the control of the compiler program if data for the program is available. Alternatively the object code is stored and the program is executed later with no involvement of the compiler.

Discussion Point:

What type of facility for language translation are you being provided with? Does your experience of using it match what has been described here?

For a programmer, the following statements can be made about the advantages and disadvantages of creating interpreted or compiled programs:

- An interpreter has advantages when a program is being developed because errors can be identified as they occur and corrected immediately without having to wait for the whole of the source code to be read and analysed.
- An interpreter has a disadvantage in that during a particular execution of the program, parts of the code which contain syntax errors may not be accessed so if errors are still present they are not discovered until later.
- An interpreter has a disadvantage when a program is error free and is distributed to users because the source code has to be sent to each user.

- A compiler has the advantage that an executable file can be distributed to users so the users have no access to the source code.

For a user, the following statements can be made about the advantages and disadvantages of using interpreted or compiled programs:

- For an interpreted program, the interpreter and the source code have to be available each time that an error-free program is run.
- For a compiled program, only the object code has to be available each time that an error-free program is run.
- Compiled object code will provide faster execution than is possible for an interpreted program.
- Compiled object code is less secure because it could contain a virus.

Whether an interpreter or a compiler is going to be used, a program can only be run on a particular computer with a particular processor if the interpreter or compiler program has been written for that processor.

Java

When the programming language Java was created, a different philosophy was applied to how it should be used. Each different type of computer has to have a Java Virtual Machine created for it. Then when a programmer writes a Java program this is compiled first of all to create what is called Java Byte Code. When the program is run, this code is interpreted by the Java Virtual Machine. The Java Byte Code can be transferred to any computer that has a Java Virtual Machine installed.

Summary

- Operating system tasks can be categorised in more than one way, for example, some are for helping the user, others are for running the system.
- Utility programs for a PC include hard disk utilities, backup programs, virus checkers and file compression utilities.
- Library programs, including Dynamic Link Library (DLL) files, are available to be incorporated into programs; they are usually subroutines and are very reliable.
- For a two-pass assembler, typical activities in the first pass are creation of a symbol table and expansion of macros; object code is generated in the second pass.
- A high-level language can be translated using an interpreter or a compiler.
- A Java compiler produces Java Byte Code which is interpreted by a Java Virtual Machine.

Exam-style Questions

1 a One of the reasons for having an operating system is to provide a user interface to a computer system.

  i Name two different types of interface that an operating system should provide. [2]

  ii Identify for each type of interface a device that could be used to enter data. [2]

b Identify and explain briefly three other management tasks carried out by an operating system. [6]

2 a A PC operating system will make available to a user a number of utility programs.

  i Identify two utility programs that might be used to deal with a hard disk problem. [2]

  ii For each of these utility programs explain why it might be needed and explain what it does. [5]

  iii Identify two other utility programs for a PC user. [2]

b Library programs are made available for programmers.

  i Explain why a programmer should use library programs. [3]

  ii Identify two examples of a library program. [2]

3 a Assemblers, compilers and interpreters are examples of translation programs.

  i State the difference between an assembler and a compiler or interpreter. [1]

  ii A 'two-pass' assembler is usually used. Give two examples of what will be done in the first pass. [2]

  iii State what will be produced in the second pass. [1]

b A programmer can choose to use an interpreter or a compiler.

  i State three differences between how an interpreter works and how a compiler works. [3]

  ii Discuss the advantages and disadvantages of an interpreter compared to a compiler. [4]

  iii If a programmer chooses Java, a special approach is used. Identify one feature of this special approach. [1]

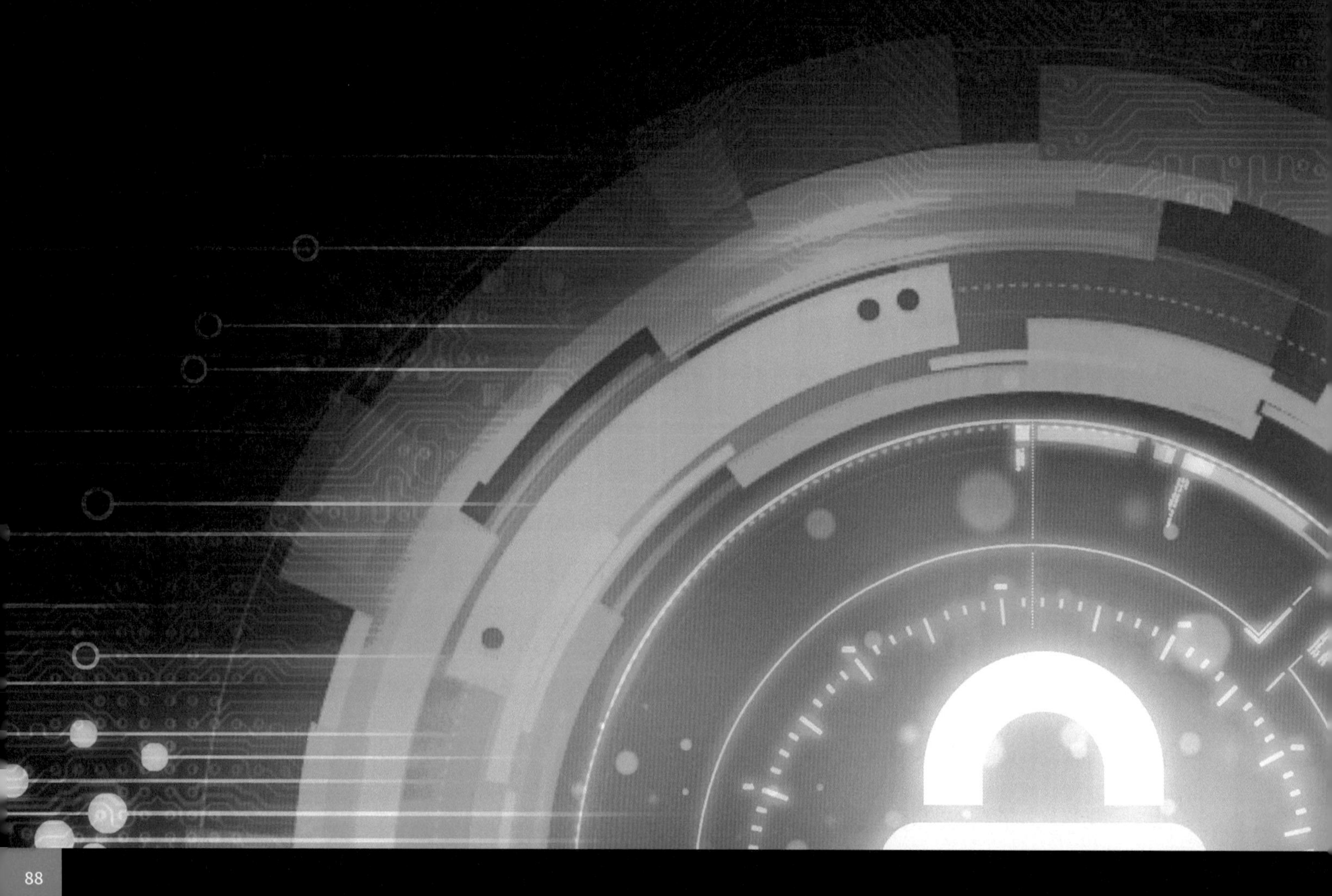

Chapter 8
Data Security, Privacy and Integrity

Learning objectives

By the end of this chapter you should be able to:

- explain the difference between the terms security, privacy and integrity of data
- show appreciation of the need for both the security of data and the security of the computer system
- describe security measures designed to protect computer systems, ranging from the stand-alone PC to a network of computers, including user accounts, firewalls and authentication techniques
- describe security measures designed to protect the security of data
- show awareness of what kind of data errors can occur and what can be done about them
- describe error detection and correction measures designed to protect the integrity of data including: data validation, data verification for data entry and data verification during data transfer.

8.01 Definitions of data integrity, privacy and security

It is easy to define integrity of data but far less easy to ensure it. Only accurate and up-to-date data has **data integrity**. Any person or organisation that stores data needs it to have integrity. Methods that can be used to give the best chance of achieving data integrity are discussed in this chapter and also in Chapter 10 (Section 10.01).

KEY TERMS

Data integrity: a requirement for data to be accurate and up to date

Data privacy: a requirement for data to be available only to authorised users

Data security: a requirement for data to be recoverable if lost or corrupted

Data privacy is about keeping data private rather than allowing it to be available in the public domain. The term 'data privacy' may be applied to a person or an organisation. Each individual has an almost limitless amount of data associated with their existence. Assuming that an individual is not engaged in criminal or subversive activities, he or she should be in control of which data about himself or herself is made public and which data remains private. An organisation can have data that is private to the organisation, such as the minutes of management meetings, but this will not be discussed further here.

For an individual there is little chance of data privacy if there is not a legal framework in place to penalise offenders who breach this privacy. Such laws are referred to as **data protection laws**. The major aspects of data protection laws relate to personal, therefore private, data that an individual supplies to an organisation. The data is supplied to allow the organisation to use it but only for purposes understood and agreed by the individual. Data protection laws oblige organisations to ensure the privacy and the integrity of this data. Unfortunately having laws does not guarantee adherence to them but they do act as a deterrent if wrong-doers can be subject to legal proceedings.

KEY TERMS

Data protection law: a law that relates to data privacy

Discussion Point:

What data protection laws are in place in your country? Are you familiar with any details of these laws?

Data protection normally applies to data stored in computer systems with the consent of the individual. Should these laws be extended to cover storage of data obtained from telephone calls or search engine usage?

Data can be said to be 'secure' if it is available for use when needed and the data made available is the data that was stored originally. The security of data has been breached if the data has been lost or corrupted.

It should be clear that **data security** is a prerequisite for ensuring data integrity and data privacy. However, by itself it cannot guarantee either.

8.02 Security measures for protecting computer systems

One of the requirements for protection of data is the security of the system used to store the data. However, system security is not needed just to protect data. There are two primary aims of system security measures. The first is to ensure system functionality. The second is to ensure that only authorised users have access to the system.

The threats to the security of a system can be categorised as being one of the following types:

- internal mismanagement
- natural disasters
- unauthorised intrusion into the system by an individual
- malicious software entering the system.

Continuity of operation is vital for large computer installations that are an integral part of the day-to-day operations of an organisation. Measures are needed to ensure that the system remains functional whatever event occurs or, if there has to be a system shut-down, at the very least to guarantee resumption of service within a very short time. Such measures come under the general heading of disaster recovery contingency planning. The contingency plan should be based on a risk assessment. The plan will have provision for an alternative system to be brought into action. If an organisation has a full system always ready to replace the normally operational one, it is referred to as a 'hot site'. By definition such a system has to be remote from the original system to allow recovery from natural disasters such as earthquake or flood.

A special case of system vulnerability arises when there is a major update of hardware and/or software. Traditionally, organisations had the luxury of installing and testing a new system over a weekend when no service was being provided. In the modern era, globally available systems are the norm: a company is never closed for business. As a result, organisations may need to have the original system and its replacement running in parallel for a period to ensure continuity of service.

Discussion Point:

Major failings of large computer systems are well documented. You could carry out research to find some examples. Find an example of where the crisis was caused by technology failure and a different example where some natural disaster was the cause.

Even if a PC is used by only one person there should be a user account set up. User accounts are, of course, essential for a multi-user (timesharing) system. The main security feature of a user account is the **authentication** of the user. The normal method is to associate a password with each account. In order for this to be effective the password needs a large number of characters including a variety of those provided in the ASCII scheme.

KEY TERMS

Authentication: verification of a user's identity

TASK 8.01

1 Create an example of a secure password using eight characters (but not one you are going to use).

2 Assuming that each character is taken from the ASCII set of graphic characters how many different possible passwords could be defined by eight characters?

3 Do you think this is a sufficient number of characters to assume that the password would not be encountered by someone trying all possible passwords in turn to access the system?

Alternative methods of authentication include biometric methods and security tokens. A biometric method might require examination of a fingerprint or the face or the eye. A security token can be a small item of hardware provided for each individual user that confirms their identity. Similar protection can be provided by software with the user required to provide further input after the password has been entered. Normal practice is to combine one of these alternative methods with the password system.

General good practice that helps to keep a personal computer secure includes not leaving the computer switched on when unattended, not allowing someone else to observe you accessing the computer and not writing down details of how you access it.

A computer system is not only accessed by users logging in. One potential problem arises from users attaching portable storage devices which can contain a virus. The safest practice is for an organisation to have a policy banning the use of such devices. Unfortunately this is not possible if normal business processes require portability of data.

The threat that is virtually unavoidable arises because of the connection of an organisation's systems to the Internet. The major potential problem is that transmissions into the system from the Internet may contain malicious software. However, a further consequence of Internet connection is that sensitive data from the system might be exported out to some other system.

The primary defence to such problems is to install a firewall. Ideally a firewall will be a hardware device that acts like a security gate at an international airport. Nothing is allowed through without it being inspected. Alternatively, a firewall might be implemented as software. The transmission must then enter the system but it can be inspected immediately. The action of a firewall might be to concentrate solely on the addresses identified in any transmission. However, in addition, a firewall might examine the data within the transmission to check for anything inappropriate.

If an incoming transmission is an email, there can be a concern about authenticating the identity of the sender. The solution is to insist on the sender attaching a digital certificate to the email. Some details of this are discussed in Chapter 21 (Section 21.02).

Security measures restricting access to a system do not guarantee success in removing all threats. It is therefore necessary to have, in addition, programs running on a system to check for problems. Options for this are:

- a virus checker which carries out regular system scans to detect any viruses and remove them or deactivate them
- an intrusion detection system that will take as input an audit record of system use and look for anomalous use.

It hardly needs saying that individuals intent on causing damage to systems are using methods that are becoming ever more sophisticated. The defence methods have to be improved continually to counter these threats.

8.03 Security measures for protecting data

There are a number of scenarios which require security methods for protecting data. The three discussed here are data loss, access to data and protection of data content.

Recovering from data loss

In addition to problems arising from malicious activity there are a variety of reasons for accidental loss of data:

- a disk or tape gets corrupted
- a disk or tape is destroyed
- the system crashes
- the file is erased or overwritten by mistake
- the location of the file is forgotten.

A system therefore needs a backup procedure to be implemented. The system administrator has to decide on the details of the procedure. The principles for the procedure traditionally followed are straightforward:

- a full backup is made at regular intervals, perhaps weekly
- at least two generations of full backup are kept in storage
- incremental backups are made on a daily basis.

For maximum security the backup disks or tapes are stored away from the system in a fire-proof and flood-proof location.

This worked well when an incremental backup was done overnight with the full backup handled at the weekend. With systems running 24/7 and therefore with data potentially changing at any time, such a simple approach to backup will leave data in an inconsistent state. One solution is to have a backup program that effectively freezes the file store while data is being copied but also records elsewhere within the system changes that are happening due to ongoing system use. The changes can then be made to the system files when the backup copy has been stored.

An alternative approach is to use a disk-mirroring strategy. In this case, data is simultaneously stored on two disk systems during the normal operation of the system. The individual disk systems might be at remote locations as part of a disaster recovery plan.

Restricting access to data

If a user has logged in they have been authorised to use the computer system but not necessarily all of it. In particular, the system administrator may recognise different categories of user with different needs with respect to the data they are allowed to see and use. The typical trivial example usually quoted is that one employee should be able to use the system to look up another employee's internal phone number. This should not allow the employee at the same time to check the salary paid to the other employee.

The solution is to have an **authorisation** policy which in general gives different access rights to different files for different individuals. For a particular file, a particular individual might have no access at all or possibly read access but not write access. In another case, an individual might have read and append access but not unrestricted write access.

KEY TERMS

Authorisation: definition of a user's access rights to system components

Protecting data content

Even with appropriate security measures in place it can happen that there is unauthorised access to a system or interception of data transmission. This can be made a futile activity for the perpetrator if the data cannot be read. Data can be encrypted to ensure this. Some details of encryption methods are discussed in Chapter 21 (Section 21.01).

8.04 Data validation and verification

Data integrity can never be absolutely guaranteed but the chances are improved if appropriate measures are taken when data originally enters a system or when it is transmitted from one system to another.

Validation and verification of data entry

The term **validation** is a somewhat misleading one. It seems to imply that data is accurate if it has been validated. This is far from the truth. If entry of a name is expected but the wrong name is entered, it will be recognised as a name and therefore accepted as valid. Validation can only prevent incorrect data if there is an attempt to input data that is of the wrong type, in the wrong format or out of range.

Data validation is implemented by software associated with a data entry interface. There are a number of different types of check that can be made. Typical examples are:

- a presence check to ensure that an entry field is not left blank
- a format check, for example a date has to be dd/mm/yyyy
- a length check, for example with a telephone number
- a range check, for example the month in a date must not exceed 12
- a type check, for example only a numeric value for the month in a date.

Verification of data means confirming what has been entered. The most common example is when a user is asked to supply a new password. There will always be a request for the password to be re-entered. Clearly, if the user entered a password but did not enter it as intended, subsequent attempts at access would fail. Verification is usually an effective process but in general it does not ensure data accuracy because the wrong data could be entered initially and in the re-entry.

KEY TERMS

Validation: a check that data entered is of the correct type and format; it does not guarantee that data is accurate

Verification: confirmation of data received by a system

Verification during data transfer

It is possible for data to be corrupted during transmission. Typically this applies at the bit level with an individual bit being flipped from 1 to 0 or vice versa. Verification techniques need to check on some property associated with the bit pattern.

The simplest approach is to use a simple one-bit parity check. This is particularly easy to implement if data is transferred in bytes using a seven-bit code. Either even or odd parity can be implemented in the eighth bit of the byte. Assuming even parity, the procedure is:

1. At the transmitting end, the number of 1s in the seven -bit code is counted.
2. If the count gives an even number, the parity bit is set to 0.
3. If the count gives an odd number, the parity bit is set to 1.
4. This is repeated for every byte in the transmission.
5. At the receiving end, the number of 1s in the eight-bit code is counted.
6. If the count gives an even number, the byte is accepted.
7. This is repeated for every byte in the transmission.

If no errors are found, the transmission is accepted. However, the transmission cannot be guaranteed to be error free. It is possible for two bits to be flipped in an individual byte. Fortunately this is rather unlikely so it is a sensible assumption to assume no error. The limitation of the method is that it can only detect the presence of an error. It cannot identify the actual bit that is in error. If an error is detected, re-transmission has to be requested.

An alternative approach is to use the checksum method. In this case at the transmitting end a block is defined as a number of bytes. Then, irrespective of what the bytes represent, the bits in each byte are interpreted as a binary number. The sum of these binary numbers in a block is calculated and supplied as a checksum value in the transmission. This is repeated for each block. The receiver does the same calculation and checks the summation value with the checksum value transmitted for each block in turn. Once again an error can be detected but its position in the transmission cannot be determined.

For a method to detect the exact position of an error and therefore be able to correct an error it has to be considerably more complex. A simple approach to this is the parity block check method. Like the checksum method this is a longitudinal parity check; it is used to check a serial sequence of binary digits contained in a number of bytes.

WORKED EXAMPLE 8.01

Using a parity block check

At the transmitting end, a program reads a group of seven bytes as illustrated in Figure 8.01. The data is represented by seven bits for each byte. The most significant bit in each byte, bit 7, is undefined so we have left it blank.

	Seven-bit codes						
	1	0	1	0	0	1	1
	0	1	1	0	0	0	1
	1	0	1	1	0	0	0
	0	0	1	1	1	0	0
	0	1	1	0	0	1	0
	0	1	1	0	0	0	1
	0	1	1	0	0	0	1

Figure 8.01 Seven bytes to be transmitted

The parity bit is set for each of the bytes, as in Figure 8.02. The most significant bit is set to achieve even parity.

Parity bits	Seven-bit codes						
0	1	0	1	0	0	1	1
1	0	1	1	0	0	0	1
1	1	0	1	1	0	0	0
1	0	0	1	1	1	0	0
1	0	1	1	0	0	1	0
1	0	1	1	0	0	0	1
1	0	1	1	0	0	0	1

Figure 8.02 Bytes with the parity bit set

An additional byte is then created and each bit is set as a parity bit for the bits at that bit position. This includes counting the parity bits in the seven bytes containing data. This is illustrated in Figure 8.03.

Parity bits	Seven-bit codes						
0	1	0	1	0	0	1	1
1	0	1	1	0	0	0	1
1	1	0	1	1	0	0	0
1	0	0	1	1	1	0	0
1	0	1	1	0	0	1	0
1	0	1	1	0	0	0	1
1	0	1	1	0	0	0	1
0	0	0	1	0	1	0	0

Figure 8.03 Parity byte added

The program then transmits the eight bytes in sequence.

At the receiving end, a program takes the eight bytes as input and checks the parity sums for the individual bytes and for the bit positions.

Note that the method is handling a serial transmission so it includes longitudinal checking but the actual checking algorithm is working on a matrix of bit values. If there is just one error in the seven bytes this method will allow the program at the receiving end to identify the position of the error. It can therefore correct the error so the transmission can be accepted.

Question 8.01

1 Assume that the seven bytes shown in Figure 8.04 contain data. The most significant bit is undefined because a seven-bit ASCII code is being used to represent character data. Choose a parity and create the appropriate parity bit for each byte, then create the eighth byte that would be used for transmission in a parity block check method.

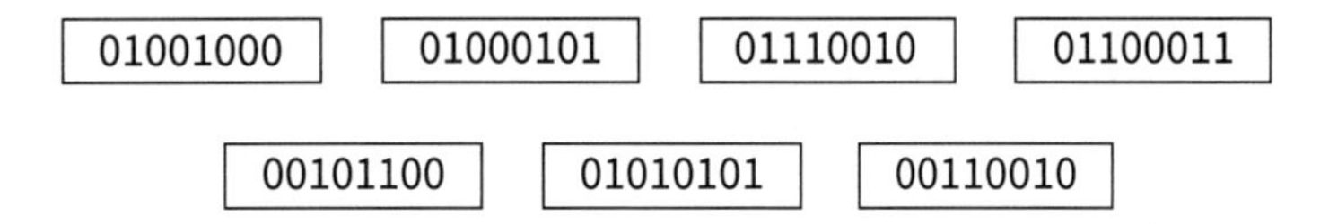

Figure 8.04 Seven bytes to be transmitted

2 The eight bytes shown in Figure 8.05 have been received in a transmission using the parity block method. The first seven bytes contain the data and the last byte contains the parity check bits.

01001000	11000101	11110001	01100011
01001010	01010101	01110010	01110010

Figure 8.05 Eight bytes received in a transmission

a Identify what has gone wrong during the transmission.

b What would happen after the transmission is checked?

Summary

- Important considerations for the storage of data are: data integrity, data privacy and data security.
- Data protection laws relate to data privacy.
- Security measures for computer systems include authentication of users, prevention of unauthorised access, protection from malware and methods for recovery following system failure.
- Security methods for data include backup procedures, user authorisation and access control.
- Data entry to a system should be subject to data validation and data verification.
- Verification for data transmission may be carried out using: a parity check, a checksum or a parity block check method.

Exam-style Questions

1 **a** It is important that data has integrity.

i Identify the missing word in the sentence 'Concerns about the integrity of data are concerns about its ....'. [1]

ii Validation and verification are techniques that help to ensure data integrity when data is entered into a system.

Explain the difference between validation and verification. [3]

iii Define a type of validation and give an example. [2]

iv Even after validation has been correctly applied data may lack integrity when it comes to be used. Explain why that might happen. [2]

b Data should be protected from being read by unauthorised individuals.

Explain two policies that can be used to provide the protection. [4]

2 **a** Security of data is an important concern for a system administrator.

i Identify three reasons why data might not be available when a user needs it. [3]

ii Describe what could be features of a policy for ensuring data security. [3]

b It is important for mission-critical systems that there is a disaster recovery contingency plan in place.

i Define what type of disaster is under consideration here. [2]

ii Define what will be a major feature of the contingency plan. [2]

c Measures to ensure security of a computer system need to be in place on a daily basis if the system is connected to the Internet.

Describe two measures that could be taken to ensure security of the system. [4]

3 **a** When data is transmitted measures need to be applied to check whether the data has been transmitted correctly.

i If data consists of seven-bit codes transmitted in bytes, describe how a simple parity check system would be used. Your account should include a description of what happens at the transmitting end and what happens at the receiving end. [5]

ii An alternative approach is to use a checksum method. Describe how this works. [3]

b For either of these two methods there are limitations as to what can be achieved by them.

Identify two of these limitations. [2]

c A different method which does not have all of these limitations is the parity block check method.

The following diagram represents eight bytes received where the parity block method has been applied at the transmitting end. The first seven bytes contain the data and the last byte contains parity bits.

Byte 1	0	1	0	1	0	0	1	1
Byte 2	1	0	1	1	0	0	0	1
Byte 3	1	1	0	1	0	0	0	0
Byte 4	1	0	0	1	1	1	0	0
Byte 5	1	0	1	1	0	0	1	0
Byte 6	1	0	1	1	0	0	0	1
Byte 7	1	0	1	1	0	0	0	1
Byte 8	0	0	0	1	0	1	0	0

Identify the problem with this received data and what would be done with it by the program used by the receiver. [4]

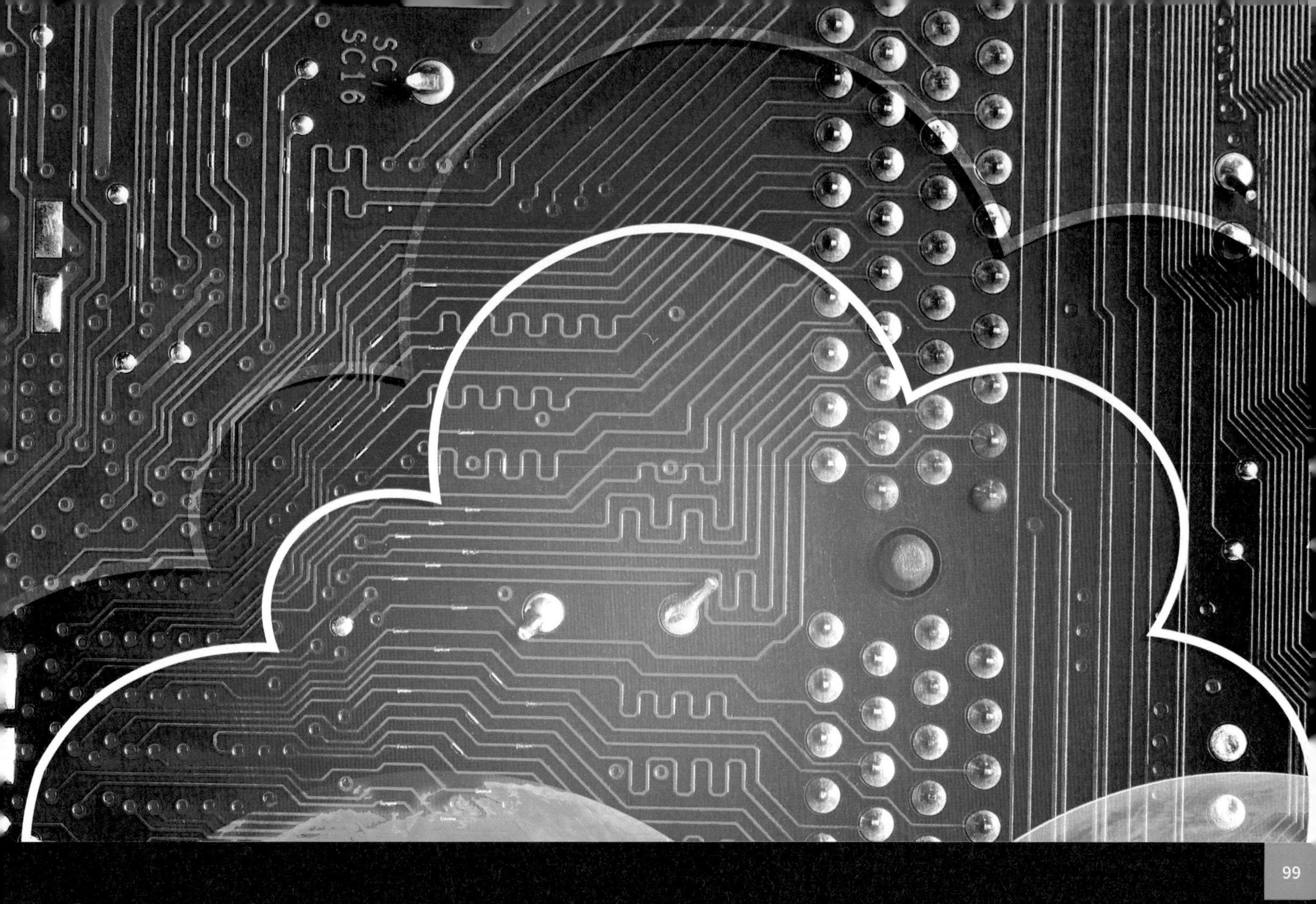

Chapter 9
Ethics and Ownership

Learning objectives

By the end of this chapter you should be able to:

- show a basic understanding of ethics
- explain how ethics may impact on the job role of the computing professional
- show understanding of the eight principles listed in the ACM/IEEE Software Engineering Code of Ethics
- demonstrate the relevance of these principles to some typical software developer workplace scenarios
- show understanding of the need for a professional code of conduct for a computer system developer
- show understanding of the concept of ownership and copyright
- describe the need for legislation to protect ownership, usage and copyright
- discuss measures to restrict access to data made available through the Internet and World Wide Web
- show understanding of the implications of different types of software licensing.

9.01 Ethics

You can find a number of definitions of what we might mean when we talk about 'ethics'. The following three sentences are representative:

- Ethics is the field of moral science.
- Ethics are the moral principles by which any person is guided.
- Ethics are the rules of conduct recognised in a particular profession or area of human life.

For present purposes we can ignore the first of these definitions. The third definition is the focus of this chapter. However, the rules of conduct must inevitably reflect, at least in part, the moral principles that are the foundation of the second definition. The following are some observations that come to mind when considering moral principles.

Moral principles concern right or wrong. The concept of virtue is often linked to what is considered to be right. What is right and wrong might be considered from one of the following viewpoints: philosophical, religious, legal or pragmatic.

Philosophical debate has been going on for well over 2000 years. Early thinkers frequently quoted in this context are Aristotle and Confucius but there are many more. Religions have sometimes incorporated philosophies already existing or have introduced their own. Laws should reflect what is right and wrong. Pragmatism could be defined as applying common sense.

This chapter is not an appropriate place to discuss religious beliefs other than to make the obvious statement that religious beliefs do have to be considered in the working environment. Legal issues clearly impact on working practices but they are rarely the primary focus in rules of conduct. What remains as the foundation for rules of conduct are the philosophical views of right and wrong and the pragmatic views of what is common sense. These will constitute a frame of reference for what follows in this chapter.

9.02 The ACM/IEEE Software Engineering Code of Ethics

The Association for Computing Machinery (ACM) and the Institute of Electrical and Electronics Engineers (IEEE) are both based in the USA but have a global perspective and global influence. It is therefore appropriate to consider the code of ethics that they have proposed but this does not signify that codes of practice published in other countries are not important.

In presenting the code, the authors make it clear that it in no way does the code represent a look-up table that will prescribe an action to be taken given a defined circumstance. They stress that the public interest is the central focus for the code. The code presents a set of fundamental principles. They advocate that a professional should make an ethical judgement based on thoughtful consideration of these fundamental principles.

The code defines eight principles. For each principle there is a one-sentence definition in the preamble. In the full version of the code, each principle is expanded into clauses. Each clause refers to a specific aspect that should be considered in the context of that principle. This is a form of checklist that gives a framework for an ethical judgement.

The eight principles are presented as follows in the preamble:

1. PUBLIC – Software engineers shall act consistently with the public interest.
2. CLIENT AND EMPLOYER – Software engineers shall act in a manner that is in the best interests of their client and employer consistent with the public interest.
3. PRODUCT – Software engineers shall ensure that their products and related modifications meet the highest professional standards possible.
4. JUDGMENT – Software engineers shall maintain integrity and independence in their professional judgment.
5. MANAGEMENT – Software engineering managers and leaders shall subscribe to and promote an ethical approach to the management of software development and maintenance.
6. PROFESSION – Software engineers shall advance the integrity and reputation of the profession consistent with the public interest.
7. COLLEAGUES – Software engineers shall be fair to and supportive of their colleagues.
8. SELF – Software engineers shall participate in lifelong learning regarding the practice of their profession and shall promote an ethical approach to the practice of the profession.

In total there are 80 clauses for these eight principles (numbered from 1.01 through to 8.09). There is little to be gained from including all of them in this book. However, you should have a copy readily available when you are studying this chapter (see https://www.acm.org/about/se-code).

Examination of some of the clauses soon makes it clear that many do not contain specific reference to software engineering but rather, relate to proper behaviour for any group of professionals. This can be illustrated by the following examples:

2.03 Use the property of a client or employer only in ways properly authorized, and with the client's or employer's knowledge and consent.

5.04 Assign work only after taking into account appropriate contributions of education and experience tempered with a desire to further that education and experience.

5.05 Ensure realistic quantitative estimates of cost, scheduling, personnel, quality and outcomes on any project on which they work or propose to work, and provide an uncertainty assessment of these estimates.

6.06 Obey all laws governing their work, unless, in exceptional circumstances, such compliance is inconsistent with the public interest.

Clauses 5.04 and 6.06 illustrate a general tendency for the clauses to be more wordy than they might have been because many of them have a qualifier. The same qualifier appears more than once. Clause 5.05 is somewhat unusual with regard to the amount of detail. You would expect a mention of realistic quantitative estimates but probably not the insistence on an uncertainty assessment.

Discussion Point:

Should clause 5.05 include an insistence on an uncertainty assessment? Are there alternative suggestions that might have been included?

Clause 6.06 advocates law-breaking to serve the public interest. Can you think of circumstances when you could agree that such action would be ethical? You might wish to consider 'whistle-blowing'.

WORKED EXAMPLE 9.01

Applying ethics to a software engineering scenario

In a real-life scenario there might be many individual clauses that should be considered when a judgement is to be made. For example, let's consider the following scenario.

You are working on a software engineering project. One day the project manager states that the project is running behind schedule. As a result, the time allocated for testing of the software will be limited to one week rather than the one month that was stated in the project plan.

You could approach your thinking by adopting a step-by-step approach.

1. You would rule out any immediate need to consider public interest.
2. You would identify the primary cause of concern as being directly addressed by clause 3.10: Ensure adequate testing, debugging, and review of software and related documents on which they work.
3. You would identify the secondary cause of concern as being one of poor management with clauses 5.01 and 5.11 being the most relevant: Ensure good management for any project on which they work, including effective procedures for promotion of quality and reduction of risk. Not ask a software engineer to do anything inconsistent with this Code.
4. You would now consider what action to take and would refer to clauses 6.11, 6.12 and 6.13: Recognize that violations of this Code are inconsistent with being a professional software engineer. Express concerns to the people involved when significant violations of this Code are detected unless this is impossible, counter-productive, or dangerous. Report significant violations of this Code to appropriate authorities when it is clear that consultation with people involved in these significant violations is impossible, counter-productive or dangerous.

Question 9.01

There are several other clauses that might be considered as relevant. Have a look at clauses 3.02, 3.05 and 7.01. Do you consider that any of these offer anything new in helping to judge what should be done?

Discussion Point:

Search the clauses for all eight principles and identify the ones that mention documentation. Why is documentation mentioned so many times?

9.03 The public good

What has been considered so far relates directly to professional working practices and therefore revolves around the third definition of ethics presented in Section 9.01. When the question of public good arises, consideration has to relate to the second definition as well. In different parts of the code there is reference to:

- the health, safety and welfare of the public
- the public interest
- the public good
- public concern.

There is no further indication of how these should be interpreted. It will be helpful to consider some individual cases to illustrate what might be considered.

Fortunately, there are very few examples which have involved loss of life and certainly none where large numbers of deaths were caused. However, there have been a number of incidents where extremely large sums of money were wasted because of rather simplistic errors.

The first example that could be mentioned is the Ariane 5 rocket which exploded 40 seconds after blast-off in 1996. To the detriment of the public good, approximately 500 million dollars were spent for no benefit at all. The problem was caused by a line of code that tried to convert a 64-bit floating point number into a 16-bit integer. The resulting overflow crashed the program and as a result also the rocket.

The second example also relates to space exploration. The NASA Mars Climate Orbiter project centred on a space probe that was due to orbit Mars to study the climate. The probe got to Mars but unfortunately failed to get into orbit. The cause of the problem was that all of the software was supposed to use the SI system of units for all calculations. One group of software engineers used the Imperial system of units. This mismatch only caused a problem at the stage when the calculations concerned with achieving orbit around Mars were executed. This time the loss to the public purse was a mere 125 million dollars.

These examples can be said to illustrate the public interest in successful software engineering. There is a strong argument that the correct application of the code of ethics with respect to specification and testing of software could have saved a lot of money.

A different type of disaster is the system that never gets built. In 2011 the UK government scrapped the National Programme for IT in the NHS (National Health Service), which had been commissioned in 2002. The project failed to produce a workable system. The estimated amount spent on the program was 12 billion pounds. The initial estimated cost was less than three billion pounds. In examples like this the software engineers are not to blame, but if correctly applied, the part of the code of ethics specifically targeted at project management would not have allowed this type of fiasco to occur.

In the three examples outlined above the public concern was solely related to the costs associated with a failed project. There was no public concern relating to the ethics of the endeavour itself. In contrast there are many areas associated with computer-based systems where there is public concern about the nature of the endeavour or at least about what it has led to. The following examples can be considered in this context:

- powerful commercial companies being able to exert pressure on less powerful companies to ensure that the powerful company's products are used when alternatives might be more suitable or less costly
- companies providing systems that do not guarantee security against unauthorised access
- organisations that try to conceal information about a security breach that has occurred in their systems
- private data transmitted by individuals to other individuals being stored and made available to security services
- social media sites allowing abusive or subversive content to be transmitted
- search engines providing search results with no concern about the quality of the content.

There is by no means a consistent public attitude to concerns like this. This makes it difficult for an individual software engineer to make a judgement with respect to public good. Even if the judgement is that a company is not acting in the public good it will always be difficult for an individual to exert any influence. There are recent examples where individuals have taken action which has resulted in their life being severely affected.

Discussion Point:

This section has deliberately been presented in generalisations. You should carry out a search for some individual examples and then consider actions that could be taken and justified as being for the public good.

9.04 Ownership and copyright

Copyright is a formal recognition of ownership. If an individual creates and publishes some work that has an element of originality, the individual becomes the owner and can therefore claim copyright. An exception is if the individual is working for an organisation. An organisation can claim copyright for a published work if it is created by one or more individuals that work for the organisation. Copyright cannot apply to an idea and it cannot apply to a component of a published work.

KEY TERMS

Copyright: a formal recognition of ownership of a created and published work

Copyright can apply to any of:

- a literary work
- a musical composition
- a film
- a music recording
- a radio or TV broadcast
- a work of art
- a computer program.

The justification for the existence of copyright has two components. The first is that the creation takes time and effort and requires original thinking. There should, therefore, be opportunity for the copyright holder to be rewarded financially for this endeavour. The second is that it is unfair for some other individual or organisation to reproduce the work and to make money from it without any compensation to the original creator.

As with the case of data protection discussed in Chapter 8 (Section 8.01), there is a need for legislation to try to deter abuses of copyright. The similarity continues in that legislation cannot ensure that no abuses occur. Different countries have different details in their legislation but there is an international agreement that copyright laws cannot be evaded by reproducing the work in a different country from where the work was created.

Typical copyright legislation will include:

- a requirement for registration recording the date of creation of the work
- a defined period when copyright will apply
- a policy to be applied if an individual holding copyright dies
- an agreed method for indicating the copyright, for example the use of the © symbol.

When copyright is in place there will be implications for how the work can be used. The copyright owner can include a statement concerning how the work might be used. For instance, the ACM has the following statement relating to the code of ethics discussed in Section 9.02:

This Code may be published without permission as long as it is not changed in any way and it carries the copyright notice. Copyright © 1999 by the Association for Computing Machinery, Inc. and the Institute for Electrical and Electronics Engineers, Inc.

This is one of several possible variations referring to permissions that are granted when the work has not been sold. If someone has bought a copy of a copyrighted product there is no restriction on copies being made provided that these are solely for the use of the individual. A general regulation relates to books in a library, where a library user can photocopy part of a book.

9.05 The consequences of the development of the Internet and World Wide Web

Before the Internet came to be a dominant feature of people's lives, breaches of copyright were routinely happening in two ways. Individuals with a music system that included a tape cassette recorder could record a radio broadcast. It also allowed a copy to be made of a friend's vinyl record. Individuals also often had unrestricted access to a photocopier in their place of work and could copy printed material.

In the modern world, the cinema, broadcast and music industries are attempting to sell their products as CDs, DVDs or Blu-ray discs. Illegal copying (known as 'piracy') now takes place through using the Internet to download or stream data that was originally released for sale on one of these optical media. As well as the change in approach, there is the significant difference that illegal copying is now happening on a major scale and thus seriously affecting the profitability of the creators.

In order for an individual or an organisation to make an illegal copy of a product available for downloading or streaming the data has to be 'ripped' from an original product. This is the process of converting the product into a form that can be stored as a computer file. The producers of the original product can use digital rights management (DRM) to attempt to counter such activity. Originally DRM was simply used to make a CD playable on a CD player but to prevent it being played on a computer system. Now DRM has to be used to prevent ripping. This might involve encryption or deliberate inclusion of damaged sectors. Unfortunately these techniques do not guarantee the prevention of piracy.

The major mechanism for piracy of media content is the widespread use of peer-to-peer file sharing, a technology discussed in Chapter 17 (Section 17.07). As a result, there are moves afoot to force ISPs to monitor the usage of this technology and to report usage to interested parties. Naturally enough there is considerable resistance to such action in that it amounts to a breach of privacy.

9.06 Software licensing

Commercial software

Commercial software almost always has to be paid for but there are a number of different options that might be available:

- A fee is paid for each individual copy of the software.
- A company might have the option of buying a site licence which allows a defined number of copies to be running at any one time.
- Special rates might be available for educational use.
- Earlier versions or limited versions might be offered free or at reduced price.

Open or free licensing

For open licensing there are two major operations under way. Both are global non-profit organisations.

The Open Source Initiative makes **open source software**, including the source code, available for free. The aim is for collaborative development of software to take place. The user of the software is free to use it, modify it, copy it or distribute it according to need.

The Free Software Foundation has similar objectives but has also incorporated what it has called 'copyleft'. This is the condition that if the software is modified the source code for the modified version must be made available under the same conditions of usage.

The two organisations are not in competition but there are some subtle differences in their philosophy. There is a different raft of products made available by each of them.

Both these organisations offer free products. Another form of free software is termed **freeware**. This is software that is distributed for free but without the source code.

Discussion Point:

How often do you think that open licence software is being used? Should it be used more often?

TASK 9.01

Carry out a search to investigate some of the software available under an open licence.

KEY TERMS

Open source software: software free with unlimited use allowed and access to source code

Shareware: software free for use for a limited period but no source code provided

Freeware: software free with unlimited use allowed but no source code provided

Shareware licensing

Shareware is commercial software which is made available on a trial basis. It might be a limited version of a full package or free to use for a trial period. A beta test version of new software might be considered to come in the shareware category.

Summary

- There are different definitions of ethics.
- The ARM/IEEE Code of Ethics has a focus on the public good.
- There is a history of software disasters that might have been prevented if sound software engineering practice had been employed.
- Copyright is formal recognition of ownership.
- Illegal copying using the Internet is a serious concern.
- Commercial software has to be paid for; alternatives are open licence or shareware which are free.

Exam-style Questions

1 The ACM and IEEE set out eight principles for ethics and professional practice. The categories, with a short explanation, are shown in this diagram.

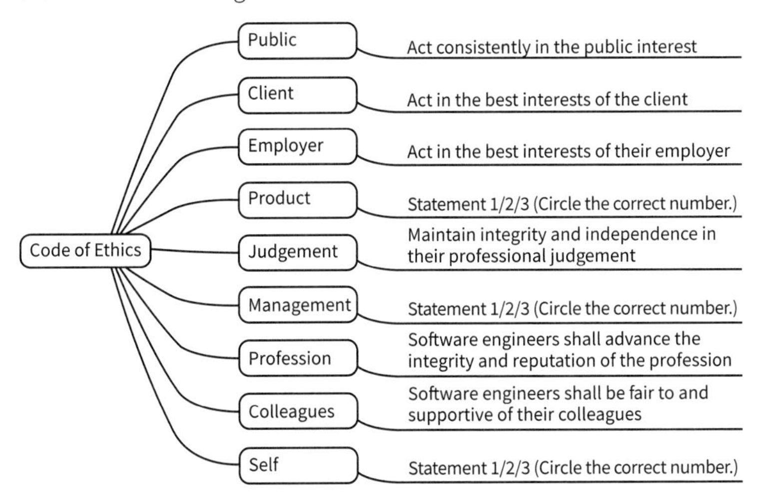

Statement 1: Team leaders should subscribe to and promote an ethical approach to the management of software development and maintenance.

Statement 2: Software engineers shall participate in lifelong learning regarding the practice of the profession.

Statement 3: Software and related modifications meet the highest possible standards.

a These three statements need to be added to the diagram. Circle the correct numbers on the diagram to indicate the positions for Statement 1, Statement 2 and Statement 3. [2]

b For each of these three workplace scenarios, unethical behaviour is demonstrated. Explain the principle(s) which are not being met.

i Workplace scenario 1

A large project is devolved to project teams, each led by a project leader. One project leader fails to inform his manager that he has major concerns that:

- their team's software contribution is taking much longer to write and test than anticipated
- they are consequently at risk of spending over their allocated budget. [3]

ii Workplace scenario 2

The software house is about to train a number of programmers in a new programming language. Two employees are refusing to attend the training. [2]

iii The company is developing some monitoring software which requires sensors placed in a nature reserve. One employee considers the sensors will be a danger to some of the wildlife, but is told by his manager that the matter is none of his concern. [2]

Cambridge International AS and A Level Computer Science 9608 Specimen Paper 1 Q6

2 a Copyright is an important consideration when something is created.

i State what copyright primarily defines. [1]

ii When copyright is registered, some data will be recorded. Identify two examples of the type of data that would be recorded. [2]

iii Copyright legislation defines two conditions that will apply to the copyrighted work. Identify one of these. [1]

iv When copyright has been established there are options for how usage will be controlled. Give two alternatives for the instructions that could be included in the copyright statement for the created item. [2]

b When software is obtained there will be an associated license defining how it can be used.

i For commercial software, describe two different ways in which the license might be applied and explain the benefits to the customer of one of these. [4]

ii Define the difference between freeware and shareware. [2]

Chapter 10
Database and Data Modelling

Learning objectives

By the end of this chapter you should be able to:

- show understanding of the limitations of using a file-based approach for the storage and retrieval of data
- describe the features of a relational database which address the limitations of a file-based approach
- show understanding of the features provided by a DBMS to address the issues of: data management, data modelling, logical schema, data integrity, data security
- show understanding of how software tools found within a DBMS are used in practice
- show awareness that high-level languages provide accessing facilities for data stored in a database
- show understanding of, and use, the terminology associated with a relational database model
- produce a relational design from a given description of a system
- use an entity–relationship diagram to document a database design
- show understanding of the normalisation process
- explain why a given set of database tables are, or are not, in 3NF and make the changes to a given set of tables to produce a solution in 3NF
- show understanding that DBMS software carries out:
  - all creation/modification of the database structure using its DDL
  - query and maintenance of data using its DML
- show understanding that the industry standard for both DDL and DML is Structured Query Language (SQL)
- show understanding of a given SQL script
- write simple SQL (DDL) commands for: creating a database, creating or changing a table definition, adding a primary or foreign key to a table
- write a SQL script for querying or modifying data (DML) which are stored in (at most two) database tables

10.01 Limitations of a file-based approach

Data integrity and data privacy concerns

Let's consider a simple scenario. A theatrical agency makes bookings for bands and is setting up a computerised system. Text files are to be used. One of these text files is to store data about individual band members. Each line of the file is to contain the following data for one band member:

Name, contact details, banking details, band name, band agent name, band agent contact details

The intention is that this file could be used if the agency needed to contact the band member directly or through the band's agent. It could also be used after a gig when the band member has to be paid. Ignoring what would constitute contact details or banking details, we can look at a snapshot of some of the data that might be stored for the member's given name, the member's family name and the band name. The file might have a thousand or more lines of text. The following is a selection of some of the data that might be contained in various lines in the file:

```
Xiangfei   Jha        ComputerKidz
Mahesh     Ravuru     ITWizz
Dylan      Stoddart
Graham     Vandana    ITWizz
Vandana    Graham     ITWizz
Mahesh     Ravuru     ITWizz
Precious   Olsen      ComputerKidz
Precious   Olsen      ITWizz
```


It is clear that there are problems with this data. It would appear that when the data for Vandana Graham was first entered her names were inserted in the wrong order. A later correct entry was made without deletion of the original incorrect data. This type of problem is not unique to a file-based system. There is no validation technique that could detect the original error. By contrast, validation should have led to the correction of the missing band name for Dylan Stoddart. The Precious Olsen data are examples of duplication of data and inconsistent data.

There is also possibly an error that is not evident from looking at the file contents. A band name could be entered here when that band doesn't exist. This shows how a file-based approach can lead to data integrity problems in an individual file. The reason is the lack of in-built control when data is entered. The database approach can prevent such problems or, at least, minimise the chances of them happening.

A different problem is a lack of data privacy. The file above was designed so that the finance section could find the banking details and the recruitment section could find contact details. The problem is that there cannot be any control of access to part of a file so staff in the recruitment section would be able to access the banking details of band members. Data privacy would be properly handled by a database system.

Mindful of this privacy problem the agency decides to store data in different files for different departments of the organisation. Table 10.01 summarises the main data to be stored in each department's file.

Department	Data items in the section's file				
Contract	Member names		Band name	Gig details	
Finance	Member names	Bank details		Gig details	
Publicity			Band name	Gig details	
Recruitment	Member names		Band name		Agent details

Table 10.01 Data to be held in the department files

There is now data duplication across the files. This is commonly referred to as **data redundancy** which doesn't mean that the data is no longer of use but rather that once data has been stored there is no need for it to be stored again. This can lead to data inconsistency because of errors in the original entry or errors in subsequent editing. This is a different cause of data lacking integrity. One of the primary aims of the database approach is the elimination of data redundancy.

KEY TERMS

Data redundancy: the same data stored more than once

Data dependency concerns

The above account has focussed on the problems associated with data storage in files. We now need to consider the problems that might occur when programs access the files.

Traditionally a programmer wrote a program and at the same time defined the data files that the program would need. For the agency each department would have its own programs which would access the department's data files. When a programmer creates a program for a department the programmer has to know how the data is organised in these files, for example, that the fourth item on a line in the file is a band name. This is an example of 'data dependency'.

It is very likely that the files used by one department might have some data which is the same as the data in the files of other departments. However, in the scenario presented above there is no plan for file sharing. A further issue is that the agency might decide that there is a need for a change in the data stored. For instance, they might see an increasing trend for bands to perform with additional session musicians. Their data will need to be entered into some files. This will require the existing files to be re-written. In turn, this will require the programs to be re-written so that the new files are read correctly. In a database scenario the existing programs could still be run even though additional data was added. The only programming change needed would be the writing of additional programs which used this additional data.

The other aspect of data dependency is that when file structures have been defined to suit specific programs they will not be suited to supporting new applications. The agency might feel the need for an information system to analyse the success or otherwise of the gigs they have organised over a number of years. Extracting the data for this from the sort of file-based system described here would be a complex task which would take considerable time to complete.

10.02 The database approach

It is vital to understand that a database is not just a collection of data. A database is an implementation according to the rules of a theoretical model. The basic concept was proposed some 40 years ago by ANSI (American National Standards Institute) in its three-level model. The three levels are:

- the external level
- the conceptual level
- the internal level.

The architecture is illustrated in Figure 10.01 in the context of a database to be set up for our theatrical agency.

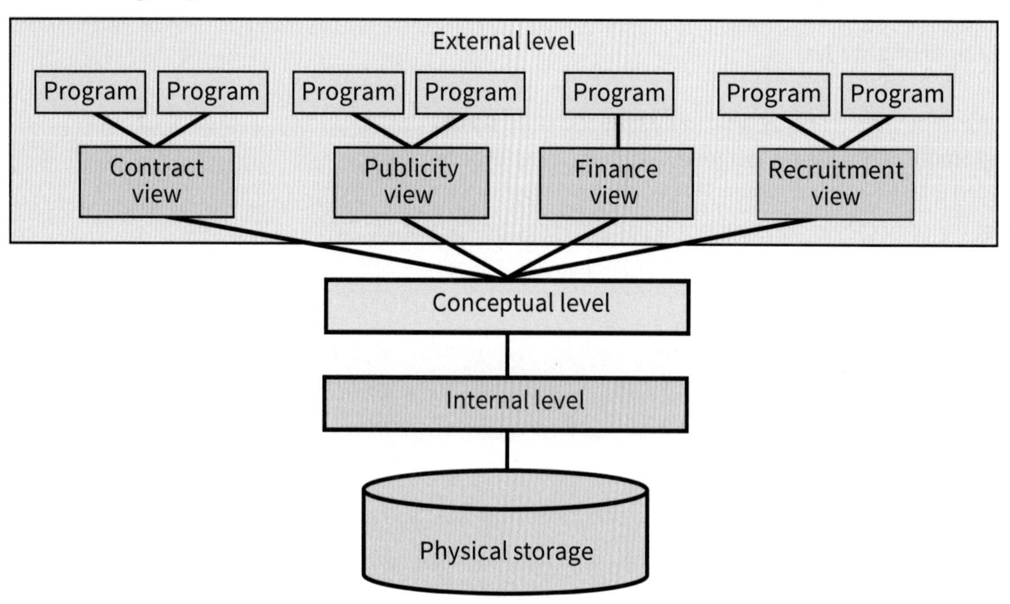

Figure 10.01 The ANSI three-level architecture for the theatrical agency database

The physical storage of the data is represented here as being on disk. The details of the storage (the internal schema) are known only at the internal level, the lowest level in the ANSI architecture. This is controlled by the **database management system (DBMS)** software. The programmers who wrote this software are the only ones who know the structure for the storage of the data on disk. The software will accommodate any changes that might be needed in the storage medium.

At the next level, the conceptual level, there is a single universal view of the database. This is controlled by the **database administrator (DBA)** who has access to the DBMS. In the ANSI architecture the conceptual level has a conceptual schema describing the organisation of the data as perceived by a user or programmer. However, this is often described as a logical schema.

At the external level there are individual user and programmer views. Each view has an external schema describing which parts of the database are accessible. A view can support a number of user programs. The DBA is responsible for setting up these views and for defining the appropriate, specific access rights. The DBMS provides facilities for a programmer to develop a user interface for a program. It also provides a query processor. The query is the mechanism for extracting and manipulating data from the database. A programmer will incorporate access to queries in a user interface. The other feature provided by the DBMS is the capability for creating a report to present formatted output.

KEY TERMS

Data management system (DBMS): software that controls access to data in a database

Database administrator (DBA): a person who uses the DBMS to customise the database to suit user and programmer requirements

Discussion Point:

How many of the above concepts are recognisable in your experience of using a database?

10.03 The relational database

In the relational database model each item of data is stored in a **relation** which is a special type of table. The strange choice of name has its origin in a mathematical theory. A relational database is a collection of relational tables.

When a table is created in a relational database it is first given a name and then the attributes are named. In a database design, a table would be given a name with the **attribute** names listed in brackets after the table name. For example, a database for the theatrical agency may contain the following tables:

Member(MemberID, MemberGivenName, MemberFamilyName, BandName, ...)

Band(BandName, AgentID, ...)

The logical view of the data in these tables is given in Table 10.02 and Table 10.03. Each attribute is associated with one column in the table and is in effect a column header. The column itself contains attribute values.

MemberID	**Member GivenName**	**Member FamilyName**	**Band Name**	**...**
0005	Xiangfei	Jha	ComputerKidz	...
0009	Mahesh	Ravuru	ITWizz	...
0001	Dylan	Stoddart	ComputerKidz	...
0025	Vandana	Graham	ITWizz	...

Table 10.02 Logical view of Member table in a relational database

BandName	**AgentID**	**...**
ComputerKidz	01	...
ITWizz	07	...

Table 10.03 Logical view of Band table in a relational database

Although some database products do allow a direct view of a table this is not the norm hence the use of the term 'logical view' here. If a user wishes to inspect all of the data in a table a query should be used.

KEY TERMS

Relation: the special type of table which is used in a relational database

Attribute: a column in a relation that contains values

A row in a relation should be referred to as a tuple but this strict nomenclature is not always used. Often a row is called a 'record' and the attribute values 'fields'. The tuple is the collection of data stored for one 'instance' of the relation. In Table 10.02, each tuple relates to one individual band member. A fundamental principle of a relational database is that a tuple is a set of atomic values; each attribute has one value or no value.

The most important feature of the relational database concept is the **primary key**. A primary key may be a single attribute or a combination of attributes. Every table must have a primary key and each tuple in the table must have a value for the primary key and that value must be unique. Once a table and its attributes have been defined the next task is to choose the primary key. In some cases there may be more than one attribute for which unique values are guaranteed. In this case, each one is a candidate key and one will be selected as the primary key. More often there is no candidate key and so a primary key has to be created. Table 10.02 shows an example of this with the introduction of the attribute MemberID as the primary key (the primary key is underlined in the logical view).

The primary key ensures 'entity integrity'. The DBMS will not allow an attempt to insert a value for a primary key when that value already exists. Therefore each tuple must be unique. This is one of the features of the relational model that helps to ensure data integrity. The primary key also provides a unique reference to any attribute value that a query is selecting.

Although it is possible for a database to contain stand-alone tables it is usually true that each table will have some relationship with another table. This relationship is implemented by using a **foreign key**.

KEY TERMS

Primary key: an attribute or a combination of attributes for which there is a value in each tuple and that value is unique

Foreign key: an attribute in one table that refers to the primary key in another table

The use of a foreign key can be discussed on the basis of the two database tables represented in Table 10.02 and Table 10.03. When the database is being created, the Band table is created first. BandName is chosen as the primary key because unique names for bands can be guaranteed. Then the Member table is created. MemberID is defined as the primary key and the attribute BandName is identified as a foreign key referencing the primary key in the Band table. Once this relationship between primary and foreign keys has been established, the DBMS will prevent any entry for BandName in the Member table being made if the corresponding value does not exist in the Band table. This provides referential integrity which is another reason why the relational database model helps to ensure data integrity.

Question 10.01

BandName is a primary key for the Band table. Does this mean that as a foreign key in the Member table it must have unique values? Explain your reasoning.

10.04 Entity–relationship modelling

The top-down, stepwise refinement (see Chapter 12, Section 12.01) approach to database design uses an entity–relationship (ER) diagram. This might be initially created and used by a systems analyst before being passed on to the database designer. Otherwise the designer has to create it. The term 'relationship' (not to be confused with a relation!) was introduced earlier in connection with the use of a foreign key. An entity (strictly speaking an entity type) could be a thing, a type of person, an event, a transaction or an organisation. Most importantly, there must be a number of 'instances' of the entity. An entity is something that will become a table in a relational database.

WORKED EXAMPLE 10.01

Creating an entity–relationship diagram for the theatrical agency

Let's consider a scenario for the theatrical agency which will be sufficient to model a part of the final database they would need. The starting point for a top-down design is a statement of the requirement:

The agency needs a database to handle bookings for bands. Each band has a number of members. Each booking is for a venue. Each booking might be for one or more bands.

Step 1: Choose the entities

You look for the nouns. You ignore 'agency' because there is only the one. You choose Booking, Band, Member and Venue. For each of these there will be more than one instance. You are aware that each booking is for a gig at a venue but you ignore this because you think that the Booking entity will be sufficient to hold the required data about a gig.

Step 2: Identify the relationships

This requires experience but the aim is not to define too many. You choose the following three:

- Booking with Venue
- Booking with Band
- Band with Member.

You ignore the fact that there will be, for example, a relationship between Member and Venue because you think that this will be handled through the other relationships that indirectly link them. You can now draw a preliminary ER diagram as shown in Figure 10.02.

Figure 10.02 A preliminary entity–relationship diagram

Step 3: Decide the cardinalities of the relationships

Now comes the crucial stage of deciding on what are known as the 'cardinalities' of the relationships. At present we have a single line connecting each pair of entities. This line actually defines two relationships which might be described as the 'forward' one and the 'backward' one on the diagram as drawn. However, this only becomes apparent at the final stage of drawing the relationship. First we have to choose one of the following descriptions for the cardinality of each relation:

- one-to-one or 1:1
- one-to-many or 1:M
- many-to-one or M:1
- many-to-many or M:M.

This can be illustrated by considering the relationship between Member and Band. We argue that one Member is a member of only one Band. (This needs to be confirmed as a fact by the agency.) We then argue that one Band has more than one Member so it has many. Therefore the relationship between Member and Band is M:1. In its simplest form, this relationship can be drawn as shown in Figure 10.03.

Figure 10.03 The M:1 relationship between Member and Band

This can be given more detail by including the fact that a member must belong to a Band and a Band must have more than one Member. To reflect this, the relationship can be drawn as shown in Figure 10.04.

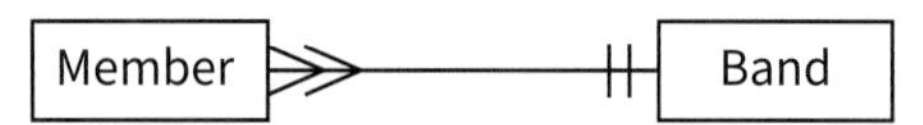

Figure 10.04 The M:1 relationship with more detail

At each end of the relationship there are two symbols. One of the symbols shows the minimum cardinality and the other the maximum cardinality. In this particular case the minimum and maximum values just happen to be the same. However, using the diagram to document that a Member must belong to a Band is important. It indicates that when the database is created it must not be possible to create a new entry in the Member table unless there is a valid entry for BandName in that table.

For the relationship between Booking and Venue we argue that one Booking is for one Venue (there must be a venue and there cannot be more than one) and that one Venue can be used for many Bookings so the relationship between Booking and Venue is M:1. However, a Venue might exist that has so far never had a booking so the relationship can be drawn as shown in Figure 10.05.

Figure 10.05 The M:1 relationship between Booking and Venue

Finally for the relationship between Band and Booking we argue that one Booking can be for many Bands and that one Band has many Bookings (hopefully!) so the relationship is M:M. However, a new band might not yet have a booking. Also there might be only one Band for a booking so the relationship can be drawn as shown in Figure 10.06.

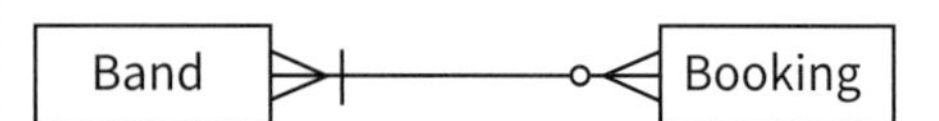

Figure 10.06 The M:M relationship between Band and Booking

Step 4: Create the full ER diagram

At this stage we should name each relationship. The full ER diagram for the limited scenario that has been considered is as shown in Figure 10.07.

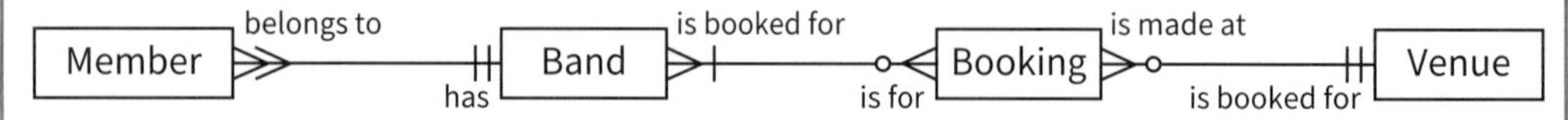

Figure 10.07 The ER diagram for the theatrical agency's booking database

To illustrate how the information should be read from such a diagram we can look at the part shown in Figure 10.08. Despite the fact that there is a many-to-many relationship, a reading of a relationship always considers just one entity to begin the sentence. So, reading forwards and then backwards, we say that:

One Band is booked for zero or many Bookings

One Booking is for one or many Bands

Band — is booked for — is for — Booking

Figure 10.08 Part of the annotated ER diagram

10.05 A logical entity–relationship model

A fully annotated ER diagram of the type developed in Section 10.04 holds all of the information about the relationships that exist for the data that is to be stored in a system. It can be defined as a conceptual model because it does not relate to any specific way of implementing a system. If the system is to be implemented as a relational database the ER diagram has to be converted to a logical model. To do this we can start with a simplified ER diagram that just identifies cardinalities.

If a relationship is 1:M, no further refinement is needed. The relationship shows that the entity at the many end needs to have a foreign key referencing the primary key of the entity at the one end.

If there were a 1:1 relationship there are options for implementation. However, such relationships are extremely rare and will not be considered further.

The problem relationship is the M:M, where a foreign key cannot be used. A foreign key attribute can only have a single value so it cannot handle the many references required. The solution for the M:M relationship is to create a link entity. For Band and Booking, the logical entity model will contain the link entity shown in Figure 10.09.

Figure 10.09 A link entity inserted to resolve a M:M relationship

Extension Question 10.01

Is it possible to annotate these relationships?

With the link entity in the model it is now possible to have two foreign keys in the link entity; one referencing the primary key of Band and one referencing the primary key of Booking.

Each entity in the logical ER diagram will become a table in the relational database. It is therefore possible to choose primary keys and foreign keys for the tables. These can be summarised in a key table. Table 10.04 shows sensible choices for the theatrical agency's booking database.

Table name	Primary key	Foreign key
Member	MemberID	BandName
Band	BandName	
Band-Booking	BandName & BookingID	BandName, BookingID
Booking	BookingID	VenueName
Venue	VenueName	

Table 10.04 A key table for the agency booking database

The decisions about the primary keys are determined by the uniqueness requirement. The link entity cannot use either BandName or BookingID alone but the combination of the two in a compound primary key will work.

TASK 10.01

Consider the following scenario. An organisation books cruises for passengers. Each cruise visits a number of ports. Create a conceptual ER diagram and convert it to a logical ER diagram. Create a key table for the database that could be implemented from the design.

10.06 Normalisation

Normalisation is a design technique for constructing a set of table designs from a list of data items. It can also be used to improve on existing table designs.

WORKED EXAMPLE 10.02

Normalising data for the theatrical agency

To illustrate the technique let's consider the document shown in Figure 10.10. This is a booking data sheet that the theatrical company might use.

Booking data sheet: 2016/023
Venue:
Cambridge International Theatre
Camside
CA1
Booking date: 23.06.2016

Bands booked	**Number of band members**	**Headlining**
ComputerKidz	5	Y
ITWizz	3	N

Figure 10.10 Example booking data sheet

The data items on this sheet (ignoring headings) can be listed as a set of attributes:

(BookingID, VenueName, VenueAddress1, VenueAddress2, Date,
(BandName, NumberOfMembers, Headlining))

The list is put inside brackets because we are starting a process of table design. The extra set of brackets around BandName, NumberOfMembers, Headlining is because they represent a **repeating group**. If there is a repeating group, the attributes cannot sensibly be put into one relational table. A table must have single rows and atomic attribute values so the only possibility would be to include tuples such as those shown in Table 10.05. There is now data redundancy here with the duplication of the bookingID, venue data and the date.

Booking ID	Venue Name	Venue Address1	Venue Address2	Date	Band Name	Number Of Members	Headlining
2016/023	Cambridge International Theatre	Camside	CA1	23.06.2016	Computer Kidz	5	Y
2016/023	Cambridge International Theatre	Camside	CA1	23.06.2016	ITWizz	3	N

Table 10.05 Data stored in an unnormalised table

Step 1: Conversion to first normal form (1NF)

The conversion to first normal form (1NF) requires splitting the data into two groups. At this stage we represent the data as table definitions. Therefore we have to choose table names and identify a primary key for each table. One table contains the non-repeating group attributes the other the repeating group attributes. For the first table a sensible design is:

Booking(BookingID, VenueName, VenueAddress1, VenueAddress2, Date)

The table with the repeating group is not so straightforward. It needs a compound primary key and a foreign key to give a reference to the first table. The sensible design is:

Band-Booking(BandName, BookingID(fk), NumberOfMembers, Headlining)

Again the primary key is underlined but also the foreign key has been identified, with (fk). Because the repeating groups have been moved to a second table, these two tables could be implemented with no data redundancy in either. This is one aspect of 1NF. Also it can be said that for each table the attributes are dependent on the primary key.

Step 2: Conversion to second normal form (2NF)

The Booking table is automatically in 2NF; only tables with repeating group attributes have to be converted. For conversion to second normal form (2NF), the process is to examine each non-key attribute and ask if it is dependent on both parts of the compound key. Any attributes that are dependent on only one of the attributes in the compound key must be moved out into a new table. In this case, NumberOfMembers is only dependent on BandName. In 2NF there are now three table definitions:

Booking(BookingID, VenueName, VenueAddress1, VenueAddress2, Date)

Band-Booking(BandName(fk), BookingID(fk), Headlining)

Band(BandName, NumberOfMembers)

Note that the Booking table is unchanged from 1NF. The Band-Booking table now has two foreign keys to provide reference to data in the other two tables. The characteristics of a table in 2NF is that it either has a single primary key or it has a compound primary key with any non-key attribute dependent on both components.

Step 3: Conversion to third normal form (3NF)

For conversion to third normal form (3NF) each table has to be examined to see if there are any non-key dependencies; that means we must look for any non-key attribute that is dependent on another non-key attribute. If there is, a new table must be defined.

In our example, VenueAddress1 and VenueAddress2 are dependent on VenueName. With the addition of the fourth table we have the following 3NF definitions:

Band(BandName, NumberOfMembers)

Band-Booking(BandName(fk), BookingID(fk), Headlining)

Booking(BookingID, Date, VenueName(fk))

Venue(VenueName, VenueAddress1, VenueAddress2)

Note that once again a new foreign key has been identified to keep a reference to data in the newly created table. These four table definitions match four of the entities in the logical ER model for which the keys were identified in Table 10.04. This will not always happen. A logical ER diagram will describe a 2NF set of entities but not necessarily a 3NF set.

KEY TERMS

Repeating group: a set of attributes that have more than one set of values when the other attributes each have a single value

To summarise, if a set of tables are in 3NF it can be said that each non-key attribute is dependent on the key, the whole key and nothing but the key.

Question 10.02

In Step 2 of Worked Example 10.02, why is the Headlining attribute not placed in the Band table?

TASK 10.02

Normalise the data shown in Figure 10.11.

Order no: 07845 **Date:** 25-06-2016

Customer no: 056 **Customer name:** CUP

Address: Cambridge square Cambridge

Sales rep no: 2 **Sales Rep name:** Dylan Stoddart

Product no	Description	Quantity	Price / unit	Total
327	Inkjet cartridges	24	$30	$720
563	Laser toner	5	$25	$125
		Total Price		$835

Figure 10.11 An order form

10.07 Structured Query Language (SQL)

SQL is the programming language provided by a DBMS to support all of the operations associated with a relational database. Even when a database package offers high-level facilities for user interaction, they use SQL.

Data Definition Language (DDL)

Data Definition Language (DDL) is the part of SQL provided for creating or altering tables. These commands only create the structure. They do not put any data into the database.

The following are some examples of DDL that could be used in creating the database for the theatrical agency:

```
CREATE DATABASE BandBooking;
CREATE TABLE Band (
    BandName varchar2(25),
    NumberOfMembers number(1));
ALTER TABLE Band ADD PRIMARY KEY (BandName);
ALTER TABLE Band-Booking ADD FOREIGN KEY (BandName REFERENCES
Band(BandName);
```

These examples show that once the database has been created the tables can be created and the attributes defined. It is possible to define a primary key and a foreign key within the `CREATE TABLE` command but the `ALTER TABLE` command can be used as shown (it can also be used to add extra attributes).

TASK 10.03

For the database defined in Worked Example 10.02, complete the DDL for creating the four tables. Use varchar2(5) for BookingID, number(1) for NumberOfMembers, date for Date, varchar2(1) for Headlining and varchar2(25) for all other data.

Data Manipulation Language (DML)

Data Manipulation Language (DML) is used when a database is first created, to populate the tables with data. It can then be used for ongoing maintenance. The following code shows a selection of the use of the commands:

```
INSERT INTO Band ('ComputerKidz', 5);
INSERT INTO Band-Booking (BandName, BookingID)
    VALUES ('ComputerKidz', '2016/023');
UPDATE Band
SET NumberOfMembers = 6;
DELETE FROM BandName
WHERE BandName = 'ITWizz';
```

The above code shows the two methods of inserting data. The first, simpler version can be used if the order of the attributes is known. The second is the safer method: the attributes are defined then the values are listed. The next two statements show a change of data and the removal of data.

The main use of DML is to obtain data from a database using a query. A query always starts with the `SELECT` command. Some examples are:

```
SELECT BandName
FROM Band
ORDER BY BandName;

SELECT BandName
FROM Band-Booking
WHERE Headlining = 'Y'
GROUP BY BandName;
```

Both of these examples select data from a single table. The first produces an ordered list of all the bands. The second produces a list of bands that have headlined a gig. The `GROUP BY` restriction ensures that the band names are not repeated.

A query can be based on a 'join condition' between data in two tables. The most frequently used is an inner join which is illustrated by:

```
SELECT VenueName, Date
FROM Booking
WHERE Band-Booking.BookingID = Booking.BookingID
AND Band-Booking.BandName = 'ComputerKidz';
```

Note the use of the full names of attributes, which include the table name. This query will find the venue and date of bookings for the band ComputerKidz.

Accessing SQL commands using a different language

Although a database can be accessed directly using SQL there is often a need to control access to a database using a different language. This makes sense because a program can access data in a file so why not in a database? Programming languages therefore have a mechanism for embedding an SQL command into a program.

A special case arises in a client–server web application as mentioned in Chapter 2 (Section 2.09). Server-side scripting using PHP can access a database associated with the server. The following is an example of some code that could be included in an HTML file:

```
<?php
// Connect to localhost using root as the username and no password
mysql_connect("localhost", "root", "");
// Select the database
mysql_select_db("BandBooking");
//Run a query
$result = mysql_query("SELECT * FROM Band")
?>
```

This code assumes that you have created a MYSQL database on a server located on your own computer.

10.08 DBMS features

There are a few important features of a DBMS which have not been mentioned. The first and most important is the data dictionary which is part of the database that is hidden from view from everyone except the DBA. It contains metadata about the data. This includes details of all the definitions of tables, attributes and so on but also of how the physical storage is organised.

There are a number of features to improve performance. Of special note is the capability to create an index for a table. This is needed if the table contains a lot of data. An index is a secondary table which is associated with an attribute that has unique values. The index table contains the attribute values and pointers to the corresponding tuple in the original table. The index can be on the primary key or on a secondary key which was a candidate key when the choice of primary key was made. Searching an index table is much quicker than searching the full table.

Finally, the DBMS controls security issues which include:

- setting access rights for users
- implementing backup procedures
- ensuring that an interrupted database transaction cannot leave the database in an undefined state.

Summary

- A database offers improved methods for ensuring data integrity compared to a file-based approach.
- A database architecture provides, for the user, a conceptual level interface to the stored data.
- A relational database comprises tables of a special type; each table has a primary key and may contain foreign keys.
- Entity–relationship modelling is a top-down approach to database design.
- Normalisation is a database design method which starts with a collection of attributes and converts them into first normal form then into second normal form and, finally, into third normal form.
- Structured Query Language (SQL) includes data definition language (DDL) commands for establishing a database and data manipulation language (DML) commands for creating queries.
- Features provided by a database management system (DBMS) include: a data dictionary, indexing capability, control of user access rights and backup procedures.

Exam-style Questions

1 a A relational database has been created to store data about subjects that students are studying. The following is a selection of some data stored in one of the tables. The data represents the student's name, the personal tutor group, the personal tutor, the subject studied, the level of study and the subject teacher but there is some data missing:

Xiangfei	3	MUB	Computing	A	DER
Xiangfei	3	MUB	Maths	A	BNN
Xiangfei	3	MUB	Physics	AS	DAB
Mahesh	2	BAR	History	AS	IJM
Mahesh	2	BAR	Geography	AS	CAB

i Define the terms used to describe the components in a relational database table using examples from this table. [2]

ii If this represented all of the data, it would have been impossible to create this table.
What is it that has not been shown here and must have been defined to allow the creation as a relational database table? Explain your answer and suggest examples of the missing data. [4]

iii Is this table in first normal form (1NF)? Explain your reason. [2]

b It has been suggested that the database design could be improved. The design suggested contains the following two tables:

Student(StudentName, TutorGroup, Tutor)

StudentSubject(StudentName, Subject, Level, SubjectTeacher)

i Identify features of this design which are characteristic of a relational database. [3]

ii Explain why the use of StudentName here is a potential problem. [2]

iii Explain why the Student table is not in third normal form (3NF). [2]

2 Consider the following scenario:

A company provides catering services for clients who need special-occasion, celebratory dinners. For each dinner, a number of dishes are to be offered. The dinner will be held at a venue. The company will provide staff to serve the meals at the venue.

The company needs a database to store data related to this business activity.

a An entity–relationship model is to be created as the first step in a database design. Identify a list of entities. [4]

b Identify pairs of entities where there is a direct relationship between them. [4]

c For each pair of entities, draw the relationship and justify the choice of cardinality illustrated by the representation. [6]

3 Consider the following booking form used by a travel agency.

Booking Number 00453

Hotel: Esplanade
Colwyn Bay
North Wales

Rating: ***

Date	**Room type**	**Number of rooms**	**Room rate**
23/06/2016	Front-facing double	2	$80
23/06/2016	Rear-facing double	1	$65
24/06/2016	Front-facing double	2	$80

a Create an unnormalised list of attributes using the data shown in this form. Make sure that you distinguish between the repeating and non-repeating attributes. [5]

b Convert the data to first normal form (1NF). Present this as designs for two tables with keys identified. [3]

c Choose the appropriate table and convert it to two tables in second normal form (2NF). Explain your choice of table to modify. Explain your identification of the keys for these two new tables. [5]

d Identify which part of your design is not in Third Normal Form (3NF). [2]

Part 2 Fundamental Problem-Solving and Programming Skills

Chapter 11 Algorithm Design and Problem-Solving

Learning objectives

By the end of this chapter you should be able to:

- show understanding that an algorithm is a solution to a problem expressed as a sequence of defined steps
- use suitable identifiers for the representation of data used by a problem and summarise identifiers using an identifier table
- show understanding that many algorithms are expressed using the four basic constructs of assignment, sequence, selection and repetition
- show understanding that simple algorithms consist of input, process, output at various stages
- document a simple algorithm using: structured English, pseudocode, program flowchart
- derive pseudocode or a program flowchart from a structured English description of a problem
- derive pseudocode from a given program flowchart
- show an appreciation of why logic statements are used to define parts of an algorithm solution
- use logic statements to define parts of an algorithm solution
- use the technical terms associated with arrays including upper and lower bound
- select a suitable data structure (1D or 2D array) to use for a given task
- write algorithms to process array data including sorting using a bubble sort and searching using a linear search.

11.01 What is an algorithm?

KEY TERMS

Algorithm: a sequence of steps that can be carried out to perform a task

We use algorithms in everyday life. If you need to change a wheel on a car, you might need to follow instructions (the algorithm) from a manual:

1. Take a spanner and loosen the wheel nuts.
2. Position a jack in an appropriate place.
3. Raise the car.
4. Take off the wheel nuts and the wheel.
5. Lift replacement wheel into position.
6. Replace wheel nuts and tighten by hand.
7. Lower the car.
8. Fully tighten wheel nuts.

This might sound all very straightforward. However, if the instructions are not followed in the correct logical sequence, the process might become much more difficult or even impossible. For example, if you tried to do Step 1 after Step 3, the wheel may spin and you can't loosen the wheel nuts. You can't do Step 4 before Step 3.

If you want to bake a cake, you follow a recipe:

1. Measure the following ingredients: 200g sugar, 200g butter, 4 eggs, 200g flour, 2 teaspoons baking powder and 2 tablespoons of milk.
2. Mix the ingredients together in a large bowl, until the consistency of the mixture is smooth.
3. Pour the mixture into a cake tin.
4. Bake in the oven at 190° C for 20 minutes.
5. Check it is fully cooked.
6. Turn cake out of the tin and cool on a wire rack.

The recipe is an algorithm. The ingredients are the input and the cake is the output. The process is mixing the ingredients and cooking the mixture in the oven.

Sometimes a step might need breaking down into smaller steps. For example Step 2 can be more detailed:

2.1 Beat the sugar and butter together until fluffy.

2.2 Add the eggs, one at a time, mixing constantly.

2.3 Sieve the flour and baking powder and stir slowly into the egg mixture.

2.4 Add milk and mix to give a creamy consistency.

Sometimes there might be different steps depending on some other conditions. For example, consider how to get from one place to another using the map of the London Underground system in Figure 11.01.

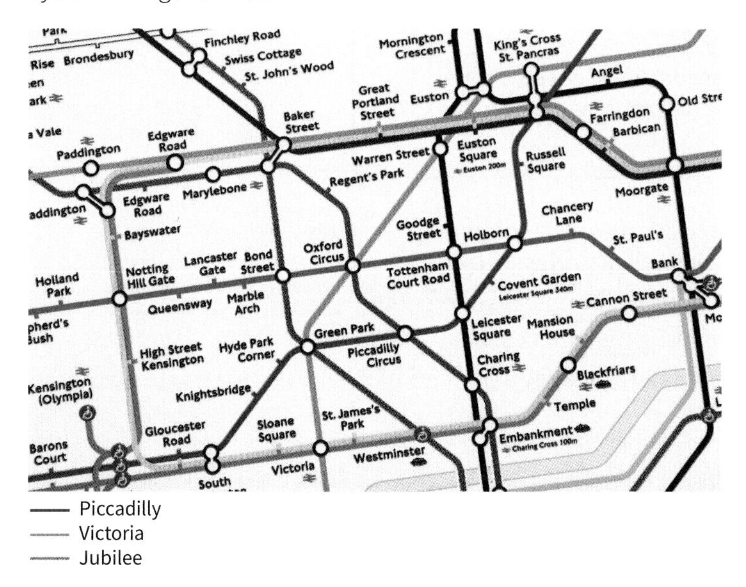

Figure 11.01 Underground map of London, UK

To travel from King's Cross St. Pancras to Westminster, we consider two routes:

- Route A: Take the Victoria Line to Green Park (4 stations); then take the Jubilee Line to Westminster (1 station).
- Route B: Take the Piccadilly Line to Green Park (6 stations); then take the Jubilee Line to Westminster (1 station).

Route A looks like the best route. If there are engineering works on the Victoria Line and trains are delayed, Route B might turn out to be the quicker route.

The directions on how to get from King's Cross St. Pancras to Westminster can be written as:

IF there are engineering works on the Victoria Line

THEN

Take the Piccadilly Line to Green Park (6 stations)

Take the Jubilee Line to Westminster (1 station)

ELSE

Take the Victoria Line to Green Park (4 stations)

Take the Jubilee Line to Westminster (1 station)

TASK 11.01

Write the steps to be followed to:

- make a sandwich
- walk from your school/college to the nearest shop
- log on to your computer.

Many problems have more than one solution. Sometimes it is a personal preference which solution to choose. Sometimes one solution will be better than another.

11.02 Expressing algorithms

TIP

Computer scientists are interested in finding good solutions. A good solution gives the correct results, takes up as little computer memory as possible and executes as fast as possible. The solution should be concise, elegant and easy to understand.

In computer science, when we design a solution to a problem we express the solution (the algorithm) using sequences of steps written in **structured English** or **pseudocode**. Structured English is a subset of the English language and consists of command statements. Pseudocode resembles a programming language without following the syntax of a particular programming language. A **flowchart** is an alternative method of representing an algorithm. A flowchart consists of specific shapes, linked together.

An algorithm consists of a sequence of steps. Under certain conditions we may wish not to perform some steps. We may wish to repeat a number of steps. In computer science, when writing algorithms, we use four basic types of construct:

KEY TERMS

Structured English: a subset of the English language that consists of command statements used to describe an algorithm

Pseudocode: a way of using keywords and identifiers to describe an algorithm without following the syntax of a particular programming language

Flowchart: shapes linked together to represent the sequential steps of an algorithm

- **Assignment:**
  a value is given a name (identifier) or the value associated with a given identifier is changed.
- **Sequence:**
  a number of steps are performed, one after the other.
- **Selection:**
  under certain conditions some steps are performed, otherwise different (or no) steps are performed.
- **Repetition:**
  a sequence of steps is performed a number of times. This is also known as iteration or looping.

Many problems we try to solve with a computer involve data. The solution involves inputting data to the computer, processing the data and outputting results (as shown in Figure 11.02).

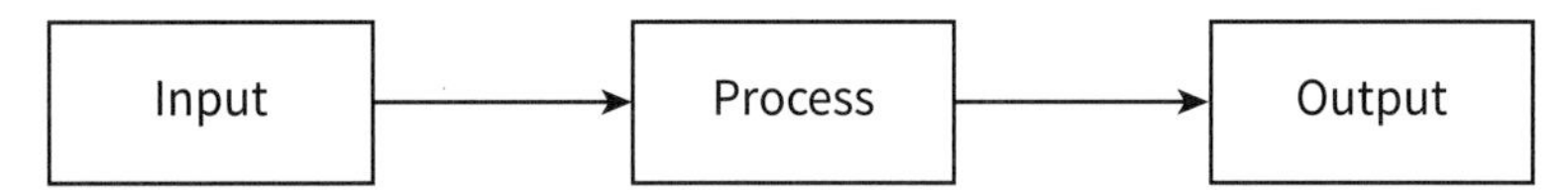

Figure 11.02 Input–process–output

We therefore also need input and output statements.

We need to know the constructs so we know how detailed our design has to be.
These constructs are represented in each of the three notations as shown in Table 11.01.

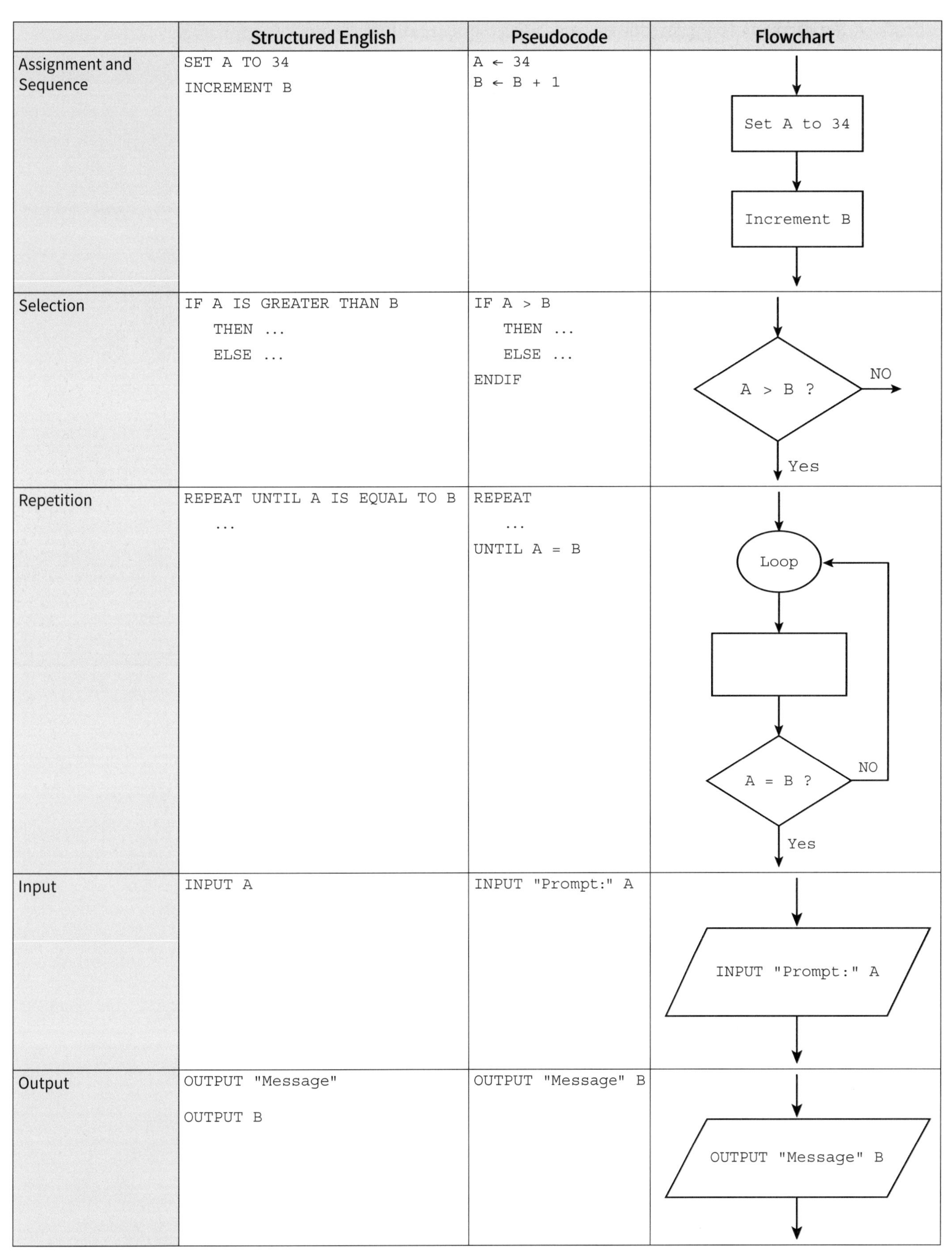

	Structured English	Pseudocode	Flowchart
Assignment and Sequence	SET A TO 34 INCREMENT B	A ← 34 B ← B + 1	Set A to 34 Increment B
Selection	IF A IS GREATER THAN B THEN ... ELSE ...	IF A > B THEN ... ELSE ... ENDIF	A > B ? NO Yes
Repetition	REPEAT UNTIL A IS EQUAL TO B ...	REPEAT ... UNTIL A = B	Loop A = B ? NO Yes
Input	INPUT A	INPUT "Prompt:" A	INPUT "Prompt:" A
Output	OUTPUT "Message" OUTPUT B	OUTPUT "Message" B	OUTPUT "Message" B

Table 11.01 Constructs for computing algorithms

In this book, algorithms and program code are typed using the `Courier` font.

11.03 Variables

When we input data for a process, individual values need to be stored in memory. We need to be able to refer to a specific memory location so that we can write statements of what to do with the value stored there. We refer to these named memory locations as variables. You can imagine these variables like boxes with name labels on them. When a value is input, it is stored in the box with the specified name (identifier) on it.

KEY TERMS

Variable: a storage location for a data value that has an identifier

For example, the variable used to store a count of how many guesses have been made might be given the identifier `NumberOfGuesses` and the player's name might be stored in a variable called `ThisPlayer`, as shown in Figure 11.03.

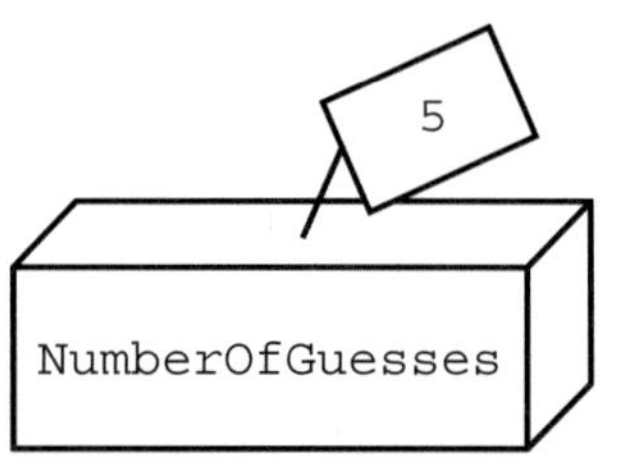

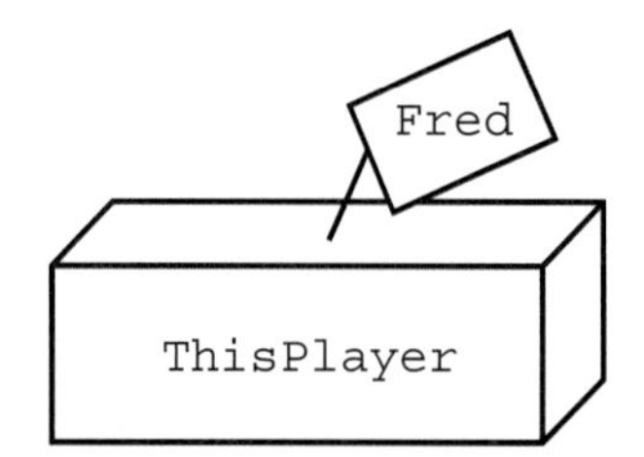

Figure 11.03 Variables

Variable identifiers should not contain spaces, only letters, digits and _ (the underscore symbol). To make algorithms easier to understand, the naming of a variable should reflect the variable's use. This means often that more than one word is used as an identifier. The formatting convention used here is known as CamelCaps. It makes an identifier easier to read.

11.04 Assignments

Assigning a value

The following pseudocode stores the value that is input (for example 15) in a variable with the identifier `Number` (see Figure 11.04(a)).

```
INPUT Number
```

The following pseudocode stores the value 1 in the variable with the identifier `NumberOfGuesses` (see Figure 11.04(b)).

```
NumberOfGuesses ← 1
```

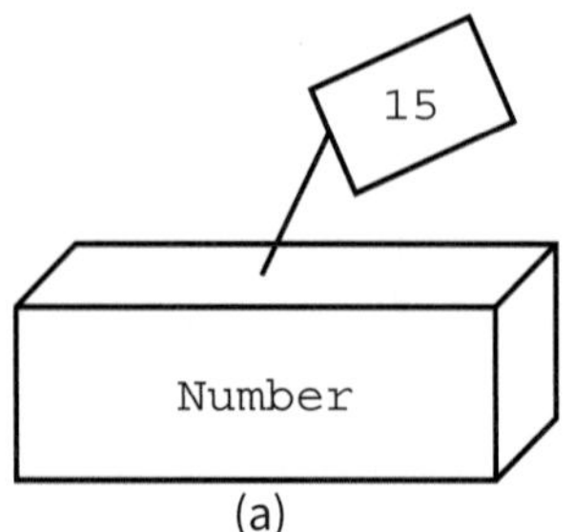

(a)

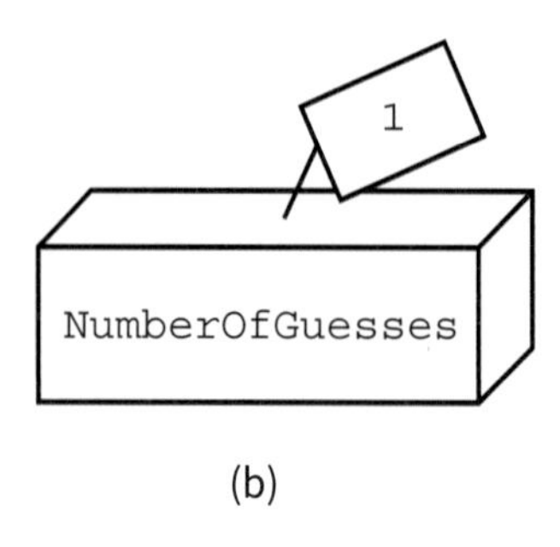

(b)

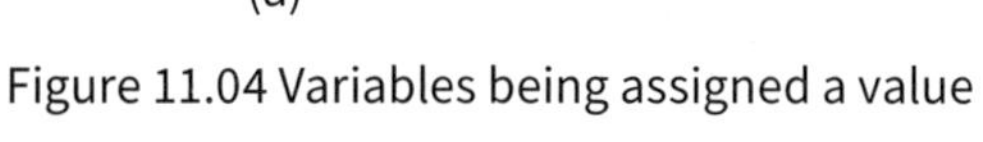

Figure 11.04 Variables being assigned a value

Updating a value

The following pseudocode takes the value stored in `NumberOfGuesses` (see Figure 11.05 (a)), adds 1 to that value and then stores the new value back into the variable `NumberOfGuesses` (see Figure 11.05 (b)).

```
NumberOfGuesses ← NumberOfGuesses + 1
```

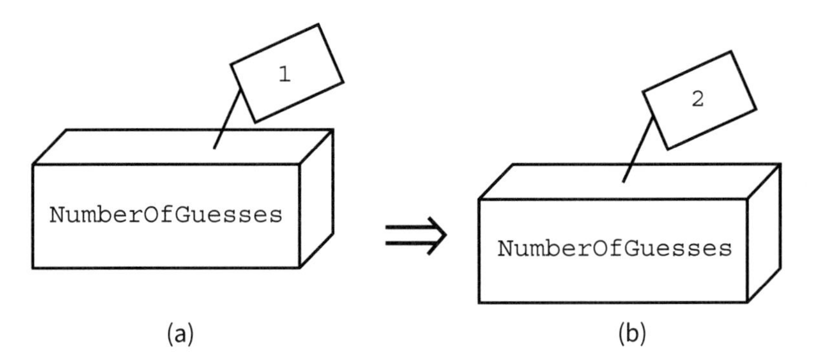

Figure 11.05 Updating the value of a variable

Copying a value

Values can be copied from one variable to another.

The following pseudocode takes the value stored in `Value1` and copies it to `Value2` (see Figure 11.06).

```
Value2 ← Value1
```

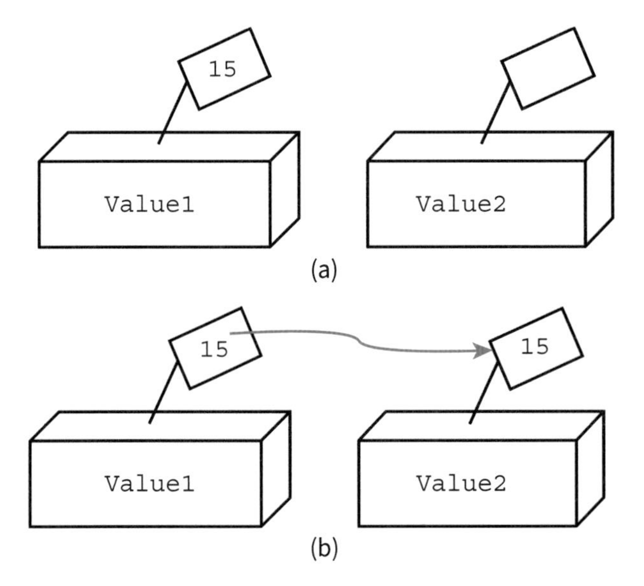

Figure 11.06 Copying the value of a variable

The value in `Value1` remains the same until it is assigned a different value.

Swapping two values

If we want to swap the contents of two variables, we need to store one of the values in another variable temporarily. Otherwise the second value to be moved will be overwritten by the first value to be moved.

In Figure 11.07(a), we copy the content from `Value1` into a temporary variable called `Temp`. Then we copy the content from `Value2` into `Value1` Figure 11.07(b)). Finally we can copy the value from `Temp` into `Value2` (Figure 11.07(c)).

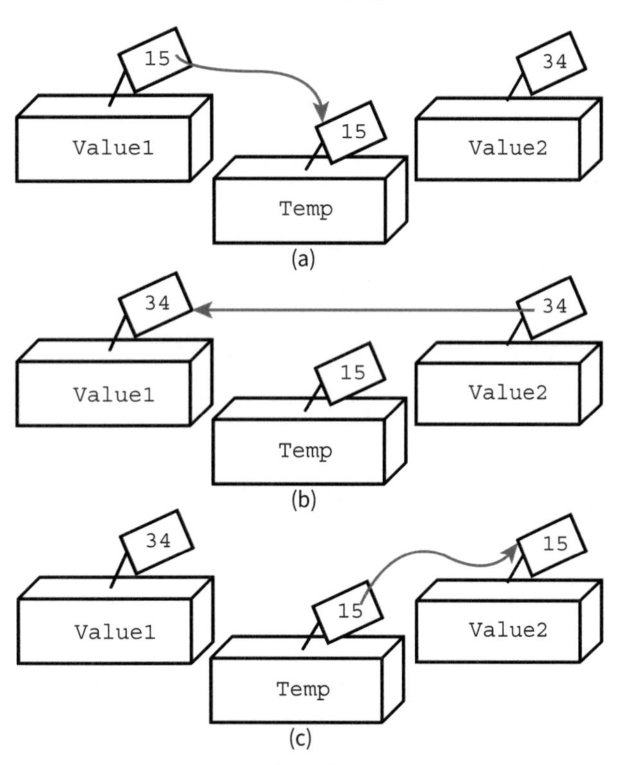

Figure 11.07 Swapping the values of two variables

Using pseudocode we write:

```
Temp ← Value1
Value1 ← Value2
Value2 ← Temp
```

WORKED EXAMPLE 11.01

Using input, output, assignment and sequence constructs

The problem to be solved: Convert a distance in miles and output the equivalent distance in km.

Step 1: Write the problem as a series of structured English statements:

```
INPUT number of miles
Calculate number of km
OUTPUT calculated result as km
```

Step 2: Analyse the data values that are needed.

We need a variable to store the original distance in miles and a variable to store the result of multiplying the number of miles by 1.61. It is helpful to construct an **identifier table** to list the variables.

Identifier	Explanation
`Miles`	Distance as a whole number of miles
`Km`	The result from using the given formula: Km = Miles * 1.61

Table 11.02 Identifier table for miles to km conversion

Step 3: Provide more detail by drawing a flowchart or writing pseudocode.

The detail given in a flowchart should be the same as the detail given in pseudocode. It should use the basic constructs listed in Table 11.01.

Figure 11.08 represents our algorithm using a flowchart and the equivalent pseudocode.

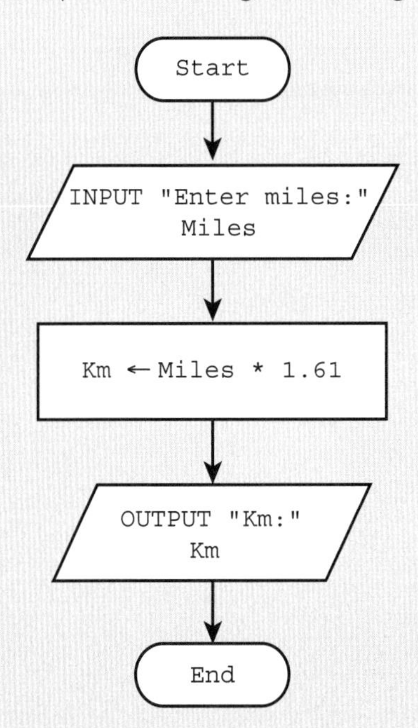


```
INPUT "Enter miles:" Miles
Km ← Miles * 1.61
OUTPUT "km:" Km
```

Figure 11.08 Flowchart and pseudocode for miles to km conversion

KEY TERMS

Identifier table: a table listing the variable identifiers required for the solution, with explanations

TASK 11.02

Consider the following algorithm steps:

1 Input a length in inches.
2 Calculate the equivalent in centimetres.
3 Output the result.

List the variables required in an identifier table.

Write pseudocode or draw a flowchart for the algorithm.

11.05 Logic statements

In Section 11.01, we looked at an algorithm with different steps depending on some other condition:

IF there are engineering works on the Victoria Line

THEN

Take the Piccadilly Line to Green Park (6 stations)

Take the Jubilee Line to Westminster (1 station)

ELSE

Take the Victoria Line to Green Park (4 stations)

Take the Jubilee Line to Westminster (1 station)

The selection construct in Table 11.01 uses a condition to follow either the first group of steps or the second group of steps (see Figure 11.09).

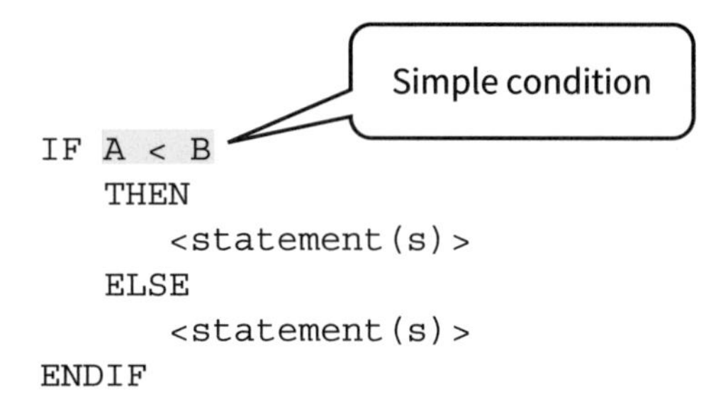

Figure 11.09 Structured English for the selection construct

A condition consists of at least one logic proposition (see Chapter 4, Section 4.01). Logic propositions use the relational (comparison) operators shown in Table 11.03.

Operator	Comparison
=	Is equal to
<	Is less than
>	Is greater than
<=	Is less than or equal to
>=	Is greater than or equal to
<>	Is not equal to

Table 11.03 Relational operators

Conditions are either TRUE or FALSE. In pseudocode, we distinguish between the relational operator = (which tests for equality) and the assignment symbol ←.

A person is classed as a child if they are under 13 and as an adult if they are over 19. If they are between 13 and 19 inclusive they are classed as teenagers. We can write these statements as logic statements:

- If Age < 13 then person is a child
- If Age > 19 then person is an adult
- If Age >= 13 AND Age <= 19 then person is a teenager

TASK 11.03

A town has a bus service where passengers under the age of 12 and over the age of 60 do not need to pay a fare. Write the logic statements for free fares.

A number-guessing game follows different steps depending on certain conditions. Here is a description of the algorithm:

- The player inputs a number to guess the secret number stored.
- If the guess was correct, output a congratulations message.
- If the number input was larger than the secret number, output message "secret number is smaller".
- If the number input was smaller than the secret number, output message "secret number is greater".

We can re-write the number-guessing game steps as an algorithm in structured English:

```
SET value for secret number
INPUT Guess
IF Guess = SecretNumber
   THEN
      OUTPUT "Well done. You have guessed the secret number"
   ELSE
      IF Guess > SecretNumber
         THEN
            OUTPUT "secret number is smaller"
         ELSE
            OUTPUT "secret number is greater"
      ENDIF
ENDIF
```

More complex conditions can be formed by using the logical operators AND, OR and NOT. For example, the number-guessing game might allow the player multiple guesses; if the player has not guessed the secret number after 10 guesses, a different message is output.

```
IF Guess = SecretNumber
   THEN
      OUTPUT "Well done. You have guessed the secret number"
   ELSE
      IF Guess <> SecretNumber AND NumberOfGuesses = 10
         THEN
            OUTPUT "You still have not guessed the secret number"
         ELSE
            IF Guess > SecretNumber
               THEN
                  OUTPUT "The secret number is smaller"
               ELSE
                  OUTPUT "The secret number is greater"
            ENDIF
      ENDIF
ENDIF
```

Complex condition

WORKED EXAMPLE 11.02

Using selection constructs

The problem to be solved: Take three numbers as input and output the largest number.

There are several different methods (algorithms) to solve this problem. Here is one method:

1. Input all three numbers at the beginning.
2. Store each of the input values in a separate variable (the identifiers are shown in Table 11.04).
3. Compare the first number with the second number and then compare the bigger one of these with the third number.
4. The bigger number of this second comparison is output.

See Worked Example 11.03 for another solution.

Identifier	Explanation
`Number1`	The first number to be input
`Number2`	The second number to be input
`Number3`	The third number to be input

Table 11.04 Identifier table for biggest number problem

The algorithm can be expressed in the following pseudocode:

```
INPUT Number1
INPUT Number2
INPUT Number3
IF Number1 > Number2
   THEN // Number1 is bigger
      IF Number1 > Number3
         THEN
            OUTPUT Number1
         ELSE
            OUTPUT Number3
      ENDIF
   ELSE // Number2 is bigger
      IF Number2 > Number3
         THEN
            OUTPUT Number2
         ELSE
            OUTPUT Number3
      ENDIF
ENDIF
```

When an `IF` statement contains another `IF` statement, we refer to these as **nested `IF` statements.**

KEY TERMS

Nested `IF` statements: conditional statements within conditional statements

Question: 11.01

What changes do you need to make to output the smallest number?

WORKED EXAMPLE 11.03

Using selection constructs (alternative method)

The problem to be solved: Take three numbers as input and output the largest number.

This is an alternative method to Worked Example 11.02.

1. Input the first number and store it in `BiggestSoFar`
2. Input the second number and compare it with the value in `BiggestSoFar`.
3. If the second number is bigger, assign its value to `BiggestSoFar`
4. Input the third number and compare it with the value in `BiggestSoFar`
5. If the third number is bigger, assign its value to `BiggestSoFar`
6. The value stored in `BiggestSoFar` is output.

The identifiers required for this solution are shown in Table 11.05.

Identifier	Explanation
`BiggestSoFar`	Stores the biggest number input so far
`NextNumber`	The next number to be input

Table 11.05 Identifier table for the alternative solution to the biggest number problem

The algorithm can be expressed in the following pseudocode:

```
INPUT BiggestSoFar
INPUT NextNumber
IF NextNumber > BiggestSoFar
   THEN
      BiggestSoFar ← NextNumber
ENDIF
INPUT NextNumber
IF NextNumber > BiggestSoFar
   THEN
      BiggestSoFar ← NextNumber
ENDIF
OUTPUT BiggestSoFar
```

Note that when we input the third number in this method the second number gets overwritten as it is no longer needed.

There are several advantages of using the method in Worked Example 11.03 compared to the method in Worked Example 11.02:

- Only two variables are used.
- The conditional statements are not nested and do not have an `ELSE` part. This makes them easier to understand.
- This algorithm can be adapted more easily if further numbers are to be compared (see Worked Example 11.04).

The disadvantage of the method in Worked Example 11.03 compared to the method in Worked Example 11.02 is that there is more work involved with this algorithm. If the second number is bigger than the first number, the value of `BiggestSoFar` has to be changed. If the third number is bigger than the value in `BiggestSoFar` then the value of `BiggestSoFar` has to be changed again. Depending on the input values, this could result in two extra assignment instructions being carried out.

11.06 Loops

Look at the pseudocode algorithm in Worked Example 11.03. The two `IF` statements are identical. To compare 10 numbers we would need to write this statement nine times. Moreover, if the problem changed to having to compare, for example, 100 numbers, our algorithm would become very tedious. If we use a repetition construct (a loop) we can avoid writing the same lines of pseudocode over and over again.

WORKED EXAMPLE 11.04

Repetition using `REPEAT...UNTIL`

The problem to be solved: Take 10 numbers as input and output the largest number.

We need one further variable to store a counter, so that we know when we have compared 10 numbers.

Identifier	Explanation
`BiggestSoFar`	Stores the biggest number input so far
`NextNumber`	The next number to be input
`Counter`	Stores how many numbers have been input so far

Table 11.06 Identifier table for the biggest number problem using `REPEAT...UNTIL`

The algorithm can be expressed in the following pseudocode:

```
INPUT BiggestSoFar
Counter ← 1
REPEAT
   INPUT NextNumber
   Counter ← Counter + 1
   IF NextNumber > BiggestSoFar
      THEN
         BiggestSoFar ← NextNumber
   ENDIF
UNTIL Counter = 10
OUTPUT BiggestSoFar
```

Question: 11.02

What changes do you need to make to the algorithm in Worked Example 11.04:

- to compare 100 numbers?
- to take as a first input the number of numbers to be compared?

There is another loop construct that does the counting for us: the `FOR...ENDFOR` loop.

WORKED EXAMPLE 11.05

Repetition using FOR...ENDFOR

The problem to be solved: Take 10 numbers as input and output the largest number.

We can use the same identifiers as in Worked Example 11.04. Note that the purpose of `Counter` has changed.

Identifier	Explanation
`BiggestSoFar`	Stores the biggest number input so far
`NextNumber`	The next number to be input
`Counter`	Counts the number of times round the loop

Table 11.07 Identifier table for biggest number problem using a FOR loop

The algorithm can be expressed in the following pseudocode:

```
INPUT BiggestSoFar
FOR Counter ← 2 TO 10
   INPUT NextNumber
   IF NextNumber > BiggestSoFar
      THEN
         BiggestSoFar ← NextNumber
   ENDIF
ENDFOR
OUTPUT BiggestSoFar
```

The first time round the loop, `Counter` is set to 2. The next time round the loop, `Counter` has automatically increased to 3, and so on. The last time round the loop, `Counter` has the value 10.

A **rogue value** is a value used to terminate a sequence of values. The rogue value is of the same data type but outside the range of normal expected values.

KEY TERMS

Rogue value: a value used to terminate a sequence of values

WORKED EXAMPLE 11.06

Repetition using a rogue value

The problem to be solved: A sequence of non-zero numbers is terminated by 0. Take this sequence as input and output the largest number.

Note: In this example the rogue value chosen is 0. It is very important to choose a rogue value that is of the same data type but outside the range of normal expected values. For example, if the input might normally include 0 then a negative value, such as –1, might be chosen.

Look at Worked Example 11.05. Instead of counting the numbers input, we need to check whether the number input is 0 to terminate the loop. The identifiers are shown in Table 11.08.

Identifier	Explanation
`BiggestSoFar`	Stores the biggest number input so far
`NextNumber`	The next number to be input

Table 11.08 Identifier table for biggest number problem using a rogue value

A possible pseudocode algorithm is:

```
INPUT BiggestSoFar
REPEAT
   INPUT NextNumber
   IF NextNumber > BiggestSoFar
      THEN
         BiggestSoFar ← NextNumber
   ENDIF
UNTIL NextNumber = 0
OUTPUT BiggestSoFar
```

This algorithm works even if the sequence consists of only one non-zero input. However, it will not work if the only input is 0. In that case, we don't want to perform the statements within the loop at all. We can use an alternative construct, the `WHILE...ENDWHILE` loop.

```
INPUT NextNumber
BiggestSoFar ← NextNumber
WHILE NextNumber <> 0 // sequence terminator not encountered
   INPUT NextNumber
   IF NextNumber > BiggestSoFar
      THEN
         BiggestSoFar ← NextNumber
   ENDIF
ENDWHILE
OUTPUT BiggestSoFar
```

Before we enter the loop we check whether we have a non-zero number. To make this work for the first number, we store it in `NextNumber` and also in `BiggestSoFar`. If this first number is zero we don't follow the instructions within the loop. For a non-zero first number this algorithm has the same effect as the algorithm using `REPEAT...UNTIL`.

WORKED EXAMPLE 11.07

Implementing the number-guessing game with a loop

Consider the number guessing game again, this time allowing repeated guesses:

1. The player repeatedly inputs a number to guess the secret number stored.
2. If the guess is correct, the number of guesses made is output and the game stops.
3. If the number input is larger than the secret number, the player is given the message to input a smaller number.
4. If the number input is smaller than the secret number, the player is given the message to input a larger number.

The algorithm is expressed in structured English, as a flowchart and in pseudocode.

Algorithm for the number-guessing game in structured English

```
SET value for secret number
REPEAT the following UNTIL correct guess
   INPUT guess
   COMPARE guess with secret number
   OUTPUT comment
```

We need variables to store the following values:

- the secret number (to be set as a random number)
- the number input by the player as a guess
- the count of how many guesses the player has made so far.

We represent this information in the identifier table shown in Table 11.09.

Identifier	Explanation
SecretNumber	The number to be guessed
NumberOfGuesses	The number of guesses the player has made
Guess	The number the player has input as a guess

Table 11.09 Identifier table for number-guessing game

Algorithm for the number-guessing game as a flowchart

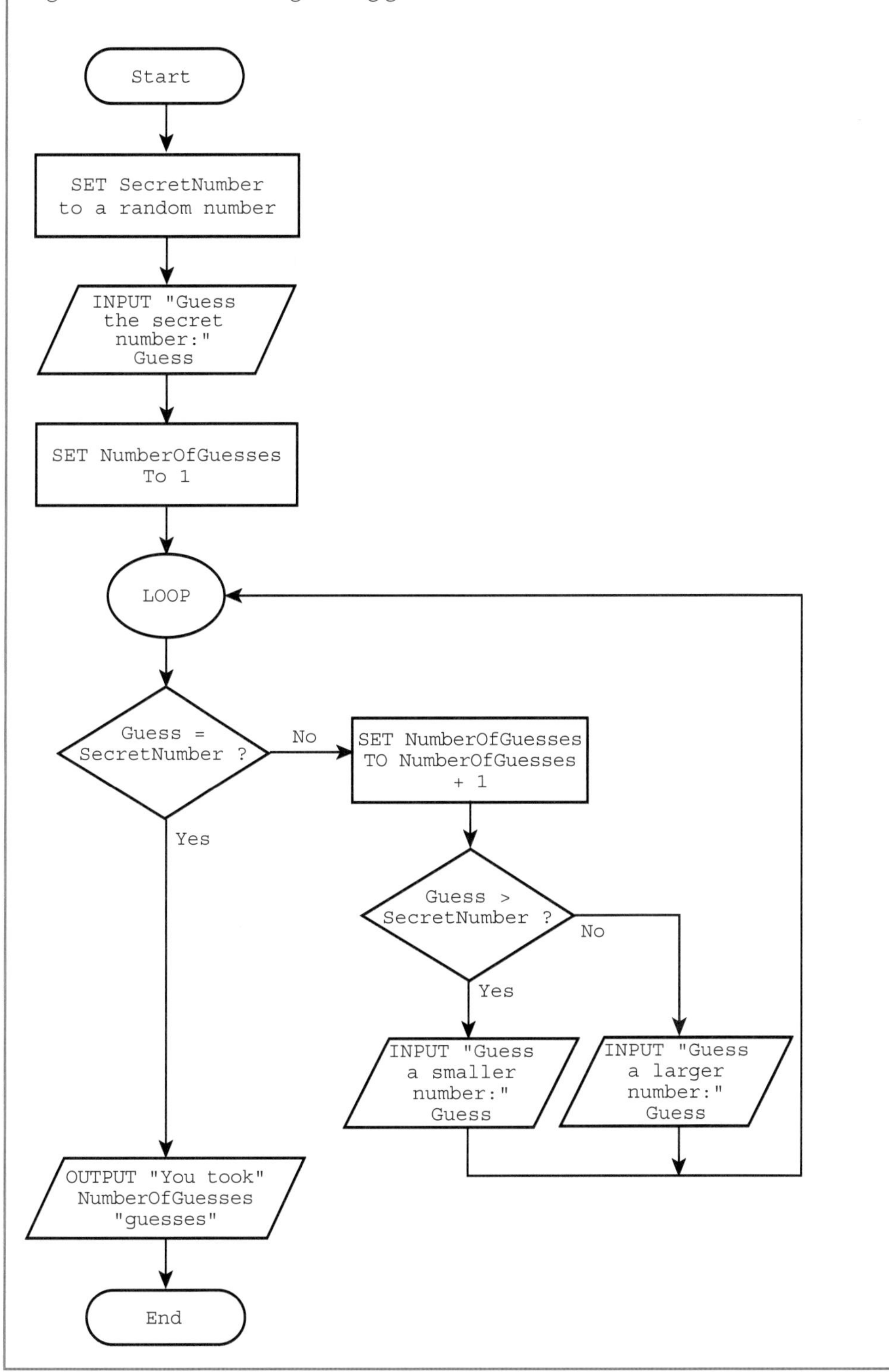

Pseudocode for the number-guessing game with a post-condition loop

```
SecretNumber ← Random
NumberOfGuesses ← 0
REPEAT
   INPUT Guess
   NumberOfGuesses ← NumberOfGuesses + 1
   IF Guess > SecretNumber
      THEN
         the player is given the message to input a smaller number
   ENDIF
   IF Guess < SecretNumber
      THEN
        the player is given the message to input a larger number
   ENDIF
UNTIL Guess = SecretNumber
```

Pseudocode for the number-guessing game with a pre-condition loop

The above solution uses a post-condition (`REPEAT...UNTIL`) loop. An alternative solution uses a pre-condition (`WHILE...ENDWHILE`) loop:

```
SecretNumber ← Random
INPUT Guess
NumberOfGuesses ← 1
WHILE Guess <> SecretNumber
   IF Guess > SecretNumber
      THEN
         the player is given the message to input a smaller number
   ENDIF
   IF Guess < SecretNumber
      THEN
        the player is given the message to input a larger number
   ENDIF
   INPUT Guess
   NumberOfGuesses ← NumberOfGuesses + 1
ENDWHILE
```


WORKED EXAMPLE 11.08

Calculating running totals and averages

The problem to be solved: Take 10 numbers as input and output the sum of these numbers and the average.

Identifier	Explanation
`RunningTotal`	Stores the sum of the numbers input so far
`Counter`	How many numbers have been input
`NextNumber`	The next number input
`Average`	The average of the numbers input

Table 11.10 Identifier table for running total and average algorithm

The following pseudocode gives a possible algorithm:

```
RunningTotal ← 0
FOR Counter ← 1 TO 10
   INPUT NextNumber
   RunningTotal ← RunningTotal + NextNumber
ENDFOR
OUTPUT RunningTotal
Average ← RunningTotal / 10
OUTPUT Average
```

It is very important that the value stored in `RunningTotal` is initialised to zero before we start adding the numbers being input.

TASK 11.04

Change the algorithm in Worked Example 11.08 so that the sequence of numbers is terminated by a rogue value of 0.

WORKED EXAMPLE 11.09

Using nested loops

The problem to be solved: Take as input two numbers and a symbol. Output a grid made up entirely of the chosen symbol, with the number of rows matching the first number input and the number of columns matching the second number input.

For example the three input values 3, 7 and &, result in the output:

```
&&&&&&&
&&&&&&&
&&&&&&&
```

We need two variables to store the number of rows and the number of columns. We also need a variable to store the symbol. We need a counter for the rows and a counter for the columns.

Identifier	Explanation
`NumberOfRows`	Stores the number of rows of the grid
`NumberOfColumns`	Stores the number of columns of the grid
`Symbol`	Stores the chosen character symbol
`RowCounter`	Counts the number of rows
`ColumnCounter`	Counts the number of columns

Table 11.11 Identifier table for the nested loop example

```
INPUT NumberOfRows
INPUT NumberOfColumns
INPUT Symbol
FOR RowCounter ← 1 TO NumberOfRows
   FOR ColumnCounter ← 1 TO NumberOfColumns
      OUTPUT Symbol // without moving to next line
   ENDFOR
   OUTPUT Newline   // move to the next line
ENDFOR
```

Each time round the outer loop (counting the number of rows) we complete the inner loop, outputting a symbol for each count of the number of columns. This type of construct is called a **nested loop.**

KEY TERMS

Nested loop: loop containing another loop

11.07 Working with arrays

WORKED EXAMPLE 11.10

Working with a one-dimensional array

The problem to be solved: Take seven numbers as input and store them for later use.

We could use seven separate variables. However, if we wanted our algorithm to work with 70 numbers, for example, then this would become very tedious. We can make use of a data structure, known as a 'linear list' or a one-dimensional (1D) array.

This array is given an identifier, for example `MyList`, and each element within the array is referred to using this identifier and its position (index) within the array. For example, `MyList[4]` refers to the fourth element in the `MyList` array.

We can use a loop to access each array element in turn. If the numbers input to the pseudocode algorithm below are 25, 34, 98, 7, 41, 19 and 5 then the algorithm will produce the result in Figure 11.10.

```
FOR Index ← 1 TO 7
   INPUT MyList[Index]
ENDFOR
```

Index	MYList
[1]	25
[2]	34
[3]	98
[4]	7
[5]	41
[6]	19
[7]	5

Figure 11.10 `MyList` array populated by a loop

TASK 11.05

Set up two arrays, one for your friends' names and one for their ages as shown in Figure 11.11.

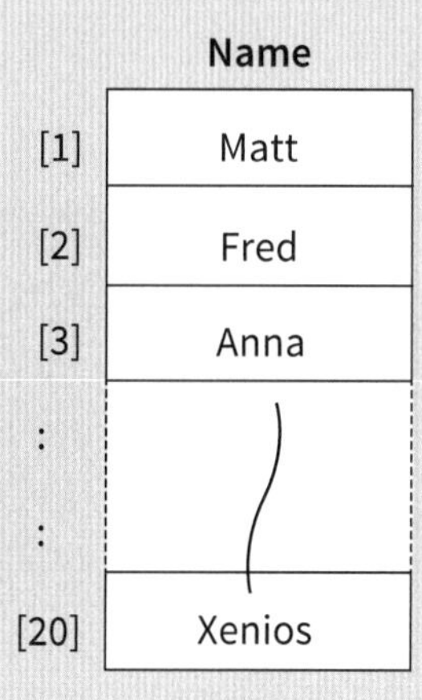

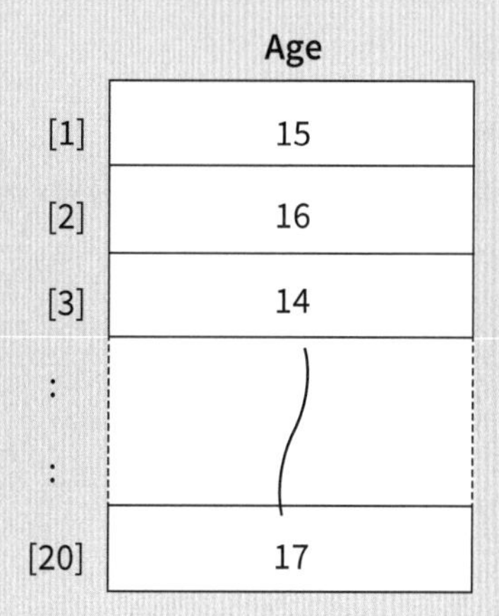

Figure 11.11 Arrays for names and ages

WORKED EXAMPLE 11.11

Searching a 1D array

The problem to be solved: Take a number as input. Search for this number in an existing 1D array of seven numbers (see Worked Example 11.10).

Start at the first element of the array and check each element in turn until the search value is found or the end of the array is reached. This method is called a **linear search**.

Identifier	Explanation
`MyList`	Data structure (1D array) to store seven numbers
`MaxIndex`	The number of elements in the array
`SearchValue`	The value to be searched for
`Found`	`TRUE` if the value has been found `FALSE` if the value has not been found
`Index`	Index of the array element currently being processed

Table 11.12 Identifier table for linear search algorithm

```
MaxIndex ← 7
INPUT SearchValue
Found ← FALSE
Index ← 0
REPEAT
   Index ← Index + 1
   IF MyList[Index]= SearchValue
      THEN
         Found ← TRUE
   ENDIF
UNTIL FOUND = TRUE OR Index >= MaxIndex
IF Found = TRUE
   THEN
      OUTPUT "Value found at location:" Index
   ELSE
      OUTPUT "Value not found"
ENDIF
```

The complex condition to the `REPEAT...UNTIL` loop allows us to exit the loop when the search value is found. Using the variable `Found` makes the algorithm easier to understand. `Found` is initialised to `FALSE` before entering the loop and set to `TRUE` if the value is found.

If the value is not in the array, the loop terminates when `Index` is greater than or equal to `MaxIndex` That means we have come to the end of the array. Note that using `MaxIndex` in the logic statement to terminate the loop makes it much easier to adapt the algorithm when the array consists of a different number of elements. The algorithm only needs to be changed in the first line, where `MaxIndex` is given a value.

KEY TERMS

Linear search: checking each element of an array in turn for a required value

TASK 11.06

Use the algorithm in Worked Example 11.11 as a design pattern to search for a friend's name and output their age.

WORKED EXAMPLE 11.12

Sorting elements in a 1D array

The simplest way to sort an unordered list of values is the following method:

1. Compare the first and second values. If the first value is larger than the second value, swap them.
2. Compare the second and third values. If the second value is larger than the third value, swap them.
3. Compare the third and fourth values. If the third value is larger than the fourth value, swap them.
4. Keep on comparing adjacent values, swapping them if necessary, until the last two values in the list have been processed.

Figure 11.12 shows what happens to the values as we work down the array, following this algorithm.

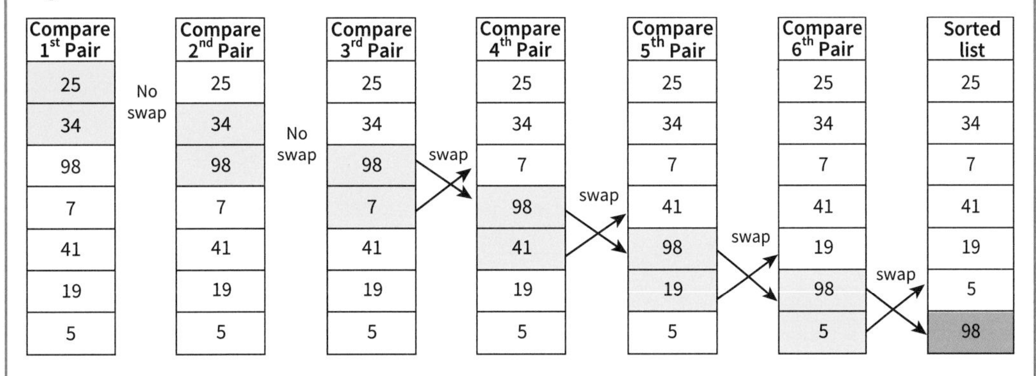

Figure 11.12 Swapping values working down the array

When we have completed the first pass through the entire array, the largest value is in the correct position at the end of the array. The other values may or may not be in the correct order.

We need to work through the array again and again. After each pass through the array the next largest value will be in its correct position, as shown in Figure 11.13.

Original list	After pass 1	After pass 2	After pass 3	After pass 4	After pass 5	After pass 6
25	25	25	7	7	7	5
34	34	7	25	19	5	7
98	7	34	19	5	19	19
7	41	19	5	25	25	25
41	19	5	34	34	34	34
19	5	41	41	41	41	41
5	98	98	98	98	98	98

Figure 11.13 States of the array after each pass

In effect we perform a loop within a loop, a nested loop. This method is known as a **bubble sort**. The name comes from the fact that smaller values slowly rise to the top, like bubbles in a liquid.
The identifiers needed for the algorithm are listed in Table 11.13.

Identifier	Explanation
`MyList[1..7]`	Data structure (1D array) to store seven numbers
`MaxIndex`	The number of elements in the array
`n`	The number of elements to compare in each pass
`i`	Counter for outer loop
`j`	Counter for inner loop
`Temp`	Variable for temporary storage while swapping values

Table 11.13 Identifier table for bubble sort algorithm

The algorithm in pseudocode is:

```
n ← MaxIndex - 1
FOR i ← 1 TO MaxIndex - 1
    FOR j ← 1 TO n
        IF MyList[j] > MyList[j + 1]
            THEN
                Temp ← MyList[j]
                MyList[j] ← MyList[j + 1]
                MyList[j + 1] ← Temp
        ENDIF
    ENDFOR
    n ← n - 1 // this means the next time round the inner loop, we don't
               // look at the values already in the correct positions.
ENDFOR
```

The values to be sorted may already be in the correct order before the outer loop has been through all its iterations. Look at the list of values in Figure 11.14. It is only slightly different from the first list we sorted.

Original list	After pass 1	After pass 2	After pass 3	After pass 4	After pass 5	After pass 6
5	5	5	5	5	5	5
34	34	7	7	7	7	7
98	7	34	19	19	19	19
7	41	19	25	25	25	25
41	19	25	34	34	34	34
19	25	41	41	41	41	41
25	98	98	98	98	98	98

Figure 11.14 States of the list after each pass

After the third pass the values are all in the correct order but our algorithm will carry on with three further passes through the array. This means we are making comparisons when no further comparisons need to be made.

If we have gone through the whole of the inner loop (one pass) without swapping any values, we know that the array elements must be in the correct order. We can therefore replace the outer loop with a conditional loop.

We can use a variable `NoMoreSwaps` to store whether or not a swap has taken place during the current pass. We initialise the variable `NoMoreSwaps to TRUE` When we swap a pair of values we set `NoMoreSwaps to FALSE`. At the end of the pass through the array we can check whether a swap has taken place.

The identifier table for this improved algorithm is shown in Table 11.14.

Identifier	Explanation
`MyList[1..7]`	Data structure (1D array) to store seven numbers
`MaxIndex`	The number of elements in the array
`n`	The number of elements to compare in each pass
`NoMoreSwaps`	`TRUE` when no swaps have occurred in current pass `FALSE` when a swap has occurred
`j`	Counter for inner loop
`Temp`	Variable for temporary storage while swapping values

Table 11.14 Identifier table for improved bubble sort algorithm

This improved algorithm in pseudocode is:

```
n ← MaxIndex - 1
REPEAT
   NoMoreSwaps ← TRUE
   FOR j ← 1 TO n
      IF MyList[j] > MyList[j + 1]
         THEN
            Temp ← MyList[j]
            MyList[j] ← MyList[j + 1]
            MyList[j + 1] ← Temp
            NoMoreSwaps ← FALSE
      ENDIF
   ENDFOR
   n ← n - 1
UNTIL NoMoreSwaps = TRUE
```

KEY TERMS

Bubble sort: a sort method where adjacent pairs of values are compared and swapped

Discussion Point:

What happens if the array elements are already in the correct order?

TASK 11.07

Rewrite the algorithm in Worked Example 11.12 to sort the array elements into descending order.

WORKED EXAMPLE 11.13

Working with two-dimensional arrays and nested loops

A 1D array is like a linear list. The *n*th element within the array `MyList` is referred to as `MyList[n]`.

A two-dimensional (2D) array is like a table or matrix. The element in row *x* and column *y* of `ThisTable` is referred to as `ThisTable[x, y]`.

For example to store the value 5 in the element in the fourth row and second column, we write:

```
ThisTable[4, 2] ← 5
```

When we want to access each element of a 1D array, we use a loop to access each element in turn. When working with a 2D array, we need a loop to access each row. Within each row we need to access each column. This means we use a loop within a loop (nested loops).

In structured English our algorithm is:

```
For each row
   For each column
      Assign the initial value to the element at the current position
```

We need the identifiers shown in Table 11.15.

Identifier	Explanation
`ThisTable[1..4, 1..6]`	Table data structure (2D array) to store values
`MaxRows`	The number of rows in the table (4 in this example)
`MaxColumns`	The number of columns in the table (6 in this example)
`Row`	Counter for the row index
`Column`	Counter for the column index

Table 11.15 Identifier table for working with a table

Using pseudocode, the algorithm to set each element of array `ThisTable` to zero is:

```
FOR Row ← 1 TO MaxRows
   FOR Column ← 1 TO MaxColumns
      ThisTable[Row, Column] ← 0
   ENDFOR
ENDFOR
```

When we want to output the contents of a 2D array, we again need nested loops. We want to output all the values in one row of the array on the same line. At the end of the row, we want to output a new line.

```
FOR Row ← 1 TO MaxRows
   FOR Column ← 1 TO MaxColumns
      OUTPUT ThisTable[Row, Column] // stay on same line
   ENDFOR
   OUTPUT Newline      // move to next line for next row
ENDFOR
```

Summary

- An algorithm is a sequence of steps that can be carried out to solve a problem.
- Algorithms are expressed using the four basic constructs of assignment, sequence, selection and repetition.
- Algorithms can be documented using structured English, pseudocode or a program flowchart.
- Logic statements use the relational operators =, <, >, <>, <= and >= and the logic operators AND, OR and NOT.
- Selection constructs and conditional loops use conditions to determine the steps to be followed.

Exam-style Questions

1 The Modulo-11 method of calculating a check digit for a sequence of nine digits is as follows:

Each digit in the sequence is given a weight depending on its position in the sequence. The leftmost digit has a weight of 10. The next digit to the right has a weight of 9, the next one 8 and so on. Values are calculated by multiplying each digit by its weight. These values are added together and the sum is divided by 11. The remainder from this division is subtracted from 11 and this value is the check digit. If this value is 10, then the check digit is X. Note that `x MOD y` gives the remainder from the division of `x` by `y`.

Complete the flowchart using the statements in the table.

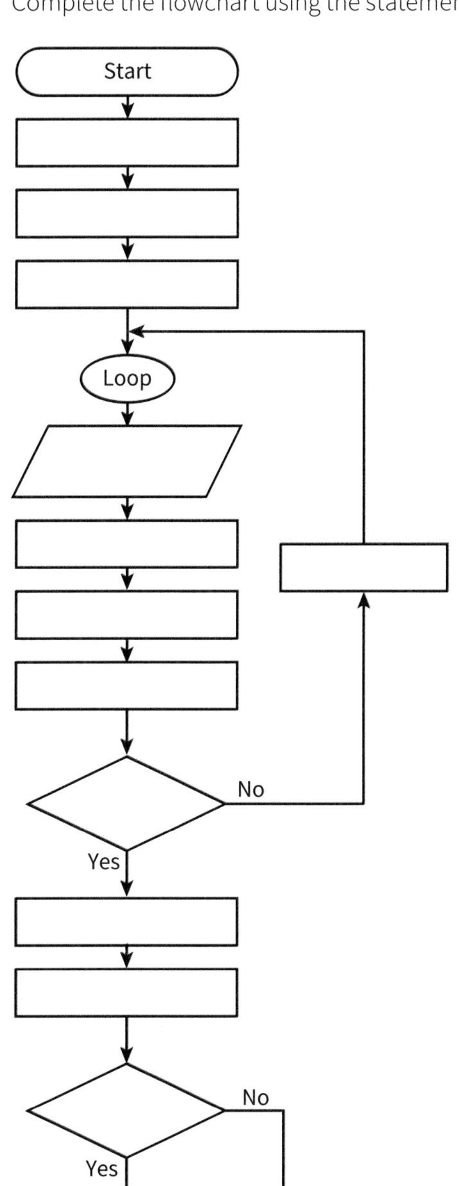

Statement number	Statement
1	`CheckDigit ← 11 - Remainder`
2	`CheckDigit ← X`
3	`CheckDigit = 10 ?`
4	`Count ← 1`
5	`Count ← Count + 1`
6	`Count = 9 ?`
7	`INPUT Digit`
8	`Remainder ← Total MOD 11`
9	`Total ← 0`
10	`Total ← Total + Value`
11	`Value ← Digit * Weighting`
12	`Weighting ← Weighting - 1`
13	`Weighting ← 10`

[9]

2 Draw a flowchart for the following problem given in structured English.

```
REPEAT the following UNTIL the number input is zero
INPUT a number
Check whether number is positive or negative
Increment positive number count if the number is positive
Increment negative number count if the number is negative
```

[7]

3 Write pseudocode from the given flowchart. Use a `WHILE` loop.

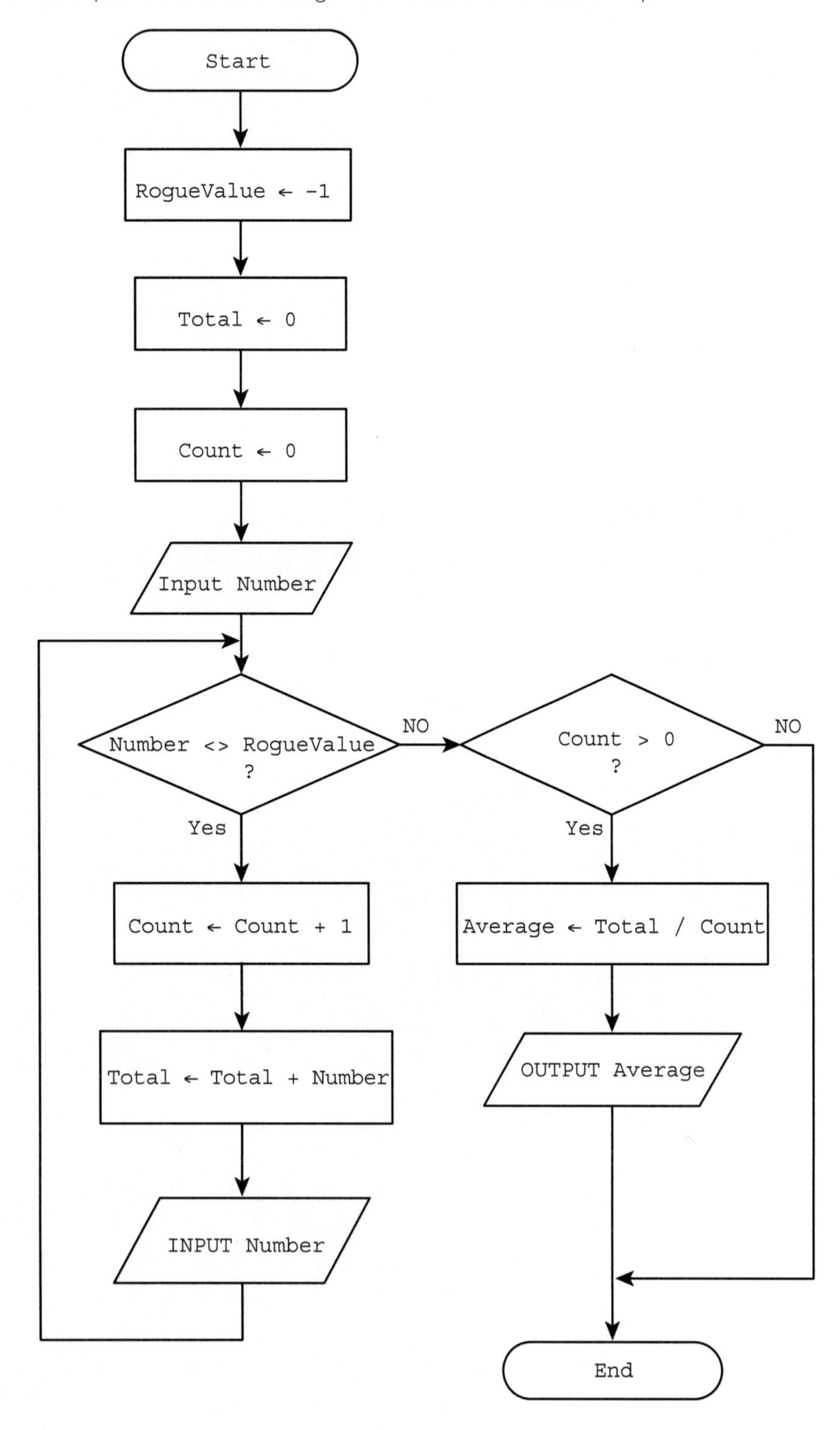

[8]

4 Alan uses two 1D arrays, `UserList` and `PasswordList`. For twenty users, he stores each user ID in `UserList` and the corresponding password in PasswordList. For example, the person with user ID `Fred12` has password `rzt456`.

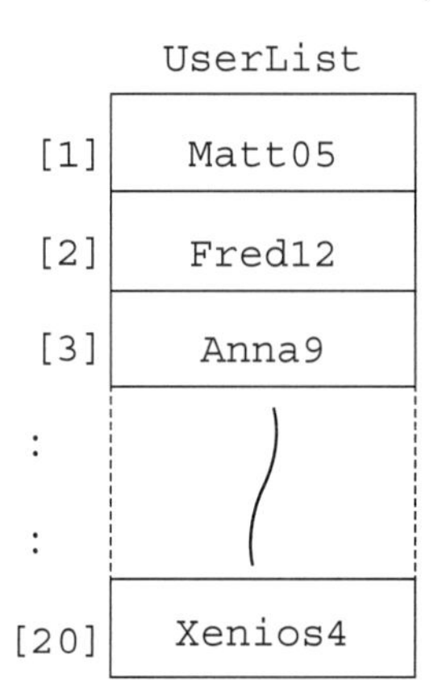

PasswordList
[1] pqklmn4
[2] rzt456
[3] jedd321
:
:
[20] wkl@tmp6

Alan wants to write an algorithm to check whether a user ID and password, entered by a user, are correct. He designs the algorithm to search `UserList` for the user ID. If the user ID is found, the password stored in `PasswordList` is to be compared to the entered password. If the passwords match, the login is successful. In all other cases, login is unsuccessful.

a Complete the identifier table. [4]

Identifier	Explanation
`UserList[1..20]`	1D array to store user IDs
....	1D array to store passwords
`MaxIndex`	Number of elements in each array
`MyUserID`	User ID entered to login
`MyPassword`	....
`UserIdFound`	`FALSE` if user ID not found in `UserList` `TRUE` if ....
`LoginOK`	`FALSE` if .... `TRUE` if ....
`Index`	Pointer to current array element

b Complete the pseudocode for Alan's algorithm:

```
MaxIndex ← 20
INPUT MyUserID
INPUT MyPassword
UserIdFound ← FALSE
LoginOK ← ..............
Index ← 0
REPEAT
   INDEX ← ..............
   IF UserList[..............] = ..............
      THEN
         UserIdFound ← TRUE
   ENDIF
UNTIL .............. OR ..............
IF UserIdFound = TRUE
   THEN
      IF PasswordList[..............] = ..............
         THEN
            LoginOK ← TRUE
      ..............
ENDIF
IF ..............
   THEN
      OUTPUT "Login successful"
   ELSE
      OUTPUT "User ID and/or password incorrect"
ENDIF
```

[10]

Chapter 12
Stepwise Refinement and Structure Charts

Learning objectives

By the end of this chapter you should be able to:

- use the process of stepwise refinement to express an algorithm to a level of detail from which the task may be programmed
- decompose a problem into sub-tasks leading to the concept of a program module (procedure/function)
- use a structure chart to express the parameters passed between the various modules/procedures/functions which are part of the algorithm design
- describe the purpose of a structure chart
- construct a structure chart for a given problem
- derive equivalent pseudocode from a structure chart.

12.01 Stepwise refinement

Many problems that we want to solve are bigger than the ones we met in Chapter 11. To make it easier to solve a bigger problem, we break the problem down into smaller steps. These might need breaking down further until the steps are small enough to solve easily.

For a solution to a problem to be programmable, we need to break down the steps of the solution into the basic constructs of sequence, assignment, selection, repetition, input and output.

We can use a method called **stepwise refinement** to break down the steps of our outline solution into smaller steps until it is detailed enough. In Section 11.01 we looked at a recipe for a cake. The step of mixing together all the ingredients was broken down into more detailed steps.

KEY TERMS

Stepwise refinement: breaking down the steps of an outline solution into smaller and smaller steps

WORKED EXAMPLE 12.01

Drawing a pyramid using stepwise refinement

The problem to be solved: Take as input a chosen symbol and an odd number. Output a pyramid shape made up entirely of the chosen symbol, with the number of symbols in the final row matching the number input.

For example the two input values A and 9 result in the following output:

```
    A
   AAA
  AAAAA
 AAAAAAA
AAAAAAAAA
```

This problem is similar to Worked Example 11.09 in Chapter 11, but the number of symbols in each row starts with one and increases by two with each row. Each row starts with a decreasing number of spaces, to create the slope effect.

Our first attempt at solving this problem using structured English is:

```
01   Set up initial values
02   REPEAT
03       Output number of spaces
04       Output number of symbols
05       Adjust number of spaces and number of symbols to be output in next row
06   UNTIL the required number of symbols have been output in one row
```

The steps are numbered to make it easier to refer to them later.

This is not enough detail to write a program in a high-level programming language. Exactly what values do we need to set?

We need as input:

- the symbol character from which the pyramid is to be formed
- the number of symbols in the final row (for the pyramid to look symmetrical, this needs to be an odd number).

We need to calculate how many spaces we need in the first row. So that the slope of the pyramid is symmetrical, this number should be half of the final row's symbols. We need to set the number of symbols to be output in the first row to 1. We therefore need the identifiers listed in Table 12.01.

Identifier	Explanation
`Symbol`	The character symbol to form the pyramid
`MaxNumberOfSymbols`	The number of symbols in the final row
`NumberOfSpaces`	The number of spaces to be output in the current row
`NumberOfSymbols`	The number of symbols to be output in the current row

Table 12.01 Identifier table for pyramid example

Using pseudocode, we now refine the steps of our first attempt. To show which step we are refining, a numbering system is used as shown.

Step 01 can be broken down as follows:

```
01   // Set up initial values expands into:
01.1 INPUT symbol
01.2 INPUT MaxNumberOfSymbols
01.3 NumberOfSpaces ← (MaxNumberOfSymbols - 1) / 2
01.4 NumberOfSymbols ← 1
```

Remember we need an odd number for `MaxNumberOfSymbols`. We need to make sure the input is an odd number. So we further refine Step 01.2:

```
01.2    // INPUT MaxNumberOfSymbols expands into:
01.2.1 REPEAT
01.2.2     INPUT MaxNumberOfSymbols
01.2.3 UNTIL MaxNumberOfSymbols MOD 2 = 1
01.2.4 // MOD 2 gives the remainder after integer division by 2
```

We can now look to refine Steps 03 and 04:

```
03     // Output number of spaces expands into:
03.1   FOR i ← 1 TO NumberOfSpaces
03.2       OUTPUT Space // without moving to next line
03.3   ENDFOR

04     // Output number of symbols expands into:
04.1   FOR i ← 1 TO NumberOfSymbols
04.2       OUTPUT Symbol // without moving to next line
04.3   ENDFOR
04.4   OUTPUT Newline // move to the next line
```

In Step 05 we need to decrease the number of spaces by 1 and increase the number of symbols by 2:

```
05   // Adjust values for next row expands into:
05.1 NumberOfSpaces ← NumberOfSpaces - 1
05.2 NumberOfSymbols ← NumberOfSymbols + 2
```

Step 06 essentially checks whether the number of symbols for the next row is now greater than the value input at the beginning.

```
06 UNTIL NumberOfSymbols > MaxNumberOfSymbols
```

We can put together all the steps and end up with a solution.

```
01         // Set Values
01.1       INPUT symbol
01.2       // Input max number of symbols (an odd number)
01.2.1   REPEAT
01.2.2       INPUT MaxNumberOfSymbols
01.2.3   UNTIL MaxNumberOfSymbols MOD 2 = 1
01.3       NumberOfSpaces ← (MaxNumberOfSymbols - 1) / 2
01.4       NumberOfSymbols ← 1
02         REPEAT
03             // Output number of spaces
03.1           FOR i ← 1 TO NumberOfSpaces
03.2               OUTPUT Space // without moving to next line
03.3           ENDFOR
04             // Output number of symbols
04.1           FOR i ← 1 TO NumberOfSymbols
04.2               OUTPUT Symbol // without moving to next line
04.3           ENDFOR
04.4           OUTPUT Newline // move to the next line
05             // Adjust Values For Next Row
05.1           NumberOfSpaces ← NumberOfSpaces - 1
05.2           NumberOfSymbols ← NumberOfSymbols + 2
06         UNTIL NumberOfSymbols > MaxNumberOfSymbols
```


TASK 12.01

Use stepwise refinement to output a hollow triangle. For example the two input values A and 9 result in the following output:

```
    A
   A A
  A   A
 A     A
AAAAAAAAA
```

A first attempt at solving this problem using structured English is:

```
01   Set up initial values
02   REPEAT
03       Output leading number of spaces
04       Output symbol, middle spaces, symbol
05       Adjust number of spaces and number of symbols to be output in next row
06   UNTIL the required number of symbols have been output in one row
```

12.02 Modules

Another method of developing a solution is to decompose the problem into sub-tasks. Each sub-task can be considered as a 'module' that is refined separately. Modules are procedures and functions.

A **procedure** groups together a number of steps and gives them a name (an identifier). We can use this identifier when we want to refer to this group of steps. When we want to perform the steps in a procedure we call the procedure by its name.

KEY TERMS

Procedure: a sequence of steps that is given an identifier and can be called to perform a sub-task

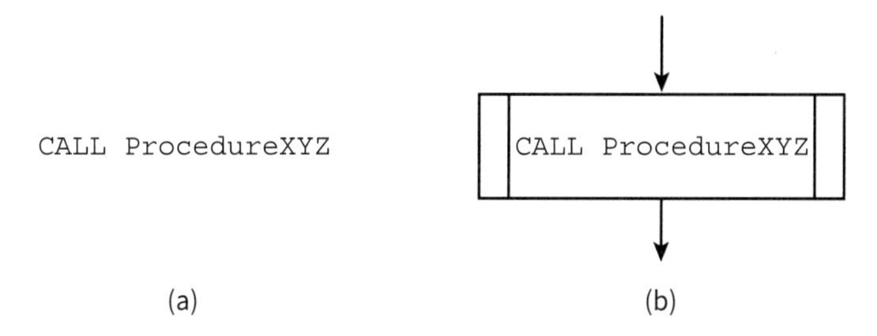

Figure 12.01 Representation of a procedure in (a) pseudocode and (b) a flowchart

The rules for module identifiers are the same as for variable identifiers (see Section 11.03)

WORKED EXAMPLE 12.02

Drawing a pyramid using modules

The problem is the same as in Worked Example 12.01.

When we want to set up the initial values, we call a procedure, using the following statement:

```
CALL SetValues
```

We can rewrite the top-level solution to our pyramid problem using a procedure for each step, as:

```
CALL SetValues
REPEAT
   CALL OutputSpaces
   CALL OutputSymbols
   CALL AdjustValuesForNextRow
UNTIL NumberOfSymbols > MaxNumberOfSymbols
```

This top-level solution calls four procedures. This means each procedure has to be defined. The procedure definitions are:

```
PROCEDURE SetValues
   INPUT symbol
   CALL InputMaxNumberOfSymbols // need to ensure it is an odd number
   NumberOfSpaces ← (MaxNumberOfSymbols - 1) / 2
   NumberOfSymbols ← 1
ENDPROCEDURE
```

```
PROCEDURE InputMaxNumberOfSymbols
   REPEAT
      INPUT MaxNumberOfSymbols
   UNTIL MaxNumberOfSymbols MOD 2 = 1
ENDPROCEDURE

PROCEDURE OutputSpaces
   FOR Count ← 1 TO NumberOfSpaces
      OUTPUT Space // without moving to next line
   ENDFOR
ENDPROCEDURE

PROCEDURE OutputSymbols
   FOR Count ← 1 TO NumberOfSymbols
      OUTPUT Symbol // without moving to next line
   ENDFOR
   OUTPUT Newline // move to the next line
ENDPROCEDURE

PROCEDURE AdjustValuesForNextRow
   NumberOfSpaces ← NumberOfSpaces - 1
   NumberOfSymbols ← NumberOfSymbols + 2
ENDPROCEDURE
```


TASK 12.02

Amend your algorithm for Task 12.01 to use modules.

WORKED EXAMPLE 12.03

Creating a program to play Connect 4

Connect 4 is a game played by two players. In the commercial version shown in Figure 12.01, one player uses red tokens and the other uses black. Each player has 21 tokens. The game board is a vertical grid of six rows and seven columns.

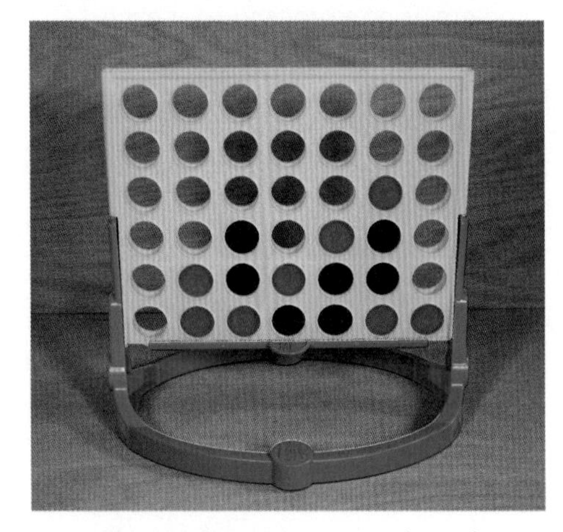

Figure 12.01 A Connect 4 board

Columns get filled with tokens from the bottom. The players take it in turns to choose a column that is not full and drop a token into this column. The token will occupy the lowest empty position in the chosen column. The winner is the player who is the first to connect four of their own tokens in a horizontal, vertical or diagonal line. If all tokens have been used and neither player has connected four tokens, the game ends in a draw.

If we want to write a program to play this game on a computer, we need to work out the steps required to 'solve the problem', that means to let players take their turn in placing tokens and checking for a winner. We will designate our players (and their tokens) by 'O' and 'X'. The game board will be represented by a 2D array. To simplify the problem, the winner is the player who is the first to connect four of their tokens horizontally or vertically.

Our first attempt in structured English is:

```
Initialise board
Set up game
Display board
While game not finished
   This Player makes a move
   Display board
   Check if this player has won
   If game not finished, swap player
```

The top-level pseudocode version using modules is:

```
01 CALL InitialiseBoard
02 CALL SetUpGame
03 CALL OutputBoard
04 WHILE GameFinished = FALSE
05    CALL ThisPlayerMakesMove
06    CALL OutputBoard
07    CALL CheckIfThisPlayerHasWon
08    IF GameFinished = FALSE
09       THEN
10          CALL SwapThisPlayer
11    ENDIF
12 ENDWHILE
```

Note that Steps 03 and 06 are the same. This means that we can save ourselves some effort. We only need to define this module once, but can call it from more than one place. This is one of the advantages of using modules.

The identifier table for the program is shown in Table 12.03.

Identifier	Explanation
`Board[1..6, 1..7]`	2D array to represent the board
`InitialiseBoard`	Procedure to initialise the board to all blanks
`SetUpGame`	Procedure to set initial values for `GameFinished` and `ThisPlayer`
`GameFinished`	`FALSE` if the game is not finished `TRUE` if the board is full or a player has won
`ThisPlayer`	`'O'` when it is Player O's turn `'X'` when it is Player X's turn
`OutputBoard`	Procedure to output the current contents of the board

ThisPlayerMakesMove	Procedure to place the current player's token into the chosen board location
CheckIfThisPlayerHasWon	Procedure to check if the token just placed makes the current player a winner
SwapThisPlayer	Procedure to change player's turn

Table 12.02 Initial identifier table for Connect 4 game

Now we can refine each procedure (module). This is likely to add some more identifiers to our identifier table. The additional entries required are shown after each procedure.

```
PROCEDURE InitialiseBoard
   FOR Row ← 1 TO 6
      FOR Column ← 1 TO 7
         Board[Row, Column] ← BLANK // use a suitable value for blank
      ENDFOR
   ENDFOR
ENDPROCEDURE
```

Identifier	Explanation
Row	Loop counter for the rows
Column	Loop counter for the columns
BLANK	A value that represents an empty board location

Table 12.03 Additional identifiers for the `InitialiseBoard` procedure

```
PROCEDURE SetUpGame
   ThisPlayer ← 'O' // Player O always starts
   GameFinished ← FALSE
ENDPROCEDURE

PROCEDURE OutputBoard
   FOR Row ← 6 DOWNTO 1
      FOR Column ← 1 TO 7
         OUTPUT Board[Row, Column] // don't move to next line
      ENDFOR
      OUTPUT Newline // move to next line
   ENDFOR
ENDPROCEDURE

PROCEDURE ThisPlayerMakesMove
   ValidColumn ← ThisPlayerChoosesColumn // a module returns column number
   ValidRow ← FindNextFreePositionInColumn // a module returns row number
   Board[ValidRow, ValidColumn] ← ThisPlayer
ENDPROCEDURE
```

Note that the modules `ThisPlayerChoosesColumn` and `FindNextFreePositionInColumn` are not procedures. These modules produce and return a value that is used in the assignment statement. We call such a module a **function**. Like a procedure, a function groups together a number of steps and gives them an identifier. But the steps of a function are to work out a single value that is returned from the function. This value is used in an expression.

Identifier	Explanation
`ValidColumn`	The column number the player has chosen
`ThisPlayerChoosesColumn`	Function to get the current player's valid choice of column
`ValidRow`	The row number that represents the first free location in the chosen column
`FindNextFreePositionInColumn`	Function to find the next free location in the chosen column

Table 12.04 Additional identifiers for the `ThisPlayerMakesMove` procedure

```
FUNCTION ThisPlayerChoosesColumn // returns a valid column number
   OUTPUT "Player " ThisPlayer "'s turn."
   REPEAT
      OUTPUT "Enter a valid column number:"
      INPUT ColumnNumber
   UNTIL ColumnNumberValid = TRUE // check whether the column number is valid
   RETURN ColumnNumber
ENDFUNCTION
```

Identifier	Explanation
`ColumnNumber`	The column number chosen by the current player
`ColumnNumberValid`	Function to check whether the chosen column is valid

Table 12.05 Additional identifiers for `ThisPlayerChoosesColumn` function

Note that we need to define the function `ColumnNumberValid`. A column is valid if it is within the range 1 to 7 inclusive and there is still at least one empty location in that column.

```
FUNCTION ColumnNumberValid // returns whether or not the column number is valid
   Valid ← FALSE
   IF ColumnNumber >= 1 AND ColumnNumber <= 7
      THEN
         IF Board[6, ColumnNumber]= BLANK // at least 1 empty space in column
            THEN
               Valid ← TRUE
         ENDIF
   ENDIF
   RETURN Valid
ENDFUNCTION
```

Identifier	Explanation
`Valid`	`FALSE` if column number is not valid `TRUE` if column number is valid

Table 12.06 Additional identifier for the `ColumnNumberValid` function

```
FUNCTION FindNextFreePositionInColumn // returns the next free position
   ThisRow ← 1
   WHILE Board[ThisRow, ValidColumn] <> BLANK // find first empty cell
      ThisRow ← ThisRow + 1
   ENDWHILE
   RETURN ThisRow
ENDFUNCTION
```

Identifier	Explanation
`ThisRow`	Points to the next row to be checked

Table 12.07 Additional identifier for the `FindNextFreePositionInColumn` function

```
PROCEDURE CheckIfThisPlayerHasWon
   WinnerFound ← FALSE
   CALL CheckHorizontalLineInValidRow
   IF WinnerFound = FALSE
      THEN
         CALL CheckVerticalLineInValidColumn
   ENDIF
   IF WinnerFound = TRUE
      THEN
         GameFinished ← TRUE
         OUTPUT ThisPlayer " is the winner"
      ELSE
         CALL CheckForFullBoard
   ENDIF
ENDPROCEDURE
```


Note that the `CheckIfThisPlayerHasWon` procedure uses three further procedures that we need to define.

Identifier	Explanation
`WinnerFound`	`FALSE` if no winning line `TRUE` if a winning line is found
`CheckHorizontalLineInValidRow`	Procedure to check if there is a winning horizontal line in the row the last token was placed in
`CheckVerticalLineInValidColumn`	Procedure to check if there is a winning vertical line in the column the last token was placed in
`CheckForFullBoard`	Procedure to check whether the board is full

Table 12.08 Additional identifiers for the `CheckIfThisPlayerHasWon` procedure

```
PROCEDURE CheckHorizontalLineInValidRow
   FOR i ← 1 TO 4
      IF Board[ValidRow, i] = ThisPlayer AND
         Board[ValidRow, i + 1] = ThisPlayer AND
         Board[ValidRow, i + 2] = ThisPlayer AND
         Board[ValidRow, i + 3] = ThisPlayer
         THEN
            WinnerFound ← TRUE
      ENDIF
   ENDFOR
ENDPROCEDURE

PROCEDURE CheckVerticalLineInValidColumn
   IF ValidRow = 4 OR ValidRow = 5 OR ValidRow = 6
     THEN
       IF Board[ValidRow, ValidColumn] = ThisPlayer AND
          Board[ValidRow - 1, ValidColumn] = ThisPlayer AND
          Board[ValidRow - 2, ValidColumn] = ThisPlayer AND
          Board[ValidRow - 3, ValidColumn] = ThisPlayer
          THEN
             WinnerFound ← TRUE
       ENDIF
       ENDIF
ENDPROCEDURE

PROCEDURE CheckForFullBoard
   BlankFound ← FALSE
   ThisRow ← 0
   REPEAT
      ThisColumn ← 0
      ThisRow ← ThisRow + 1
      REPEAT
         ThisColumn ← ThisColumn + 1
         IF Board[ThisRow, ThisColumn] = BLANK
            THEN
               BlankFound ← TRUE
         ENDIF
      UNTIL ThisColumn = 7 OR BlankFound = TRUE
   UNTIL ThisRow = 6 OR BlankFound = TRUE
   IF BlankFound = FALSE
      THEN
         OUTPUT "It is a draw"
         GameFinished ← TRUE
   ENDIF
ENDPROCEDURE
```

Identifier	Explanation
`BlankFound`	`FALSE` if no blank location found on the board `TRUE` if a blank location found on the board
`ThisRow`	Loop counter for rows
`ThisColumn`	Loop counter for columns

Table 12.09 Additional identifiers for the `CheckForFullBoard` procedure

```
PROCEDURE SwapThisPlayer
   IF ThisPlayer = 'O'
      THEN
         ThisPlayer ← 'X'
      ELSE
         ThisPlayer ← 'O'
   ENDIF
ENDPROCEDURE
```

The complete identifier table for the Connect 4 program is shown in Table 12.11.

Identifier	Explanation
`Board[1..6, 1..7]`	2D array to represent the board
`InitialiseBoard`	Procedure to initialise the board to all blanks
`SetUpGame`	Procedure to set initial values for `GameFinished` and `ThisPlayer`
`GameFinished`	`FALSE` if the game is not finished `TRUE` if the board is full or a player has won
`ThisPlayer`	`'O'` when it is Player O's turn `'X'` when it is Player X's turn
`OutputBoard`	Procedure to output the current contents of the board
`ThisPlayerMakesMove`	Procedure to place the current player's token into the chosen board location
`CheckIfThisPlayerHasWon`	Procedure to check if the token just placed makes the current player a winner
`SwapThisPlayer`	Procedure to change player's turn
`Row`	Loop counter for the rows
`Column`	Loop counter for the columns
`BLANK`	A value that represents an empty board location
`ValidColumn`	The column number the player has chosen
`ThisPlayerChoosesColumn`	Function to get the current player's valid choice of column
`ValidRow`	The row number that represents the first free location in the chosen column
`FindNextFreePositionInColumn`	Function to find the next free location in the chosen column
`ColumnNumber`	The column number chosen by the current player
`ColumnNumberValid`	Function to check whether the chosen column is valid
`Valid`	`FALSE` if column number is not valid `TRUE` if column number is valid

`ThisRow`	Points to the next row to be checked
`WinnerFound`	`FALSE` if no winning line `TRUE` if a winning line is found
`CheckHorizontalLineInValidRow`	Procedure to check if there is a winning horizontal line in the row the last token was placed in
`CheckVerticalLineInValidColumn`	Procedure to check if there is a winning vertical line in the column the last token was placed in
`CheckForFullBoard`	Procedure to check whether the board is full
`BlankFound`	`FALSE` if no blank location is found on the board `TRUE` if a blank location is found on the board
`ThisRow`	Loop counter for rows
`ThisColumn`	Loop counter for columns

Table 12.10 Complete identifier table for Connect 4 game

KEY TERMS

Function: a sequence of steps that is given an identifier and returns a single value; function call is part of an expression

Note that some of the identifiers in Table 12.10 are for variables that are used only within a single module. We call such a variable a **local variable** (see Chapter 14, Section 14.03). In Table 12.10, the local variables are highlighted. The other variables in Table 12.10 are used by several sub-tasks. Variables available to all modules are known as **global variables** (see Chapter 14, Section 14.03).

KEY TERMS

Local variable: a variable that is only accessible within the module in which it is declared

Global variable: a variable that is accessible from all modules

12.03 Structure charts

An alternative approach to modular design is to choose the sub-tasks and then construct a **structure chart** to show the interrelations between the modules. Each box of the structure chart represents a module. Each level is a refinement of the level above.

A structure chart also shows the interface between modules, the variables. These variables are referred to as 'parameters'. A **parameter** supplying a value to a lower-level module is shown as a downwards pointing arrow. A parameter supplying a new value to the module at the next higher level is shown as an upward pointing arrow.

KEY TERMS

Structure chart: a graphical representation of the modular structure of a solution

Parameter: a value passed between modules

Figure 12.02 shows a structure chart for a module that calculates the average of two numbers. The top-level box is the name of the module, which is refined into the three sub-tasks of Level 1. The input numbers (parameters Number1 and Number2) are passed into the 'Calculate Average' sub-task and then the Average parameter is passed into the 'OUTPUT Average' sub-task. The arrows show how the parameters are passed between the modules. This parameter passing is known as the 'interface'.

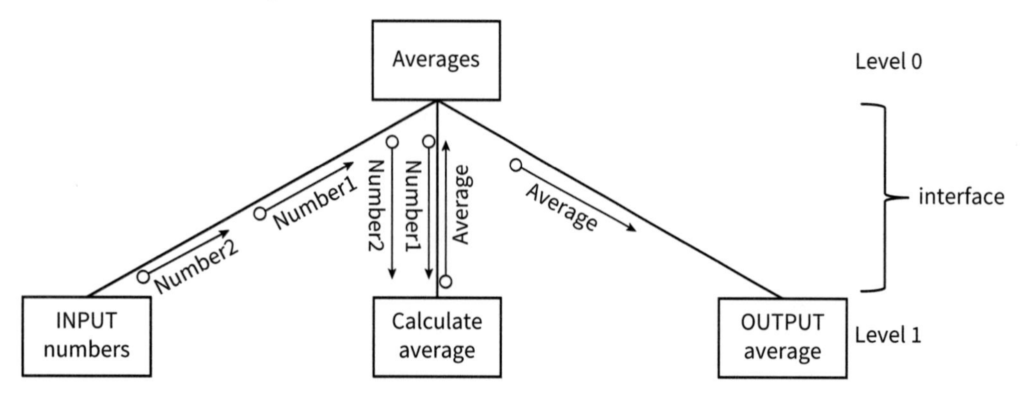

Figure 12.02 Structure chart for a module that calculates the average of two numbers

TASK 12.03

Draw a structure chart for the following module: Input a number of km, output the equivalent number of miles.

Structure charts can also show control information: selection and repetition.

The simple number-guessing game that was introduced in Chapter 11 (Section 11.05) could be modularised and presented as a structure chart, as shown in Figure 12.03.

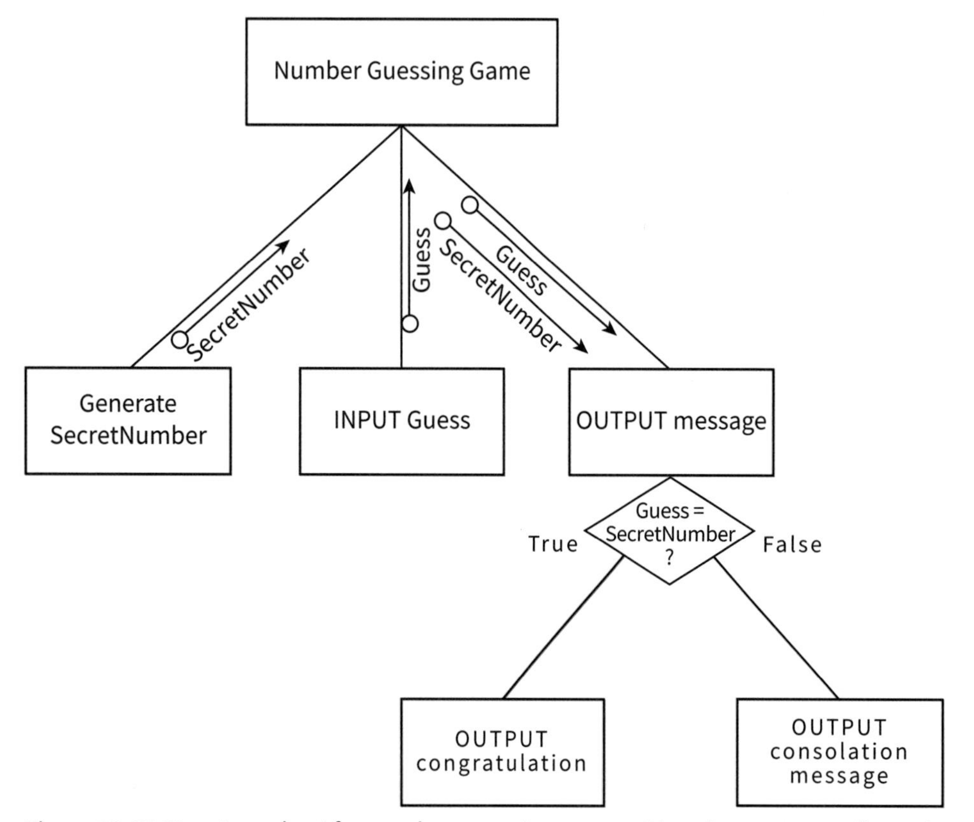

Figure 12.03 Structure chart for number-guessing game with only one guess allowed

The diamond shape shows a condition that is either True or False. So either one branch or the other will be followed.

Figure 12.04 shows the structure chart for the pyramid-drawing program from Worked Example 12.01. The semi-circular arrow represents repetition of the modules below the arrow. The label shows the condition when repetition occurs.

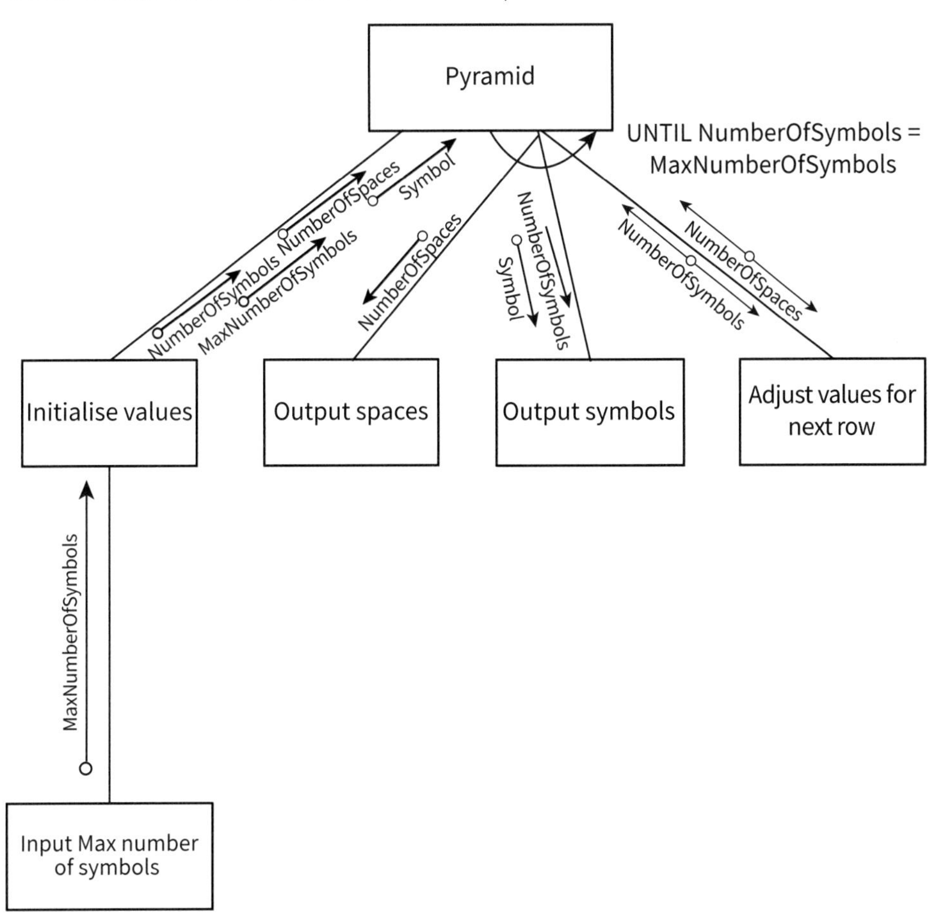

Figure 12.04 Structure chart for pyramid-drawing program

TASK 12.04

Amend the structure chart for the number-guessing game (Figure 12.03) to include repeated guesses until the player guesses the secret number. The output should include the number of guesses made.

TASK 12.05

Draw a structure chart for the following problem: A user attempts to log on with a user ID. User IDs and passwords are stored in two 1D arrays (lists). The algorithm searches the list of user IDs and looks up the password in the password list. The user is given three chances to input the correct password. if the correct password is entered, a suitable message is output. If the third attempt is incorrect, a warning message is output.

Structure charts help programmers to visualise how modules are interrelated and how they interface with each other. When looking at a larger problem this becomes even more important. Figure 12.05 shows a structure chart for the Connect 4 program. It uses the following symbols:

- An arrow with a solid round end shows that the value transferred is a flag (a Boolean value).
- A double-headed arrow shows that the variable value is updated within the module.

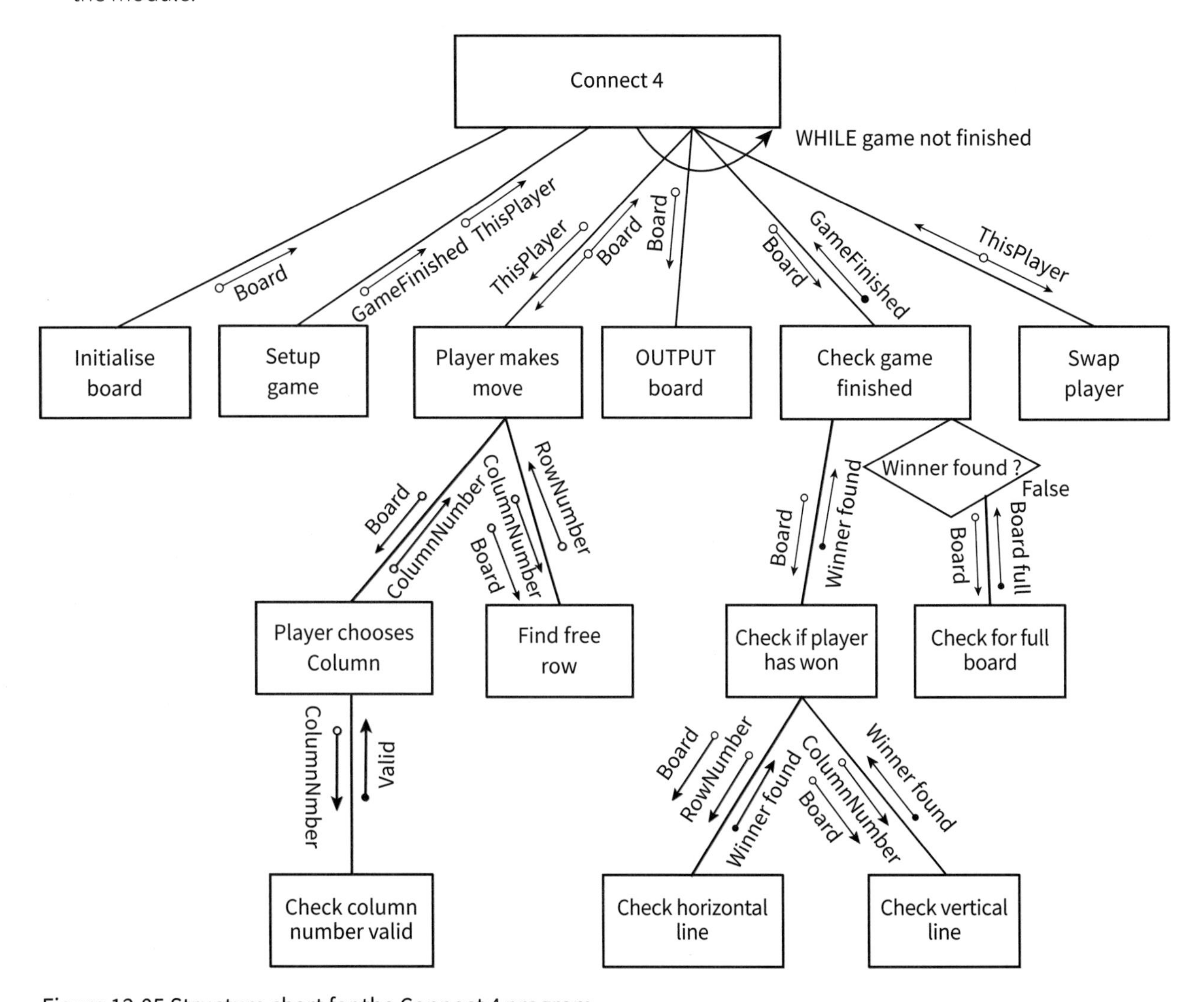

Figure 12.05 Structure chart for the Connect 4 program

12.04 Deriving pseudocode from a structure chart

Let's look at the pyramid problem again (Figure 12.04). In Worked Example 12.02, a modular solution was created without using a structure chart and all variables were global. Now we are going use local variables and parameters. The reason for using local variables and parameters is that modules are then self-contained and any changes to variables do not have accidental effects on a variable value elsewhere.

The top-level module, Pyramid, calls four modules. When a module is called, we supply the parameters in parentheses after the module identifier. This gives the following pseudocode:

```
MODULE Pyramid
   CALL SetValues(NumberOfSymbols, NumberOfSpaces, Symbol, MaxNumberOfSymbols)
   REPEAT
      CALL OutputSpaces(NumberOfSpaces)
      CALL OutputSymbols(NumberOfSymbols, Symbol)
      CALL AdjustValuesForNextRow(NumberOfSpaces, NumberOfSymbols)
   UNTIL NumberOfSymbols > MaxNumberOfSymbols
ENDMODULE

PROCEDURE SetValues(NumberOfSymbols, NumberOfSpaces, Symbol, MaxNumberOfSymbols)
   INPUT Symbol
   CALL InputMaxNumberOfSymbols
   NumberOfSpaces ← (MaxNumberOfSymbols - 1) / 2
   NumberOfSymbols ← 1
ENDPROCEDURE

PROCEDURE InputMaxNumberOfSymbols(MaxNumberOfSymbols)
   REPEAT
      INPUT MaxNumberOfSymbols
   UNTIL MaxNumberOfSymbols MOD 2 = 1
ENDPROCEDURE

PROCEDURE OutputSpaces(NumberOfSpaces)
   FOR Count ← 1 TO NumberOfSpaces
      OUTPUT Space // without moving to next line
   ENDFOR
ENDPROCEDURE

PROCEDURE OutputSymbols(NumberOfSymbols, Symbol)
   FOR Count ← 1 TO NumberOfSymbols
      OUTPUT Symbol // without moving to next line
   ENDFOR
   OUTPUT Newline // move to the next line
ENDPROCEDURE

PROCEDURE AdjustValuesForNextRow(NumberOfSpaces, NumberOfSymbols)
   NumberOfSpaces ← NumberOfSpaces - 1
   NumberOfSymbols ← NumberOfSymbols + 2
ENDPROCEDURE
```

Discussion Point:

The full rules of Connect 4 are that a diagonal of four tokens also is a winning line. Where in Figure 12.05 should the module to check for a diagonal be added? What parameters are required for this module? Does this additional module require further stepwise refinement?

Summary

- Stepwise refinement involves breaking down the steps of an outline solution into smaller and smaller steps (sub-tasks).
- Stepwise refinement is used to produce a solution that can be stated in terms of the four basic constructs of sequence, assignment, selection and repetition.
- Each sub-task can be written as a module.
- Modules are either procedures or functions.
- A procedure is a sequence of steps that are given an identifier. A procedure can be called whenever this sequence of steps should be followed.
- A function is a sequence of steps that are given an identifier. This sequence of steps results in a single value that is returned from the function. A function call is part of an expression or assignment.
- Local variables are variables that are used within a single module.
- Global variables are variables that are used throughout the solution.
- Structure charts are graphical representations of the modular structure of solutions.
- A structure chart shows the interface between modules: parameters passed between the calling module and the module being called.
- Structure charts show selection, where a module is called only under certain conditions.
- Structure charts show repetition, where modules are called repeatedly.

Exam-style Questions

1 A random number generator is to be tested to see whether all numbers within the range 1 to 20 are generated equally frequently. The structured English version of the algorithm is

```
Initialise a tally for the numbers 1 to 20
Repeatedly generate numbers in range 1 to 20
For each number generated, increment the relevant count
Calculate how often each number should be generated (expected
frequency)
Output expected frequency
Output the list of numbers as a table with actual frequency
```

The identifiers required are:

Identifier	Explanation
`Tally[1..20]`	1D array to store the count of how many times each number has been generated
`RandomNumber`	The random number generated
`NumberOfTests`	The number of times a random number is to be generated (1000 in this example)
`ExpectedFrequency`	The number of times any one number would be generated if all numbers are generated equally frequently (1000/20 in this example)

a Complete the structure chart below by naming the labels A to E: [5]

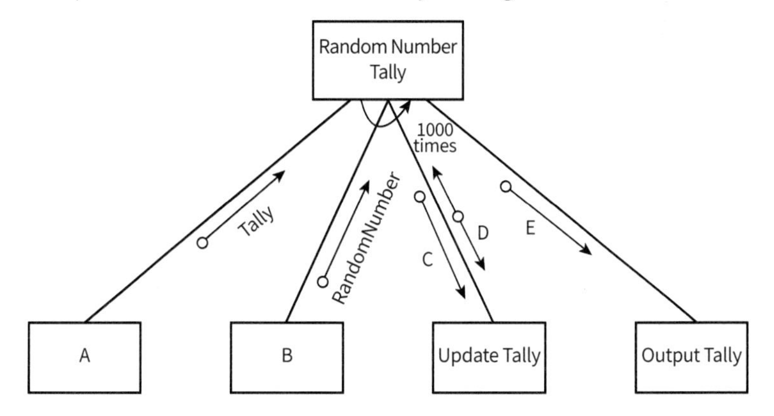

b Produce pseudocode from the structure chart. [12]

2 A game to test players' memory is played as follows:

- There are 64 square cards with 32 different pictures.
- Each picture is on two different cards.
- The cards are placed face down in random order as an 8 × 8 grid pattern.
- Two players take turns.
- When it is a player's turn, the player chooses two cards and turns them face up so the pictures show.
- If the pictures are the same, the player takes the pair of cards, gains a point and has another go.
- If the pictures are not the same, the cards are turned face down again.
- All players can see the up-turned pictures and memorise their grid positions.
- The game finishes when all cards have been paired.
- The player with the most points is the winner.

The problem is to design an algorithm that

- puts 64 cards into random positions into an 8 × 8 table
- after the input of two sets of co-ordinates shows the chosen cards for a short time
- removes the cards if there is a match
- updates the player's points
- outputs the number of points for both players when there are no more cards (the game has finished).

For the purpose of this algorithm:

- The pictures are to be represented by the numbers 1 to 32.
- A grid position with no card is to be represented by 0.

The identifiers required are:

Identifier	**Explanation**
`Grid[1..8, 1..8]`	Table to store the card values
`Points[1..2]`	List to store the points for player 1 and player 2
`ThisPlayer`	The number of the current player (1 or 2)
`GameEnd`	`FALSE` while there are cards left in the grid `TRUE` when all cards have been taken
`x1, y1` `x2, y2`	The co-ordinate pairs of the two cards chosen by the current player

Top-level algorithm:

```
01   CALL SetUpEmptyGrid
02   CALL RandomlyDistributeCards
03   CALL SetUpPlayers
04   GameEnd ← FALSE
05   REPEAT
06      CALL GetPlayersCoordinates
07      CALL DisplayGrid
08      CALL TestForMatch
09      CALL TestForEndGame
10   UNTIL GameEnd = TRUE
11   CALL OutputResults
```

a What is the name given to the method of breaking the above steps down into smaller steps? [1]

b Complete the following procedures:

```
PROCEDURE SetUpEmptyGrid
   FOR i ← 1 TO 8
      FOR j ← 1 TO 8
         ............................................ // assign grid elements
      ENDFOR
   ENDFOR
ENDPROCEDURE

PROCEDURE RandomlyDistributeCards
   FOR Number ← 1 TO 32
      CALL GetEmptyGridPosition
      Grid[x, y] ← Number       // place first card with this number
      CALL GetEmptyGridPosition
      ................... // place second card with this number
   ENDFOR
ENDPROCEDURE

PROCEDURE GetEmptyGridPosition
   REPEAT
      x ← RandomNumber(1,8) // generate a random number between 1 and 8
      y ← RandomNumber(1,8) // generate another random number
   UNTIL ................... // find a grid position without a card
ENDPROCEDURE

PROCEDURE SetUpPlayers
   Points[1] ← 0 // both players start with 0 points
   ...................................................................
   ThisPlayer ← 1
ENDPROCEDURE

PROCEDURE GetPlayersCoordinates
   REPEAT
      INPUT x1, y1
   UNTIL Grid[x1, y1] > 0 // check grid position has a card
   CALL DisplayGrid
   REPEAT
      INPUT x2, y2
      // check grid position has a card and is not in the same position as first card
   UNTIL (...................) AND (...................)
ENDPROCEDURE
```

```
PROCEDURE DisplayGrid
   FOR i ← 1 TO 8
      FOR j ← 1 TO 8
         IF (i = x1) AND (j = y1)   // it is the chosen card
            THEN
               OUTPUT ..............................................
            ELSE
               IF Grid[i, j] = 0   // the card in this position has been removed
                  THEN
                     OUTPUT ..............................................
                  ELSE   // back of card to be shown as ' ? '
                     OUTPUT ..............................................
               ENDIF
         ENDIF
      ENDFOR
   ENDFOR
ENDPROCEDURE

PROCEDURE TestForMatch
   IF Grid[x1, y1] = Grid[x2, y2]
      THEN
         // match found, remove cards
         Grid[x1, y1] ← ........................
         Grid[x2, y2] ← ........................
         // increment points
         Points[ThisPlayer] ← ........................
      ELSE
         CALL SwapPlayers
   ENDIF
ENDPROCEDURE

PROCEDURE SwapPlayers
   ...............................................................
   ...............................................................
   ...............................................................
   ...............................................................
   ...............................................................
   ...............................................................
ENDPROCEDURE

PROCEDURE TestForEndGame
   IF Points[1] + Points[2] = 32
      THEN
         GameEnd ← ........................
   ENDIF
ENDPROCEDURE

PROCEDURE OutputResults
   ...............................................................
   ...............................................................
ENDPROCEDURE
```

[18]

c Draw a structure chart for this problem. [15]

Chapter 13
Programming and Data Representation

Learning objectives

By the end of this chapter you should be able to:

- write a program in a high-level language (Python, Visual Basic console mode, Pascal/Delphi console mode)
- implement and write a program from a given design presented as either a program flowchart or pseudocode
- write program statements for:
  - the declaration of variables and constants
  - the assignment of values to variables and constants
  - expressions involving any of the arithmetic or logical operators
  - input from the keyboard and output to the console
- select appropriate data types for a problem solution (integer, real, char, string, Boolean, date)
- show understanding of how character and string data are represented by software including the ASCII and Unicode character sets
- use an 'IF' structure including the 'ELSE' clause and nested IF statements
- use a 'CASE' structure
- use a loop ('count controlled', 'post-condition', 'pre-condition')
- justify why one loop structure may be better suited to a problem than the others
- select a suitable data structure (1D or 2D array) to use for a given task
- write program code to process array data (including bubble sort and linear search)
- recognise the basic control structures in a high-level language other than the one chosen to be studied in depth
- use a subset of the built-in functions and library routines supported by the chosen programming language, including those used for string/character manipulation, formatting of numbers, random number generator
- use the information provided in technical documentation describing functions/procedures
- show understanding of why files are needed and write pseudocode and program code for simple file handling of a text file, consisting of several lines of text.

13.01 Programming languages

Chapters 11 and 12 introduced the concept of solving a problem and representing a solution using a flowchart, pseudocode or a structure chart. We expressed our solutions using the basic constructs: assignment, sequence, selection, iteration, input and output.

To write a computer program, we need to know the syntax of these basic constructs in our chosen programming language. This chapter introduces syntax for Python, Visual Basic console mode and Pascal/Delphi console mode.

You only need learn to program in one of the three languages covered in this book. However, you should be able to recognise the basic control structures in a high-level language other than the one chosen to be studied in depth. So do read the sections covering the other two programming languages.

Python

Python was conceived by Guido van Rossum in the late 1980s. Python 2.0 was released in 2000 and Python 3.0 in 2008. Python is a multi-paradigm programming language. It fully supports both object-oriented programming and structured programming. Many other paradigms, including logic programming, are supported using extensions. These paradigms are covered in Chapters 26, 27 and 29.

The Python programs in this book have been prepared using Python 3 (see www.python.org for a free download) and Python's Integrated DeveLopment Environment (IDLE).

Key characteristics of Python are:

- Every statement must be on a separate line.
- Indentation is significant. This is known as the 'off-side rule'.
- Keywords are written in lower case.
- Python is case sensitive: the identifier `Number1` is seen as different from `number1` or `NUMBER1`.
- Everything in Python is an object (see Chapter 27).
- Code makes extensive use of a concept called 'slicing' (see Section 13.08).
- Programs are interpreted (see Chapter 7, Section 7.05 for information on interpreted and compiled programs).

You can type a statement into the Python Shell and the Python interpreter will run it immediately (see Figure 13.01).

Python Shell
File Edit Shell Debug Options Windows Help

```
Python 3.2.3 (default, Apr 11 2012, 07:12:16) [MSC v.1500 64 bit (AMD64)] on win32
Type "copyright", "credits" or "license()" for more information.
>>> print("Hello World!")
Hello World!
>>> |
```

Ln: 5 Col: 4

Figure 13.01 Running a statement in the Python Shell

You can also type program code into a Python editor (such as IDLE), save it with a .py extension and then run the program code from the Run menu in the editor window (see Figure 13.02).

Figure 13.02 (a) A saved program in the Python editor window and (b) running in the Python shell

Visual Basic Console Mode (VB.NET)

VB.NET is a multi-paradigm, high-level programming language, implemented on the .NET Framework. Microsoft launched VB.NET in 2002 as the successor to its original Visual Basic language. Microsoft's integrated development environment (IDE) for developing in VB.NET is Visual Studio. Visual Studio Express and Visual Studio Community are freeware.

The Visual Basic programs in this book have been prepared using Microsoft Visual Basic 2010 Express Console Application. (Free download available from www.visualstudio.com/products/visual-studio-express-vs)

Key characteristics of VB.NET are:

- Every statement should be on a separate line. Statements can be typed on the same line with a colon (:) as a separator. However, this is not recommended.
- Indentation is good practice.
- VB.NET is not case sensitive. Modern VB.NET editors will automatically copy the case from the first definition of an identifier.
- The convention is to use CamelCaps (also known as PascalCaps) for identifiers and keywords.
- Programs need to be compiled (see Chapter 7, Section 7.05 for information on interpreted and compiled programs).

You type your program code into the Integrated Development Environment (IDE) as shown in Figure 13.03 (a), save the program code and then click on the Run button (▷). This invokes the compiler. If there are no syntax errors the compiled program will then run. Output will be shown in a separate console window (see Figure 13.03 (b)).

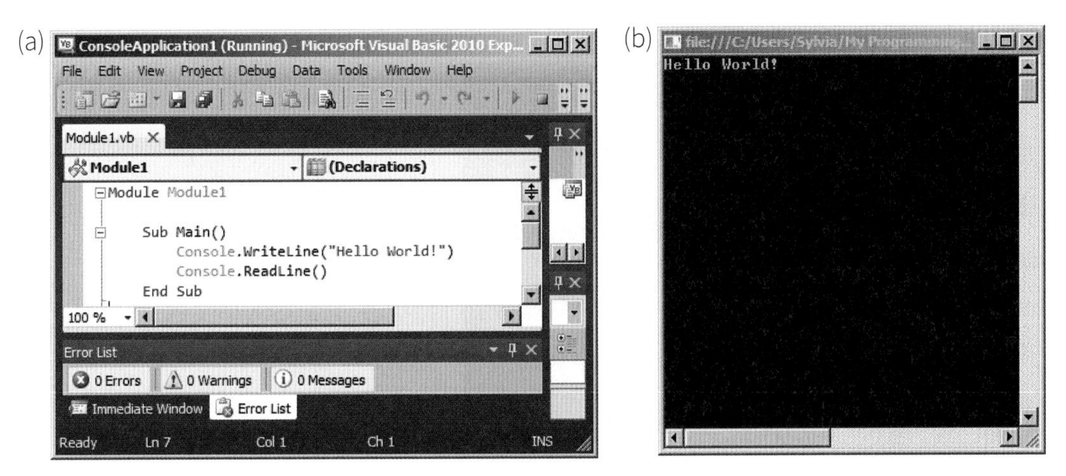

Figure 13.03 (a) A saved program in the VB.NET editor and (b) running in the program execution (console) window

Note that the console window shuts when the program has finished execution. To keep it open, so you can see the output, the last statement of your program should be `Console.ReadLine()` (see Figure 13.03(a)).

Pascal/Delphi Console Mode (Pascal)

Designed by Niklaus Wirth as a small and efficient language, Pascal was intended to encourage good programming practice using structured programming. Pascal was published in 1970. A derivative known as Object Pascal for object-oriented programming was developed in 1985. Delphi was originally developed by Borland and uses Object Pascal. Since 2008, Delphi has been owned by Embarcadero Technologies.

The Pascal programs in this book have been prepared using Borland Delphi 7 Console Application. Other Pascal/Delphi IDEs will work in a similar way (for example, the free version from www.lazarus.freepascal.org).

Key characteristics of Pascal are:

- Every statement ends with a semicolon (;). More than one statement can go on a single line, but this is not recommended.
- Indentation is good practice.
- Pascal is not case sensitive.
- The convention is to use CamelCaps (also known as PascalCaps) for identifiers and lower case for keywords.
- A compound statement consists of a sequence of statements enclosed between the keywords `begin` and `end`.
- Whenever Pascal syntax requires a statement, a compound statement can be used. For an example see Table 13.28.
- Programs need to be compiled (see Chapter 7, Section 7.05 for information on interpreted and compiled programs).

You type your program statements into the Integrated Development Environment (IDE) as shown in Figure 13.04 (a), save the program code and then click on the Run button (▷). This invokes the compiler. If there are no syntax errors the compiled program code will then run. Output will be shown in a separate (console) window (see Figure 13.04 (b).

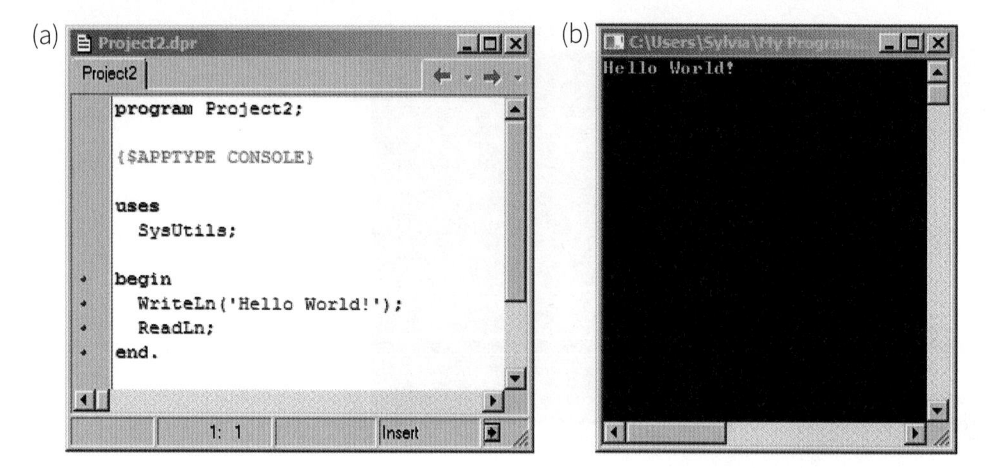

Figure 13.04 (a) A Pascal program in the Delphi editor and (b) running in the program execution (console) window

Note that the console window shuts when the program has finished execution. To keep it open, so you can see the output, the last statement of your program should be `ReadLn;` (see Figure 13.04(a)).

13.02 Programming basics

Declaration of variables

Most programming languages require you to declare the type of data to be stored in a variable, so the correct amount of memory space can be reserved by the compiler. A variable declared to store a whole number (integer) cannot then be used to store alphanumeric characters (strings) or vice versa. Pascal and VB.NET require variables to be declared before they are used.

Python handles variables differently to most programming languages. It tags values. This is why Python does not have variable declarations. However, it is good programming practice to include a comment about the variables you are planning to use and the type of data you will store in them.

In pseudocode, variable declarations are written as:

```
DECLARE <identifier> : <dataType>
```

For example, you may declare the following variables:

```
DECLARE Number1 : INTEGER // this declares Number1 to store a whole number
DECLARE YourName : STRING // this declares YourName to store a sequence of
                          // alphanumeric characters
DECLARE N1, N2, N3 : INTEGER  // declares 3 integer variables
DECLARE Name1, Name2 : STRING // declares 2 string variables
```

Syntax definitions

The syntax of variable declarations in language code is as follows:

Python	Python does not have variable declarations
VB.NET	`Dim <identifier>[, <identifier] As <dataType>` Each line of declarations must start with the keyword `Dim`.
Pascal	`var <identifier>[, <identifier>] : <dataType>;` The keyword **`var`** starts declarations.

Code examples

Python	`# Number1 of type Integer`
	`# YourName of type String`
	`# N1, N2, N3 of type integer;`
	`# Name1, Name2 of type string;`
		There are no declarations, but comments should be made at the beginning of a module (see the section about comments at the end of Section 13.02).

VB.NET	`Dim Number1 As Integer`
	`Dim YourName As String`
	`Dim N1, N2, N3 As Integer`
	`Dim Name1, Name2 As String`
		You can group more than one variable of the same type on the same line.

Pascal	`var Number1 : integer;`
	`var YourName : string;`
	`var N1, N2, N3 : integer;`
	`    Name1, Name2 : string;`
		The keyword **`var`** can be repeated on each line or omitted for further lines of declarations. You can group more than one variable of the same type on the same line.

Declaration and assignment of constants

Sometimes we use a value in a solution that never changes, for example, the value of the mathematical constant pi (π). Instead of using the actual value in program statements, it is good practice and helps readability, if we give a constant value a name and declare it at the beginning of the program.

In pseudocode, constant declarations are written as:

```
CONSTANT <identifier> = <value>
```

For example:

```
CONSTANT Pi = 3.14
```

Syntax definitions

Python	`<identifier> = <value>`
VB.NET	`Const <identifier> = <value>` Each line of declarations must start with the keyword `Const`.
Pascal	`Const <identifier> = <value>;` The keyword `const` must be used to start the declarations.

Code examples

Python	`PI = 3.14`	Python convention is to write constant identifiers using all capital letters. The values can be changed, although you should treat constants as not changeable.
VB.NET	`Const Pi = 3.14`	The value of a constant in VB.NET cannot be altered within the program.
Pascal	`Const Pi = 3.14;`	The value of a constant in Pascal cannot be altered within the program.

Assignment of variables

Once we have declared a variable, we can assign a value to it (See Chapter 11, Section 11.04).

In pseudocode, assignment statements are written as:

```
<identifier> ← <expression>
```

Syntax definitions and code examples

Python	`<identifier> = <expression>`	`A = 34` `B = B + 1`	The assignment operator is =
VB.NET	`<identifier> = <expression>`	`A = 34` `B = B + 1`	The assignment operator is =
Pascal	`<identifier> := <expression>;`	`A := 34;` `B := B + 1;`	The assignment operator is a combination of a colon and an equals sign without a space in between (:=)

VB.NET allows you to initialise a variable as part of the declaration statement, for example:

```
Dim Number1 As Integer = 0
```

VB.NET and Python allow increment statements such as `B = B + 1` to be written as `B += 1`.

Arithmetic operators

Assignments don't just give initial values to variables. We also use an assignment when we need to store the result of a calculation. The arithmetic operators used for calculations are shown in Table 13.01.

Operation	Pseudocode	Python	VB.NET	Pascal
Addition	+	+	+	+
Subtraction	-	-	-	-
Multiplication	*	*	*	*
Division	/	/	/	/
Exponent	^	**	^	Not available
Integer division	DIV	//	\	Div
Modulus	MOD	%	Mod	Mod

Table 13.01 Arithmetic operators

When more than one operator appears in an expression, the order of evaluation depends on the mathematical **rules of precedence**: parentheses, exponentiation, multiplication, division, addition, subtraction.

KEY TERMS

Rules of precedence: define the order of the calculations to be performed

Question 13.01

Evaluate each of the following expressions:

4 * 3 – 3 ^ 2

(4 * 3 – 3) ^ 2

4 * (3 – 3) ^ 2

4 * (3 – 3 ^ 2)

Outputting information to the screen

In pseudocode, output statements are written as:

```
OUTPUT <string>
OUTPUT <identifier(s)>
```

When outputting text and data to the console screen, we can list a mixture of output strings and variable values in the print list.

Syntax definitions

Python	`print(<printlist>)` `print(<printlist>, end = '')`	Print list items are separated by commas (,). To avoid moving onto the next line after the output, use `end = ''`.
VB.NET	`Console.WriteLine(<printlist>)` `Console.Write(<printlist>)`	Print list items are joined using &. `Console.WriteLine` will move onto the next line after the output; `Console.Write` will remain on the same line.
Pascal	`WriteLn(<printlist>);` `Write(<printlist>);`	Print list items are separated by commas (,). `WriteLn` will move onto the next line after the output; `Write` will remain on the same line.

Code examples

In the examples below, the print list consists of four separate items:
"Hello " and ". Your number is " are strings and
YourName and Number1 are variables, for which we print the value.

```
OUTPUT "Hello ", YourName, ". Your number is ", Number1 // newline
OUTPUT "Hello " // no new line
```

In pseudocode, we can indicate whether a new line should be output at the end by a comment at the end of the statement.

Python	`print("Hello ", YourName,`
	`   ". Your number is ", Number1)`
	`print("Hello ", end= '')`

VB.NET	`Console.WriteLine("Hello " & YourName &`
	`   ". Your number is " & Number1)`
	`Console.Write("Hello")`

Pascal	`WriteLn('Hello ', YourName,`
	`   '. Your number is ', Number1);`
	`Write('Hello ');`

In the code examples above you can see how output statements can be spread over more than one line when they are very long. You must break the line between two print list items. You cannot break in the middle of a string, unless you make the string into two separate strings.

In Python and VB.NET you can also use the placeholder method for output: the variables to be printed are represented by sequential numbers in { } in the message string and the variables are listed in the correct order after the string, separated by commas:

Python	`print ("Hello {0}. Your number is {1}".format(YourName, Number1))`
VB.NET	`Console.WriteLine("Hello {0}. Your number is {1}", YourName, Number1)`

Getting input from the user

When coding an input statement, it is good practice to prompt the user as to what they are meant to enter. For example, consider the pseudocode statement:

```
INPUT "Prompt: " A
```

Note the space between the colon and the closing quote. This is significant. It gives a space before the user types their input.

Python	`A = input("Prompt: ")`	The prompt is provided as a parameter to the input function. Single quotes are also accepted. All input is taken to be a string; if you want to use the input as a number the input string has to be converted using a function (see Section 13.03).
VB.NET	`Console.Write("Prompt: ")` `A = Console.ReadLine()`	The prompt has to be supplied as an output statement separately.
Pascal	`Write('Prompt: ');` `ReadLn(A);`	The prompt has to be supplied as an output statement separately. Note the single quotes around the message text. The `ReadLn` procedure returns as a parameter the value entered by the user. An alternative procedure, `Read` exists but its use is very specialised as it does not remove the new line character from the input string.

Comments

It is good programming practice to add comments to explain code where necessary.

Python	`# this is a comment` `# this is another comment`
VB.NET	`// this is a comment` `// this is another comment`

Pascal	`// this is a comment`
	`// this is another comment`
	`{this is a multi-line`
	`   comment}`

TASK 13.01

Use the IDE of your chosen programming language (in future just referred to as 'your language'). Type the program statements equivalent to the following pseudocode (you may need to declare the variable `YourName` first):

```
INPUT "What is your name? " YourName
OUTPUT "Have a nice day, " YourName
```

Save your program as Example1 and then run it. Is the output as you expected?

13.03 Data types

Every programming language has built-in data types. Table 13.02 gives a subset of those available. The number of bytes of memory allocated to a variable of the given type is given in brackets for VB.NET and Pascal.

Description of data	Pseudocode	Python	VB.NET	Pascal
Whole signed numbers	`INTEGER`	`int`	`Integer` (4 bytes)	`Integer` (4 bytes)
Signed numbers with a decimal point	`REAL`	`float`	`Single` (4 bytes) `Double` (8 bytes)	`Real` (8 bytes)
A single alphanumeric character	`CHAR`	`Not available`	`Char` (2 bytes – Unicode)	`Char` (1 byte – ASCII)
A sequence of alphanumeric characters (a string)	`STRING` Use single (') or double (") quotation marks to delimit a string.	`str` (stored as ASCII but Unicode strings are also available) Use single ('), double (") or triple (''' or """) quotation marks to delimit a string.	`String` (2 bytes per character) Use double (") quotation marks to delimit a string.	`String` (1 byte per character plus 1) Use single (') quotation marks to delimit a string.
Logical values: `True` (represented as 1) and `False` (represented as 0)	`BOOLEAN`	`bool`	`Boolean` (2 bytes)	`Boolean` (1 byte)

Table 13.02 Simple data types

In Python, a single alphanumeric character is represented as a string of length 1.

See Chapter 1 (Sections 1.02 and 1.03) on how integers and characters are represented inside the computer. Chapter 16 (Section 16.03) covers the internal representation of real (single, double, float) numbers.

The string data type is known as a structured type because it is essentially a sequence of characters. A special case is the empty string: a value of data type string, but with no characters stored in it. In VB.NET, each character in a string requires two bytes of memory and each character is represented in memory as Unicode (in which, the values from 1 to 127 correspond to ASCII).

In Pascal, a string occupies as many bytes as its maximum length plus one. The first byte contains the current length of the string and the following bytes contain the characters of the string (stored as ASCII). Because the largest unsigned integer that can be stored in a byte is 255, the maximum length of a string is 255 characters.

Date and currency have various internal representations but are output in conventional format (except in Pascal where you have to do a string conversion for dates).

Description of data	Pseudocode	Python	VB.NET	Pascal
Date value	`DATE`	Not available as a built-in data type	`Date` (8 bytes)	`TDateTime` (8 bytes)
Monetary value	`CURRENCY`	Not available	`Decimal` (16 bytes)	`Currency` (8 bytes)

Table 13.03 Further data types

In Python, date and currency are not available as built-in data types. A date is stored as the number of days after 1/1/0001, using the `datetime` class (see Section 13.08). For currency, use `float`.

VB.NET stores dates and times from 1.1.0001 (0 hours) to 31.12.9999 (23:59:59 hours) with a resolution of 100 nanoseconds (this unit is called a 'tick'). Floating-point (decimal) numbers are stored in binary-coded decimal format (see Section 1.02).

Pascal stores dates and times internally as a real number: the whole number part represents the days since 30/12/1899 and the fractional part represents the part of the day that has elapsed (time). Currency values are stored internally as a scaled and signed 64-bit integer with the least significant four digits implicitly representing four decimal places.

There are many more data types. Programmers can also design and declare their own data types (see Chapter 16 (Section 16.01) and Chapter 26 (Section 26.02).

TASK 13.02

1 Look at the identifier tables in Chapter 11 (Tables 11.02 and 11.04 to 11.12). Decide which data type from your language is appropriate for each variable listed.

2 Write program code to implement the pseudocode from Worked Example 11.01 in Chapter 11.

13.04 Boolean expressions

In Chapter 11 (Section 11.05), we covered logic statements. These were statements that included a condition. Conditions are also known as Boolean expressions and evaluate to either True or False. True and False are known as Boolean values.

Simple Boolean expressions involve comparison operators (Table 13.04). Complex Boolean expressions also involve Boolean operators (Table 13.05).

Operation	Pseudocode	Python	VB.NET	Pascal
equal	`=`	`==`	`=`	`=`
not equal	`<>`	`!=`	`<>`	`<>`
greater than	`>`	`>`	`>`	`>`
less than	`<`	`<`	`<`	`<`
greater than or equal to	`>=`	`>=`	`>=`	`>=`
less than or equal to	`<=`	`<=`	`<=`	`<=`

Table 13.04 Comparison operators

Operation	Pseudocode	Python	VB.NET	Pascal
AND (logical conjunction)	AND	and	And	AND
OR (logical inclusion)	OR	or	Or	OR
NOT (logical negation)	NOT	not	Not	NOT

Table 13.05 Boolean operators

13.05 Selection

IF...THEN statements

In pseudocode the IF...THEN construct is written as:

```
IF <Boolean expression>
   THEN
      <statement(s)>
ENDIF
```

Syntax definitions

Python	if <Boolean expression>: <statement(s)>	Note that the THEN keyword is replaced by a colon (:). Indentation is used to show which statements form part of the conditional statement.

VB.NET	If <Boolean expression> Then
	   <statement(s)>
	End If
		Note the position of Then on the same line as the Boolean expression. The End If keywords should line up with the If keyword.

Pascal	if <Boolean expression> then <statement>;	If more than one statement is required as part of the conditional statement, the statements must be put between begin and end keywords.

Code examples

Pseudocode example:

```
IF x < 0
   THEN
      OUTPUT "Negative"
ENDIF
```

Python	if x < 0: print("Negative")

VB.NET	If x < 0 Then
	   Console.WriteLine("Negative")
	End If

Pascal	if x < 0
	   then
	      WriteLn('Negative');

TASK 13.03

Write program code to implement the pseudocode from Worked Example 11.03 in Chapter 11.

IF...THEN...ELSE statements

In pseudocode, the IF...THEN...ELSE construct is written as:

```
IF <Boolean expression>
   THEN
      <statement(s)>
   ELSE
      <statement(s)>
ENDIF
```

Syntax definitions

Python	if <Boolean expression>:
	   <statement(s)>
	else:
	   <statement(s)>
		Indentation is used to show which statements form part of the conditional statement the `else` keyword must line up with the corresponding `if` keyword.

VB.NET	If <Boolean expression> Then
	   <statement(s)>
	Else
	   <statement(s)>
	End If
		The `Else` keyword is on its own on a separate line. It is good programming practice to line it up with the corresponding `If` keyword and indent the statements within the conditional statement.

Pascal	**if** <Boolean expression>
	   then
	      <statement>
	   else
	      <statement>;
		If more than one statement is required in the **`else`** part of the statement, the statements must be placed between **`begin`** and **`end`**.
		Note the convention for indentation.
		Do not include a semicolon before the **`else`**.

Code examples

Pseudocode example:

```
IF x < 0
   THEN
      OUTPUT "Negative"
   ELSE
      OUTPUT "Positive"
ENDIF
```

<table>
<tr><td>Python</td><td><pre>if x < 0:
   print("Negative")
else:
   print("Positive")</pre></td></tr>
<tr><td>VB.NET</td><td><pre>If x < 0 Then
   Console.WriteLine("Negative")
Else
   Console.WriteLine("Positive")
End If</pre></td></tr>
<tr><td>Pascal</td><td><pre>if x < 0
   then
     WriteLn('Negative')
   else
     WriteLn('Positive');</pre></td></tr>
</table>

Nested IF statements

In pseudocode, the nested IF statement is written as:

```
IF <Boolean expression>
   THEN
      <statement(s)>
   ELSE
      IF <Boolean expression>
         THEN
            <statement(s)>
         ELSE
            <statement(s)>
      ENDIF
ENDIF
```

Syntax definitions

<table>
<tr><td>Python</td><td><pre>if <Boolean expression>:
   <statement(s)>
elif <Boolean expression>:
   <statement(s)>
else:
   <statement(s)></pre></td><td>Note the keyword <code>elif</code> (an abbreviation of <code>else if</code>). This keyword must line up with the corresponding <code>if</code>.

There can be as many <code>elif</code> parts to this construct as required.</td></tr>
<tr><td>VB.NET</td><td><pre>If <Boolean expression> Then
   <statement(s)>
ElseIf
   <statement(s)>
Else
   <statement(s)>
End If</pre></td><td>If <code>ElseIf</code> is used as one word, only one <code>End If</code> is required at the end of this construct.

There can be as many <code>ElseIf</code> parts as required.</td></tr>
<tr><td>Pascal</td><td><pre>if <Boolean expression>
   then
      <statement>
   else
      if <Boolean expression>
         then
            <statement>
         else
            <statement>;</pre></td><td>Repeated indentation can make nested if statements quite awkward. However, without careful indentation, the overview can be lost. Whenever possible, a CASE statement is preferable (see the next section).</td></tr>
</table>

Code examples

Pseudocode example:

```
IF x < 0
   THEN
      OUTPUT "Negative"
   ELSE
      IF x = 0
         THEN
            OUTPUT "Zero"
         ELSE
            OUTPUT "Positive"
      ENDIF
ENDIF
```

<table>
<tr><td>Python</td><td><pre>if x < 0:
   print("Negative")
elif x = 0:
   print("Zero")
else:
   print("Positive")</pre></td></tr>
<tr><td>VB.NET</td><td><pre>If x < 0 Then
   Console.WriteLine("Negative")
ElseIf x = 0 Then
   Console.WriteLine("Zero")
Else
   Console.WriteLine("Positive")
End If</pre></td></tr>
<tr><td>Pascal</td><td><pre>if x < 0
   then
      WriteLn('Negative')
   else
      if x = 0
         then
            WriteLn('Zero')
         else
            WriteLn('Positive');</pre></td></tr>
</table>

TASK 13.04

Write program code to implement the pseudocode from Worked Example 11.02 in Chapter 11.

CASE statements

An alternative selection construct is the CASE statement. Each considered CASE condition can be:

- a single value
- single values separated by commas
- a range.

In pseudocode, the CASE statement is written as:

```
CASE OF <expression>

   <value1>               : <statement(s)>
   <value2>,<value3>      : <statement(s)>
   <value4> TO <value5>   : <statement(s)>
   .
   .
   OTHERWISE <statement(s)>
ENDCASE
```

The value of `<expression>` determines which statements are executed. There can be as many separate cases as required. The `OTHERWISE` clause is optional and useful for error trapping.

Syntax definitions

<table>
<tr><td>Python</td><td>Python does not have a CASE statement. You need to use nested If statements instead.</td></tr>
<tr><td>VB.NET</td><td><pre>Select Case <expression>
   Case value1
      <statement(s)>
   Case value2,value3
      <statement(s)>
   Case value4 To value5
      <statement(s)>
   .
   .
   .
   Case Else
      <statement(s)>
End Select</pre></td></tr>
<tr><td>Pascal</td><td><pre>case <expression> of
   value1: <statement>;
   value2, value3: <statement>;
   value4..value5: <statement>;
   .
   .
   .
else
   <statement>;
end;</pre></td></tr>
</table>

Code examples

In pseudocode, an example CASE statement is:

```
CASE OF Grade
   "A"      : OUTPUT "Top grade"
   "F","U"  : OUTPUT "Fail"
   "B".."E" : OUTPUT "Pass"
   OTHERWISE
      OUTPUT "Invalid grade"
ENDCASE
```

<table>
<tr><td>Python</td><td><pre>if Grade == "A":
   print("Top grade")
elif Grade == "F" or Grade == "U":
   print("Fail")
elif Grade in ("B","C","D","E"):
   print("Pass")
else:
   print("Invalid grade")</pre></td></tr>
<tr><td>VB.NET</td><td><pre>Select Case Grade
   Case "A"
      Console.WriteLine("Top grade")
   Case "F","U"
      Console.WriteLine("Fail")
   Case "B" To "E"
      Console.WriteLine("Pass")
   Case Else
      Console.WriteLine("Invalid grade")
End Select</pre></td></tr>
<tr><td>Pascal</td><td><pre>case Grade of
   'A'   : WriteLn('Top grade');
   'F','U' : WriteLn('Fail');
   'B'..'E' : WriteLn('Pass');
else
   WriteLn('Invalid grade');
end;</pre></td></tr>
</table>

TASK 13.05

The problem to be solved: the user enters the number of the month and year. The output is the number of days in that month. The program has to check if the year is a leap year for February.

The pseudocode solution is:

```
INPUT MonthNumber
INPUT Year
Days ← 0
CASE OF MonthNumber
   CASE 1,3,5,7,8,10,12: Days ← 31
   CASE 4,6,9,11: Days ← 30
   CASE 2: Days ← 28
       If Year MOD 400 = 0
          THEN // it is a leap year
             Days ← 29
       ENDIF
       IF (Year MOD 4 = 0) AND (Year MOD 100 > 0)
          THEN // it is a leap year
             Days ← 29
       ENDIF
   OTHERWISE: OUTPUT "Invalid month number"
ENDCASE
OUTPUT Days
```

Write program code to implement the pseudocode above.

13.06 Iteration

Count-controlled (for) loops

In pseudocode, a count-controlled loop is written as:

```
FOR <control variable> ← s TO e STEP i // STEP is optional
   <statement(s)>
ENDFOR
```

The control variable starts with value `s`, increments by value `i` each time round the loop and finishes when the control variable reaches the value `e`.

Syntax definitions

Python	for <control variable> in range(s, e, i): <statement(s)>	The values s, e and i must be of type integer. The loop finishes when the control variable is just below e. The values for s and i can be omitted and they default to 0 and 1, respectively.
VB.NET	For <control variable> = s To e Step i <statement(s)> Next	The values s, e and i can be of type integer or float.
Pascal	**for** <control variable> := s **to** e **do** <statement>;	The control variable can be of type integer or char. Intervals other than 1 are not available.

Code examples

Python	for x in range(5): print(x, end=' ')	The start value of x is 0 and it increases by 1 on each iteration. Output: 0 1 2 3 4
	for x in range(2, 14, 3): print(x, end=' ')	Output: 2 5 8 11
	for x in range(5, 1, -1): print(x, end=' ')	The start value of x is 5 and it decreases by 1 on each iteration. Output: 5 4 3 2
	for x in ["a","b","c"]: print(x, end='')	The control variable takes the value of each of the group elements in turn. Output: abc
VB.NET	For x = 1 To 5 Console.Write(x) Next	Output: 1 2 3 4 5
	For x = 2 To 14 Step 3 Console.Write(x) Next	Output: 2 5 8 11 14
	For x = 5 To 1 Step -1 Console.Write(x) Next	Output: 5 4 3 2 1
	For x = 1 To 2.5 Step 0.5 Console.WriteLine(x) Next	Output: 1 1.5 2 2.5

	For Each x In {"a", "b", "c"} Console.Write(x) Next	The control variable takes the value of each of the group elements in turn. Output: abc
Pascal	for x := 1 to 5 do write(x);	Output: 1 2 3 4 5
	for x := 5 downto 1 do write(x);	Output: 5 4 3 2 1
	for x := 'a' to 'c' do write(x);	Output: abc

TASK 13.06

1 Write program code to implement the pseudocode from Worked Example 11.05 in Chapter 11.
2 Write program code to implement the pseudocode from Worked Example 11.08 in Chapter 11.
3 Write program code to implement the pseudocode from Worked Example 11.09 in Chapter 11.

Post-condition loops

A post-condition loop, as the name suggests, executes the statements within the loop at least once. When the condition is encountered, it is evaluated. As long as the condition evaluates to False the statements within the loop are executed again. When the condition evaluates to True, execution will go to the next statement after the loop.

When coding a post-condition loop, you must ensure that there is a statement within the loop that will at some point change the end condition to True. Otherwise the loop will execute forever.

In pseudocode, the post-condition loop is written as:

```
REPEAT
   <statement(s)>
UNTIL <condition>
```

Syntax definitions

Python	Post-condition loops are not available in Python. Use a pre-condition loop instead.
VB.NET	Do <statement(s)> Loop Until <condition>
Pascal	**repeat** <statement(s)>; **until** <condition>;

Code examples

Pseudocode example:

```
REPEAT
   INPUT "Enter Y or N: " Answer
UNTIL Answer = "Y"
```

VB.NET	`Do`
	`   Console.Write("Enter Y or N: ")`
	`   Answer = Console.ReadLine()`
	`Loop Until Answer = "Y"`

Pascal	`repeat`
	`   Write('Enter Y or N: ');`
	`   ReadLn(Answer);`
	`until Answer = 'Y';`

TASK 13.07

1. Write program code to implement the pseudocode from Worked Example 11.04 in Chapter 11.
2. Write program code to implement the first algorithm from Worked Example 11.06 in Chapter 11.

Pre-condition loops

Pre-condition loops, as the name suggests, evaluate the condition before the statements within the loop are executed. Pre-condition loops will execute the statements within the loop as long as the condition evaluates to True. When the condition evaluates to False, execution will go to the next statement after the loop. Note that any variable used in the condition must not be undefined when the loop structure is first encountered.

When coding a pre-condition loop, you must ensure that there is a statement within the loop that will at some point change the value of the controlling condition. Otherwise the loop will execute forever.

In pseudocode the pre-condition loop is written as:

```
WHILE <condition>
   <statement(s)>
ENDWHILE
```

Syntax definitions

Python	`while <condition>:` `   <statement(s)>`	Note that statements within the loop must be indented by a set number of spaces. The first statement after the loop must be indented less.

VB.NET	`Do While <condition>`
	`   <statement(s)>`
	`Loop`
	`Do Until <condition>`
	`   <statement(s)>`
	`Loop`
		Note the keyword `Loop` indicates the end of the loop.
		
		VB.NET also has a pre-condition `Until` loop. This will execute the statements within the loop as long as the condition evaluates to False. If the condition evaluates to True when the loop is first encountered, the statements within the loop are not executed at all.

Pascal	`while <condition> do` `   <statement>;`	

Code examples

Pseudocode example,

```
Answer ← ""
WHILE Answer <> "Y"
   INPUT "Enter Y or N: " Answer
ENDWHILE
```

<table>
<tr><td>Python</td><td><pre>Answer = ''
while Answer != 'Y':
   Answer = input('Enter Y or N: ')</pre></td><td></td></tr>
<tr><td>VB.NET</td><td><pre>Dim Answer As String = ""
Do While Answer <> "Y"
   Console.Write("Enter Y or N: ")
   Answer = Console.ReadLine()
Loop
Answer = ""
Do Until Answer = "Y"
   Console.Write("Enter Y or N: ")
   Answer = Console.ReadLine()
Loop</pre></td><td></td></tr>
<tr><td>Pascal</td><td><pre>Answer := '';
while Answer <> 'Y' do
   begin
      Write('Enter Y or N: ');
      ReadLn(Answer);
   end;</pre></td><td>Note the use of the compound statement, enclosed between the keywords <code>begin</code> and <code>end</code>. These keywords are not required if there is only a single statement within the loop. For example:<pre>while x < 10 do
   x := x + 1;</pre></td></tr>
</table>

TASK 13.08

Write program code to implement the second algorithm from Worked Example 11.06 in Chapter 11.

Which loop structure to use?

If you know how many times around the loop you need to go when the program execution gets to the loop statements, use a count-controlled loop. If the termination of the loop depends on some condition determined by what happens within the loop, then use a conditional loop. A pre-condition loop has the added benefit that the loop may not be entered at all, if the condition does not require it.

13.07 Arrays

Traditionally, an array is a static data structure. This means the array is declared with a specified number of elements of one specified data type and this does not change after compilation. However, many programming languages now allow an array to be dynamic. This means the array can grow in size if required.

Creating 1D arrays

When we write a list on a piece of paper and number the individual items, we would normally start the numbering with 1. You can view a 1D array like a numbered list of items. VB.NET and Python number array elements from 0 (the lower bound). Depending on the problem to be solved, it might make sense to ignore element 0. Pascal allows you to choose your lower bound to be any integer. The upper bound is the largest number used for numbering the elements of an array.

In pseudocode, a 1D array declaration is written as:

```
DECLARE <arrayIdentifier> : ARRAY[<lowerBound>:<upperBound>] OF <dataType>
```

Syntax definitions

Python	In Python, there are no arrays. The equivalent data structure is called a list. A list is an ordered sequence of items that do not have to be of the same data type. Python's lists are dynamic.
VB.NET	Dim <arrayIdentifier>(<upperBound>) As <dataType>
Pascal	**var** <arrayIdentifier> : **array**[lowerBound..upperBound] **of** <dataType>;

Code examples

Pseudocode example:

```
DECLARE List1 : ARRAY[1:3]   OF STRING  // 3 elements in this list
DECLARE List2 : ARRAY[0:5]   OF INTEGER // 6 elements in this list
DECLARE List3 : ARRAY[1:100] OF INTEGER // 100 elements in this list
DECLARE List4 : ARRAY[0:25]  OF STRING  // 26 elements in this list
```

Python	List1 = [] List1.append("Fred") List1.append("Jack") List1.append("Ali")	As there are no declarations, the only way to generate a list is to initialise one. You can append elements to an existing list.
	List2 = [0, 0, 0, 0, 0, 0]	You can enclose the elements in [ ].
	List3 = [0 for i in range(100)]	You can use a loop.
	AList = [""] * 26	You can provide an initial value, multiplied by number of elements required.
VB.NET	Dim List1 As String () = {"","",""} Dim List2(5) As Integer Dim List3(100) As Integer Dim AList(0 To 25) As String	You can initialise an array at declaration time (as with List1). Note that List3 has 101 elements. You can use a range as an array dimension (as with AList) however the lower bound must be 0.
Pascal	**var** List1 : **array**[1..3] of **string**; **var** List2 : **array**[10..15] of **integer**; **var** NList : **array**[1..100] of **integer**; **var** AList : **array**['A'..'Z'] of **string**;	The dimension can be an integer range or a char range. Ranges can start with any value.

Accessing 1D arrays

A specific element in an array is accessed using an index value. In pseudocode, this is written as:

```
<arrayIdentifier>[x]
```

Code examples

Pseudocode example:

```
NList[25] = 0   // set 25th element to zero
AList[3] = "D" // set 4th element to letter D
```

Python	`NList[24] = 0` `AList[3] = "D"`	
VB.NET	`NList(25) = 0` `AList(3) = "D"`	We ignore element 0, so the 25th element is `NList(25)`.
Pascal	`NList[24] := 0` `AList['D'] := 'D'`	

In Python, you can print the whole contents of a list using `print(List)`. In VB.NET and Pascal, you need to use a loop to print one element of an array at a time.

TASK 13.09

1. Write program code to implement the pseudocode from Worked Example 11.10 in Chapter 11.
2. Write program code to implement the pseudocode from Worked Example 11.11 in Chapter 11.
3. Write program code to implement the improved algorithm from Worked Example 11.12 in Chapter 11.

Creating 2D arrays

When we write a table of data (a matrix) on a piece of paper and want to refer to individual elements of the table, the convention is to give the row number first and then the column number. When declaring a 2D array, the number of rows is given first, then the number of columns. Again we have lower and upper bounds for each dimension. VB.NET and Python number all elements from 0.

In pseudocode, a 2D array declaration is written as:

```
DECLARE <identifier> : ARRAY[<lBound1>:<uBound1>,
<lBound2>:<uBound2>] OF <dataType>
```

Syntax definitions

Python	In Python, there are no arrays. The equivalent data structure is a list of lists.
VB.NET	`Dim <arrayIdentifier>(<uBound1, uBound2>) As <dataType>`
Pascal	`var <arrayIdentifier> : array[lBound1..uBound1, lBound2..uBound2] of <dataType>;`

Code examples

To declare a 2D array to represent a game board of six rows and seven columns, the pseudocode statement is:

```
Board[1:6, 1:7] OF INTEGER
```

Python	`Board = [[0, 0, 0, 0, 0, 0, 0],`
	`[0, 0, 0, 0, 0, 0, 0],`
	`[0, 0, 0, 0, 0, 0, 0],`
	`[0, 0, 0, 0, 0, 0, 0],`
	`[0, 0, 0, 0, 0, 0, 0],`
	`[0, 0, 0, 0, 0, 0, 0]]`
	`Board = [[0 for i in range(7)]`
	`for j in range(6)]`
	`Board = [[0] * 7] * 6`
		2D lists can be initialised in a similar way to 1D lists. Remember that elements are numbered from 0.
		These are alternative ways of initialising a 6 × 7 list. The rows are numbered 0 to 5 and the columns 0 to 6.
		The upper value of the range is not included.

VB.NET	`Dim Board(6, 7) As Integer`	Elements are numbered from 0 to the given number. This declaration has one row and one column too many. However, the algorithm may be such that it is easier to convert to program code if row 0 and column 0 are ignored.
Pascal	`var Board : array[1..6, 1..7] of integer;`	Similar to 1D arrays, 2D array ranges can start with any value and can be of type integer or char.

Accessing 2D arrays

A specific element in a table is accessed using an index pair. In pseudocode this is written as:

```
<arrayIdentifier>[x, y]
```

Code examples

Pseudocode example:

```
Board[3,4] = 0 // sets the element in row 3 and column 4 to zero
```

The following code examples demonstrate how to access elements in each of the three languages.

Python	`Board[2][3] = 0`	Elements are numbered from 0 in Python, so [3] gives access to the fourth element.
VB.NET	`Board(3, 4) = 0`	We are ignoring row 0 and column 0.
Pascal	`Board[3, 4] := 0`	When the array was declared, the elements were numbered from 1.

TASK 13.10

Write program code to implement the pseudocode from Worked Example 11.13; first initialise the table and then output its contents.

13.08 Built-in functions

Programming environments provide many built-in functions. Some of them are always available to use; some need to be imported from specialist module libraries.

Discussion Point:

Investigate your own programming environment and research other library routines.

String manipulation functions

Table 13.06 contains some useful functions for manipulating strings.

Description	Pseudocode	Python	VB.NET	Pascal
Access a single character using its position P in a string	`ThisString[P]` Counts from 1	`ThisString[P]` Counts from 0	`ThisString(P)` Counts from 0	`ThisString[P]` Counts from 1
Return the character associated with the specified character code	`CHAR(i)`	`chr(i)`	`Chr(i)`	`Chr(i)`
Return an integer value representing the character code of the specified character	`ASCII(ch)`	`ord(ch)`	`Asc(ch)`	`Ord(ch)`
Return an integer that contains the number of characters in string `S`	`LENGTH(S)`	`len(S)`	`len(S)`	`Length(S)`
Return a substring of length L from the left of string `S`	`LEFT(S, L)`	`S[0:L]` See the next section, on slicing	`Left(S, L)`	Uses the StrUtils library `LeftStr(S, L)`
Return a substring of length `L` from the right of string `S`	`RIGHT(S, L)`	`S[-L:]` See the next section, on slicing	`Right(S, L)`	Uses the StrUtils library `RightStr(S, L)`
Return a substring of length `L` from position `P` in string `S`	`MID(S, P, L)`	`S[P : P + L]` See the next section, on slicing	`mid(S, P, L)`	Uses the StrUtils library `MidStr(S, P, L)`
Join strings	`CONCAT(S1, S2)` `S1 & S2`	`S = S1 + S2`	`S = S1 + S2` `S = S1 & S2`	`S := Concat(S1, S2);` `S := S1 + S2;`

Table 13.06 Some useful string manipulation functions

Slicing in Python

In Python a subsequence of any sequence type (e.g. lists and strings) can be created using 'slicing'.

A slice is a substring of a string. For example, to get a substring of length L from position P in string S we write S[P : P + L].

Figure 13.05 shows a representation of `ThisString`. If we want to return a slice of length 3 starting at position 3, we use `ThisString[3 : 6]` to give 'DEF'. Position is counted from 0 and the position at the upper bound of the slice is not included in the substring.

Figure 13.05 A representation of `ThisString`

If you imagine the numbering of each element to start at the left-hand end (as shown in Figure 13.05), then it is easier to see how the left element (the lower bound) is included, but the right element (the upper bound) is excluded. Table 13.07 shows some other useful slices in Python.

Expression	Result	Explanation
`ThisString[2:]`	`CDEFG`	If you do not state the upper bound, the slice includes all characters to the end of the string.
`ThisString[:2]`	`AB`	If you do not state the lower bound, the slice includes all characters from the beginning of the string.
`ThisString[-2:]`	`FG`	A negative lower bound means that it takes the slice starting from the end of the string.
`ThisString[:-2]`	`ABCDE`	A negative upper bound means that it terminates the string at that position.

Table 13.07 Some useful slices in Python

Rounding numbers

Sometimes we need to round numbers after a calculation involving real numbers. Rounding is done away from zero. This means that 0.5 is rounded to 1 and –0.5 is rounded to –1.0.

Python	`round(x[, ndigits])`	The floating-point value `x` is rounded to `ndigits` after the decimal point. If `ndigits` is omitted, it defaults to zero. The result is a floating point number.
VB.NET	`Math.Round(x)`	The value of `x` is rounded to the nearest whole number.
Pascal	`Round(x)`	The value of `x` is rounded to the nearest whole number.

Truncating numbers

Instead of rounding, sometimes we just want the whole number part of a real number. This is known as 'truncation'.

Python	`int(x)`	If `x` is a floating-point number, the conversion truncates towards zero.
VB.NET	`Math.Truncate(x)`	The whole number part of the real number `x` is returned.
Pascal	`Trunc(x)`	The whole number part of the real number `x` is returned.

Converting a string to a number

Sometimes a whole number may be held as a string. To use such a number in a calculation, we first need to convert it to an integer. For example, these functions return the integer value 5 from the string `"5"`:

Python	`int(S)`
VB.NET	`CInt(S)`
Pascal	`StrToInt(S)`

Sometimes a number with a decimal point may be held as a string. To use such a number in a calculation, we first need to convert it to a real (float). For example, these functions return the real number 75.43 from the string `"75.43"`:

Python	`float(x)`	The returned value is a floating-point number.
VB.NET	`CDbl(S)`	The returned value is of type double.
Pascal	`StrToFloat(S)`	The returned value is a floating-point number.

Formatting numbers for output

When we want to present output in a tabulated way, we need to format the output statement.

Python	`print("N1:{0:>10}|N2:{1:^10}|N3:{2:<10}|${3:.2f}".format(N1, N2, N3, Price))`	When using the placeholder method for a print statement in Python, you can format the output. Within {}, you give the number of the item in the print list, then a colon (:) and then these codes: `^` centres the value `<` align the value on the left `>` aligns the value on the right `w` a number giving the overall character width of the value `xf` where `x` is the number of decimal places for a floating point number

VB.NET	`Dim N1 As Decimal = 21.457`
	`Dim N2 As Double = 3.14159`
	`Console.WriteLine("Price:{0:C}", N1)`
	`Console.WriteLine("Pi:{0:F}", N2)`
		`:C` outputs the value as currency: $21.46.
		`:F` outputs a double as fixed point (with two decimal places): 3.14.

Pascal	`Write(<printlistitem>:W:D);` `WriteLn(Pi:5:2);`	Print list items can be formatted using a field width, W, and the number of decimal places, D.

Random number generator

Random numbers are often required for simulations. Most programming languages have various random number generators available. As the random numbers are generated through a program, they are referred to as 'pseudo-random' numbers.

Python	`# in the random library:` `randint(1, 6)`	This code produces a random number between 1 and 6 inclusive.

VB.NET	`Dim RandomNumber As New Random`
	`Dim x As Integer`
	`x = RandomNumber.Next(1, 6)`
		You have to set up a `RandomNumber` object (see Chapter 27). This code generates an integer between 1 (inclusive) and 6 (exclusive).

Pascal	`Random(6)`	The simplest option returns a random number between 0 (inclusive) and 6 (exclusive).
	`Randomize;`	This code initialises the random number generator.
	`RandSeed := <integer value>`	It can be useful, particularly during testing, to produce the same sequence of random numbers each time the program executes.
	`RandomRange(1, 6)`	There is a function in the `Math` library that returns a random number between two values, in this case 1 (inclusive) and 6 (exclusive).

TASK 13.11

1. Write program code to generate 20 random numbers in the range 1 to 10 inclusive.
2. Write program code to implement the pseudocode using a pre-condition loop from Worked Example 11.07 in Chapter 11.

Date and time functions

Sometimes we want to work with the current time and date. The system clock can provide this. There are many functions available to manipulate dates and times. Most are beyond the scope of this book. Here are just a few basic functions.

Python	`from datetime import *` `SomeDate = date(2015,3,15)`	Import the library. Convert the separate integers for year, month and day into a date.
	`Today = date.today()`	The system clock can be read.
	`print(SomeDate)` `print(Today)`	Date values con be output without conversion.
	`SomeDate = SomeDate + timedelta(1)`	Adding `timedelta(1)` moves the date on by 1 day.
VB.NET	`Dim SomeDate, Today As Date` `SomeDate = #3/15/2015#`	Declare date variables. The format of the string is MM/DD/YYYY.
	`Today = Now()`	The system clock can be read. The value returned is of type Date.
	`Console.WriteLine(SomeDate)` `Console.WriteLine(Today)`	Date type values can be output without conversion.
	`SomeDate = SomeDate.AddDays(1)`	Add a value to a date to increment it by a number of days.

Pascal	`var SomeDate, Today : TDateTime;`
	`var DateString : String;`
	`DateString := '15/03/2015';`
	`SomeDate := StrToDate(DateString);`
		Declare date variables.
		A date stored as a string can be converted to store it in a variable of type `TDateTime`.

	`Today := Date();`	The system clock can be read. The value returned is of type `TDateTime`.

	`DateString := DateToStr(SomeDate);`
	`WriteLn(DateString);`
	`DateString := DateToStr(Today);`
	`WriteLn(DateString);`
		A date must be converted to a string for output.

	`SomeDate := SomeDate + 1;`	Adding 1 to a date produces the next day's date.

TASK 13.12

Write program code to get today's date from the system clock and output it with a suitable message. Also output tomorrow's date with a suitable message. Will your program give the correct information, regardless of which day it is executed?

Extend your program to output yesterday's date.

Discussion Point:

What other useful functions can you find? Which module libraries have you searched?

13.09 Text files

Data need to be stored permanently. One approach is to use a file. For example, any data held in an array while your program is executing will be lost when the program stops. You can save the data out to file and read it back in when your program requires it on subsequent executions.

A text file consists of a sequence of characters formatted into lines. Each line is terminated by an end-of-line marker. The text file is terminated by an end-of-file marker.

Note: you can check the contents of a text file (or even create a text file required by a program) by using a text editor such as NotePad.

Writing to a text file

Writing to a text file usually means creating a text file.

The following pseudocode statements provide facilities for writing to a file:

```
OPENFILE <filename> FOR WRITE          // open the file for writing
WRITEFILE <filename>, <stringValue>   // write a line of text to the file
CLOSEFILE                             // close file
```

The following code examples demonstrate how to open, write to and close a file called `SampleFile.TXT` in each of the three languages. If the file already exists, it is overwritten as soon as the file handle is assigned by the 'open file' command.

Python	`FileHandle = open("SampleFile.TXT", "w")`
	`FileHandle.write(LineOfText)`
	`FileHandle.close()`
		You specify the filename and mode ('w' for write) when you call the `open` function. The line of text to be written to the file must contain the newline character `"\n"` to move to the next line of the text file.

VB.NET	`Dim FileHandle As IO.StreamWriter`
	`Dim LineOfText As String`
	`FileHandle = New`
	`IO.StreamWriter("SampleFile.TXT")`
	`FileHandle.WriteLine(LineOfText)`
	`FileHandle.Close()`
		The file is accessed through an object (see Chapter 27) called a `StreamWriter`.

Pascal	`var LineOfText : String;`
	`var FileHandle : TextFile;`
	`AssignFile(FileHandle, 'SampleFile.TXT');`
	`Rewrite(FileHandle);`
	`WriteLn(FileHandle, LineOfText);`
	`CloseFile(FileHandle);`
		The `TextFile` data type enables append access to a file. Note that the `AssignFile` procedure simply connects the variable with the filename; the `Rewrite` procedure opens the file.

Reading from a text file

An existing file can be read by a program. The following pseudocode statements provide facilities for reading from a file:

```
OPENFILE <filename> FOR READ              // open file for reading
READFILE <filename>, <stringVariable>    // read a line of text from the file
CLOSEFILE                                // close file
```

The following code examples demonstrate how to open, read from and close a file called `SampleFile.TXT` in each of the three languages.

Python	`FileHandle = open("SampleFile.TXT", "r")`
	`LineOfText = FileHandle.readline()`
	`FileHandle.close`
		You specify the filename and mode ('r' for read) when you call the `open` function.

VB.NET	`Dim LineOfText As String`
	`Dim FileHandle As System.`
	`IO.StreamReader`
	`FileHandle = New System.`
	`IO.StreamReader("SampleFile.TXT")`
	`LineOfText = FileHandle.ReadLine()`
	`FileHandle.Close()`
		The file is accessed through an object (see Chapter 27) called a `StreamReader`.

Pascal	`var FileHandle : TextFile;`
	`var LineOfText : String;`
	`AssignFile(FileHandle, 'SampleFile.TXT');`
	`Reset(FileHandle);`
	`ReadLn(FileHandle, LineOfText);`
	`CloseFile(FileHandle);`
		The `TextFile` data type enables read access to a file. Note that the `Reset` procedure opens the file for reading.

Appending to a text file

Sometimes we may wish to add data to an existing file rather than creating a new file. This can be done in Append mode. It adds the new data to the end of the existing file.

The following pseudocode statements provide facilities for appending to a file:

```
OPENFILE <filename> FOR APPEND       // open file for append
WRITEFILE <filename>, <stringValue> // write a line of text to the file
CLOSEFILE                           // close file
```

The following code examples demonstrate how to open, append to and close a file called `SampleFile.TXT` in each of the three languages.

Python	`FileHandle = open("SampleFile.TXT", "a")`
	`FileHandle.write(LineOfText)`
	`FileHandle.close()`
		You specify the filename and mode ('a' for append) when you call the `open` function.

VB.NET	`Dim FileHandle As IO.StreamWriter`
	`FileHandle = New IO.StreamWriter("SampleFile.TXT", True)`
	`FileHandle.WriteLine(LineOfText)`
	`FileHandle.Close()`
		The file is accessed through a `StreamWriter`. The extra parameter, `True`, tells the system to append to the object.

Pascal	`var LineOfText : String;`
	`var FileHandle : TextFile;`
	`AssignFile(FileHandle, 'SampleFile.TXT');`
	`Append(FileHandle);`
	`WriteLn(FileHandle, LineOfText);`
	`CloseFile(FileHandle);`
		The `TextFile` data type enables append access to a file. Note that the `Append` procedure opens the file for appending.

The end-of-file (EoF) marker

If we want to read a file from beginning to end we can use a conditional loop. Text files contain a special marker at the end of the file that we can test for. Testing for this special end-of-file marker is a standard function in programming languages. Every time this function is called it will test for this marker. The function will return FALSE if the end of the file is not yet reached and will return TRUE if the end-of-file marker has been reached.

In pseudocode we call this function `EOF()`. We can use the construct `REPEAT...UNTIL EOF()`. If it is possible that the file contains no data, it is better to use the construct `WHILE NOT EOF()`.

For example, the following pseudocode statements read a text file and output its contents:

```
OPENFILE "Test.txt" FOR READ
WHILE NOT EOF("Test.txt")
   READFILE "Test.txt", TextString
   OUTPUT TextString
ENDWHILE
CLOSEFILE "Test.txt"
```

The following code examples demonstrate how to output the contents of a file in each of the three languages.

<table>
<tr><td>Python</td><td><pre>FileHandle = open("Test.txt", "r")
LineOfText = FileHandle.readline()
while len(LineOfText) > 0:
   LineOfText = FileHandle.readline()
   print(LineOfText)
FileHandle.close()</pre></td><td>There is no explicit EOF function. However, when a line of text has been read that only consists of the end-of-file marker, the line of text is of length 0.</td></tr>
<tr><td>VB.NET</td><td><pre>Dim LineOfText As String
Dim FileHandle As System.IO.StreamReader
FileHandle = New
System.IO.StreamReader("Test.txt")
Do Until FileHandle.EndOfStream
   LineOfText = FileHandle.ReadLine()
   Console.WriteLine(LineOfText)
Loop
FileHandle.Close()</pre></td><td>When the end-of-file marker is detected, the <code>EndOfStream</code> method returns the value True and so the loop will end.</td></tr>
<tr><td>Pascal</td><td><pre>var FileHandle : TextFile;
var LineOfText : String;
AssignFile(FileHandle, 'Test.txt');
Reset(FileHandle);
while not EoF(Filehandle) do
   begin
     ReadLn(FileHandle, LineOfText);
     WriteLn(LineOfText);
   end;
CloseFile(FileHandle);</pre></td><td>The <code>EoF</code> function returns the value True when the end-of-file marker is detected.</td></tr>
</table>

Summary

- Programming constructs in Python, VB.NET and Pascal have been introduced:
  - declaration and assignment of constants and variables
  - the basic constructs of assignment, selection, repetition, input and output
  - built-in data types and functions
  - declaring arrays and using them in a program.
- Code should be commented where it helps understanding.
- Boolean expressions are needed for conditions.
- Text files can be written to and read from within a program.

Exam-style Questions

1 Matt wants a program to output a conversion table for ounces to grams (1 ounce is 28.35 grams). He writes an algorithm:

```
OUTPUT "Ounces Grams"
FOR Ounces ← 1 TO 30
   Grams ← Rounded(Ounces * 28.35) // whole number of grams only
   OUTPUT Ounces, Grams
ENDFOR
```

Write program code to implement the algorithm. Include formatting, so that the output is tabulated. [7]

2 Write program code to accept an input string `UserID`. The program is to test the `UserID` format. A valid format `UserID` consists of three upper case letters and four digits. The program is to output a message whether `UserID` is valid or not. [5]

3 Fred surveys the students at his college to find out their favourite hobby. He wants to present the data as a tally chart.

Fred plans to enter the data into the computer as he surveys the students. After data entry is complete, he wants to output the total for each hobby.

1	Reading books	\\\
2	Play computer games	\\\\\\\\
3	Sport	\\\\\
4	Programming	\\
5	Watching TV	\\\\\\\\\\\

He starts by writing an algorithm:

```
Initialise Tally array
REPEAT
   INPUT Choice // 1 for Reading, 2 for computer games,
                // 3 for Sport, 4 for Programming, 5 for TV
                // 0 to end input
   Increment Tally[Choice]
UNTIL Choice = 0
FOR Index = 1 TO 5
   OUTPUT Tally[Index]
ENDFOR
```

a Write program code to declare and initialise the array `Tally[1:5] OF INTEGER`. [5]

b Write program code to implement the algorithm above. [7]

c Write program code to declare an array to store the hobby titles and rewrite the `FOR` loop of your program in part (b) so that the hobby title is output before each tally. [4]

d Write program code to save the array data in a text file. [5]

e Write program code to read the data from the text file back into the initialised array. [5]

Chapter 14
Structured Programming

Learning objectives

By the end of this chapter you should be able to:

- use a procedure and explain where in the construction of an algorithm it is appropriate to use a procedure
- show understanding of passing parameters by reference and by value
- use a function and explain where in the construction of an algorithm it is appropriate to use a function
- use the terminology associated with procedures and functions: procedure/function header, procedure/function interface, parameter, argument, return value
- show understanding that a function is used in an expression
- write programs containing several components and showing good use of resources.

14.01 Terminology

Different programming languages use different terminology for their subroutines, as listed in Table 14.01.

Pseudocode	PROCEDURE	FUNCTION
Python	void function	fruitful function
VB	Subroutine	Function
Pascal	procedure	function

Table 14.01 Programming language terminology for subroutines

14.02 Procedures

In Chapter 12 (Section 12.02), we used procedures as a means of giving a group of statements a name. When we want to program a procedure we need to define it before the main program. We call it in the main program when we want the statements in the procedure body to be executed.

In pseudocode, a procedure definition is written as:

```
PROCEDURE <procedureIdentifier>() // this is the procedure header
   <statement(s)>                 // these statements are the procedure body
ENDPROCEDURE
```

This procedure is called using the pseudocode statement:

```
CALL <procedureIdentifier>()
```

Syntax definitions

Python	`def <identifier>():`
	
	`   <statement(s)>`

VB.NET	`Sub <identifier>()`
	
	`   <statement(s)>`
	
	`End Sub`

Pascal	`procedure <identifier>;`
	
	`begin`
	
	`   <statement(s)>;`
	
	`end;`

When programming a procedure, note where the definition is written and how the procedure is called from the main program.

Code examples

Here is an example pseudocode procedure definition:

```
PROCEDURE InputOddNumber()
   REPEAT
      INPUT "Enter an odd number: " Number
   UNTIL Number MOD 2 = 1
ENDPROCEDURE
```

This procedure is called using the `CALL` statement:

```
CALL InputOddNumber()
```

Python

ProcedureExample.py - C:/Users/Sylvia/My Programming/CIE B...

File Edit Format Run Options Windows Help

```
def InputOddNumber():
    Number = 0
    while Number % 2 == 0:
        Number = int(input("Enter an odd number: "))

# ********* main program starts here **************
InputOddNumber()
```

Ln: 9 Col: 0

Figure 14.01 The Python editor with a procedure

The Python editor colour-codes the different parts of a statement. This helps when you are typing your own code. The indentation shows which statements are part of the loop.

The built-in function `input` returns a string, which must be converted to an integer before it can be used as a number.

VB.NET

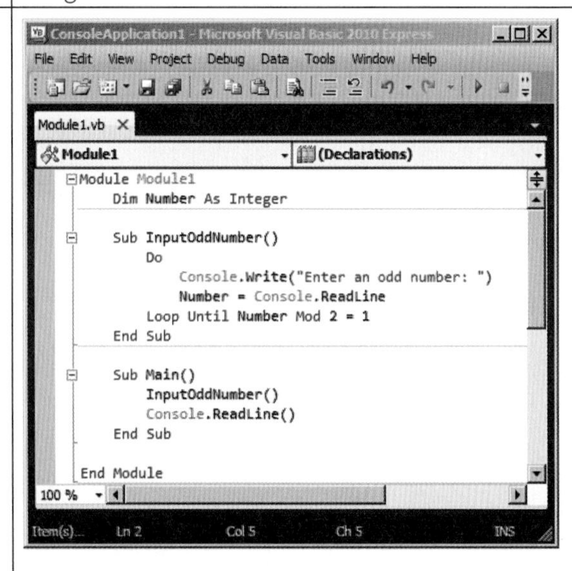
ConsoleApplication1 - Microsoft Visual Basic 2010 Express
File Edit View Project Debug Data Tools Window Help
Module1.vb
Module1
(Declarations)
Module Module1
Dim Number As Integer
Sub InputOddNumber()
Do
Console.Write("Enter an odd number: ")
Number = Console.ReadLine
Loop Until Number Mod 2 = 1
End Sub
Sub Main()
InputOddNumber()
Console.ReadLine()
End Sub
End Module
100 %
Item(s)...
Ln 2
Col 5
Ch 5
INS

Figure 14.02 The Visual Basic Express editor with a procedure

The Visual Basic Express editor colour-codes different parts of the statement, so it is easy to see if syntax errors are made. The editor also auto-indents and capitalises keywords.

Variables need to be declared before they are used. The editor will follow the capitalisation of the variable declaration when you type an identifier without following your original capitalisation.

The editor is predictive: pop-up lists will show when you type the first part of a statement.

When you execute the Main program, `Console.ReadLine()` keeps the run-time window open.

Pascal

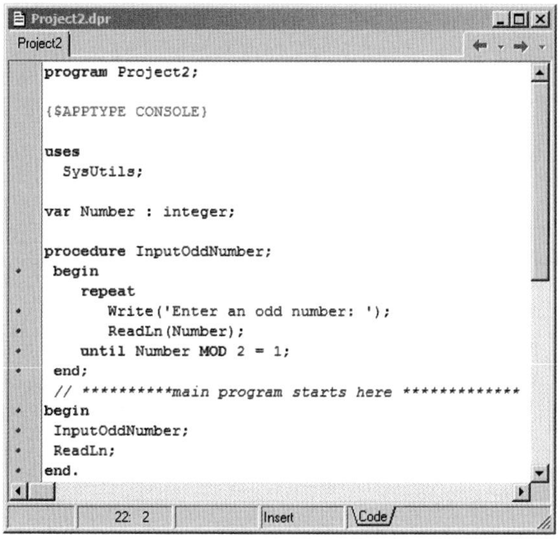

```
Project2.dpr
Project2
program Project2;

{$APPTYPE CONSOLE}

uses
  SysUtils;

var Number : integer;

procedure InputOddNumber;
 begin
    repeat
       Write('Enter an odd number: ');
       ReadLn(Number);
    until Number MOD 2 = 1;
 end;
 // **********main program starts here *************
begin
 InputOddNumber;
 ReadLn;
end.
22: 2   Insert   Code
```

Figure 14.03 The Pascal editor with a procedure

The Pascal editor automatically emboldens keywords.

The procedure body is enclosed within `begin` and `end` statements.

There is no semicolon after the keywords `begin` or `repeat`.

Variables need to be declared before they are used.

When you execute the main program, `ReadLn` keeps the run-time window open. The main program finishes with `end`. (note the full stop).

TASK 14.01

Write program code to implement the pseudocode from Worked Example 12.02 in Chapter 12.

14.03 Functions

In Chapter 13 (Section 13.08), we used built-in functions. These are useful subroutines written by other programmers and made available in module libraries. The most-used ones are usually in the system library, so are available without having to explicitly import them.

You can write your own functions. Any function you have written can be used in another program if you build up your own module library.

A function is used as part of an expression. When program execution gets to the statement that includes a function call as part of the expression, the function is executed. The value returned from this function call is then used in the expression.

When writing your own function, ensure you always return a value as part of the statements that make up the function (the function body). You can have more than one RETURN statement if there are different paths through the function body.

In pseudocode, a function definition is written as:

```
FUNCTION <functionIdentifier>() RETURNS <dataType> // function header
   <statement(s)> // function body
   RETURN <value>
ENDPROCEDURE
```

Syntax definitions

Python	def <functionIdentifier>(): <statement(s)> return <value>
VB.NET	Function <functionIdentifier>() As <dataType> <statement(s)> <functionIdentifier> = <value> 'Return <value> End Function

Pascal	**function** <functionIdentifier>() : <dataType>;
	begin
	   <statement(s);
	   result := <value>; // <functionIdentifier> := <value>;
	end;

When programming a function, the definition is written in the same place as a procedure. The function is called from within an expression in the main program, or in a procedure.

Code example

We can write the example procedure from Section 14.02 as a function. In pseudocode, this is:

```
FUNCTION InputOddNumber() RETURNS INTEGER
   REPEAT
      INPUT "Enter an odd number: " Number
   UNTIL Number MOD 2 = 1
   RETURN Number
ENDFUNCTION
```

Python	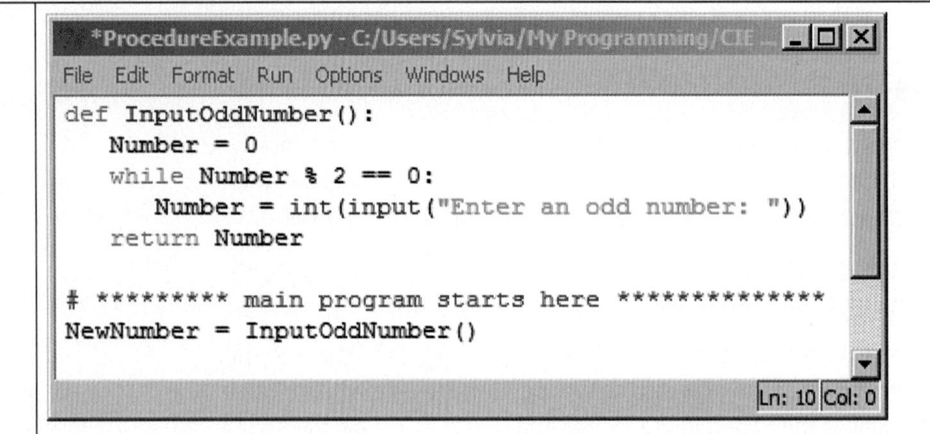 Figure 14.04 The Python editor with a function and local variable The variable `Number` in Figure 14.04 is not accessible in the main program. Python's variables are local unless declared to be global.

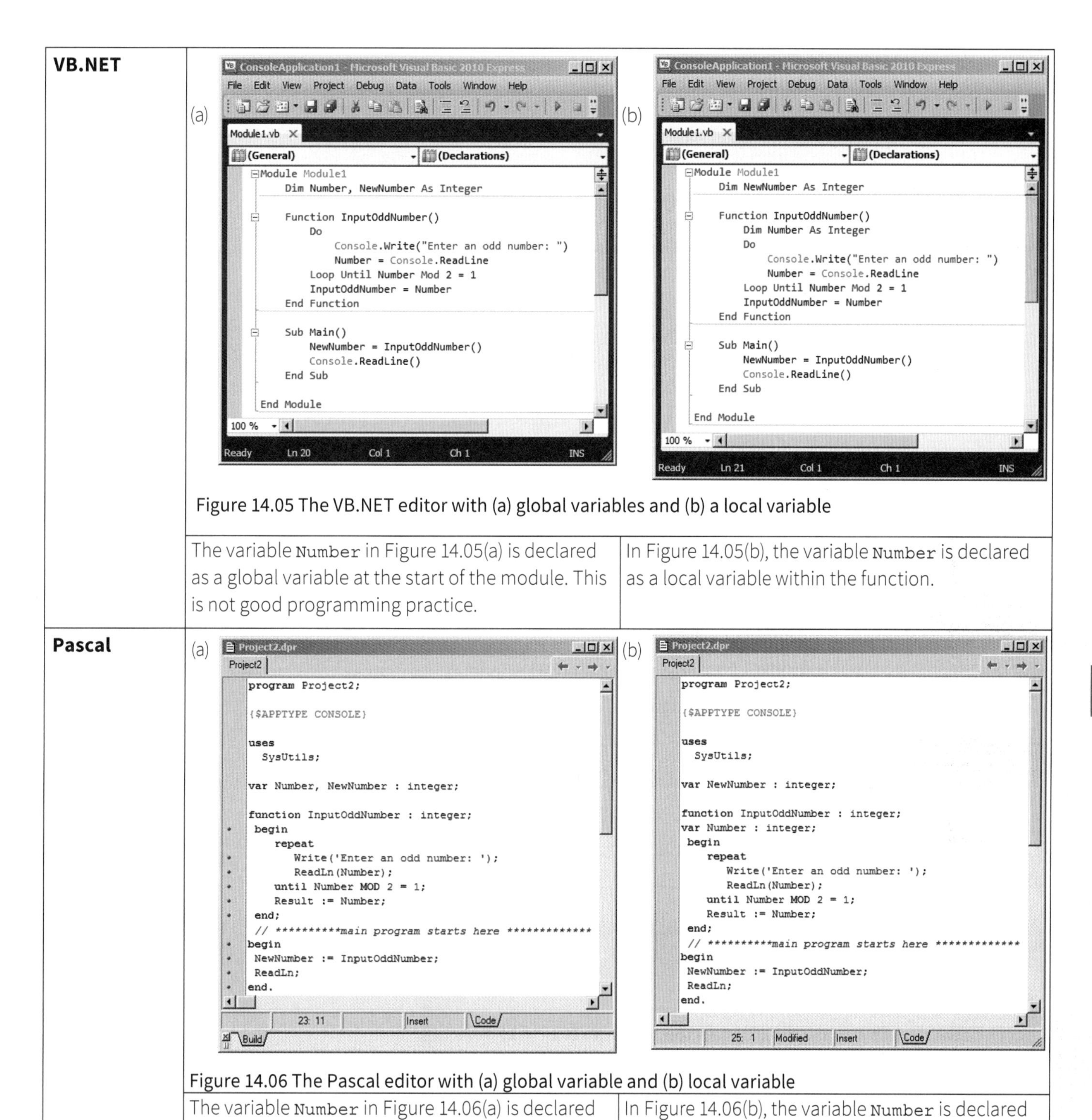

Figure 14.05 The VB.NET editor with (a) global variables and (b) a local variable

The variable `Number` in Figure 14.05(a) is declared as a global variable at the start of the module. This is not good programming practice.	In Figure 14.05(b), the variable `Number` is declared as a local variable within the function.

Figure 14.06 The Pascal editor with (a) global variable and (b) local variable

The variable `Number` in Figure 14.06(a) is declared as a global variable, outside the function. This is not good programming practice.	In Figure 14.06(b), the variable `Number` is declared as a local variable within the function.

A global variable is available in any part of the program code. It is good programming practice to declare a variable that is only used within a subroutine as a local variable.

In Python, every variable is local, unless it is overridden with a `global` declaration. In VB.NET and Pascal, you need to write the declaration statement for a local variable within the subroutine.

TASK 14.02

Write program code to implement the pseudocode from Worked Example 12.03 in Chapter 12. The global and local variables are listed in Table 12.10.

14.04 Passing parameters to subroutines

When a subroutine requires one or more values from the main program, we supply these as arguments to the subroutine at call time. This is how we use built-in functions. We don't need to know the identifiers used within the function when we call a built-in function.

When we define a subroutine that requires values to be passed to the subroutine body, we use a parameter list in the subroutine header. When the subroutine is called, we supply the arguments in brackets. The arguments supplied are assigned to the corresponding parameter of the subroutine (note the order of the parameters in the parameter list must be the same as the order in the list of arguments). This is known as the subroutine interface.

14.05 Passing parameters to functions

The function header is written in pseudocode as:

```
FUNCTION <functionIdentifier> (<parameterList>) RETURNS <dataType>
```

where `<parameterList>` is a list of identifiers and their data types, separated by commas.

Here is an example pseudocode function definition that uses parameters:

```
FUNCTION SumRange(FirstValue : INTEGER, LastValue : INTEGER) : INTEGER
DECLARE Sum, ThisValue : INTEGER
   Sum ← 0
   FOR ThisValue ← FirstValue TO LastValue
      Sum ← Sum + ThisValue
   ENDFOR
   RETURN Sum
ENDFUNCTION
```

ProcedureExample.py - C:/Users/Sylvia/My Programming/CIE Book/...

File Edit Format Run Options Windows Help

```
def SumRange(FirstValue, LastValue):
   Sum = 0
   for ThisValue in range(FirstValue, LastValue + 1):
      Sum = Sum + ThisValue
   return Sum

# ********* main program starts here **************
NewNumber = SumRange(1, 5)
print(NewNumber)
```

Ln: 14 Col: 0

Figure 14.07 The `SumRange()` function in Python

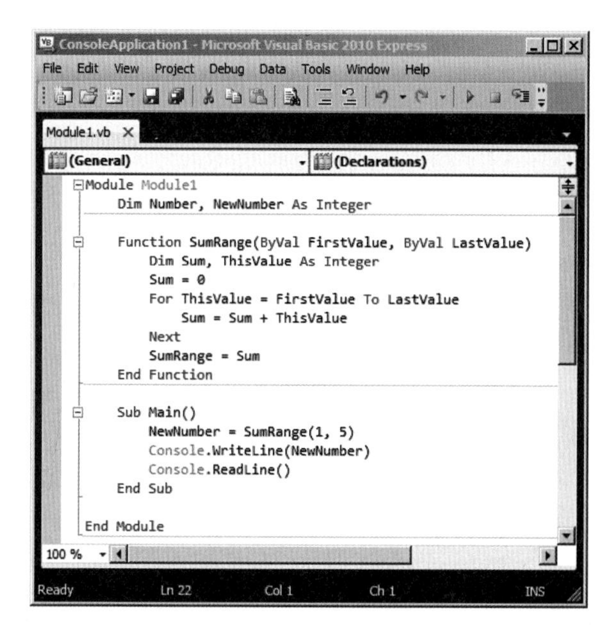

Figure 14.08 The `SumRange()` function in VB.NET

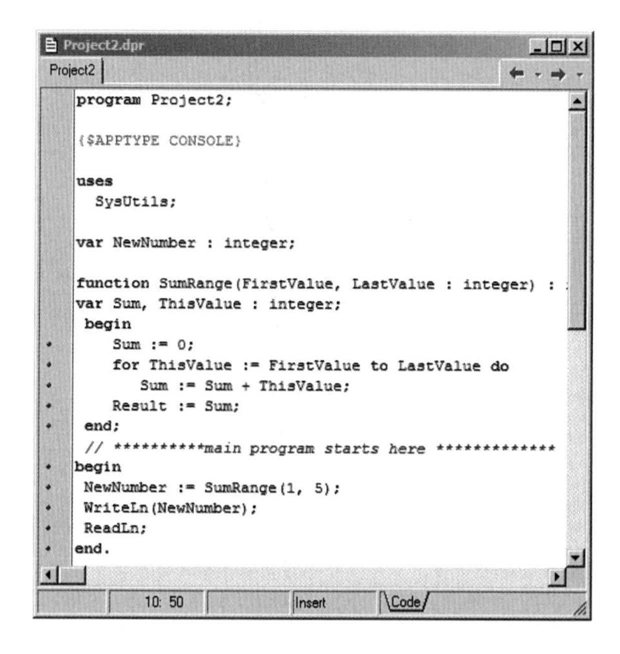

Project2.dpr
Project2
program Project2;
{$APPTYPE CONSOLE}
uses
SysUtils;
var NewNumber : integer;
function SumRange(FirstValue, LastValue : integer) :
var Sum, ThisValue : integer;
begin
Sum := 0;
for ThisValue := FirstValue to LastValue do
Sum := Sum + ThisValue;
Result := Sum;
end;
// **********main program starts here *************
begin
NewNumber := SumRange(1, 5);
WriteLn(NewNumber);
ReadLn;
end.
10: 50 Insert Code

Figure 14.09 The `SumRange()` function in Pascal

TASK 14.03

Write a function to implement the following pseudocode:

```
FUNCTION Factorial (Number : INTEGER) : INTEGER
DECLARE Product : INTEGER
   Product ← 1
   FOR n ← 2 TO Number
      Product ← Product * n
   ENDFOR
   RETURN Product
ENDFUNCTION
```

14.06 Passing parameters to procedures

If a parameter is passed **by value**, at call time the argument can be an actual value (as we showed in Section 14.04). If the argument is a variable, then a copy of the current value of the variable is passed into the subroutine. The value of the variable in the calling program is not affected by what happens in the subroutine.

For procedures, a parameter can be passed **by reference**. At call time, the argument must be a variable. A pointer to the memory location of that variable is passed into the procedure. Any changes that are applied to the variable's contents will be effective outside the procedure in the calling program/module.

KEY TERMS

By value: the actual value is passed into the procedure
By reference: the address of the variable is passed into the procedure

Note that neither of these methods of parameter passing applies to Python. In Python, the method is called pass by object reference. This is basically an object-oriented way of passing parameters and is beyond the scope of this chapter (objects are dealt with in Chapter 27). The important point is to understand how to program in Python to get the desired effect.

The full procedure header is written in pseudocode, in a very similar fashion to that for function headers, as:

```
PROCEDURE <ProcedureIdentifier> (<parameterList>)
```

The parameter list needs more information for a procedure definition. In pseudocode, a parameter in the list is represented in one of the following formats:

```
BYREF <identifier1> : <dataType>
BYVAL <identifier2> : <dataType>
```

Passing parameters by value

The pseudocode for the pyramid example in Chapter 12 (Section 12.04) includes a procedure definition that uses two parameters passed by value. We can now make that explicit:

```
PROCEDURE OutputSymbols(BYVAL NumberOfSymbols : INTEGER, BYVAL Symbol : CHAR)
DECLARE Count : INTEGER
   FOR Count ← 1 TO NumberOfSymbols
      OUTPUT Symbol // without moving to next line
   ENDFOR
   OUTPUT NewLine
ENDPROCEDURE
```

In Python (Figure 14.10), all parameters behave like local variables and their effect is as though they are passed by value.

ProcedureExample.py - C:/Users/Sylvia/My Programming/CIE Book/...

File Edit Format Run Options Windows Help

```python
def OutputSymbols(NumberOfSymbols, Symbol):
   for Count in range(NumberOfSymbols):
      print(Symbol, end='')
   print()

# ********* main program starts here **************
OutputSymbols(5, '*')
```

Ln: 9 Col: 0

Figure 14.10 Parameters passed to a Python subroutine

In VB.NET (Figure 14.11), parameters default to passing by value. The keyword `ByVal` is automatically inserted by the editor.

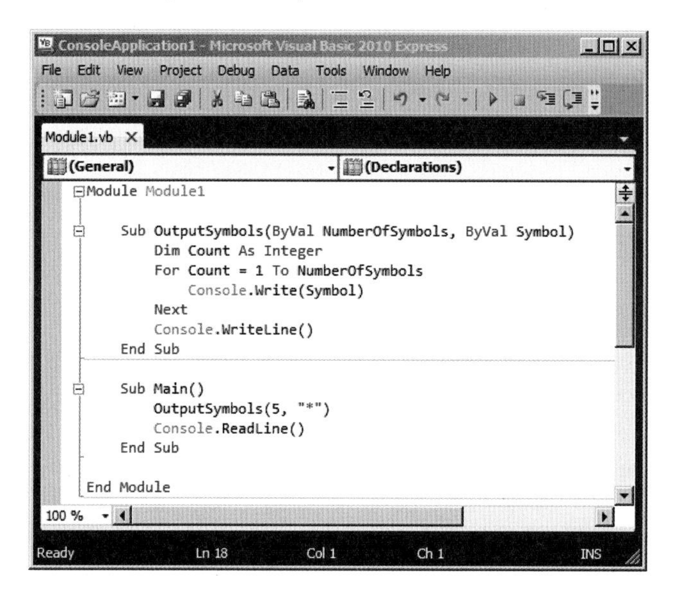

Figure 14.11 Parameters passed by value to a VB.NET procedure

In Pascal (Figure 14.12), there is no keyword for passing by value. This is the default method.

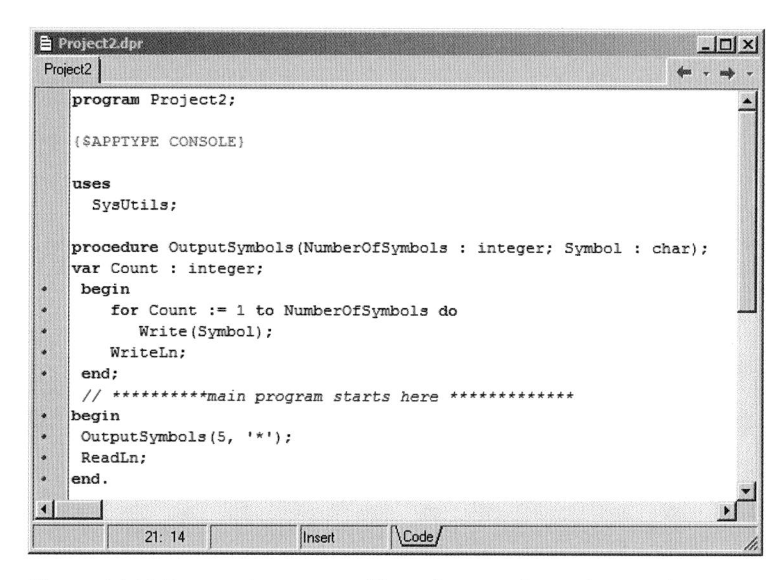

Project2.dpr
Project2
program Project2;
{$APPTYPE CONSOLE}
uses
SysUtils;
procedure OutputSymbols(NumberOfSymbols : integer; Symbol : char);
var Count : integer;
begin
for Count := 1 to NumberOfSymbols do
Write(Symbol);
WriteLn;
end;
// **********main program starts here *************
begin
OutputSymbols(5, '*');
ReadLn;
end.
21: 14
Insert
Code

Figure 14.12 Parameters passed by value to a Pascal procedure

Passing parameters by reference

The pseudocode for the pyramid example generated in Chapter 12 (Section 12.04) includes a procedure definition that uses two parameters passed by reference. We can now make that explicit:

```
PROCEDURE AdjustValuesForNextRow(BYREF Spaces : INTEGER,
      BYREF Symbols : INTEGER)
   Spaces ← Spaces – 1
   Symbols ← Symbols + 2
ENDPROCEDURE
```

The pseudocode statement to call the procedure is:

```
CALL AdjustValuesForNextRow(NumberOfSpaces, NumberOfSymbols)
```

Python does not have a facility to pass parameters by reference. Instead the subroutine behaves as a function and returns multiple values (see Figure 14.13). Note the order of the variables as they receive these values in the main part of the program.

procedure3.py - C:/Users/Sylvia/My Programming/CIE Book/Ch13/python/procedure3.py

File Edit Format Run Options Windows Help

```python
def AdjustValuesForNextRow(Spaces, Symbols):
    Spaces = Spaces - 1
    Symbols = Symbols + 2
    return Spaces, Symbols

#*********main program starts here ***************************
NumberOfSpaces = int(input())
NumberOfSymbols = int(input())
NumberOfSpaces, NumberOfSymbols = AdjustValuesForNextRow(NumberOfSpaces, NumberOfSymbols)
print(NumberOfSpaces)
print(NumberOfSymbols)
```

Ln: 6 Col: 62

Figure 14.13 Multiple values returned from a Python subroutine

This way of treating a multiple of values as a unit is called a 'tuple'. This concept is beyond the scope of this book. You can find out more by reading the Python help files.

In VB.NET (Figure 14.14), the `ByRef` keyword is placed in front of each parameter to be passed by reference.

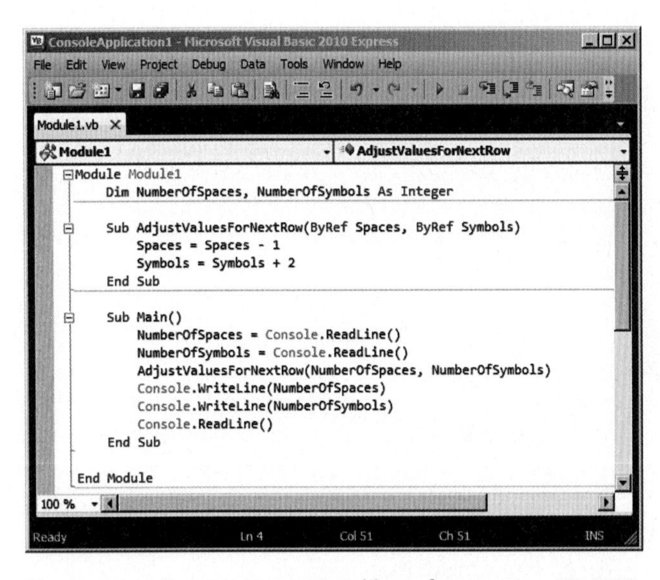
ConsoleApplication1 - Microsoft Visual Basic 2010 Express
File Edit View Project Debug Data Tools Window Help
Module1.vb
Module1
AdjustValuesForNextRow
Module Module1
Dim NumberOfSpaces, NumberOfSymbols As Integer
Sub AdjustValuesForNextRow(ByRef Spaces, ByRef Symbols)
Spaces = Spaces - 1
Symbols = Symbols + 2
End Sub
Sub Main()
NumberOfSpaces = Console.ReadLine()
NumberOfSymbols = Console.ReadLine()
AdjustValuesForNextRow(NumberOfSpaces, NumberOfSymbols)
Console.WriteLine(NumberOfSpaces)
Console.WriteLine(NumberOfSymbols)
Console.ReadLine()
End Sub
End Module
100 %
Ready
Ln 4
Col 51
Ch 51
INS

Figure 14.14 Parameters passed by reference to a VB.NET procedure

In Pascal (Figure 14.15), The keyword `var` is placed in front of the declaration of parameters to be passed by reference.

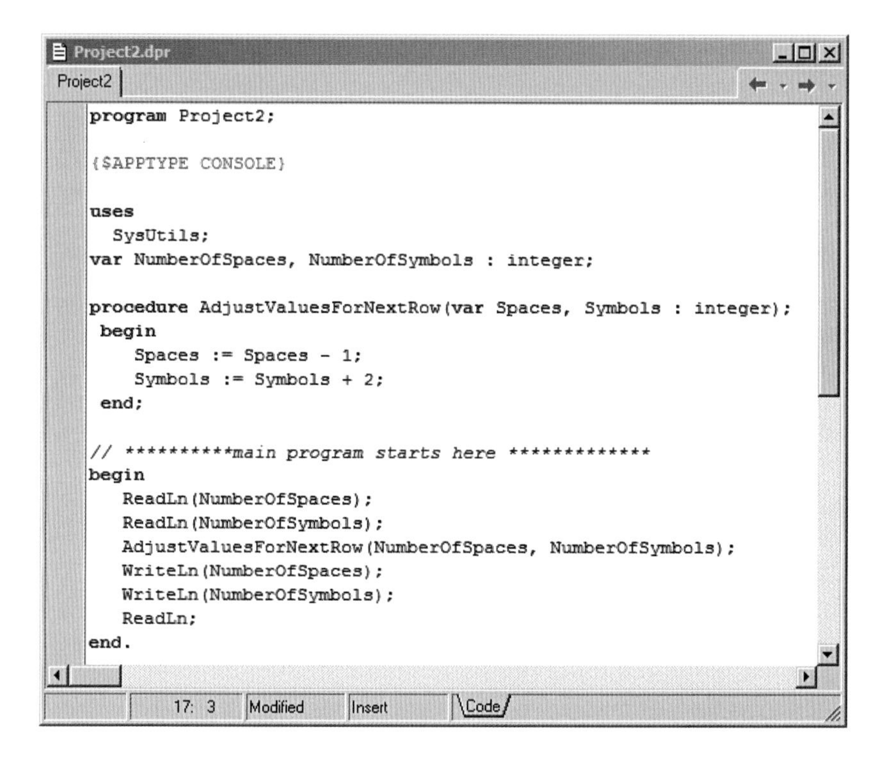

```
program Project2;

{$APPTYPE CONSOLE}

uses
  SysUtils;
var NumberOfSpaces, NumberOfSymbols : integer;

procedure AdjustValuesForNextRow(var Spaces, Symbols : integer);
 begin
    Spaces := Spaces - 1;
    Symbols := Symbols + 2;
 end;

// **********main program starts here *************
begin
   ReadLn(NumberOfSpaces);
   ReadLn(NumberOfSymbols);
   AdjustValuesForNextRow(NumberOfSpaces, NumberOfSymbols);
   WriteLn(NumberOfSpaces);
   WriteLn(NumberOfSymbols);
   ReadLn;
end.
```


Figure 14.15 Parameters passed by reference to a Pascal procedure

TASK 14.04

1. Write program code to implement the structure chart from Figure 12.02 in Chapter 12 (for the average of two numbers).
2. Write program code to implement the structure chart from Figure 12.03 in Chapter 12 (for the number-guessing game).
3. Amend your program code from Task 14.02 to implement the interface shown in the structure chart from Figure 12.05 in Chapter 12.

14.07 Putting it all together

The programs in this section are full solutions to the pyramid-drawing program developed in Chapter 12 (Section 12.04).

The parameters of the subroutines have different identifiers from the variables in the main program. This is done deliberately, so that it is quite clear that the parameters and local variables within a subroutine are separate from those in the calling program or module. If a parameter is passed by reference to a procedure, the parameter identifier within the procedure references the same memory location as the variable identifier passed to the procedure as argument.

The pyramid-drawing program in Python VB.NET and Pascal

<table>
<tr><td>Python</td><td>

```
SPACE = ' '  # constant to give a space a name
def InputMaxNumberOfSymbols():
   Number = 0
   while Number % 2 == 0:
      print("How many symbols make the base?")
      Number = int(input("Input an odd number: "))
   return Number

def SetValues():
   Symbol = input("What symbol do you want to use? ")
   MaxSymbols = InputMaxNumberOfSymbols()
   Spaces = (MaxSymbols + 1) // 2
   Symbols = 1
   return Symbol, MaxSymbols, Spaces, Symbols

def OutputChars(Number, Symbol):
   for Count in range (Number):
      print(Symbol, end='')

def AdjustValuesForNextRow(Spaces, Symbols):
   Spaces = Spaces - 1
   Symbols = Symbols + 2
   return Spaces, Symbols

def main():
   ThisSymbol, MaxNumberOfSymbols, NumberOfSpaces, NumberOfSymbols = SetValues()
   while NumberOfSymbols <= MaxNumberOfSymbols:
      OutputChars(NumberOfSpaces, SPACE)
      OutputChars(NumberOfSymbols, ThisSymbol)
      print()  # move to new line
      NumberOfSpaces, NumberOfSymbols = AdjustValuesForNextRow(NumberOfSpaces, NumberOfSymbols)
main()
```

</td></tr>
<tr><td>VB.NET</td><td>

```
Module Module1
   Const Space = " " 'constant to give a space a name
   Dim NumberOfSpaces, NumberOfSymbols As Integer
   Dim MaxNumberOfSymbols As Integer
   Dim ThisSymbol As Char

Sub InputMaxNumberOfSymbols(ByRef Number As Integer)
   Do
      Console.WriteLine("How many symbols make the base?")
      Console.Write("Input an odd number: ")
      Number = Console.ReadLine()
   Loop Until (Number Mod 2 = 1)
End Sub

Sub SetValues(ByRef Symbol, ByRef MaxSymbols, ByRef Spaces, ByRef Symbols)
   Console.Write("What symbol do you want to use? ")
   Symbol = Console.ReadLine()
   InputMaxNumberOfSymbols(MaxSymbols)
   Spaces = (MaxSymbols + 1) \ 2
   Symbols = 1
End Sub
```

</td></tr>
</table>

	<pre>Sub OutputChars(ByVal Number, ByVal Symbol)
	   Dim Count As Integer
	   For Count = 1 To Number
	      Console.Write(Symbol)
	   Next
	End Sub
	
	Sub AdjustValuesForNextRow(ByRef Spaces, ByRef Symbols)
	   Spaces = Spaces - 1
	   Symbols = Symbols + 2
	End Sub
	
	Sub Main()
	   SetValues(ThisSymbol, MaxNumberOfSymbols, NumberOfSpaces, NumberOfSymbols)
	   Do
	      OutputChars(NumberOfSpaces, Space)
	      OutputChars(NumberOfSymbols, ThisSymbol)
	      Console.WriteLine() 'move to new line
	      AdjustValuesForNextRow(NumberOfSpaces, NumberOfSymbols)
	   Loop Until NumberOfSymbols > MaxNumberOfSymbols
	   Console.ReadLine()
	End Sub
	
	End Module</pre>

Pascal	<pre>program Project2;
	
	{$APPTYPE CONSOLE}
	
	uses
	   SysUtils;
	   const Space = ' '; // constant to give a space a name
	   var NumberOfSpaces, NumberOfSymbols : integer;
	   var MaxNumberOfSymbols : integer;
	   var SymbolsThisSymbol : char;
	procedure InputMaxNumberOfSymbols(var Number : integer);
	begin
	   repeat
	      WriteLn('How many symbols make the base?');
	      Write('Input an odd number: ');
	      ReadLn(Number);
	   until Number MOD 2 = 1;
	end;
	
	procedure SetValues(var Symbol : char; var MaxSymbols, Spaces, Symbols : integer);
	begin
	   Write('What symbol do you want to use? ');
	   ReadLn(Symbol);
	   InputMaxNumberOfSymbols(MaxSymbols);
	   Spaces := (MaxSymbols + 1) DIV 2;
	   Symbols := 1;
	end;</pre>

```
procedure OutputChars(Number : integer; Symbol : char);
var Count : integer;
begin
   for Count := 1 to Number do
      Write(Symbol);
end;

procedure AdjustValuesForNextRow(var Spaces, Symbols : integer);
begin
   Spaces := Spaces - 1;
   Symbols := Symbols + 2;
end;

// ********** main program starts here *************
begin
   SetValues(ThisSymbol, MaxNumberOfSymbols, NumberOfSpaces, NumberOfSymbols);
   repeat
      OutputChars(NumberOfSpaces, Space);
      OutputChars(NumberOfSymbols, ThisSymbol);
      WriteLn; // move to new line
      AdjustValuesForNextRow(NumberOfSpaces, NumberOfSymbols);
   until NumberOfSymbols > MaxNumberOfSymbols;
   ReadLn;    // to keep the window open
end.
```


Discussion Point:

Can you see how the two procedures `OutputSpaces` and `OutputSymbols` have been replaced by a single procedure `OutputChars` without changing the effect of the program?

Summary

- Declaration of subroutines (functions and procedures) is done before the main program body.
- Calling a procedure is a program statement.
- Calling a function is done within an expression, for example an assignment.
- VB.NET and Pascal functions return exactly one value.
- Parameters can be passed to a subroutine. This is known as the interface.
- VB.NET and Pascal pass parameters by value, as a default, but can return one or more values via parameters if they are declared as reference parameters.
- In Python, parameters can only pass values into a subroutine. The only way to update a value of a variable in the calling program is to return one or more values from a function.
- When a subroutine is defined, parameters are the 'placeholders' for values passed into a subroutine.
- Arguments are the values passed to the subroutine when it is called.

Exam-style Questions

1 Write program code for a procedure `OutputTimesTable` that takes one integer parameter, `n`, and outputs the times table for `n`. For example the procedure call `OutputTimesTable(5)` should produce:

```
 1 x 5 = 5
 2 x 5 = 10
 3 x 5 = 15
 4 x 5 = 20
 5 x 5 = 25
 6 x 5 = 30
 7 x 5 = 35
 8 x 5 = 40
 9 x 5 = 45
10 x 5 = 50
```

[6]

2 Write program code for a function `isDivisible()` that takes two integer parameters, `x` and `y`. The function is to return the value True or False to indicate whether `x` is exactly divisible by `y`. For example, `isDivisible(24, 6)` should return True and `isDivisible(24, 7)` should return False. [6]

3 A poultry farm packs eggs into egg boxes. Each box takes six eggs. Boxes must not contain fewer than six eggs.

Write program code for a procedure `EggsIntoBoxes` that takes an integer parameter, `NumberOfEggs`. The procedure is to calculate how many egg boxes can be filled with the given number of eggs and how many eggs will be left over. The procedure is to return two values as parameters, `NumberOfBoxes` and `EggsLeftOver`. [9]

Chapter 15
Software Development

Learning objectives

By the end of this chapter you should be able to:

- show understanding of the design, coding and testing stages in the program development cycle
- show understanding of how to write, translate, test and run a high-level language program
- describe features found in a typical Integrated Development Environment (IDE):
  - for coding, including context-sensitive prompts
  - for initial error detection, including dynamic syntax checks
  - for presentation, including prettyprint, expand and collapse code blocks
  - for debugging, including: single stepping, breakpoints, variables/expressions report window
- show understanding of ways of exposing faults in programs and ways of avoiding faults
- locate and identify the different types of errors (syntax errors, logic errors and run-time errors)
- correct identified errors
- choose suitable data for black-box testing
- understand the need for stub testing
- perform white-box testing by selecting suitable data and using a trace table
- identify any error(s) in the algorithm by using the completed trace table and amend the algorithm if required
- make amendments to an algorithm and data structure in response to specification changes
- analyse an existing program and make amendments to enhance functionality.

15.01 Stages in the program development cycle

Problem solving

The first step in solving a problem is to define it clearly. This is usually done in structured English (See Chapter 11, Section 11.02) and is known as a 'specification'.

The next step is planning a solution. Sometimes there is more than one solution. You need to decide which is the most appropriate.

The third step is to decide how to solve the problem:

- bottom-up: start with a small sub-problem and then build on this
- top-down: stepwise refinement using pseudocode, flowcharts or structure charts.

Design

You have a solution in mind. How do you design the solution in detail? Chapter 11 (Section 11.04) showed that an identifier table is a good starting point. This leads you to thinking about data structures: do you need a 1D array or a 2D array to store data while it is processed? Do you need a file to store data long-term?

Plan your algorithm by drawing a flowchart or writing pseudocode.

Coding

When you have designed your solution you may need to choose a suitable high-level programming language. If you know more than one programming language, you have to weigh up the pros and cons of each one. Looking at Chapter 13, you need to decide which programming language would best suit the problem you are trying to solve and which language you are most familiar with.

You implement your algorithm by converting your pseudocode into program code. Depending on your editor you may have some helpful facilities (for features to expect see Section 15.02).

Some syntax errors may be flagged up by your editor, so you can correct these as you go along. A **syntax error** is a 'grammatical' error, in which a program statement does not follow the rules of the high-level language constructs.

KEY TERMS

Syntax error: an error in which a program statement does not follow the rules of the language

Translation

Some syntax errors may only become apparent when you are using an interpreter or compiler to translate your program. Interpreters and compilers work differently (see Chapter 7, Section 7.05, and Chapter 20, Section 20.05). When a program compiles successfully, you know there will be no syntax errors remaining.

This is not the case with interpreted programs. Only statements that are about to be executed will be syntax checked. So, if your program has not been thoroughly tested, it may even have syntax errors remaining.

Figure 15.01 gives an example of how a compiler flags a syntax error. The compiler stops when it first notices a syntax error. The error is often on the previous line. The compiler can't tell until it gets to the next line of code and finds an unexpected keyword.

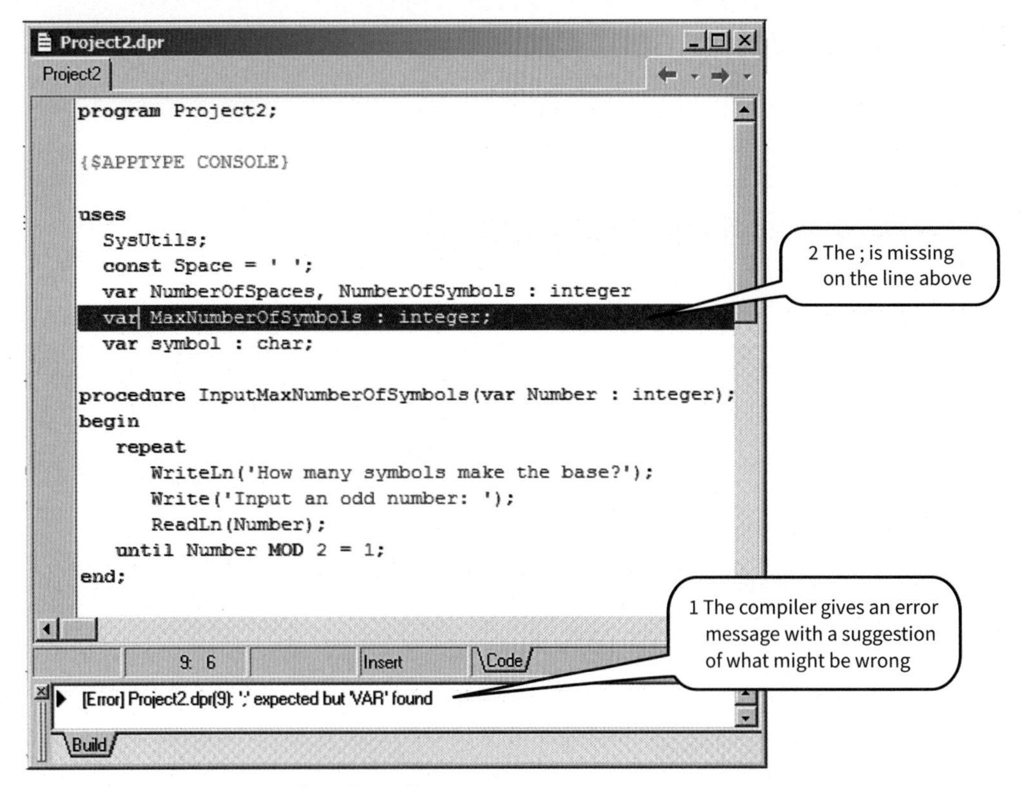

Figure 15.01 Syntax error in a Pascal program

Execution

When you start writing programs you may find it takes several attempts before the program compiles. When it finally does, you can execute it. It may 'crash', meaning that it stops working. In this case, you need to debug the code. The program may run and give you some output. This is the Eureka moment: 'it works!!!!'. But does the program do what it was meant to do?

Testing

Only thorough testing can ensure the program really works under all circumstances (see Sections 15.03 to 15.05).

Discussion Point:

Do you think that all programs can be totally error-free?

15.02 Features found in a typical Integrated Development Environment (IDE)

Prettyprinting

Prettyprint refers to the presentation of the program code typed into an editor. It includes indentation, colour-coding of keywords and comments.

Python

IDLE (see Figure 15.02) automatically colour-codes keywords, built-in function calls, comments, strings and the identifier in a function header. Indentation is automatic. When you need to unindent after a block of statements, delete the spaces provided.

```
ProcedureExample.py - C:/Users/Sylvia/My Programming/CIE Book/...
File  Edit  Format  Run  Options  Windows  Help

def OutputSymbols(NumberOfSymbols, Symbol):
    for Count in range(NumberOfSymbols):
        print(Symbol, end='')
    print()

# ********* main program starts here **************
OutputSymbols(5, '*')

Ln: 9 Col: 0
```

Figure 15.02 Prettyprint in IDLE

VB.NET

The editor provided by Visual Studio (see Figure 15.03) automatically colour-codes keywords, object references (such as `Console`), comments and strings. The editor automatically indents blocks of code correctly.

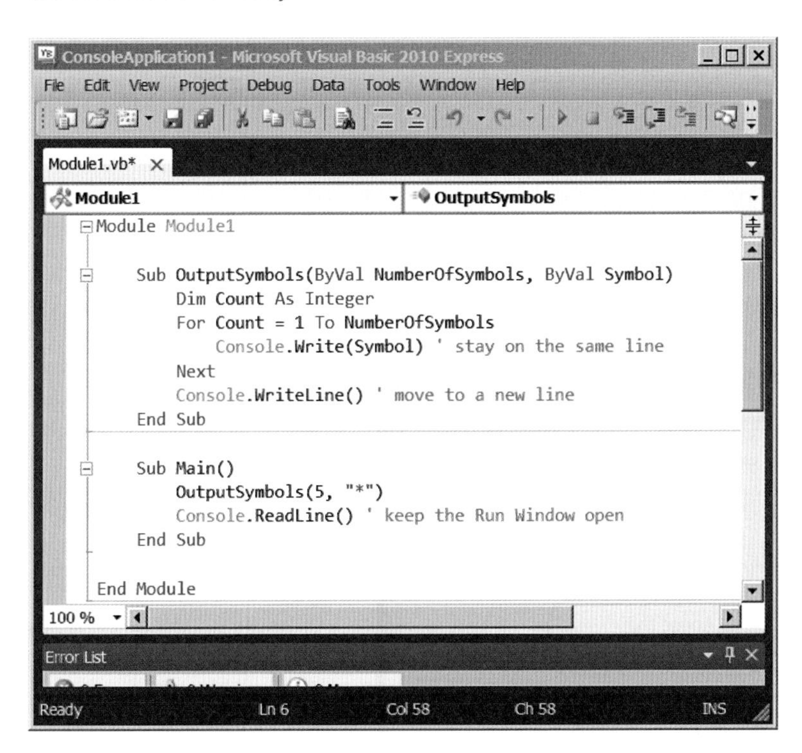
ConsoleApplication1 - Microsoft Visual Basic 2010 Express
File Edit View Project Debug Data Tools Window Help
Module1.vb*
Module1
OutputSymbols
Module Module1
Sub OutputSymbols(ByVal NumberOfSymbols, ByVal Symbol)
Dim Count As Integer
For Count = 1 To NumberOfSymbols
Console.Write(Symbol) ' stay on the same line
Next
Console.WriteLine() ' move to a new line
End Sub
Sub Main()
OutputSymbols(5, "*")
Console.ReadLine() ' keep the Run Window open
End Sub
End Module
100 %
Error List
Ready
Ln 6
Col 58
Ch 58
INS

Figure 15.03 Prettyprint in Visual Studio

Pascal

This Delphi editor (see Figure 15.04) emboldens keywords and colour-codes strings, comments and system directives (such as {APPTYPE CONSOLE}). When the programmer indents a line of code, the next line is automatically indented by the same amount.

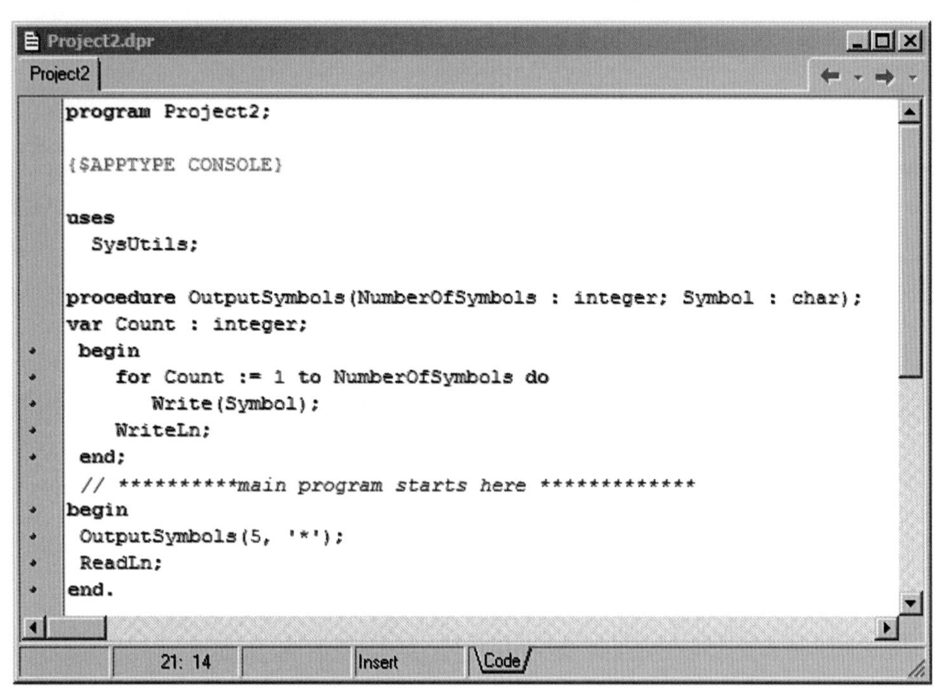

Project2.dpr
Project2
program Project2;
{$APPTYPE CONSOLE}
uses
SysUtils;
procedure OutputSymbols(NumberOfSymbols : integer; Symbol : char);
var Count : integer;
begin
for Count := 1 to NumberOfSymbols do
Write(Symbol);
WriteLn;
end;
// **********main program starts here *************
begin
OutputSymbols(5, '*');
ReadLn;
end.
21: 14
Insert
Code

Figure 15.04 Prettyprint in the Delphi editor

Context-sensitive prompts

This feature displays hints or a choice of keywords and available identifiers appropriate at the current insertion point of the program code.

Figure 15.05 shows an example of the Visual Studio editor responding to text typed in by the programmer.

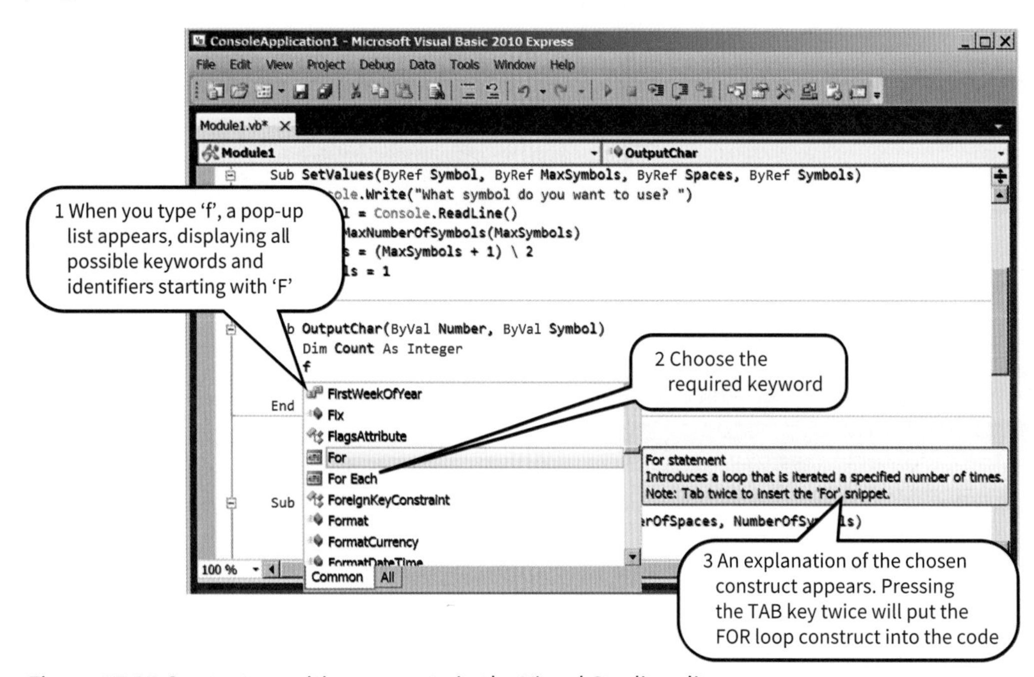

Figure 15.05 Context-sensitive prompts in the Visual Studio editor

In Figure 15.06, the Python editor, IDLE, shows the required parameters after a function identifier has been typed in by the programmer.

```
*procedure3.py - C:/Users/Sylvia/My Programming/CIE Book/Ch13/python/proced...
File Edit Format Run Options Windows Help
SPACE = ' '  # constant to give a space a name
def InputMaxNumberOfSymbols():
   Number = 0
   while Number % 2 == 0:
      print("How many symbols make the base?")
      Number = int(input("Input an odd number: "))
   return Number

def SetValues():
   Symbol = input("What symbol do you want to use? ")
   MaxSymbols = InputMaxNumberOfSymbols()
   Spaces = (MaxSymbols + 1) // 2
   Symbols = 1
   return Symbol, MaxSymbols, Spaces, Symbols

def OutputChar(Number, Symbol):
   for Count in range(Number):
      print(
         print(value, ..., sep=' ', end='\n', file=sys.stdout)
Ln: 18 Col: 12
```

Pop-up text shows that print list elements are separated by commas and the parameters that you can specify (the separator (sep) and how a line should end)

Figure 15.06 Context-sensitive prompts in IDLE

Dynamic syntax checks

When a line has been typed, some editors perform syntax checks and alert the programmer to errors.

Figure 15.07 shows an example of the Visual Studio editor responding to a syntax error.

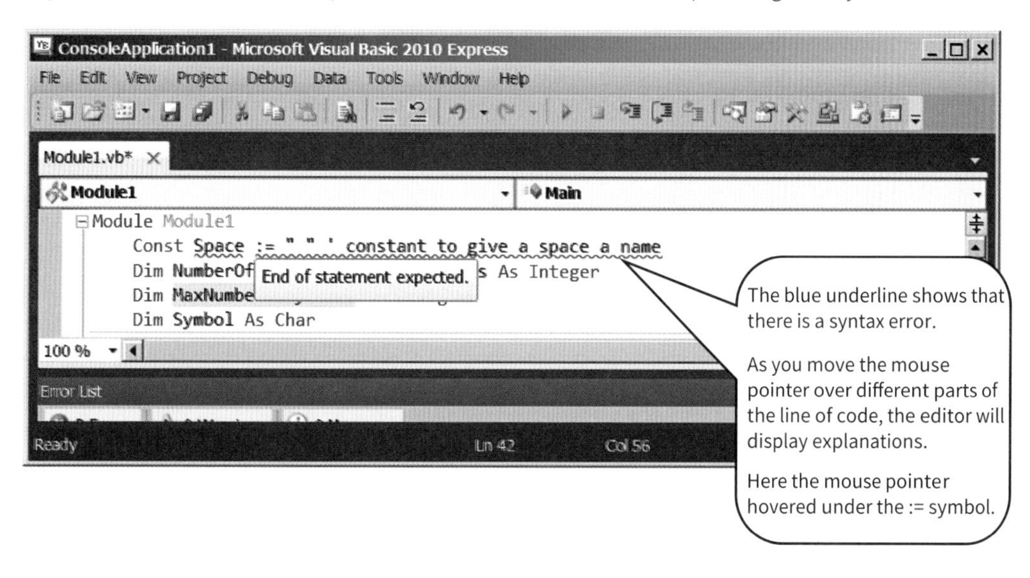

Figure 15.07 Dynamic syntax check in the Visual Studio editor

Expanding and collapsing code blocks

When working on program code consisting of many lines of code, it saves excessive scrolling if you can collapse blocks of statements.

Figure 15.08 shows the Visual Studio editor window with the procedures collapsed, so the programmer can see the global variable declarations and the main program body. The procedure headings are still visible to help the programmer supply the correct arguments when calling one of these procedures from the main program.

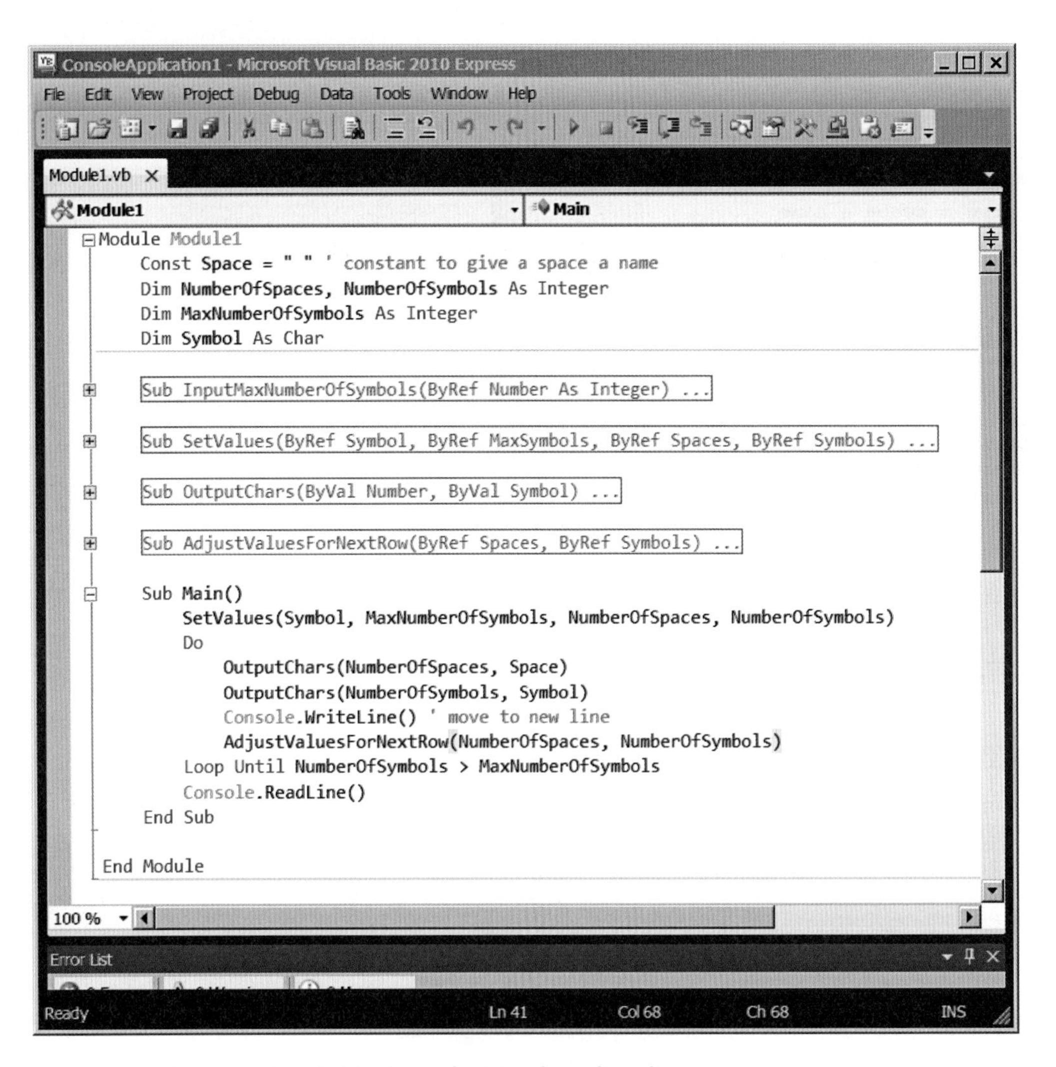
ConsoleApplication1 - Microsoft Visual Basic 2010 Express
File Edit View Project Debug Data Tools Window Help
Module1.vb
Module1
Main
Module Module1
Const Space = " " ' constant to give a space a name
Dim NumberOfSpaces, NumberOfSymbols As Integer
Dim MaxNumberOfSymbols As Integer
Dim Symbol As Char
Sub InputMaxNumberOfSymbols(ByRef Number As Integer) ...
Sub SetValues(ByRef Symbol, ByRef MaxSymbols, ByRef Spaces, ByRef Symbols) ...
Sub OutputChars(ByVal Number, ByVal Symbol) ...
Sub AdjustValuesForNextRow(ByRef Spaces, ByRef Symbols) ...
Sub Main()
SetValues(Symbol, MaxNumberOfSymbols, NumberOfSpaces, NumberOfSymbols)
Do
OutputChars(NumberOfSpaces, Space)
OutputChars(NumberOfSymbols, Symbol)
Console.WriteLine() ' move to new line
AdjustValuesForNextRow(NumberOfSpaces, NumberOfSymbols)
Loop Until NumberOfSymbols > MaxNumberOfSymbols
Console.ReadLine()
End Sub
End Module
100 %
Error List
Ready
Ln 41
Col 68
Ch 68
INS

Figure 15.08 Collapsed code blocks in the Visual Studio editor

TASK 15.01

Investigate the facilities in the editors you have available. If you have a choice of editors, you may like to use the editor with the most helpful facilities.

15.03 Testing strategies

Finding syntax errors is easy. The compiler/interpreter will find them for you and usually gives you a hint as to what is wrong.

Much more difficult to find are **logic errors** and **run-time errors**. A run-time error occurs when program execution comes to an unexpected halt or 'crash' or it goes into an infinite loop and 'freezes'.

KEY TERMS

Logic error: an error in the logic of the solution that causes it not to behave as intended

Run-time error: an error that causes program execution to crash or freeze

Both of these types of error can only be found by careful testing. The danger of such errors is that they may only manifest themselves under certain circumstances. If a program crashes every time it is executed, it is obvious there is an error. If the program is used frequently and appears to work until a certain set of data causes a malfunction, that is much more difficult to discover without perhaps serious consequences.

Stub testing

When you develop a user interface, you may wish to test it before you have implemented all the facilities. You can write a 'stub' for each procedure (see Figure 15.09). The procedure body only contains an output statement to acknowledge that the call was made. Each option the user chooses in the main program will call the relevant procedure.

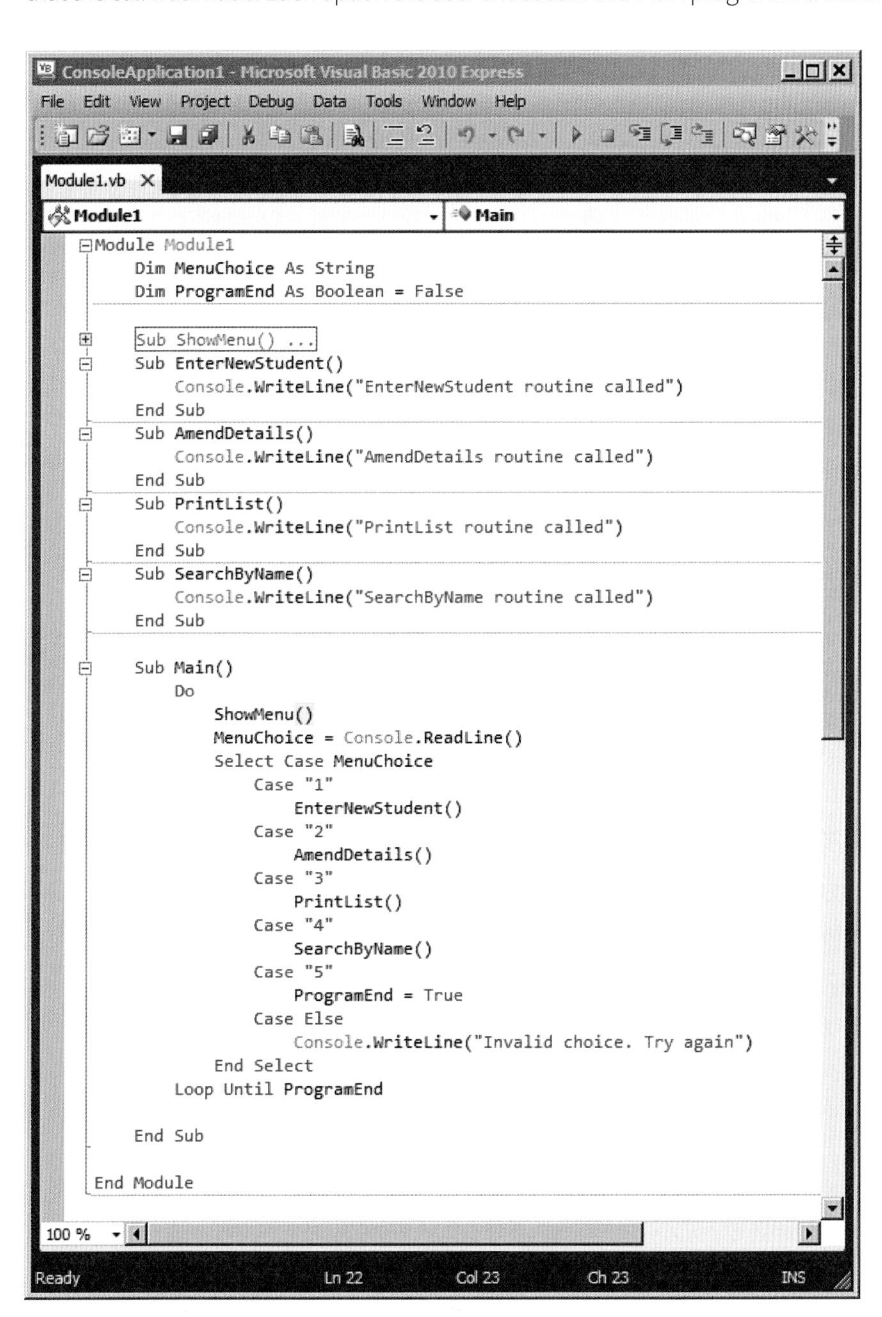


```
Module Module1
    Dim MenuChoice As String
    Dim ProgramEnd As Boolean = False

    Sub ShowMenu() ...
    Sub EnterNewStudent()
        Console.WriteLine("EnterNewStudent routine called")
    End Sub
    Sub AmendDetails()
        Console.WriteLine("AmendDetails routine called")
    End Sub
    Sub PrintList()
        Console.WriteLine("PrintList routine called")
    End Sub
    Sub SearchByName()
        Console.WriteLine("SearchByName routine called")
    End Sub

    Sub Main()
        Do
            ShowMenu()
            MenuChoice = Console.ReadLine()
            Select Case MenuChoice
                Case "1"
                    EnterNewStudent()
                Case "2"
                    AmendDetails()
                Case "3"
                    PrintList()
                Case "4"
                    SearchByName()
                Case "5"
                    ProgramEnd = True
                Case Else
                    Console.WriteLine("Invalid choice. Try again")
            End Select
        Loop Until ProgramEnd

    End Sub

End Module
```

Figure 15.09 VB.NET stub testing

Black-box testing

As the programmer, you can see your program code and your testing will involve knowledge of the code (see the next section, about white-box testing).

As part of thorough testing, a program should also be tested by other people, who do not see the program code and don't know how the solution was coded.

Such program testers will look at the program specification to see what the program is meant to do, devise **test data** and work out expected results. Test data usually consists of normal data values, boundary data values and erroneous data values.

The tester then runs the program with the test data and records their results. This method of testing is called **black-box testing** because the tester can't see inside the program code: the program is a 'black box'.

Where the actual results don't match the expected results, a problem exists. This needs further investigation by the programmer to find the reason for this discrepancy and correct the program (see Section 15.06). Once black-box testing has established that there is an error, other methods (see Sections 15.04 and 15.05) have to be employed to find the lines of code that need correcting.

KEY TERMS

Test data: carefully chosen values that will test a program

Black-box testing: comparing expected results with actual results when a program is run

White-box testing

How can we check that code works correctly? We choose suitable test data that checks every path through the code.

KEY TERMS

White-box testing: testing every path through the program code

WORKED EXAMPLE 15.01

White-box testing of pseudocode

This is the pseudocode from Worked Example 11.02 in Chapter 11:

```
INPUT Number1
INPUT Number2
INPUT Number3
IF Number1 > Number2
   THEN              // Number1 is bigger
      IF Number1 > Number3
         THEN
            OUTPUT Number1
         ELSE
            OUTPUT Number3
      ENDIF
   ELSE              // Number2 is bigger
      IF Number2 > Number3
         THEN
            OUTPUT Number2
         ELSE
            OUTPUT Number3
      ENDIF
ENDIF
```

To test it, we need four sets of numbers with the following characteristics:

- The first number is the largest.
- The first number larger than the second number; the third number is the largest.
- The second number is the largest.
- The second number is larger than the first number; the third number is the largest.

Note that it does not matter what exact values are chosen as test data. The important point is that the values differ in such a way that each part of the nested `IF` statement is checked. Table 15.01 lists four sets of test data and the results from them. The parts of the algorithm not entered for a particular set of data are greyed out. This makes it easier to see that each part has been checked after all four tests have been done.

Line of algorithm	Test 1	Test 2	Test 3	Test 4
`INPUT Number1`	15	12	12	8
`INPUT Number2`	12	8	15	12
`INPUT Number3`	8	15	8	15
`IF Number1 > Number2`	TRUE	TRUE	FALSE	FALSE
`THEN` `IF Number1 > Number3`	TRUE	FALSE		
`THEN` `OUTPUT Number1`	Output 15			

`ELSE`
`OUTPUT Number3`
`ENDIF`
		Output 15		

`ELSE` `IF Number2 > Number3`			TRUE	FALSE
`THEN` `OUTPUT Number2`			Output 15	

`ELSE`
`OUTPUT Number3`
`ENDIF`
`ENDIF`
				Output 15

Table 15.01 Testing the validity of the nested IF statement

For more white-box testing methods see Sections 15.04 and 15.05.

15.04 Program testing using the IDE

Debugging is the action of finding and correcting errors ('bugs') in a program. An IDE often contains features to help with debugging.

KEY TERMS

Debugging: finding and correcting errors in a program

Python

To debug using IDLE, from the Python Shell (see Figure 15.10), choose Debugger from the Debug menu.

Open the source program from the File menu. To set a breakpoint, right-click on the line you want to set the breakpoint on.

Start running the program by clicking the Go button in the Debug Control window. The program stops at the breakpoint (Figure 15.11(a)). Then click the Step button to execute one instruction at a time.

The Debug Control window (Figure 15.11(b)) shows which line number is about to be executed (line 4 in the example). The contents of all variables are also displayed in the Debug Control window.

```
*Python Shell*
File  Edit  Shell  Debug  Options  Windows  Help
Python 3.2.3 (default, Apr 11 2012, 07:12:16) [MSC v.1500 64 bit (AMD64)] on win
32
Type "copyright", "credits" or "license()" for more information.
>>>
[DEBUG ON]
>>> ================================ RESTART ================================
[DEBUG ON]
>>>
7
8
                                                                 Ln: 10 Col: 0
```

Figure 15.10 Python Shell with Debugger switched on

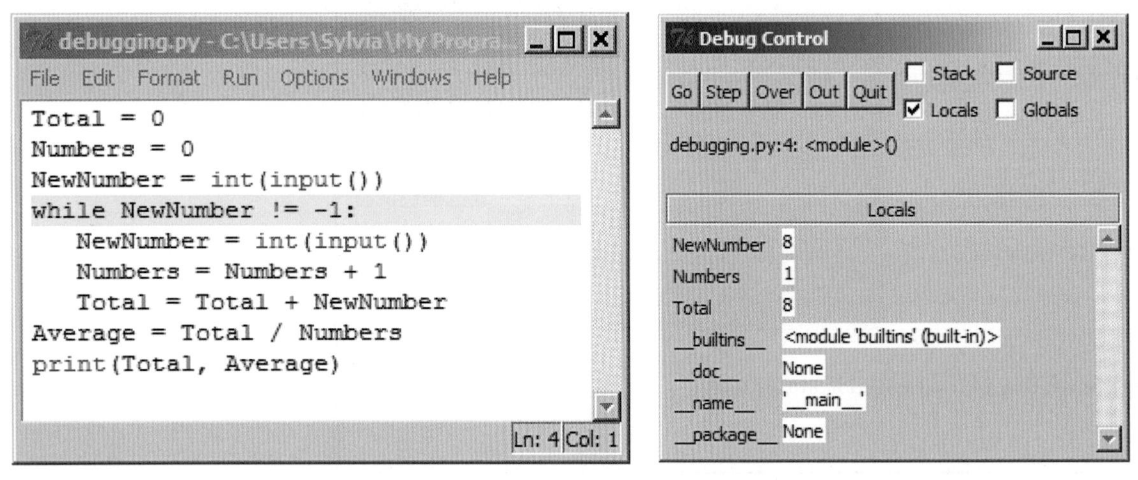

Figure 15.11 (a) Python program showing a breakpoint and (b) the Debug Control window

VB.NET

In Visual Studio (see Figure 15.12(a)), you can set breakpoints by clicking in the left margin of the editor.

Click on Run to run the program and enter data (see Figure 15.12(b)). When your program reaches the breakpoint, use the 'Step Into' button ( ) to single-step through your program.

To set up a variable watch window, select Windows from the Debug menu and choose Watch. A table is displayed at the bottom of the editor (see Figure 15.12(a)) and you can type in the variable names you want to inspect.

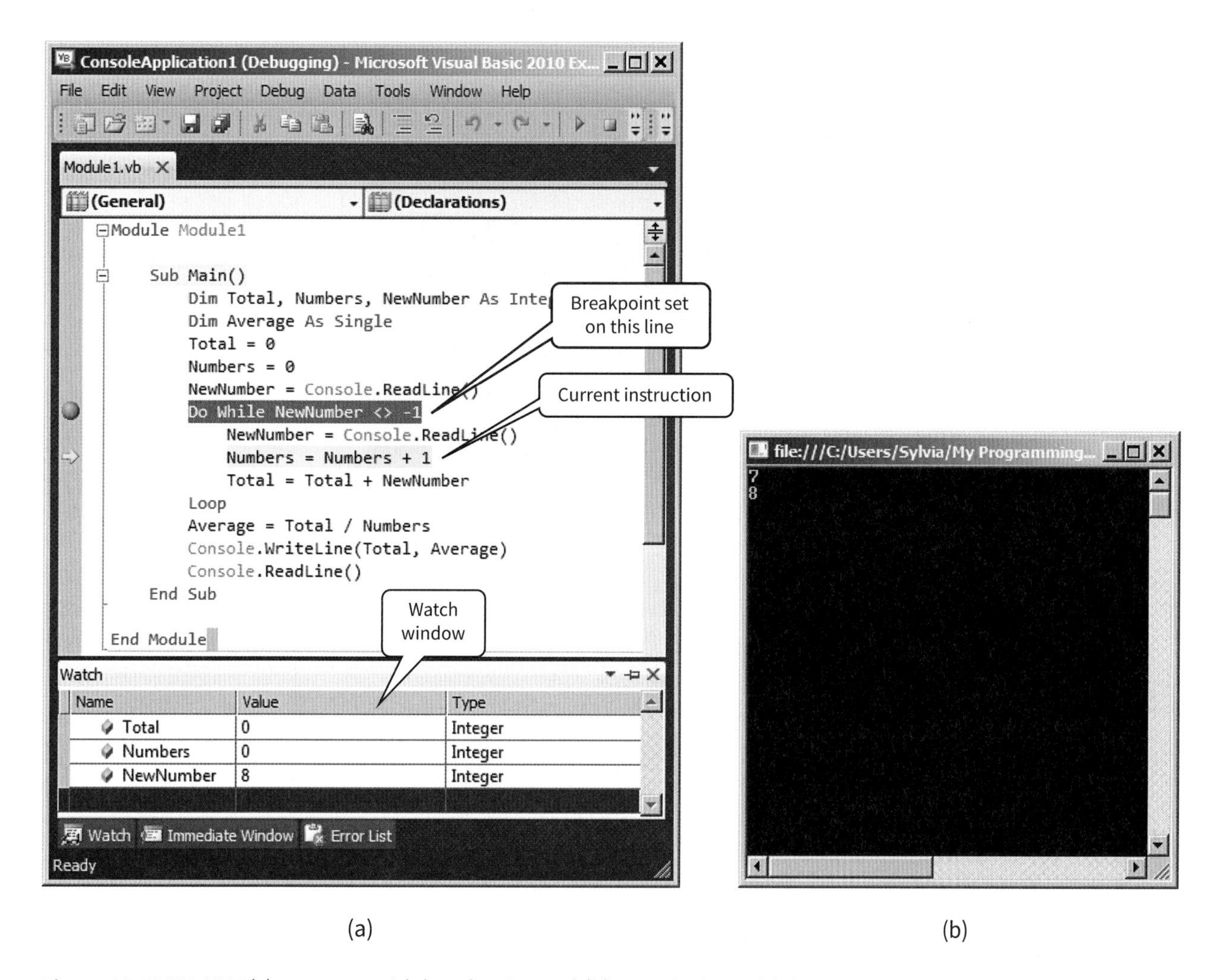

Figure 15.12 VB.NET (a) program with breakpoint and (b) run window with input

Pascal

In the Delphi editor, you need to switch the debugger on before compiling your program: in the Tools menu, select Debugger Options and ensure the Integrated Debugger option is ticked.

You can now set breakpoints by clicking in the left margin of the editor (see Figure 15.13(a)).

Click on Run. When your program reaches the breakpoint, use the 'Trace into' button ( ) to single-step through your program, entering data (see Figure 15.13(b)).

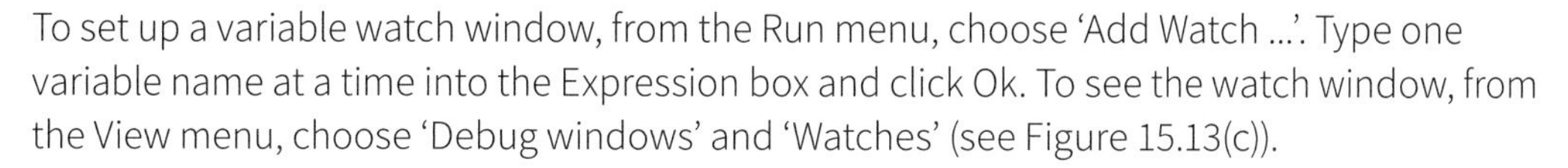

To set up a variable watch window, from the Run menu, choose 'Add Watch ...'. Type one variable name at a time into the Expression box and click Ok. To see the watch window, from the View menu, choose 'Debug windows' and 'Watches' (see Figure 15.13(c)).

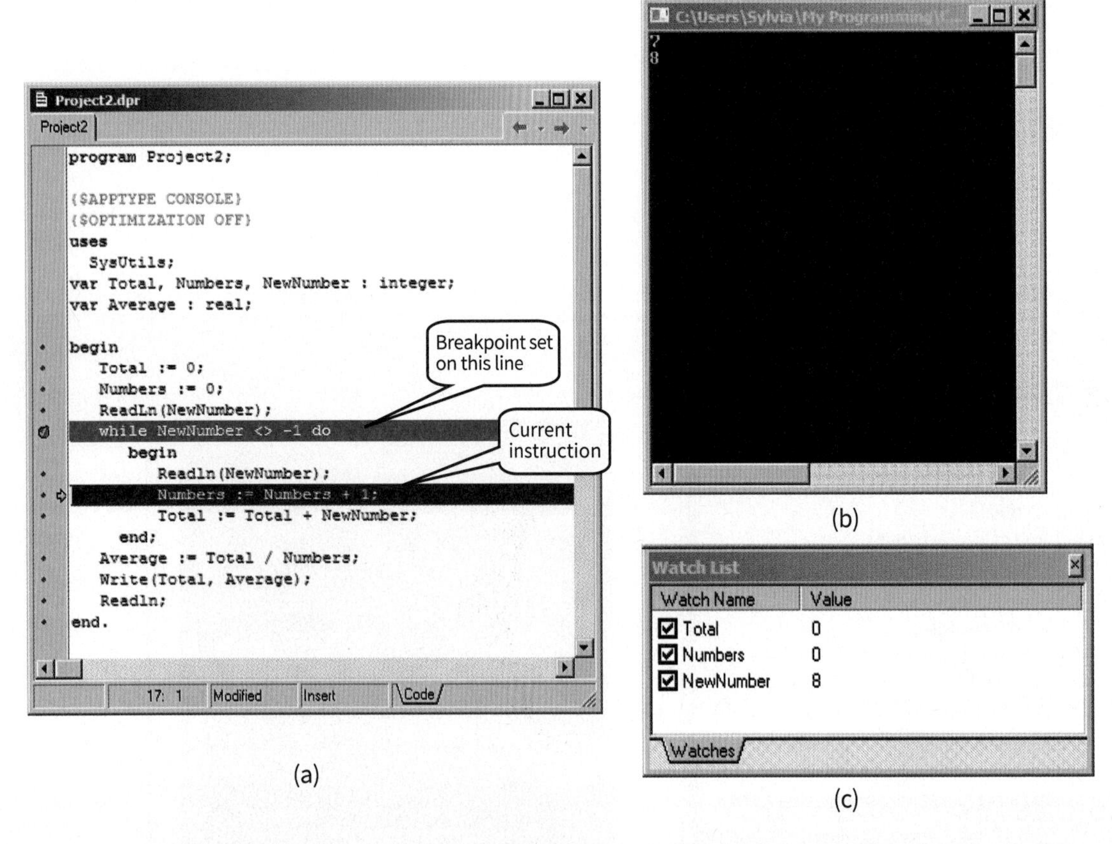

Figure 15.13 Pascal (a) program with breakpoint, (b) run window with input and (c) watch window

15.05 Dry-running an algorithm

A good way of checking that an algorithm works as intended is to **dry-run** the algorithm using a **trace table** and different test data.

The idea is to write down the current contents of all variables and conditional values at each step of the algorithm.

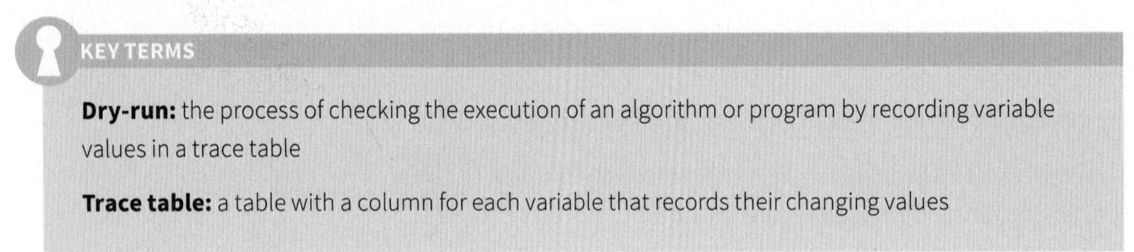

KEY TERMS

Dry-run: the process of checking the execution of an algorithm or program by recording variable values in a trace table

Trace table: a table with a column for each variable that records their changing values

WORKED EXAMPLE 15.02

Tracing an algorithm

Here is the algorithm of the number-guessing game:

```
SecretNumber ← 34
INPUT "Guess a number: " Guess
NumberOfGuesses ← 1
REPEAT
   IF Guess = SecretNumber
      THEN
         OUTPUT "You took" NumberOfGuesses "guesses"
      ELSE
         IF Guess > SecretNumber
            THEN
               INPUT "Guess a smaller number: " Guess
            ELSE
               INPUT "Guess a larger number: " Guess
         ENDIF
         NumberOfGuesses ← NumberOfGuesses + 1
   ENDIF
UNTIL Guess = SecretNumber
```

To test the algorithm, construct a trace table (Table 15.02) with one column for each variable used in the algorithm and also for the condition `Guess > SecretNumber`

Now carefully look at each step of the algorithm and record what happens. Note that we do not tend to write down values that don't change. Here `SecretNumber` does not change after the initial assignment, so the column is left blank in subsequent rows.

SecretNumber	Guess	NumberOfGuesses	Guess > SecretNumber	Message
34	5	1	FALSE	...larger...
	55	2	TRUE	...smaller...
	30	3	FALSE	...larger...
	42	4	TRUE	...smaller...
	36	5	TRUE	...smaller...
	33	6	FALSE	...larger...
	34	7		... 7 guesses

Table 15.02 Trace table for number-guessing game

We only make an entry in a cell when an assignment occurs. Values remain in variables until they are overwritten. So a blank cell means that the value from the previous entry remains.

It is important to start filling in a new row in the trace table for each iteration (each time round the loop).

WORKED EXAMPLE 15.03

Tracing an algorithm

To test the improved algorithm of Worked Example 11.12 (bubble sort), dry-run the algorithm by completing the trace table (Table 15.03).

```
MaxIndex ← 7
n ← MaxIndex - 1
REPEAT
   NoMoreSwaps ← TRUE
   FOR j ← 1 TO n
      IF MyList[j] > MyList[j + 1]
         THEN
            Temp ← MyList[j]
            MyList[j] ← MyList[j + 1]
            MyList[j + 1] ← Temp
            NoMoreSwaps ← FALSE
      ENDIF
   ENDFOR
   n ← n - 1
UNTIL NoMoreSwaps = TRUE
```

Max Index	n	NoMoreSwaps	j	MyList[j] > MyList[j + 1]	Temp	MyList						
						[1]	[2]	[3]	[4]	[5]	[6]	[7]
7	6					5	34	98	7	41	19	25
		TRUE	1	FALSE								
			2	FALSE								
		FALSE	3	TRUE	98			7	98			
			4	TRUE	98				41	98		
			5	TRUE	98					19	98	
			6	TRUE	98						25	98
	5	TRUE	1	FALSE								
		FALSE	2	TRUE	34		7	34				
			3	FALSE								
			4	TRUE	41				19	41		
			5	TRUE	41					25	41	
	4	TRUE	1	FALSE								
			2	FALSE								
		FALSE	3	TRUE	34			19	34			
			4	TRUE	34				25	34		
	3	TRUE	1	FALSE								
			2	FALSE								
			3	FALSE								
	2											

Table 15.03 Trace table for improved bubble sort algorithm

TASK 15.02

Design a trace table for the following algorithm:

```
FUNCTION ConvertFromHex(HexString : STRING) RETURNS INTEGER
   DECLARE ValueSoFar, HexValue, HexLength, i : INTEGER
   DECLARE HexDigit : CHAR
   ValueSoFar ← 0
   HexLength ← Length(HexString)
   FOR i ← 1 TO HexLength

      HexDigit ← HexString[i]
      CASE OF HexDigit
         'A': HexValue ← 10
         'B': HexValue ← 11
         'C': HexValue ← 12
         'D': HexValue ← 13
         'E': HexValue ← 14
         'F': HexValue ← 15
         OTHERWISE HexValue ← StringToInt(HexDigit)
      ENDCASE
      ValueSoFar ← ValueSoFar * 16 + HexValue
   ENDFOR
   RETURN ValueSoFar
ENDFUNCTION
```

Dry-run the function call `ConvertFromHex('A5')` by completing the trace table.

15.06 Corrective maintenance

Maintaining programs is not like maintaining a mechanical device. It doesn't need lubricating and parts don't wear out. **Corrective maintenance** of a program refers to the work required when a program is not working correctly due to a logic error or because of a run-time error. Sometimes program errors don't become apparent for a long time because it is only under very rare circumstances that there is an unexpected result or the program crashes. These circumstances might arise because part of the program is not used often or because the data on an occasion includes extreme values.

KEY TERMS

Corrective maintenance: correcting identified errors

When a problem is reported, the programmer needs to find out what is causing the bug. To find a bug, a programmer either uses the features found in an IDE (see Section 15.04) or a trace table (see Section 15.05).

TASK 15.03

Design a trace table for the following algorithm:

```
INPUT BinaryString
StringLength ← Length(BinaryString)
FOR i ← 1 TO StringLength
   Bit ← BinaryString[i]
   BitValue ← IntegerValue(Bit) // convert string to integer
   DenaryValue ← DenaryValue + 2 + BitValue
ENDFOR
```

1 Dry-run the algorithm using `'101'` as the input. Complete the trace table.

2 The result should be 5. Can you find the error in the code and correct it?

15.07 Adaptive maintenance

Programs often get changed to make them perform functions they were not originally designed to do.

For example, the Connect 4 game introduced in Chapter 12 (Worked Example 12.03) allows two players, O and X, to play against each other. An amended version would be for one player to be the computer. This would mean a single player could try and win against the computer.

Adaptive maintenance is the action of making amendments to a program to enhance functionality or in response to specification changes.

KEY TERMS

Adaptive maintenance: amending a program to enhance functionality or in response to specification changes

TASK 15.04

Design the algorithm to simulate the computer playing the part of Player X in Connect 4.

Summary

- The stages of the program development cycle include design, coding and testing.
- Features of a typical integrated development environment (IDE) include context-sensitive prompts, dynamic syntax checks, prettyprint formatting and collapsible code blocks.
- Testing strategies include stub testing, black-box testing and white-box testing.
- Locating and correcting logic errors and run-time errors can be done by dry-running an algorithm using a trace table or using a debugger.
- Corrective maintenance means fixing bugs that have come to light during use of the program.
- Adaptive maintenance involves altering an algorithm and data structure in response to required changes.

Exam-style Questions

1 Consider this code for a function:

```
FUNCTION Binary(Number : INTEGER) : STRING
   DECLARE BinaryString : STRING
   DECLARE PlaceValue : INTEGER
   BinaryString ← '' // empty string
   PlaceValue ← 8
   REPEAT
      IF Number >= PlaceValue
         THEN
            BinaryString ← BinaryString & '1' // concatenates two strings
            Number ← Number - PlaceValue
         ELSE
            BinaryString ← BinaryString & '0'
            PlaceValue ← PlaceValue DIV 2
   UNTIL Number = 0
   RETURN BinaryString
ENDFUNCTION
```

a Dry-run the function call `Binary(11)` by completing the given trace table.

Number	BinaryString	PlaceValue	Number >= PlaceValue
11	''	8	

What is the return value? [5]

b **i** Now dry-run the function call `Binary(10)` by completing the given trace table.

Number	BinaryString	PlaceValue	Number >= PlaceValue
10	''	8	

What is the return value? [3]

ii The algorithm is supposed to convert a denary integer into the equivalent binary number, stored as a string of 0s and 1s. Explain the result of each dry-run and what needs changing in the given algorithm. [3]

Part 3 Advanced Theory

Chapter 16
Data Representation

Learning objectives

By the end of this chapter you should be able to:

- show understanding of why user-defined types are necessary
- define composite and non-composite types
- show understanding of methods of file organisation and of file access
- select an appropriate method of file organisation and file access for a given problem
- describe the format of binary floating-point real numbers
- normalise floating-point numbers and show understanding of the reasons for normalisation
- show understanding of the effects of changing the allocation of bits to mantissa and exponent in a floating-point representation
- convert binary floating-point real numbers into denary and vice versa
- show understanding of the consequences of a binary representation only being an approximation to the real number it represents and that binary representations can give rise to rounding errors
- show understanding of how underflow and overflow can occur.

16.01 User-defined data types

This chapter must start with a clarification. It is generally accepted that a programmer writes a program which is to be used by a 'user' in the same way that an operating system provides a 'user' interface. However, in the activity of programming the programmer now becomes the 'user' of the programming language. The term 'user-defined data type' applies to this latter type of user.

Non-composite user-defined data types

A non-composite data type has a definition which does not involve a reference to another type. The simple built-in types such as integer or real are obvious examples. When a programmer uses a simple built-in type the only requirement is for an identifier to be named with a defined type. A user-defined type has to be explicitly defined before an identifier can be created. Two examples are discussed here.

Enumerated data type

An **enumerated data type** defines a list of possible values. The following pseudocode shows two examples of type definitions:

```
TYPE
TDirections = (North, East, South, West)
TDays = (Monday, Tuesday, Wednesday, Thursday, Friday, Saturday, Sunday)
```

Variables can then be declared and assigned values, for example:

```
DECLARE Direction1 : TDirections
DECLARE StartDay : TDays
Direction1 ← North
StartDay ← Wednesday
```

It is important to note that the values of the enumerated type look like string values but they are not. They must not be enclosed in quote marks.

The values defined in an enumerated data type are ordinal. This means that they have an implied order of values. This makes the second example much more useful because the ordering can be put to many uses in a program. For example, a comparison statement can be used with the values and variables of the enumerated data type:

```
DECLARE Weekend : Boolean
DECLARE Day : TDays
Weekend = TRUE IF Day > Friday
```

KEY TERMS

Enumerated data type: a list of possible data values

Pointer data type

A pointer data type is used to reference a memory location. It may be used to construct dynamically varying data structures.

The pointer definition has to relate to the type of the variable that is being pointed to. The pseudocode for the definition of a pointer is illustrated by:

```
TYPE
TMyPointer = ^<Type name>
```

Declaration of a variable of pointer type does not require the caret symbol (^) to be used:

```
DECLARE MyPointer : TMyPointer
```

A special use of a pointer variable is to access the value stored at the address pointed to. The pointer variable is said to be 'dereferenced':

```
ValuePointedTo ← MyPointer^
```

Composite user-defined data types

A composite user-defined data type has a definition with reference to at least one other type. Three examples are considered here.

Record data type

A **record data type** is the most useful and therefore most widely used. It allows the programmer to collect together values with different data types when these form a coherent whole.

KEY TERMS

Record data type: a data type that contains a fixed number of components, which can be of different types

As an example, a record could be used for a program using employee data. Pseudocode for defining the type could be:

```
TYPE
TEmployeeRecord
    DECLARE EmployeeFirstName : STRING
    DECLARE EmployeeFamilyName : STRING
    DECLARE DateEmployed : DATE
    DECLARE Salary : CURRENCY
ENDTYPE
```

An individual data item can then be accessed using a dot notation:

```
Employee1.DateEmployed ← #16/05/2017#
```

A particular use of a record is for the implementation of a data structure where one or possibly two of the variables defined are pointer variables.

Set data type

A set data type allows a program to create sets and to apply the mathematical operations defined in set theory. The following is a representative list of the operations to be expected:

- union
- difference
- intersection

- include an element in the set
- exclude an element from the set
- check whether an element is in a set.

Objects and classes

In object-oriented programming, a program defines the classes to be used – they are all user-defined data types. Then for each class the objects must be defined. Chapter 27 (Section 27.03) has a full discussion of this subject.

Why are user-defined data types necessary?

When object-oriented programming is not being used a programmer may choose not to use any user-defined data types. However, for any reasonably large program it is likely that their use will make a program more understandable and less error-prone. Once the programmer has decided because of this advantage to use a data type that is not one of the built-in types then user-definition is inevitable. The use of, for instance, an integer variable is the same for any program. However, there cannot be a built-in record type because each different problem will need an individual definition of a record.

16.02 File organisation

In everyday computer usage, a wide variety of file types is encountered. Examples are graphic files, word-processing files, spreadsheet files and so on. Whatever the file type, the content is stored using a defined binary code that allows the file to be used in the way intended.

For the very specific task of storing data to be used by a computer program, there are only two defined file types. A file is either a text file or a **binary file**. A text file, as discussed in Chapter 13 (Section 13.09), contains data stored according to a defined character code as defined in Chapter 1 (Section 1.03). It is possible, by using a text editor, to create a text file. A binary file stores data in its internal representation, for example an integer value might be stored in two bytes in two's complement representation. This type of file will be created using a specific program.

The organisation of a binary file is based on the concept of a **record**. A file contains records and each record contains fields. Each field consists of a value.

KEY TERMS

Binary file: a file designed for storing data to be used by a computer program

Record: a collection of fields containing data values

Discussion Point:

A record is a user-defined data type. It is also a component of a file. Can there be or should there be any relationship between these two concepts?

Serial files

A serial file contains records which have no defined order. A typical use of a serial file would be for a bank to record transactions involving customer accounts. A program would be running. Each time there was a withdrawal or a deposit the program would receive the details as data input and would record these in a transaction file. The records would enter the file in chronological order but otherwise the file would have no ordering of the records.

A text file can be considered to be a type of serial file but it is different because the file has repeating lines which are defined by an end-of-line character or characters. There is no end-of-record character. A record in a serial file must have a defined format to allow data to be input and output correctly.

Sequential files

A sequential file has records that are ordered. It is the type of file suited to long-term storage of data. As such it should be the type of file that is considered as an alternative to a database. The discussion in Chapter 10 (Section 10.01) compared a text file with a database but the arguments for using a database remain the same if a sequential file is used for the comparison. In the banking scenario, a sequential file could be used as a master file for an individual customer account. Periodically, the transaction file would be read and all affected customer account master files would be updated.

In order to allow the sequential file to be ordered there has to be a key field for which the values are unique and sequential but not necessarily consecutive. It is worth emphasising the difference between key fields and primary keys in a database table, where the values are required to be unique but not to be sequential. In a sequential file, a particular record is found by sequentially reading the value of the key field until the required value is found.

Direct-access files

Direct-access files are sometimes referred to as 'random-access' files but, as with random-access memory, the randomness is only that the access is not defined by a sequential reading of the file. For large files, direct access is attractive because of the time that would be taken to search through a sequential file. In an ideal scenario, data in a direct-access file would be stored in an identifiable record which could be located immediately when required. Unfortunately, this is not possible. Instead, data is stored in an identifiable record but finding it may involve an initial direct access to a nearby record followed by a limited serial search.

The choice of the position chosen for a record must be calculated using data in the record so that the same calculation can be carried out when subsequently there is a search for the data. The normal method is to use a hashing algorithm. This takes as input the value for the key field and outputs a value for the position of the record relative to the start of the file. The hashing algorithm must take into account the potential maximum length of the file, that is, the number of records the file will store. A simple example of a hashing algorithm, if the key field has a numeric value, is to divide the value by a suitably large number and use the remainder from the division to define the position. This method will not create unique positions. If a hash position is calculated that duplicates one already calculated by a different key, the next position in the file is used. This is why a search will involve a direct access possibly followed by a limited serial search.

File access

Once a file organisation has been chosen and the data has been entered into a file, the question now to be considered is how this data is to be used. If an individual data item is to be read then the access method for a serial file is to successively read record by record until the required data is found. If the data is stored in a sequential file the process is similar but only the value in the key field has to be read. For a direct-access file, the value in the key field is submitted to the hashing algorithm which then provides the same value for the position in the file that was provided when the algorithm was used at the time of data input.

File access might also be needed to delete or edit data. The normal approach with a sequential file is to create a new version of the file. Data is copied from the old file to the new file until the record is reached which needs deleting or editing. If deletion is needed, reading and copying of the old file continues from the next record. If a record has changed, an edited version of the record is written to the new file and then the remaining records are copied to the new file. For a direct-access file there is no need to create a new file (unless the file has become full). A deleted record can have a flag set so that in a subsequent reading process the record is skipped over.

Serial file organisation is well suited to batch processing or for backing up data on magnetic tape. However, if a program needs a file in which individual data items might be read, updated or deleted then direct-access file organisation is the most suitable and serial file organisation the least suitable.

16.03 Real numbers

A real number is one with a fractional part. When we write down a value for a real number in the denary system we have a choice. We can use a simple representation or we can use an exponential notation (sometimes referred to as scientific notation). In this latter case we have options. For example, the number 25.3 might alternatively be written as:

$$.253 \times 10^2 \quad \text{or} \quad 2.53 \times 10^1 \quad \text{or} \quad 25.3 \times 10^0 \quad \text{or} \quad 253 \times 10^{-1}$$

For this number, the simple expression is best but if a number is very large or very small the exponential notation is the only sensible choice.

Floating-point and fixed-point representations

A binary code must be used for storing a real number in a computer system. One possibility is to use a fixed-point representation. In this option, an overall number of bits is chosen with a defined number of bits for the whole number part and the remainder for the fractional part. The alternative is a **floating-point representation**. The format for a floating-point number can be generalised as:

$$\pm M \times R^E$$

In this option a defined number of bits are used for what is called the significand or mantissa, ±M. The remaining bits are used for the exponent or exrad, E. The radix, R is not stored in the representation; it has an implied value of 2.

KEY TERMS

Floating-point representation: a representation of real numbers that stores a value for the mantissa and a value for the exponent

To illustrate the differences between the two representations a very simple example can be used. Let's consider that a real number is to be stored in eight bits.

For the fixed-point option, a possible choice would be to use the most significant bit as a sign bit and the next five bits for the whole number part leaving two bits for the fractional part.

Some important non-zero values in this representation are shown in Table 16.01. (The bits are shown with a gap to indicate the implied position of the binary point.)

Description	Binary code	Denary equivalent
Largest positive value	011111 11	31.75
Smallest positive value	000000 01	0.25
Smallest **magnitude** negative value	100000 01	–0.25
Largest **magnitude** negative value	111111 11	–31.75

Table 16.01 Example fixed-point representations (using sign and magnitude)

For a floating-point representation, a possible choice would be four bits for the mantissa and four bits for the exponent with each using two's complement representation. The exponent is stored as a signed integer. The mantissa has to be stored as a fixed-point real value. The question now is where the binary point should be.

Two of the options for the mantissa being expressed in four bits are shown in Table 16.02(a) and Table 16.02(b). In each case, the denary equivalent is shown and the position of the implied binary point is shown by a gap. Table 16.02(c) shows the three largest magnitude positive and negative values for integer coding that will be used for the exponent.

a)

First bit pattern for a real value	Real value in denary
011 1	3.5
011 0	3.0
010 1	2.5
101 0	–3.0
100 1	–3.5
100 0	–4.0

b)

Second bit pattern for a real value	Real value in denary
0 111	.875
0 110	.75
0 101	.625
1 010	–.75
1 001	–.875
1 000	–1.0

c)

Integer bit pattern	Integer value in denary
0111	7
0110	6
0101	5
1010	–6
1001	–7
1000	–8

Table 16.02 Coding a fixed-point real value in eight bits (four for the mantissa and four for the exponent)

It can be seen that having the mantissa with the implied binary point immediately following the sign bit produces smaller spacing between the values that can be represented. This is the preferred option for a floating-point representation. Using this option, the most important non-zero values for the floating-point representation are shown in Table 16.03. (The implied binary point and the mantissa exponent separation are shown by a gap.)

Description	Binary code	Denary equivalent
Largest positive value	0 111 0111	$.875 \times 2^{7} = 112$
Smallest positive value	0 001 1000	$.125 \times 2^{-8} = 1/2048$
Smallest magnitude negative value	1 111 1000	$-.125 \times 2^{-8} = -1/2048$
Largest magnitude negative value	1 000 0111	$-1 \times 2^{7} = -128$

Table 16.03 Example floating-point representations

The comparison between the values in Tables 16.01 and 16.03 illustrate the greater range of positive and negative values available if floating-point representation is used.

Extension question 16.01

1 Using the methods suggested in Chapter 1 (Section 1.01) can you confirm for yourself that the denary equivalents of the binary codes shown in Tables 16.02 and Table 16.03 are as indicated?

2 Can you also confirm that conversion from positive to negative or vice versa for a fixed-format real value still follows the rules defined in Chapter 1 (Section 1.02) for two's complement representation.

Precision and normalisation

In principle a decision has to be made about the format of a floating-point representation both with regard to the total number of bits to be used and the split between those representing the mantissa and those representing the exponent. In practice, a choice for the total number of bits to be used will be available as an option when the program is written. However, the split between the two parts of the representation will have been determined by the floating-point processor. If you did have a choice you would base a decision on the fact that increasing the number of bits for the mantissa would give better precision for a value stored but would leave fewer bits for the exponent so reducing the range of possible values.

In order to achieve maximum precision, it is necessary to normalise a floating-point number. (This normalisation is totally unrelated to the process associated with designing a database.) Since precision increases with an increasing number of bits for the mantissa it follows that optimum precision will only be achieved if full use is made of these bits. In practice, that means using the largest possible magnitude for the value represented by the mantissa.

To illustrate this we can consider the eight-bit representation used in Table 16.03. Table 16.04 shows possible representations for denary 2 using this representation.

Denary representation	Floating-point binary representation
0.125×2^4	0 001 0100
0.25×2^3	0 010 0011
0.5×2^2	0 100 0010

Table 16.04 Alternative representations of denary 2 using four bits each for mantissa and exponent.

For a negative number we can consider representations for –4 as shown in Table 16.05.

Denary representation	Floating-point binary representation
-0.25×2^4	1 110 0100
-0.5×2^3	1 100 0011
-1.0×2^2	1 000 0010

Table 16.05 Alternative representations of denary –4 using four bits each for mantissa and exponent.

It can be seen that when the number is represented with the highest magnitude for the mantissa, the two most significant bits are different. This fact can be used to recognise that a number is in a normalised representation. The values in these tables also show how a number could be normalised. For a positive number, the bits in the mantissa are shifted left until the most significant bits are 0 followed by 1. For each shift left the value of the exponent is reduced by 1.

The same process of shifting is used for a negative number until the most significant bits are 1 followed by 0. In this case, no attention is paid to the fact that bits are falling off the most significant end of the mantissa.

Conversion of representations

In Chapter 1 (Section 1.01), a number of methods for converting numbers into different representations were discussed. The ideas presented there now need a little expansion.

Let's start by considering the conversion of a simple real number, such as 4.75, into a simple fixed-point binary representation. This looks easy because 4 converts to 100 in binary and .75 converts to .11 in binary so the binary version of 4.75 should be:

100.11

However, we now remember that a positive number should start with 0. Can we just add a sign bit? For a positive number we can. Denary 4.75 can be represented as 0100.11 in binary.

For negative numbers we still want to use two's complement form. So, to find the representation of −4.75 we can start with the representation for 4.75 then convert it to two's complement as follows:

0100.11 converts to 1011.00 in one's complement

then to 1011.01 in two's complement

To check the result, we can apply Method 2 from Worked Example 1.01 in Chapter 1. 1011 is the code for −8 + 3 and .01 is the code for .25; −8 + 3 + .25 = −4.75.

We can now consider the conversion of a denary value expressed as a real number into a floating-point binary representation. The first thing to realise is that most fractional parts do not convert to a precise representation. This is because the binary fractional parts represent a half, a quarter, an eighth, a sixteenth and so on. Unless a denary fraction is a sum of a collection of these values, there cannot be an accurate conversion. In particular, of the values from .1 through to .9 only .5 converts accurately. This was mentioned in Chapter 1 (Section 1.02) in the discussion about storing currency values.

The method for conversion of a positive value is as follows:

1. Convert the whole-number part using the method described in Chapter 1 (Section 1.01).
2. Add the 0 sign bit.
3. Convert the fractional part using the method described in Worked Example 16.01.
4. Combine the two, with the exponent expressed as zero.
5. Adjust the position of the binary point and change the exponent accordingly to achieve a normalised form.

WORKED EXAMPLE 16.01

Converting a denary value to a floating-point representation

Example 1

Let's consider the conversion of 8.75:

1. The 8 converts to 1000, adding the sign bit gives 01000.
2. The .75 can be recognised as being .11 in binary.
3. The combination gives 01000.11 which has exponent value zero.

4 Shifting the binary point gives 0.100011 which has exponent value denary 4.

5 The next stage depends on the number of bits defined for the mantissa and the exponent; if ten bits are allocated for the mantissa and four bits are allocated for the exponent the final representation becomes 0100011000 for the mantissa and 0100 for the exponent.

Example 2

Let's consider the conversion of 8.63. The first step is the same but now the .63 has to be converted by the 'multiply by two and record whole number parts' method. This works as follows:

.63 x 2 = 1.26 so 1 is stored to give the fraction .1

.26 x 2 = .52 so 0 is stored to give the fraction .10

.52 x 2 = 1.04 so 1 is stored to give the fraction .101

.04 x 2 = .08 so 0 is stored to give the fraction .1010

At this stage it can be seen that multiplying .08 by 2 successively is going to give a lot of zeros in the binary fraction before another 1 is added so the process can be stopped. What has happened is that .63 has been approximated as .625. So, following Steps 3–5 in Example 1, the final representation becomes 0100010100 for the mantissa and 0100 for the exponent.

TASK 16.01

Convert the denary value –7.75 to a floating-point binary representation with ten bits for the mantissa and four bits for the exponent. Start by converting 7.75 to binary (make sure you add the sign bit!). Then convert to two's complement form. Finally, choose the correct value for the exponent to leave the implied position of the binary point after the sign bit. Convert back to denary to check the result.

Problems with using floating-point numbers

As illustrated above, the conversion of a real value in denary to a binary representation almost guarantees a degree of approximation. This is then added to by the restriction of the number of bits used to store the mantissa.

Many uses of floating-point numbers are in extended mathematical procedures involving repeated calculations. Examples of such use would be in weather forecasting using a mathematical model of the atmosphere or in economic forecasting. In such programming there is a slight approximation in recording the result of each calculation. These so-called rounding errors can become significant if calculations are repeated enough times. The only way of preventing this becoming a serious problem is to increase the precision of the floating-point representation by using more bits for the mantissa. Programming languages therefore offer options to work in 'double precision' or 'quadruple precision'.

The other potential problem relates to the range of numbers that can be stored. Referring back to the simple eight-bit representation illustrated in Table 16.03, the highest value represented is denary 112. A calculation can easily produce a value higher than this. As Chapter 5 (Section 5.02) illustrated, this produces an overflow error condition. However, for floating-point values there is also a possibility that if a very small number is divided by a number greater than 1 the result is a value smaller than the smallest that can be stored. This is an underflow error condition. Depending on the circumstances, it may be possible for a program to continue running by converting this very small number to zero but clearly this must involve risk.

Summary

- Examples of non-composite user-defined data types include enumerated and pointer data types.
- Record, set and class are examples of composite user-defined data types.
- File organisation allows for serial, sequential or direct access.
- Floating-point representation for a real number allows a wider range of values to be represented.
- A normalised floating-point representation achieves optimum precision for the value stored.
- Stored floating-point values rarely give an accurate representation of the denary equivalent.

Exam-style Questions

1 A programmer may choose to use a user-defined data type when writing a program.

a Give an example of a non-composite user-defined data type and explain why its use by a programmer is different to the use of an in-built data type. [3]

b A program is to be written to handle data relating to the animals kept in a zoo. The programmer chooses to use a record user-defined data type.

i Explain what a record user-defined data type is. [2]

ii Explain the advantage of using a record user-defined data type. [2]

iii Write pseudocode for the definition of a record type which is to be used to store: animal name, animal age, number in zoo and location in the zoo. [5]

2 a A binary file is to be used to store data for a program.

i What are the terms used to describe the components of such a file. [2]

ii Explain the difference between a binary file and a text file. [3]

b A binary file might be organised for serial, sequential or direct access.

i Explain the difference between the three types of file organisation. [4]

ii Give an example of file use for which a serial file organisation would be suitable. Justify your choice. [3]

iii Give an example of file use when direct access would be advantageous. Justify your choice. [3]

3 A file contains binary coding. The following are four successive bytes in the file:

10010101	00110011		11001000	00010001

a The four bytes represent two numbers in floating-point representation. The first byte in each case represents the mantissa. Each byte is stored in two's complement representation.

i Give the name for what the second byte represents in each case. [1]

ii State whether the representations are for two positive numbers or two negative numbers and explain why. [2]

iii One of the numbers is in a normalised representation. State which one it is and give the reason why. [2]

iv State where the implied binary point is in a normalised representation and explain why a normalised representation gives better precision for the value represented. [3]

v If two bytes were still to be used but the number of bits for each component was going to be changed by allocating more to the mantissa, what effect would this have on the numbers that could be represented? Explain your answer. [2]

b Using the representation described in part (a), Show the representation of denary 12.43 as a floating-point binary number. [5]

Chapter 17
Communication and Internet Technologies

Learning objectives

By the end of this chapter you should be able to:

- show understanding of a bus or star topology network
- show understanding of circuit switching and where it is applicable
- show understanding of packet switching and explain how it is used to pass messages across a network
- explain how hardware is used to support a LAN
- show understanding of why a protocol is essential for communication between computers
- show understanding of how protocol implementation can be viewed as a stack
- show understanding of the function of each layer of the TCP/IP protocol suite and the application of the suite when a message is sent from one host to another on the internet
- show understanding of the function of a router in packet switching
- show awareness of other protocols (HTTP, FTP, POP3, SMTP) and their purposes
- show understanding of Ethernet and how collision detection and avoidance works
- show understanding of how the BitTorrent protocol provides peer-to-peer file sharing
- show understanding of a wireless network.

17.01 Isolated network topologies

There are five requirements for a data communications system: a sender, a receiver, a transmission medium, a message and a protocol. Here, a 'message' is a general term to describe any type of transmitted data. A message can only be transmitted if there is an agreed protocol. Protocols are discussed in later sections of this chapter.

A data communications system may consist of an isolated network. There are several possible topologies for an isolated network. The simplest possible network is where two end-systems are connected by a network link as shown in Figure 17.01. This is an example of a point-to-point connection for which there is a dedicated link.

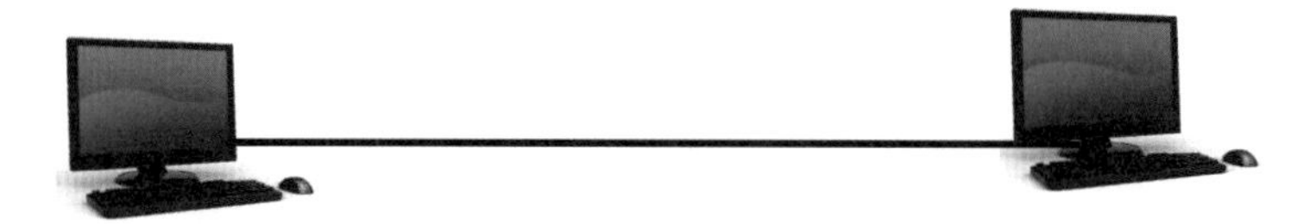

Figure 17.01 A point-to-point network

A bus topology also has only one link but it is shared by a number of end-systems and is therefore described as a multi-point connection. The configuration is shown in Figure 17.02. This configuration has a major difference in that there is no direct connection between any pair of end-systems.

Figure 17.02 A bus network

A ring topology is shown in Figure 17.03(a). In this configuration, each end-system has a point-to-point connection to the two adjacent end-systems.

An example of a fully-connected mesh topology is shown in Figure 17.03(b). In this configuration, each end-system has a point-to-point connection to each of the other end-systems.

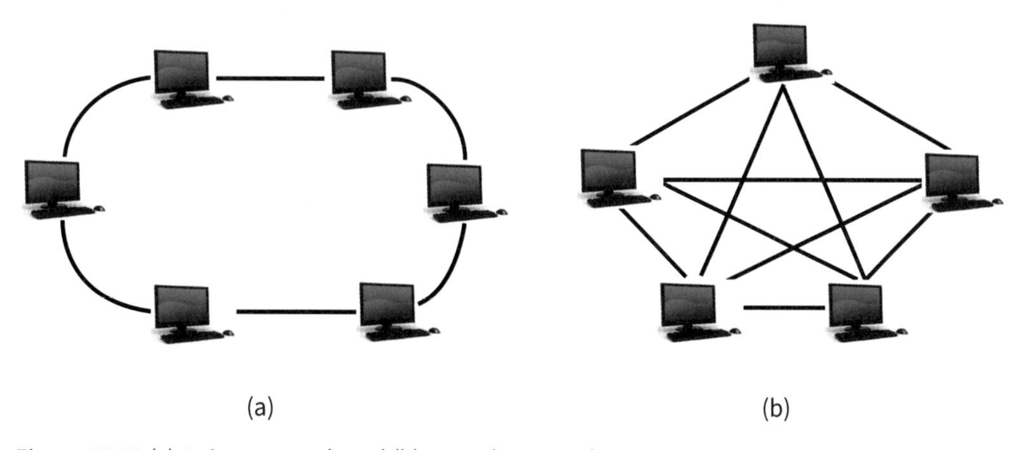

Figure 17.03 (a) A ring network and (b) a mesh network

The final possibility is a star topology which is shown in Figure 17.04. This could have been drawn so that it looked like a star but it is better drawn to represent the physical configuration that is used in an actual installation. In a star topology, each end-system has a point-to-point connection to the 'central' device.

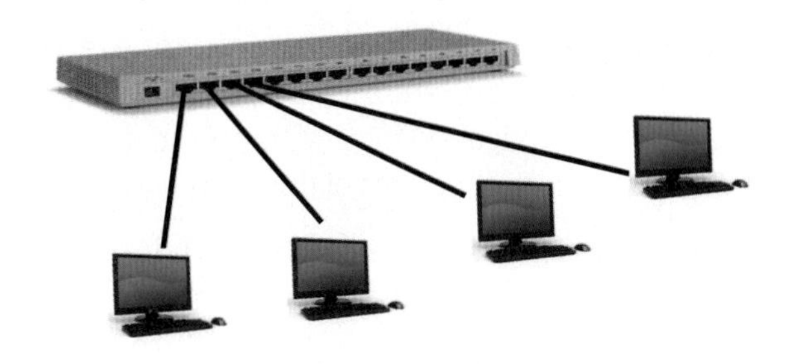

Figure 17.04 A star topology

The ring and bus topologies were used in early networks. Most of the end-systems would have been user workstations; the others would have been servers. With regard to the end-systems the same applies to a fully-connected mesh network but this was never a realistic configuration because of the amount of cabling required.

In the star topology, the end-systems may again be user workstations or servers but the central device is different. The star topology is nowadays the dominant configuration for an individual network. There are several reasons for this. The most important is that the central device can be used to connect the network to other networks and, in particular, to the Internet. A specialised application is to use the star topology to function logically as a ring. With the appropriate software installed, each end-system can function as though it has just two directly connected neighbours.

Discussion Point:

Which network topologies have you used? You may wish to defer this discussion until you have read about network devices later in this chapter.

17.02 Communication and transmission concepts

There are several concepts relating to the use of a network for communication and data transmission.

Data flow modes

The data flow along an individual link is simplex, half duplex or full duplex. In simplex mode the flow is one-way. In a duplex mode flow is both ways but only occurs simultaneously in full-duplex mode.

Message types

When a message is sent it can be as a broadcast, a multicast or a unicast. Broadcasting is a one-to-all communication (as used traditionally for radio and television). Multicasting is from one source to many destinations. Unicasting is a one-to-one communication.

Transmission modes

For communication over an internetwork there are two possible approaches: circuit switching or packet switching. Circuit switching is the method used in the traditional telephone system. Because the Public Switched Telephone Networks (PTSNs) have now largely converted to digital technology, the same method can be provided for data transfer rather than voice communication. Typically this is provided in a leased line service. The concept is illustrated in Figure 17.05, which shows end-systems connected to local exchanges which have a switching function and which are connected via a number of intermediate nodes with a switching function.

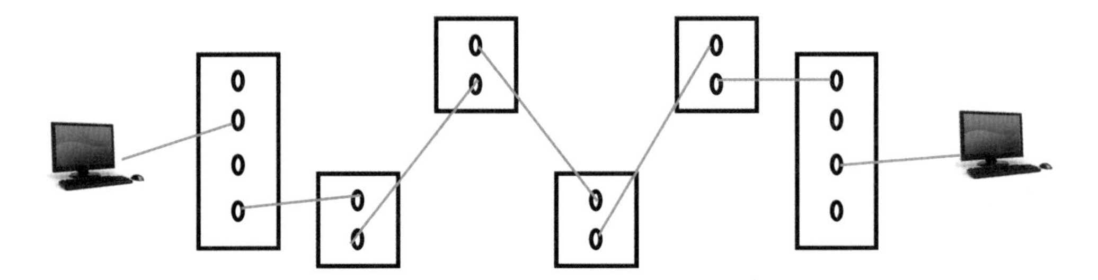

Figure 17.05 Circuit-switched data transmission

For data transfer to take place, the following has to happen:

1 The sender provides the identity of the intended receiver.
2 The system checks whether or not the receiver is ready to accept data.
3 If the receiver is available, a sequence of links is established across the network.
4 The data is transferred.
5 The links are removed.

It is not necessary for this discussion to define what could constitute a node in a circuit-switched network. The links that are provided between the nodes are dedicated channels in shared transmission media that guarantee unimpeded transmission. When a telephone call is made there is a definite end of the call with removal of the links. However, for a leased-line data connection there might be a permanent circuit established.

The packet-switching method allows data transmission without a circuit being established. Data cannot be sent in a continuous stream. Instead data is packaged in portions inside packets. A packet consists of a header which contains instructions for delivery plus the data body. The method is similar to that used by the postal service but rather more complex! The network schematic shown in Figure 17.05 is still appropriate to describe packet switching except that the links used are not defined at the time a packet is transmitted by the sender.

Packet-switching services

When packet switching is used there are two ways that the network can provide a service: connectionless service or connection-oriented service.

If a connectionless service is provided, a packet is dispatched with no knowledge of whether or not the receiver is ready to accept it. In a connection-oriented service the first packet sent includes a request for an acknowledgement. If this is received, the sender transmits further packets. If no acknowledgement is received the sender tries again with the first packet.

17.03 Hardware connection devices

An end-system on an Ethernet LAN needs a network interface card (NIC). Each NIC has a unique 'physical' address. This is sometimes referred to as the MAC address as explained in Section 17.06. The end-system itself has no identification on the network. If the NIC is removed and inserted into a different end-system, it takes the address with it.

The simplest device that can be used at the 'centre' of a star topology LAN is a hub. A hub ensures that any incoming communication is broadcast to all connected end-systems. However, the use of a hub is not restricted to supporting an isolated network. One possibility is to have a hierarchical configuration with one hub connected to other hubs, which support individual LANs. Another possibility is for a hub to have a built-in broadband modem. This allows all of the end-user systems on the LAN to have an Internet connection when this modem is connected to a telephone line.

A switch can function as a hub but it is a more intelligent device and, in particular, can keep track of the addresses of connected devices. This allows a switch to send an incoming transmission to a specific end-system as a unicast. This facility obviously reduces the amount of network traffic compared to that generated by a hub.

A router is the most intelligent of the connecting devices. It is in effect a small computer. It can function as a switch but the router can make a decision about which device it will transmit a received transmission to. As was mentioned in Chapter 2 (Section 2.04), the main use of routers is in the backbone fabric of the Internet. Nearer to the end-systems, a router may function as a gateway, as a network address translation box (described in Chapter 2 (Section 2.07)) or be combined with a firewall. There is further discussion of routers in Section 17.04.

17.04 The TCP/IP protocol suite

Protocols are essential for successful transmission of data over a network. Each **protocol** defines a set of rules that must be agreed between sender and receiver. At the simplest level, a protocol could define that a positive voltage represents a bit with value 1. At the other extreme, a protocol could define the format of the first 40 bytes in a packet.

KEY TERMS

Protocol: a set of rules for data transmission which are agreed by sender and receiver

The complexity of networking requires a very large number of protocols. A protocol suite is a collection of related protocols. TCP/IP is the dominant protocol suite for Internet usage. TCP/IP can be explained on the basis of the network model shown in Figure 17.06.

Figure 17.06 shows a stack of layers for the protocols where:

- Each layer except the physical layer represents software installed on an end-system or on a router.
- The software for each layer must provide the capability to receive and to transmit data in full-duplex mode to an adjacent layer.
- A protocol in an upper layer is serviced by the protocols in lower layers.

As a result, an application run on one end-system can behave as though there was a direct connection with an application running on a different end-system. To achieve this, the application layer protocol on the sender end-system sends a 'message' to the transport layer protocol on the same system. The transport layer protocol then initiates a process which results in the identical 'message' being delivered to the receiver end-system. Finally, on the receiver end-system, the transport layer protocol delivers the 'message' to the application layer protocol.

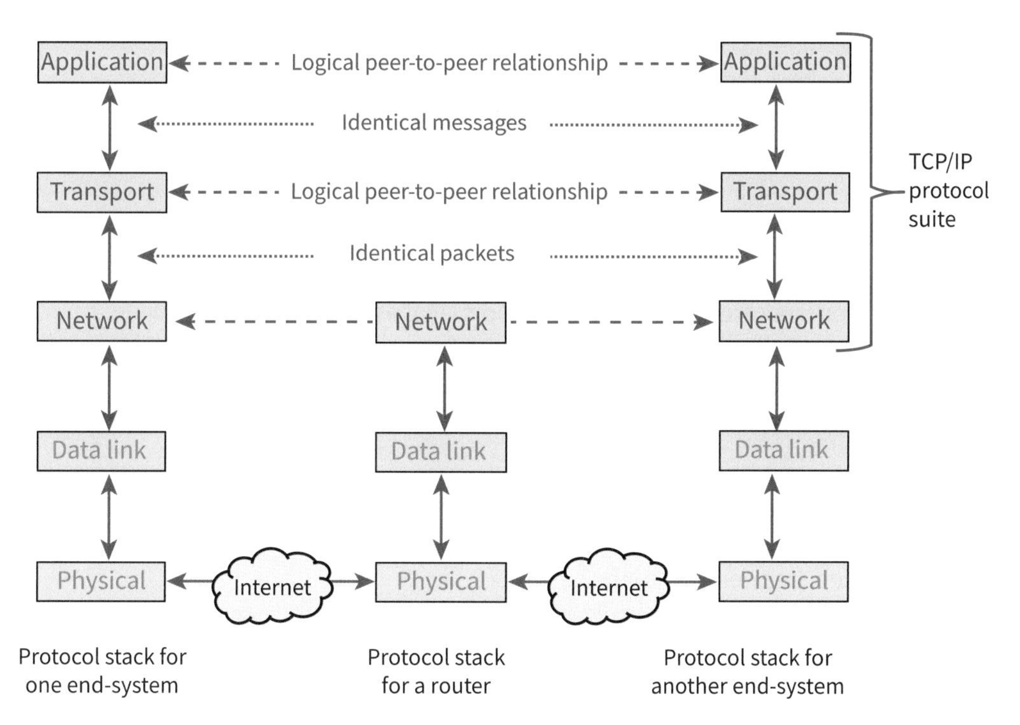

Figure 17.06 A network model relating to the TCP/IP protocol suite

The TCP/IP protocol suite only operates at the top three layers. The lower layers operate with a different protocol suite, such as Ethernet. A router has no awareness of the two highest layers.

The TCP/IP suite comprises a number of protocols, including the following:

- Application layer: HTTP, SMTP, DNS, FTP, POP3
- Transport layer: TCP, UDP, SCTP
- Network layer: IP, IGMP, ICMP, ARP

The selection has been chosen to illustrate that the TCP/IP suite encompasses a very wide range of protocols which is still evolving. Some of the listed protocols will not be considered further.

TCP (Transmission Control Protocol)

If an application is running on an end-system where a 'message' is to be sent to a different end-system the application will be controlled by an application layer protocol (see Section 17.05). The protocol will transmit the user data to the transport layer. The TCP protocol operating in the transport layer now has to take responsibility for ensuring the safe delivery of the 'message' to the receiver. To do this it creates sufficient packets to hold all of the data. Each packet consists of a header plus the user data.

As well as needing to ensure safe delivery, TCP also has to ensure that any response is directed back to the application protocol. Thus one item in the header is the port number which identifies the application layer protocol. For example, for HTTP the port number is 80. The packet must also include the port number for the application layer protocol at the receiving end-system. However, TCP is not concerned with the address of the receiving end-system. If the packet is one of a sequence, a sequence number is included to ensure eventual correct reassembly of the user data.

The TCP protocol is connection-oriented. As described in Section 17.02, initially just one packet of a sequence is sent to the network layer. Once the connection has been established, TCP sends the other packets and receives response packets containing acknowledgements. This allows missing packets to be identified and re-sent.

IP (Internet Protocol)

The function of the network layer, and in particular of the IP protocol, is to ensure correct routing over the Internet. To do this it takes the packet received from the transport layer and adds a further header. This header contains the IP addresses of both the sender and the receiver. To find the IP address of the receiver, it is very likely to use the DNS system to find the address corresponding to the URL supplied in the user data. This aspect was discussed in some detail in Chapter 2 (Section 2.08).

The IP packet, which is usually called a 'datagram', is sent to the data-link layer and therefore to a different protocol suite. The data-link layer assembles datagrams into 'frames'. At this stage, transmission can begin. Once the IP packet has been sent to the data-link layer, IP has no further duty. IP functions as a connectionless service. If IP receives a packet which contains an acknowledgement of a previously sent packet, it will simply pass the packet on to TCP with no awareness of the content.

The router

As Figure 17.06 shows, the frame sent by the data-link layer will arrive at a router during transmission (more likely at several routers!). At this stage, the datagram content of the frame is given back to IP. It is now the function of the router software to choose the next target host in the transmission. The software has access to a routing table appropriate to that router. The size and complexity of the Internet prohibits a router from having a global routing table. IP then passes the datagram back to the data-link layer at the router.

The distinction between a switch and a router was discussed earlier. A further point to note here is that when a frame arrives at a switch, it is transmitted on without any routing decision. A switch operates in the data-link layer, not in the network layer.

17.05 Application-layer protocols associated with TCP/IP

There are very many application-layer protocols. This discussion will consider only a few of the protocols that were introduced early in the use of TCP/IP.

HTTP (HyperText Transfer Protocol)

Because HTTP (HyperText Transfer Protocol) underpins the World Wide Web it has to be considered to be the most important application-layer protocol. Every time a user accesses a website using a browser, HTTP is used but its functionality is hidden from view.

HTTP is a transaction-oriented, client–server protocol. The transaction involves the client sending a 'request' message and the server sending back a 'response' message. The HTTP protocol defines the format of the message. The first line of a request message is the 'request line'. Optionally this can be followed by header lines. All of this uses ASCII coding. The format of the request line is:

```
<Method> <URL> <Version>CRLF
```

where CR and LF are the ASCII carriage return and line feed characters. The request line usually has GET as the method. However, there are several alternatives to the GET method which makes HTTP potentially a more widely applicable protocol than just being used for webpage access. The version has to be specified because HTTP has evolved so there is more than one version in use.

In Chapter 2 (Section 2.09), a sequence of events was described for when a browser accesses a webpage. This can now be presented as a sequence of protocol actions. The following is an abbreviated version:

1 HTTP transmits a request message to TCP.
2 TCP creates one or more packets and sends the first one to IP using port 80 for the destination port and a temporary port number for the sending port.
3 IP uses the URL in the message to get an IP address using DNS and sends a datagram.
4 At the server, IP forwards the datagram to TCP.
5 The server TCP sends an acknowledgement.
6 When a connection has been established, TCP sends the remaining packets, if any, to IP which then forwards them through the server IP and TCP to the server application layer.
7 HTTP transmits a response message which is transmitted via TCP, IP, IP and TCP to the client browser application.

All of this can happen with just one click on a bookmark item in a browser!

Email protocols

The traditional method of sending and receiving emails is schematically illustrated in Figure 17.07. It can be seen that three individual client–server interactions are involved. The client has a connection to a mail server which then has to function as a client in the transmission to the mail server used by the receiver.

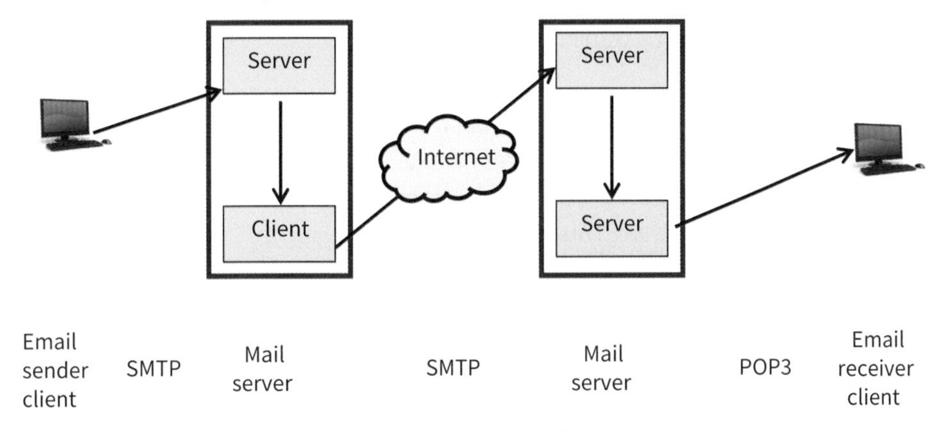

Figure 17.07 An email message being transmitted from a sender to a receiver

SMTP (Simple Mail Transfer Protocol) is a 'push' protocol. POP3 (Post Office Protocol version 3) is a 'pull' protocol. There is a more recent alternative to POP3, which is IMAP (Internet Message Access Protocol). IMAP offers the same facilities as POP3 but also a lot more.

This approach has been largely superseded by the use of web-based mail. A browser is used to access the email application, so HTTP is now the protocol used. However, SMTP remains in use for transfer between the mail servers.

FTP (File Transfer Protocol)

For routine transfers of files from one user to another the most likely method is to attach the file to an email. However, this is not always a suitable method. FTP (File Transfer Protocol) is the application-layer protocol that can handle any file transfer between two end-systems. File transfer can be less than straightforward if the end-systems have different operating systems with different file systems. FTP handles this by separating the control process from the data-transfer process.

17.06 Ethernet protocol

Ethernet is the other dominant protocol in the modern networked world. It is primarily focused on LANs. Although Ethernet was first devised in the 1970s independently of any organisation, it was later adopted for standardisation by the Institute of Electrical and Electronics Engineers (IEEE). In particular it was their 802 committee (obviously one of many!) that took responsibility for the development of the protocol. The standard for a wired network is denoted as IEEE 802.3 which can be considered to be a synonym for Ethernet. The standard has evolved through five generations: standard or traditional, fast, gigabit, 10 gigabit and 100 gigabit. The gigabit part of the name indicates the transfer speed capability.

Ethernet transmits data in frames. Each frame contains a source address and a destination address. The address is the physical or MAC address, which uniquely defines one NIC, as described in Section 17.03. The reason that a unique address can be guaranteed is that 48 bits are used for the definition. The address is usually written in hexadecimal notation, for example:

4A:30:12:24:1A:10

Standard Ethernet was implemented on a LAN configured either as a bus or as a star with a hub as the central device. In either topology, a transmission was broadcast in a connectionless service.

Extension Question 17.01

In a star topology LAN with a hub as the central device, why must a transmission be broadcast?

Because of the broadcast transmission, there was a need for the access to the shared medium by end-systems to be controlled. If there were no control, two messages sent at the same time would 'collide' and each message would be corrupted. The method adopted was CSMA/CD (carrier sense multiple access with collision detection). This relied on the fact that if a frame was being transmitted there was a voltage level on the Ethernet cable which could be detected by an end-system. If this was the case, the protocol defined a time that the end-system had to wait before it tried again. However, because two end-systems could have waited then both decided to transmit at the same time collisions could still happen. Thus there was also a need to incorporate a means for an end-system to detect a collision and to discontinue transmission if a collision occurred.

Although there might be some legacy standard Ethernet LANs still operating, the modern implementation of Ethernet is switched. The star configuration has a switch as the central device. The switch controls transmission to specific end-systems. Each end-system is connected to the switch by a full-duplex link so no collision is possible along that link. Since collisions are now impossible, CSMA/CD is no longer needed.

Ethernet is the most likely protocol to be operating in the data-link layer defined in the TCP/IP protocol stack. Referring back to Figure 17.06, the diagram shows IP in the network layer sending a datagram to the data-link layer. When the data-link layer uses Ethernet, the protocol defines two sub-layers. The upper of these is the logical link-control layer, which handles flow control, error control and part of the framing process. The lower is the media access control (MAC) sublayer which completes the framing process and defines the access method. The MAC layer transmits the frames that contain the physical addresses for sender and receiver. This is the reason that these addresses are often referred to as MAC addresses.

17.07 Peer-to-peer (P2P) file sharing

The network traffic generated by peer-to-peer (P2P) file sharing has come to be a dominant feature of Internet usage. It is an architecture that has no structure and no controlling mechanism. Peers act as both clients and servers and each peer is just one end-system.

The BitTorrent protocol is the most used protocol because it allows fast sharing of files. There are three basic problems to solve if end-systems are to be confident in using BitTorrent:

- How does a peer find others that have the wanted content?
- How do peers replicate content to provide high-speed downloads for everyone?
- How do peers encourage other peers to provide content rather just using the protocol to download for themselves?

The answer provided by BitTorrent to the first question is to get every content provider to provide a content description, called a torrent, which is a file that contains the name of the tracker (a server that leads peers to the content) and a list of the chunks that make up the content. The torrent file is at least three orders of magnitude smaller than the content so can be transferred quickly. The tracker is a server that maintains a list of all the other peers (the 'swarm') actively downloading and uploading the content.

The answer to the second question involves peers simultaneously downloading and uploading chunks but peers have to exchange lists of chunks and aim to download rare chunks for preference. Each time a rare chunk is downloaded it automatically becomes less rare!

The answer to the third question requires dealing with the free-riders or 'leechers' who only download. The solution is for a peer to initially randomly try other peers but then to only continue to upload to those peers that provide regular downloads. If a peer is not downloading or only downloading slowly, it will eventually be isolated or 'choked'.

It is worth noting that the language of BitTorrent is somewhat esoteric and there are other terms used which have not been mentioned. Fortunately the principles are straightforward.

17.08 Wireless networks

All of the previous discussion in this chapter has related to transmission using a cable medium. In today's world, this is no longer the dominant technology. The following brief discussion considers four important examples of wireless technology discussed in order of increasing scale of operation.

Bluetooth

Bluetooth has been standardised as IEEE 802.15. Communication is by short-range radio transmission in a confined area. A Bluetooth LAN is an ad hoc network. This means that there is no defined infrastructure and network connections are created spontaneously. There is an almost limitless range of applications that use Bluetooth; some are very simple, such as using a wireless keyboard or mouse.

WiFi

WiFi (WLAN in some countries) is a term used by the public to describe what is sometimes called wireless Ethernet but is formally IEEE 802.11. This is a wireless LAN protocol which uses radio frequency transmission. Most often a WiFi LAN is centred on a wireless access point in an 'infrastructure' network (i.e. not an ad hoc network). The wireless access point communicates wirelessly with any end-systems that have connected to the device. It also has a wired connection to the Internet.

WiMAX

WiMAX (Worldwide Interoperability for Microwave Access) or IEEE 802.16 is a protocol for a MAN or WAN. It is designed for use by PSTNs to provide broadband access to the Internet without having to lay underground cables. Local subscribers connect to the antenna of a local base station using a microwave signal.

Cellular networks

A mobile phone is often called a 'cell phone' because of the fundamental infrastructure provided for mobile phone users. This is illustrated in Figure 17.08.

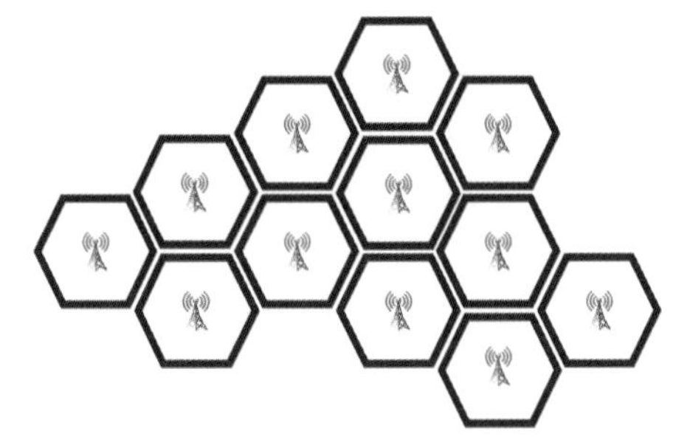

Figure 17.08 A collection of mobile phone cells

Each cell has at its centre a base station. The system works because each cell has a defined frequency for transmission which is different from the frequencies used in adjacent cells.

The technology available in a mobile phone has progressed dramatically through what are described as generations:

- 1G was designed for voice communication using analogue technology.
- 2G went digital.
- 3G introduced multimedia and serious Internet connection capability.
- 4G introduced smartphones with high-bandwidth broadband connectivity.

Summary

- Possible topologies for an isolated network are: single link, bus, ring, star or mesh.
- Circuit switching requires a dedicated circuit to be established between sender and receiver before transmission can start.
- In packet switching, packets can be transmitted without any circuit being created.
- Hardware network-connecting devices include network interface cards, hubs, switches and routers.
- The TCP/IP protocol suite is implemented as a layered stack.
- Examples of application-layer protocols are HTTP, SMTP, POP3 and FTP.
- The dominant LAN protocol is Ethernet.
- Peer-to-peer file sharing on the Internet uses the BitTorrent protocol.
- The four major wireless technologies are Bluetooth, WiFi, WiMAX and cellular networks.

Exam-style Questions

1 **a** There are five requirements for a data communication system. State the five requirements. [3]

b An isolated wired network is to be used as a data communication system.

i Draw two possible topologies. [2]

ii For each topology, explain why there is or is not direct point-to-point connections between the end-systems. [4]

c Each end-system is fitted with a network interface card (NIC).

i Explain why the NIC is needed. [3]

ii Explain what would happen if the NIC in an end-system was replaced by a newer version. [2]

2 One end-system with an Internet connection has a file. A user on another end-system connected to the Internet needs a copy of the file. There are different methods that might be used to enable the user to obtain a copy of the file.

a Identify three possible methods with a brief explanation for each. [6]

b Identify the application-layer protocols that each method will use with a brief explanation for each one. [8]

3 **a** Standard Ethernet is a term used to describe the original version of Ethernet.
CSMA/CD was a feature of standard Ethernet.

i Describe, with the aid of a diagram, a network topology that could be used with standard Ethernet. [3]

ii Describe the CSMA/CD method and explain its use. [4]

b Ethernet can be used in conjunction with the TCP/IP protocol suite.

i Draw a diagram to illustrate how the combination of Ethernet and the TCP/IP suite provides support for data communication. [5]

ii Explain the meaning of the term 'MAC address'. [3]

Chapter 18
Boolean Algebra and Logic Circuits

Learning objectives

By the end of this chapter you should be able to:

- show understanding of Boolean algebra
- show understanding of De Morgan's Laws
- perform Boolean algebra using De Morgan's Laws
- simplify a logic circuit/expression using Boolean algebra
- produce truth tables for common logic circuits
- show understanding of how to construct a flip-flop
- describe the role of flip-flops as data storage elements
- show understanding of Karnaugh Maps and the benefits of using them
- solve logic problems using Karnaugh Maps.

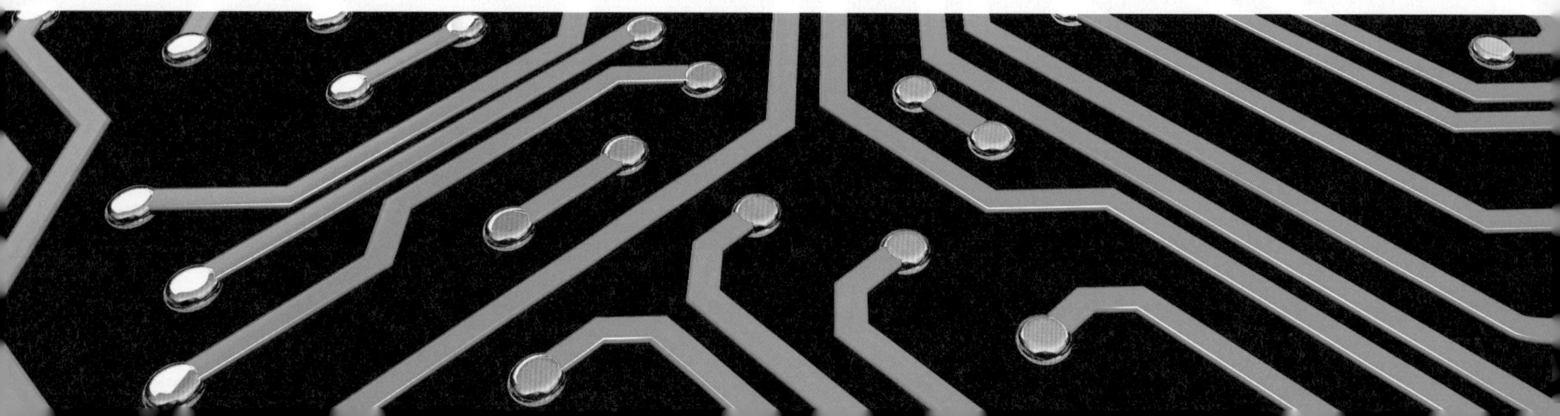

18.01 Boolean algebra basics

Chapter 4 (Section 4.01) introduced logic expressions consisting of logic propositions combined using Boolean operators. Boolean algebra provides a simplified way of writing a logic expression and a set of rules for manipulating an expression.

Whenever a form of algebra is used it is vital that there is an understanding of its meaning. As a simple example we can consider the following four interpretations of the meaning of 1 + 1:

$$1 + 1 = 2$$
$$1 + 1 = 10$$
$$1 + 1 = 0$$
$$1 + 1 = 1$$

The first shows denary arithmetic, the second binary arithmetic and the third bit arithmetic. The last one applies if Boolean algebra is being used. This is because in Boolean algebra 1 represents TRUE, 0 represents FALSE, and + represents OR. Therefore the fourth statement represents the logic statement:

TRUE OR TRUE is TRUE

There are options for the representation of Boolean algebra. For example, the symbols for AND and OR are sometimes represented as $\wedge$ and $\vee$. There is the option of writing A.B or AB for AND. The dot notation is used in this book. Finally, there are options for how NOT A (the inverse of A) can be represented. $\bar{A}$ is used here.

Having established the notation for Boolean algebra we have to consider the rules that apply. These can formally be described as 'laws' or 'identities'. Table 18.01 contains a full listing.

Identity/Law	AND form	OR form
Identity	1.A = A	0+A = A
Null	0.A = 0	1+A = 1
Idempotent	A.A = A	A+A = A
Inverse	$A.\bar{A} = 0$	$A+\bar{A} = 1$
Commutative	A.B = B.A	A+B = B+A
Associative	(A.B).C = A.(B.C)	(A+B)+C = A+(B+C)
Distributive	A+B.C = (A+B).(A+C)	A.(B+C) = A.B+A.C
Absorption	A.(A+B) = A	A+A.B = A
De Morgan's	$\overline{(A.B)} = \bar{A} + \bar{B}$	$\overline{(A + B)} = \bar{A}.\bar{B}$
Double Complement	$\bar{\bar{A}} = A$	

Table 18.01 Boolean algebra identities (laws)

Some of the names used for the identities may be unfamiliar to you. This is not a concern. You should note that for all but one of the identities there is an AND form and an OR form. Furthermore, it is important to note that an identity written in one form can be transformed into the other by interchanging each 0 or 1 and each AND and OR. For example, 0.A = 0 which reads FALSE AND A is FALSE transforms into TRUE OR A is TRUE, written in the algebra as 1+A = 1.

It can also be seen that some of the identities look like those applying in normal algebra with AND functioning as multiplication and OR functioning as addition. Thus it is allowed for the terms 'product' and 'sum' to be used in the context of Boolean algebra.

TASK 18.01

It is vital that you can interpret a Boolean expression correctly. Go through Table 18.01 item by item and in each case read out the full meaning. For example:

1+A = 1 can be read as 'one plus A equals 1'

but must be understood as 'TRUE OR A is TRUE'

Although De Morgan's laws look complicated at first glance, they can be rationalised easily. The inverse of a Boolean product becomes the sum of the inverses of the individual values in the product. The inverse of a Boolean sum is the product of the individual inverses.

Unfortunately, using the algebra to simplify expressions is not something which can be learnt as a routine. It almost inevitably requires a little lateral thinking as Worked Example 18.01 will show.

WORKED EXAMPLE 18.01

Using Boolean algebra to simplify an expression

Let's consider a simple example:

$A+\bar{A}.B$ can be simplified to $A+B$

In order to simplify the expression we have to first make it more complicated! This is where the lateral thinking comes in. The OR form of the absorption identity is A+A.B = A. This can be used in reverse to replace A by A+A.B to produce the following:

$$A+A.B+\bar{A}.B$$

Applying the AND form of the commutative law and the OR form of the distributive law in reverse we can see that:

$A.B+\bar{A}.B$ is the same as $B.A+B.\bar{A}$ which converts to $B.(A+\bar{A})$

This allows us to use the OR form of the inverse identity which converts $A+\bar{A}$ to 1. As a result the expression has become:

$$A+B.1$$

When the OR form of the commutative law and the AND form of the identity law are applied to the B.1 term, it then becomes A+B.

18.02 Logic circuits

Chapter 4 introduced the symbols for logic gates that are used in logic circuits and discussed the relationships between logic circuits, truth tables and logic expressions. This chapter introduces some specific circuits that are used to construct components that provide functionality in computer hardware.

The half adder

A fundamental operation in computing is binary addition. The result of adding two bits is either 1 or 0. However, when 1 is added to 1 the result is 0 but there is a carry bit equal to 1. This cannot be ignored if two numbers with several bits in each are being added.

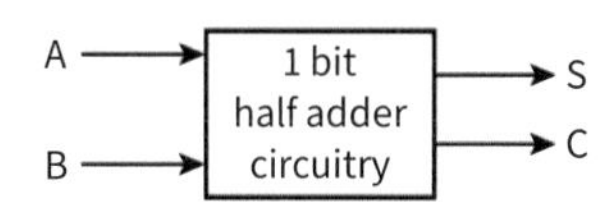

Figure 18.01 A half adder

The simplest circuit that can be used for binary addition is the half adder. This can be represented by the diagram in Figure 18.01. The circuit takes two input bits and outputs a sum bit (S) and a carry bit (C).

The circuit required can be considered in the context of the truth table which is shown as Table 18.02.

Input		Output	
A	**B**	**S**	**C**
0	0	0	0
0	1	1	0
1	0	1	0
1	1	0	1

Table 18.02 The truth table for a half adder

One possible circuit can be defined directly by examination of the truth table. It can be seen that the only combination of inputs that produces a 1 for the carry bit is when two 1 bits are input. The truth table for the C output is in fact the AND truth table. The truth table for the S output can be seen to match that for the XOR operator which is shown in Figure 4.02 in Chapter 4 (Section 4.04). Therefore, one circuit that would produce the half adder functionality would contain an AND gate and an XOR gate with each gate receiving input from A and B.

This is only one of several circuits that would provide the functionality. As was explained in Chapter 4 (Section 4.05), circuit manufacturers prefer to use either NAND or NOR gates. The circuit shown in Figure 18.02 consisting only of NAND gates has the correct logic to produce the C and S outputs and is a likely choice for implementation.

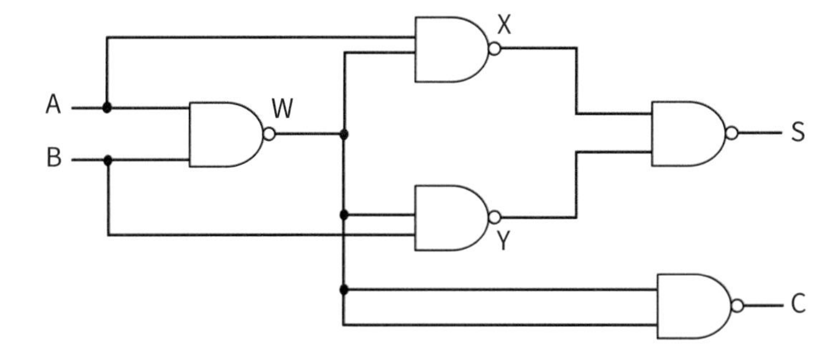

Figure 18.02 A half adder circuit constructed from NAND gates

Question 18.01

In Figure 18.02, can you identify the individual circuits that represent the AND operator and the XOR operator?

TASK 18.02

Use the intermediate points labelled W, X and Y to construct a truth table for the circuit shown in Figure 18.02. Check that this reproduces the truth table shown as Table 18.02.

The full adder

If two numbers expressed in binary with several bits are to be added, the addition must start with the two least significant bits and then proceed to the most significant bits. At each stage the carry from the previous addition has to be incorporated into the current addition. If a half adder is used each time, there has to be separate circuitry to handle the carry bit because the half adder only takes two inputs.

The full adder is a circuit that has three inputs including the previous carry bit. The truth table is shown as Table 18.03.

One possible circuit for implementation contains two half adder circuits and an OR gate as shown in Figure 18.03.

Input			Output	
A	B	Cin	S	Cout
0	0	0	0	0
0	0	1	1	0
0	1	0	1	0
0	1	1	0	1
1	0	0	1	0
1	0	1	0	1
1	1	0	0	1
1	1	1	1	1

Table 18.03 The truth table for a full adder

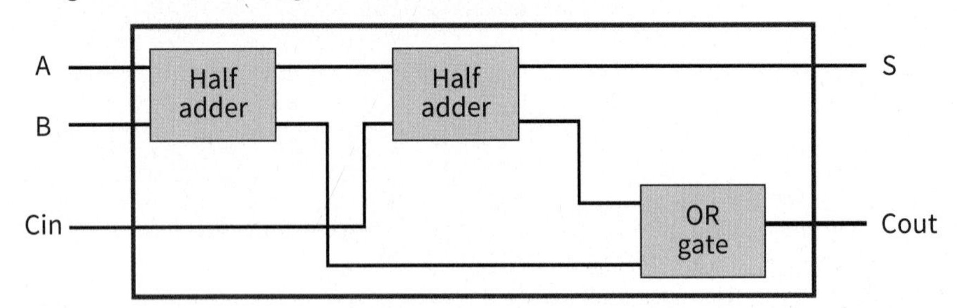

Figure 18.03 A possible implementation of a full adder

As before, it is possible to construct the circuit entirely from NAND gates as shown in Figure 18.04.

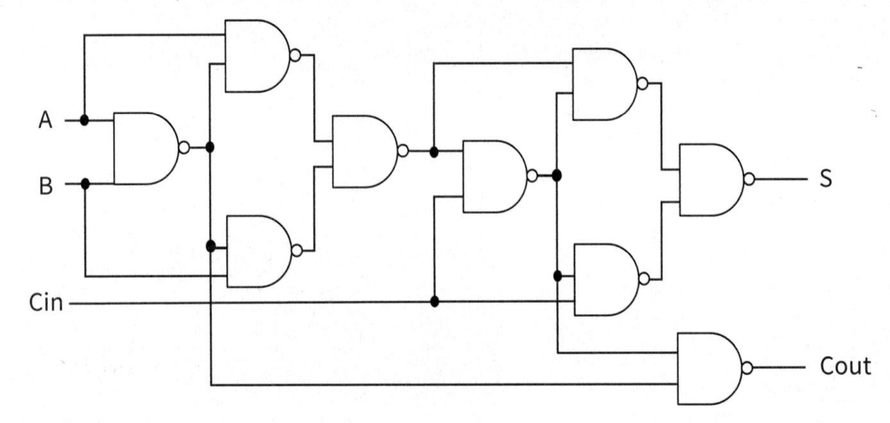

Figure 18.04 A full adder circuit constructed from NAND gates

Discussion Point:

Can you see how full adders could be combined to handle addition of, for example, four-bit binary numbers? What happens to the carry input for the first addition?

The SR flip-flop

All of the circuits so far encountered in this book have been **combinational circuits**. For such a circuit the output is dependent only on the input values. An alternative type of circuit is a **sequential circuit** where the output depends on the input and on the previous output.

KEY TERMS

Combinational circuit: a circuit in which the output is dependent only on the input values

Sequential circuit: a circuit in which the output depends on the input values and the previous output

The SR flip-flop or 'latch' is a simple example of a sequential circuit. It can be constructed with two NAND gates or two NOR gates. Figure 18.05 shows the version with two NOR gates. The flip-flop is a two-state device. Either it has Q set to 1 and Q' set to 0 or it has the reverse.

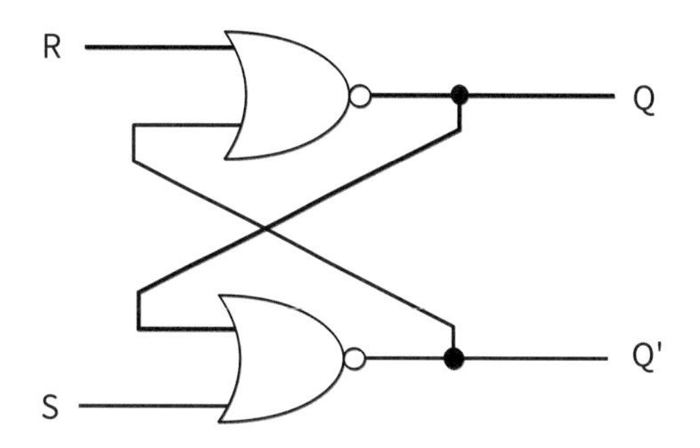

Figure 18.05 A circuit for an SR flip-flop using NOR gates

The truth table for the circuit can be presented as shown in Table 18.04. The two lines of the truth table where both S and R are input as 0 produce no change in the values set for Q or Q'. This is the condition when no signal is input to the flip-flop. Input of S = 1 and R = 0 always produces Q = 1 and Q' = 0. Input of S = 0 and R = 1 always produces the reverse.

This explains why the SR flip-flop can be used as a storage device for 1 bit and therefore could be used as a component in RAM because a value is stored but can be altered. The circuit must be protected from receiving input on R and S simultaneously because this leads to an invalid state with both Q and Q' set to 0.

Input signals		Initial state		Final state	
S	R	Q	Q'	Q	Q'
0	0	1	0	1	0
1	0	1	0	1	0
0	1	1	0	0	1
0	0	0	1	0	1
1	0	0	1	1	0
0	1	0	1	0	1

Table 18.04 A representation of a truth table for an SR flip-flop

The JK flip-flop

In addition to the possibility of entering an invalid state there is also the potential for a circuit to arrive in an uncertain state if inputs do not arrive quite at the same time. In order to prevent this, a circuit may include a clock pulse input to give a better chance of synchronising inputs. The JK flip-flop is an example.

The JK flip-flop can be illustrated by the symbol shown in Figure 18.06(a). A possible circuit is shown in Figure 18.06(b).

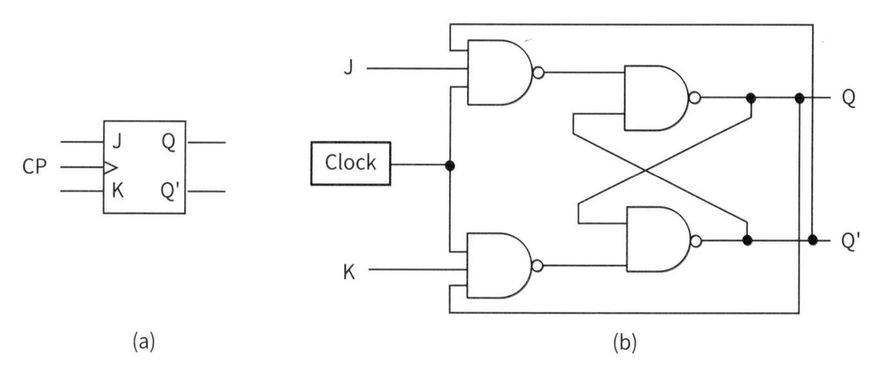

Figure 18.06 (a) A symbol for a JK flip-flop and (b) a possible circuit

The workings of the circuit are viewed in terms of the value of the Q output immediately after the circuit detects a clock pulse. The J input acts as a set input and the K as a clear so there is some similarity to the functioning of the SR flip-flop. However, if both J and K are input as a 1 then Q always switches value. The significant part of the truth table is shown as Table 18.05.

J	K	Clock	Q
0	0	↑	Q unchanged
1	0	↑	1
0	1	↑	0
1	1	↑	Q toggles

Table 18.05 Part of the truth table for a JK flip-flop

18.03 Boolean algebra applications

The Boolean algebra representation of a truth table

One approach to creating a Boolean algebra expression for a particular problem is to start with the truth table and apply the sum of products method. This establishes a minterm for each row of the table that results in a 1 for the output.

This can be illustrated using the truth table for the half adder circuit shown in Figure 18.02. The only row of the table creating a 1 output for C has a 1 input for A and for B. The product becomes A.B and the sum has only this one term so we have:

$$C = A.B$$

For the S output, there are two rows that produce a 1 output so there is a sum of two minterms:

$$S = \bar{A}.B + A.\bar{B}$$

Note that the 0 in a row is represented by the inverse of the input symbol.

The Boolean algebra representation of a logic circuit

This approach can also be used as part of the process of creating a Boolean algebra logic expression from a circuit diagram. The truth tables for the individual logic gates are used and then some algebraic simplification is applied.

WORKED EXAMPLE 18.02

Creating a Boolean algebra logic expression from a half adder circuit

For convenience Figure 18.02 is reproduced here as Figure 18.07. Examination of the figure shows inputs A and B to a NAND gate with output W.

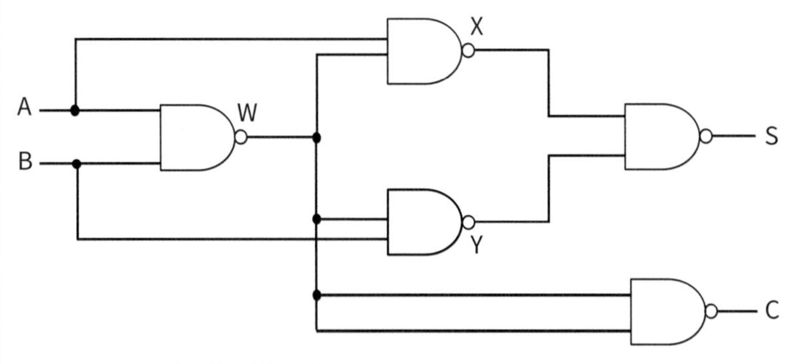

Figure 18.07 A half adder circuit

The first three rows of the NAND truth table produce a 1 output so the sum of products has three minterms:

$$W = \bar{A}.\bar{B} + \bar{A}.B + A.\bar{B}$$

We can now consider the input of W to a NAND gate with A as the other input to produce the X output. The NAND gate operates as an AND gate followed by a NOT gate. The result of the AND operation is the product of the inputs so:

$$X = A.(\bar{A}.\bar{B} + \bar{A}.B + A.\bar{B})$$

Applying the distributive and inverse laws now gives:

$$X = 0 + 0 + A.A.\bar{B} \text{ which is simply } A.\bar{B}$$

We have to take the inverse of this to complete the NAND operation. This is where we need the AND version of De Morgan's law, which transforms the $A.\bar{B}$ into $\bar{A}+B$.

The same laws applied to the output Y from the other intermediate NAND gate to give

$$Y = A+\bar{B}$$

Finally, we need to consider $A+\bar{B}$ and $\bar{A}+B$ being input to the final NAND gate. Again we can consider the AND operation first as the product of the inputs:

$$S = (A+\bar{B}).(\bar{A}+B)$$

If we pause to think we will not multiply this out but instead we will apply De Morgan's law directly to this to perform the inverse operation to complete the NAND operation. This gives:

$$S = \bar{A}.B + A.\bar{B}$$

This is the value obtained directly from the truth table so the algebra has been used correctly.

Extension question 18.01

Worked Example 18.02 did not show that the circuit produced the correct output for C. Also a shortcut was used to reach the final form of S. Can you use Boolean algebra to find the form of C from the circuit and can you convert the expression for S if you start by using the distributive law before applying De Morgan's law?

18.04 Karnaugh maps (K-maps)

A Karnaugh map is a method of creating a Boolean algebra expression from a truth table. It can make the process much easier than if you use sum-of-products to create minterms. The truth table for an OR gate, shown as Table 18.06, can be used to illustrate the method.

A	B	X
0	0	0
0	1	1
1	0	1
1	1	1

Table 18.06 The truth table for the OR operand

Using the sum-of-products approach gives the following expression for X:

$$X = \bar{A}.B + A.\bar{B} + A.B$$

This is not instantly recognisable as A+B but, with a little effort, using Boolean algebra laws it could be shown to be the same.

The Karnaugh map approach is simpler. The corresponding K-map is shown in Figure 18.08. Each cell in a Karnaugh map shows the value of the output X for a combination of input values for A and B.

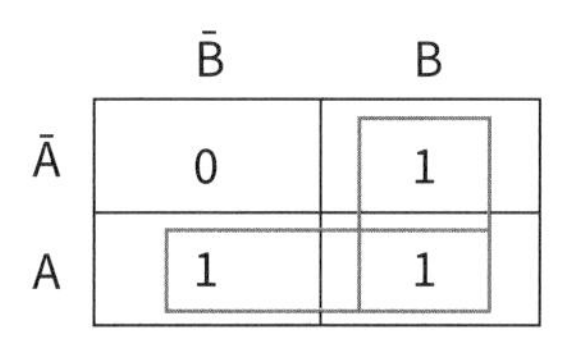

Figure 18.08 A K-map of the truth table in Table 18.06

The interpretation of a Karnaugh map follows these rules:

- Only cells containing a 1 are considered.
- Groups of cells containing 1s are identified where possible, with a group being a row, a column or a rectangle.
- Groups must contain 2, 4, 8 and so on cells.
- Each group should be as large as possible.
- Groups can overlap.
- If an individual cell cannot be contained in any group it is treated as being a group.
- Within each group, the only input values retained are those which retain a constant value throughout the group.

These rules define a column and a row group as indicated by the blue outlines. In the column group, B remains unchanged but A changes so B is retained. In the row group, it is A that remains unchanged. The Boolean algebra expression is then just the sum of these retained values:

$$X = A+B$$

Thus the Karnaugh map has found the OR expression without using any algebra.

WORKED EXAMPLE 18.03

Using a K-map to interpret a three-input problem

Let's consider the truth table shown in Table 18.07.

A	B	C	X
0	0	0	1
0	0	1	0
0	1	0	1
0	1	1	1
1	0	0	0
1	0	1	0
1	1	0	1
1	1	1	1

Table 18.07 A sample truth table with three inputs

Before starting any application of a method it is always worth looking to see if there are any trends. In this case you can see that whenever B = 1 the output for X is 1. This means that the final algebra should have B + something.

Applying sum of products gives the following five-minterm expression:

$$\bar{A}.\bar{B}.\bar{C} + \bar{A}.B.\bar{C} + \bar{A}.B.C + A.B.\bar{C} + A.B.C$$

There are options for how the K-map is presented. We will choose to combine input values in the columns. Figure 18.09 shows the result. This follows the convention of having the rows corresponding to values of A and the columns to combinations of values for B and C.

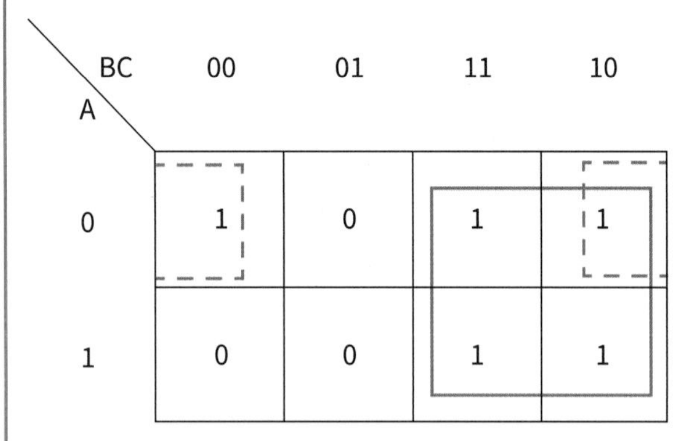

Figure 18.09 A K-map representation of the truth table shown in Table 18.07

It is important to note that the labelling of the columns does not follow a binary value pattern. Instead it follows the Gray coding sequence, where only one bit changes value each time.

Following the rules stated above, the first group to identify is the square of four cells with a value 1 as identified by the blue rectangle in the diagram. For these it can be seen that A has different values, B has a constant value but C changes values. So, only B is retained. Note this was anticipated from the initial inspection of the truth table.

This apparently only leaves the top left cell. It looks like an isolated cell but it is not because K-maps wrap round. The cell is defined by BC = 00. This has two adjacent cells under Gray coding rules. One is immediately obvious – BC = 01 but this contains 0 so can be ignored. The other adjacent cell is the BC = 10 combination. Thus, there is a row group containing BC = 00 and BC = 10, indicated by the dotted line partial group outlines. Note that we cannot include the 11 cell in the same row because a group cannot contain three members. For this row, the value $\bar{A}$ remains unchanged, B changes but $\bar{C}$ remains unchanged so the product $\bar{A}.\bar{C}$ results. So by adding this to the B for the other group the final expression becomes:

$$\bar{A}.\bar{C} + B$$

This is much simpler than the expression with five minterms derived directly from the truth table.

Extension question 18.02

Consider the Karnaugh map shown in Figure 18.10. This corresponds to a problem with four inputs. It wraps round horizontally and vertically. Use the map to create a Boolean algebra expression.

AB \ CD	00	01	11	10
00	1	0	1	1
01	0	0	1	1
11	0	0	1	1
10	1	0	0	0

Figure 18.10 A K-map for a four input problem

Summary

- There are Boolean algebra laws that can be used to simplify logic expressions.
- Binary addition can be carried out using a half adder or a full adder circuit.
- SR or JK flip-flop circuits can be used to store a bit value.
- The sum-of-products method can be used to create an equivalent logic expression containing minterms from a truth table.
- A Karnaugh map is a representation of a truth table that allows a simplified logic expression to be derived from a truth table.

Exam-style Questions

1 a Consider the following circuit:

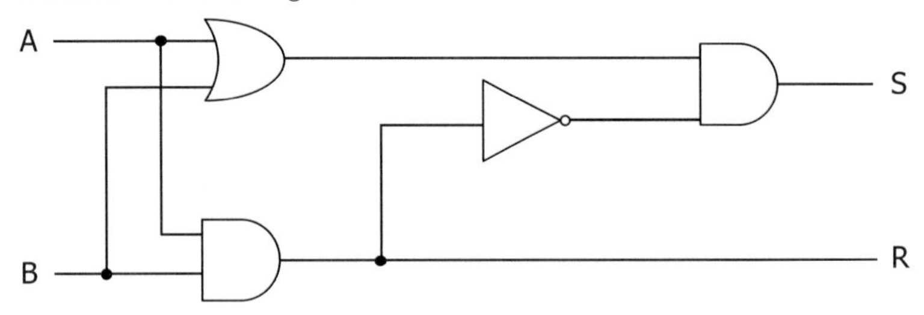

i Identify the three different logic gates used. [2]

ii Complete the following truth table for the circuit for the inputs shown for A and B: [5]

Inputs		Working space	Outputs	
A	B		S	R
0	0			
0	1			
1	0			
1	1			

b For the circuit shown in part (a), identify the type of circuit and what the outputs represent. [3]

2 a Consider the following truth table:

A	B	X
0	0	1
0	1	0
1	0	1
1	1	1

i Using the sum-of-products approach, create a Boolean expression that matches the logic. [3]

ii For the rows that have A = 1, the output for X is 1. Explain how this would be reflected in a simplified form of Boolean expression matching the truth table. [2]

b Consider the following circuit:

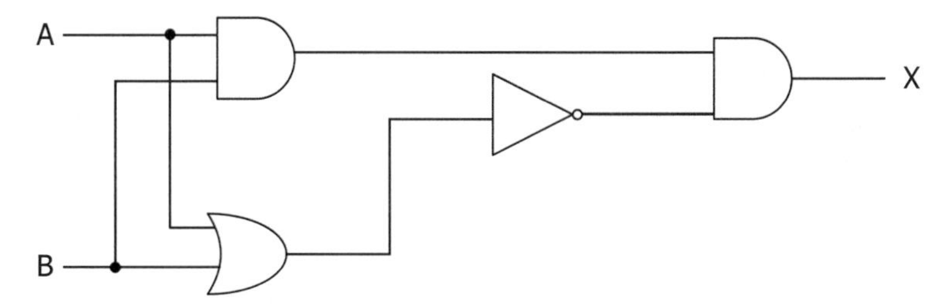

i Using your knowledge of the truth table for an AND gate, create a Boolean algebra expression for the output from the first AND gate. [2]

ii Carry out the same exercise for the OR gate in the circuit. [3]

iii Using De Morgan's law, create the logic expression for the output from the NOT gate. [4]

3 a Consider the following truth table:

A	B	X
0	0	1
0	1	0
1	0	1
1	1	1

i Create a Karnaugh map to match this truth table. [4]

ii Use the Karnaugh map to create a Boolean algebra expression for this logic. [3]

b Consider the truth table shown in **3 a**.

i Use the sum-of-products method to create a Boolean algebra expression from the truth table. [3]

ii Use Boolean algebra to show that this expression can be simplified to give the same expression created from the Karnaugh map. (Hint: you might wish to use the fact that $A.\bar{B} = A.\bar{B} + A.\bar{B}$). [4]

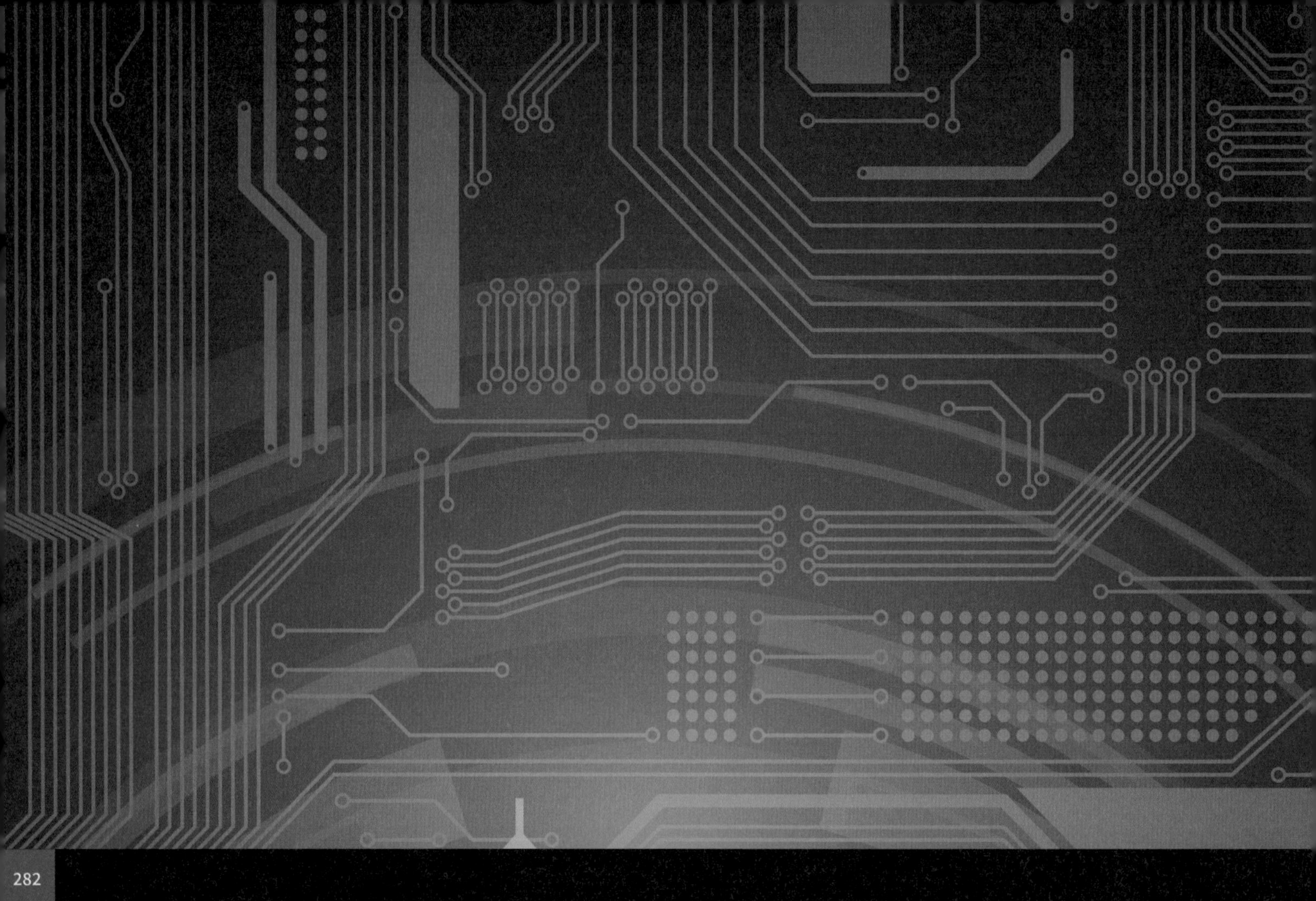

Chapter 19
Processor and Computer Architecture

Learning objectives

By the end of this chapter you should be able to:

- show understanding of the differences between RISC and CISC processors
- show understanding of the importance/use of pipelining and registers in RISC processors
- show understanding of interrupt handling on CISC and RISC processors
- show awareness of the four basic computer architectures: SISD, SIMD, MISD, MIMD
- show awareness of the characteristics of massively parallel computers.

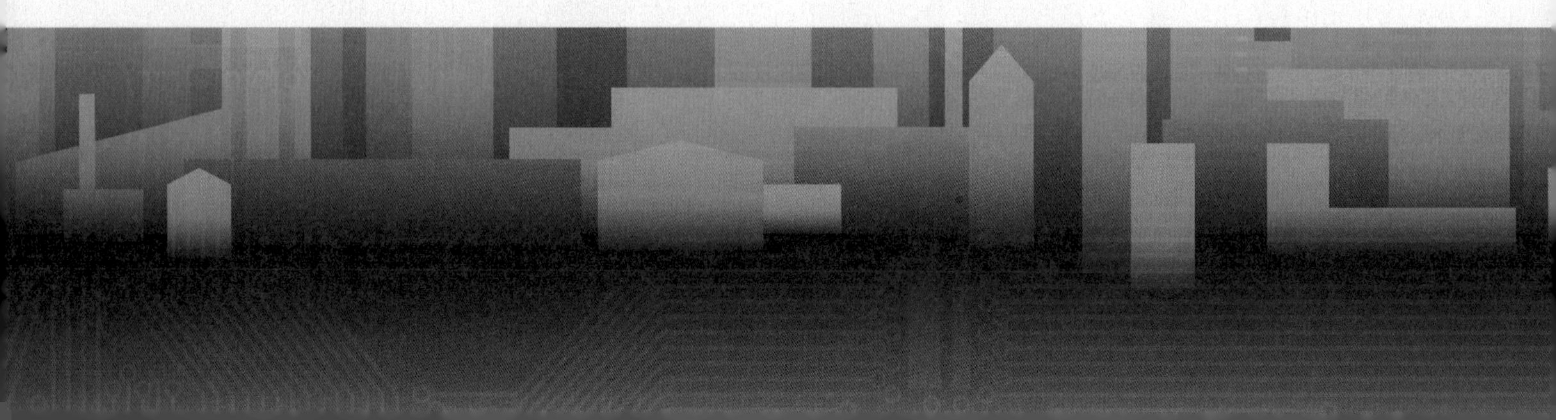

19.01 The control unit

While a program is being executed, the CPU is receiving a sequence of machine-code instructions. It is the responsibility of the control unit within the CPU to ensure that each machine instruction is handled correctly. There are two ways that a control unit can be designed to allow it to perform its function.

One method is for the control unit to be constructed as a logic circuit. This is called the hard-wired solution. The machine-code instructions are handled directly by hardware.

The alternative is for the control unit to use microprogramming. In this approach, the control unit contains a ROM component in which is stored the microinstructions or microcode for microprogramming. This is often referred to as firmware. The choice of which method is used is largely dependent on the type of processor.

19.02 CISC and RISC processors

The 'architecture' of a processor can be defined in a number of ways. From the point of view of a sophisticated programmer, the architecture involves the following:

- the instruction set
- the instruction format
- the addressing modes
- the registers accessible by instructions.

The choice of the instruction set is the main factor in deciding on a suitable architecture. One view is that the instruction set should be chosen so that it can be clearly applied to important problems, that only simple equipment is required and that important problems are handled speedily. An opposing view is that it should be chosen to suit the needs of high-level languages.

Early developments in computing led to the latter view becoming dominant. Computer systems contained what would now be referred to as CISC (Complex Instruction Set Computers) processors with the complexity increasing with the advent of new systems. However, the philosophy began to be challenged in the late 1970s. It was argued that RISC (Reduced Instruction Set Computers) would be a better approach. Table 19.01 contains a number of features that distinguish RISC from CISC.

RISC	CISC
Fewer instructions	More instructions
Simpler instructions	More complex instructions
Small number of instruction formats	Many instruction formats
Single-cycle instructions whenever possible	Multi-cycle instructions
Fixed-length instructions	Variable-length instructions
Only load and store instructions to address memory	Many types of instructions to address memory
Fewer addressing modes	More addressing modes
Multiple register sets	Fewer registers
Hard-wired control unit	Microprogrammed control unit
Pipelining easier	Pipelining more difficult

Table 19.01 Comparison of RISC with CISC

It can be seen that 'reduced' affects more than just the number of instructions. The simplicity of the instructions allows data to be stored in registers and manipulated in them with no resource to memory access other than that necessary for initial loading and possible final storing. The simplicity also allows hard-wiring inside the control unit with limited complexity required.

In contrast, the specialised instructions that can be part of a CISC architecture often require repeated memory access. The complexity of some of the instructions makes hard-wiring extremely difficult so microprogramming is the norm. However, the increased complexity of instructions for CISC is often because they more closely match high-level language constructs. This means that compiler writing becomes much easier for a CISC processor.

Extension question 19.01

Can you find out whether the processors in any systems you are using are described as RISC or CISC?

One of the major driving forces for creating RISC processors was the opportunity they would provide for efficient **pipelining**. Pipelining is a form of parallelism applied specifically to instruction execution. Other forms of parallelism are discussed in Section 19.03.

KEY TERMS

Pipelining: instruction-level parallelism

The underlying principle of pipelining is that the fetch–decode–execute cycle described in Chapter 5 (Section 5.04) can be separated into a number of stages. One possibility is a five-stage model consisting of:

- instruction fetch (IF)
- instruction decode (ID)
- operand fetch (OF)
- instruction execute (IE)
- result write back (WB).

Figure 19.01 shows how pipelining would work with this five-stage breakdown of instruction handling. For pipelining to be implemented, the construction of the processor must have five independent units, with each handling one of the five stages identified. This explains the need for a RISC processor to have many register sets; each processor unit must have access to its own set of registers. Figure 19.01 uses the representation 1.1, 1.2 and so on to define the instruction and the stage of the instruction. Initially only the first stage of the first instruction has entered the pipeline. At clock cycle 6 the first instruction has left the pipeline, the last stage of instruction 2 is being handled and instruction 6 has just entered.

Processor units / Clock cycles	1	2	3	4	5	6	7
IF	1.1	2.1	3.1	4.1	5.1	6.1	7.1
ID		1.2	2.2	3.2	4.2	5.2	6.2
OF			1.3	2.3	3.3	4.3	5.3
IE				1.4	2.4	3.4	4.4
WB					1.5	2.5	3.5

Figure 19.01 Pipelining for five-stage instruction handling

It can be seen that once under way the pipeline is handling five stages of five individual instructions. In particular, at each clock cycle the complete processing of one instruction has finished. Without the pipeline the processing time would be five times longer.

One issue that has to be dealt with regarding a pipelined processor is interrupt handling. The discussion in Chapter 5 (Section 5.06) referred to a processor with instructions handled sequentially. In the pipelined system described above there will be five instructions in the pipeline when an interrupt occurs. One option for handling the interrupt is to erase the pipeline contents for the latest four instructions to have entered. Then the normal interrupt-handling routine can be applied to the remaining instruction. The other option is to construct the individual units in the processor with individual program counter registers. This allows current data to be stored for all of the instructions in the pipeline while the interrupt is handled.

Discussion Point:

Consider the two consecutive instructions:

```
ADD R1, R2, R3
ADD R5, R1, R4
```

These are typical three-register instructions favoured for RISC. The first adds the contents of registers R2 and R3 and stores the result in R1. The next instruction is similar but uses the value stored in R1. In a pipelined structure, the second instruction will be reading the contents of R1 before the previous instruction has placed the value there. How could this potential problem be overcome?

19.03 Parallel processing

Parallel processor systems

One computer can have multiple processors running in parallel.

In principle, there are four categories of system:

- SISD (Single Instruction Single Data stream)
- SIMD (Single Instruction Multiple Data stream)
- MISD (Multiple Instruction Single Data stream)
- MIMD (Multiple Instruction Multiple Data stream).

SISD (Single Instruction Single Data stream) is the typical arrangement found in early personal computers. There is a single processor so no processor parallelism. The single data stream just means one memory.

SIMD (Single Instruction Multiple Data stream) describes how an array or vector processor works. The multiple processors each have their own memory. One instruction is input and each processor executes this instruction using data available in its dedicated memory.

MISD (Multiple Instruction Single Data stream) isn't implemented in commercial products.

MIMD (Multiple Instruction Multiple Data stream) has examples in modern personal computers which are of the symmetric multiprocessor type using identical processors. In this case, each processor executes a different individual instruction. The multiple data stream can be provided by a single memory suitably partitioned. Each processor might have a dedicated cache memory.

Parallel computer systems

Examples of one type of multicomputer system are called massively parallel computers. These are the systems used by large organisations for computations involving highly complex mathematical processing. They are the latest in an evolution of what have traditionally been called 'supercomputers'. The major difference in architecture is that instead of having a bus structure to support multiple processors there is a network infrastructure to support multiple computer units. The programs running on the different computers can communicate by passing messages using the network.

An alternative type of multicomputer system is cluster computing, where a very large number of PCs are networked.

Summary

- A control unit can be hard-wired or microprogrammed.
- RISC (Reduced Instruction Set Computers) processors have a number of advantages compared to CISC (Complex Instruction Set Computers).
- Pipelining is one of the reasons for choosing a RISC architecture.
- Parallelism can be based at the instruction level, processor level or computer level.

Exam-style Questions

1 a Computer systems are now often constructed with RISC processors.

i State what the acronym RISC stands for. [1]

ii State four characteristics to be expected of a RISC system. [4]

b A RISC processor is likely to be 'hard-wired'.

i Explain what this term means and which specific part of the processor will be hard-wired. [3]

ii State what the alternative to hard-wiring is and what hardware component is needed to be part of the processor to allow this alternative to be implemented. [2]

2 a Parallelism can be achieved in a number of ways.

i Identify three different types of parallelism. [3]

ii Identify which type pipelining belongs to. [1]

iii Using a diagram, explain how pipelining works. [5]

b Interrupt handling is not so straightforward in a pipelined system. Explain why this is so and give a brief account of how problems can be avoided. [3]

Chapter 20
System Software

Learning objectives

By the end of this chapter you should be able to:

- show understanding of how an operating system can maximise the use of resources
- describe the ways in which the user interface hides the complexities of the hardware from the user
- show understanding of processor management including: the concepts of a process, multitasking and an interrupt and the need for scheduling
- show understanding of paging for memory management including: the concepts of paging and virtual memory, the need for paging, how pages can be replaced and how disk thrashing can occur
- show understanding of the concept of a virtual machine and give examples of the role of virtual machines and their benefits and limitations
- show understanding of how an interpreter can execute programs without producing a translated version
- show understanding of the various stages in the compilation of a program
- show understanding of how the grammar of a language can be expressed using syntax diagrams or Backus-Naur Form (BNF) notation
- show understanding of how Reverse Polish Notation (RPN) can be used to carry out the evaluation of expressions.

20.01 The purposes of an operating system (OS)

Before considering the purposes of an operating system (OS), we need to present the context in which it runs. A computer system needs a program that begins to run when the system is first switched on. At this stage, the operating system programs are stored on disk so there is no operating system. However, the computer has stored in ROM a basic input output system (BIOS) which starts a bootstrap program. It is this bootstrap program that loads the operating system into memory and sets it running.

An operating system can provide facilities to have more than one program stored in memory. Only one program can access the CPU at any given time but others are ready when the opportunity arises. This is described as multi-programming. This will happen for one single user. Some systems are designed to have many users simultaneously logged in. This is a time-sharing system.

The purposes of an operating system can usefully be considered from two viewpoints: an internal viewpoint and an external viewpoint. The internal viewpoint concerns how the activities of the operating system are organised to best use the resources available. The external viewpoint concerns the facilities made available for system usage. Chapter 7 (Section 7.02) contained a categorised summary of the various activities that an operating system engages in. This chapter discusses some of them in more detail.

Resource management

The three fundamental resources in a computer system are:

- the CPU
- the memory
- the I/O (input/output) system.

Resource management relating to the CPU concerns scheduling to ensure efficient usage. The methods used are described in Section 20.03. These methods consider the CPU as a single unit; specific issues relating to a multiprocessor system are not considered. Resource management relating to the memory concerns optimum usage of main memory.

The I/O system does not just relate to input and output that directly involves a computer user. It also includes input and output to storage devices while a program is running. Figure 20.01 shows a schematic diagram that illustrates the structure of the I/O system.

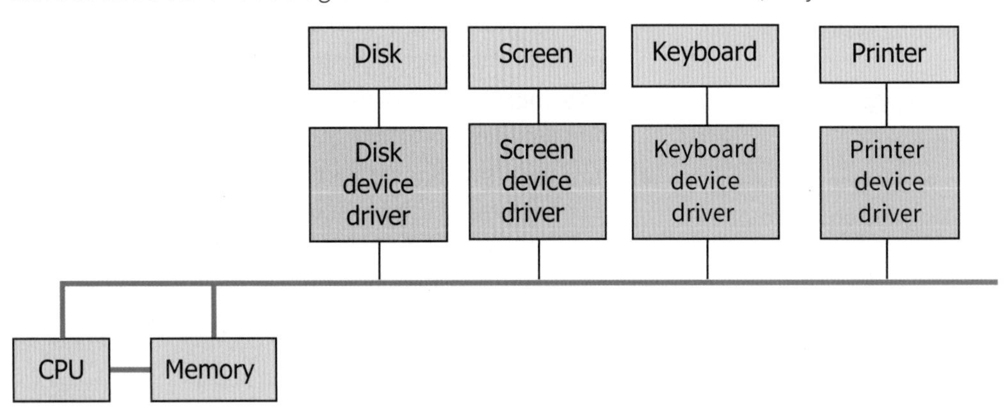

Figure 20.01 Main components associated with the I/O system

The bus structure in Figure 20.01 shows that there can be an option for the transfer of data between an I/O device and memory. The operating system can ensure that I/O passes via the

CPU but for large quantities of data the operating system can ensure direct transfer between memory and an I/O device.

To understand the issues associated with I/O management, some discussion of timescales is required. It must be understood that one second is a very long time for a computer system. A CPU typically operates at GHz frequencies. One second sees more than one trillion clock cycles. Some typical speeds for I/O are given in Table 20.01.

Device	Data rate	Time for transfer of 1 byte
Keyboard	10 Bps	0.1 s
Screen	50 MBps	2×10^{-8} s
Disk	5 MBps	2×10^{-7} s

Table 20.01 Typical rates and times for data transfer

The slow speed of I/O compared to a typical CPU clock cycle shows that management of CPU usage is vital to ensure that the CPU does not remain idle while I/O is taking place.

Operating system facilities provided for the user

The user interface may be made available as a command line, a graphical display or a voice recognition system but the function is always to allow the user to interact with running programs. When a program involves use of a device, the operating system provides the device driver: the user just expects the device to work. (You might, however, wish to argue that printers do not always quite fit this description.)

The operating system will provide a file system for a user to store data and programs. The user has to choose filenames and organise a directory (folder) structure but the user does not have to organise the physical data storage on a disk. If the user is a programmer, the operating system supports the provision of a programming environment. This allows a program to be created and run without the programmer being familiar with how the processor functions.

When a program is running it can be considered to be a type of user. The operating system provides a set of system calls that provide an interface to the services it offers. For instance, if a program specifies that it needs to read data from a file, the request for the file is converted into a system call that causes the operating system to take charge, find the file and make it available to the program. An extension of this concept is when an operating system provides an application programming interface (API). Each API call fulfils a specific function such as creating a screen icon. The API might use one or more system calls. The API concept aims to provide portability for a program.

Operating system structure

An operating system has to be structured in order to provide a platform for both resource management and the provision of facilities for users. The logical structure of the operating system provides two modes of operation. User mode is the one available for the user or an application program. The alternative has a number of different names of which the most often used are 'privileged mode' or 'kernel mode'. The difference between the two is that kernel mode has sole access to part of the memory and to certain system functions that user mode cannot access.

It is now normal for the operating system to be separated into a kernel which runs all of the time and the remainder which runs in user mode. One possibility then is to use a layered structure as illustrated in Figure 20.02.

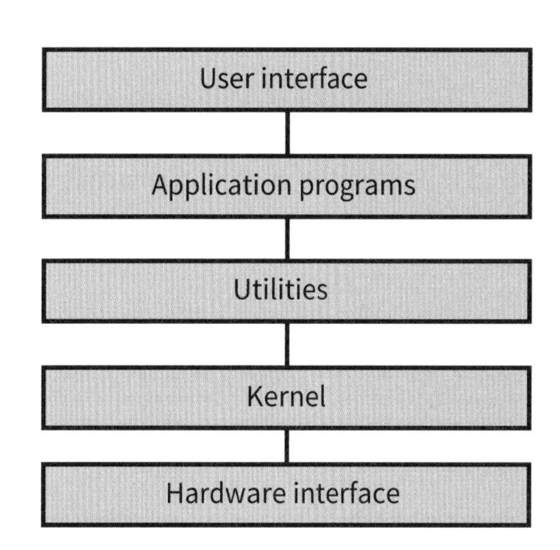

Figure 20.02 Layered structure for an operating system

In this model, application programs or utility programs could make system calls to the kernel. However, to work properly each higher layer needs to be fully serviced by a lower layer (as in a network protocol stack).

This is hard to achieve in practice. A more flexible approach uses a modular structure, illustrated in Figure 20.03. The structure works by the kernel calling on the individual services when required. It could possibly be associated with a micro-kernel structure where the functionality in the kernel is reduced to the absolute minimum.

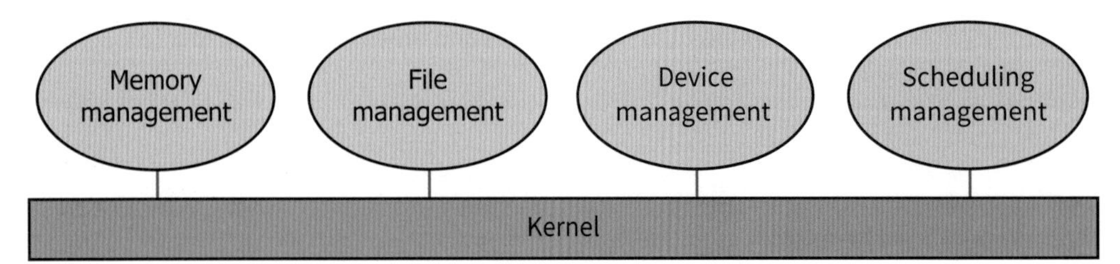

Figure 20.03 Modular structure for an operating system

20.02 Process scheduling

Programs that are available to be run on a computer system are initially stored on disk. In a time-sharing system a user could submit a program as a 'job' which would include the program and some instructions about how it should be run. Figure 20.04 shows an overview of the components involved when a program is run.

A long-term or high-level scheduler program controls the selection of a program stored on disk to be moved into main memory. Occasionally a program has to be taken back to disk due to the memory getting overcrowded. This is controlled by a medium-term scheduler. When the program is installed in memory, a short-term or low-level scheduler controls when it has access to the CPU.

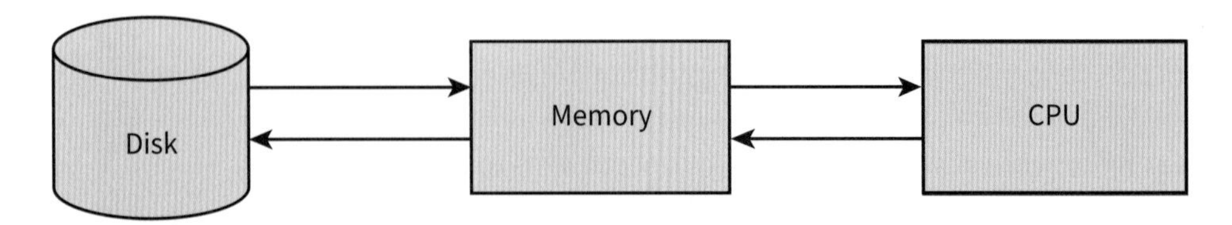

Figure 20.04 Components involved in running a program

Process states

In Chapter 7 (Section 7.02), it was stated that a **process** can be defined as 'a program being executed'. This definition is perhaps better slightly modified to include the state when the program first arrives in memory. At this stage a **process control block (PCB)** can be created in memory ready to receive data when the process is executed. Once in memory the state of the process can change.

The transitions between the states shown in Figure 20.05 can be described as follows:

- A new process arrives in memory and a PCB is created; it changes to the ready state.
- A process in the ready state is given access to the CPU by the dispatcher; it changes to the running state.
- A process in the running state is halted by an interrupt; it returns to the ready state.
- A process in the running state cannot progress until some event has occurred (I/O perhaps); it changes to the waiting state (sometimes called the 'suspended' or 'blocked' state).

- A process in the waiting state is notified that an event is completed; it returns to the ready state.
- A process in the running state completes execution; it changes to the terminated state.

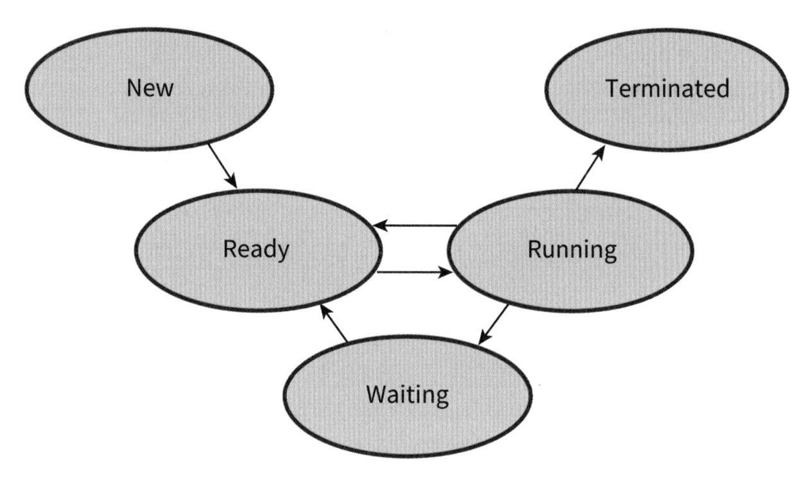

Figure 20.05 The five states defined for a process being executed

It is possible for a process to be separated into different parts for execution. The separate parts are called **threads.** If this has happened, each thread is handled as though it were a process.

KEY TERMS

Process: a program in memory that has an associated process control block

Process control block (PCB): a complex data structure containing all data relevant to the running of a process

Thread: part of a process being executed

Interrupts

Some interrupts are caused by errors that prematurely terminate a running process. Otherwise there are two reasons for interrupts:

- Processes consist of alternating periods of CPU usage and I/O usage. I/O takes far too long for the CPU to remain idle waiting for it to complete. The interrupt mechanism is used when a process in the running state makes a system call requiring an I/O operation and has to change to the waiting state.
- The scheduler decides to halt the process for one of several reasons, discussed in the next section ('Scheduling algorithms').

Whatever the reason for an interrupt, the OS kernel must invoke an interrupt-handling routine. This may have to decide on the priority of an interrupt. One required action is that the current values stored in registers must be recorded in the process control block. This allows the process to continue execution when it eventually returns to the running state.

Discussion Point:

What would happen if an interrupt was received while the interrupt-handling routine was being executed by the CPU? Does this require a priority being set for each interrupt?

Scheduling algorithms

Although the long-term or high-level scheduler will have decisions to make when choosing which program should be loaded into memory, we concentrate here on the options for the short-term or low-level scheduler.

A scheduling algorithm can be preemptive or non-preemptive. A preemptive algorithm can halt a process that would otherwise continue running undisturbed. If an algorithm is preemptive it may involve prioritising processes.

The simplest possible algorithm is first come first served (FCFS). This is a non-preemptive algorithm and can be implemented by placing the processes in a first-in first-out (FIFO) queue. It will be very inefficient if it is the only algorithm employed but it can be used as part of a more complex algorithm.

A round-robin algorithm allocates a time slice to each process and is therefore preemptive, because a process will be halted when its time slice has run out. It can be implemented as a FIFO queue. It normally does not involve prioritising processes. However, if separate queues are created for processes of different priorities then each queue could be scheduled using a round-robin algorithm.

A priority-based scheduling algorithm is more complicated. One reason for this is that every time a new process enters the ready queue or when a running process is halted, the priorities for the processes may have to be re-evaluated. The other reason is that whatever scheme is used to judge priority level it will require some computation. Possible criteria are:

- estimated time of process execution
- estimated remaining time for execution
- length of time already spent in the ready queue
- whether the process is I/O bound or CPU bound.

More than one of these criteria might be considered. Clearly, estimating a time for execution may not be easy. Some processes require extensive I/O, for instance printing wage slips for employees. There is very little CPU usage for such a process so it makes sense to allocate it a high priority so that the small amount of CPU usage can take place. The process will then change to the waiting state while the printing takes place.

20.03 Memory management

The term memory management embraces a number of aspects. One aspect concerns the provision of protected memory space for the OS kernel. Another is that the loading of a program into memory requires defining the memory addresses for the program itself, for associated procedures and for the data required by the program. In a multiprogramming system, this might not be straightforward. The storage of processes in main memory can get fragmented in the same way as happens for files stored on a hard disk. There may be a need for the medium-term scheduler to move a process out of main memory to ease the problem.

One memory management technique is to partition memory with the aim of loading the whole of a process into one partition. Dynamic partitioning allows the partition size to match the process size. An extension of this idea is to divide larger processes into segments, with each segment loaded into a dynamic partition. Alternatively, a paging method can be used. The process is divided into equal-sized pages and memory is divided into frames of the same size. All of the pages are loaded into memory at the same time.

The most flexible approach to memory management is to use **virtual memory** based on paging but with no requirement for all pages to be in memory at the same time. In a virtual memory system, the address space that the CPU uses is larger than the physical main memory space. This requires the CPU to transfer address values to a memory management unit that allocates a corresponding address on a page.

KEY TERMS

Virtual memory: a paging mechanism that allows a program to use more memory addresses than are available in main memory

The starting situation is that the set of pages comprising the process are stored on disk. One or more of these pages is loaded into memory when the process is changing to the ready state. When the process is dispatched to the running state, the process starts executing. At some stage, it will need access to pages still stored on disk which means that a page needs to be taken out of memory first. This is when a page replacement algorithm is needed. A simple algorithm would use a first-in first-out method. A more sensible method would be the least-recently-used page but this requires statistics of page use to be recorded.

One of the advantages of the virtual memory approach is that a very large program can be run when an equally large amount of memory is unavailable. Another advantage is that only part of a program needs to be in memory at any one time. For example, the index tables for a database could be permanently in memory but the full tables could be brought in only when required.

The system overhead in running virtual memory can be a disadvantage. The worst problem is 'disk thrashing', when part of a process on one page requires another page which is on disk. When that page is loaded it almost immediately requires the original page again. This can lead to almost perpetual loading and unloading of pages. Algorithms have been developed to guard against this but the problem can still occur, fortunately only rarely.

20.04 Virtual machine

Although virtual memory could be used in a system running a virtual machine, the two are completely different concepts that must not be confused. Also note that the Java virtual machine discussed in Chapter 7 (Section 7.05) is based on a different underlying concept.

The principle of a virtual machine is that a process interacts directly with a software interface provided by the operating system. The kernel of the operating system handles all of the interactions with the actual hardware of the host system. The software interface provided for the virtual machine provides an exact copy of the hardware. The logical structure is shown in Figure 20.06.

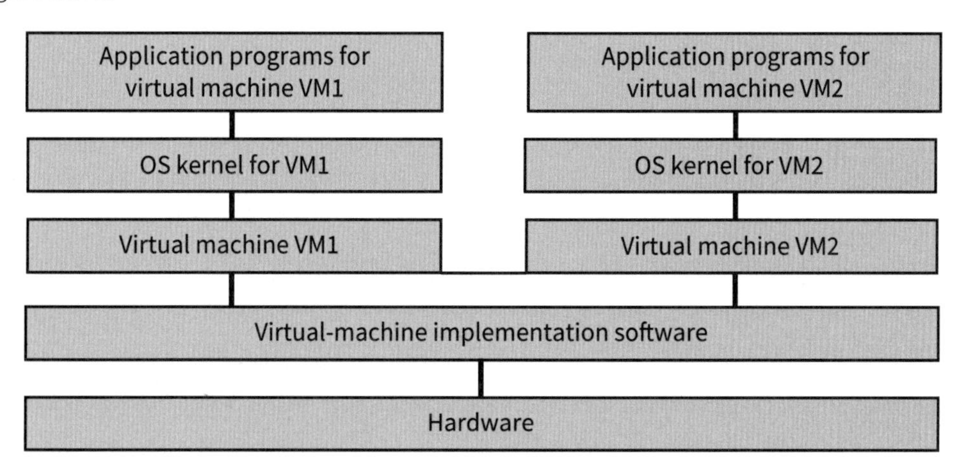

Figure 20.06 Logical structure for a virtual machine implementation

The advantage of the virtual machine approach is that more than one different operating system can be made available on one computer system. This is particularly valuable if an organisation has legacy systems and wishes to continue to use the software but does not wish to keep the aged hardware. Alternatively, the same operating system can be made available many times. This is done by companies with large mainframe computers that offer server consolidation facilities. Different companies can be offered their own virtual machine running as a server.

One drawback to using a virtual machine is the time and effort required for implementation. Another is the fact that the implementation will not offer the same level of performance that would be obtained on a normal system.

20.05 Translation software

An overview of how a compiler or an interpreter is used was presented in Chapter 7 (Section 7.05). This section will consider some details of how a compiler works with a brief reference to the workings of an interpreter.

A compiler can be described as having a 'front end' and a 'back end'. The front-end program performs analysis of the source code and produces an intermediate code that expresses completely the semantics (the meaning) of the source code. The back-end program then takes this intermediate code as input and performs synthesis of object code. This analysis–synthesis model is represented in Figure 20.07.

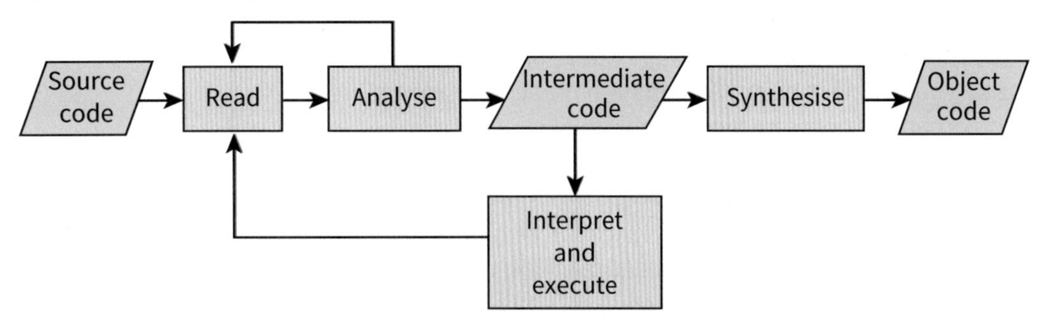

Figure 20.07 Analysis–synthesis model for a compiler

For simplicity, Figure 20.07 assumes no error in the source code. There is a repetitive process in which the source code is read line-by-line. For each line, the compiler creates matching intermediate code. Figure 20.07 also shows how an interpreter program would have the same analysis front-end: In this case, however, once a line of source code has been converted to intermediate code, it is executed.

Front-end analysis stages

The four stages of front-end analysis, shown in Figure 20.08, are:

- lexical analysis
- syntax analysis
- semantic analysis
- intermediate code generation.

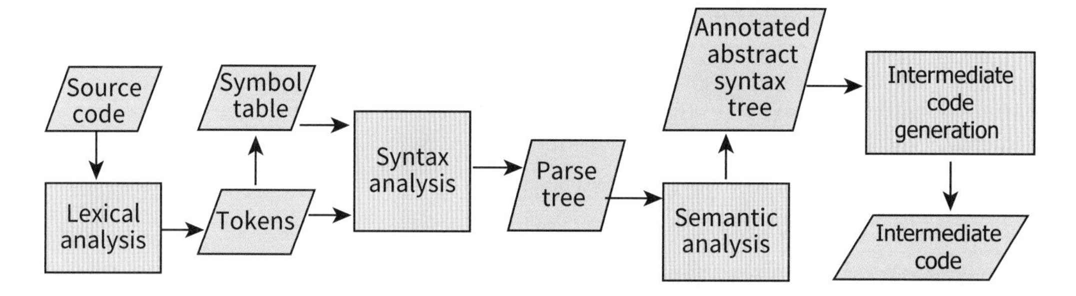

Figure 20.08 Front-end analysis

In lexical analysis each line of source code is separated into tokens. This is a pattern-matching exercise. It requires the analyser to have knowledge of the components that can be found in a program written in the particular programming language.

For example, the declaration statement:

```
Var Count : integer;
```

would be recognised as containing five tokens:

```
Var  Count  :  integer  ;
```

The assignment statement:

```
PercentMark[Count] :=  Score * 10
```

would be recognised as containing eight tokens:

```
PercentMark  [  Count  ]  :=  Score  *  10
```

The analyser must categorise each token. For instance, in the first example, `Var` and `integer` must be recognised as keywords. The non-alphanumeric characters such as `[` or `*` must be categorised. The `:=` is a special case; the analyser must recognise that this is one operator with two characters that must not be separated.

Finally, all identifiers such as `Count` and `PercentMark` must be recognised as such and an entry for each must be made in the **symbol table** (which could have been called the identifier table). The symbol table contains identifier attributes such as the data type, where it is declared and where it is assigned a value. The symbol table is an important data structure for a compiler. Although Figure 20.08 shows it only being used by the syntax analysis program, it is also used by later stages of compilation.

KEY TERMS

Symbol table: a data structure in which each record contains the name and attributes of an identifier

Syntax analysis, which is also known as parsing, involves analysis of the program constructs. The results of the analysis are recorded as a syntax or parse tree. Figure 20.09 shows the parse tree for the following assignment statement:

```
y := 2 * x + 4
```

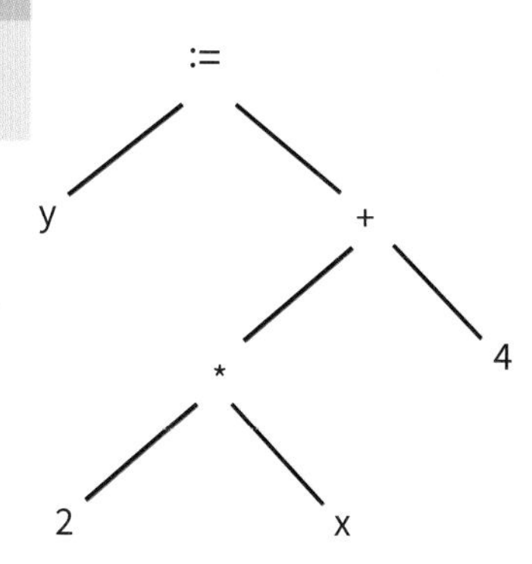

Figure 20.09 Parse tree for an assignment statement

Note that the hierarchical structure of the tree, if correctly interpreted, ensures that the multiplication of 2 by x is carried out before the addition of 4.

Semantic analysis is about establishing the full meaning of the code. An annotated abstract syntax tree is constructed to record this information. For the identifiers in this tree an associated set of attributes is established including, for example, the data type. These attributes are also recorded in the symbol table.

An often-used intermediate code created by the last stage of front-end analysis is a three-address code. As an example the following assignment statement has five identifiers requiring five addresses:

```
y := a + (b * c - d) / e
```

This could be converted into the following four statements, each requiring at most three addresses:

```
temp := b * c

temp := temp - d

temp := temp / e

y := a + temp
```

Representation of the grammar of a language

For each programming language, there is a defined grammar. This grammar must be understood by a programmer and also by a compiler writer.

One method of presenting the grammar rules is a syntax diagram. Figure 20.10 represents the grammar rule that an identifier must start with a letter which can be followed by any combination of none or more letters or digits. The convention used here is that options are drawn above the main flow line and repetitions are drawn below it.

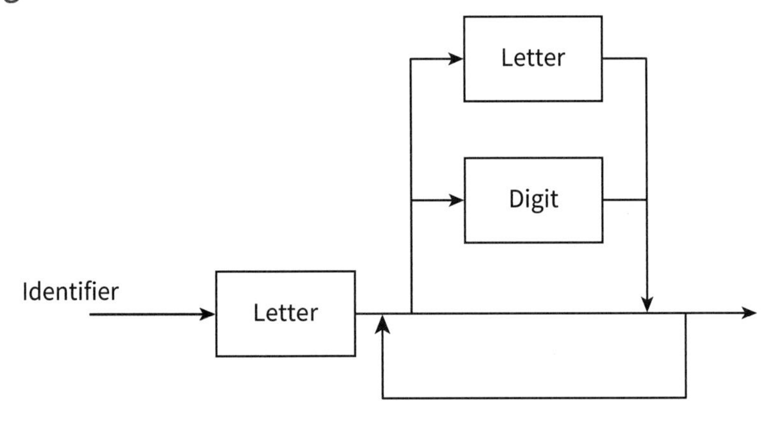

Figure 20.10 Syntax diagram defining an identifier

An alternative approach is to use Backus–Naur Form (BNF). A possible format for a BNF definition of an identifier is:

<Identifier> ::= <Letter>|<Identifier><Letter>|<Identifier><Digit>

<Digit> ::= 0|1|2|3|4|5|6|7|8|9

<Letter> ::= <UpperCaseLetter>|<LowerCaseLetter>

<UpperCaseLetter> ::= A|B|C|D|E|F|G|H|I|J|K|L|M|N|O|P|Q|R|S|T|U|V|W|X|Y|Z

<LowerCaseLetter> ::= a|b|c|d|e|f|g|h|i|j|k|l|m|n|o|p|q|r|s|t|u|v|w|x|y|z

The use of | is to separate individual options. The ::= characters can be read as 'is defined as'. Note the recursive definition of <Identifier> in this particular version of BNF. Without the use of recursion the definition would need to be more complicated to include all possible combinations following the initial <Letter>.

A syntax diagram is only used in the context of a language. It has limited use because it cannot be incorporated into a compiler program as an algorithm. By contrast, BNF is a general approach which can be used to describe any assembly of data. Furthermore, it can be used as the basis for an algorithm.

Back-end synthesis stages

If the front-end analysis has established that there are syntax errors, the only back-end process is the presentation of a list of these errors. For each error, there will be an explanation and the location within the program source code.

In the absence of errors, the main back-end stage is machine code generation from the intermediate code. This may involve optimisation of the code. The aim of optimisation is to create an efficient program; the methods that can be used are diverse. One type of optimisation focuses on features that were inherent in the original source code and have been propagated into the intermediate code. As a simple example, consider these successive assignment statements:

```
x := (a + b) * (a - b)

y := (a + 2 * b) * (a - b)
```

The most efficient code would be:

```
temp := (a - b)

x := (a + b) * temp

y := x + temp * b
```

Question 20.01

Check the maths for the efficient code defined above.

Another example is when a statement inside a loop, which is therefore executed for each repetition of the loop, does the same thing each time. Optimisation would place the statement immediately before the loop.

The other type of optimisation is instigated when the machine code has been created. This type of optimisation may involve efficient use of registers or of memory.

Evaluation of expressions

An assignment statement often has an algebraic expression defining a new value for an identifier. The expression can be evaluated by firstly converting the infix representation in the code to Reverse Polish Notation (RPN). RPN is a postfix representation which never requires brackets and has no rules of precedence.

WORKED EXAMPLE 20.01

Manually converting an expression between RPN and infix

Converting an expression to RPN

We consider a very simple expression:

```
a + b * c
```

The conversion to RPN has to take into account operator precedence so the first step is to convert `b * c` to get the intermediate form:

```
a + b c *
```

We then convert the two terms to give the final RPN form:

```
a b c * +
```

If the original expression had been `(a + b) * c` (where the brackets were essential) then the conversion to RPN would have given:

```
a b + c *
```

Converting an expression from RPN

Consider this more complicated example of an RPN expression:

```
x 2 * y 3 * + 6 /
```

The process is as follows. The RPN is scanned until two identifiers are followed by an operator. This combination is converted to give an intermediate form (brackets are used for clarification):

```
(x * 2) y 3 * + 6 /
```

This process is repeated to give the following successive versions:

```
(x * 2)(y * 3) + 6 /
(x * 2) + (y * 3) 6 /
((x * 2) + (y * 3)) / 6
```

Because of the precedence rules, some of the brackets are unnecessary; the final version could be written as:

```
(x * 2 + y * 3) / 6
```


WORKED EXAMPLE 20.02

Using a syntax tree to convert an expression to RPN

In the syntax analysis stage, an expression is represented as a syntax tree. The expression `a + b * c` would be presented as shown in Figure 20.11.

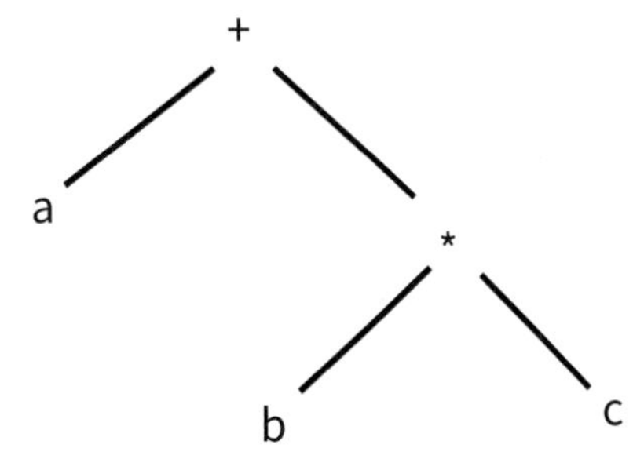

Figure 20.11 Syntax tree for an infix expression

To create this tree, the lowest precedence operator (+) is positioned at the root. If there are several with the same precedence, the first one is used. The RPN form of the expression can now be extracted by a post-order traversal. This starts at the lowest leaf to the left of the root and then uses left–right–root ordering which ensures, in this case, that the RPN representation is:

```
a b c * +
```

WORKED EXAMPLE 20.03

Using a stack with an RPN expression

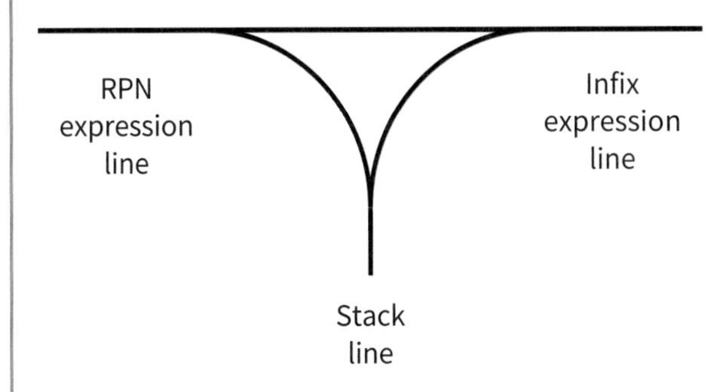

Figure 20.12 Shunting-yard algorithm

To convert an infix expression to RPN using a stack, the shunting-yard algorithm is used (Figure 20.12).

Converting an expression to RPN

The rules of the algorithm are to consider the string of tokens representing the infix expression. These represent the railroad waggons that are to be shunted from the infix line to the RPN line. The tokens are examined one by one. For each one, the rules are:

- If it is an identifier, it passes straight through to the RPN expression line.
- If it is an operator, there are two options:
  - If the stack line is empty or contains a lower precedence operator, the operator is diverted into the stack line.
  - If the stack line contains an equal or higher preference operator, then that operator is popped from the stack into the RPN expression line and the new operator takes its place on the stack line.
- When all tokens have left the infix line, the operators remaining on the stack line are popped one by one from the stack line onto the RPN expression line.

Consider the infix expression `a + b * c`. Table 20.02 traces the conversion process. The first operator to enter the stack line is the + so when the higher precedence * comes later it too enters the stack line. At the end the * is popped followed by the +.

Infix line	Stack line	RPN line
a + b * c		
+ b * c		a
b * c	+	a
* c	+	a b
c	+ *	a b
	+ *	a b c
	+	a b c *
		a b c * +

Table 20.02 Trace of the conversion process

Had the infix expression been `a * b + c then` * would have been first to enter the stack line but it would have been popped from the stack before + could enter.

Evaluating an RPN expression

A stack can be used to evaluate an RPN expression. Let's consider the execution of the following RPN expression when x has the value 3 and y has the value 4:

```
x 2 * y 3 * + 6 /
```

The rules followed here are that the values are added to the stack in turn. The process is interrupted if the next item in the RPN expression is an operator. This causes the top two items to be popped from the stack. Then the operator is used to create a new value from these two and the new value is added to the stack. The process then continues. Figure. 20.13 shows the successive contents of the stack with an indication of when an operator has been used. The intermediate states of the stack when two values have been popped are not shown.

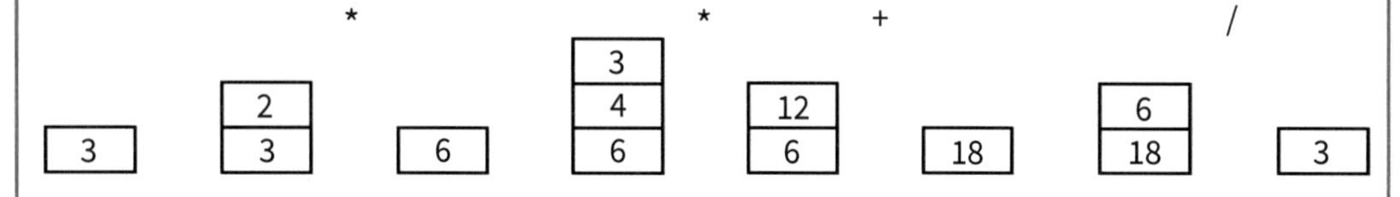

Figure 20.13 Evaluating a Reverse Polish expression using a stack

TASK 20.01

Practise your understanding of RPN.

1 Convert the following infix expressions into RPN using the methods described in Worked Examples 20.01, 20.02 and 20.03:

```
(x - y) / 4

3 * (2 + x / 7)
```

2 Convert the following RPN expressions into the corresponding infix expressions:

```
4 a b + c + d + e + *

y 2 ^ z 3 ^ + 6/
```

Note that the caret (^) symbol represents 'to the power of'.

3 Using simple values for each variable in part 2, use the infix version to evaluate the expression. Then use the stack method to evaluate the RPN expression and check that you get the same result.

It needs to be understood that the use of RPN would be of little value if the simple processor with a limited instruction set discussed in Chapter 6 (Section 6.04) was being used. Modern processors will have instructions in the instruction set that handle stack operations, so a compiler can convert expressions into RPN knowing that conversion to machine code can utilise these and allow stack processing in program execution.

Summary

- The operating system provides resource management including scheduling of processes, memory management and control of the I/O system.
- For the user, the operating system provides an interface, a file system and application programming interfaces.
- A modular approach provides a flexible structure for the operating system.
- There are five states for a process: new, ready, running, waiting and terminated.
- A process may be interrupted by an error, a need for an I/O activity or the scheduling algorithm.
- In a virtual machine, a process interacts with a software interface provided by the operating system.
- Compiler operation has a front-end program providing analysis and a back-end program providing synthesis.
- Backus–Naur form is used to represent the rules of a grammar.
- Reverse Polish Notation is used for the evaluation of expressions.

Exam-style Questions

1 **a** In a multiprogramming environment, the concept of a process has been found to be very useful in controlling the execution of programs.

i Explain the concept of a process. [2]

ii In one model for the execution of a program, there are five defined process states. Identify three of them and explain the meaning of each. [6]

b The transition of processes between states is controlled by a scheduler.

i Identify two scheduling algorithms and for each classify its type. [4]

ii A scheduling algorithm might be chosen to use prioritisation. Identify two criteria that could be used to assign a priority to a process. [2]

2 **a** Three memory management techniques are partitioning, scheduling and paging.

i Give definitions of them. [3]

ii Identify two ways in which they might be combined. [2]

b Some systems use virtual memory.

i Identify which of the techniques in part (a) is used to create virtual memory. [1]

ii Explain two advantages of using virtual memory. [4]

iii Explain one problem that can occur in a virtual memory system. [2]

3 a A compiler is used to translate a program into machine code.

i A compiler is modelled as containing a front end and a back end. State the overall aim of the front end and of the back end. [2]

ii Identify two processes which are part of the front end. [2]

iii Identify two processes which are part of the back end. [2]

b Complete the following Backus–Naur definition of a signed integer:

<Digit> ::= ....

<Sign> ::= ....

<Unsigned integer> ::= ....

<Signed integer> ::= .... [4]

c Convert the expression `(a + 6) + b / c` into Reverse Polish Notation. [2]

d Convert the Reverse Polish Notation expression `a 3 b * 6 c * - +` into infix notation. [2]

Chapter 21
Security

Learning objectives

By the end of this chapter you should be able to:

- show understanding of the terms: public key, private key, plain text, cipher text, encryption and asymmetric key cryptography
- show understanding of how the keys can be used to send:
  - a private message from the public to an individual/organisation
  - a verified message to the public
- show understanding of how a digital certificate is acquired and used to produce digital signatures
- show awareness of the purpose of Secure Socket Layer (SSL)/Transport Layer Security (TLS); its use in client–server communication and situations where its use would be appropriate
- show understanding of malware: viruses, worms, phishing and pharming
- describe vulnerabilities that the various types of malware can exploit
- describe methods that can be used to restrict the effect of malware.

21.01 Encryption fundamentals

Encryption can be used as a routine procedure when storing data within a computing system. However, the focus in this chapter is on the use of encryption when transmitting data over a network.

The use of encryption is illustrated in Figure 21.01.The process starts with original data referred to as **plaintext**, whatever form it takes. This is encrypted by an encryption algorithm which makes use of a key. The product of the encryption is **ciphertext**, which is transmitted to the recipient. When the transmission is received it is decrypted using a decryption algorithm and a key to produce the original plaintext.

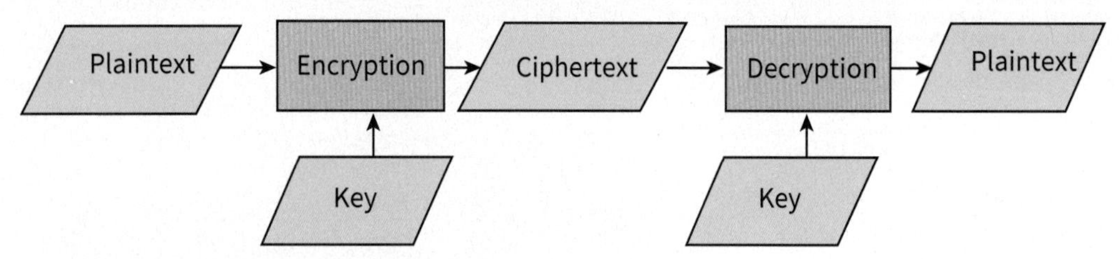

Figure 21.01 Overview of encryption and decryption

KEY TERMS

Plaintext: data before encryption

Ciphertext: the result of applying an encryption algorithm to data

Security concerns

There are a number of security concerns relating to a transmission:

- Confidentiality: Only the intended recipient should be able to decrypt the ciphertext.
- Authenticity: The receiver must be certain who sent the ciphertext.
- Integrity: The ciphertext must not be modified during transmission.
- Non-repudiation: Neither sender nor receiver should be able to deny involvement in the transmission.
- Availability: Nothing should happen to prevent the receiver from receiving the transmission.

This chapter will consider only confidentiality, authenticity and integrity.

The confidentiality concern arises because a message could be intercepted during transmission and the contents read by an unauthorised person. The concern about integrity reflects the fact that the transmission might be interfered with deliberately but also that there might be accidental corruption of the data during transmission.

Encryption methods

The fundamental principle of encryption is that the encryption algorithm must not be a secret: it must be in the public domain. In contrast, an encryption key must be secret. However, this is not quite the full story. There are two alternative approaches. One is symmetric key encryption; the other is asymmetric key encryption.

In symmetric key encryption there is just one key which is used to encrypt and then to decrypt. This key is a secret shared by the sender and the receiver of a message. In asymmetric key encryption two different keys are used, one for encryption and a different one for decryption. Only one of these is a secret.

So, how does this work? What happens at the sending end is straightforward. The sender has a key which is used to encrypt some plaintext and the ciphertext produced is transmitted to the receiver. The question is, how does the receiver get to have the key needed for decryption? If symmetric key encryption is used, there needs to be a secure method for the sender and receiver to be provided with the secret key.

Using asymmetric key encryption, the process actually starts with the receiver. The receiver must be in possession of two keys. One is a public key which is not secret. The other is a private key which is secret and known only to the receiver. The receiver can send the public key to a sender, who uses the public key for encryption and sends the ciphertext to the receiver. The receiver is the only person who can decrypt the message because the private and public keys are a matched pair. The public key can be provided to any number of different people allowing the receiver to receive a private message from any of them. Note, however, that if two individuals require two-way communication, both communicators need a private key and must send the matching public key to the other person.

There are two requirements to ensure confidentiality should the transmission be intercepted and the message extracted: the encryption algorithm must be complex and the number of bits used to define the key must be large.

Extension Question 21.01

The details of encryption algorithms are beyond the scope of this book. However, you might wish to investigate the type of approach used in established examples, such as DES or RSA. Also, you might wish to consider the number of different combinations for a 64-bit or 128-bit key.

The above account does not completely answer the question of how encryption works. The missing factor is an organisation to provide keys and to ensure their safe delivery to individuals using them.

21.02 Digital signatures and digital certificates

Using asymmetric encryption, the decryption–encryption works if the keys are used the other way round. An individual can encrypt a message with a private key and send this to many recipients who have the corresponding public key and can therefore decrypt the message. This approach would not be used if the content of a message was confidential. However, it could be used if it was important to verify who the sender was. Only the sender has the private key and the public keys only work with that one specific private key. Therefore, used this way, the message has a digital signature identifying the sender.

There is a disadvantage in using this method of applying a digital signature in that it is associated with an encryption of the whole of a message. An alternative is to use a cryptographic one-way hash function which creates from the message a number, uniquely defined for the particular message, called a 'digest'. The private key is used as a signature for this digest. This speeds up the process of confirming the sender's identity. The process at the sender's end of the transmission is outlined in Figure 21.02. A public one-way hash function is used.

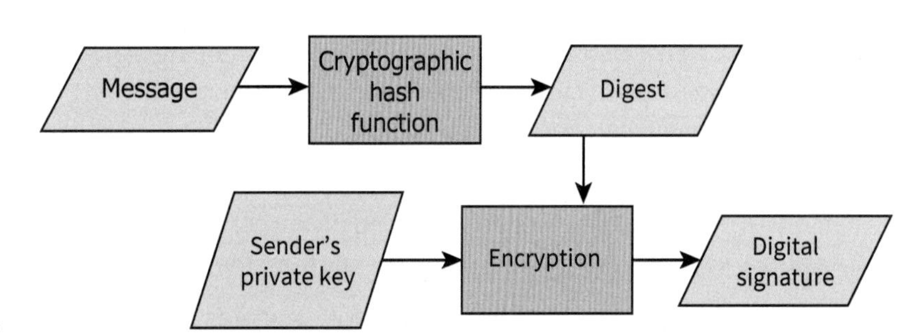

Figure 21.02 Sender using a one-way hash function to send a digital signature

We will assume that the message is transmitted as plaintext together with the digital signature as a separate file. The processes that take place at the receiver end are outlined in Figure 21.03. The same public hash key function is used that was used by the sender so the same digest is produced if the message has been transmitted without alteration.

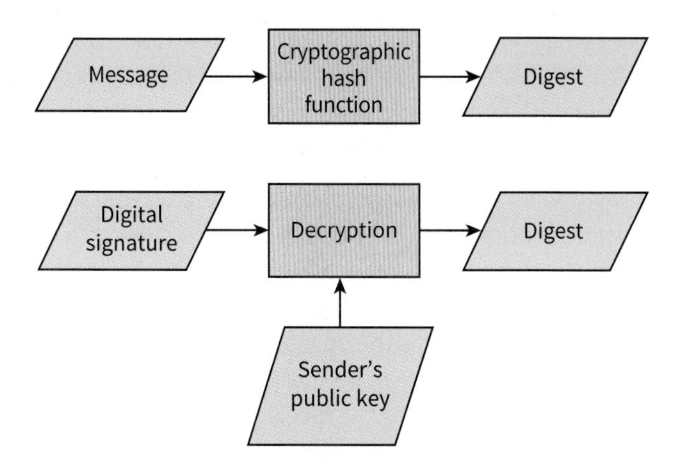

Figure 21.03 Checking received transmissions

The decryption of the digital signature produces an identical digest if the message was genuinely sent by the original owner of the public key that the receiver has used. This approach has allowed the receiver to be confident that the message is both authentic and unaltered.

This sounds good but unfortunately it does not consider the fact that someone might forge a public key and pretend to be someone else. Therefore, there is a need for a more rigorous means of ensuring authentication. This can be provided by a Certification Authority (CA) provided as part of a Public Key Infrastructure (PKI).

Let's consider a would-be receiver who has a public–private key pair. This individual wishes to be able to receive secure messages from other individuals. The public key must be made available in a way that ensures authentication. The steps taken by the would-be receiver to obtain a digital certificate to allow safe public key delivery are illustrated in Figure 21.04. The process can be summarised as follows:

- An individual (person A) who is a would-be receiver and has a public–private key pair contacts a local CA.
- The CA confirms the identity of person A.
- Person A's public key is given to the CA.
- The CA creates a public-key certificate (a digital certificate) and writes person A's public key into this document.
- The CA uses encryption with the CA's private key to add a digital signature to this document.
- The digital certificate is given to person A.
- Person A posts the digital certificate on a website.

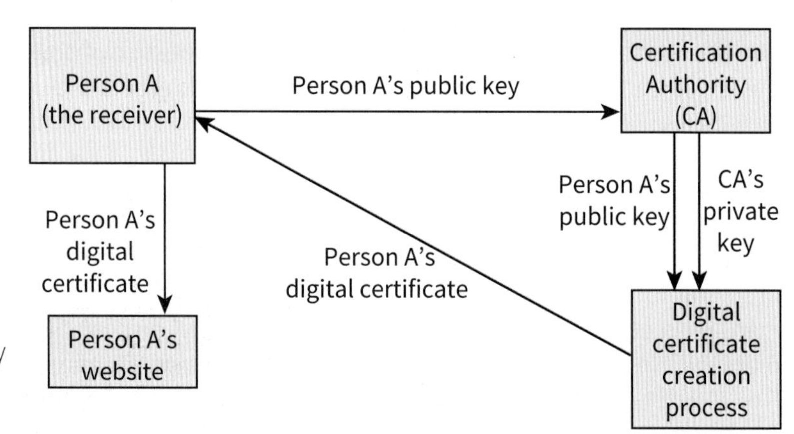

Figure 21.04 Processes involved in obtaining a digital certificate

Figure 21.04 has person A placing the digital certificate on that person's website but another option is to post it on a website designed specifically for keeping digital certificate data. Alternatively, a digital certificate might be used solely for authenticating emails as was suggested in Chapter 8 (Section 8.02).

Once a signed digital certificate has been posted on a website, any other person wishing to use person A's public key downloads the signed digital certificate from the website and uses the CA's public key to extract person A's public key from the digital certificate.

For this overall process to work there is a need for standards to be defined. As ever, the name for the standard, X.509, is not very memorable.

21.03 SSL and TLS

Secure Socket Layer (SSL) and Transport Layer Security (TLS) are two closely related protocols providing security in using the Internet. TLS is a slightly modified version of SSL. We concentrate on SSL here. The main context for the use of SSL is a client–server application. As described in Chapter 17 (Section 17.04), the interface between an application and TCP uses a port number. In the absence of a security protocol, TCP services an application using the port number. The combination of an IP address and a port number is called a 'socket'. When the Secure Socket Layer protocol is implemented it functions as an additional layer between TCP in the transport layer and the application layer. When the SSL protocol is in place, the application protocol HTTP becomes HTTPS. Note that although SSL is referred to as a protocol, it is in fact a protocol suite.

The starting point for SSL implementation is a connection between the client and the server being established by TCP. The Handshake Protocol from the SSP suite is used to create a session to allow the client and the server to communicate. Once the session has been established, the client and server can agree which encryption algorithms are to be used and can define the values for the session keys that are to be used. This interchange may involve checking digital certificates. For the transmission, SSL provides encryption, compression of the data and integrity checking. When the transmission is complete the session is closed and all records of the encryption disappear.

An application running HTTPS can guarantee secure communication allowing users to send confidential information such as credit card details in an ecommerce transaction. The user is completely unaware of the processes involved in ensuring confidential transmission with data integrity assured.

Discussion Point:

Chapter 8 (Section 8.01) discussed security and privacy issues. The use of encryption has always been a controversial subject. There are two important aspects to this. The first is whether powerful, unbreakable encryption algorithms should be made available to the public. The second relates to the key escrow scheme, which allows governments access to all secret keys. You may wish to revisit your Chapter 8 discussions.

21.04 Malware

Types of malware

Malware is the colloquial name for malicious software. Malicious software is software that is introduced into a system for a harmful purpose. One category of malware is where program code is introduced to a system. The various types of malware-containing program code are:

- virus: tries to replicate itself inside other executable code
- worm: runs independently and propagates to other network hosts
- logic bomb: lies dormant until some condition is met
- Trojan horse: replaces all or part of a previously useful program
- spyware: collects information and transmits it to another system
- bot: takes control of another computer and uses it to launch attacks.

The differences between the different types are not large and what is always called an 'anti-virus' package will detect all of the different types. The virus category is often subdivided according to the software that the virus attaches itself to. Examples are boot sector viruses and macro viruses.

Malware can also be classified in terms of the activity involved:

- phishing: sending an email or electronic message from an apparently legitimate source requesting confidential information
- pharming: setting up a bogus website which appears to be a legitimate site
- keylogger: recording keyboard usage by the legitimate user of the system.

System vulnerabilities

Many system vulnerabilities are associated directly with the activities of legitimate users of a system. Malware can be introduced inadvertently by the user in a number of ways:

- attaching a portable storage device
- opening an email attachment
- accessing a website
- downloading a file from the Internet.

Alternatively, a legitimate user with a grievance might introduce malware deliberately.

Other vulnerabilities are indirectly associated with the activities of legitimate users. By far the most significant is the use of weak passwords and particularly those which have a direct connection to the user. A poor choice of password gives the would-be hacker a strong chance of being able to gain unauthorised access. Other examples include a legitimate user not recognising a phishing or pharming attack and, as a result, disclosing sensitive information.

Systems inherently lack optimum security. Operating systems are notorious for lacking good security. There is a tendency for operating systems to increase in complexity which tends to offer the potential for more insecurity. The regular updates are often required because of a newly discovered security vulnerability. In the past, commonly used application packages have allowed macro viruses to flourish but this particular problem is largely under control.

A very specific vulnerability is buffer overflow. Programs written in the C programming language, of which there are very many, do not automatically carry out array bound checks. A program can be written to deliberately write code to the part of memory that is outside the address range defined for the array implemented as a buffer. This will overwrite what is stored there so when a subsequent program reads this overwritten section it will not execute as it should. This might just cause minor disruption but if cleverly engineered it could lead to an attacker gaining unauthorised access to the system and causing serious problems.

Chapter 8 (Section 8.02) has a discussion of the standard security measures for computer systems such as firewalls and anti-virus software.

Summary

- Alternatives for encryption are symmetric, using one key, or asymmetric, using two different keys.
- Encryption converts plaintext to ciphertext; decryption reverses the process.
- The five main security concerns when transmitting messages are: confidentiality, authenticity, integrity, non-repudiation and availability.
- Authentication can be achieved using a digital signature and a digital certificate.
- A digital certificate is provided by a certification authority within a public key infrastructure.
- Secure Socket Layer (SSL) and Transport Layer Security (TLS) protocols provide security for transmissions using the Internet.
- The following are types of malware: virus, worm, logic bomb, Trojan horse, spyware and bot.
- Malicious activities include pharming, phishing, keylogging and hacking.
- Malware can inadvertently enter a system through a user attaching a portable storage device, opening an email attachment, accessing a website or downloading a file from the Internet.

Exam-style Questions

1 **a** When transmitting data across a network three concerns relate to: confidentiality, authenticity and integrity.

Explain each of these terms. [4]

b Encryption and decryption can be carried out using a symmetric or an asymmetric key method.

Explain how keys are used in each of these methods. You are not required to describe the algorithms used. Your account must include reference to a public key, a private key and a secret key. [6]

c Digital signatures and digital certificates are used in message transmission.

Give an explanation of their use. [5]

2 Malware is a serious concern for computer system users.

a Give the names of two types of malware which involve some malicious code being input into a system. [2]

b Explain the difference between the two types of code. [3]

c Identify and explain two approaches for preventing malicious code from entering a computer system. [4]

d Explain the terms 'phishing' and 'pharming'. [3]

e Identify one possible policy for reducing the threat from phishing or pharming. [2]

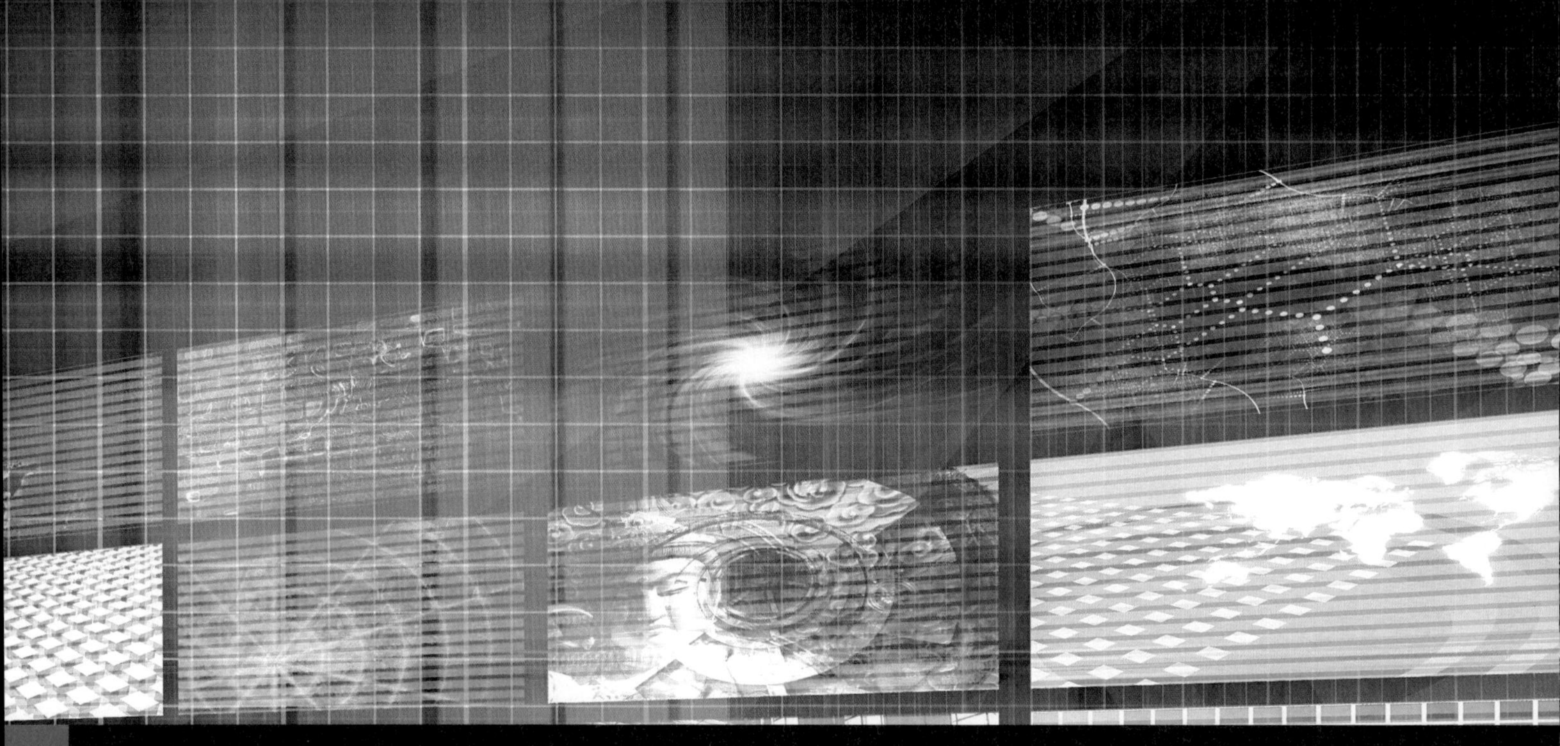

Chapter 22
Monitoring and Control Systems

Learning objectives

By the end of this chapter you should be able to:

- show understanding of the difference between a monitoring system and a control system
- show understanding of sensors and actuators and their usage
- show understanding of the additional hardware required to build these systems
- show understanding of the importance of feedback in a control system
- show understanding of the software requirements of these systems
- show understanding of how bit manipulation can be used to monitor/control a device
- carry out bit manipulations
- show understanding of how to make use of appropriate bit manipulation in monitoring systems and control systems.

22.01 Logistics

Monitoring can be used to describe a very wide range of activities but all are characterised by the measurement of some physical property. Typical examples of the physical property could be temperature, pressure, light intensity, flow rate or movement.

Let's consider temperature as an example. If this was being monitored under human control, the measurement could be made with a standard mercury thermometer. However, in this chapter we are interested in systems where a computer or microprocessor is being used. In this scenario, monitoring requires a measuring device that records a value which can be transmitted to the computer. Such a measuring device is a called a **sensor**. For monitoring temperature, a sensor could contain a thermocouple which outputs a temperature-dependent voltage.

There can only be one of two reasons to monitor a system:

- to check whether or not the monitored value is within acceptable limits; in a safety system, if the measured property has reached a dangerous level, some immediate action is required.
- to ensure routinely and continuously that the monitored property is as required; if the value measured indicates that a change has occurred, then the control part of the system may have to take measures to reverse this change.

The control element of a monitoring and control system needs a device, called an **actuator**. Figure 22.01 shows a schematic diagram of a computer-controlled environment.

KEY TERMS

Sensor: a hardware device that measures a property and transmits a value to a controlling computer

Actuator: a hardware device that receives a signal from a computer and adjusts the setting of a controlling device

Figure 22.01 includes an analogue-to-digital converter (ADC) and a digital-to-analogue converter (DAC) as separate components but they are likely to be integral to the device in the controlled environment. It should be noted that the diagram also shows an actuator as a single component. This is a simplification. An actuator is an electric motor that drives a controlling device which is not shown.

The system shown in Figure 22.01 involves a continuous process where a measurement is made and then, if needed, a control action is initiated. Following this control action, a measurement is taken again. There is therefore an element of feedback in the system.

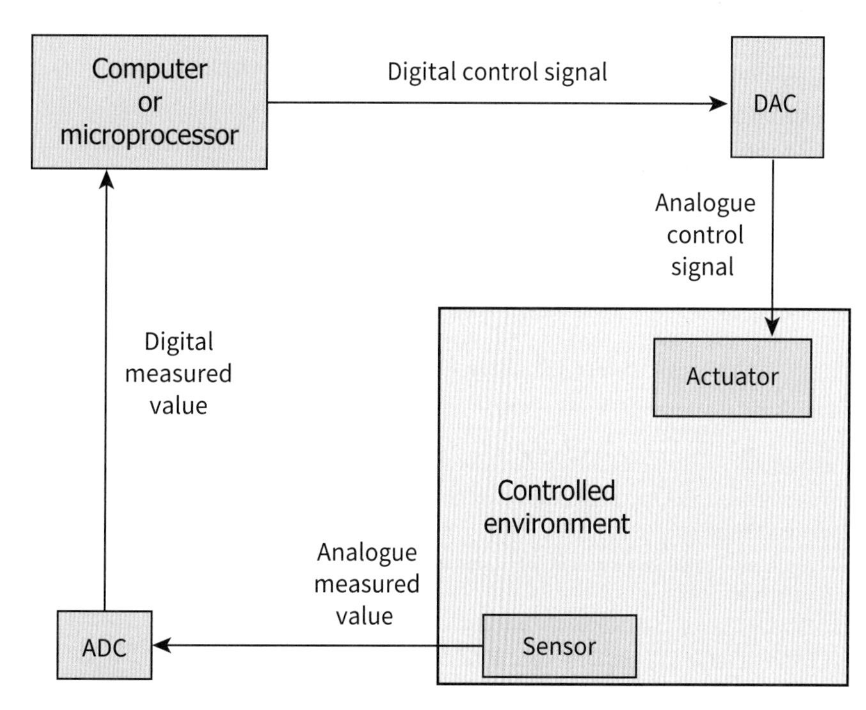

Figure 22.01 Computer-controlled environment

A closed-loop feedback control system is a special type of monitoring and control system where the feedback directly controls the operation. Figure 22.02 shows a schematic diagram of such a system. A microprocessor functions as the controller. This compares the value for the actual output, as read by the sensor, with the desired output. It then transmits a value to the actuator which depends on the difference calculated.

22.02 Real-time programming

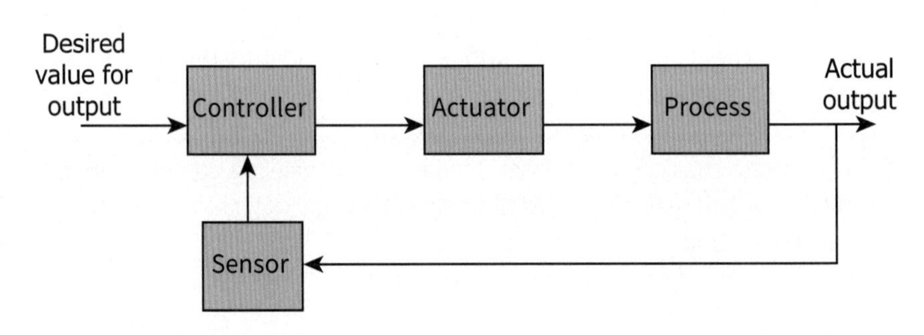

Figure 22.02 Closed-loop feedback control system

Monitoring and control systems require real-time programming. Whether a program is just monitoring or is monitoring and controlling, it must incorporate a structure for repetitive sensor reading. This must continue for the whole duration of the period that the system is switched on. A simple loop structure will achieve this but reading sensor values every clock cycle of a processor is unnecessarily frequent. The program must control the timing of the repetitions. This might be done by creating a timed sequence for reading values or possibly by including a time delay inside a loop.

Extension question 22.01

Research the capabilities for controlling the timing sequence for continuous running in your chosen programming language. Which ones would be best suited to a monitoring and control program?

An example monitoring program

Consider the following fragment of pseudocode:

```
EndReadingSensor ← FALSE
ReadingOutOfRange ← FALSE
REPEAT
   CALL SensorRead(SensorValue)
   IF SensorValue > MaximumAllowed
      THEN
         ReadingOutOfRange ← TRUE
         Reading ← 'H'
      ELSE
         IF SensorValue < MinimumAllowed
            THEN
               ReadingOutOfRange ← TRUE
               Reading ← 'L'
         ENDIF
   ENDIF
   IF ReadingOutOfRange
      THEN
         CALL WarningDisplay(Reading)
   ENDIF
   ReadingOutOfRange ← FALSE
   FOR TimeFiller ← 1 TO 999999
   ENDFOR
UNTIL EndReadingSensor
```

Note the following features of the program:

- There is an infinite loop.
- The loop finishes with another loop that does nothing other than create a delay before the outer loop repeats.
- When the sensor reading indicates a problem, the loop calls a procedure to handle whatever notification method is to be used.
- Following this call, the loop continues so the Boolean variable has to be reset to prevent the warning procedure being repetitively called.

An example monitoring and control program

Consider a system which is controlling an enclosed environment. The environment has a sensor to monitor a property and an actuator to control that property. The following fragment of code might be used:

```
EndReadingSensor ← FALSE
READ DesiredOutputLevel
REPEAT
   CALL SensorRead(SensorValue)
   SensorDifference ← DesiredOutputLevel - SensorValue
   IF ABS(SensorDifference) < DesiredOutputLevel/100
      THEN
         SensorDifference ← 0
   ENDIF
   IF SensorDifference > 0
      THEN
         ActuatorAdjustmentFactor ← SensorDifference/DesiredOutputLevel
         AdjustmentDirection ← 'up'
         CALL ActivateActuator(AdjustmentDirection, ActuatorAdjustmentFactor)
   ENDIF
   IF SensorDifference < 0
      THEN
         ActuatorAdjustmentFactor ← ABS(SensorDifference)/DesiredOutputLevel
         AdjustmentDirection ← 'down'
         CALL ActivateActuator(AdjustmentDirection, ActuatorAdjustmentFactor)
   ENDIF
   FOR TimeFiller ← 1 TO 999999
   ENDFOR
UNTIL EndReadingSensor
```

Note the following features of the program:

- A procedure is called to activate the actuator only if the sensor reading shows a significant change.
- The code will only work properly if it can be guaranteed that the activation of the actuator has caused a change in the property before the sensor reading in the next iteration of the loop.

22.03 Bit manipulation

The two fragments of code in Section 22.02 have a direct call to a procedure to take some action. A slightly different approach would be to set values for Boolean variables subject to what the sensors detect. For instance if a controlled environment had two properties to be monitored and controlled, four Boolean variables could be used. Values could be set by assignment statements such as:

```
IF SensorDifference1 > 0 THEN Sensor1HighFlag ← TRUE
IF SensorDifference1 < 0 THEN Sensor1LowFlag ← TRUE
IF SensorDifference2 > 0 THEN Sensor2HighFlag ← TRUE
IF SensorDifference2 < 0 THEN Sensor2LowFlag ← TRUE
```

Another part of the monitoring and control program would be checking whether any of the four flags were set. The machine code for running such a program could use individual bits to represent each flag. The way that flags could be set and read are illustrated by the following assembly language code fragments in which the three least significant bits (positions 0, 1 and 2) of the byte are used as flags:

`LDD 0034`	Loads a byte into the accumulator from an address
`AND #B00000000`	Uses a bitwise AND operation of the contents of the accumulator with the operand to convert each bit to 0
`STO 0034`	Stores the altered byte in the original address
⋮	
`LDD 0034`	
`XOR #B00000001`	Uses a bitwise XOR operation of the contents of the accumulator with the operand to toggle the value of the bit stored in position 0. This changes the value of the flag it represents.
`STO 0034`	
⋮	
`LDD 0034`	
`AND #B00000010`	Uses a bitwise AND operation of the contents of the accumulator with the operand to leave the value in position 1 unchanged but to convert every other bit to 0. A subsequent instruction can now compare the value of the byte with denary 2 to see if the flag represented by this bit position is set.
`STO 0034`	
⋮	
`LDD 0034`	
`OR #B00000100`	Uses a bitwise OR operation of the contents of the accumulator with the operand to set the flag represented by the bit in position 2. All other bit positions remain unchanged.
`STO 0034`	

Summary

- A monitoring system requires sensors; a monitoring and control system also requires actuators.
- A program used for a monitoring and control system has to operate in real time with an infinite loop that accepts input from the sensors at timed intervals.
- The program transmits signals to the actuators if the values received from the sensors indicate a need for control measures to be taken.
- Bit manipulation can be used within an assembly language program to monitor or control devices.

Exam-style Questions

1 A zoo reptile house has sixteen tanks which accommodate its reptiles. Each tank has to have its own microclimate where the appropriate levels of heat and humidity are crucial. The zoo implements a computer system which supplies the conditions in each of the tanks to a terminal in a central area. Warning messages are flashed up on the screen if any condition arises which requires the intervention of a zoo-keeper.

a State the name of the type of computing system described. [1]

b State **two** items of hardware which need to be present in the tanks for this system to function correctly. [2]

c This is the polling routine which is used to run the system indefinitely:

```
01 REPEAT
02    FOR i ← 1 TO ..............
03       READ Condition1, Condition2 in tank (i)
04       IF Condition1 < Extreme[i,1] OR Condition1 > Extreme[i,2]
05          THEN
06             OUTPUT "Warning! Problem in Tank ", i
07       ENDIF
08       IF Condition2 < Extreme[i,3] OR Condition3 > Extreme[i,4]
09          THEN
10             OUTPUT "Warning! Problem in Tank ", i
11       ENDIF
12    ENDFOR
13
14    FOR i ← 1 TO 999999
15    ENDFOR
16 UNTIL ............................
```

i Fill in the gaps in the pseudocode. [2]

ii Explain what is stored in the array `Extreme`. [2]

iii Explain what happens in lines 04 to 11. [3]

iv Explain the purpose of the loop in lines 14 to 15. [1]

d The zoo decides that the computer system needs to be updated. The computer system will now make use of actuators. These actuators will operate devices which adjust the microclimate.

Actuators can be in two states, on or off. Whether an actuator is on or off is determined by a single bit value (0 means off, 1 means on) in a specific 8-bit memory location.

The actuators to control the climate in Tank 4 use memory location 0804. Bit 5 of this memory location controls the heater.

7	6	5	4	3	2	1	0	bit number
0	0	1	1	0	1	0	1	value

Use some of the assembly language instructions to write the instructions that will ensure bit 5 of location 0804 is set to 1. [6]

Instruction		**Explanation**
Op Code	**Operand**	
`LDM #n`		Immediate addressing. Load the number n to ACC
`LDD <address>`		Direct addressing. Load the contents of the given address to ACC
`STO <address>`		Store the contents of ACC at the given address
`OUT`		Output to the screen the character whose ASCII value is stored in ACC
`AND #n`		Bitwise AND operation of the contents of ACC with the operand
`AND <address>`		Bitwise AND operation of the contents of ACC with the contents of <address>
`XOR #n`		Bitwise XOR operation of the contents of ACC with the operand
`OR #n`		Bitwise OR operation of the contents of ACC with the operand

Cambridge International AS and A Level Computer Science 9608 Specimen Paper 3 Q 3

Part 4 Further Problem-Solving and Programming Skills

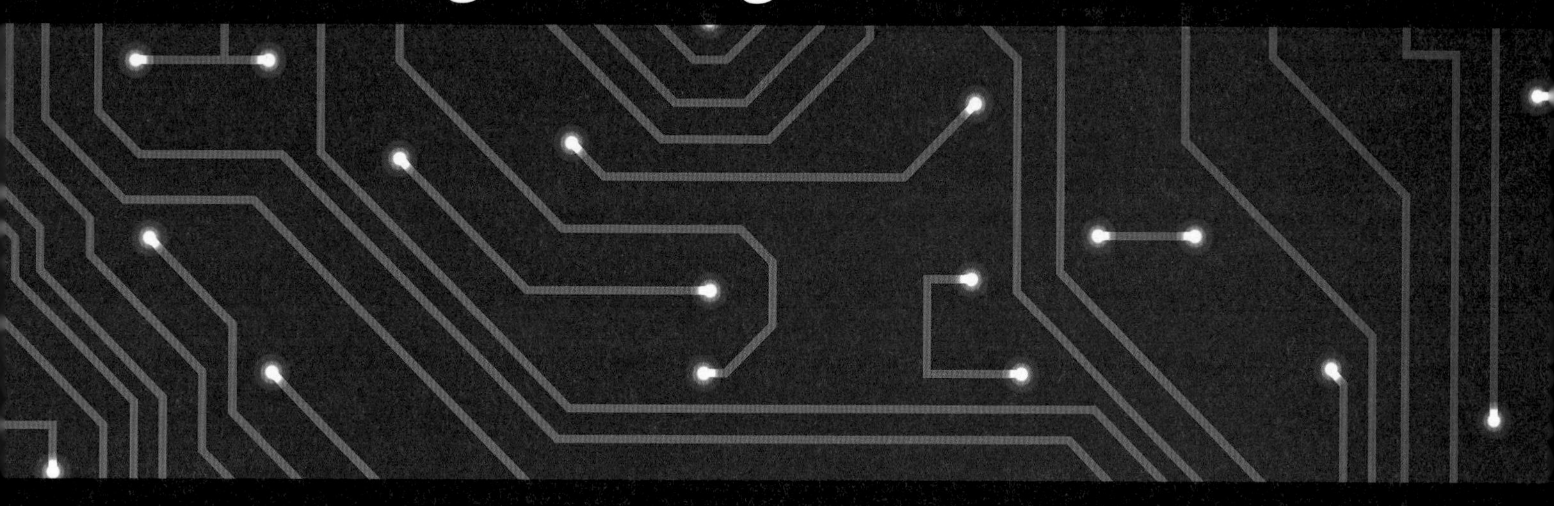

Chapter 23
Computational Thinking and Problem-Solving

Learning objectives

By the end of this chapter you should be able to:

- show understanding of how to model a complex system by only including essential details
- write a binary search algorithm to solve a particular problem
- show understanding of the conditions necessary for the use of a binary search
- show understanding of how the performance of a binary search varies according to the number of data items
- write algorithms to:
  - implement an insertion sort
  - implement a bubble sort
  - find an item in each of the following: linked list, binary tree, hash table
  - insert an item into each of the following: stack, queue, linked list, binary tree, hash table
  - delete an item from each of the following: stack, queue, linked list
- show understanding that performance of a sort routine may depend on the initial order of the data and the number of data items
- show understanding that different algorithms which perform the same task can be compared by using criteria such as time taken to complete the task and memory used
- show understanding that an abstract data type (ADT) is a collection of data and a set of operations on those data
- show understanding that data structures not available as built-in types in a particular programming language need to be constructed from those data structures which are built-in within the language
- show how it is possible for ADTs to be implemented from another ADT
- describe the following ADTs and demonstrate how they can be implemented from appropriate built-in types or other ADTs: stack, queue, linked list, dictionary, binary tree.

23.01 What is computational thinking?

We have already been thinking computationally in Chapters 11 to 15. Here is the formal definition:

Computational thinking is a problem-solving process where a number of steps are taken in order to reach a solution, rather than relying on rote learning to draw conclusions without considering these conclusions.

Computational thinking involves abstraction, decomposition, data modelling, pattern recognition and algorithm design.

Abstraction

Abstraction involves filtering out information that is not necessary to solving the problem. There are many examples in everyday life where abstraction is used. In Chapter 11 (Section 11.01), we saw part of the underground map of London, UK. The purpose of this map is to help people plan their journey within London. The map does not show a geographical representation of the tracks of the underground train network nor does it show the streets above ground. It shows the stations and which train lines connect the stations. In other words, the information that is not necessary when planning how to get from Kings Cross St. Pancras to Westminster is filtered out. The essential information we need to be able to plan our route is clearly represented.

Abstraction gives us the power to deal with complexity. An algorithm is an abstraction of a process that takes inputs, executes a sequence of steps, and produces outputs. An abstract data type defines an abstract set of values and operations for manipulating those values.

Decomposition

Decomposition means breaking tasks down into smaller parts in order to explain a process more clearly. Decomposition is another word for step-wise refinement (covered in Chapter 12, Section 12.01). This led us to structured programming using procedures and functions with parameters, covered in Chapter 14 (Section 14.03 to 14.05).

Data modelling

Data modelling involves analysing and organising data. In Chapter 13 we met simple data types such as integer, character and Boolean. The string data type is a composite type: a sequence of characters. When we have groups of data items we used one-dimensional (1D) arrays to represent linear lists and two-dimensional (2D) arrays to represent tables or matrices. We stored data in text files. In Chapter 10, we used data modelling to design database tables.

We can set up abstract data types to model real-world concepts, such as records, queues or stacks. When a programming language does not have such data types built-in, we can define our own by building them from existing data types (see Section 23.03). There are more ways to build data models. In Chapter 27 we cover object-oriented programming where we build data models by defining classes. In Chapter 29 we model data using facts and rules. In Chapter 26 we cover random files.

Pattern recognition

Pattern recognition means looking for patterns or common solutions to common problems and exploiting these to complete tasks in a more efficient and effective way. There are many standard algorithms to solve standard problems, such as insertion sort or binary search (see Section 23.02).

Algorithm design

Algorithm design involves developing step-by-step instructions to solve a problem (see Chapter 11).

23.02 Standard algorithms

Bubble sort

In Chapter 11, we developed the algorithm for a bubble sort (Worked Example 11.12).

Discussion Point:

What were the essential features of a bubble sort?

TASK 23.01

Write program code for the most efficient bubble sort algorithm. Assume that the items to be sorted are stored in a 1D array with n elements.

Insertion sort

Imagine you have a number of cards with a different value printed on each card. How would you sort these cards into order of increasing value?

You can consider the pile of cards as consisting of a sorted part and an unsorted part. Place the unsorted cards in a pile on the table. Hold the sorted cards as a pack in your hand. To start with only the first (top) card is sorted. The card on the top of the pile on the table is the next card to be inserted. The last (bottom) card in your hand is your current card.

Figure 23.01 shows the sorted cards in your hand as blue and the pile of unsorted cards as white. The next card to be inserted is shown in red. Each column shows the state of the pile as the cards are sorted.

Position number						
1	47	6	6	6	6	6
2	6	47	47	17	17	17
3	54	54	54	47	47	28
4	17	17	17	54	54	47
5	93	93	93	93	93	54
6	28	28	28	28	28	93

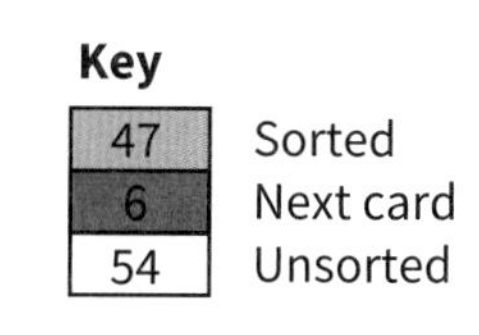

Figure 23.01 Sorting cards

Repeat the following steps until all cards in the unsorted pile have been inserted into the correct position:

1 Repeat until the card to be inserted has been placed in its correct position.

1.1 Compare the current card with the card to be inserted.

1.2 If the card to be inserted is greater than the current card, insert it below the current card.

1.3 Otherwise, if there is a card above the current card in your hand, make this your new current card.

1.4 If there is no new current card, place the card to be inserted at the top of the sorted pile.

What happens when you work through the sorted cards to find the correct position for the card to be inserted? In effect, as you consider the cards in your hand, you move the current card down a position. If the value of the card to be inserted is smaller than the last card you considered, then the card is inserted at the top of the pile (position 1).

This method is known as an insertion sort. It is a standard sort method.

We can write this algorithm using pseudocode. Assume the values to be sorted are stored in a 1D array, `List`:

```
FOR Pointer ← 2 TO NumberOfitems
    ItemToBeInserted ← List[Pointer]
    CurrentItem ← Pointer - 1 // pointer to last item in sorted part of list
    WHILE (List[CurrentItem] > ItemToBeInserted) AND (CurrentItem > 0)
        List[CurrentItem + 1]← List[CurrentItem]// move current item down
        CurrentItem ← CurrentItem - 1 // look at the item above
    ENDWHILE
    List[CurrentItem + 1]← ItemToBeInserted // insert item
ENDFOR
```


TASK 23.02

1 Dry-run the insertion sort algorithm using a trace table. Assume the list consists of the following six items in the order given: 53, 21, 60, 18, 42, 19.

2 Write program code for the insertion sort algorithm. Assume that the items to be sorted are stored in a 1D array with n elements.

Extension question 23.01

Investigate the performances of the insertion sort and the bubble sort by:

- varying the initial order of the items
- increasing the number of items to be sorted.

Binary search

In Chapter 11 we developed the algorithm for a linear search (Worked Example 11.11). This is the only way we can systematically search an unordered list. However, if the list is ordered, then we can use a different technique.

Consider the following real-world example.

If you want to look up a word in a dictionary, you are unlikely to start searching for the word from the beginning of the dictionary. Suppose you are looking for the word 'quicksort'. You look at the middle entry of the dictionary (approximately) and find the word 'magnetic'. 'quicksort' comes after 'magnetic', so you look in the second half of the dictionary. Again you look at the entry in the middle of this second half of the dictionary (approximately) and find the word 'report'. 'quicksort' comes before 'report', so you look in the third quarter. You can keep looking at the middle entry of the part which must contain your word, until you find the word. If the word does not exist in the dictionary, you will have no entries in the dictionary left to find the middle of.

This method is known as a **binary search**. It is a standard method.

KEY TERMS

Binary search: repeated checking of the middle item in an ordered search list and discarding the half of the list which does not contain the search item

We can write this algorithm using pseudocode. Assume the values are sorted in ascending order and stored in a 1D array, `List` of size `MaxItems`.

```
Found ← FALSE
SearchFailed ← FALSE
First ← 1
Last ← MaxItems // set boundaries of search area
WHILE NOT Found AND NOT SearchFailed
   Middle ← (First + Last) DIV 2 // find middle of current search area
   IF List[Middle] = SearchItem
      THEN
         Found ← TRUE
      ELSE
         IF First >= Last // no search area left
            THEN
               SearchFailed ← TRUE
            ELSE
               IF List[Middle] > SearchItem
                  THEN // must be in first half
                     Last ← Middle - 1  // move upper boundary
                  ELSE // must be in second half
                     First ← Middle + 1  // move lower boundary
               ENDIF
         ENDIF
   ENDIF
ENDWHILE
IF Found = TRUE
   THEN
      OUTPUT Middle // output position where item was found
   ELSE
      OUTPUT "Item not present in array"
ENDIF
```

TASK 23.03

Dry-run the binary search algorithm using a trace table. Assume the list consists of the following 20 items in the order given: 7, 12, 19, 23, 27, 33, 37, 41, 45, 56, 59, 60, 62, 71, 75, 80, 84, 88, 92, 99.

Search for the value 60. How many times did you have to execute the `While` loop?

Dry-run the algorithm again, this time searching for the value 34. How many times did you have to execute the `While` loop?

Discussion Point:

Compare the binary-search algorithm with the linear-search algorithm. If the array contains n items, how many times on average do you need to test a value when using a binary search and how many times on average do you need to test a value when using a linear search? Can you describe how the search time varies with increasing n?

23.03 Abstract data types (ADTs)

An **abstract data type** is a collection of data. When we want to use an abstract data type, we need a set of basic operations:

- create a new instance of the data structure
- find an element in the data structure
- insert a new element into the data structure
- delete an element from the data structure
- access all elements stored in the data structure in a systematic manner.

KEY TERMS

Abstract data type: a collection of data with associated operations

The remainder of this chapter describes the following ADTs: stack, queue, linked list, binary tree, hash table and dictionary. It also demonstrates how they can be implemented from appropriate built-in types or other ADTs.

23.04 Stacks

What are the features of a stack in the real world? To make a stack, we pile items on top of each other. The item that is accessible is the one on top of the stack. If we try to find an item in the stack and take it out, we are likely to cause the pile of items to collapse.

Figure 23.02 shows how we can represent a stack when we have added four items in this order: A, B, C, D. Note that the slots are shown numbered from the bottom as this is more intuitive.

The `BaseOfStackPointer` will always point to the first slot in the stack. The `TopOfStackPointer` will point to the last element pushed onto the stack. When an element is removed from the stack, the `TopOfStackPointer` will decrease to point to the element now at the top of the stack.

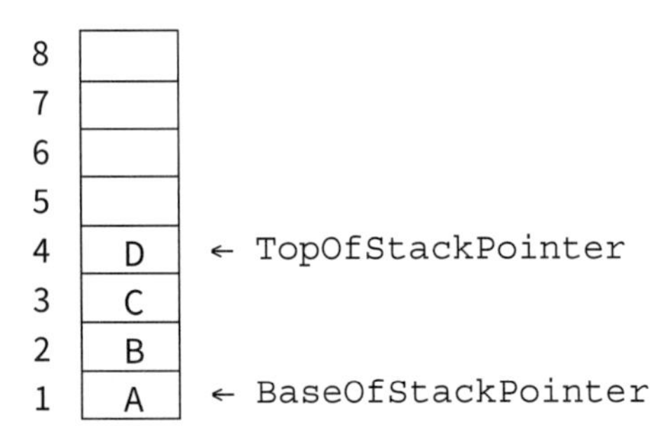

Figure 23.02 A stack

23.05 Queues

What are the features of a queue in the real world? When people form a queue, they join the queue at the end. People leave the queue from the front of the queue. If it is an orderly queue, no-one pushes in between and people don't leave the queue from any other position.

Figure 23.03 shows how we can represent a queue when five items have joined the queue in this order: A, B, C, D, E.

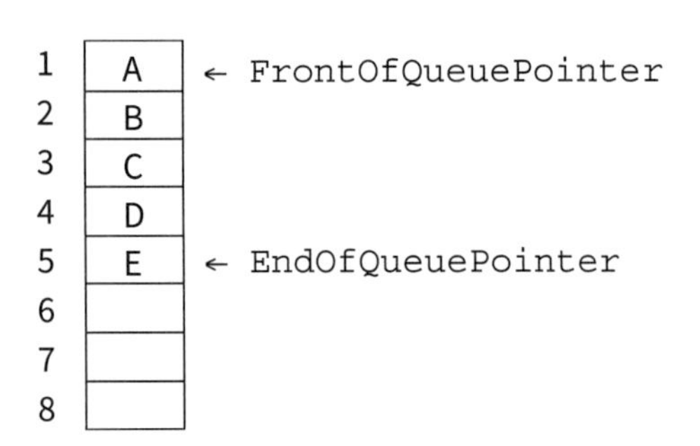

Figure 23.03 A queue

When the item at the front of the queue leaves, we need to move all the other items one slot forward. This would involve a lot of moving of data. A more efficient way to make use of the slots is the concept of a 'circular' queue. Pointers show where the front and end of the queue are. Eventually the queue will 'wrap around' to the beginning. Figure 23.04 shows a circular queue after 11 items have joined and five items have left the queue.

1	I	
2	J	
3	K	← EndOfQueuePointer
4		
5		
6	F	← FrontOfQueuePointer
7	G	
8	H	

Figure 23.04 A circular queue

23.06 Linked lists

In Chapter 11 we used an array as a linear list. In a linear list, the list items are stored in consecutive locations. This is not always appropriate. Another method is to store an individual list item in whatever location is available and link the individual item into an ordered sequence using pointers.

An element of a list is called a **node**. A node can consist of several data items and a **pointer**, which is a variable that stores the address of the node it points to.

A pointer that does not point at anything is called a **null pointer.** It is usually represented by Ø. A variable that stores the address of the first element is called a **start pointer.**

KEY TERMS

Node: an element of a list

Pointer: a variable that stores the address of the node it points to

Null pointer: a pointer that does not point at anything

Start pointer: a variable that stores the address of the first element of a linked list

In Figure 23.05, the data value in the node box represents the key field of that node. There are likely to be many data items associated with each node. The arrows represent the pointers. It does not show at which address a node is stored, so the diagram does not give the value of the pointer, only where it conceptually links to.

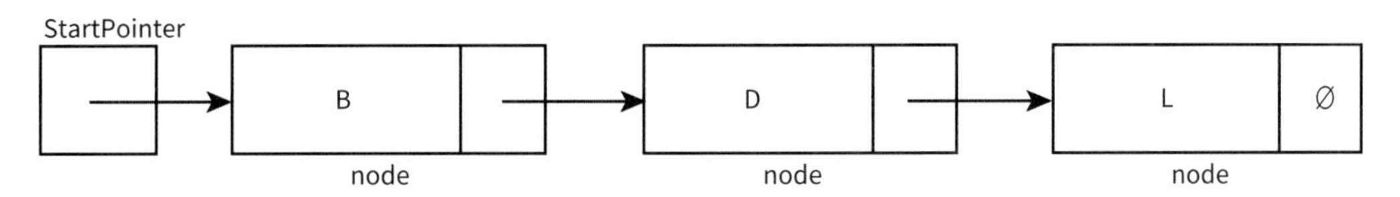

Figure 23.05 Conceptual diagram of a linked list

A new node, A, is inserted at the beginning of the list. The content of `StartPointer` is copied into the new node's pointer field and `StartPointer` is set to point to the new node, A.

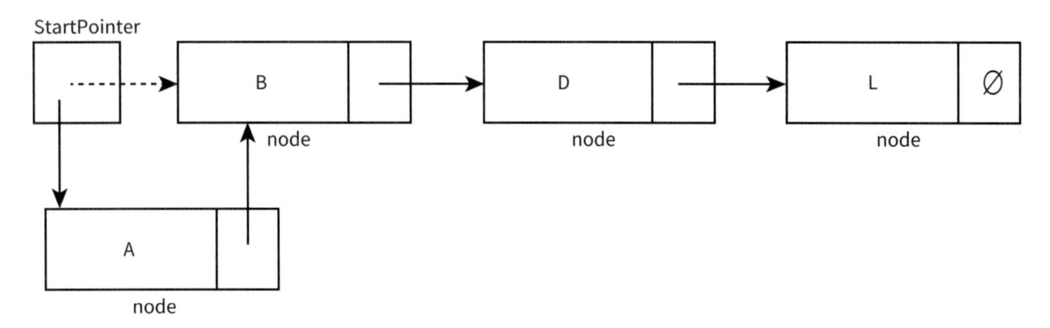

Figure 23.06 Conceptual diagram of adding a new node to the beginning of a linked list

In Figure 23.07, a new node, P, is inserted at the end of the list. The pointer field of node L points to the new node, P. The pointer field of the new node, P, contains the null pointer.

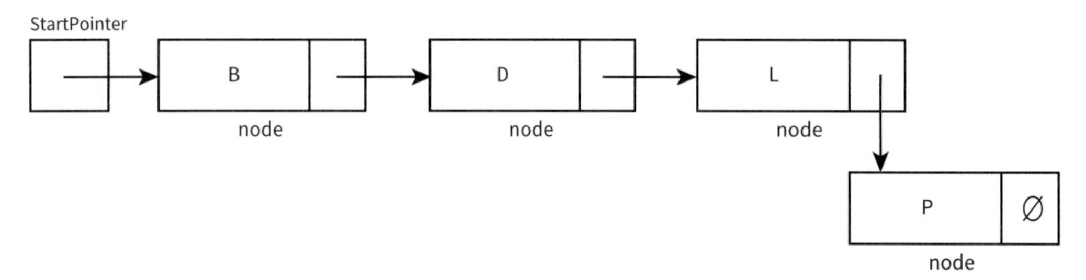

Figure 23.07 Conceptual diagram of adding a new node to the end of a linked list

To delete the first node in the list (Figure 23.08), we copy the pointer field of the node to be deleted into `StartPointer`.

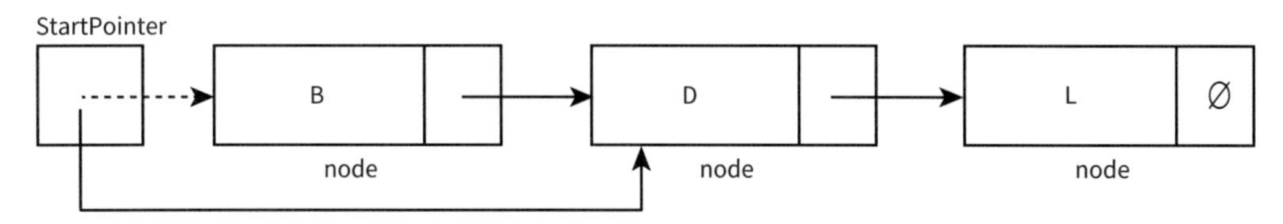

Figure 23.08 Deleting the first node in a linked list

To delete the last node in the list (Figure 23.09), we set the pointer field for the previous node to the null pointer.

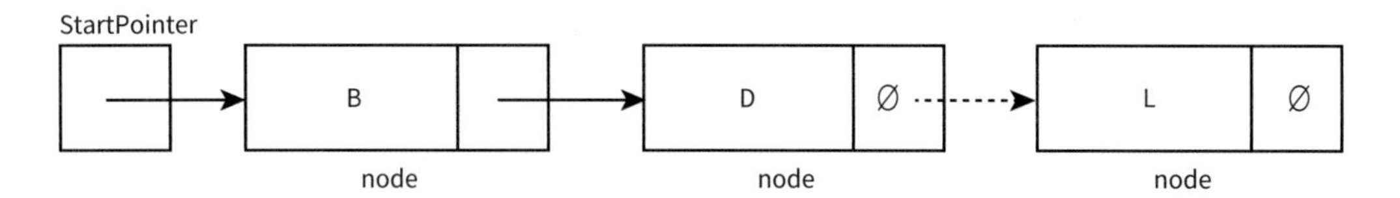

Figure 23.09 Conceptual diagram of deleting the last node of a linked list

Sometimes the nodes are linked together in order of key field value to produce an ordered linked list. This means a new node may need to be inserted or deleted from between two existing nodes.

To insert a new node, C, between existing nodes, B and D (Figure 23.10), we copy the pointer field of node B into the pointer field of the new node, C. We change the pointer field of node B to point to the new node, C.

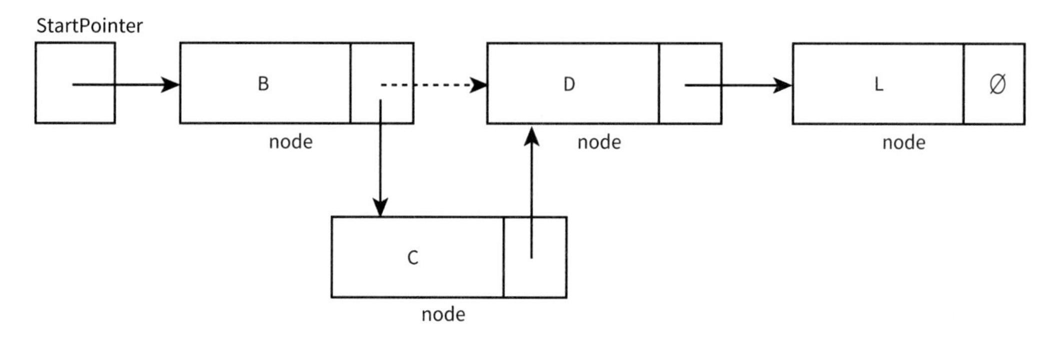

Figure 23.10 Conceptual diagram of adding a new node into a linked list

To delete a node, D, within the list (Figure 23.11), we copy the pointer field of the node to be deleted, D, into the pointer field of node B.

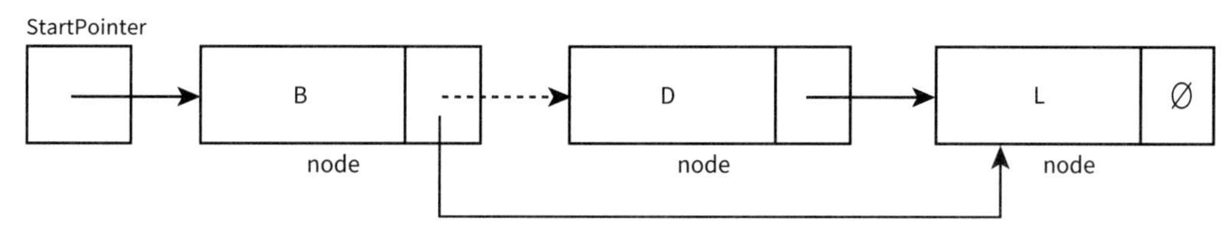

Figure 23.11 Conceptual diagram of deleting a node within a linked list

Remember that, in real applications, the data would consist of much more than a key field and one data item. This is why linked lists are preferable to linear lists. When list elements need reordering, only pointers need changing in a linked list. In a linear list, all data items would need to be moved.

Using linked lists saves time, however we need more storage space for the pointer fields.

In Chapter 16 we looked at composite data types, in particular the user-defined record type. We grouped together related data items into record data structures. To use a record variable, we first define a record type. Then we declare variables of that record type.

We can store the linked list in an array of records. One record represents a node and consists of the data and a pointer. When a node is inserted or deleted, only the pointers need to change. A pointer value is the array index of the node pointed to.

Unused nodes need to be easy to find. A suitable technique is to link the unused nodes to form another linked list: the free list. Figure 23.12 shows our linked list and its free list.

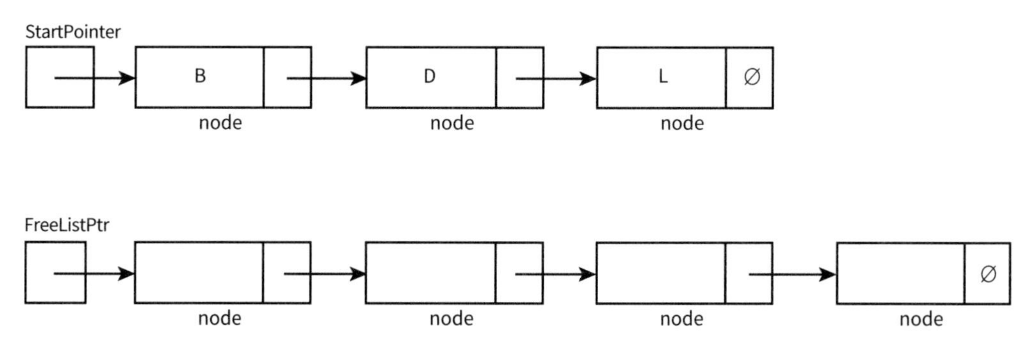

Figure 23.12 Conceptual diagram of a linked list and a free list

When an array of nodes is first initialised to work as a linked list, the linked list will be empty. So the start pointer will be the null pointer. All nodes need to be linked to form the free list. Figure 23.13 shows an example of an implementation of a linked list before any data is inserted into it.

StartPointer: ∅

FreeListPtr: 1

List

	Data	Pointer
[1]		2
[2]		3
[3]		4
[4]		5
[5]		6
[6]		7
[7]		∅

Figure 23.13 A linked list before any nodes are used

We now code the basic operations discussed using the conceptual diagrams in Figures 23.05 to 23.12.

Create a new linked list

```
// NullPointer should be set to -1 if using array element with index 0
CONSTANT NullPointer = 0
// Declare record type to store data and pointer
TYPE ListNode
   DECLARE Data    : STRING
   DECLARE Pointer : INTEGER
ENDTYPE
DECLARE StartPointer : INTEGER
DECLARE FreeListPtr : INTEGER
DECLARE List[1 : 7] OF ListNode

PROCEDURE InitialiseList
   StartPointer ← NullPointer    // set start pointer
   FreeListPtr ← 1               // set starting position of free list
   FOR Index ← 1 TO 6            // link all nodes to make free list
      List[Index].Pointer ← Index + 1
   ENDFOR
   List[7].Pointer ← NullPointer // last node of free list
ENDPROCEDURE
```

Insert a new node into an ordered linked list

```
PROCEDURE InsertNode(NewItem)
   IF FreeListPtr <> NullPointer
      THEN  // there is space in the array
         // take node from free list and store data item
         NewNodePtr ← FreeListPtr
         List[NewNodePtr].Data ← NewItem
         FreeListPtr ← List[FreeListPtr].Pointer
         // find insertion point
         ThisNodePtr ← StartPointer            // start at beginning of list
         WHILE ThisNodePtr <> NullPointer          // while not end of list
               AND List[ThisNodePtr].Data < NewItem
            PreviousNodePtr ← ThisNodePtr               // remember this node
                                        // follow the pointer to the next node
            ThisNodePtr ← List[ThisNodePtr].Pointer
         ENDWHILE
         IF PreviousNodePtr = StartPointer
            THEN  // insert new node at start of list
               List[NewNodePtr].Pointer ← StartPointer
               StartPointer ← NewNodePtr
            ELSE  // insert new node between previous node and this node
               List[NewNodePtr].Pointer ← List[PreviousNodePtr].Pointer
               List[PreviousNodePtr].Pointer ← NewNodePtr
         ENDIF
   ENDIF
ENDPROCEDURE
```


After three data items have been added to the linked list, the array contents are as shown in Figure 23.14.

StartPointer: 1

FreeListPtr: 4

List	Data	Pointer
[1]	B	2
[2]	D	3
[3]	L	∅
[4]		5
[5]		6
[6]		7
[7]		∅

Figure 23.14 Linked list of three nodes and free list of four nodes

Find an element in an ordered linked list

```
FUNCTION FindNode(DataItem) RETURNS INTEGER  // returns pointer to node
   CurrentNodePtr ← StartPointer  // start at beginning of list
   WHILE CurrentNodePtr <> NullPointer  // not end of list
         AND List[CurrentNodePtr].Data <> DataItem  // item not found
      // follow the pointer to the next node
      CurrentNodePtr ← List[CurrentNodePtr].Pointer
   ENDWHILE
   RETURN CurrentNodePtr  // returns NullPointer if item not found
ENDFUNCTION
```

Delete a node from an ordered linked list

```
PROCEDURE DeleteNode(DataItem)
   ThisNodePtr ← StartPointer                    // start at beginning of list
   WHILE ThisNodePtr <> NullPointer               // while not end of list
         AND List[ThisNodePtr].Data <> DataItem  // and item not found
      PreviousNodePtr ← ThisNodePtr  // remember this node
                                     // follow the pointer to the next node
      ThisNodePtr ← List[ThisNodePtr].Pointer
   ENDWHILE
   IF ThisNodePtr <> NullPointer  // node exists in list
      THEN
         IF ThisNodePtr = StartPointer  // first node to be deleted
            THEN
               StartPointer ← List[StartPointer].Pointer
            ELSE
               List[PreviousNodePtr] ← List[ThisNodePtr].Pointer
         ENDIF
         List[ThisNodePtr].Pointer ← FreeListPtr
         FreeListPtr ← ThisNodePtr
   ENDIF
ENDPROCEDURE
```

Access all nodes stored in the linked list

```
PROCEDURE OutputAllNodes
   CurrentNodePtr ← StartPointer // start at beginning of list
   WHILE CurrentNodePtr <> NullPointer  // while not end of list
      OUTPUT List[CurrentNodePtr].Data
      // follow the pointer to the next node
      CurrentNodePtr ← List[CurrentNodePtr].Pointer
   ENDWHILE
ENDPROCEDURE
```


TASK 23.04

Convert the pseudocode for the linked-list handling subroutines to program code. Incorporate the subroutines into a program and test them.

Note that a stack ADT and a queue ADT can be treated as special cases of linked lists. The linked list stack only needs to add and remove nodes from the front of the linked list. The linked list queue only needs to add nodes to the end of the linked list and remove nodes from the front of the linked list.

TASK 23.05

Write program code to implement a stack as a linked list. Note that the adding and removing of nodes is much simpler than for an ordered linked list.

TASK 23.06

Write program code to implement a queue as a linked list. You may find it helpful to introduce another pointer that always points to the end of the queue. You will need to update it when you add a new node to the queue.

23.07 Binary trees

In the real world, we draw tree structures to represent hierarchies. For example, we can draw a family tree showing ancestors and their children. A binary tree is different to a family tree because each node can have at most two 'children'.

In computer science binary trees are used for different purposes. In Chapter 20 (Section 20.05), you saw the use of a binary tree as a syntax tree. In this chapter, you will use an ordered binary tree ADT (such as the one shown in Figure 23.15) as a binary search tree.

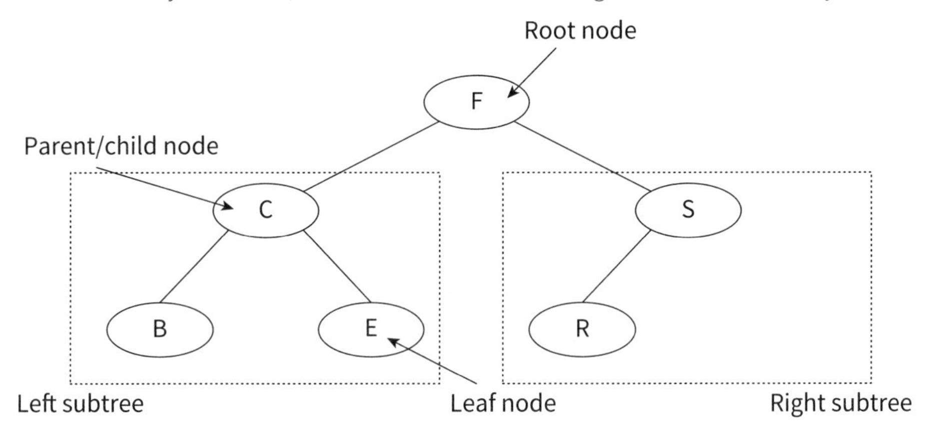

Figure 23.15 Conceptual diagram of an ordered binary tree

Nodes are added to an ordered binary tree in a specific way:

Start at the root node as the current node.
Repeat
If the data value is greater than the current node's data value, follow the right branch.
If the data value is smaller than the current node's data value, follow the left branch.
Until the current node has no branch to follow.
Add the new node in this position.

For example, if we want to add a new node with data value D to the binary tree in Figure 23.15, we execute the following steps:

1. Start at the root node.
2. D is smaller than F, so turn left.
3. D is greater than C, so turn right.
4. D is smaller than E, so turn left.
5. There is no branch going left from E, so we add D as a left child from E (see Figure 23.16).

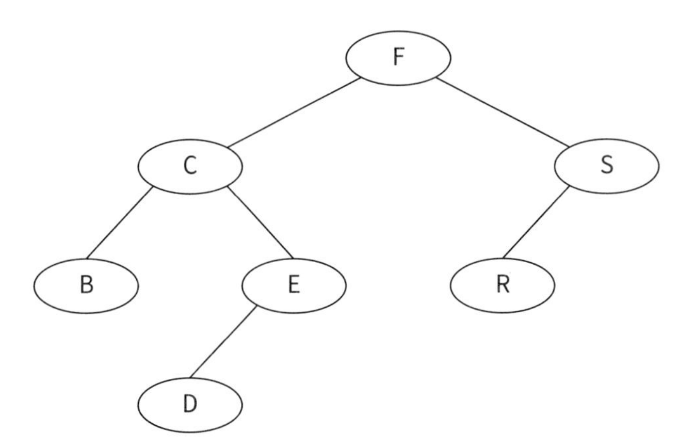

Figure 23.16 Conceptual diagram of adding a node to an ordered binary tree

This type of tree has a special use as a search tree. Just like the binary search applied to an ordered linear list, the binary search tree gives the benefit of a faster search than a linear search or searching a linked list. The ordered binary tree also has a benefit when adding a new node: other nodes do not need to be moved, only a left or right pointer needs to be added to link the new node into the existing tree.

We can store the binary tree in an array of records (see Figure 23.17). One record represents a node and consists of the data and a left pointer and a right pointer. Unused nodes are linked together to form a free list.

RootPointer: Ø

FreePtr: 1

Tree

	LeftPointer	Data	RightPointer
[1]	2		
[2]	3		
[3]	4		
[4]	5		
[5]	6		
[6]	7		
[7]	Ø		

Figure 23.17 Binary tree before any nodes are inserted

Create a new binary tree

```
// NullPointer should be set to -1 if using array element with index 0
CONSTANT NullPointer = 0
// Declare record type to store data and pointers
TYPE TreeNode
   DECLARE Data : STRING
   DECLARE LeftPointer : INTEGER
   DECLARE RightPointer : INTEGER
ENDTYPE
DECLARE RootPointer : INTEGER
DECLARE FreePtr : INTEGER
DECLARE Tree[1 : 7] OF TreeNode
PROCEDURE InitialiseTree
   RootPointer ← NullPointer  // set start pointer
   FreePtr ← 1                // set starting position of free list
   FOR Index ← 1 TO 6         // link all nodes to make free list
      Tree[Index].LeftPointer ← Index + 1
   ENDFOR
   Tree[7].LeftPointer ← NullPointer // last node of free list
ENDPROCEDURE
```

Insert a new node into a binary tree

```
PROCEDURE InsertNode(NewItem)
   IF FreePtr <> NullPointer
      THEN  // there is space in the array
         // take node from free list, store data item and set null pointers
         NewNodePtr ← FreePtr
         FreePtr ← Tree[FreePtr].LeftPointer
         Tree[NewNodePtr].Data ← NewItem
         Tree[NewNodePtr].LeftPointer ← NullPointer
         Tree[NewNodePtr].RightPointer ← NullPointer
         // check if empty tree
         IF RootPointer = NullPointer
            THEN  // insert new node at root
               RootPointer ← NewNodePtr
            ELSE  // find insertion point
               ThisNodePtr ← RootPointer   // start at the root of the tree
               WHILE ThisNodePtr <> NullPointer   // while not a leaf node
                  PreviousNodePtr ← ThisNodePtr  // remember this node
                  IF Tree[ThisNodePtr].Data > NewItem
                     THEN  // follow left pointer
                        TurnedLeft ← TRUE
                        ThisNodePtr ← Tree[ThisNodePtr].LeftPointer
                     ELSE // follow right pointer
                        TurnedLeft ← FALSE
                        ThisNodePtr ← Tree[ThisNodePtr].RightPointer
                  ENDIF
               ENDWHILE
               IF TurnedLeft = TRUE
                  THEN
                     Tree[PreviousNodePtr].LeftPointer ← NewNodePtr
                  ELSE
                     Tree[PreviousNodePtr].RightPointer ← NewNodePtr
               ENDIF
         ENDIF
   ENDIF
ENDPROCEDURE
```

Find a node in a binary tree

```
FUNCTION FindNode(SearchItem) RETURNS INTEGER  // returns pointer to node
   ThisNodePtr ← RootPointer     // start at the root of the tree
   WHILE ThisNodePtr <> NullPointer   // while a pointer to follow
         AND Tree[ThisNodePtr].Data <> SearchItem // and search item not found
      IF Tree[ThisNodePtr].Data > SearchItem
         THEN  // follow left pointer
            ThisNodePtr ← Tree[ThisNodePtr].LeftPointer
         ELSE // follow right pointer
            ThisNodePtr ← Tree[ThisNodePtr].RightPointer
      ENDIF
   ENDWHILE
   RETURN ThisNodePtr // will return null pointer if search item not found
ENDFUNCTION
```

TASK 23.07

Write program code to implement a binary search tree.

23.08 Hash tables

If we want to store records in an array and have direct access to records, we can use the concept of a hash table.

The idea behind a hash table is that we calculate an address (the array index) from the key value of the record and store the record at this address. When we search for a record, we calculate the address from the key and go to the calculated address to find the record. Calculating an address from a key is called 'hashing'.

Finding a hashing function that will give a unique address from a unique key value is very difficult. If two different key values hash to the same address this is called a 'collision'. There are different ways to handle collisions:

- chaining: create a linked list for collisions with start pointer at the hashed address
- using overflow areas: all collisions are stored in a separate overflow area, known as 'closed hashing'
- using neighbouring slots: perform a linear search from the hashed address to find an empty slot, known as 'open hashing'.

WORKED EXAMPLE 23.01

Calculating addresses in a hash table

Assume we want to store customer records in a 1D array `HashTable[0 : n]`. Each customer has a unique customer ID, an integer in the range 10001 to 99999.

We need to design a suitable hashing function. The result of the hashing function should be such that every index of the array can be addressed directly. The simplest hashing function gives us addresses between 0 and n:

```
FUNCTION Hash(Key) RETURNS INTEGER
   Address ← Key MOD(n + 1)
   RETURN Address
ENDFUNCTION
```

For illustrative purposes, we choose n to be 9. Our hashing function is:

```
Index ← CustomerID MOD 10
```

We want to store records with customer IDs: 45876, 32390, 95312, 64636, 23467. We can store the first three records in their correct slots, as shown in Figure 23.18.

[0]	[1]	[2]	[3]	[4]	[5]	[6]	[7]	[8]	[9]
32390		95312				45876			

Figure 23.18 A hash table without collisions

The fourth record key (64636) also hashes to index 6. This slot is already taken; we have a collision. If we store our record here, we lose the previous record. To resolve the collision, we can choose to store our record in the next available space, as shown in Figure 23.19.

[0]	[1]	[2]	[3]	[4]	[5]	[6]	[7]	[8]	[9]
32390		95312				45876	64636		

Figure 23.19 A hash table with a collision resolved by open hashing

The fifth record key (23467) hashes to index 7. This slot has been taken up by the previous record, so again we need to use the next available space (Figure 23.20).

[0]	[1]	[2]	[3]	[4]	[5]	[6]	[7]	[8]	[9]
32390		95312				45876	64636	23467	

Figure 23.20 A hash table with two collisions resolved by open hashing

When searching for a record, we need to allow for these out-of-place records. We know if the record we are searching for does not exist in the hash table when we come across an unoccupied slot.

We will now develop algorithms to insert a record into a hash table and to search for a record in the hash table using its record key.

- The hash table is a 1D array `HashTable[0 : Max] OF Record`.
- The records stored in the hash table have a unique key stored in field `Key`.

Insert a record into a hash table

```
PROCEDURE Insert(NewRecord)
   Index ← Hash(NewRecord.Key)
   WHILE HashTable[Index] NOT empty
      Index ← Index + 1 // go to next slot
      IF Index > Max // beyond table boundary?
         THEN // wrap around to beginning of table
            Index ← 1
      ENDIF
   ENDWHILE
   HashTable[Index] ← NewRecord
ENDPROCEDURE
```

Find a record in a hash table

```
FUNCTION FindRecord(SearchKey) RETURNS Record
   Index ← Hash(SearchKey)
   WHILE (HashTable[Index].Key <> SearchKey) AND (HashTable[Index] NOT empty)
      Index ← Index + 1 // go to next slot
      IF Index > Max // beyond table boundary?
         THEN // wrap around to beginning of table
            Index ← 0
      ENDIF
   ENDWHILE
   IF HashTable[Index] NOT empty // if record found
      THEN
         RETURN HashTable[Index] // return the record
   ENDIF
ENDFUNCTION
```

23.09 Dictionaries

A real-world dictionary is a collection of key–value pairs. The key is the term you use to look up the required value. For example, if you use an English–French dictionary to look up the English word 'book', you will find the French equivalent word 'livre'. A real-world dictionary is organised in alphabetical order of keys.

An ADT dictionary in computer science is implemented using a hash table, so that a value can be looked up using a direct-access method.

Python has a built-in ADT dictionary. The hashing function is determined by Python. For VB and Pascal, we need to implement our own.

Here are some examples of Python dictionaries:

```
EnglishFrench = {} # empty dictionary
EnglishFrench["book"] = "livre" # add a key-value pair to the dictionary
EnglishFrench["pen"] = "stylo"

print(EnglishFrench["book"]) # access a value in the dictionary

# alternative method of setting up a dictionary
ComputingTerms = {"Boolean" : "can be TRUE or FALSE", "Bit" : "0 or 1"}

print(ComputingTerms["Bit"])
```

There are many built-in functions for Python dictionaries. These are beyond the scope of this book. However, we need to understand how dictionaries are implemented. The following pseudocode shows how to create a new dictionary.


```
TYPE DictionaryEntry
   DECLARE Key   : STRING
   DECLARE Value : STRING
ENDTYPE
DECLARE EnglishFrench[0 : 999] OF DictionaryEntry  // empty dictionary
```

TASK 23.08

Write pseudocode to:

- insert a key–value pair into a dictionary
- look up a value in a dictionary.

Use the hashing function from Worked Example 23.01.

Summary

- Computational thinking is a problem-solving process.
- Standard algorithms include bubble sort, insertion sort, linear search and binary search.
- Abstract data types (ADTs) include records, stacks, queues, linked lists, binary trees, hash tables and dictionaries.
- Basic operations required for an ADT include creating an ADT and inserting, finding or deleting an element of an ADT.

Exam-style Questions

1 **a** Complete the algorithm for a binary search function `FindName`.

The data being searched is stored in the array `Names[0 : 50]`.
The name to be searched for is passed as a parameter.

```
FUNCTION FindName(s : STRING) RETURNS INTEGER
   Index ← -1
   First ← 0
   Last ← 50
   WHILE (Last >= First) AND .....................................
      Middle ← (First + Last) DIV 2
      IF Names[Middle] = s
         THEN
            Index ← Middle
         ELSE
            IF .......................................................
               THEN
                  Last  ← Middle + 1
               ELSE
                  ....................................................
            ENDIF
      ENDIF
   ENDWHILE
ENDFUNCTION
```
[3]

b The binary search does not work if the data in the array being searched is................................ [1]

c What does the function `FindName` return when:

i the name searched for exists in the array

ii the name searched for does not exist in the array? [2]

2 A queue Abstract Data Type (ADT) is to be implemented as a linked list of nodes. Each node is a record, consisting of a data field and a pointer field. The queue ADT also has a `FrontOfQueue` pointer and an `EndOfQueue` pointer associated with it. The possible queue operations are: `JoinQueue` and `LeaveQueue`.

a **i** Add labels to the diagram to show the state of the queue after three data items have been added to the queue in the given order: Apple, Pear, Banana. [5]

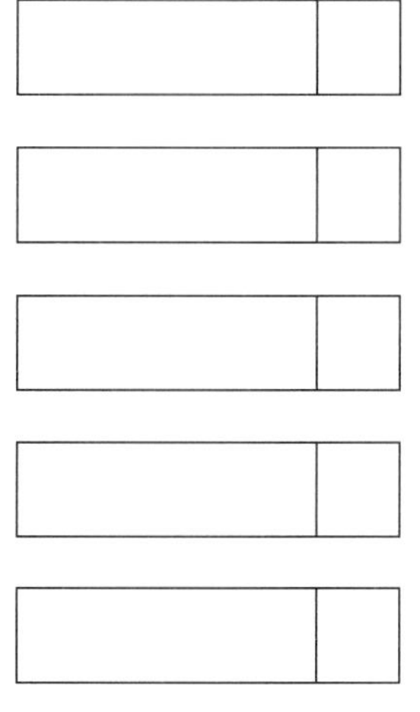

ii Add labels to the diagram to show how the unused nodes are linked to form a list of free nodes. This list has a `StartOfFreeList` pointer associated with it. [2]

b **i** Using program code, declare the record type `Node`. [3]

ii Write program code to create an array `Queue` with 50 records of type `Node.` Your solution should link all nodes and initialise the pointers `FrontOfQueue, EndOfQueue` and `StartOfFreeList`. [7]

c The pseudocode algorithm for the queue operation `JoinQueue` is written as a procedure with the header:

```
PROCEDURE JoinQueue(NewItem)
```

where `NewItem` is the new value to be added to the queue. The procedure uses the variables shown in the following identifier table:

Identifier	Data type	Description
NullPointer	INTEGER	Constant set to –1
		Array to store queue data
	STRING	Value to be added
		Pointer to next free node in array
		Pointer to first node in queue
		Pointer to last node in queue
		Pointer to node to be added

i Complete the identifier table. [7]

ii Complete the pseudocode using the identifiers from the table in part (i). [6]

```
PROCEDURE JoinQueue(NewItem : STRING)
   // Report error if no free nodes remaining
   IF StartOfFreeList = ............................
      THEN
         Report Error
      ELSE
         // new data item placed in node at start of free list
         NewNodePointer ← StartOfFreeList
         Queue[NewNodePointer].Data ← NewItem
         // adjust free list pointer
         StartOfFreeList ← Queue[NewNodePointer].Pointer
         Queue[NewNodePointer].Pointer ← NullPointer
         // if first item in queue then adjust front of queue pointer
         IF FrontOfQueue = NullPointer
            THEN
               .................... ← ..............................
         ENDIF
         // new node is new end of queue
         Queue[....................].Pointer ← ....................
         EndOfQueue ← ..............................................
   ENDIF
ENDPROCEDURE
```

Chapter 24

Algorithm Design Methods

Learning objectives

By the end of this chapter you should be able to:

- describe the purpose of a decision table
- construct a decision table with a maximum of three conditions and simplify it by removing redundancies
- construct a JSP structure diagram showing repetition
- construct a JSP structure diagram showing selection
- write equivalent pseudocode from JSP structure charts
- construct a JSP structure diagram to describe a data structure
- construct a JSP data structure diagram using sequence, selection, iteration
- construct a JSP diagram for a program design
- use state-transition diagrams to document an algorithm and show the behaviour of an object.

24.01 Decision tables

A **decision table** is a precise way of modelling logic. Each possible combination of conditions is considered in turn and what action is required.

KEY TERMS

Decision table: a precise way of modelling logic

A decision table has the format shown in Figure 24.01.

Conditions	Condition alternatives
Actions	Action entries

Figure 24.01 The four quadrants of a decision table

Example

Students in a particular college take an end-of-year test. Any student with 90 marks or more gets a distinction. Students with fewer than 20 marks fail. All other students get a pass.

We set up a decision table by allowing one row for each condition and one row for each possible action. We need one column for every possible combination of conditions. Two conditions require four columns; three conditions require eight columns. Table 24.01 shows the decision table for awarding grades.

Conditions	>= 90 marks	Y	Y	N	N
	< 20 marks	Y	N	Y	N
Actions	Distinction	–	X		
	Pass	–			X
	Fail	–		X	

Table 24.01 Decision table example

Note that Y means true and N means false. X means this action is to be performed. A dash is added where the condition alternatives are irrelevant or impossible: a student cannot have fewer than 20 marks and at the same time at least 90 marks.

The real power of decision tables becomes apparent when the conditions and resulting actions are more complex. Inspection of the action entries sometimes shows redundancies and the decision table can be simplified. This means the program code to be written will also be simplified.

WORKED EXAMPLE 24.01

Creating a decision table

Consider an online order company that charges $5 for delivery of packages. If the order value is over $50, the package is small and the customer has a promotion code, the delivery is free. If the order value is over $50 and the package is small, the delivery charge is $1. If the order value is over $50 and the customer has a promotion code, the delivery charge is $1.

We complete the conditions in a decision table for the order form in the systematic manner shown. Table 24.02 shows the delivery charge conditions.

Conditions	order value over $50	Y	Y	Y	Y	N	N	N	N
	small package	Y	Y	N	N	Y	Y	N	N
	promotion code	Y	N	Y	N	Y	N	Y	N

Table 24.02 Delivery charge conditions

Next, we look at each combination of conditions in turn and decide which action needs to be taken and mark those with X (see Table 24.03).

Conditions	order value over $50	Y	Y	Y	Y	N	N	N	N
	small package	Y	Y	N	N	Y	Y	N	N
	promotion code	Y	N	Y	N	Y	N	Y	N
Actions	free delivery	X							
	$1 charge		X	X					
	$5 charge				X	X	X	X	X

Table 24.03 Delivery charge decision table

To find redundancies, we look at each action and then check whether the conditions are required:

Free delivery only applies if all 3 conditions are true. There are no redundancies here.

The $1 charge applies if condition 1 is true and either condition 2 or condition 3 is true. There are no redundancies here either.

The $5 charge applies in all cases where condition 1 is false. The redundant conditions are shown by the shaded cells. We can therefore simplify the table (see Table 24.04) We put a dash in the cells where the condition can be true or false – the action will be the same. The dash is sometimes referred to as the 'don't care' symbol.

Conditions	order value over $50	Y	Y	Y	Y	N
	small package	Y	Y	N	N	–
	promotion code	Y	N	Y	N	–
Actions	free delivery	X				
	$1 charge		X	X		
	$5 charge				X	X

Table 24.04 Simplified delivery charge decision table

Decision tables can also be used to define outputs dependent on inputs so can be a basis for testing a program.

24.02 Jackson structured programming (JSP)

When designing a program using Jackson structured programming (JSP), we set up a structure based on the structure of the data the intended program is to handle.

A structure can consist of elementary components (they have no parts) and composite components (sequence, selection or iteration). A sequence has two or more components. Selection consists of two or more parts, only one of which is selected. Iteration consists of one part that repeats zero or more times.

WORKED EXAMPLE 24.02

Designing a program using JSP

Consider a company's order form template:

Parts Order Form				
Customer Name:				
Customer Address:				
Product ID	**Description**	**Quantity**	**Unit Price**	**Price**
			Postage & Packing	
			Total Price	
Payment by:	Cheque/Bank card	(delete as appropriate)		
Bank Card Number:				

Figure 24.02 Order form

The first stage of designing a program to process the data in this order form is to draw a data structure diagram of the data.

Using the top-down approach, at the top level the order form consists of these components: the header, the order body, the totals and the payment method.

- The header is a sequence composite component containing customer name and address.
- The body is an iteration composite component containing repeated products and their quantity, etc.
- The payment method is a selection composite component containing either cheque or bank card.

On the data structure diagram (see Figure 24.03):

- Repetition is shown by an asterisk (*) in the corner of components that are repeated.
- Selection is shown by a circle in the corner of components where only one is chosen.

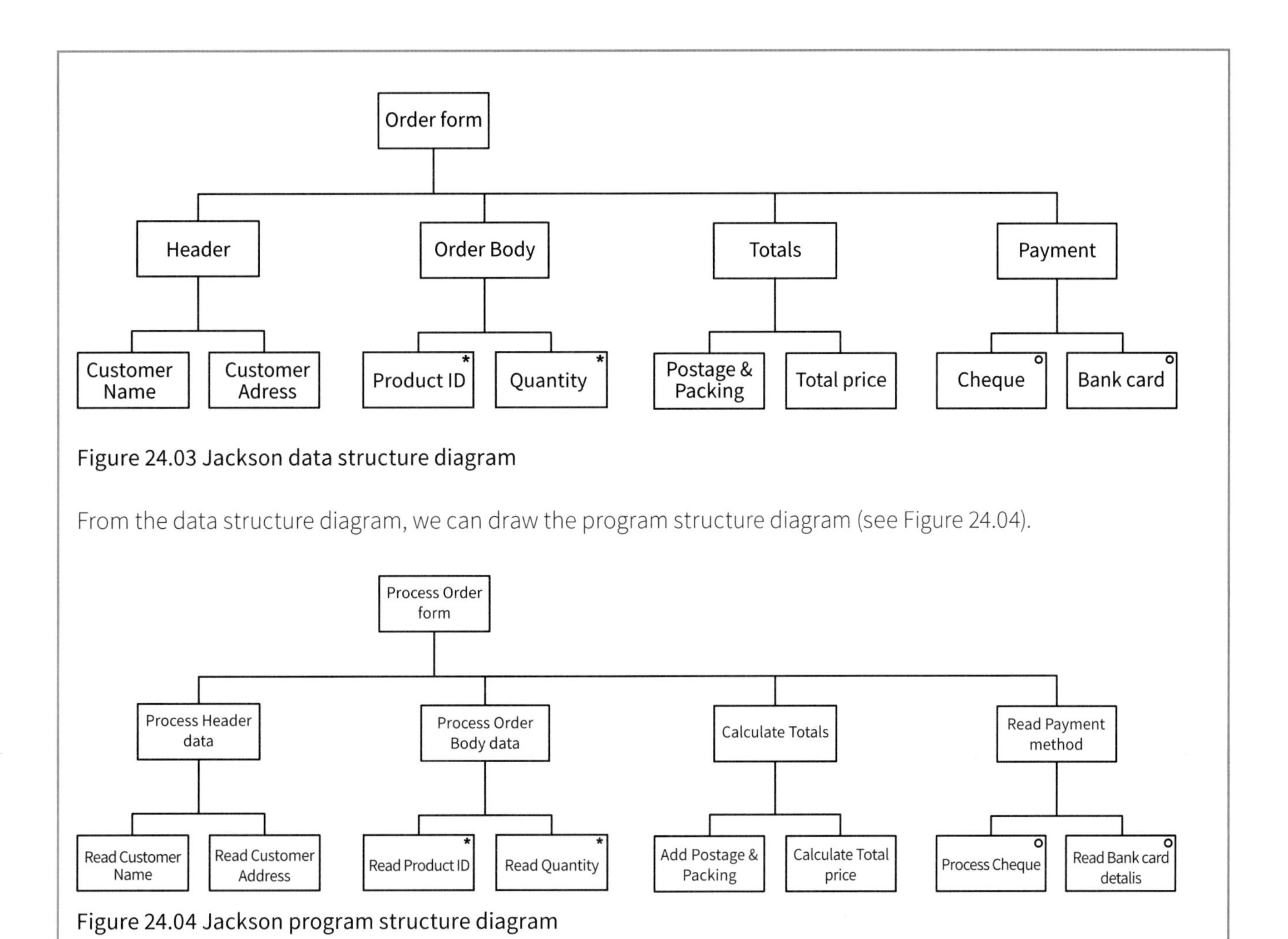

Figure 24.03 Jackson data structure diagram

From the data structure diagram, we can draw the program structure diagram (see Figure 24.04).

Figure 24.04 Jackson program structure diagram

TASK 24.01

Write pseudocode from the Jackson program structure diagram in Figure 24.04.

In more complicated systems, the output data can be subjected to the same analysis, possibly leading to conflicts to be resolved.

24.03 State-transition diagrams

A computer system can be seen as a **finite state machine (FSM)**. An FSM has a start state. An input to the FSM produces a transformation from one state to another state.

The information about the states of an FSM can be presented in a **state-transition table**.

KEY TERMS

Finite state machine (FSM): a machine that consists of a fixed set of possible states with a set of inputs that change the state and a set of possible outputs

State-transition table: a table that gives information about the states of an FSM

Table 24.05 shows an example FSM represented as a state-transition table.

- If the FSM is in state S1, an input of a causes no change of state.
- If the FSM is in state S1, an input of b transforms S1 to S2.
- If the FSM is in state S2, an input of b causes no change of state.
- If the FSM is in state S2, an input of a transforms S2 to S1.

		current state	
		S1	S2
input	a	S1	S1
	b	S2	S2

Table 24.05 State-transition table

A **state-transition diagram** can be used to describe the behaviour of an FSM. Figure 24.05 shows the start state as S1 (denoted by ●——➤). If the FSM has a final state (also known as the halting state), this is shown by a double-circled state (S1 in the example).

KEY TERMS

State-transition diagram: a diagram that describes the behaviour of an FSM

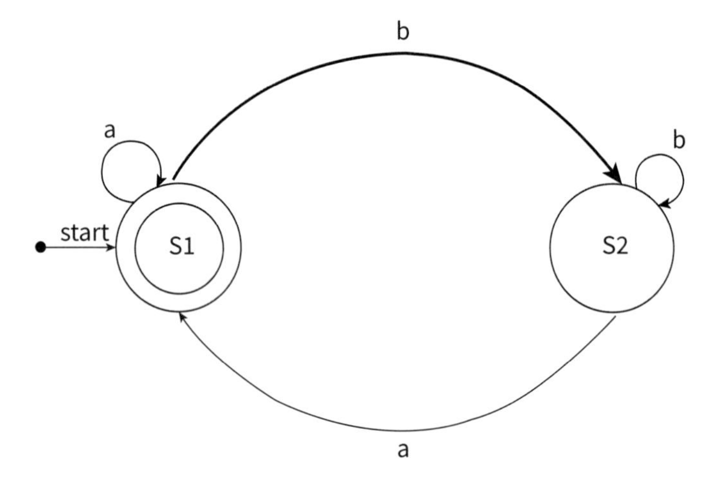

Figure 24.05 State-transition diagram

If an input causes an output this is shown by a vertical bar (as in Figure 24.06). For example, if the current state is S1, an input of b produces output c and transforms the FSM to state S2.

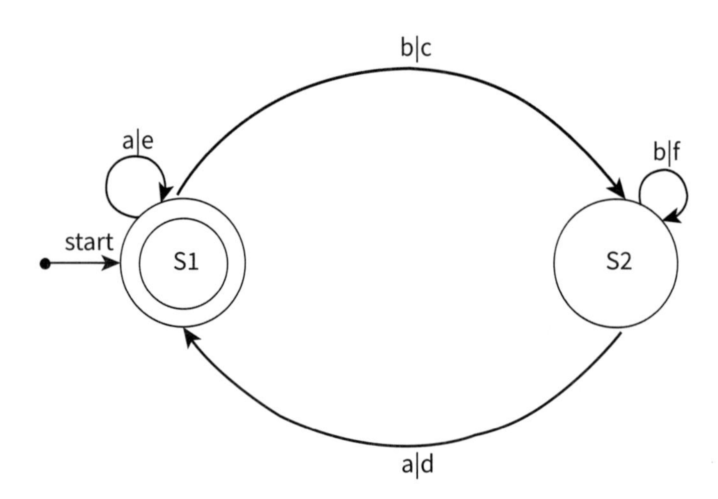

Figure 24.06 State-transition diagram with outputs

WORKED EXAMPLE 24.03

Creating a state-transition diagram for an intruder detection system

A program is required that simulates the behaviour of an intruder detection system.

Description of the system: The system has a battery power supply. The system is activated when the start button is pressed. Pressing the start button when the system is active has no effect. To de-activate the system, the operator must enter a PIN. The system goes into alert mode when a sensor is activated. The system will stay in alert mode for two minutes. If the system has not been de-activated within two minutes an alarm bell will ring.

We can complete a state-transition table (Table 24.06) using the information from the system description.

Current state	Event	Next state
System inactive	Press start button	System active
System active	Enter PIN	System inactive
System active	Activate sensor	Alert mode
System active	Press start button	System active
Alert mode	Enter PIN	System inactive
Alert mode	2 minutes pass	Alarm bell ringing
Alert mode	Press start button	Alert mode
Alarm bell ringing	Enter PIN	System inactive
Alarm bell ringing	Press start button	Alarm bell ringing

Table 24.06 State-transition table for intruder detection simulation

The start state is 'System inactive'. We can draw a state-transition diagram (Figure 24.07) from the information in Table 24.06.

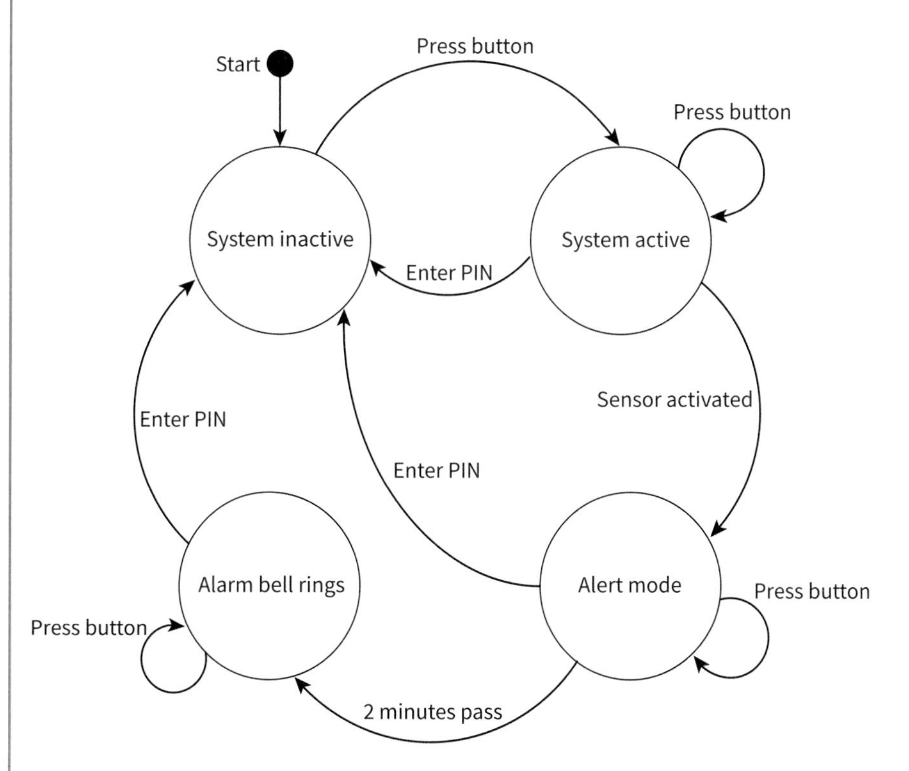

Figure 24.07 State-transition diagram for intruder alarm system

WORKED EXAMPLE 24.04

Creating a state-transition diagram for a two's complement FSM

A finite state machine has been designed that will take as input a positive binary integer, one bit at a time, starting with the least significant bit. The FSM converts the binary integer into the two's complement negative equivalent. The method to be used is:

1 Output the bits input up to and including the first 1.

2 Output the other bits following this scheme:

2.1 For each 1, output a 0

2.2 For each 0, output a 1.

This information is represented in the state-transition table shown in Table 24.07.

Current state	S1	S1	S2	S2
Input bit	0	1	0	1
Next state	S1	S2	S2	S2
Output bit	0	1	1	0

Table 24.07 State-transition table with outputs

This method can be represented as the state-transition diagram in Figure 24.08.

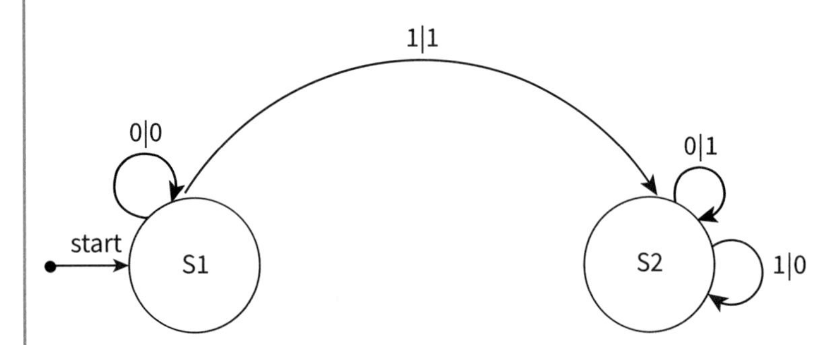

Figure 24.08 State-transition diagram for a two's complement FSM

TASK 24.02

Write a program that simulates the intruder alarm system in Worked Example 24.03.

Question 24.01

What is the output from the FSM represented by the state-transition diagram in Figure 24.08, when the input is `0101`?

Extension Question 24.01

Does the FSM in Figure 24.08 work for converting a negative binary number into its positive equivalent?

Summary

- A decision table shows all possible combinations of conditions and the resulting actions. A decision table may show redundancies that result in a simplified decision table.
- Jackson structured programming (JSP) is modelled on the structure of the data.
- JSP structures consist of elementary and composite components.
- Composite components represent sequence, selection or iteration.
- A finite state machine (FSM) has a start state.
- A state-transition table shows each state of a FSM and the events that produce a transformation from one state to another state.
- A state-transition diagram is another way of representing the states and transformations of a FSM.

Exam-style Questions

1 A toll road is a road on which motor vehicle drivers have to pay to drive. The payment is calculated as follows: Motor vehicles pay a standard charge. If passenger vehicles (cars and buses) use the road during off-peak times (not within 06:00 hrs to 19:00 hrs), the charge is reduced. Passenger vehicles with more than three occupants do not get charged.

a Complete the decision table. [6]

Conditions	passenger vehicle								
	between 06:00 and 19:00								
	more than 3 occupants								
Actions	standard charge								
	reduced charge								
	Free								

b Simplify your solution by removing redundancies. [3]

2 A bank uses a data file to print a monthly statement for a bank account. The file consists of a header (account number and name of account holder), followed by a statement body (repeated transactions detailing date of payment, recipient and amount), followed by a trailer (final balance and message if overdrawn).

Complete the JSP data structure diagram: [5]

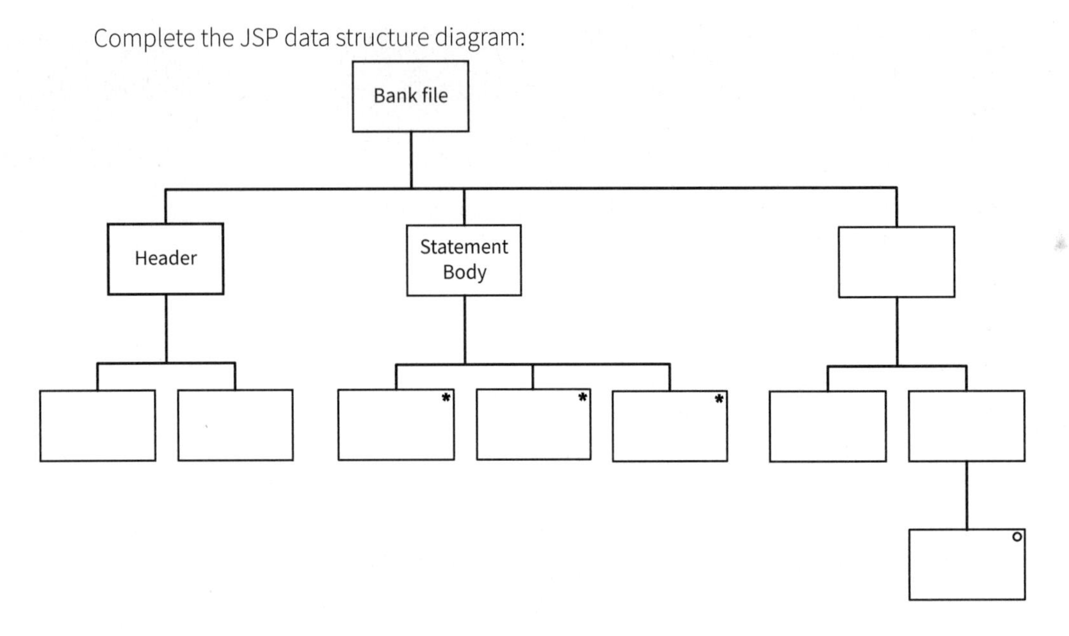

3 A car park has a barrier at the exit. The starting position of the barrier is lowered. When a car wants to exit the car park, the driver has to insert a coin into a coin slot at the barrier. The barrier raises and allows the car to drive out of the car park. After the car has passed through the barrier, the barrier lowers. In case of emergency, a member of staff can open the barrier using a remote control. The barrier will remain open until the remote control is used again to lower the barrier.

The barrier has three states: lowered, raised and open. The transition from one state to another is as shown in the state-transition table:

Current state	Event	Next state
Barrier lowered	Coin inserted	Barrier raised
Barrier lowered	Open remotely	Barrier open
Barrier open	Close remotely	Barrier lowered
Barrier raised	Car has exited	Barrier lowered

Complete the state-transition diagram for the barrier:

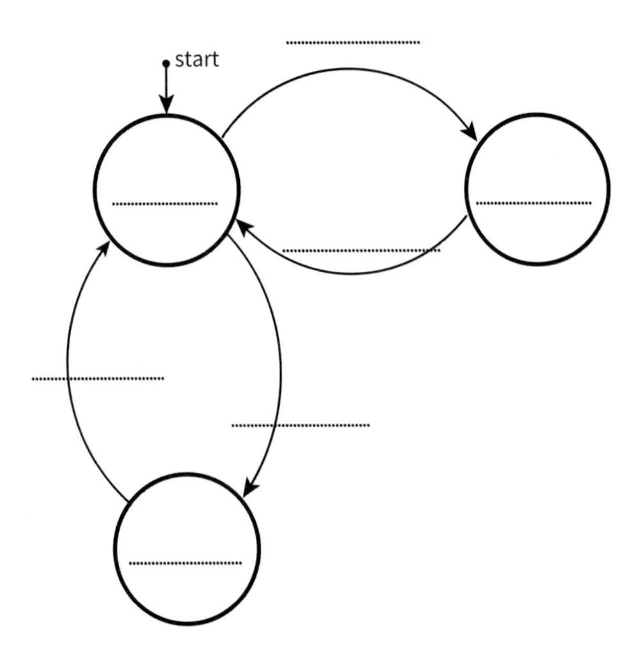

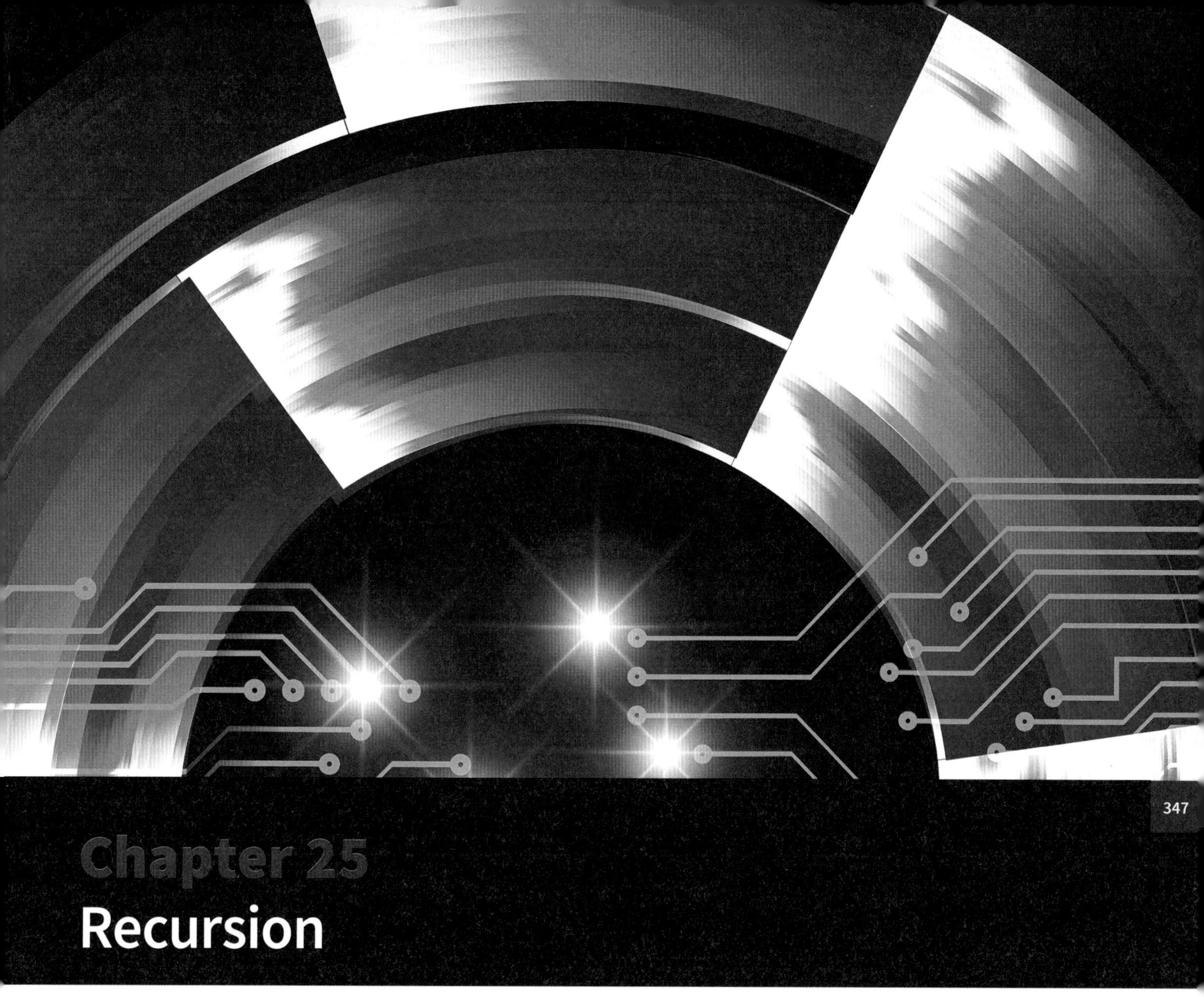

Chapter 25
Recursion

Learning objectives

By the end of this chapter you should be able to:

- show understanding of the essential features of recursion
- show understanding of how recursion is expressed in a programming language
- trace recursive algorithms
- write recursive algorithms
- show understanding of when the use of recursion is beneficial
- show awareness of what a compiler has to do to implement recursion in a programming language.

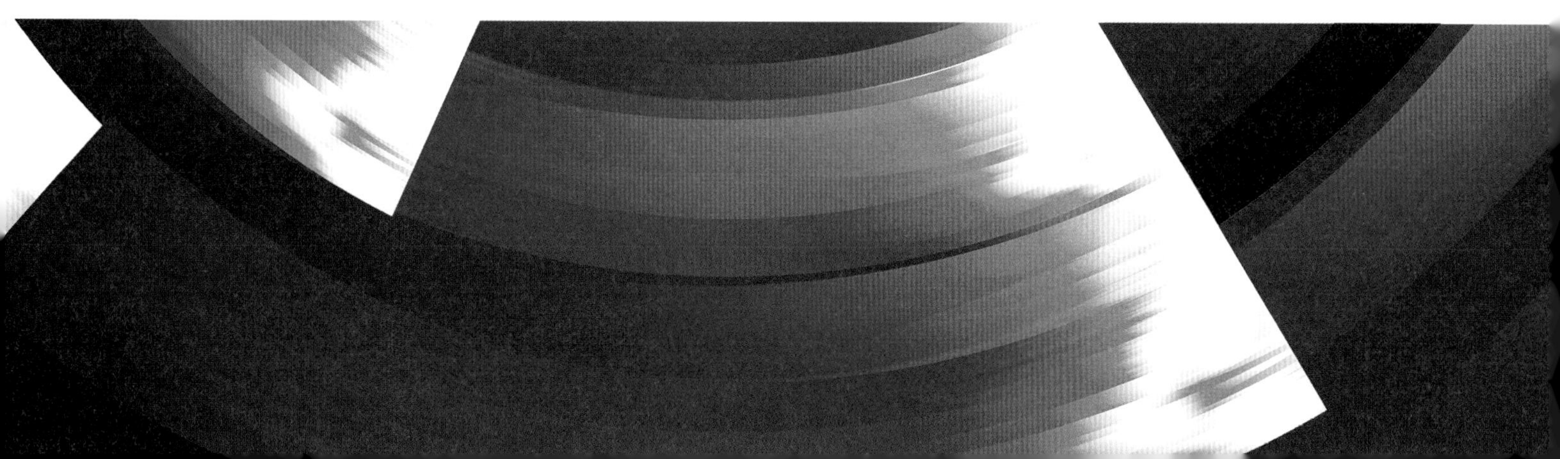

25.01 Concept of recursion

In mathematical logic and computer science, a function or procedure is said to be a **recursive routine** if it is defined in terms of itself.

KEY TERMS

Recursive routine: a function or procedure defined in terms of itself

The classic mathematical example is the factorial function, n!, which is defined in Figure 25.01. This definition holds for all positive whole numbers.

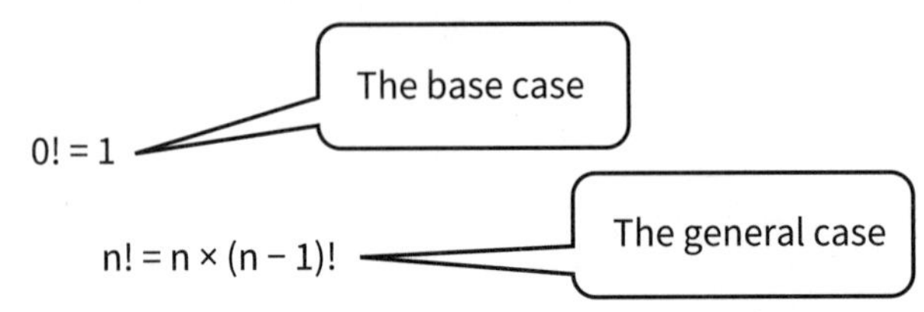

Figure 25.01 Mathematical definition of the factorial function

Figure 25.02 shows expressions of the factorial function for the first four numbers.

Here is the recursive function, with a smaller number (3)

$4! = 4 \times (4 - 1)! = 4 \times 3!$

$3! = 3 \times (3 - 1)! = 3 \times 2!$

$2! = 2 \times (2 - 1)! = 2 \times 1!$

$1! = 1 \times (1 - 1)! = 1 \times 0!$

The number for the recursive function keeps getting smaller, until we reach 0!, which is explicitly defined.

Figure 25.02 Expressions of the factorial function

Because 0! = 1:

$$4! = 4 \times 3 \times 2 \times 1 \times 1 = 24$$

Recursive solutions have a **base case** and a **general case**. The base case gives a result without involving the general case. The general case is defined in terms of the definition itself. It is very important that the general case must come closer to the base case with each recursion, for any starting point.

KEY TERMS

Base case: an explicit solution to a recursive function

General case: a definition of a recursive function in terms of itself

25.02 Programming a recursive subroutine

WORKED EXAMPLE 25.01

Coding the factorial function

We could program the function Factorial iteratively, using a loop:

```
FUNCTION Factorial(n : INTEGER) RETURNS INTEGER
   Result ← 1
   FOR i ← 1 TO n
      Result ← Result * i
   ENDFOR
   RETURN Result
ENDFUNCTION
```

Alternatively, we can define the function Factorial recursively (Figure 25.03).

```
FUNCTION Factorial(n : INTEGER) RETURNS INTEGER
   IF n = 0
      THEN
         Result ← 1
      ELSE
         Result ← n * Factorial(n-1)
   ENDIF
   RETURN Result
ENDFUNCTION
```

This is the base case
This is the general case
This is the recursive call

Figure 25.03 The factorial function coded recursively

The recursive pseudocode resembles the original mathematical definition of the factorial function. The dry run in Table 25.02 (Section 25.03) shows how this works.

Discussion Point:

Carefully examine the two solutions to the factorial function. What happens if the iterative function is called with parameter 0? What happens if the recursive function is called with parameter 0? What changes would need to be made so the mathematical definition holds for all values of n?

When writing a recursive subroutine, there are three rules you must observe. A recursive subroutine must:

- have a base case
- have a general case
- reach the base case after a finite number of calls to itself.

TASK 25.01

Write program code to implement the recursive algorithm for the `Factorial` function.

Question 25.01

What happens when the function is called with `Factorial(-2)`? Which rule is not satisfied?

WORKED EXAMPLE 25.02

Coding a recursive procedure

Consider a procedure to count down from a given integer. We can write the solution as an iterative algorithm:

```
PROCEDURE CountDownFrom(n : INTEGER)
   FOR i ← n DOWNTO 0
     OUTPUT i
   ENDFOR
ENDPROCEDURE
```

We can also write the solution as a recursive algorithm. Consider what happens after the first value has been output. The remaining numbers follow the same pattern of counting down from the next smaller value. The base case is when n reaches 0. 0 will be output but no further numbers. The general case is outputting n and then counting down from (n-1). This can be written using pseudocode:


```
PROCEDURE CountDownFrom(n : INTEGER)
   OUTPUT n
   IF n > 0
      THEN
         CALL CountDownFrom(n-1)
   ENDIF
ENDPROCEDURE
```

25.03 Tracing a recursive subroutine

Tracing a recursive procedure

Dry-running the recursive procedure from Worked Example 25.02, we can complete a trace table as shown in Table 25.01.

Call number	Procedure call	OUTPUT	n > 0
1	CountDownFrom(3)	3	TRUE
2	CountDownFrom(2)	2	TRUE
3	CountDownFrom(1)	1	TRUE
4	CountDownFrom(0)	0	FALSE

Table 25.01 Trace table for `CALL CountDownFrom(3)`

It is more complex to trace a subroutine that contains statements to execute after the recursive call. Look at the slightly modified algorithm:

```
PROCEDURE CountUpTo(n : INTEGER)
    IF n > 0
       THEN
          CALL CountUpTo(n-1)
    ENDIF
    OUTPUT n
ENDPROCEDURE
```

Note that the statements after `CALL CountUpTo(n-1)` are not executed until control returns to this statement as the recursive calls unwind.

What is the effect of moving the `OUTPUT` statement to the end of the procedure? Figure 25.04 traces the execution of `CALL CountUpTo(3)`

Call number	Procedure call	n > 0	OUTPUT
1	CountUpTo(3)	TRUE	
2	CountUpTo(2)	TRUE	
3	CountUpTo(1)	TRUE	
4	CountUpTo(0)	FALSE	0
(3)	CountUpTo(1)	TRUE	1
(2)	CountUpTo(2)	TRUE	2
(1)	CountUpTo(3)	TRUE	3

Figure 25.04 Trace table for `CALL CountUpTo(3)`

When the base case is reached, the fourth call of the procedure is complete and the procedure is exited. Control then passes back to the third call and so on. Note how we show the trace as the recursive calls unwind. Don't go back up the table and fill in the OUTPUT column as this will not make it clear enough when the output occurred.

Tracing a recursive function

A recursive function has a statement after the recursive call to itself: the `RETURN` statement. Again we show what happens when the recursive calls unwind by filling in more rows in the trace table. Let's consider the factorial function again.

```
FUNCTION Factorial(n : INTEGER) RETURNS INTEGER
    IF n = 0
       THEN
          Result ← 1
       ELSE
          Result ← n * Factorial(n-1)
    ENDIF
    RETURN Result
ENDFUNCTION
```

Call number	Procedure call	n = 0	Result	Return value
1	Factorial(4)	FALSE	4 * Factorial(3)	
2	Factorial(3)	FALSE	3 * Factorial(2)	
3	Factorial(2)	FALSE	2 * Factorial(1)	
4	Factorial(1)	FALSE	1 * Factorial(0)	
5	Factorial(0)	TRUE	1	1
(4)	Factorial(1)	FALSE	1 * 1	1
(3)	Factorial(2)	FALSE	2 * 1	2
(2)	Factorial(3)	FALSE	3 * 2	6
(1)	Factorial(4)	FALSE	4 * 6	24

Figure 25.05 Trace table for `CALL Factorial(4)`

Another way to illustrate how the function calls unwind is by framing each call with a box (see Figure 25.06). When the inner-most box is completed the result is fed to the next outer one. And so on until the outermost box has been completed.

```
Factorial(4)
   Result ← 4 * Factorial(3)
      Factorial(3)
         Result ← 3 * Factorial(2)
            Factorial(2)
               Result ← 2 * Factorial(1)
                  Factorial(1)
                     Result ← 1 * Factorial(0)
                        Factorial(0)
                           Result ← 1
                           Result 1
                     Return 1
               Return 2
         Return 6
   Return 24
```

Figure 25.06 Diagrammatic view of recursive calls of `Factorial`

TASK 25.02

Consider the following recursive algorithm:

```
PROCEDURE X(n : INTEGER)
   IF (n = 0) OR (n = 1)
      THEN
         OUTPUT n
      ELSE
         CALL X(n DIV 2)
         OUTPUT(n MOD 2)
   ENDIF
ENDPROCEDURE
```

Dry-run the procedure call `X(19)` by completing a trace table. What is the purpose of this algorithm?

25.04 Running a recursive subroutine

Recursive subroutines can only be executed if the compiler produces object code that uses a stack to push return addresses and local variables when calling a subroutine repeatedly.

WORKED EXAMPLE 25.03

Running the factorial function

Consider the following program, written in pseudocode:

```
010  PROGRAM
020
030  FUNCTION Factorial(n : INTEGER) RETURNS INTEGER
040     IF n = 0
050        THEN
060           Result ←  1
070        ELSE
080           Result ← n * Factorial(n - 1)
090     ENDIF
```

```
100      RETURN Result
110   ENDFUNCTION
120
130   // main program
140
150   DECLARE Answer : INTEGER
160   Answer ← Factorial(Number)
170   OUTPUT Answer
180
190   ENDPROGRAM
```

The first program statement to be executed is line 160. The actual parameter `n` has the value 3. The function call causes the return address to be put on the stack, as shown in Figure 25.07. Program execution jumps to line 30.

When line 80 is reached, the function call causes the return address to be stored on the stack, together with the current contents of the local variables. The locations used to store these values are referred to as a stack frame (represented by the blue borders in Figure 25.07). Each recursive call will add another stack frame to the stack until the base case is reached.

When the base case is reached, the result of the function call `Factorial(0)` is returned by pushing it onto the stack. The result is popped off the stack by the previous invocation of the function. With each return from a function call, the corresponding stack frame is taken off and the values of the local variables are restored. Eventually, control is returned to line 160 with the result of the function call on the top of the stack. The value of Answer is output in line 170.

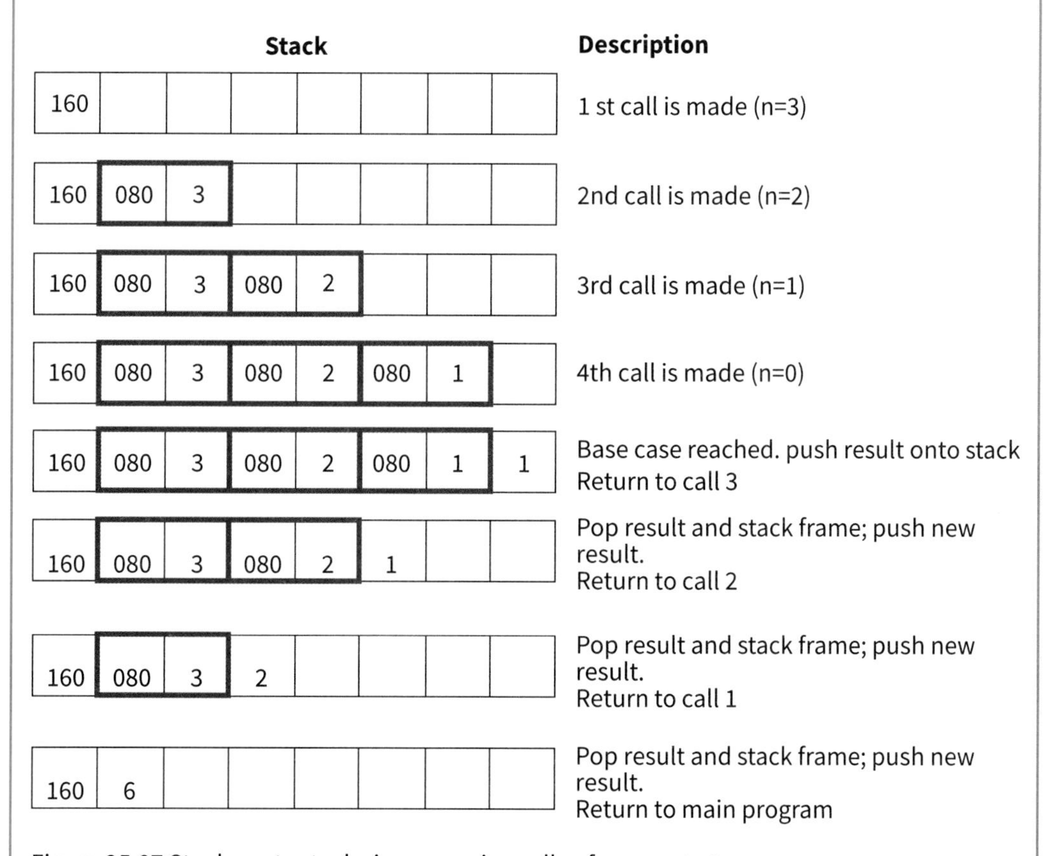

Figure 25.07 Stack contents during recursive calls of `Factorial`

TASK 25.03

Use your program code from Task 25.01 and add the main program as shown in Worked Example 25.03.

Amend your code in the following ways (line numbers are relative to the pseudocode in Worked Example 25.03):

- Add a global integer variable `CallNumber`.
- Initialise `CallNumber` to zero (line `155`).
- Increment `CallNumber` (line `35`).
- Add a statement to output the values of `CallNumber` and `n` (line `36`).
- Add a statement to output the value of `Result` (line `95`).

Run the program and study the output.

25.05 Benefits and drawbacks of recursion

Recursion is an important technique in different programming paradigms (See Chapter 29, Section 29.08). When designing a solution to a mathematical problem that is inherently recursive, the easiest way to write a solution is to implement the recursive definition.

Recursive solutions are often more elegant and use less program code than iterative solutions. However, repeated recursive calls can carry large overheads in terms of memory usage and processor time (see Section 25.04). For example, the procedure call `CountDownFrom(100)` will require 100 stack frames before it completes.

Summary

- A recursive subroutine is defined in terms of itself.
- A recursive subroutine must have a base case and a general case.
- A recursive subroutine must reach the base case after a finite number of calls to itself.
- Each time a subroutine is called, a stack frame is pushed onto the stack.
- A stack frame consists of the return address and the values of the local variables.
- When a subroutine completes, the corresponding stack frame is popped off the stack.

Exam-style Questions

1 a Distinguish between iteration and recursion. [2]

b Give **one** advantage and **one** disadvantage of using recursive subroutines. [2]

2 The following is a recursively defined function which calculates the result of $Base^{Exponent}$.
For example, 2^3 is 8.

```
FUNCTION Power(Base: INTEGER, Exponent : INTEGER) RETURNS INTEGER
   IF Exponent = 0
      THEN
         Result ← 1
      ELSE
         Result ← Base * Power(Base, Exponent - 1)
   ENDIF
   RETURN Result
ENDFUNCTION
```

a What is meant by 'recursively defined'? [1]

b Trace the execution of the function call `Power(2,4)` showing for each re-entry into the Power function, the values passed to the function and the results returned. [6]

c Explain the role of the stack in the execution of the Power function. [3]

d Write a pseudocode non-recursive (iterative) version of the Power function. [6]

e **i** Give **one** reason why a non-recursive Power function may be preferred to a recursive one. [1]

ii Give one reason why a recursive Power function may be preferred to a non-recursive one. [1]

3 The following is a recursively defined function which calculates the *n* th integer in the sequence of Fibonacci numbers.

```
01  FUNCTION Fibonacci(n : INTEGER) RETURNS INTEGER
02     IF (n = 0) OR (n = 1)
03        THEN
04           Result ←1
05        ELSE
06           Result ← Fibonacci(n - 1) + Fibonacci(n - 2)
07     ENDIF
08     RETURN Result
09  ENDFUNCTION
```

a **i** Which line is the base case? [1]

ii Which line is the general case? [1]

b Dry-run the function call `Fibonacci(4)`. [7]

Chapter 26
Further Programming

Learning objectives

By the end of this chapter you should be able to:

- show understanding of what is meant by a programming paradigm
- show understanding of the characteristics of a number of programming paradigms
  (low-level, imperative, object-oriented, declarative)
- write code to define a record structure
- write code to perform file-processing operations: open or close a file; read or write a record to a file
- use pseudocode for random file handling
- write code to perform file-processing operations on serial, sequential and random files
- show understanding of an exception and the importance of exception handling
- show understanding of when it is appropriate to use exception handling
- write code to use exception handling in practical programming
- describe features in editors that benefit programming
- know when to use compilers and interpreters
- describe facilities available in debuggers and how and when they should be deployed.

26.01 Programming paradigms

A programming paradigm is a fundamental style of programming. Each paradigm will support a different way of thinking and problem solving. Paradigms are supported by programming language features. Some programming languages support more than one paradigm. There are many different paradigms, not all mutually exclusive. Here are just a few different paradigms.

Low-level programming paradigm

The features of low-level programming languages give us the ability to manipulate the contents of memory addresses and registers directly and exploit the architecture of a given processor. We solve problems in a very different way when we use the low-level programming paradigm than if we use a high-level paradigm. See Chapter 6 and Chapter 28 for low-level programming examples. Note that each different type of processor has its own programming language. There are 'families' of processors that are designed with similar architectures and therefore use similar programming languages. For example, the Intel processor family (present in many PC-type computers) uses the x86 instruction set.

Imperative programming paradigm

Imperative programming involves writing a program as a sequence of explicit steps that are executed by the processor. Most of the programs in this book use imperative programming (Chapters 11 to 15 and Chapters 23 to 26). An imperative program tells the computer *how* to get a desired result, in contrast to declarative programming where a program describes *what* the desired result should be. Note that the procedural programming paradigm belongs to the imperative programming paradigm. There are many imperative programming languages, Pascal, C and Basic to name just a few.

Object-oriented programming paradigm

The object-oriented paradigm is based on objects interacting with one another. These objects are data structures with associated methods (see Chapter 27). Many programming languages that were originally imperative have been developed further to support the object-oriented paradigm. Examples include Pascal (under the name Delphi or Object Pascal) and Visual Basic (the .NET version being the first fully object-oriented version). Newer languages, such as Python and Java, were designed to be object-oriented from the beginning.

Declarative programming paradigm

Declarative programs are expressed as formal logic and computations are deductions from the formal logic statements (see Chapter 29). Declarative programming languages include SQL (see Chapter 10, Section 10.07) and Prolog (Chapter 29).

26.02 Records

We used records in Chapter 23 (Section 23.06 onwards) to declare nodes. Records are user-defined types (discussed in Chapter 16, Section 16.01).

WORKED EXAMPLE 26.01

Using records

A car manufacturer and seller wants to store details about cars. These details can be stored in a record structure:

```
TYPE CarRecord
   DECLARE VehicleID            : STRING   // unique identifier and record key
   DECLARE Registration         : STRING
   DECLARE DateOfRegistration   : DATE
   DECLARE EngineSize           : INTEGER
   DECLARE PurchasePrice        : CURRENCY
ENDTYPE
```

To declare a variable of that type we write:

```
DECLARE ThisCar : CarRecord
```

Note that we can declare arrays of records. If we want to store the details of 100 cars, we declare an array of type `CarRecord`

```
DECLARE Car[1:100] OF CarRecord
```


Python

Python does not have a record type. However, we can use a class definition (see Chapter 27 for more about classes).

The pseudocode example of a car record described in Worked Example 26.01 can be programmed as follows:

```
class CarRecord:          # declaring a class without other methods
   def __init__(self):    # constructor
      self.VehicleID = ""
      self.Registration = ""
      self.DateOfRegistration = None
      self.EngineSize = 0
      self.PurchasePrice = 0.00

ThisCar = CarRecord() # instantiates a car record
ThisCar.EngineSize = 2500 # assigning a value to a field

ThisCar = CarRecord() # instantiates a car record
Car = [ThisCar for i in range(100)] # make a list of 100 car records
Car[1].EngineSize = 2500 # assigning value to a field of the 2nd car in list
```

VB.NET

```
Structure CarRecord
   Dim VehicleID As String
   Dim Registration As String
   Dim DateOfRegistration As Date
   Dim EngineSize As Integer
   Dim PurchasePrice As Decimal
End Structure
Dim ThisCar As CarRecord  ' declare a variable of CarRecord type
Dim Car(100) As CarRecord ' declare an array of CarRecord type

ThisCar.EngineSize = 2500  ' assign value to a field
Car(2).EngineSize = 2500   ' assign value to a field of 2nd car in array
```

Pascal

```
type
   CarRecord = record
      VehicleID : string[20];
      Registration : string[10];
      DateOfRegistration : TDateTime;
      EngineSize : integer;
      PurchasePrice : currency;
   end;
var ThisCar : CarRecord; // declare a variable of CarRecord type
var Car : array[1..100] of CarRecord; // declare an array of CarRecord type
ThisCar.EngineSize := 2500; // assign value to a field
Car[2].EngineSize := 2500; // assign value to a field of 2nd car in array
```

26.03 File processing

In Chapter 13 (Section 13.09) we used text files to store and read lines of text. Text files only allow us to write strings in a serial or sequential manner. We can append strings to the end of the file.

When we want to store records in a file, we create a binary file (see Chapter 16, Section 16.02). We can store records serially or sequentially. We can also store records using direct access to a **random file**. Table 26.01 lists the operations we use for processing files.

KEY TERMS

Random file: a file that stores records at specific addresses that can be accessed directly

Structured English	**Pseudocode**
Create a file and open it for writing	`OPENFILE <filename> FOR WRITE`
Open a file for reading	`OPENFILE <filename> FOR READ`
Open a file for random access	`OPENFILE <filename> FOR RANDOM`
Close a file	`CLOSEFILE <filename>`
Write a record to a file	`PUTRECORD <filename>, <identifier>`
Read a record from a file	`GETRECORD <filename>, <identifier>`
Move to a specific disk address within the file	`SEEK <filename>, <address>`
Test for end of file	`EOF(<filename>)`

Table 26.01 Operations for file processing

Sequential file processing

If we have an array of records, we may want to store the records on disk before the program quits, so that we don't lose the data. We can open a binary file and write one record after another to the file. We can then read the records back into the array when the program is run again.

WORKED EXAMPLE 26.02

Processing records in a sequential file

Table 26.02 shows the pseudocode for storing the car records from Worked Example 26.01 in a sequential file and accessing them.

Saving contents of array	Restoring contents of array

`OPENFILE "CarFile" FOR WRITE`
`FOR i ← 1 TO MaxRecords`
`   PUTRECORD "CarFile", Car[i]`
`ENDFOR`
`CLOSEFILE "CarFile"`
	`OPENFILE "CarFile" FOR READ`
	`FOR i ← 1 TO MaxRecords`
	`   GETRECORD "CarFile", Car[i]`
	`ENDFOR`
	`CLOSEFILE "CarFile"`

Table 26.02 Pseudocode for processing records

Processing records sequentially in Python, VB.NET and Pascal

Python

```
import pickle # this library is required to create binary files
ThisCar = CarRecord()
Car = [ThisCar for i in range(100)]

CarFile = open('Cars.DAT','wb') # open file for binary write

for i in range(100):  # loop for each array element
   pickle.dump(Car[i], CarFile) # write a whole record to the binary file

CarFile.close()  # close file

CarFile = open('Cars.DAT','rb')  # open file for binary read


Car = []  # start with empty list
while True:  # check for end of file
   Car.append(pickle.load(CarFile))  # append record from file to end of list

CarFile.close()
```

VB.NET

```
Option Explicit On
Imports System.IO


Dim CarFileWriter As BinaryWriter
Dim CarFileReader As BinaryReader
Dim CarFile As FileStream
Dim Car(100) As CarRecord ' declare an array of CarRecord type

'link file to the filename
CarFile = New FileStream("CarFile.DAT", FileMode.Create)
' create a new file and open it for writing
CarFileWriter = New BinaryWriter(CarFile)
```

	``
	For i = 1 To 100 ' loop for each array element
	   CarFileWriter.Write(Car(i).VehicleID) ' write a field to the binary file
	   CarFileWriter.Write(Car(i).Registration)
	   CarFileWriter.Write(Car(i).DateOfRegistration)
	   CarFileWriter.Write(Car(i).EngineSize)
	   CarFileWriter.Write(Car(i).PurchasePrice)
	Next
	
	CarFileWriter.Close() 'close file channel
	CarFile.Close()
	
	'link file to the filename
	CarFile = New FileStream("CarFile.DAT", FileMode.Open)
	' create a new file and open it for reading
	CarFileReader = New BinaryReader(CarFile)
	
	' loop until end of binary file reached
	Do While CarFile.Position < CarFile.Length
	   ' read fields from the binary file
	   Car(i).VehicleID = CarFileReader.ReadString()
	   Car(i).Registration = CarFileReader.ReadString()
	   Car(i).DateOfRegistration = CarFileReader.ReadString()
	   Car(i).EngineSize = CarFileReader.ReadInt32()
	   Car(i).PurchasePrice = CarFileReader.ReadDecimal()
	   i = i + 1
	Loop
	
	CarFileReader.Close() 'close file channel
	
	CarFile.Close()
	``

Pascal	```
	var
	   CarFile : file of CarRecord; // declare a file channel to take car records
	   Car : array[1..100] of CarRecord; // declare an array of CarRecord type
	
	AssignFile(CarFile, 'CarFile.DAT'); // link the file channel to the filename
	Rewrite(CarFile); // create a new file and open it for writing
	
	for i := 1 to 100 do // loop for each array element
	   Write(CarFile, Car[i]); // write a whole record to the binary file
	CloseFile(CarFile); // close file channel
	
	AssignFile(CarFile, 'CarFile.DAT'); // link the file channel to the filename
	Reset(CarFile); // open file for reading
	
	i := 1;
	
	while not Eof(CarFile) do // check for end of file
	   begin
	      Read(CarFile, Car[i]); // read a record from file into record variable
	      i := i + 1;
	   end;
	
	CloseFile(CarFile); // close file channel
	``

TASK 26.01

1 Write a complete program to save several car records to a sequential file.

2 Write another program to read the file and display the contents on screen.

Random-access file processing

Instead of storing records in an array, we may want to store each record in a binary file as the record is created. We can then update the record in situ (read it, change it and save it back in the same place). Note that this only works for fixed-length records. We can use a hashing function to calculate an address from the record key and store the record at the calculated address in the file (this is similar to using a hash table, see Chapter 23, Section 23.08). Just as with a hash table, collisions may occur and records need to be stored in the next free record space.

WORKED EXAMPLE 26.03

Processing records in a random-access file

Table 26.03 shows the pseudocode for storing a car record from Worked Example 26.01 in a random-access file and accessing it.

Saving a record	Retrieving a record
`OPENFILE "CarFile" FOR RANDOM`	`OPENFILE "CarFile" FOR RANDOM`
`Address ← Hash(ThisCar.VehicleID)`	`Address ← Hash(ThisCar.VehicleID)`
`SEEK "CarFile", Address`	`SEEK "CarFile", Address`
`PUTRECORD "CarFile", ThisCar`	`GETRECORD "CarFile", ThisCar`
`CLOSEFILE "CarFile"`	`CLOSEFILE "CarFile"`

Table 26.03 Pseudocode for random-access file operations

`SEEK` moves a pointer to the given record address. The `PUTRECORD` and `GETRECORD` commands access the record at that address. After the command has been executed the pointer points to the next record in the file.

Processing random-access records in Python, VB.NET and Pascal

Python

```
import pickle  # this library is required to create binary files
ThisCar = CarRecord()

CarFile = open('Cars.DAT','rb+')  # open file for binary read and write
Address = hash(ThisCar.VehicleID)
CarFileseek(Address)
pickle.dump(ThisCar, CarFile)  # write a whole record to the binary file

CarFile.close()  # close file

CarFile = open('Cars.DAT','rb')  # open file for binary read
```

	``` Address = hash(VehicleID) CarFile.seek(Address) ThisCar = pickle.load(CarFile) # load record from file CarFile.close() ``` In Python, the hash function needs to allow for the record size in bytes. For example, if the record size is 58 bytes, then the second record slot starts at position 59. The *n* th record slot starts at position (n – 1) × 58 + 1.
VB.NET	(see code below)

```
Dim CarFileWriter As BinaryWriter
Dim CarFileReader As BinaryReader
Dim CarFile As FileStream
Dim ThisCar, MyCar As CarRecord
' link the file to the filename
CarFile = New FileStream("CarFile.DAT", FileMode.Open)

' create a new file and open it for writing
CarFileWriter = New BinaryWriter(CarFile)
' get starting address for record
CarFile.Position = Hash(ThisCar.VehicleID)

' write fields to the binary file

CarFileWriter.Write(ThisCar.VehicleID)
CarFileWriter.Write(ThisCar.Registration)
CarFileWriter.Write(ThisCar.DateOfRegistration)
CarFileWriter.Write(ThisCar.EngineSize)
CarFileWriter.Write(ThisCar.PurchasePrice)

CarFileWriter.Close()  'close file channel
CarFile.Close()

CarFile = New FileStream("CarFile.DAT", FileMode.Open)
CarFileReader = New BinaryReader(CarFile)
' get starting address for record
CarFile.Position = Hash(VehicleID)

' read fields from the binary file
MyCar.VehicleID = CarFileReader.ReadString()
MyCar.Registration = CarFileReader.ReadString()
MyCar.DateOfRegistration = CarFileReader.ReadString()
MyCar.EngineSize = CarFileReader.ReadInt32()
MyCar.PurchasePrice = CarFileReader.ReadDecimal()

CarFileReader.Close()  'close file channel
CarFile.Close()
```

In VB.NET, the hash function needs to allow for the record size in bytes. For example, if the record size is 58 bytes, then the second record slot starts at position 59. The *n* th record slot starts at position (n - 1) × 58 + 1.

Pascal	

```
var
   CarFile : file of CarRecord;  // declare a file channel to take car records
   ThisCar : CarRecord;        // declare a variable of car record type

AssignFile(CarFile, 'CarFile.DAT');  // link the file channel to the filename
Reset(CarFile);  // open file for updating (file must already exist)

Address := Hash(ThisCar.VehicleID);
Seek(CarFile, Address);
Write(CarFile, ThisCar);  // write a whole record to the binary file

CloseFile(CarFile);  // close file channel
AssignFile(CarFile, 'CarFile.DAT');  // link the file channel to the filename
Reset(CarFile);  // open file for reading

Address := Hash(ThisCar.VehicleID);
Seek(CarFile, Address);
Read(CarFile, ThisCar);  // read a record from file into record variable
CloseFile(CarFile);  // close file channel
```

In Pascal, the file is of the given record type and the addresses for the records are slot addresses where each slot has the required number of bytes to accommodate the record.

TASK 26.02

Write a complete program to save several car records to a random-access file. Write another program to find a record in the random-access file using the record key. Display the record data on screen.

26.04 Exception handling

Run-time errors can occur for many reasons. Some examples are division by zero, invalid array index or trying to open a non-existent file. Run-time errors are called 'exceptions'. They can be handled (resolved) with an error subroutine (known as an 'exception handler'), rather than let the program crash.

Using pseudocode, the error-handling structure is:

```
TRY
   <statementsA>
EXCEPT
   <statementsB>
ENDTRY
```

Any run-time error that occurs during the execution of `<statementsA>` is caught and handled by executing `<statementsB>`. There can be more than one `EXCEPT` block, each handling a different type of exception. Sometimes a `FINALLY` block follows the exception handlers. The statements in this block will be executed regardless of whether there was an exception or not.

VB.NET and Delphi are designed to treat exceptions as abnormal and unpredictable erroneous situations. Python is designed to use exception handling as flow-control structures. You may find you need to include exception handling in the code for Worked Example 26.02. Otherwise the end of file is encountered and the program crashes.

Python distinguishes between different types of exception, such as:

- `IOError`: for example, a file cannot be opened
- `ImportError`: Python cannot find the module
- `ValueError`: an argument has an inappropriate value
- `KeyboardInterrupt`: the user presses Ctrl+C or Ctrl+Del
- `EOFError`: a file-read meets an end-of-file condition
- `ZeroDivisionError`.

WORKED EXAMPLE 26.04

Here is a simple example of exception handling. Asking the user to key in an integer could result in a non-integer input. This should not crash the program.

Python

```
NumberString = input("enter an integer: ")
try:
   n = int(NumberString)
   print(n)
except:
   print("This was not an integer")
```

VB.NET

```
NumberString = Console.ReadLine()
Try
   n = Int(NumberString)
   Console.WriteLine(n)
Catch
   Console.WriteLine("this was not an integer")
End Try
```

Pascal

The integrated debugger must be switched off for exception handling to work. In the Tools menu, select Debugger Options and ensure the Integrated Debugger option is not ticked.

```
ReadLn(NumberString);
try
   n := StrToInt(NumberString);
except
   WriteLn('this was not an integer');
end;
```

TASK 26.03

Add exception-handling code to your programs for Task 26.01 or Task 26.02. Test your code handles exceptions without the program crashing.

26.05 Programming environments

Programming environments for Python, VB.NET and Pascal were introduced in Chapter 15. Section 15.02 covered the features found in a typical integrated development environment (IDE). Section 15.04 described the use of a debugger.

Chapter 7 (Section 7.05) discussed the operation of compilers and interpreters and their relative merits. In theory, the ideal situation would be to use an interpreter while developing a program, because partial programs can be tested and no time is wasted waiting for compilation. When the program is finished the compiled object code could be distributed without having to divulge the source code. Compiled code also runs faster than a program executed using an interpreter. Compiled code will not contain any syntax errors. Unless every line of an interpreted program has been executed, it is possible that there are syntax errors still present in the source code.

In practice, this choice rarely exists. Pascal programs can only be executed once compiled. Similarly, VB.NET has to be compiled before it can be executed. Python programs, on the other hand, run under an interpreter. Internally, Python source code is always translated into a bytecode representation and this bytecode is then executed by the Python virtual machine.

Summary

- **Programming paradigms include low-level, imperative, procedural, object-oriented and declarative.**
- **Records are user-defined types.**
- **Records can be stored in files in a serial, sequential or random (direct access) manner.**
- **Exception handling is advisable to avoid program crashes due to run-time errors.**
- **Pascal and VB.NET programs must be compiled before they can be executed.**
- **Python programs are executed using an interpreter (the Python virtual machine).**

Exam-style Questions

1 A company stores details about their customers in a binary file of records.

- The key field of a customer record is the customer ID (a number between 100001 and 999999).
- The name of the customer is stored in a 30-character field.
- The customer's telephone number is stored in a 14-character field.
- The total value of orders so far is stored in a currency (decimal) field.

a **i** Declare the record data type `CustomerRecord` required to store the data. Write program code. [6]

ii Declare an array `CustomerData[0 : 999]` to store customer records. [2]

b The array `CustomerData` is to be used as a hash table to store customer records.
The function `Hash` is used to calculate the address where a record is to be stored.

```
FUNCTION Hash(CustomerID : INTEGER) RETURNS INTEGER
   Address ← CustomerID MOD 1000
   RETURN Address
ENDFUNCTION
```

i Write program code to implement the function `Hash`. [3]

ii Write a procedure `AddRecord(Customer : CustomerRecord)` to add a customer record to the hash table `CustomerData`. Your solution should handle collisions by using the next available slot in the hash table. [7]

iii Write a function `FindRecord(CustomerID : INTEGER)` that returns the index of the hash table slot where the record for the customer with `CustomerID` is stored. [7]

c Before the program stops, the hash table records must be stored in a sequential file, so that the records can be restored to the array when the program is re-entered.

Write program code to store the records of the array `CustomerData` sequentially into a binary file `CustomerData.DAT` [6]

d Instead of using a hash table, the company decide they want to store customer records in a direct-access binary file.

Explain what changes need to be made to your program to do this. [6]

2 A program allows a user to enter a filename for accessing a data file. If the user types in a filename that does not exist, the program crashes. Write program code that includes exception handling to replace the following pseudocode: [5]

```
OUTPUT "Which file do you want to use? "
INPUT FileName
OPENFILE FileName FOR RANDOM
```

Chapter 27
Object-oriented Programming (OOP)

Learning objectives

By the end of this chapter you should be able to:

- solve a problem by designing appropriate classes
- write code that demonstrates the use of classes, inheritance, polymorphism and containment (aggregation).

27.01 Concept of OOP

Chapters 14 and 26 covered programming using the procedural aspect of our programming languages. Procedural programming groups related programming statements into subroutines. Related data items are grouped together into record data structures. To use a record variable, we first define a record type. Then we declare variables of that record type.

OOP goes one step further and groups together the record data structure and the subroutines that operate on the data items in this data structure. Such a group is called an 'object'. The feature of data being combined with the subroutines acting on the data is known as **encapsulation**.

To use an object, we first define an object type. An object type is called a **class**.

KEY TERMS

Encapsulation: combining data and subroutines into a class
Class: a type that combines a record with the methods that operate on the properties in the record

Example of using a record

A car manufacturer and seller wants to store details about cars. These details can be stored in a record structure (see Chapter 16, Section 16.01 and Chapter 26, Section 26.02):

```
TYPE CarRecord
   DECLARE VehicleID            : STRING
   DECLARE Registration         : STRING
   DECLARE DateOfRegistration   : DATE
   DECLARE EngineSize           : INTEGER
   DECLARE PurchasePrice        : CURRENCY
ENDTYPE
```

We can write program code to access and assign values to the fields of this record. For example:

```
PROCEDURE UpdateRegistration(BYREF ThisCar : CarRecord,
                             BYVAL NewRegistration)
   ThisCar.Registration ← NewRegistration
ENDPROCEDURE
```

We can call this procedure from anywhere in our program. This seems a well-regulated way of operating on the data record. However, we can also access the record fields directly from anywhere within the scope of `ThisCar`:

```
ThisCar.EngineSize ← 2500
```

Classes in OOP

The idea behind classes in OOP is that attributes can only be accessed through methods written as part of the class definition and validation can be part of these methods. The direct path to the data is unavailable. **Attributes** are referred to as 'private'. The **methods** to access the data are made available to programmers, so these are 'public'.
Classes are templates for **objects**. When a class type has been defined it can be used to create one or more objects of this class type.

KEY TERMS

Attributes: the data items of a class

Methods: the subroutines of a class

Object: an instance of a class

The first stage of writing an object-oriented program to solve a problem is to design the classes. This is part of **object-oriented design**. From this design, a program can be written using an object-oriented programming (OOP) language.

The programming languages the syllabus prescribes can be used for OOP: Python 3, VB.NET and Delphi/ObjectPascal.

Advantages of OOP over procedural languages

The advantage of OOP is that it produces robust code. The attributes can only be manipulated using methods provided by the class definition. This means the attributes are protected from accidental changes. Classes provided in module libraries are thoroughly tested. If you use tried and tested building blocks to construct your program, you are less likely to introduce bugs than when you write code from scratch.

27.02 Designing classes and objects

When designing a class, we need to think about the attributes we want to store. We also need to think about the methods we need to access the data and assign values to the data of an object. A data type is a blueprint when declaring a variable of that data type. A class definition is a blueprint when declaring an object of that class. Creating a new object is known as 'instantiation'.

Any data that is held about an object must be accessible, otherwise there is no point in storing it. We therefore need methods to access each one of these attributes. These methods are usually referred to as getters. They get an attribute of the object.

When we first set up an object of a particular class, we use a constructor. A **constructor** instantiates the object and assigns initial values to the attributes.

Any properties that might be updated after instantiation will need subroutines to update their values. These are referred to as setters. Some properties get set only at instantiation. These don't need setters. This makes an object more robust, because you cannot change properties that were not designed to be changed.

KEY TERMS

Constructor: a special type of method that is called to create a new object and initialise its attributes

WORKED EXAMPLE 27.01

Creating a class

Consider the car data from Section 27.01.

When a car is manufactured it is given a unique vehicle ID that will remain the same throughout the car's existence. The engine size of the car is fixed at the time of manufacture. The registration ID will be given to the car when the car is sold.

In our program, when a car is manufactured, we want to create a new car object. We need to instantiate it using the constructor. Any attributes that are already known at the time of instantiation can be set with the constructor. In our example, `VehicleID` and `EngineSize` can be set by the constructor. The other attributes are assigned values at the time of purchase and registration. So we need setters for them. The identifier table for the `Car` class is shown in Table 27.01.

Identifier	Description
`Car`	Class identifier
`VehicleID`	Unique ID assigned at time of manufacture
`Registration`	Unique ID assigned after time of purchase
`DateOfRegistration`	Date of registration
`EngineSize`	Engine size assigned at time of manufacture
`PurchasePrice`	Purchase price assigned at time of purchase
`Constructor()`	Method to create a `Car` object and set properties assigned at manufacture
`SetPurchasePrice()`	Method to assign purchase price at time of purchase
`SetRegistration()`	Method to assign registration ID
`SetDateOfRegistration()`	Method to assign date of registration
`GetVehicleID()`	Method to access vehicle ID
`GetRegistration()`	Method to access registration ID
`GetDateOfRegistration()`	Method to access date of registration
`GetEngineSize()`	Method to access engine size
`GetPurchasePrice()`	Method to access purchase price

Table 27.01 Identifier table for `Car` class

We can represent this information as a class diagram in Figure 27.01.

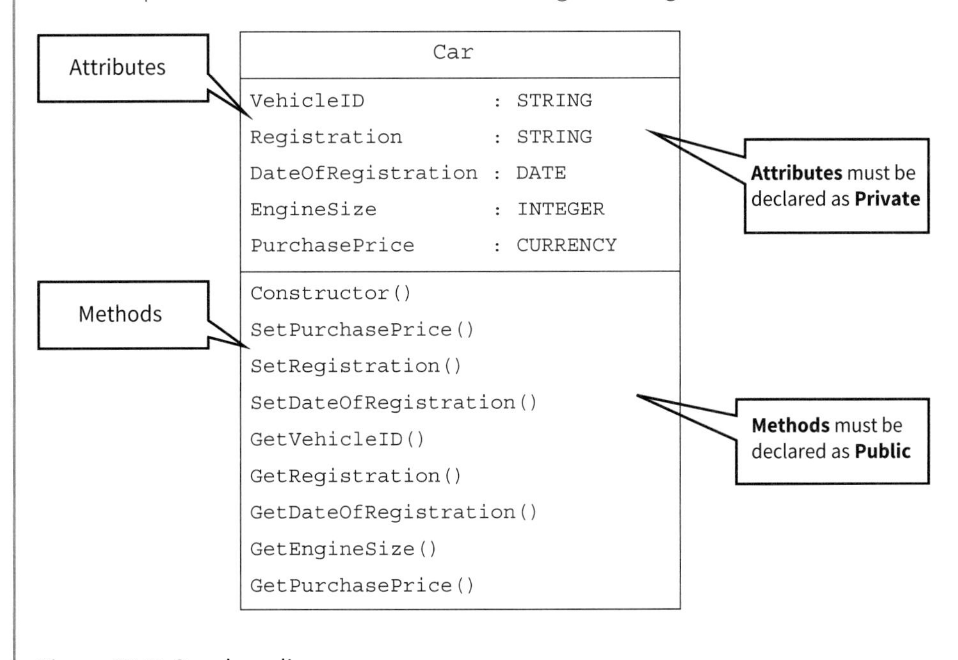

Figure 27.01 Car class diagram

27.03 Writing object-oriented code

Declaring a class

Attributes should always be declared as 'Private'. This means they can only be accessed through the class methods. So that the methods can be called from the main program, they have to be declared as 'Public'. There are other modifiers (such as 'Protected'), but they are beyond the scope of this book.

The syntax for declaring classes is quite different for the different programming languages. We will look at the three chosen languages. You are expected to write programs in one of these.

Python and VB.NET include the method body within the class declaration.

Declaring a class in Python

The code below shows how a constructor is declared in Python.

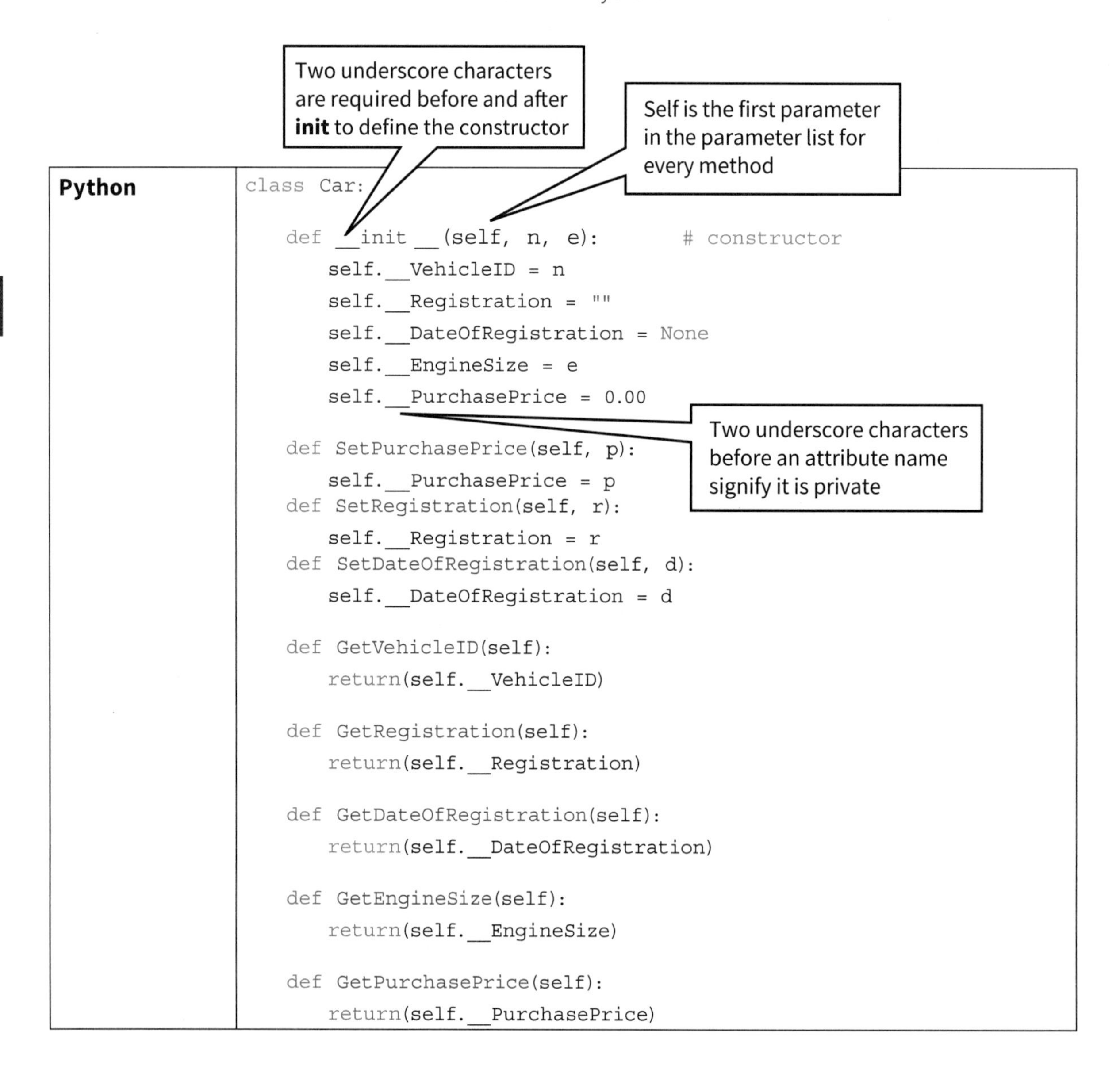
Two underscore characters are required before and after **init** to define the constructor
Self is the first parameter in the parameter list for every method
Two underscore characters before an attribute name signify it is private

Python

```
class Car:

    def __init__(self, n, e):          # constructor
        self.__VehicleID = n
        self.__Registration = ""
        self.__DateOfRegistration = None
        self.__EngineSize = e
        self.__PurchasePrice = 0.00

    def SetPurchasePrice(self, p):
        self.__PurchasePrice = p
    def SetRegistration(self, r):
        self.__Registration = r
    def SetDateOfRegistration(self, d):
        self.__DateOfRegistration = d

    def GetVehicleID(self):
        return(self.__VehicleID)

    def GetRegistration(self):
        return(self.__Registration)

    def GetDateOfRegistration(self):
        return(self.__DateOfRegistration)

    def GetEngineSize(self):
        return(self.__EngineSize)

    def GetPurchasePrice(self):
        return(self.__PurchasePrice)
```

Declaring a class in VB.NET

The code below shows how properties and the constructor are declared in VB.NET.

Each attribute must be preceded by **Private**

Every public method header must start with **Public**

The constructor always has identifier **New**

VB.NET

```
Class Car
   Private VehicleID As String
   Private Registration As String = ""
   Private DateOfRegistration As Date = #1/1/1900#
   Private EngineSize As Integer
   Private PurchasePrice As Decimal = 0.0

   Public Sub New(ByVal n As String, ByVal e As String)
      VehicleID = n
      EngineSize = e
   End Sub

   Public Sub SetPurchasePrice(ByVal p As Decimal)
      PurchasePrice = p
   End Sub

   Public Sub SetRegistration(ByVal r As String)
      Registration = r
   End Sub

   Public Sub SetDateOfRegistration(ByVal d As Date)
      DateOfRegistration = d
   End Sub

   Public Function GetVehicleID() As String
      Return (VehicleID)
   End Function

   Public Function GetRegistration() As String
      Return (Registration)
   End Function

   Public Function GetDateOfRegistration() As Date
      Return (DateOfRegistration)
   End Function

   Public Function GetEngineSize() As Integer
      Return (EngineSize)
   End Function

   Public Function GetPurchasePrice() As Decimal
      Return (PurchasePrice)
   End Function

End Class
```

Declaring a class in Pascal

Pascal includes only the headers of the functions and procedures within the class definition. The full method code follows the class definition. Note that the class name is included when the method is coded after the class declaration.

The code below shows how properties and the constructor are declared in Pascal.

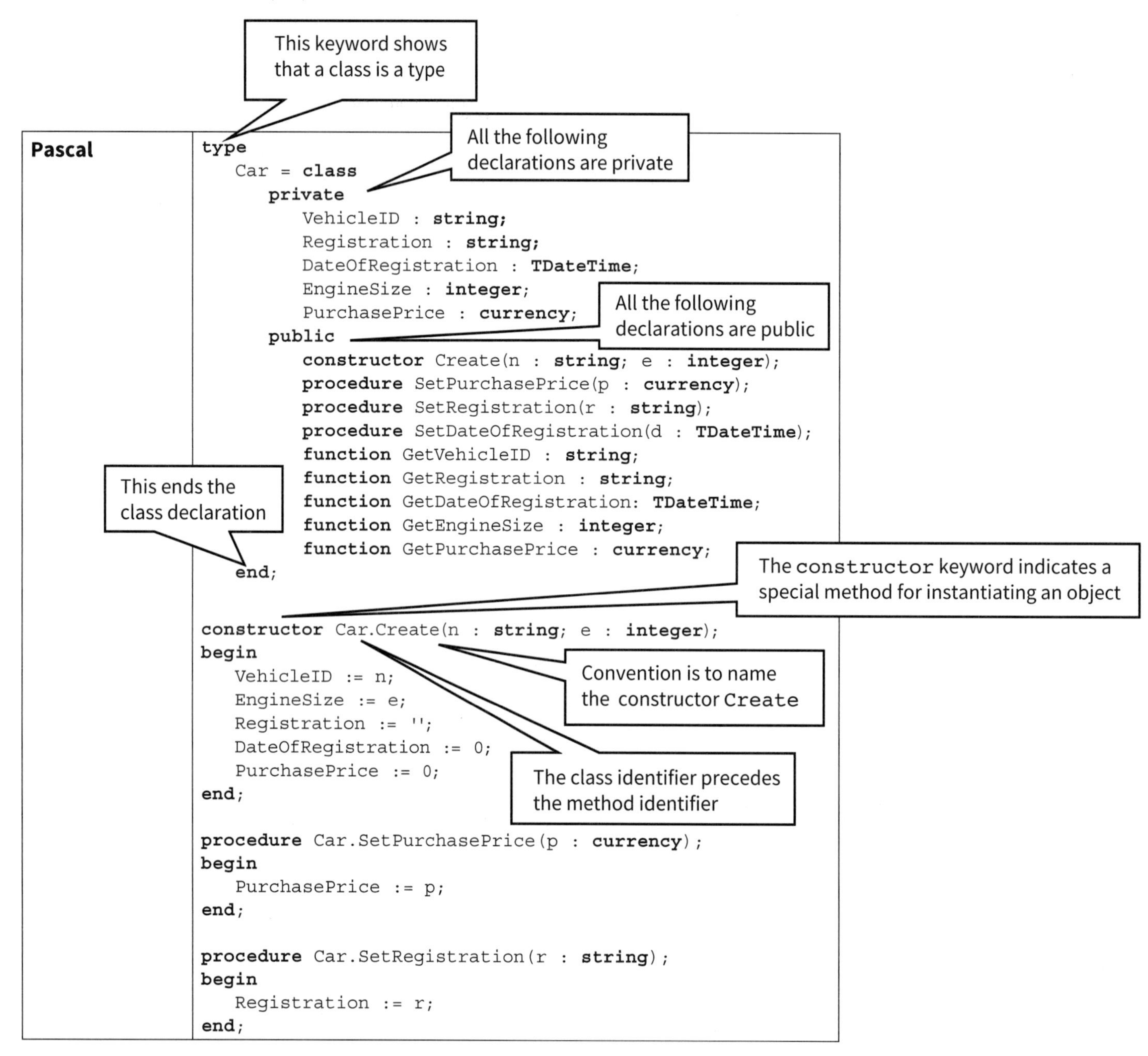

Pascal

```
type
   Car = class
      private
         VehicleID : string;
         Registration : string;
         DateOfRegistration : TDateTime;
         EngineSize : integer;
         PurchasePrice : currency;
      public
         constructor Create(n : string; e : integer);
         procedure SetPurchasePrice(p : currency);
         procedure SetRegistration(r : string);
         procedure SetDateOfRegistration(d : TDateTime);
         function GetVehicleID : string;
         function GetRegistration : string;
         function GetDateOfRegistration: TDateTime;
         function GetEngineSize : integer;
         function GetPurchasePrice : currency;
   end;

constructor Car.Create(n : string; e : integer);
begin
   VehicleID := n;
   EngineSize := e;
   Registration := '';
   DateOfRegistration := 0;
   PurchasePrice := 0;
end;

procedure Car.SetPurchasePrice(p : currency);
begin
   PurchasePrice := p;
end;

procedure Car.SetRegistration(r : string);
begin
   Registration := r;
end;
```

This keyword shows that a class is a type
All the following declarations are private
All the following declarations are public
This ends the class declaration
The constructor keyword indicates a special method for instantiating an object
Convention is to name the constructor Create
The class identifier precedes the method identifier

	`procedure Car.SetDateOfRegistration(d : TDateTime);`
	`begin`
	`   DateOfRegistration := d;`
	`end;`
	
	`function Car.GetVehicleID : string;`
	`begin`
	`   GetVehicleID := VehicleID;`
	`end;`
	
	`function Car.GetRegistration : string;`
	`begin`
	`   GetRegistration := Registration;`
	`end;`
	
	`function Car.GetDateOfRegistration : TDateTime;`
	`begin`
	`   GetDateOfRegistration := DateOfRegistration;`
	`end;`
	
	`function Car.GetEngineSize : integer;`
	`begin`
	`   GetEngineSize := EngineSize;`
	`end;`
	
	`function Car.GetPurchasePrice : currency;`
	`begin`
	`   GetPurchasePrice := PurchasePrice;`
	`end;`

Instantiating a class

To use an object of a class type in a program the object must first be instantiated. This means the memory space must be reserved to store the attributes.

The following code instantiates an object `ThisCar` of class `Car`.

Python	`ThisCar = Car("ABC1234", 2500)`
VB.NET	`Dim ThisCar As New Car("ABC1234", 2500)`
Pascal	`var ThisCar : Car;` `ThisCar := Car.Create('ABC1234', 2500);`

Using a method

To call a method in program code, the object identifier is followed by the method identifier and the parameter list.

The following code sets the purchase price for an object `ThisCar` of class `Car`.

Python	`ThisCar.SetPurchasePrice(12000)`
VB.NET	`ThisCar.SetPurchasePrice(12000)`
Pascal	`ThisCar.SetPurchasePrice(12000);`

The following code gets and prints the vehicle ID for an object `ThisCar` of class `Car`.

Python	`print(ThisCar.GetVehicleID())`
VB.NET	`Console.WriteLine(ThisCar.GetVehicleID())`
Pascal	`WriteLn(ThisCar.GetVehicleID);`

TASK 27.01

1 Copy the `Car` class definition into your program editor and write a simple program to test that each method works.

2 A business wants to store data about companies they supply. The data to be stored includes: company name, email address, date of last contact.

(a) Design a class `Company` and draw a class diagram.

(b) Write program code to declare the class. Company name and email address are to be set by the constructor and will never be changed.

(c) Instantiate one object of this class and test your class code works.

27.04 Inheritance

The advantage of OOP is that we can design a class (a base class or a superclass) and then derive further classes (subclasses) from this base class. This means that we write the code for the base class only once and the subclasses make use of the attributes and methods of the base class, as well as having their own attributes and methods. This is known as **inheritance** and can be represented by an inheritance diagram (Figure 27.02).

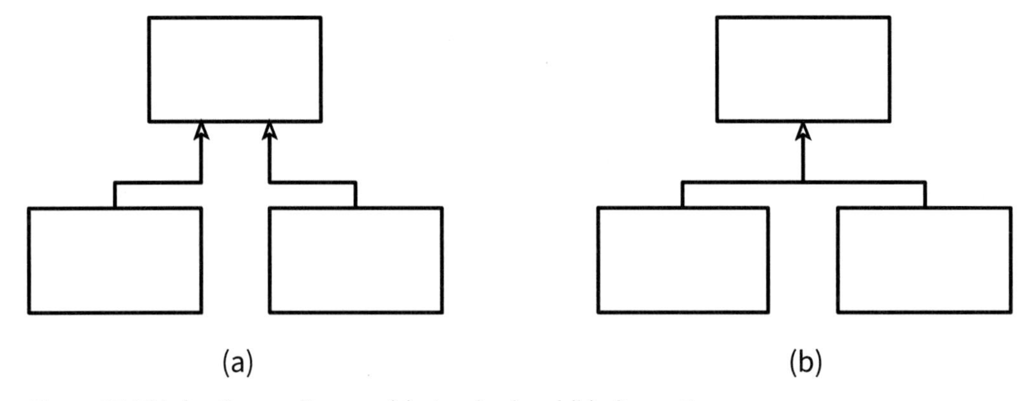

Figure 27.02 Inheritance diagram (a) standard and (b) alternative

KEY TERMS

Inheritance: all attributes and methods of the base class are copied to the subclass

WORKED EXAMPLE 27.02

Implementing a library system

Consider the following problem:

- A college library has items for loan.
- The items are currently books and CDs.
- Items can be borrowed for three weeks.
- If a book is on loan, it can be requested by another borrower.

Table 27.02 shows the information to be stored.

Library item	
Book	**CD**
Title of book*	Title of CD*
Author of book*	Artist of CD*
Unique library reference number*	Unique library reference number*
Whether it is on loan*	Whether it is on loan*
The date the book is due for return*	The date the CD is due for return*
Whether the book is requested by another borrower	The type of music on the CD (genre)

Table 27.02 Library system information

The information to be stored about books and CDs needs further analysis. Note that we could have a variable `Title`, which stores the book title or the CD title, depending on which type of library item we are working with. There are further similarities (marked * in Table 27.02).

There are some items of data that are different for books and CDs. Books can be requested by a borrower. For CDs, the genre is to be stored.

We can define a class `LibraryItem` and derive a `Book` class and a `CD` class from it. We can draw the inheritance diagrams for the `LibraryItem`, `Book` and `CD` classes as in Figure 27.03.

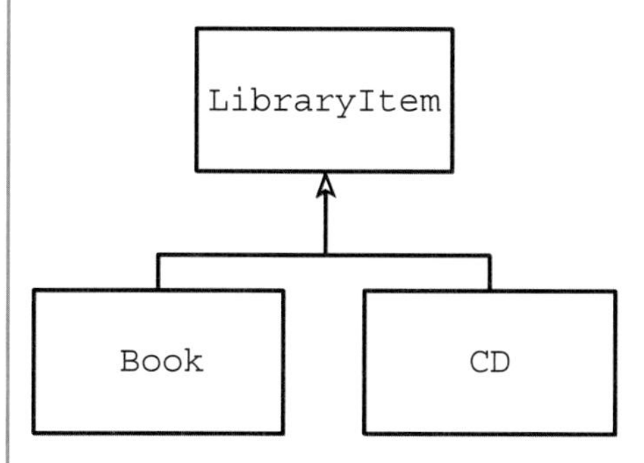

Figure 27.03 Inheritance diagram for Library Item, Book and CD classes

Analysing the attributes and methods required for all library items and those only required for books and only for CDs, we arrive at the class diagram in Figure 27.04.

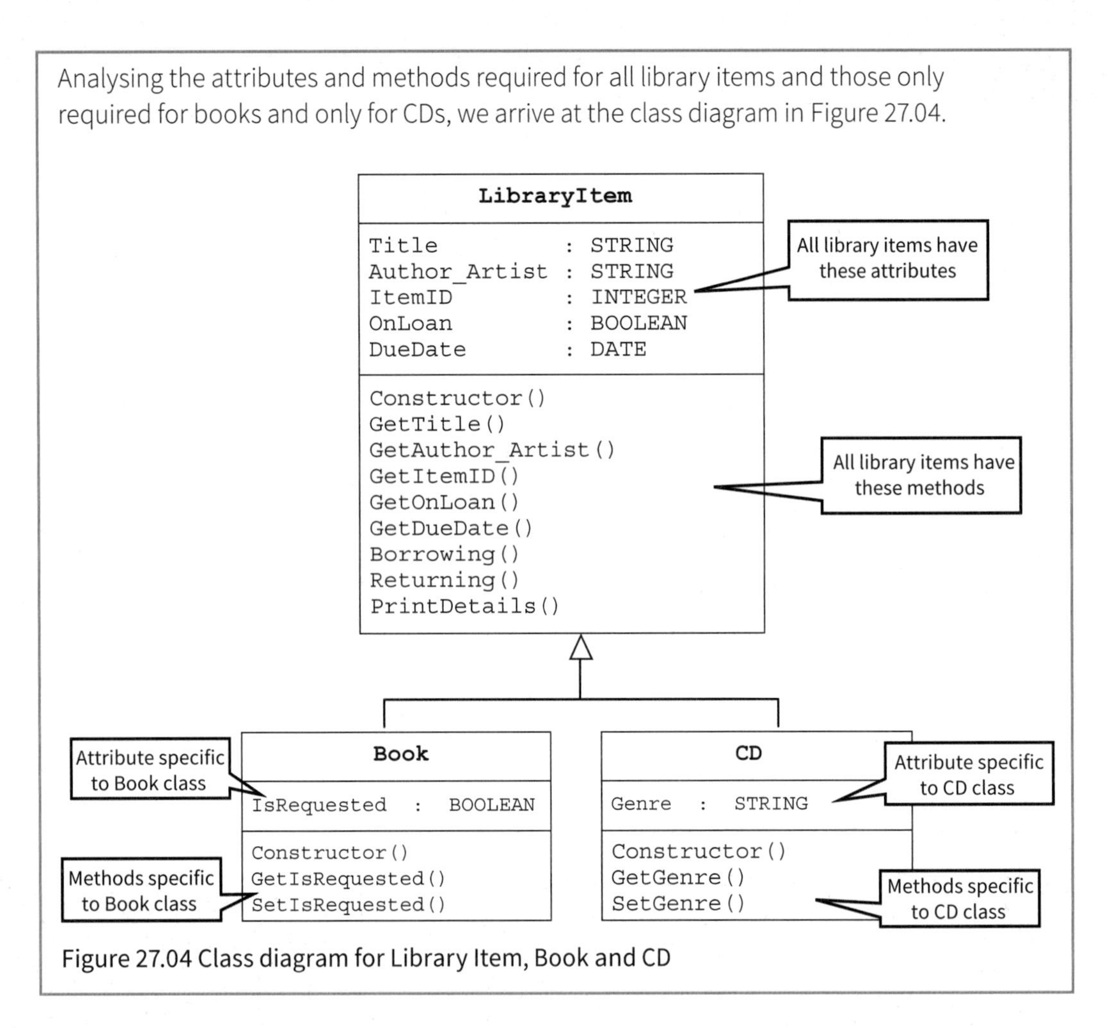

Figure 27.04 Class diagram for Library Item, Book and CD

A base class that is never used to create objects directly is known as an **abstract class**. `LibraryItem` is an abstract class.

KEY TERMS

Abstract class: a base class that is never used to create objects directly

Declaring a base class and derived classes (subclasses) in Python

The code below shows how a base class and its subclasses are declared in Python.

The base class definition

Python

```
import datetime
class LibraryItem:
   def __init__(self, t, a, i):          # initialiser method
      self.__Title = t
      self.__Author__Artist = a
      self.__ItemID = i
      self.__OnLoan = False
      self.__DueDate = datetime.date.today()

   def GetTitle(self):
      return(self.__Title)

# other Get methods go here

   def Borrowing(self):
      self.__OnLoan = True
      self.__DueDate = self.__DueDate + datetime.timedelta(weeks=3)

   def Returning(self):
      self.__OnLoan = False

   def PrintDetails(self):
      print(self.__Title,'; ', self.__Author__Artist,'; ', end='')
      print(self.__ItemID,'; ', self.__OnLoan,'; ', self.__DueDate)

class Book(LibraryItem):
   def __init__(self, t, a, i):          # initialiser method
      LibraryItem.__init__(self, t, a, i)
      self.__IsRequested = False
      self.__RequestedBy = 0
  def GetIsRequested(self):
      return(self.__IsRequested)

   def SetIsRequested(self):
      self.__IsRequested = True

class CD(LibraryItem):
   def __init__(self, t, a, i):          # initialiser method
      LibraryItem.__init__(self, t, a, i)
      self.__Genre = ""

   def GetGenre(self):
      return(self.__Genre)

   def SetGenre(self, g):
      self.__Genre = g
```

A subclass definition

This statement calls the constructor for the base class

Declaring a base class and derived classes (subclasses) in VB.NET

The code below shows how a base class and its subclasses are declared in VB.NET.

VB.NET

```
Class LibraryItem
    Private Title As String
    Private Author_Artist As String
    Private ItemID As Integer
    Private OnLoan As Boolean = False
    Private DueDate As Date = Today

    Sub Create(ByVal t As String, ByVal a As String, ByVal i As Integer)
        Title = t
        Author_Artist = a
        ItemID = i
    End Sub

    Public Function GetTitle() As String
        Return (Title)
    End Function

    ' other Get methods go here

    Public Sub Borrowing()
        OnLoan = True
        DueDate = DateAdd(DateInterval.Day, 21, Today()) '3 weeks from today
    End Sub


    Public Sub Returning()
        OnLoan = False
    End Sub

    Sub PrintDetails()
        Console.WriteLine(Title & "; " & ItemID & "; " & OnLoan & "; " & DueDate)
    End Sub
End Class

Class Book
    Inherits LibraryItem
    Private IsRequested As Boolean = False

    Public Function GetIsRequested() As Boolean
        Return (IsRequested)
    End Function

    Public Sub SetIsRequested()
        IsRequested = True
    End Sub
End Class
```

The base class definition

A subclass definition

The Inherits statement is the first statement of a subclass definition

	``
	Class CD
	    Inherits LibraryItem
	    Private Genre As String = ""
	
	    Public Function GetGenre() As String
	        Return (Genre)
	    End Function
	
	    Public Sub SetGenre(ByVal g As String)
	        Genre = g
	    End Sub
	End Class
	``

Declaring a base class and derived classes (subclasses) in Pascal

The code below shows how a base class and its subclasses are declared in Pascal.

Pascal

```
type
   LibraryItem = class
      private
         Title : STRING;
         Author_Artist : STRING;
         ItemID : INTEGER;
         OnLoan : BOOLEAN;
         DueDate : TDATETIME;
      public
         constructor Create(t, a : STRING; i : INTEGER); virtual;
         function GetTitle : STRING;
         function GetAuthor_Artist : STRING;
         function GetItemID : INTEGER;
         function GetOnLoan : BOOLEAN;
         function GetDueDate : TDATETIME;
         procedure Borrowing;
         procedure Returning;
         procedure PrintDetails;
      end;

  Book = class(LibraryItem)
      private
         IsRequested : BOOLEAN;
      public
         constructor Create(t, a : STRING; i : INTEGER); override;
         function GetIsRequested : BOOLEAN;
         procedure SetIsRequested;
      end;

   CD = class(LibraryItem)
      private
         Genre : STRING;
      public
         constructor Create(t, a : STRING; i : INTEGER); override;
         function GetGenre : STRING;
         procedure SetGenre(g : STRING);
      end;
```

Base class definition

The keyword virtual allows a subclass to redefine the constructor

Subclass definition shows the base class in brackets

The keyword override shows that the constructor is redefined

```
// implementation of methods

constructor LibraryItem.Create(t, a : STRING; i : INTEGER);
begin
   Title := t;
   Author_Artist := a;
   ItemID := i;
   OnLoan := FALSE;
   DueDate := 0;
end;

function LibraryItem.GetTitle : STRING;
begin
   GetTitle := Title;
end;

// other Get methods go here

procedure LibraryItem.Borrowing;
begin
   OnLoan := TRUE;
   DueDate := Date() + 21;
end;

procedure LibraryItem.Returning;
begin
   OnLoan := FALSE;
end;

procedure LibraryItem.PrintDetails;
begin
   Write(Title,'; ', ItemID,'; ', OnLoan,'; ', DateToStr(DueDate))
end;

constructor Book.Create(t, a : STRING; i : INTEGER);
begin
   inherited Create(t, a, i);
   IsRequested := FALSE;
end;

procedure Book.SetIsRequested;
begin
   IsRequested := TRUE;
end;
function Book.GetIsRequested : BOOLEAN;
begin
   GetIsRequested := IsRequested;
end;
```

The subclass constructor

This statements calls the constructor for the base class

```
constructor CD.Create(t, a : STRING; i : INTEGER);
begin
   inherited Create(t, a, i);
   Genre := g;
end;

function CD.GetGenre : STRING;
begin
   GetGenre := Genre;
end;

procedure CD.SetGenre(g : STRING);
begin
   Genre := g;
end;
```

Instantiating a subclass

Creating an object of a subclass is done in the same way as with any class (See Section 27.03).

Python	`ThisBook = Book(Title, Author, ItemID)` `ThisCD = CD(Title, Artist, ItemID)`

VB.NET	`Dim ThisBook As New Book()`
	`Dim ThisCD As New CD()`
	`ThisBook.Create(Title, Author, ItemID)`
	`ThisCD.Create(Title, Artist, ItemID)`

Pascal	`var ThisBook : Book;`
	`var ThisCD : CD;`
	`ThisBook := Book.Create(Title, Author, ItemID);`
	`ThisCD := CD.Create(Title, Artist, ItemID);`

Using a method

Using an object created from a subclass is exactly the same as an object created from any class.

TASK 27.02

Copy the class definitions for `LibraryItem`, `Book` and `CD` into your program editor. Write the additional get methods. Write a simple program to test that each method works.

TASK 27.03

Write code to define a Borrower class as shown in the class diagram in Figure 27.05.

Borrower
BorrowerName : STRING EmailAddress : STRING BorrowerID : INTEGER ItemsOnLoan : INTEGER
Constructor() GetBorrowerName() GetEmailAddress() GetBorrowerID() GetItemsOnLoan() UpdateItemsOnLoan() PrintDetails()

Figure 27.05 Borrower class diagram

The constructor should initialise `ItemsOnLoan` to `0`. `UpdateItemsOnLoan()` should increment `ItemsOnLoan` by an integer passed as parameter.

Write a simple program to test the methods.

27.05 Polymorphism

Look at Worked Example 27.02 and the code that implements it in Section 27.04. The constructor method of the base class is redefined in the subclasses. The constructor for the `Book` class calls the constructor of the `LibraryItem` class and also initialises the `IsRequested` attribute. The constructor for the `CD` class calls the constructor of the `LibraryItem` class and also initialises the `Genre` attribute.

The `PrintDetails` method is currently only defined in the base class. This means we can only get information on the attributes that are part of the base class. To include the additional attributes from the subclass, we need to declare the method again. Although the method in the subclass will have the same identifier as in the base class, the method will actually behave differently. This is known as **polymorphism**.

KEY TERMS

Polymorphism: the method behaves differently for different classes in the hierarchy

The way the programming languages re-define a method varies.

The code shown here includes a call to the base class method with the same name. You can completely re-write the method if required.

Python

```
# define the print details method for Book
def PrintDetails(self):
   print("Book Details")
   LibraryItem.PrintDetails(self)   <- This line calls the base class method with the same name.
   print(self.__IsRequested)
```

VB.NET

```
' in base class, add the keyword Overridable
' to the method to be redefined
Overridable Sub PrintDetails()

' in subclass, add the redefined method:
Public Overrides Sub PrintDetails()
   Console.WriteLine("Book Details")
   MyBase.PrintDetails()   <- This line calls the base class method with the same name.
   Console.WriteLine(IsRequested)
End Sub
```

Pascal

```
// in base class, add the keyword virtual
// to method header to be redefined:
procedure PrintDetails; virtual;

// add the procedure header to the Book class
procedure PrintDetails; override;

// define the method
procedure Book.PrintDetails;
begin
   WriteLn('Book Details');
   inherited;   <- This line calls the base class method with the same name.
   WriteLn(IsRequested);
end;
```

TASK 27.04

Use your program code from Task 27.02. Re-define the `PrintDetail` methods for the `Book` class and the `CD` class. Test your code.

TASK 27.05

Use your program code from Task 27.03. Add another attribute, `BorrowerID`, to the `LibraryItem` class so that the item being loaned can have the borrower recorded.

Change the `LibraryItem.LoanItem` and `LibraryItem.ReturnItem` methods, so that `LoanItem.BorrowerID` and `Borrower.ItemsOnLoan` are updated when a library item is borrowed or returned.

TASK 27.06

Use your code from Task 27.02 or Task 27.04. Add another attribute, `RequestedBy`, to the `Book` class so that the borrower making the request can be recorded.

Change the method `Book.RequestBook`, so that `Book.RequestedBy` is updated when a book is requested.

TASK 27.07

Use your code from Task 27.06 to write the complete program to implement a simplified library system.

Write code to provide the user with a menu to choose an option. An example of a menu that would be suitable is shown in Figure 27.06.

```
1 - Add a new borrower
2 - Add a new book
3 - Add a new CD
4 - Borrow a book
5 - Return a book
6 - Borrow a CD
7 - Return a CD
8 - Request book
9 - Print all details
99 - Exit program
Enter your menu choice:
```

Figure 27.06 Library system menu

27.06 Garbage collection

When objects are created they occupy memory. When they are no longer needed, they should be made to release that memory, so it can be re-used. If objects do not let go of memory, we eventually end up with no free memory when we try and run a program. This is known as 'memory leakage'.

How do our programming languages handle this?

Table 27.03 Garbage collection strategies

Python	Memory management involves a private heap containing all Python objects and data structures. The management of the Python heap is performed by the interpreter itself. The programmer does not need to do any housekeeping.
VB.NET	A garbage collector automatically reclaims memory from objects that are no longer referred to by the running program.
Pascal	When an object is no longer required, the programmer can use the method `.Free`. For example, `ThisBook.Free`.

27.07 Containment (aggregation)

In Section 27.04 we covered how a subclass inherits from a base class. This can be seen as generalisation and specialisation. The base class is the most general class, subclasses derived from this base class are more specialised.

We have other kinds of relationships between classes. **Containment** means that one class contains other classes. For example, a car is made up of different parts and each part will be an object based on a class. The wheels are objects of a different class to the engine object. The engine is also made up of different parts. Together, all these parts make up one big object.

KEY TERMS

Containment: a relationship in which one class has a component that is of another class type

The containment relationship is shown in Figure 27.07.

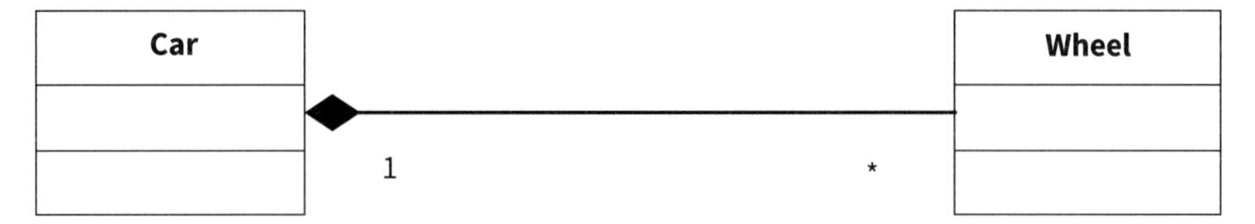

Figure 27.07 Containment (aggregation) class diagram

WORKED EXAMPLE 27.03

Using containment

A college runs courses of up to 50 lessons. A course may end with an assessment. Object-oriented programming is to be used to set up courses. The classes required are shown in Figure 27.08.

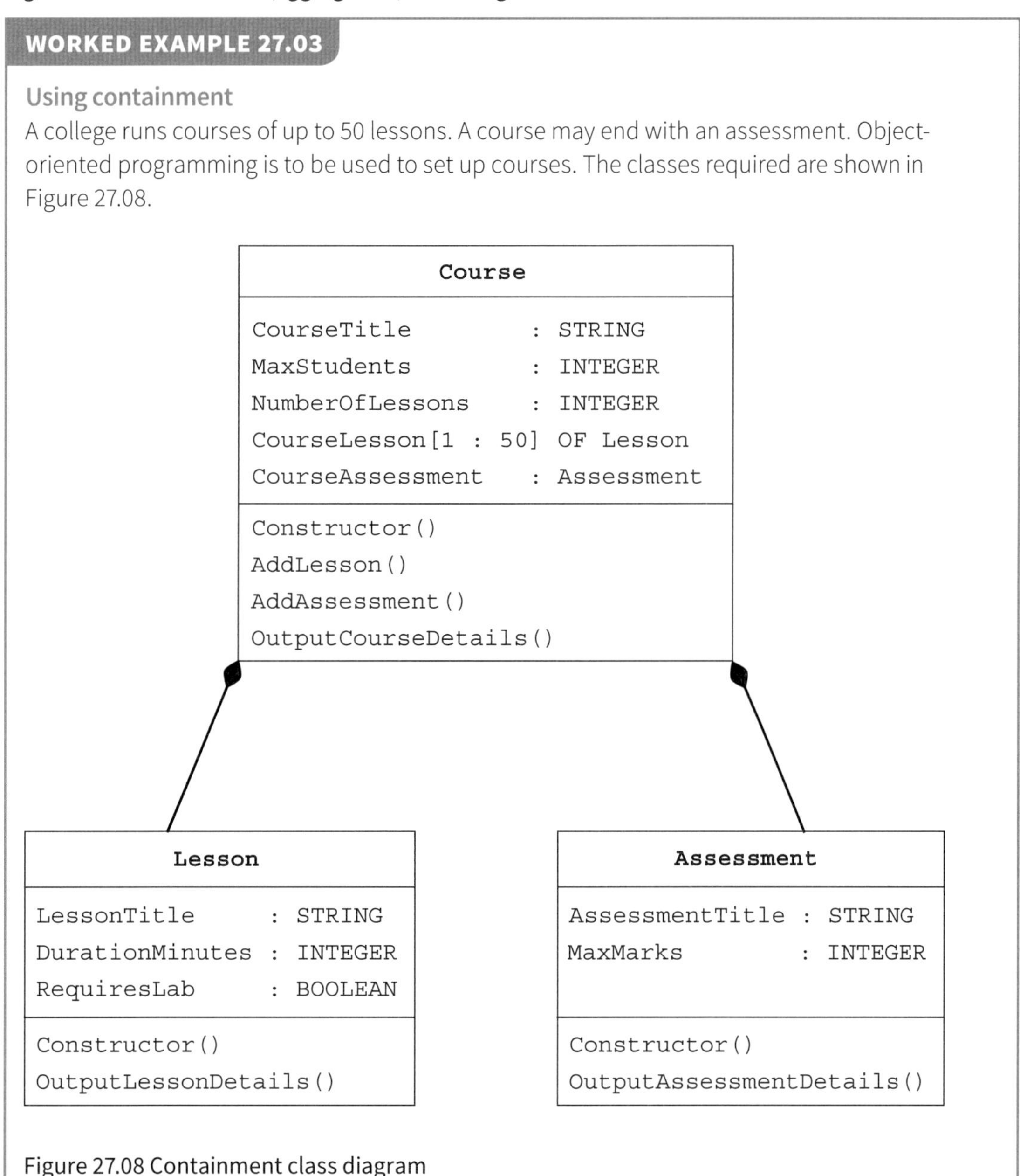

Figure 27.08 Containment class diagram

Assuming that all attributes for the `Lesson` and `Assessment` class are set by values passed as parameters to the constructor, the code for declaring the `Lesson` and `Assessment` classes are straightforward.

The code below shows how the `Course` class is declared.

Python Course class declaration

```
class Course:
   def __init__(self, t, m): # sets up a new course
      self.__CourseTitle = t
      self.__MaxStudents = m
      self.__NumberOfLessons = 0
      self.__CourseLesson = []
      self.__CourseAssessment = Assessment

   def AddLesson(self, t, d, r):
      self.__NumberOfLessons = self.__NumberOfLessons + 1
      self.__CourseLesson.append(Lesson(t, d, r))

   def AddAssessment(self, t, m):
      self.__CourseAssessment = Assessment(t, m)

   def OutputCourseDetails(self):
      print(self.__CourseTitle, "Maximum number: ", self.__MaxStudents)
      for i in range(self.__NumberOfLessons):
         print(self.__CourseLesson[i].OutputLessonDetails())
```


VB.NET Course class declaration

```
Class Course
    Private CourseTitle As String
    Private MaxStudents As Integer
    Private NumberOfLessons As Integer = 0
    Private CourseLesson(50) As Lesson
    Private CourseAssessment As Assessment

    Public Sub Create(ByVal t As String, ByVal m As Integer)
        CourseTitle = t
        MaxStudents = m
    End Sub

    Sub AddLesson(ByVal t As String, ByVal d As Integer, ByVal r As Boolean)
        NumberOfLessons = NumberOfLessons + 1
        CourseLesson(NumberOfLessons) = New Lesson
        CourseLesson(NumberOfLessons).Create(t, d, r)
    End Sub

    Public Sub AddAssessment(ByVal t As String, ByVal m As Integer)
        CourseAssessment = New Assessment
        CourseAssessment.Create(t, m)
    End Sub

    Public Sub OutputCourseDetails()
        Console.WriteLine(CourseTitle & "Maximum number: " & MaxStudents)
        For i = 1 To NumberOfLessons
            CourseLesson(i).OutputLessonDetails()
        Next
    End Sub
End Class
```

Pascal Course class declaration

```
Course = class
   private
      CourseTitle : string;
      MaxStudents : integer;
      NumberOfLessons : integer;
      CourseLesson : [1..50] of Lesson;
      CourseAssessment Array: Assessment;

   public
      constructor Create(t : string; m : integer);
      procedure AddLesson(t : string; d : integer; r : boolean);
      procedure AddAssessment(t : string; m : integer);
      procedure OutputCourseDetails;
end;

// *** class implementation starts here *******

constructor Create(t : string; m : integer);
begin
   CourseTitle := t;
   MaxStudents := m;
end;

procedure Course.AddLesson(t : string; d : integer; r : boolean);
begin
   NumberOfLessons := NumberOfLessons + 1;
   CourseLesson[NumberOfLessons] := Lesson.Create(t, d, r);
end;

procedure Course.AddAssessment(t : string; m : integer);
begin
   CourseAssessment := Assessment.Create(t, m);
end;

procedure Course.OutputCourseDetails;
var i : integer;
begin
   WriteLn(CourseTitle, '  Maximum number: ', MaxStudents);
   for i := 1 to NumberOfLessons do
   WriteLn(CourseLesson[i].LessonTitle);
end;
```

Here are simple test programs to check it works.

Python test program

```
def Main():
   MyCourse = Course("Computing", 10) # sets up a new course

   MyCourse.AddAssessment("Programming", 100) # adds an assignment

   # add 3 lessons
   MyCourse.AddLesson("Problem Solving", 60, False)
   MyCourse.AddLesson("Programming", 120, True)
   MyCourse.AddLesson("Theory", 60, False)

   # check it all works
   MyCourse.OutputCourseDetails()
```

VB.NET test program

```
Dim MyCourse As New Course
MyCourse.Create("Computing", 10) ' sets up a new course

MyCourse.AddAssessment("Programming", 100) ' adds an assessment

' add 3 lessons
MyCourse.AddLesson("Problem Solving", 60, False)
MyCourse.AddLesson("Programming", 120, True)
MyCourse.AddLesson("Theory", 60, False)

'check it all works
MyCourse.OutputCourseDetails()
Console.ReadLine()
```

Pascal test program

```
var MyCourse : Course;
begin
  MyCourse := Course.Create('Computing', 10); // sets up a new course

  MyCourse.AddAssessment('Programming', 100); // adds an assessment

  // add 3 lessons
  MyCourse.AddLesson('Problem Solving',60, FALSE);
  MyCourse.AddLesson('Programming',120, TRUE);
  MyCourse.AddLesson('Theory',60, FALSE);

  // check it all works
  MyCourse.OutputCourseDetails;
  ReadLn;
  MyCourse.Free;  // free memory
end.
```


TASK 27.08

Write the code required for the `Lesson` and `Assessment` classes. Add the code for the `Course` class and test your program with the appropriate simple program from Worked Example 27.03.

Summary

- A class has attributes (declared as private) and methods (declared as public) that operate on the attributes. This is known as encapsulation.
- A class is a blueprint for creating objects.
- An object is an instance of a class.
- A constructor is a method that instantiates a new object.
- A class and its attributes and methods can be represented by a class diagram.
- Classes (subclasses) can inherit from another class (the base class or superclass). This relationship between a base class and its subclasses can be represented using an inheritance diagram.
- A subclass has all the attributes and methods of its base class. It also has additional attributes and/or methods.
- Polymorphism describes the different behaviour of a subclass method with the same name as the base class method.
- Containment is a relationship between two classes where one class has a component that is of the other class type. This can be represented using a containment diagram.

Exam-style Questions

1 A program is to be written using an object-oriented programming language. A bank account class is designed. Two subclasses have been identified:

- `PersonalAccount`: the account holder pays a monthly fee and may overdraw the account up to an agreed overdraft limit.
- `SavingsAccount`: the account holder must maintain a positive balance and gets paid interest on the balance at an agreed interest rate.

a Draw an inheritance diagram for these classes. [3]

The design for the `BankAccount` class consists of:

- **attributes:**
  - `AccountHolderName`
  - `IBAN`: International Bank Account Number
- **methods**
  - `CreateNewAccount`
  - `SetAccountHolderName`
  - `GetAccountHolderName`
  - `GetIBAN`

b Write **program code** for the class definition of the superclass `BankAccount`. [5]

c **i** State the attributes and/or methods required for the subclass `PersonalAccount` [4]

ii State the attributes and/or methods required for the subclass `SavingsAccount.` [4]

iii Name the feature of object-oriented program design that combines the attributes and methods into a class. [1]

2 A bus company in a town has two types of season ticket for their regular customers: pay-as-you-go and contract. All season ticket holders have their name and email address recorded.

A pay-as-you-go ticket holder pays a chosen amount into their account. Each time the ticket holder makes a journey on the bus, the price of the fare is deducted from the amount held in the account. They can top up the amount at any time.

A contract ticket holder pays a fixed fee per month. They can then make unlimited journeys on the bus.

The bus company wants a program to process the season ticket data. The program will be written using an object-oriented programming language.

a Complete the class diagram showing the appropriate attributes and methods.

SeasonTicketHolder
PRIVATE TicketHolderName: STRING ....
PUBLIC Constructor () ....

Pay-As-You-Go-TicketHolder	ContractTicketHolder
....	....
....	Constructor (Name: STRING, email : STRING, Fee : CURRENCY) ....

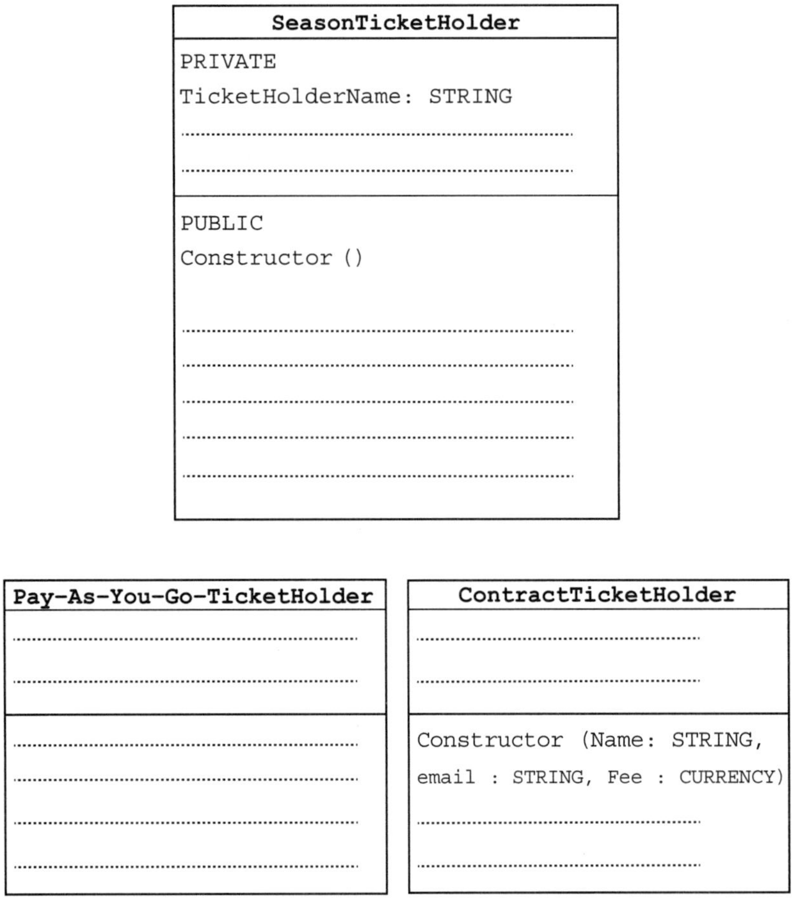

[7]

b Attributes and methods can be declared as either public or private.

i Explain why the `SeasonTicketHolder` attributes are declared as private. [2]

ii Explain why the `SeasonTicketHolder` methods have been declared as public. [2]

c Write program code to create a new instance of `ContractTicketHolder` with:

- Identifier: `NewCustomer`
- name: A. Smith
- email address: xyz@abc.xx
- monthly fee: $10

[3]

3 A queue abstract data type (ADT) is to be implemented using object-oriented programming. Two classes have been identified: `Queue` and `Node`. The class diagrams are as follows:

QueueClass
Queue : ARRAY[0 : 50] OF NodeClass Head : INTEGER Tail : INTEGER
Constructor() JoinQueue(NewItem : NodeClass) LeaveQueue() : STRING

NodeClass
Data : STRING Pointer : INTEGER
Constructor() SetData(d : STRING) SetPointer(x : INTEGER) GetData() : STRING GetPointer() : INTEGER

a State the relationship between these two classes. [1]

b The `NodeClass` constructor is to

- create a new node
- initialise the `Data` attribute to the empty string
- initialise the `Pointer` attribute to -1.

Write program code to define `NodeClass`, including the get and set methods. [10]

c The `QueueClass` constructor is to

- create a new queue
- initialise the `Head` and `Tail` attributes to -1.

Write program code to define the constructor for `QueueClass`. [3]

d The `JoinQueue` method is to

- create a new object, `Node`, of `NodeClass`
- assign the value passed as parameter to the `Data` attribute of `Node`
- assign `Node` to the end of `Queue`.

Write program code to define the `JoinQueue` method. [5]

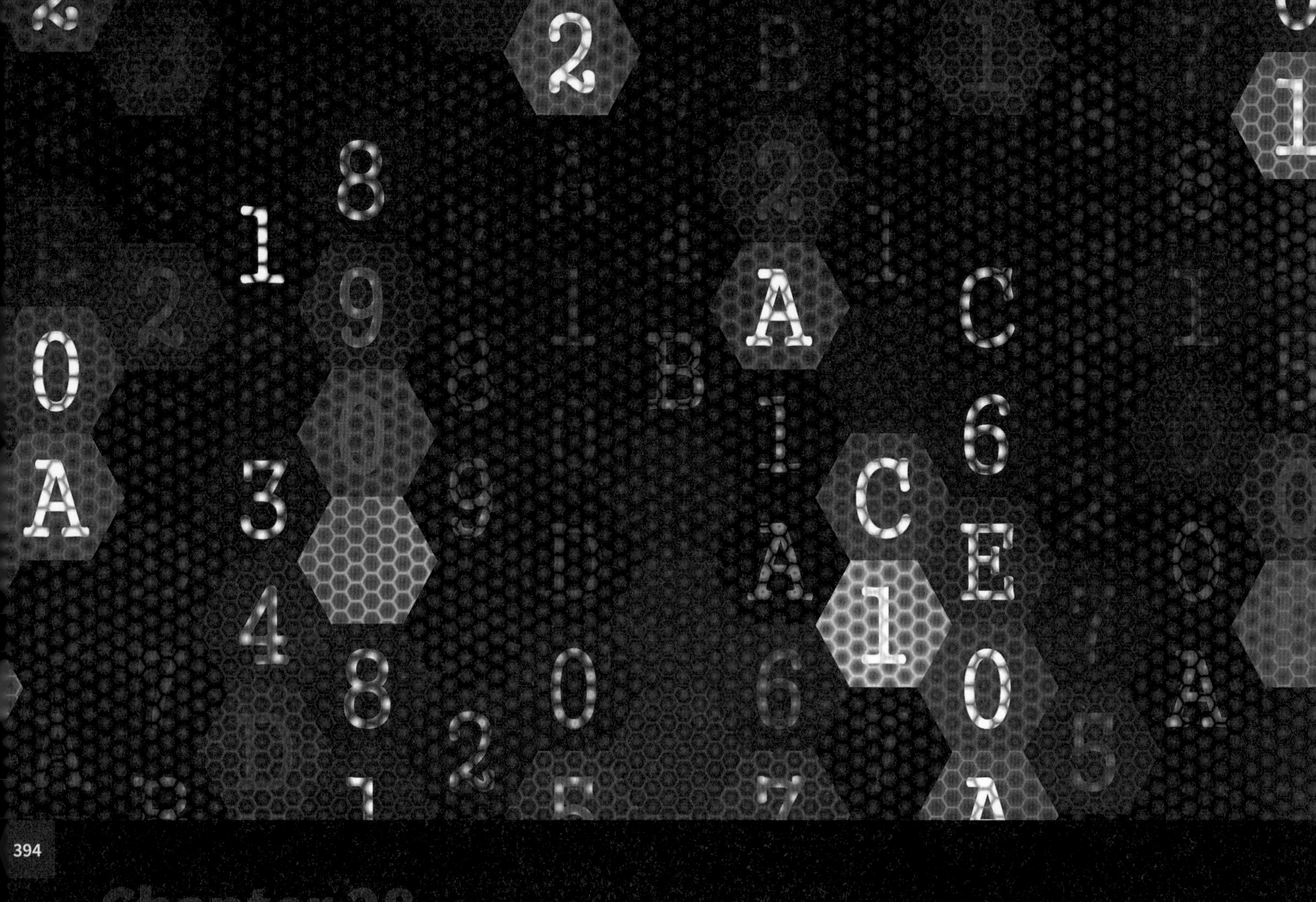

Chapter 28

Low-level Programming

Learning objectives

By the end of this chapter you should be able to:

- write low-level code that uses various address modes: immediate, direct, indirect, indexed and relative.

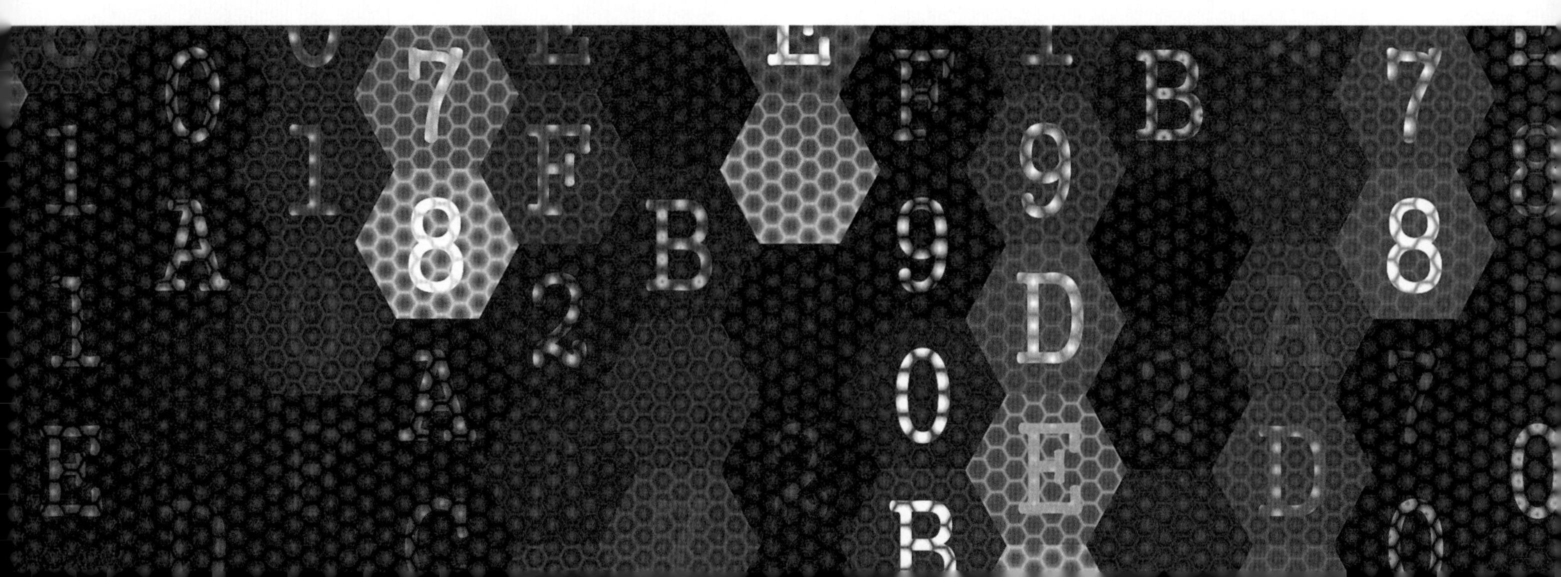

28.01 Processor instruction set

For the purposes of this chapter, the instruction set used is given in Table 28.01.

Instruction			Explanation
Label	Op code	Operand	
Data movement instructions			
	LDM	#n	Immediate addressing. Load the number *n* to ACC
	LDD	<address>	Direct addressing. Load the contents of the location at the given address to ACC
	LDI	<address>	Indirect addressing. The address to be used is at the given address. Load the contents of this second address to ACC
	LDX	<address>	Indexed addressing. Form the address from <address> + the contents of the index register. Copy the contents of this calculated address to ACC
	LDR	#n	Immediate addressing. Load the number *n* to IX
	STO	<address>	Store the contents of ACC at the given address
	STX	<address>	Indexed addressing. Form the address from <address> + the contents of the index register. Copy the contents from ACC to this calculated address
	STI	<address>	Indirect addressing. The address to be used is at the given address. Store the contents of ACC at this second address
Arithmetic operations			
	ADD	<address>	Add the contents of the given address to the ACC
	INC	<register>	Add 1 to the contents of the register (ACC or IX)
	DEC	<register>	Subtract 1 from the contents of the register (ACC or IX)
Comparison and jump instructions			
	JMP	<address>	Jump to the given address
	CMP	<address>	Compare the contents of ACC with the contents of <address>
	CMP	#n	Compare the contents of ACC with number *n*
	JPE	<address>	Following a compare instruction, jump to <address> if the compare was True
	JPN	<address>	Following a compare instruction, jump to <address> if the compare was False

Input/output instructions			
	IN		Key in a character and store its ASCII value in ACC
	OUT		Output to the screen the character whose ASCII value is stored in ACC
Bit manipulation instructions			
	AND	#n	Bitwise AND operation of the contents of ACC with the operand
	AND	<address>	Bitwise AND operation of the contents of ACC with the contents of <address>
	XOR	#n	Bitwise XOR operation of the contents of ACC with the operand
	XOR	<address>	Bitwise XOR operation of the contents of ACC with the contents of <address>
	OR	#n	Bitwise OR operation of the contents of ACC with the operand
	OR	<address>	Bitwise OR operation of the contents of ACC with the contents of <address>
	LSL	#n	Bits in ACC are shifted *n* places to the left. Zeros are introduced on the right hand end
	LSR	#n	Bits in ACC are shifted *n* places to the right. Zeros are introduced on the left hand end
Other			
	END		Return control to the operating system
<label>:	<opcode>	<operand>	Labels an instruction
<label>:	<data>		Gives a symbolic address <label> to the memory location with contents <data>

Table 28.01 Processor instruction set

In the assembly code in this chapter:

- ACC denotes the Accumulator.
- IX denotes the Index Register.
- # denotes immediate addressing.
- B denotes a binary number, e.g. B01001010.
- & denotes a hexadecimal number, e.g. &4A.
- <address> can be an absolute address or a symbolic address.

The data movement, arithmetic operation, comparison and jump instructions were introduced in Chapter 6. The bit-wise manipulation instructions were introduced in Chapter 22.

To write useful programs, we need instructions for input and output. IN and OUT are provided here to input and output single characters, represented internally by their ASCII codes.

28.02 Symbolic addresses

A label is a symbolic name for the memory location that it represents. You can treat it like a variable name. When writing low-level programs, we can give absolute addresses of memory locations. This is very restrictive, especially if we want to change the program by adding extra instructions. Writing low-level instructions using symbolic addresses (labels), allows us to think at a higher level. The assembler will allocate absolute addresses during the assembly process (see Chapter 7, Section 7.05).

28.03 Problem-solving and assembly-language programs

When writing a solution to a problem using low-level programming, we need to break down the problem into simple steps that can be programmed using the instruction set available.

One approach is to think in terms of the basic constructs we discussed for high-level languages. You can use the following examples as design patterns.

Assignment

Table 28.02 shows some examples of assembly language assignments that match the pseudocode.

Pseudocode examples	Assembly code examples	Explanation
`A ← 34`	`LDM #34` `STO A`	To store a value in a memory location, the value must first be generated in the accumulator

`B ← B + 1`	`LDD B`
	`INC ACC`
	`STO B`
		To increment the value stored at a memory location: first load the value into the accumulator, increment the value and then store the contents of the accumulator back to the memory location

`B ← B + A`	`LDD B`
	`ADD A`
	`STO B`
		To calculate a value: load the first value from a memory location into the accumulator, then add the value stored at the second memory location to the accumulator and then store the contents of the accumulator to the required memory location

`A ← -A`	`LDD A`
	`XOR #&FF`
	`INC ACC`
	`STO A`
		Load the value (assuming eight bits), `XOR` with `11111111` to produce the one's complement. Add 1 to get the two's complement.

Table 28.02 Using assignment instructions

TASK 28.01

Write assembly code instructions for this sequence of pseudocode statements:

```
A ← 2
B ← 10
C ← A + B
D ← A - B
```

Selection

Table 28.03 shows some examples of assembly language selections that match the pseudocode.

Pseudocode examples	Assembly code examples	Explanation

`IF A = 0`
`THEN`
`B ← B + 1`
`ENDIF`
	`LDD A`
	`CMP #0`
	`JPN ENDIF`
	`THEN: LDD B`
	`INC ACC`
	`STO B`
	`ENDIF: ...`
		Load the contents of the memory location to be tested. Compare it with the required value (in this example 0).
		If the comparison result is false (A does not equal 0), a jump over the **THEN** part is required; if the comparison result is true (A = 0) then the following instructions are executed. For ease of understanding, the labels **THEN** and **ENDIF** are used.

`IF A = B`
`THEN`
`OUTPUT "Y"`
`ELSE`
`OUTPUT "N"`
`ENDIF`
	`LDD A`
	`XOR #&FF`
	`INC ACC`
	`ADD B`
	`CMP #0`
	`JPN ELSE`
	`THEN: LDM #89`
	`OUT`
	`JMP ENDIF`
	`ELSE: LDM #78`
	`OUT`
	`ENDIF: ...`
		Load the contents of A.
		Get the negative equivalent.
		
		Add B.
		If the result is zero, A = B.
		If the comparison result is false (A does not equal B), jump to the **ELSE** part; if the comparison result is true (A = B) the instructions following the **THEN** label are executed.
		Note that a jump over the **ELSE** part is required.

Table 28.03 Using selection instructions

TASK 28.02

Write assembly code instructions for this sequence of pseudocode statements:

```
IF A <> 0
   THEN
      B ← A
   ELSE
       B ← B - 1
```

Repetition

Table 28.04 shows an example of repetition in assembly language that matches the pseudocode.

Pseudocode examples	Assembly code examples	Explanation

`A = 0`
`REPEAT`
`OUTPUT "*"`
`A ← A + 1`
`UNTIL A = 5`
	`LDM #0`
	`STO A`
	`LOOP: LDM #42`
	`OUT`
	`LDD A`
	`INC ACC`
	`STO A`
	`CMP #5`
	`JPN LOOP`
		Store the initial value of the counter in A.
		Generate the ASCII code for the character "*" and output it.
		Load the counter value,
		increment the counter,
		save it,
		test for final value.
		If final value has not been reached, jump back to beginning of loop.

Table 28.04 Using repetition instructions

TASK 28.03

Write assembly code instructions for this sequence of pseudocode statements:

```
Number ← 1
Total ← 0
Max ← 5
REPEAT
    Total ← Total + Number
    Number ← Number + 1
UNTIL Number = Max
```

Input/output

Table 28.05 shows some examples of input and output in assembly language that match the pseudocode.

Pseudocode examples	Assembly code examples	Explanation
`INPUT A`	`IN` `STO A`	Store a character input from the keyboard at memory location A

`OUTPUT B`	`LDR #-1`
	`LOOP: INC IX`
	`LDX B`
	`OUT`
	`CMP #13`
	`JPN LOOP`
		To output a string of characters stored in consecutive locations, a loop and indexed addressing are used.
		The first time round the loop the index register is 0 and the character in memory location B will be loaded into the accumulator and output to the screen. Then a check is made for the end of the string (the carriage return character with ASCII code 13). If it is not the end of the string, jump back to the beginning of the loop.
		To output a number, the number must first be changed into its equivalent string and stored in consecutive memory locations. Then the above method can be used.

`INPUT A`	`LDR #-1`
	`LOOP: INC IX`
	`IN`
	`STX A`
	`CMP #13`
	`JPN LOOP`
		Store a string of characters input from the keyboard into consecutive memory locations starting from A.

Table 28.05 Using input and output instructions

TASK 28.04

Write assembly code instructions for this sequence of pseudocode statements:

```
Count ← 0
REPEAT
    Count ← Count + 1
    INPUT Character
UNTIL Character = "N"
```

TASK 28.05

Modify your assembly code instructions from Task 28.04 to implement this sequence of pseudocode statements:

```
Count ← 0
REPEAT
   Count ← Count + 1
   INPUT Character
UNTIL Character = "N"
OUTPUT Count
```

28.04 Absolute and relative addressing

An absolute address is the numeric address of a memory location. A program using absolute addresses cannot be loaded anywhere else in memory. Some assemblers produce relative addresses, so that the program can be loaded anywhere in memory.

Relative addresses are addresses relative to a base address, for example the first instruction of the program. When the program is loaded into memory the base address is stored in a base register `BR`. Instructions that refer to addresses then use the value in the base register, modified by the offset. For example, `STO [BR] + 10` will store the contents of the accumulator at the address calculated from (contents of the base register) + 10.

Table 28.06 shows an example of instructions using symbolic, relative and absolute addressing.

Symbolic addressing		Offset from base (START)	Relative addressing (base address stored in base register)	Absolute addressing	
START:	LDM #0	0	LDM #0	100	LDM #0
	STO A	1	STO [BR] + 10	201	STO 210
LOOP:	LDM #42	2	LDM #42	202	LDM #42
	OUT	3	OUT	203	OUT
	LDD A	4	LDD [BR] + 10	204	LDD 210
	INC ACC	5	INC ACC	205	INC ACC
	STO A	6	STO [BR] + 10	206	STO 210
	CMP #5	7	CMP #5	207	CMP #5
	JPN LOOP	8	JPN [BR] + 2	208	JPN 202
	END	9	END	209	END
A:	0	10	0	210	0

Table 28.06 Symbolic, relative and absolute addressing

It is very important that, at the end of the program, control is passed back to the operating system. Otherwise the binary pattern held in the next memory location will be interpreted as an instruction. If the content of that memory location does not correspond to a valid instruction, the processor will crash. The instruction `END` signals the end of the program instructions.

28.05 Indirect addressing

Indirect addressing is useful if the memory address to be used in an instruction is changed during the execution of the program.

One example is when programming subroutines to which parameters are passed by reference (this is beyond the scope of this book).

Another use of indirect addressing is for a pointer variable.

WORKED EXAMPLE 28.01

Writing a program for a simple queue

At the top level, we can write the problem using structured English:

```
Add a character to the queue:
1     Store the contents of the accumulator in the memory location
      pointed to by the tail pointer.
2     Increment the tail pointer.
Remove a character from the queue:
1     Load contents of the memory location at the head of the queue.
2     Increment the head pointer.
```

Table 28.07 shows an example of instructions that implement the above queue-processing algorithms.

Instruction			Explanation
Label	Op code	Operand	
JOINQ:	STI	TAILPTR	Store contents of ACC in the memory location pointed to by the tail pointer
	LDD	TAILPTR	Increment the tail pointer
	INC	ACC	
	STO	TAILPTR	
	JMP	ENDQ	
LEAVEQ:	LDI	HEADPTR	Load contents of memory location at the head of the queue
	OUT		Output the character
	LDD	HEADPTR	Increment the head pointer
	INC	ACC	
	STO	HEADPTR	
	JMP	ENDQ	
ENDQ:			
HEADPTR:	QSTART		Pointer to start of queue
TAILPTR:	QSTART		Pointer to next free location in queue
QSTART:	""		Start of memory reserved for queue, currently empty

Table 28.07 Queue processing

Note that the value shown in Table 28.07 at the memory locations labelled HEADPTR and TAILPTR is the address of the start of the memory locations reserved for the queue. As values are added to the queue, the TAILPTR value will increase to point to the memory location at the end of the queue data. When a value is taken from the queue, the HEADPTR value will increase to point to the memory location at the head of the queue data.

TASK 28.06

Write instructions to reverse a word entered at the keyboard. This requires access to an area of memory treated as a stack.

Summary

- A problem to be solved must be broken down into simple steps that can be programmed using the processor's given instruction set.
- A value must be copied into the accumulator before it can be processed.
- Processing includes:
  - o arithmetic: adding, incrementing, decrementing
  - o comparison: equal or not equal
  - o bitwise operations: AND, OR, XOR, shifting
  - o output to screen.
- To set a value in the accumulator it can be:
  - o input from the keyboard
  - o created using immediate addressing
  - o loaded from a memory location using direct, relative, indirect or indexed addressing.
- An address can be absolute (a number) or symbolic (a label).

Exam-style Questions

1 The instruction set of a processor with one general-purpose register, the accumulator, includes the following instructions.

Instruction			Explanation
Label	Op code	Operand	
	LDD	<address>	Direct addressing. Load the contents of the location at the given address to ACC
	STO	<address>	Store the contents of ACC at the given address
	ADD	<address>	Add the contents of the given address to the ACC
	IN		Key in a character and store its ASCII value in ACC
	AND	<address>	Bitwise AND operation of the contents of ACC with the contents of <address>
	LSL	#n	Bits in ACC are shifted *n* places to the left. Zeros are introduced on the right hand end
	END		Return control to the operating system
<label>:	<data>		Gives a symbolic address <label> to the memory location with contents <data>

- ACC denotes the Accumulator.
- # denotes immediate addressing.
- & denotes a hexadecimal number, e.g. &4A.
- <address> can be an absolute address or a symbolic address.

a Explain the operation of the AND instruction. [1]

b The ASCII code for '0' is the binary value 00110000. The ASCII code for '1' is the binary value 00110001.
Write an AND instruction to convert any numeric digit stored in ACC in the form of an ASCII code to its eight-bit binary integer equivalent. [1]

c Write the assembly code instructions to convert a two-digit number keyed in at the keyboard to its BCD representation. Store the result in the memory location labelled Result. [7]

Instruction			Explanation
Label	Op code	Operand	
			Input first digit
			Convert from ASCII to its digit value
			Move to upper nibble
			Store in location Result
			Input second digit
			Convert from ASCII to its digit value
			Combine the two values
			Store result
			End of program
Mask:			Mask to convert from ASCII to digit equivalent
Result:	&00		Memory location for result

2 A given processor has one general-purpose register, the accumulator ACC, and one index register, IX. Part of the instruction set for this processor is as follows. [8]

Instruction			Explanation
Label	Op code	Operand	
	LDM	#n	Immediate addressing. Load the number *n* to ACC
	LDD	<address>	Direct addressing. Load the contents of the location at the given address to ACC
	LDX	<address>	Indexed addressing. Form the address from <address> + the contents of the index register. Copy the contents of this calculated address to ACC
	LDR	#n	Immediate addressing. Load the number *n* to IX
	STO	<address>	Store the contents of ACC at the given address
	STX	<address>	Indexed addressing. Form the address from <address> + the contents of the index register. Copy the contents from ACC to this calculated address
	ADD	<address>	Add the contents of the given address to the ACC

	INC	<register>	Add 1 to the contents of the register (ACC or IX)
	JMP	<address>	Jump to the given address
	CMP	<address>	Compare the contents of ACC with the contents of <address>
	CMP	#n	Compare the contents of ACC with number *n*
	JPE	<address>	Following a compare instruction, jump to <address> if the compare was True
	JPN	<address>	Following a compare instruction, jump to <address> if the compare was False
	IN		Key in a character and store its ASCII value in ACC
	END		Return control to the operating system
<label>:	<op code>	<operand>	Labels an instruction
<label>:	<data>		Gives a symbolic address <label> to the memory location with contents <data>

- # denotes immediate addressing.
- <address> can be an absolute address or a symbolic address.

Write an assembly language program that takes a sequence of characters as input from the keyboard and stores each character in successive locations, starting at the location labelled: STRING. Input ends when the input character is '!' (ASCII code 33).

Instruction			Explanation
Label	Op code	Operand	
			set index register to zero
			input character
			store it at STRING (modified by index register)
			increment index register
			is this character the ! key?
			No – jump to beginning of loop
			End of program
STRING:			store input characters from here onwards

Chapter 29
Declarative Programming

Learning objectives

By the end of this chapter you should be able to:

- solve a problem by writing appropriate facts and rules based on supplied information
- write code that can satisfy a goal using facts and rules.

29.01 Imperative and declarative programming languages

Programming languages such as Pascal, VB and Python are referred to as 'imperative programming languages' because the programmer writes sequences of statements that reflect *how* to solve the problem. When a programmer uses a declarative programming language, the programmer writes down (in the language of logic) a declarative specification that describes the situation of interest: *what* the problem is. The programmer doesn't tell the computer what to do. To get information, the programmer poses a query (sets a goal). It's up to the logic programming system to work out how to get the answer.

Declarative languages include database query languages (such as SQL, see Chapter 10, Section 10.07), regular expressions, logic programming and functional programming.

Prolog is a logic programming language widely used for artificial intelligence and expert systems.

The Prolog programs in this chapter have been prepared using the SWI-Prolog environment shown in Figure 29.01 (see www.swi-prolog.org for a free download).

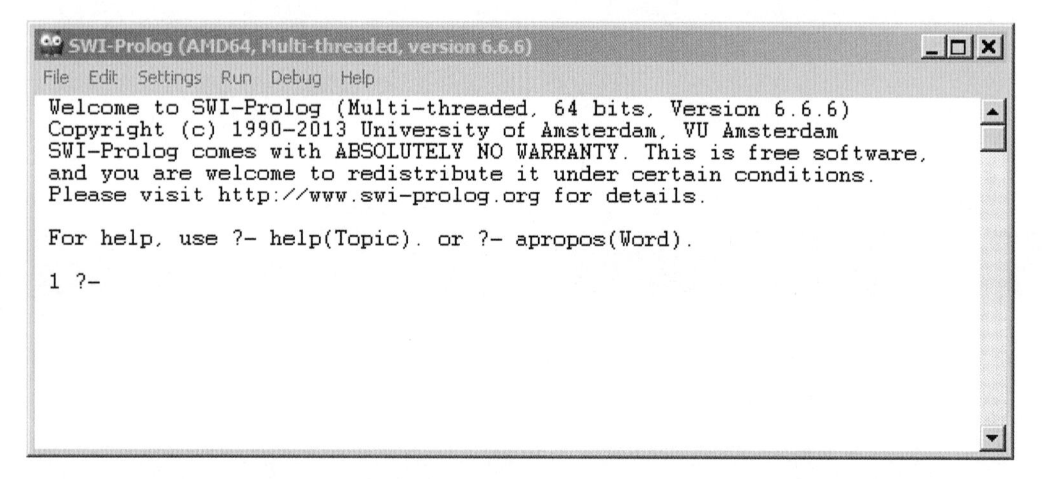
SWI-Prolog (AMD64, Multi-threaded, version 6.6.6)
File Edit Settings Run Debug Help
Welcome to SWI-Prolog (Multi-threaded, 64 bits, Version 6.6.6)
Copyright (c) 1990-2013 University of Amsterdam, VU Amsterdam
SWI-Prolog comes with ABSOLUTELY NO WARRANTY. This is free software,
and you are welcome to redistribute it under certain conditions.
Please visit http://www.swi-prolog.org for details.
For help, use ?- help(Topic). or ?- apropos(Word).
1 ?-

Figure 29.01 SWI-Prolog environment

29.02 Prolog basics

There are three basic constructs in Prolog: facts, rules and queries.

The program logic is expressed using clauses (facts and rules). Problems are solved by running a query (goal).

A collection of clauses is called a 'knowledge base'. Writing a Prolog program means writing a knowledge base as a collection of clauses. We use the program by writing queries.

A clause is of the form:

```
Head :- Body.
```

Note that a clause always terminates with a full stop (.)

Prolog has a single data type, called a 'term'. A term can be:

- an atom, a general-purpose name with no inherent meaning that always starts with a lower case letter
- a number, integer or float (real)

- a variable, denoted by an identifier that starts with a capital letter or an underscore (_)
- a compound term, a predicate, consisting of an atom and a number of arguments in parentheses.

The arguments themselves can be compound terms. A predicate has an arity (that is, the number of arguments in parentheses).

Prolog is case sensitive.

29.03 Facts in Prolog

A clause without a body is a fact, for example:

```
01   capitalCity(paris).
02   capitalCity(berlin).
03   capitalCity(cairo).
```

The meaning of clause `01` is: Paris is a capital city.

`capitalCity(paris)` is a compound term. Both `capitalCity` and `paris` are atoms. `capitalCity` is called a predicate and `paris` is the argument.

`capitalCity` has arity 1, as it has just one argument. This can be written as `capitalCity/1`, the `/1` showing that it takes one argument.

TASK 29.01

Launch the editor (File, New ...) from the SWI-Prolog environment. Enter the three clauses above, as shown in Figure 29.02. Then save the file (File, Save buffer) as Ex1.

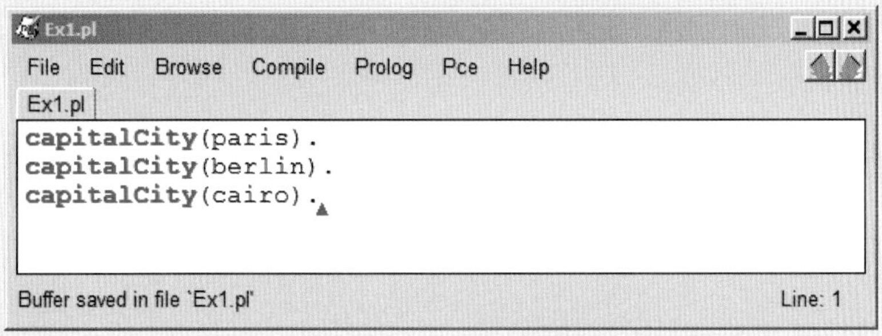

Ex1.pl
File Edit Browse Compile Prolog Pce Help
Ex1.pl

```
capitalCity(paris).
capitalCity(berlin).
capitalCity(cairo).
```

Buffer saved in file `Ex1.pl' Line: 1

Figure 29.02 Example facts in SWI-Prolog editor

Clauses 01 to 03 are a knowledge base. We can run a query on this knowledge base.

To ask the question whether Paris is a capital city, we write:

```
capitalCity(paris).
```

Prolog answers `true.`

This means: yes, Paris is a capital city.

To ask the question whether London is a capital city, we write:

```
capitalCity(london).
```

Prolog answers `false.`

This means: no, London is not a capital city.

This is because the fact that London is a capital city has not been included in our knowledge base.

TASK 29.02

Run your own queries. You first need to consult the knowledge base (File, Consult ...) from within the Prolog environment. Note that SWI-Prolog uses the prompt ?- (see Figure 29.03).

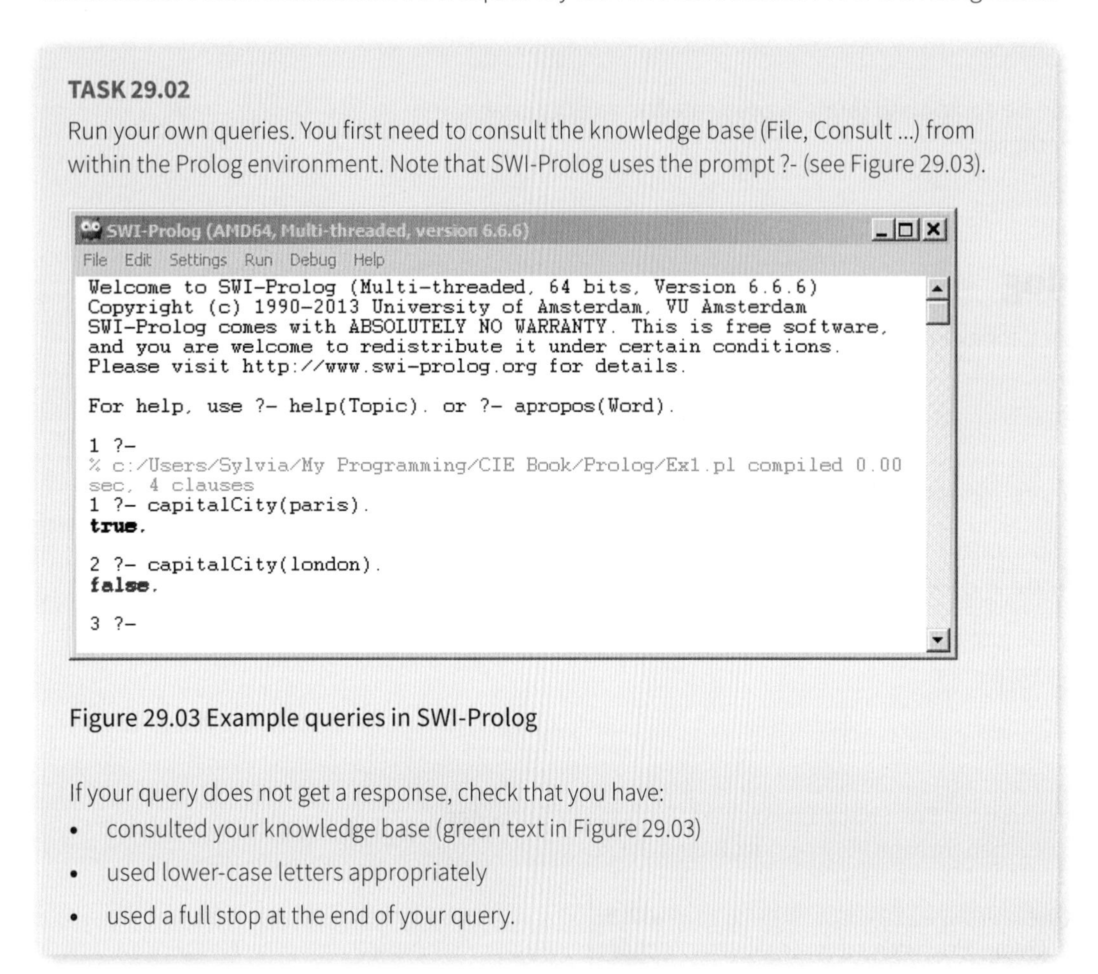
SWI-Prolog (AMD64, Multi-threaded, version 6.6.6)
File Edit Settings Run Debug Help
Welcome to SWI-Prolog (Multi-threaded, 64 bits, Version 6.6.6)
Copyright (c) 1990-2013 University of Amsterdam, VU Amsterdam
SWI-Prolog comes with ABSOLUTELY NO WARRANTY. This is free software,
and you are welcome to redistribute it under certain conditions.
Please visit http://www.swi-prolog.org for details.
For help, use ?- help(Topic). or ?- apropos(Word).
1 ?-
% c:/Users/Sylvia/My Programming/CIE Book/Prolog/Ex1.pl compiled 0.00 sec, 4 clauses
1 ?- capitalCity(paris).
true.
2 ?- capitalCity(london).
false.
3 ?-

Figure 29.03 Example queries in SWI-Prolog

If your query does not get a response, check that you have:

- consulted your knowledge base (green text in Figure 29.03)
- used lower-case letters appropriately
- used a full stop at the end of your query.

29.04 Prolog variables

Let's add some more facts to our knowledge base. Comments in Prolog are enclosed in /* and */.

```
04  cityInCountry(paris, france). /* Paris is a city in France */
05  cityInCountry(berlin, germany).
06  cityInCountry(cairo, egypt).
07  cityInCountry(munich, germany).
```

To find out which country Berlin is in, we can run the query (see Figure 29.04):

```
cityInCountry(berlin, Country).
```

Note that `Country` is a variable (it starts with a capital letter).

To find out which cities are in Germany, we can run the query (see Figure 29.04):

```
cityInCountry(City, germany).
```

```
SWI-Prolog (AMD64, Multi-threaded, version 6.6.6)
File  Edit  Settings  Run  Debug  Help
% c:/Users/Sylvia/My Programming/CIE Book/Prolog/Ex1.pl compiled 0.00
sec, 8 clauses
1 ?- cityInCountry(berlin,Country).
Country = germany.

2 ?- cityInCountry(City, germany).
City = berlin ;
City = munich.

3 ?-
```

Figure 29.04 Instantiations of a variable

Note how Prolog responds when running a query that includes a variable. When there is more than one answer, you need to type a semicolon after the first answer and Prolog will give the second answer. The semicolon has the meaning OR. First `City` is instantiated to `berlin` and then `City` is instantiated to `munich`.

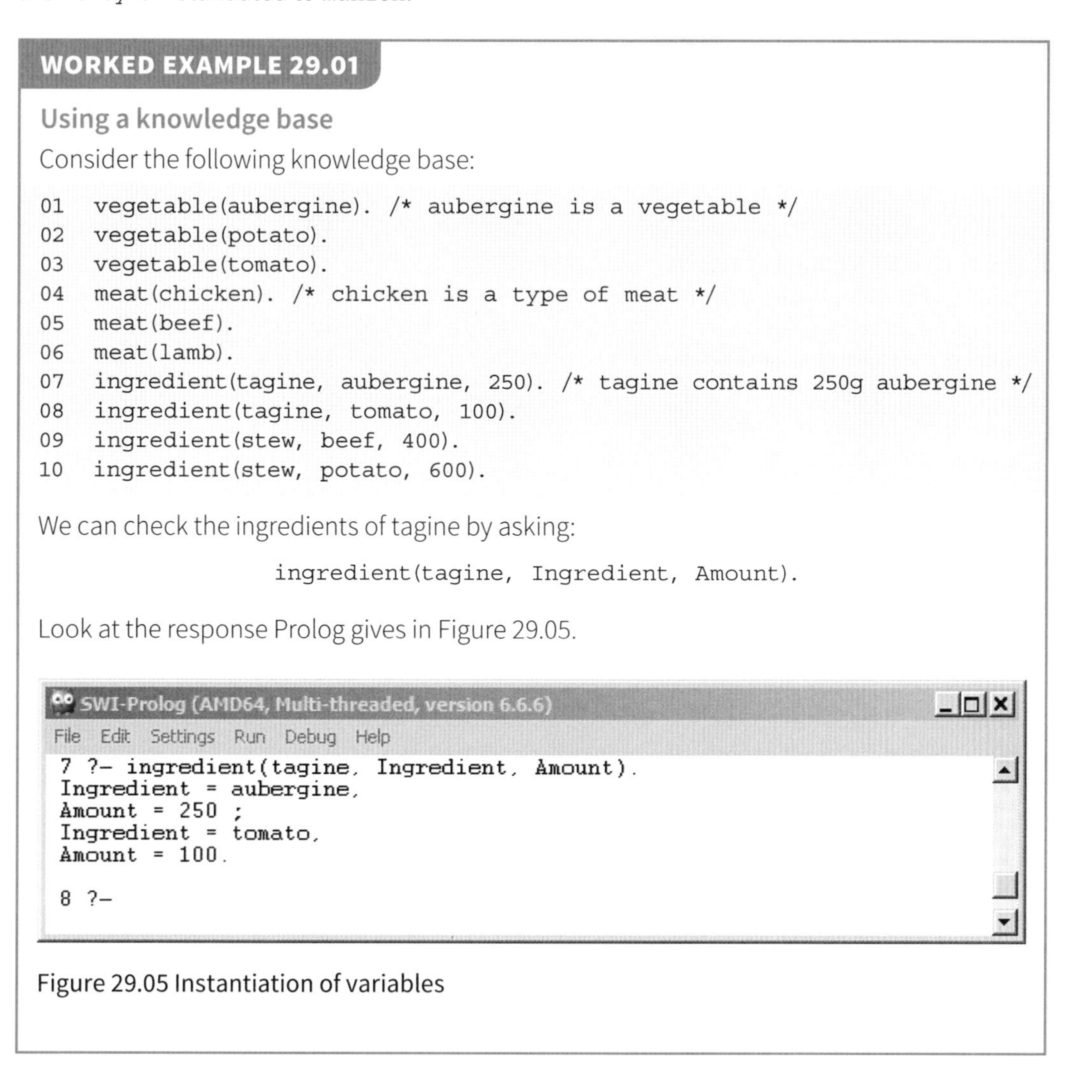

WORKED EXAMPLE 29.01

Using a knowledge base

Consider the following knowledge base:

```
01  vegetable(aubergine). /* aubergine is a vegetable */
02  vegetable(potato).
03  vegetable(tomato).
04  meat(chicken). /* chicken is a type of meat */
05  meat(beef).
06  meat(lamb).
07  ingredient(tagine, aubergine, 250). /* tagine contains 250g aubergine */
08  ingredient(tagine, tomato, 100).
09  ingredient(stew, beef, 400).
10  ingredient(stew, potato, 600).
```

We can check the ingredients of tagine by asking:

```
ingredient(tagine, Ingredient, Amount).
```

Look at the response Prolog gives in Figure 29.05.

```
SWI-Prolog (AMD64, Multi-threaded, version 6.6.6)
File  Edit  Settings  Run  Debug  Help
7 ?- ingredient(tagine, Ingredient, Amount).
Ingredient = aubergine,
Amount = 250 ;
Ingredient = tomato,
Amount = 100.

8 ?-
```

Figure 29.05 Instantiation of variables

29.05 The anonymous variable

Consider the knowledge base from Worked Example 29.01. If we are not interested in the amount of each ingredient, we can use the anonymous variable (represented by the underscore character). The query then becomes

```
ingredient(tagine, Ingredient, _ ).
```

29.06 Rules in Prolog

Remember a clause is of the form `Head :- Body.`

A rule's body consists of calls to predicates, which are called the rule's goals. A predicate is either true or false, based on its terms. If the body of the rule is true, then the head of the rule is true too.

WORKED EXAMPLE 29.02

Using rules in a knowledge base

Consider the following knowledge base:

```
01  parent(fred, jack). /* Fred is the father of Jack */
02  parent(fred, alia).
03  parent(fred, paul).
04  parent(dave, fred).
```

We know that G is a grandparent of S, if G is a parent of P and P is a parent of S.

We could write this as a rule:

```
grandparent(G, S) IF parent(G, P) AND parent(P, S).
```

However, in Prolog the `IF` is replaced by `:-` and the `AND` is replaced with a comma:

```
grandparent(G, S) :- parent(G, P), parent(P, S).
```

A person has a sibling (brother or sister) if they have the same parent. We can write this as the Prolog rule:

```
sibling(A, B) :-
   parent(P, A),
   parent(P, B).
```

If we run the query `sibling(jack, X).`, we get the answers we expect, but we also get the answer that Jack is his own sibling. To avoid this we modify the query to ensure that A is not equal to B:

```
sibling(A, B) :-
   parent(P, A),
   parent(P, B),
   not(A=B).
```

Question 29.01

What answer do you expect to get from Prolog to the following query:

```
sibling(dave, X).
```

TASK 29.03

Write a knowledge base for your own family. You can include more predicates, for example:

Predicate	Meaning
`male(fred).`	Fred is male
`female(alia).`	Alia is female

Write a rule for father.

Test your program.

WORKED EXAMPLE 29.03

Adding a rule to a knowledge base

Using the knowledge base from Worked Example 29.01, we want to know which dishes contain meat. We are not interested how much meat, so we don't need to know the value of the third argument of the predicate `ingredient/3`. We can write the rule:

```
containsMeat(X) :-
   ingredient(X, Meat, _ ),
   meat(Meat).
```

The query `containsMeat(X).` returns `X = stew.`

29.07 Instantiation and backtracking

Prolog responds to a query with an answer, such as the one in Worked Example 29.03: `X = stew.`

The = sign is not an assignment as in imperative programs. The = sign shows instantiation.

How does Prolog use the knowledge base to arrive at the answers? One way to see exactly what Prolog is doing is to use the graphical debugger.

WORKED EXAMPLE 29.04

Use the knowledge base from Worked Example 29.03. After consulting the knowledge base, start the debugger (Debug, Graphical debugger) from the Prolog environment. Then type: `trace.` and then the goal as shown in Figure 29.06.

```
SWI-Prolog (AMD64, Multi-threaded, version 6.6.6)
File  Edit  Settings  Run  Debug  Help
Welcome to SWI-Prolog (Multi-threaded, 64 bits, Version 6.6.6)
Copyright (c) 1990-2013 University of Amsterdam, VU Amsterdam
SWI-Prolog comes with ABSOLUTELY NO WARRANTY. This is free software,
and you are welcome to redistribute it under certain conditions.
Please visit http://www.swi-prolog.org for details.

For help, use ?- help(Topic). or ?- apropos(Word).

1 ?-
% c:/Users/Sylvia/My Programming/CIE Book/Prolog/Ex3.pl compiled 0.00
sec, 12 clauses
% The graphical front-end will be used for subsequent tracing
1 ?- trace.
true.

[trace] 1 ?- containsMeat(X).
```

Figure 29.06 Switching on the trace facility

The graphical debugger window opens as shown in Figure 29.07.

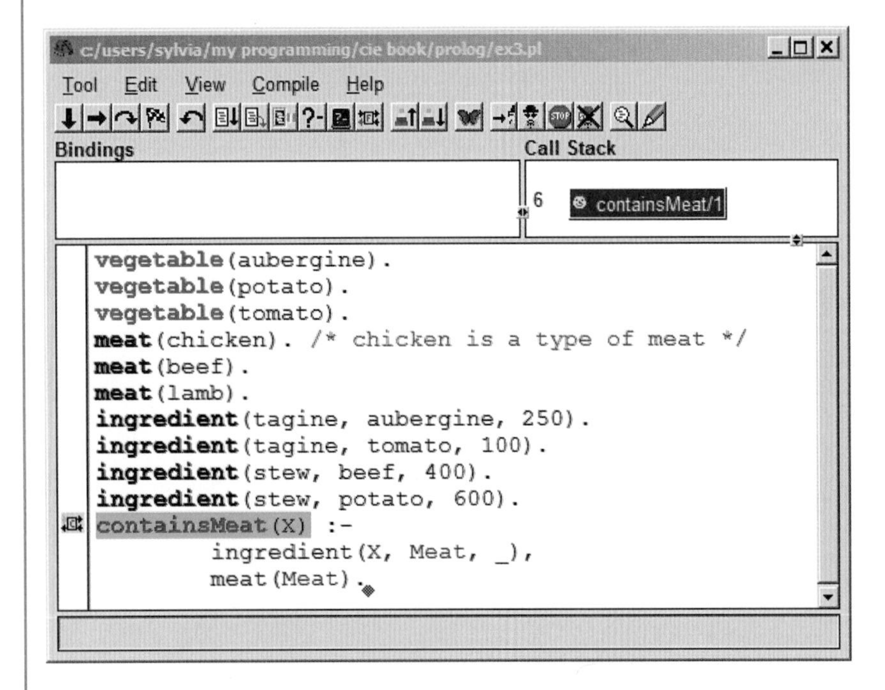

Figure 29.07 Graphical debugger

Using the space bar you can step through the program. When Prolog gives an answer in the Prolog Environment window, remember to input a semicolon, so that Prolog will go and check for another possible answer.

If you don't use the graphical debugger but type `trace.` you can see the trace in the SWI-Prolog window, as shown in Figure 29.08.

```
SWI-Prolog -- c:/Users/Sylvia/My Programming/CIE Book/Prolog/Ex3.pl
File Edit Settings Run Debug Help
1 ?-
% c:/Users/Sylvia/My Programming/CIE Book/Prolog/Ex3.pl compiled 0.00
sec, 1 clauses
1 ?- trace.
true.

[trace] 1 ?- containsMeat(X).
   Call: (6) containsMeat(_G464) ? creep
   Call: (7) ingredient(_G464, _G536, _G537) ? creep
   Exit: (7) ingredient(tagine, aubergine, 250) ? creep
   Call: (7) meat(aubergine) ? creep
   Fail: (7) meat(aubergine) ? creep
   Redo: (7) ingredient(_G464, _G536, _G537) ? creep
   Exit: (7) ingredient(tagine, tomato, 100) ? creep
   Call: (7) meat(tomato) ? creep
   Fail: (7) meat(tomato) ? creep
   Redo: (7) ingredient(_G464, _G536, _G537) ? creep
   Exit: (7) ingredient(stew, beef, 400) ? creep
   Call: (7) meat(beef) ? creep
   Exit: (7) meat(beef) ? creep
   Exit: (6) containsMeat(stew) ? creep
X = stew ;
   Redo: (7) ingredient(_G464, _G536, _G537) ? creep
   Exit: (7) ingredient(stew, potato, 600) ? creep
   Call: (7) meat(potato) ? creep
   Fail: (7) meat(potato) ? creep
   Fail: (6) containsMeat(_G464) ? creep
false.

[trace] 2 ?-
```

Figure 29.08 SWI-Prolog trace of goal `containsMeat(X)`.

The following terminology is used when discussing a trace:

- `Call` is the initial entry to a predicate.
- `creep` indicates that Prolog is moving to the next predicate.
- `Exit` is a successful return.
- `Redo` indicates that the predicate is backed into for another answer.
- `Fail` indicates that Prolog can find no more solutions.

29.08 Recursion

Recursion for imperative languages is covered in Chapter 25. Recursion for declarative languages is where a rule is defined by itself, or more precisely, a rule uses itself as a sub-goal.

Let us expand the Family knowledge base from Worked Example 29.02.

We want a rule that defines whether person A is an ancestor of person B. If A is a parent of B, then A is an ancestor of B. Similarly, if person A is the parent of P, who is the parent of B, then A is an ancestor of B. This is true for the parent of a parent of a parent of B. In general, if A is a parent of X and X is an ancestor of B, then A is an ancestor of B. We can write this information as the rules shown in Figure 29.09.

```
ancestor(A, B) :- parent(A, B).                        The base case
ancestor(A, B) :- parent(A, X), ancestor(X, B).        The general case
```

Figure 29.09 Recursive rules

Note that recursion in declarative programming must follow the equivalent rules that imperative programming must follow. A recursive rule must:

- have a base case
- have a general case
- reach the base case after a finite number of calls to itself.

TASK 29.04

Add the ancestor rules to the Family knowledge base and check that the following query gives the correct results:

```
ancestor(A, jack).
```

WORKED EXAMPLE 29.05

Creating the Factorial function in Prolog

In Chapter 25, Worked Example 25.01, we programmed the factorial function using recursion with imperative programming. We can also program this function using recursion in Prolog.

```
factorial(0, 1).                         /* base case: 0! = 1       */
factorial(N, Result) :-                  /* Result = N!             */
   M is N - 1,                           /* assign N-1 to M         */
   factorial(M, PartResult),             /* PartResult  =  (N-1)!   */
   Result is PartResult * N.             /* Result = N *  (N-1)!    */
```

TASK 29.05

Enter the code from Worked Example 29.05 into the Prolog editor. Save it and consult it. Then pose the following query:

```
factorial(5, Answer).
```

Do you get the correct answer?

29.09 Lists

A list is an ordered collection of terms. It is denoted by square brackets with the terms separated by commas or in the case of the empty list, []. For example [1, 2, 3] or [red, green, blue]. An element can be any type of Prolog object. Different types can be mixed within one list. Lists are used in Prolog where arrays may be used in procedural languages.

Any non-empty list can be thought of as consisting of two parts: the head and the tail. The head is the first item in the list; the tail is the list that remains when we take the first element away. This means that the tail of a list is always a list.

Lists are manipulated by separating the head from the tail. The separator used is a vertical line (a bar):|

If Prolog tries to match `[H|T]` to `[car, lorry, boat, ship]`, it will instantiate `H` to `car` and `T` to `[lorry, boat, ship]`.

The clause definition `showHeadAndTail([H|T], H, T).` can be used to pose the query:

```
showHeadAndTail([fred, jack, emma], Head, Tail).
```

Prolog responds with:

```
Head = fred,
Tail = [jack, emma].
```

The clause definition `myList([1,2,3]).` can be used to pose the query:

```
myList([H|T]).
```

Prolog responds with:

```
H = 1,
T = [2, 3].
```

The clause definition `emptyList(A) :- A = [].` can be used to pose the query:

```
emptyList([1]).
```

Prolog responds with:

```
false.
```

List-processing predicate: `append`

The built-in predicate `append(A, B, C)` joins list A and list B and produces list C.

```
append([a, b], [c, d], MyList).
```

produces `MyList = [a, b, c, d].`

```
append(FirstList, [c, d], [a, b, c, d]).
```

produces `FirstList = [a, b].`

List-processing predicate: `member`

The built-in predicate `member(A, B)` returns true if item A is in list B.

```
member(c, [a, b, c, d, e]).
```

produces:

```
true.
```

```
member(X,[a, b, c, d]).
```

produces:

```
X = a ;
X = b ;
X = c ;
X = d.
```

List-processing predicates: `write` and `read`

The built-in predicate `write(A)` outputs A to the screen.

`write('message: ').` outputs `message:` .

`write(X).` outputs the value currently instantiated with the variable X.

The built-in predicate `read(A)` reads a value from the keyboard into variable A.

`read(Name).` waits for an atom to be input from the keyboard and instantiates the variable `Name` with that value.

Note that the input must start with a lower case letter and not have spaces or be enclosed in quotes.

`nl` moves the output to a new line.

We can write user-friendly programs using the `read` and `write` predicates.

WORKED EXAMPLE 29.06

Using the `read` and `write` predicates

Note how the interface with the user in the code below is written as a rule with the separate steps separated by commas (representing AND).

`assert/1` adds the clause given as the argument to the knowledge base.

`retractall/1` takes the given clause out of the knowledge base, so the next time the program is run, the new facts will be added and used in the goal.

```
/* Weather knowledge base */
weather(good):-
   temp(high),
   humidity(dry),
   sky(sunny).
weather(bad):-
   (humidity(wet);
   temp(low);
   sky(cloudy)).

/* interface */
go:-
   write('Is the temperature high or low?'),
   read(Temp), nl,
   write('Is the sky sunny or cloudy?'),
   read(Sky), nl,
   write('Is the humidity dry or wet?'),
   read(Humidity), nl,
   assert(temp(Temp)),
   assert(sky(Sky)),
   assert(humidity(Humidity)),
   weather(Weather),
   write('The weather is '), write(Weather),
   retractall(temp(_)),
   retractall(sky(_)),
   retractall(humidity(_)).
```

To run the program, type `go`.

TASK 29.06

Test the recursively defined rule `writelist/1` to output the elements of a list.

```
writeList([]).
writeList([H|T]):-write(H), nl, writeList(T).
```

Summary

- Imperative programs reflect the steps of *how* to solve a problem.
- Declarative programs reflect *what* the problem is.
- A knowledge base consists of two types of clause: facts and rules.
- Clauses are sometimes referred to as predicates.
- The arity of a predicate shows how many arguments it takes.
- To solve a problem, the user of the knowledge base poses a query.
- A recursive rule is defined in terms of itself.
- In logic programming, a list is manipulated by separating the head from the tail ([H|T]).

Exam-style Questions

1 A logic programming language is used to represent, as a set of facts and rules, details of cities of the world. The set of facts and rules are shown below in clauses labelled 1 to 17.

```
01  capital(vienna).
02  capital(london).
03  capital(santiago).
04  capital(caracas).
05  capital(tokyo).
06  cityIn(vienna, austria).
07  cityIn(santiago, chile).
08  cityIn(salzburg, austria).
09  cityIn(maracaibo, venezuela).
10  continent(austria, europe).
11  continent(chile, southAmerica).
12  continent(uk, europe).
13  continent(argentina, southAmerica).
14  iVisited(vienna).
15  iVisited(tokyo).
16  capitalOf(City, Country) IF capital(City) AND cityIn(City, Country).
17  europeanCity(City)
        IF cityIn(City, Country) AND continent(Country, europe).
```

These clauses have the following meanings:

Clause	Meaning
01	Vienna is a capital.
06	Vienna is in Austria.
10	Austria is in the continent of Europe.
14	I visited the city of Vienna.
16	`City` is the capital of `Country` if `City` is a capital and it is in `Country`.
17	`City` is a city in Europe if `City` is in `Country` and `Country` is in Europe.

a Write down the extra clauses needed to express the following facts:

i London is in the UK. [1]

ii I visited the city of Strasbourg. [1]

b The clause `cityIn(City, austria)` would return the result: `vienna, salzburg.`

Write down the result returned by the clause:
`continent(Country, southAmerica).` [2]

c Complete the rule to list countries that I have visited

`countriesIVisited(Country) IF ...` [3]

2 In a particular country, to become a qualified driver you must:

- have a licence: there is a minimum age at which a person can be issued with a licence and it is different for cars and trucks
- pass a theory test: it is the same test for cars and trucks
- pass a driving test for a specific vehicle (car or truck).

A declarative programming language is to be used to represent the knowledge base shown below:

```
01  minimumAge(car, 18).
02  minimumAge(truck, 21).
03  age(fred, 19).
04  age(jack, 22).
05  age(mike, 17).
06  age(jhon, 20).
07  age(emma, 22).
08  age(sheena, 19).
09  hasLicence(fred).
10  hasLicence(jack).
11  hasLicence(mike).
12  hasLicence(jhon).
13  hasLicence(emma).
14  hasLicence(sheena).
15  allowedToDrive(X, V)
       IF hasLicence(X) AND minimumAge(V, L)
          AND age(X, A)
          AND A >= L.
16  passedTheoryTest(jack).
17  passedTheoryTest(emma).
18  passedTheoryTest(jhon).
19  passedTheoryTest(fred).
20  passedDrivingTest(jhon, car).
21  passedDrivingTest(fred, car).
22  passedDrivingTest(jack, car).
23  passedDrivingTest(jack, truck).
24  passedDrivingTest(sheena, car).
25  qualifiedDriver(X, V)
       IF allowedToDrive(X, V)
          AND passedTheoryTest(X)
          AND passedDrivingTest(X, V).
```

These clauses have the following meanings:

Clause	Meaning
01	The minimum age for a car licence is 18.
03	Fred is aged 19.
09	Fred has a licence.
15	Person `X` is able to drive vehicle `V` if person `X` has a licence and the age `A` of person `X` is greater than or equal to the minimum age `L` to drive vehicle `V`.

a **i** give **one** example of a fact in this knowledge base. [1]

ii Give **one** example of a rule in this knowledge base. [1]

b Show the output produced from these clauses:

i `passedDrivingTest(Who, truck).` [1]

ii `allowedToDrive(mike, car).` [1]

iii `NOT(hasLicence(sheena)).` [1]

c Write a clause to output:

i all qualified car drivers [2]

ii all drivers who have passed the theory test but not a driving test. [3]

d To produce the output from a clause, the inference engine uses a process called backtracking.

Consider the clause:

```
AllowedToDrive(mike, car).
```

List the order in which clauses are used to produce the output. For each clause, describe the result that it returns. [5]

Chapter 30
Software Development

Learning objectives

By the end of this chapter you should be able to:

- show understanding of the possible role of program generators and program libraries in the development process
- show awareness of why errors occur
- show understanding of how testing can expose possible errors
- appreciate the significance of testing throughout software development
- show understanding of the methods of testing available: dry run, walkthrough, white-box, black-box, integration, alpha, beta, acceptance
- show understanding of the need for a test strategy and test plan and their likely contents
- choose appropriate test data (normal, abnormal and extreme/boundary) for a test plan
- show understanding that large developments will involve teams
- show understanding of the need for project management
- show understanding of project planning techniques including the use of Gantt and Program Evaluation and Review Technique (PERT) charts
- describe the information that Gantt and PERT charts provide
- construct and edit Gantt and PERT charts.

30.01 Program generators and program libraries

The first computers had to be programmed using machine code. This is a very tedious method for writing programs. Assemblers were invented to generate a computer program in machine code from assembly code instructions. Later interpreters and compilers were invented to generate low-level code from high-level programs written by people. So you can see that **program generators** have been around for a very long time.

Development is ongoing to invent program generators that will take ever more abstract models and translate them into executable code. An integrated development environment (IDE) for a modern high-level language provides facilities for software development, such as a source code editor with intelligent code completion, build automation and a debugger. Some IDEs have more advanced forms of code generation. For example, programmers can design GUIs interactively or generate code from a wizard or template. Computer-aided software engineering (CASE) tools are also used to generate code.

In Chapter 13 (Section 13.08) we covered built-in functions. These are part of a **program library**.

KEY TERMS

Program generator: a computer program that can be used to create other computer programs

Program library: a collection of pre-compiled routines or modules that a program can use

30.02 Why errors occur and how to find them

Software may not perform as expected for a number of reasons:

- The programmer has made a coding mistake.
- The requirement specification was not drawn up correctly.
- The software designer has made a design error.
- The user interface is poorly designed and the user makes mistakes.
- Computer hardware experiences failure.

How are errors found? The end user may report an error. This is not good for the reputation of the software developer. Testing software before it is released for general use is essential. Research has shown that the earlier an error can be found, the cheaper it is to fix it. It is very important that software is tested throughout its development.

The purpose of testing is to discover errors. Edsger Dijkstra, a famous Dutch computer scientist, said 'Program testing can be used to show the presence of bugs, but never to show their absence!'.

30.03 Testing methods

We covered logic errors and run-time errors in Chapter 15. In Section 15.03 we discussed black-box and white-box testing. In Section 15.04 we used debugging facilities in an IDE. In Section 15.05 we worked through program code by dry-running it and recording the steps in a trace table. Dry-running program code is also sometimes referred to as a 'walkthrough'.

These testing methods are used early on in software development, for example when individual modules are written. Sometimes programmers themselves use these testing methods. In larger software development organisations, separate software testers will be employed.

Discussion Point:

Do you think that a program tester will find errors the programmer did not know about? You can try out the idea by letting your friends test a program that you think works perfectly.

Software often consists of many modules, sometimes written by different programmers. Each individual module may have passed all the tests, but when modules are joined together into one program, it is vital that the whole program is tested. This is known as **integration testing**. Integration testing is usually done incrementally. This means that a module at a time is added and further testing is carried out before the next module is added.

Software will be tested in-house by software testers before being released to customers. This type of testing is called **alpha testing**.

Bespoke software (written for a specific customer) will then be released to the customer. The customer will check that it meets their requirements and works as expected. This stage is referred to as **acceptance testing**. It is generally part of the hand-over process. On successful acceptance testing, the customer will sign off the software.

When software is not bespoke but produced for general sale, there is no specific customer to perform acceptance testing and sign off the software. So, after alpha testing, a version is released to a limited audience of potential users, known as 'beta testers'. These beta testers will use the software and test it in their own environments. This early release version is called a beta version and the chosen users perform **beta testing**. During beta testing, the users will feed back to the software house any problems they have found, so that the software house can correct any reported faults.

KEY TERMS

Integration testing: individually tested modules are joined into one program and tested to ensure the modules interact correctly

Alpha testing: testing of software in-house by dedicated testers

Acceptance testing: testing of software by customers before sign-off

Beta testing: testing of software by a limited number of chosen users before general release

30.04 Test plans and test data

During the design stage of a software project, a suitable testing strategy must be worked out to ensure rigorous testing of the software from the very beginning. Consideration should be given to which testing methods are appropriate for the project in question. A carefully designed test plan has to be produced.

It is important to recognise that large programs cannot be exhaustively tested but it is important that systematic testing finds as many errors as possible. We therefore need a test plan. In the first instance, an outline plan is designed, for example:

- flow of control: does the user get appropriate choices and does the chosen option go to the correct module?
- validation of input: has all data been entered into the system correctly?

- do loops and decisions perform correctly?
- is data saved into the correct files?
- does the system produce the correct results?

This outline test plan needs to be made into a detailed test plan.

How can we carry out these tests? We need to select data that will allow us to see whether it is handled correctly. This type of data is called 'test data'. It differs from real, live data because it is specifically chosen with a view of testing different possibilities. We distinguish between different types of test data, listed in Table 30.01.

Type of test data	Explanation
Normal (valid)	Typical data values that are valid
Abnormal (erroneous)	Data values that the system should not accept
Boundary (extreme)	Data values that are at a boundary or an extreme end of the range of normal data; test data should include values just within the boundary (that is, valid data) and just outside the boundary (that is, invalid data)

Table 30.01 Types of test data

WORKED EXAMPLE 30.01

Designing test data

Look at the Pyramid Problem (code shown in Section 14.07). This is a simple program, but we can use it to illustrate how to choose test data. There are just two user inputs: the number of symbols that make up the base and the symbol that is to be used to construct the pyramid. Let's consider just the test data for the number of symbols (Table 30.02).

Type of test data	Example test values	Explanation
Normal (valid)	7	7 is an odd integer, so should be accepted. Any odd positive integer would be suitable as test data. However, it should be bigger than 1 to check that the pyramid is correctly formed. More than one different value to test would be a good idea.
Abnormal (erroneous)	 -7 8 7.5 '*'	Any number that is not a positive odd integer. This will require several tests to ensure that the following types of data are not accepted: • negative integer • even integer • real number • non-numeric input You should not take shortcuts and choose one negative even integer or one negative real number and think you can test two things at the same time. You will not know whether the test fails for just one reason or both.

Boundary (extreme)	1	What is a boundary value? The smallest possible pyramid is a single symbol. So the value 1 is just within the boundary. Sometimes choosing test data throws up some interesting questions that need to be considered when designing the solution:
	0	• Should 0 be accepted? Is 0 an even number? Is it outside the boundary because a pyramid of 0 symbols is not really a pyramid? • Is there just one boundary? Should the program reject numbers that are too large?
	79 81	The output would not look like a pyramid if there is a wrap-around. So the program really should check how many symbols fit onto one line and not allow the user to input a number greater than this. If the number of characters across the screen is 80, then 79 would be just within the boundary but 81 would be outside the boundary, and should not be accepted. Note that by testing with values within the boundary you are also testing normal data, albeit at the extreme ends of the normal range.

Table 30.02 Test data for the pyramid problem

TASK 30.01

Look at the programs you wrote in Chapter 14 (Task 14.04).

1. Design test data for the number-guessing game.
2. Design test data for the Connect 4 game.

30.05 How to prevent errors

The best way to write a program that works correctly is to prevent errors in the first place. How can we minimise the errors in a program? A major cause of errors is poor requirements analysis. When designing a solution it is very important that we understand the problem and what the user of the system wants or needs. We should use:

- tried and tested design techniques such as structured programming or object-oriented design
- conventions such as identifier tables, data structures and standard algorithms
- tried and tested modules or objects from program libraries.

30.06 Project management

If you embark on writing a large program, you may wish to map out stages and a schedule when you should achieve certain milestones. This is especially important if you are working to a deadline.

Commercial software consists of very large programs that require many people to work on them. Usually there are programmers to write code designed by senior program designers. There will be software testers and document writers. If new hardware is required, there will be engineers and installers. To manage people and resources and schedule activities, a project manager is usually appointed.

Discussion Point:

Explore the job titles of people involved in producing computer software.

The first task of a project management team is to break down the project into individual activities that need to be completed to produce the final product. These activities will take a certain amount of time and will need to be done in a certain order. Some activities can only start when other activities have been completed. This is where scheduling becomes very important.

Project managers can use various methods to help them. They can make use of the Program Evaluation and Review Technique (PERT) to establish the critical path. Then they can use a Gantt chart to schedule activities.

PERT charts

PERT was developed for the US Navy to simplify the planning and scheduling of a large and complex project. It is a method to analyse the activities required to complete a project, especially the time required to complete each activity. It also helps to identify the minimum time needed to complete the project (critical path analysis).

An activity may result in a document, a report or some other building block of the project. Such a building block is called a **deliverable**.

A **milestone** is a scheduled event signifying the completion or submission of a deliverable.

KEY TERMS

Deliverable: the result of an activity, such as a document or a report

Milestone: a scheduled event signifying the completion or submission of a deliverable

WORKED EXAMPLE 30.02

Reading a PERT chart

A software developer is to produce software for a customer. The activities, deliverables and milestones in Table 30.03 have been identified.

Activity	Description	Weeks to complete	Deliverables	Milestone
			Start	1
A	Identify requirements	1	Requirement specification	2
B	Produce design	2	Program design	3
C	Write program code	8	Complete program code	4
D	Test modules	5	Tested program modules	5
E	Integration testing	2	Tested integrated software	6
F	Install software	1	Software ready to use	7
G	Acceptance testing	2	Software signed off	8
H	Write documentation	4	Technical documentation	9
J	Write training material	2	User documentation	8
K	Train users	3	Users trained	10
L	Go live	1	Finish	11

Table 30.03 Breakdown of project into activities, deliverables and milestones

The project manager produces the PERT chart shown in Figure 30.01 for this project.

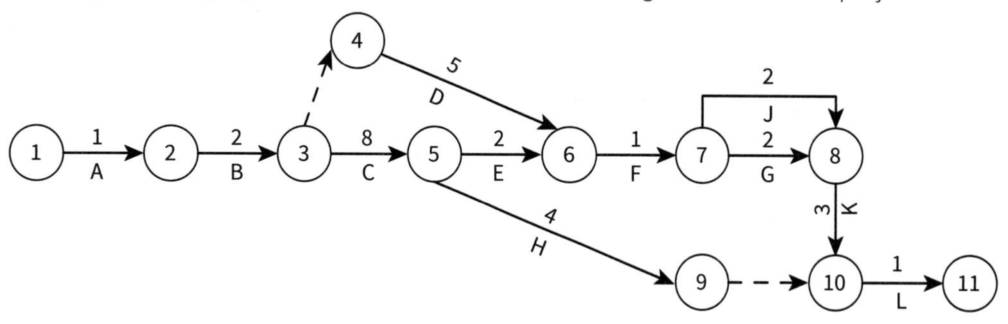

Figure 30.01 PERT chart

Figure 30.01 demonstrates the following features:

- Milestones are shown as numbered nodes.
- Activities are represented by arrows linking the milestones. The arrows are labelled with the activity code below the arrow and the duration above the arrow.
- Nodes 1, 2, 3, 5, 6, 7, 8, 10 and 11 are joined by solid arrows. These activities must be completed in sequence; they are called 'dependent activities'.
- Activities that must be completed in sequence but that don't require resources or completion time are represented by dotted lines and are called 'dummy activities'. The dotted line between milestones 3 and 4 indicates that the program modules must be tested before software installation can begin, but the time required to do the testing is on another path (path D).

Critical path

The **critical path** is the longest possible continuous pathway from Start to Finish. It determines the shortest time required to complete the project. Any time delays along the critical path will delay the final milestone.

KEY TERMS

Critical path: the longest possible continuous pathway from Start to Finish

In Worked Example 30.02, the critical path is A, B, C, E, F, G, K, L. This means the shortest possible time to complete the project is 20 weeks.

Question 30.01

What would be the effect of Activity H taking six weeks instead of the original four weeks? Explain.

Gantt charts

A Gantt chart is a horizontal bar chart developed by Henry Gantt. It is a graphical representation of a project schedule and helps to plan specific activities in a project.

Gantt charts can be produced on paper, in spreadsheet software or in specific project management software.

WORKED EXAMPLE 30.03

Reading a Gantt chart

Following on from Worked Example 30.02, the Gantt chart for the project is shown in Figure 30.02.

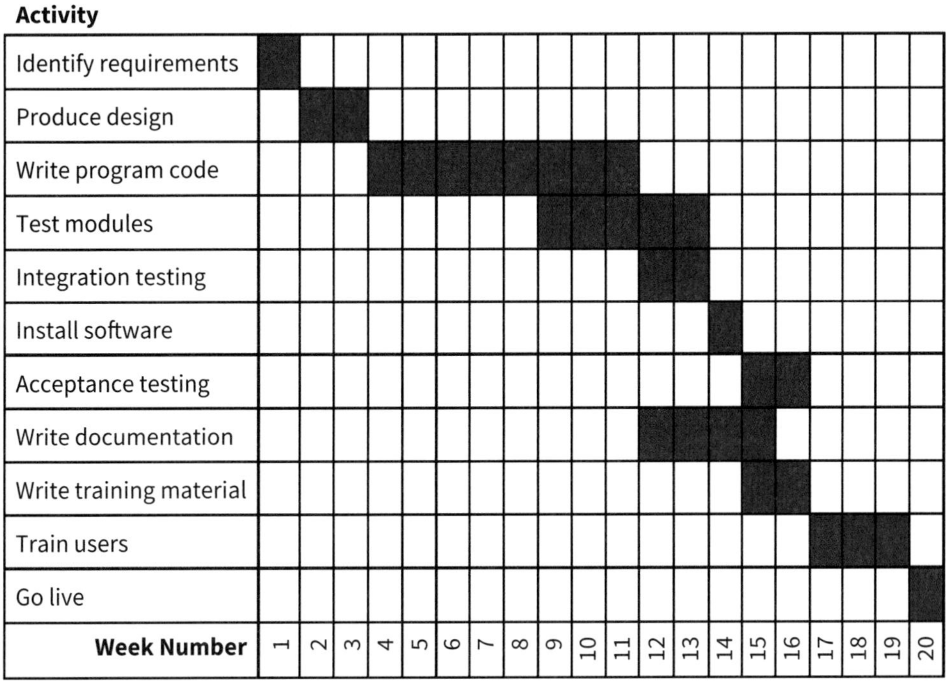

Activity																				
Identify requirements	■																			
Produce design		■	■																	
Write program code				■	■	■	■	■	■	■	■									
Test modules									■	■	■	■	■							
Integration testing												■	■							
Install software														■						
Acceptance testing															■	■				
Write documentation												■	■	■	■					
Write training material															■	■				
Train users																	■	■	■	
Go live																				■
Week Number	1	2	3	4	5	6	7	8	9	10	11	12	13	14	15	16	17	18	19	20

Figure 30.2 Gantt chart

Figure 30.02 demonstrates the following features:

- The horizontal axis represents time. In this example the schedule is worked out in weekly steps. This could be done on a daily or monthly basis, depending on the overall length of the project.
- Individual activities are shown as horizontal bars, one activity per row.
- Activities can overlap. In this example, module testing can begin before all the program code has been written. The documentation can be started before all the testing has been completed.
- Some activities can only begin when others have been completed. In this example, integration testing can only start after all modules have been successfully tested. Software can only be installed after integration testing has been successfully completed.

If any activities take longer than planned, the chart may need to be modified to represent the revised schedule. For example, if serious problems are encountered during acceptance testing, further design, program coding, module testing and integration testing may be required.

Question 30.02

Redraw the Gantt chart from Figure 30.02 to show the position if the acceptance testing failed and an extra week of design, two extra weeks of coding, one week of module testing and a further week of integration testing are required before the software can be re-installed.

Summary

- A program generator is a computer program to create other computer programs.
- A program library is a collection of tried and tested pre-compiled routines.
- The purpose of program testing is to find errors.
- The types of test data are: normal (valid), abnormal (erroneous) and boundary or extreme data.
- Structured programming and object-oriented design minimise programming errors.
- Project management use PERT charts and Gantt charts to schedule project activities.
- PERT charts show activities, their duration and milestones.
- A Gantt chart is a horizontal bar chart, showing the individual activities including their start and end times.

Exam-style Questions

1 A procedure to output a row in a tally chart has been written using pseudocode:

```
PROCEDURE OutputTallyRow(NumberToDraw : INTEGER)
   IF Count > 0
      THEN
         FOR Count ← 1 TO NumberToDraw
            IF (Count MOD 5) = 0
               THEN
                  OUTPUT('\') // every 5th bar slants the other way
               ELSE
                  OUTPUT('/')
            ENDIF
         ENDFOR
   ENDIF
   OUTPUT NewLine // move to next row
ENDPROCEDURE
```

Design suitable test data that will test the procedure adequately. Justify your choices in each case. [9]

2 A business approaches a software house for a bespoke system. The systems analyst for this project has drawn up the following outline activities:

Activity	Description	Weeks to complete	dependent on activity
A	Identify requirements	1	
B	Produce program design	5	A
C	Produce hardware requirements	3	A
D	Programming	10	B
E	Order hardware	4	C
G	Module testing	7	D
M	Technical documentation	5	D
F	Install hardware	1	E
P	Convert data files	1	F
H	Integration testing	2	G
J	Alpha testing	3	H
L	Acceptance testing	2	J
N	User documentation	2	J
K	Train users	4	N
Q	Go live	1	K, L, P

a **i** Complete the PERT chart, showing all activities and durations. [8]

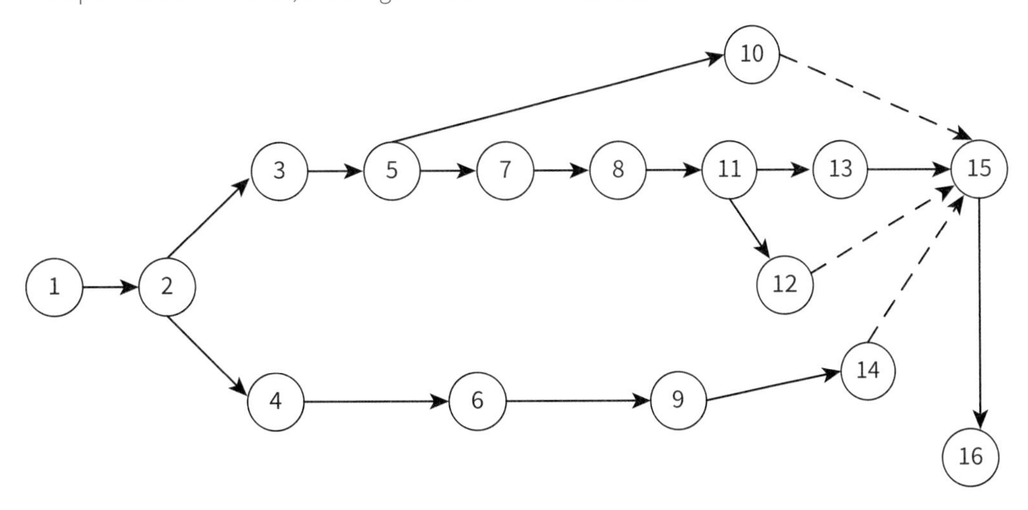

ii Use the PERT chart to work out the critical path. [3]

b **i** Draw a Gantt chart from the information in the above table. [8]

ii Using the information from the Gantt chart, calculate the time required for the project from start to completion. [3]

Glossary

Abstract class: a base class that is never used to create objects directly

Abstract data type: a collection of data with associated operations

Acceptance testing: testing of software by customers before sign-off

Accumulator: a general-purpose register that stores a value before and after the execution of an instruction by the ALU

Actuator: a hardware device that receives a signal from a computer and adjusts the setting of a controlling device

Adaptive maintenance: amending a program to enhance functionality or in response to specification changes

Address bus: a component that carries an address to the memory controller to identify a location in memory which is to be read from or written to

Algorithm: a sequence of steps that can be carried out to perform a task

Alpha testing: testing of software in-house by dedicated testers

Attribute: a column in a relation that contains values

Attributes: the data items of a class

Authentication: verification of a user's identity

Authorisation: definition of a user's access rights to system components

Base case: an explicit solution to a recursive function

Beta testing: testing of software by a limited number of chosen users before general release

Binary file: a file designed for storing data to be used by a computer program

Binary search: repeated checking of the middle item in an ordered search list and discarding the half of the list which does not contain the search item

Black-box testing: comparing expected results with actual results when a program is run

Bubble sort: a sort method where adjacent pairs of values are compared and swapped

By reference: the address of the variable is passed into the procedure

By value: the actual value is passed into the procedure

Byte: a group of eight bits treated as a single unit

Capacitive touch screen: a rigid surface above a conductive layer which undergoes a change in electrical state when a finger touches the screen

Ciphertext: the result of applying an encryption algorithm to data

Combinational circuit: a circuit in which the output is dependent only on the input values

Constructor: a special type of method that is called to create a new object and initialise its properties

Containment: a relationship in which one class has a component that is of another class type

Copyright: a formal recognition of ownership of a created and published work

Corrective maintenance: correcting identified errors

Critical path: the longest possible continuous pathway from Start to Finish

Data bus: a component that carries data to and from the processor

Data integrity: a requirement for data to be accurate and up to date

Data management system (DBMS): software that controls access to data in a database

Data privacy: a requirement for data to be available only to authorised users

Data protection law: a law that relates to data privacy

Data redundancy: the same data stored more than once

Data security: a requirement for data to be recoverable if lost or corrupted

Database administrator (DBA): a person who uses the DBMS to customise the database to suit user and programmer requirements

Debugging: finding and correcting errors in a program

Deliverable: the result of an activity, such as a document or a report

Directive: an instruction to the assembler program

Domain name system (DNS): a hierarchical distributed database installed on domain name servers that is responsible for mapping a domain name to an IP address

Dry-run: the process of checking the execution of an algorithm or program by recording variable values in a trace table

Enumerated data type: a list of possible data values

Finite state machine (FSM): a machine that consists of a fixed set of possible states with a set of inputs that change the state and a set of possible outputs

Floating-point representation: a representation of real numbers that stores a value for the mantissa and a value for the exponent

Flowchart: shapes linked together to represent the sequential steps of an algorithm

Foreign key: an attribute in one table that refers to the primary key in another table

Freeware: software free with unlimited use allowed but no source code provided

Function: a sequence of steps that is given an identifier and returns a single value; function call is part of an expression

Gateway: a device that connects networks of different underlying technologies

General case: a definition of a recursive function in terms of itself

Gibi: a prefix representing the factor 230 written as the symbol Gi

Global variable: a variable that is accessible from all modules

Identifier table: a table listing the variable identifiers required for the solution, with explanations

Inheritance: all properties and methods of the base class are copied to the subclass

Integration testing: individually tested modules are joined into one program and tested to ensure the modules interact correctly

IPv4 address: a 32-bit long, hierarchical address of a device on the Internet

Kibi: a prefix representing the factor 210 (1024) written as the symbol Ki

Linear search: checking each element of an array in turn for a required value

Liquid-crystal display (LCD): a screen back-lit by light-emitting diodes and with liquid crystal cells sandwiched between polarisers

Local variable: a variable that is only accessible within the module in which it is declared

Logic error: an error in the logic of the solution that causes it not to behave as intended

Logic expression: logic propositions combined using Boolean operators, which may be written with a defined outcome

Logic gate: a component of a logic circuit that has an operation matching that of a Boolean operator

Logic proposition: a statement that is either TRUE or FALSE

Lossless compression: coding techniques that allow subsequent decoding to recreate exactly the original file

Lossy compression: coding techniques that cause some information to be lost so that the exact original file cannot be recovered in subsequent decoding

Machine code instruction: a binary code with a defined number of bits that comprises an opcode and, most often, one operand

Mebi: a prefix representing the factor 220 (1048 576) written as the symbol Mi

Methods: the subroutines of a class

Milestone: a scheduled event signifying the completion or submission of a deliverable

Nested IF **statements**: conditional statements within conditional statements

Nested loop: loop containing another loop

Node: an element of a list

Null pointer: a pointer that does not point at anything

Object: an instance of a class

One's complement: the binary number obtained by subtracting each digit in a binary number from 1

Open source software: software free with unlimited use allowed and access to source code

Operating system: a software platform that provides facilities for programs to be run which are of benefit to a user

Parameter: a value passed between modules

Picture element (pixel): the smallest identifiable component of a bitmap image, defined by just two properties: its position in the bitmap matrix and its colour

Pipelining: instruction-level parallelism

Plaintext: data before encryption

Pointer: a variable that stores the address of the node it points to

Polymorphism: the method behaves differently for different classes in the hierarchy

Primary key: an attribute or a combination of attributes for which there is a value in each tuple and that value is unique

Problem statement: an informal definition of an outcome which is dependent on one logic proposition or a combination of two or more logic propositions

Procedure: a sequence of steps that is given an identifier and can be called to perform a sub-task

Process control block (PCB): a complex data structure containing all data relevant to the running of a process

Process: a program in memory that has an associated process control block

Process: a program that has begun execution

Protocol: a set of rules for data transmission which are agreed by sender and receiver

Pseudocode: a way of using keywords and identifiers to describe an algorithm without following the syntax of a particular programming language

Random-access memory (RAM): volatile memory that can be read from or written to any number of times

Read-only memory (ROM): non-volatile memory that cannot be written to but can be read from any number of times

Record data type: a data type that contains a fixed number of components, which can be of different types

Record: a collection of fields containing data values

Recursive routine: a function or procedure defined in terms of itself

Relation: the special type of table which is used in a relational database

Repeating group: a set of attributes that have more than one set of values when the other attributes each have a single value

Resistive touch screen: a flexible surface which causes contact between electrically resistive layers beneath when touched

Rogue value: a value used to terminate a sequence of values

Router: a device that acts as a node on the Internet

Rules of precedence: define the order of the calculations to be performed

Run-time error: an error that causes program execution to crash or freeze

Sensor: a hardware device that measures a property and transmits a value to a controlling computer

Sequential circuit: a circuit in which the output depends on the input values and the previous output

Server: a device that provides services via a network

Shareware: software free for use for a limited period but no source code provided

Start pointer: a variable that stores the address of the first element of a linked list

State-transition diagram: a diagram that describes the behaviour of an FSM

State-transition table: a table that gives information about the states of an FSM

Stepwise refinement: breaking down the steps of an outline solution into smaller and smaller steps

Structure chart: a graphical representation of the modular structure of a solution

Structured English: a subset of the English language that consists of command statements used to describe an algorithm

Symbol table: a data structure in which each record contains the name and attributes of an identifier

Syntax error: an error in which a program statement does not follow the rules of the language

Test data: carefully chosen values that will test a program

Thread: part of a process being executed

Trace table: a table with a column for each variable that records their changing values

Two's complement: the one's complement of a binary number plus 1

Validation: a check that data entered is of the correct type and format; it does not guarantee that data is accurate

Variable: a storage location for a data value that has an identifier

Vector graphic: a graphic consisting of components defined by geometric formulae and associated properties, such as line colour and style

Verification: confirmation of data received by a system

Virtual memory: a paging mechanism that allows a program to use more memory addresses than are available in main memory

White-box testing: testing every path through the program code

Word: a small number of bytes handled as a unit by the computer system

Index

Acknowledgements

The authors and publishers acknowledge the following sources of copyright material and are grateful for the permissions granted. While every effort has been made, it has not always been possible to identify the sources of all the material used, or to trace all copyright holders. If any omissions are brought to our notice, we will be happy to include the appropriate acknowledgements on reprinting.

p. 101 - ACM/IEEE Software Engineering Code of Ethics, adapted with permission. www.acm.org/about/se-code

pp. 107-108, 316 questions from Cambridge International AS and A Level Computer Science 9608 Specimen papers 1 and 3 are reproduced by permission of Cambridge International Examinations

Images:

p. 2 polygraphus/Shutterstock; p. 18 dgbomb/Shutterstock; p. 19 Galushko Sergey/Shutterstock; p. 19 Solomonkein/Shutterstock; p. 36 Pingingz/ Shutterstock; p. 47 photo by Frank Wojciechowski, used with permission of Michael McAlpine and Princeton University; p. 49 agsandrew/Shutterstock; p. 59 Raimundas/Shutterstock; pp. 69, 155, 212, 356, 405 Mclek/Shutterstock; p. 78 Toria/Shutterstock; p. 88 deepadesigns/ Shutterstock; p. 99 R. Gino Santa Maria/ Shutterstock; p. 109 kubais/Shutterstock; pp. 125, 258 bluebay/Shutterstock; p. 127 Thinglass/Shutterstock; p. 160 digitalreflections/Shutterstock; pp. 176, 246 Kheng Guan Toh/Shutterstock; p. 228 wongwean/Shutterstock; p. 270 James Steidl/Shutterstock; p. 282 Lukas Rs/ Shutterstock; pp. 287, 310, 337 kentoh/Shutterstock; p. 303 jijomathaidesigners/ Shutterstock; p. 317 mistery/ Shutterstock; p. 347 Titima Ongkantong/Shutterstock; p. 368 Mike McDonald/ Shutterstock; p. 394 Tashatuvango/Shutterstock; p. 420 Mario7/ Shutterstock